The Yale Edition of the Complete Works of St. Thomas More

VOLUME 11

THE ANSWER TO A POISONED BOOK

Published by the St. Thomas More Project, Yale University,
under the auspices of Gerard L. Carroll and Joseph B. Murray,
Trustees of the Michael P. Grace, II, Trust,
and with the support of the Editing Program of the
National Endowment for the Humanities
and the Knights of Columbus

ℭ The answere to the fyrst parte

of the poysened booke,
Whych a namelesse
heretyke hath
named
the souper of the lorde.

By syr Thomas More knyght.

Henry

Title page, *The Answer to a Poisoned Book*

The Complete Works of
ST. THOMAS MORE

VOLUME 11

Edited by

STEPHEN MERRIAM FOLEY
and
CLARENCE H. MILLER

Yale University Press, New Haven and London

Published with assistance from
the National Endowment for the Humanities

Set in Baskerville type.
Printed in the United States of America by
Vail-Ballou Press, Binghamton, New York.

Library of Congress catalog number: 63-7949
International standard book number: 0-300-03129-7

The paper in this book meets the guidelines
for permanence and durability of the
Committee on Production Guidelines
for Book Longevity of the Council on
Library Resources.

10   9   8   7   6   5   4   3   2   1

For Virgil Chrysostom Dechant
Supreme Knight
of the
Knights of Columbus

ACKNOWLEDGMENTS

This edition of *The Answer to a Poisoned Book* is the fruit of several years of friendly collaboration in the office of the St. Thomas More project at Yale. Clarence Miller is primarily responsible for the text, Stephen Foley for the commentary, but the effort of making the book whole has been gladly shared. Alone among the Yale editors, we have had the privilege of working together at the same place at the same time in one of the world's best libraries, and our work has been easier and happier for it. We are also endebted to the Yale editors whose work has preceded ours, for *The Answer* was the last book published by More in his lifetime, and their fine research on its predecessors has made our burden lighter. The memory of Richard Sylvester may be seen in all these volumes, and our personal memories of this good man—his kindness, his hard work, and his determination—have been a sustaining inspiration to us as we worked on *The Answer*.

Like all our fellow editors, we are thankful for the devoted and meticulous labors of the More project staff: Katherine Gardner, Shane Gasbarra, Po-chia Hsia, Daniel Kinney, Rosemarie McGerr, Michelle Margetts, James Warren and Nancy Wright. The learning and wit of Ralph Keen, assistant research editor at the project, have been invaluable. Louis Martz has, as ever, provided warm, patient support and encouragement. We should also like to thank Emmett McLaughlin of Yale, who read our edition in typescript; Anne Hawthorne, our expert copy-editor for the Yale University Press; Maureen McGrogan and Jay Williams of the Press, who have guided our book through to publication; and Constance Smith of the Pius XII Memorial Library, St. Louis University, who supplied valuable bibliographical assistance.

Stephen Foley would like to thank his wife, Mary Jo, and his parents, Virginia and Donald, for their love and kindness; he is thankful (for many reasons) that his son Nicholas was born just as his work on this book was nearing completion. Clarence Miller would like to thank members of his family who gave him encouragement in New Haven and elsewhere and made his life easier while he worked on this edition: his brothers George and Roger Miller, his sister, Georgina Holt, and especially his mother, Theresa Wöss Miller.

Finally, we are grateful to the Knights of Columbus for their generous support of our project.

Providence, R.I.   New Haven, Conn.   S. M. F. and C. H. M.

CONTENTS

ILLUSTRATIONS

INTRODUCTION

I. THE SHAPE OF THE EUCHARISTIC CONTROVERSY

The Controversy in Switzerland, Germany, and England: 1524–1533

In December 1533, Thomas More released for publication both *The Answer to a Poisoned Book*, which he had just completed, and his *Letter against Frith*, which he had withheld from publication for nearly a year. In these two books, More addressed a subject he had not treated at length in his earlier polemical works: the real presence of the body and blood of Christ in the eucharist. More knew of the continental controversy over the real presence from the first explosive denials of the doctrine by Karlstadt, Zwingli, and Oecolampadius in 1524 and 1525. He had often accused English radicals like William Roye and Jerome Barlowe of taking Zwingli's or Oecolampadius' side, and he had long suspected William Tyndale of denying the real presence. But not until John Frith wrote the first clear and credible English exposition of the new eucharistic theology and circulated his piece in manuscript did More devote an entire work to the subject, *A Letter against Frith*.[1] And not until Frith secretly read More's *Letter* and prepared to publish a rebuttal did More release it for publication. At the same time More published his *Answer to a Poisoned Book*, a refutation of the anonymous *Souper of the Lorde* (probably by George Joye), an inflammatory pamphlet based upon a Latin tract of Zwingli's. *The Answer to a Poisoned Book* turned out to be the last work by More published in his lifetime. When he published his eucharistic treatises late in 1533, he faced an issue that threatened to draw England, along with the rest of Europe, into destructive and lasting argument.

The doctrine of Christ's physical presence in the eucharist—as well as

---

[1] *A letter of syr Tho. More knyght impugnynge the erronyouse wrytyng of Iohan Fryth agaynst the blessed sacrament of the aultare* (London, William Rastell, 1533 [1532]); cited hereafter as *A Letter against Frith*; no. 18090 in *A Short-Title Catalogue of Books Printed in England, Scotland, & Ireland, and of English Books Printed Abroad, 1475–1640*, ed. W. A. Jackson, F. S. Ferguson, and Katharine F. Pantzer, vol. 2 (London, 1976), a revised edition of *A Short-Title Catalogue . . . 1475–1640*, ed. A. W. Pollard and G. R. Redgrave (London, 1926; cited hereafter as "*STC²*" and "*STC*" by number). *A Letter against Frith* was reprinted in Elizabeth Frances Rogers, ed., *The Correspondence of Sir Thomas More* (Princeton, 1947), no. 190 (cited hereafter as "Rogers"). *A Letter against Frith* is no. 66 in R. W. Gibson and J. Max Patrick, *St. Thomas More: A Preliminary Bibliography of His Works and of Moreana to the Year 1750* (New Haven and London, 1961; cited hereafter as "Gibson").

disagreement about the way he is present—has a long and venerable history.[1] Ambrose, for example, propounded an early realistic theology of the eucharist, stressing the physical change of the bread and wine. Augustine stressed the spiritual reception of the eucharist—his *crede et manducasti*[2] became a byword—and he was interested in the rich relation between *res* and *signum* in the sacrament. Yet precisely what the early church meant by such important (and unstable) terms as *sacramentum, figura, mysterium,* or *corporaliter* remains a vexing question.[3] Christ's presence in the eucharist did not become a divisive issue, however, until the ninth century, when Paschasius Radbertus' identification of Christ's eucharistic body with his historical body drew the opposition of Ratramnus, who challenged what he saw as an undue emphasis upon Christ's material presence alone, drawing a distinction between the real body of the sacrament and the historical body, which is present in the sacrament only figuratively. The controversy resumed and reached a high pitch during the eleventh century in the exchanges between the skillful dialectician Lanfranc, archbishop of Canterbury, who argued that the bread and wine were converted essentially into Christ's body and blood while retaining their natural appearance, and Berengarius of Tours, who argued that Christ's historical body had been resurrected and could not be present and that the bread and wine remain bread and wine even though filled with Christ's presence through a sacramental change. Debate over the issue continued in the schools, where Lanfranc's position was elaborated by Guitmond of Aversa and Alger of Liège and found a place in the sacramental systems of theologians like Peter Lombard.

---

[1] For surveys of eucharistic theology, see P. Batiffol, "L'Eucharistic, la présence réele, et la transsubstantiation" in *Études d'histoire et de théologie positive,* 2me série, 2 vols., 7th ed. (Paris, 1920); C. W. Dugmore, *The Mass and the English Reformers* (London, 1958); Josef Rupert Geiselmann, *Die Eucharistielehre der Vorscholastik,* Forschungen zur christlichen Literatur– und Dogmengeschichte 15/1–3 (Paderborn, 1926) and *Die Abendmahlslehre an der Wende der christlichen Spätantike zum Frühmittelalter: Isidor von Sevilla und das Sakrament der Eucharistie* (Munich, 1933); Henri de Lubac, *Corpus mysticum: L'eucharistie et l'eglise au moyen age* (Paris, 1944); A. J. MacDonald, *The Evangelical Doctrine of Holy Communion* (Cambridge, 1930); Jean de Montclos, *Lanfranc et Bérenger: La controverse eucharistique du XIᵉ siècle,* Spicilegium Sacrum Lovaniense, Études et documents 37 (Louvain, 1971); Jaroslav Pelikan, *The Christian Tradition: A History of the Development of Doctrine,* 4 vols. (Chicago and London, 1971–), *1,* 167–71, 305–07; *3,* 74–80, 184–204; (cited hereafter as "Pelikan, *The Christian Tradition*"); Darwell Stone, *A History of the Doctrine of the Holy Eucharist* (London, 1909).

[2] *In Iohannis evangelium tractatus* 25.12, in *Patrologiae Cursus Completus: Series Latina,* ed. J.–P. Migne, 221 vols. (Paris, 1844–64), *35,* 1602 (cited hereafter as *PL*).

[3] See de Lubac, *Corpus mysticum,* pp. 45–64, 97, 129, 142, 351–64; Joseph de Ghellinck, *Pour l'histoire du mot " sacramentum,"* Spicilegium Sacrum Lovaniense, Études et Documents 3 (Louvain, 1924).

The word *transubstantiatio* is first recorded in the mid-twelfth century.[1] Transubstantiation was accepted as an article of faith by the Fourth Lateran Council in 1215,[2] and the doctrine soon received its familiar definition in the works of the great thirteenth-century doctors, the Angelic Thomas Aquinas and the Subtle Duns Scotus. The feast of Corpus Christi was instituted in 1264, with a liturgy drawn up by Thomas Aquinas, and by the fourteenth century the cult of the host became widespread, and sometimes extravagant. Eucharistic questions were investigated with growing complexity in the works of many fourteenth- and fifteenth-century theologians, Scotist, Thomist, and nominalist alike. A work like Gabriel Biel's *Canonis Missae expositio* could define a subtle new position with elaborate references to the entire preceding controversy.[3] Berengarius, whose recantation entered canon law,[4] acquired a reputation as the father of eucharistic heresy. When Ockham, Wyclif, or the Albigensians departed from received doctrine on the eucharist, their beliefs were often identified with Berengarius, whether or not the connection was strictly justified. And Thomas More, like other Catholic apologists of the sixteenth century, saw the sacramentarianism of Zwingli and Oecolampadius as the contemporary legacy of this persistent heresy.[5] The sacramentarians themselves, on the other hand, favored the view that they were returning to the doctrines of the early church. The sacramentarian controversy clearly belongs in the context of earlier eucharistic debates. But the intellectual origins of positions taken by both sides cannot always be traced with much accuracy. John Fisher (to cite only one example of the possible confusion) summons to the support of his orthodox position both Paschasius and his determined opponent Ratramnus.[6]

Even the immediate origins of the sacramentarianism of Karlstadt, Zwingli, and Oecolampadius are difficult to trace. Eucharistic discussion was widespread in the fifteenth century. And despite the scholastic complication of eucharistic issues like the sacrifice of the mass, the working of the mass *ex opere operantis* or *ex opere operato*, and the physics of the real presence, eucharistic theology was important to the faith and liturgical life not only of the learned clergy but also of the ordinary Christian. The

---

[1] See Dugmore, *The Mass and English Reformers*, p. 37.

[2] See Commentary at 169/26–29.

[3] Biel's treatise has been edited by H. A. Oberman and W. J. Courtenay (Wiesbaden, 1963).

[4] De consecratione 2.42, in Emil L. Richter and Emil A. Friedberg, eds., *Corpus Iuris Canonici*, 2 vols. (Leipzig, 1879; reprinted Graz, 1959), *1*, 1328–29 (cited hereafter as "*CIC*").

[5] See the text and Commentary at 179/15–16.

[6] Fisher, *De veritate corporis et sanguinis Christi in Eucharistia* (Cologne, Peter Quentel, 1527), sig. P₅ (cited hereafter as "Fisher, *De veritate*").

eucharist was central to the sacramental constitution of the church, and
eucharistic theology could affect such practical matters as private masses
or the reservation of the sacrament or communion in both kinds, as well
as such larger issues as the power of the clergy or works versus faith. As
the Lutheran reform gained strength after 1517, questions concerning the
eucharist were raised with increasing urgency. In 1520, for example, an
old Dutch lawyer with humanist interests, Cornelius Hoen, wrote a short
letter to Luther on the eucharist, setting forth the notion, later adopted
by Zwingli, that *est* means *significat* in the phrase *hoc est corpus meum*.[1]
Hoen's interest had been drawn to the eucharist by a chance reading of
some treatises by Wessel Gansfort,[2] a fifteenth-century theologian trained
at Deventer by the Brethren of the Common Life. Hoen's treatise presents
many topics that were common in Gansfort and other earlier eucharistic
writers, but Hoen simplifies and makes more radical their understanding
of eucharistic symbolism. To Hoen the eucharistic meal is like a wedding
feast. Christ the bridegroom gives his ring, the bread, as a pledge to his
bride the church. The bread represents the eternal unity of Christ and his
church. The true believer in the redemptive power of Christ's death eats
the body of the Lord and drinks his blood through belief, not through
ingestion, for Christ can no more be bread or wine than he can be a vine
or a door. The eucharist is not a sacrifice but a commemoration, and the
bread and wine are only symbols.[3] Hoen was too old to make the pilgrim-
age to Luther in Wittenberg himself, and he sent a friend, Hinne Rode, to
see Luther in early 1521.[4] Luther, about to depart for Worms to take his
stand against the emperor, was not receptive either to Hoen's letter or to
the copies of Gansfort's works that the Dutchman brought along.

The question of the eucharist was again raised by Luther's ambitious

---

[1] The letter was published by Zwingli in 1525; it has been edited in *Huldreich Zwinglis
Sämtliche Werke*, ed. E. Egli, G. Finsler, W. Köhler, and O. Farner, Corpus Reformatorum
88–101 (Leipzig, 1905–59), *4*, 505–19 (hereafter cited as *CRZ*). An English translation
appears in H. A. Oberman, *Forerunners of the Reformation* (New York, 1966), pp. 269–78. For
one view that there is a direct relation between fifteenth-century Dutch theology and
sixteenth-century sacramentarianism, see George Huntston Williams, *The Radical Reformation*
(London, 1962), pp. 30–37 (cited hereafter as " Williams, *The Radical Reformation* ").

[2] Hoen came to know Gansfort's work through a coincidence. An old friend from his
school days in Utrecht, Martin van Dorp, the stolid epistolary opponent of More and
Erasmus, asked Hoen to examine a library that contained many of Gansfort's treatises (see
Williams, *The Radical Reformation*, pp. 35–36). For a study of Gansfort's theology, see M. van
Rijn, *Wessel Gansfort* ('s–Gravenhage, 1917), pp. 156–63.

[3] *CRZ 4*, 512–18.

[4] See Otto Clemen, " Hine Rode in Wittenberg, Basel, Zürich, und die frühesten Ausga-
ben Wesselcher Schriften," *Zeitschrift für Kirchengeschichte, 18* (1897), 346–72.

lieutenant, Andreas Bodenstein von Karlstadt,[1] who had pushed his way through the university ranks to become dean of the theological faculty at Wittenberg. Karlstadt was always looking for ways to make his mark, and the theme of the eucharist was one of many that he seized upon. Luther's departure for Worms in April 1521 and his ten months of hiding at the Wartburg gave Karlstadt an opportunity to test his talents as a leader, for during Luther's absence Karlstadt emerged as the principal spokesman for the Lutheran faction. After a brief and unsuccessful mission of reform to Denmark, Karlstadt launched a vigorous series of sermons and pamphlets in Wittenberg. As the spirit of reform reached a riotous pitch in late 1521, Karlstadt took the radical step of celebrating the first protestant communion. On Christmas Day 1521 he entered the chancel at the cathedral without vestments and celebrated communion in both kinds. The consecration was delivered in German; the host was not elevated; and no mention was made of the sacrifice of the mass. In January the town council of Wittenberg issued an ordinance that gave sanction to the communion service Karlstadt had celebrated. Violent demonstrations of zeal erupted throughout the city. One of the interlocutors in William Barlowe's *Dyaloge . . . of . . . Lutheran faccyons* (1531) reports: "I sawe many wonderfull alteracyons as destroyeng of monasteryes, pluckyng down of churches, castynge out of ymages, breakynge of aultares, & caryeng the consecrate stones to the buyldynge of theyr bull warkes."[2] In March 1522 Luther returned to Wittenberg to calm the rage of reform. He restored the Latin mass with communion in one kind only and slowed the pace of iconoclastic innovation. Karlstadt retired to the rural parish of Orlamunde but continued to preach sermons that stressed a spiritualist theology of the inner life of belief and departed more and more from the Lutheran program. Karlstadt and Luther were never again on good terms with one another.

The decisive break came in August 1524.[3] Luther was visiting parish churches on a campaign against false preachers. When he spoke in Orlamunde, Karlstadt himself was among the congregation, and Karlstadt later attempted to defend himself against Luther at a meeting in the Black Bear Tavern at Jena. In the midst of the discussion Luther extracted a gold coin and threw it at Karlstadt, who caught it, brand-

---

[1] There is a full biography by Hermann Barge, *Andreas Bodenstein von Karlstadt*, 2 vols. (Leipzig, 1905), and also a lucid and fresh account by Gordon Rupp in *Patterns of Reformation* (Philadelphia, 1969), pp. 49–153 (cited hereafter as "Rupp").

[2] London, 1531, sig. l₁v; *STC* 1461.

[3] The encounter is described by Martin Reinhard in *Acta Ienensia* in *D. Martin Luthers Werke*, 94 vols. (Weimar, 1883–), *15*, 327–41 (cited hereafter as "*WA*").

ished it before the audience, and placed it in his purse. The coin, like a gauntlet, symbolized a challenge given and accepted. Karlstadt was soon exiled from Saxony as a dangerous rebel. He launched his campaign against Luther from Basel, catching the public eye and winning considerable European notoriety through his opinion on the eucharist.[1] In a series of German tracts published in Basel in October and November 1524, Karlstadt denied the real presence, denied even that the bread and the wine are sacramental signs.[2] The most lively of these tracts is a dialogue between a zealous, intelligent layman and two somewhat pedantic priests—one devoted to *sola scriptura* and the other leaning toward scholasticism. As the two clerics haggle over the words of the consecration, the layman interrupts to say that he could never believe Christ was referring to the bread when he uttered the words *hoc est corpus meum*. Must not he have meant his own physical body? Could he not have been pointing to himself, saying, "*This* is my body"? The layman knows this to be true because he has heard it himself through the inward voice of the holy spirit—the same voice that we all must listen to if we wish to receive Christ spiritually. Merely eating is something outward. One achieves true communion with Christ only by the passionate remembrance of his suffering and love for sinful man.[3]

At nearly the same time that Karlstadt came to his denial of the real presence, a second and different strain of sacramentarianism grew up in Switzerland.[4] There Hinne Rode found a favorable reception for his views.[5] In January 1523 he traveled to Basel, where he stayed with Andreas Cratander, who hoped to publish an edition of Gansfort's works. At Cratander's house he dined with Johannes Oecolampadius, the scholarly friend of Erasmus who had left the Brigittine order only a year

---

[1] The chronology of Karlstadt's eucharistic views is in dispute. Barge (*Karlstadt 2*, 151) and Williams (*The Radical Reformation*, p. 43) believe that he had begun to deny the real presence as early as 1523. Rupp (p. 142) finds no evidence of this before the Basel pamphlets of 1524.

[2] See Ernst Freys and Hermann Barge, "Verzeichnis der gedruckten Schriften des Andreas Bodenstein von Karlstadt," *Zentralblatt für Bibliothekswesen*, 21 (1904), 305–19, nos. 124, 126, 129, 131, 135 (cited hereafter as "Freys and Barge"). On the chronology of Karlstadt's eucharistic pamphlets see Freys and Barge, pp. 327–28.

[3] *Dialogus oder ein gesprechbüchlin von dem grewlichen vnnd abgöttischen missbrauch, des hochwirdigsten sacraments Iesu Christi* (Basel, Cratander, 1524), Freys and Barge, no. 126, reprinted in *Karlstadts Schriften aus den Jahren 1523–25*, ed. Erich Hertzsch, Neudrucke deutscher Literaturwerke des 16. und 17. Jahrhunderts no. 325 (Halle/Saale, 1956–57), pt. 2, pp. 6–49.

[4] On the sacramentarian movement in Switzerland, see Walther Köhler, *Zwingli und Luther: Ihr Streit über das Abendmahl nach seinen politischen und religiösen Beziehungen*, 2 vols. (Leipzig, 1924–53) (cited hereafter as "Köhler").

[5] See Williams, *The Radical Reformation*, pp. 86–89.

before. There were already strong undercurrents of sacramentarianism in Basel; indeed Oecolampadius' own views approached those of Hoen. Oecolampadius welcomed the chance to discuss eucharistic theology with Rode. His only regret was that he could not do more for the cause: " I am sorry that I am in such circumstances that I cannot help those whom I would like to help on Christ's behalf. May He then help them."[1] But Oecolampadius encouraged Rode to travel on to Zürich to discuss his views with Ulrich Zwingli.

To Zwingli, Hoen's letter to Luther was a clarifying light. He later had it published (anonymously in order to protect its author) and he described his readings of the letter as a turning point: " In it I discovered the lucky pearl that *est* is here to be taken as *significat*. When I was constrained to expound my opinion openly . . . it seemed wiser to open up the word under which the trope lay hidden with this key than simply to say ' This is a trope.' . . . If you say six hundred times ' This is a trope ' and you do not open up the trope, you're offering an unbroken nut to a boy."[2] Zwingli was perhaps already inclining toward a sacramentarian position—indeed Rode felt him out on the subject before speaking with him about it—but even after the visit from Rode he was unwilling to make a public statement. In January 1523 he had rejected the mass as sacrifice and communion in one kind only and had called for a reform of the canon of the mass.[3] But early in June 1523 he was still willing to affirm the orthodox doctrine of transubstantiation, which Luther had rejected in 1520. Only later that month, in a private letter, did he begin to acknowledge his inclination toward the sacramentarian position.

When Karlstadt's pamphlets on the eucharist came out in October and November 1524 and Zürich seemed in danger of falling under radical influence, Zwingli made public his sacramentarian views, carefully distinguishing his position from Karlstadt's and Luther's. His first sacramentarian tract, an open letter to the Lutheran preacher Matthew Alber,[4] was widely tested in manuscript before it was committed to print in March 1525. Zürich soon moved officially into reform under his leadership. During Holy Week of 1525 the celebration of the Roman mass was

---

[1] See Ernst Staehelin, ed., *Briefe und Akten zum Leben Oekolampads*, 2 vols. (Leipzig, 1927 and 1934), *1*, 204, no. 142 (cited hereafter as " Staehelin, *Briefe und Akten* ").

[2] " In ea foelicem hanc margaritam ' est ' pro ' significat ' hic accipi inveni. Cumque hanc sententiam cogeremur . . . palam exponere, consultius videbatur, ipsam vocem, in qua tropus latet, adperire sua ista clave, quam solummodo dicere: ' Tropus est.' . . . Sexcenties enim dicas: ' Tropus est,' nec tropum adperias, infractam nucem puero praebueris " (*CRZ 4*, 560–61).

[3] See George R. Potter, *Zwingli* (Cambridge, 1976), pp. 150–55.

[4] *CRZ 3*, 322–54.

forbidden, and on Maundy Thursday the first evangelical communion service was held. Zwingli's key to the eucharist was the definition of *est* as *significat*; his chief theological points were that the true eating of Christ's body as represented in communion was the belief of the communicant— *edere, credere*—and that the distinction between Christ's natural body and his glorified body made his corporeal presence in the eucharist impossible. His chief scriptural authority was John 6:64: "Spiritus est qui vivificat; caro non prodest quidquam." Over the next two years, apart from German treatises and translations, Zwingli published five Latin sacramentarian tracts totalling about 350 pages in the modern edition of his complete works.[1] A long eucharistic section of Zwingli's *De vera et falsa religione commentarius* became the principal source for *The Souper of the Lorde*,[2] the "poisoned book" that provoked More's *Answer*.

In the summer of 1525, Oecolampadius published a compendium of patristic passages that became a handbook of the eucharistic controversy, *De genuina verborum Domini " Hoc est corpus meum " iuxta vetustissimos auctores expositione liber*.[3] Thereafter the controversy quickly spread. Zwingli was challenged by opponents in Zürich, and in Swabia a group of Lutheran preachers composed a *Swabian Syngramma* in response.[4] Luther himself did not reply formally to the Swiss until late in 1526, when he lumped Zwingli together with the radicals Karlstadt, Münzer, and Schwenkfeld in his *Sermon von dem Sakrament des Leibes und Blutes Christi, wider die Schwarmgeister*.[5] A confusing array of eucharistic views spread through Protestant theology as one man after another entered the controversy: Leo Jud, Pellicanus, Bibliander, Bullinger, Bucer, Bugenhagen, Billicanus, Capito, Pirckheimer, Melanchthon. The Protestant side was divided—to the delight of the Catholics, who could rely on the overwhelming unanimity of the massive defenses of orthodox eucharistic thought written by Josse Clichtove and John Fisher.[6]

Zürich, the only declared Protestant city in the Swiss confederacy, was outnumbered and isolated. When Catholics called for a public discussion of the controversy, they were able to set their own terms, and they profited

---

[1] *CRZ 3*, 773–820; *4*, 440–504, 546–76, 880–941; *5*, 548–758.

[2] See Appendix A, pp. 297–340.

[3] Ernst Staehelin, "Oekolampad-Bibliographie: Verzeichnis der im 16. Jahrhundert erschienenen Oekolampaddrucke," *Basler Zeitschrift für Geschichte und Altertumskunde, 17* (1918), 1–119 (reprint, Nieuwkoop, 1963), no. 113, p. 55 (cited hereafter as "Staehelin, 'Oekolampad-Bibliographie'").

[4] See Köhler, *1*, 126–27, 293, 299.

[5] *WA 19*, 474–523; the sermon repeats and expands views Luther had expressed in a letter of January 4, 1526, which (though not intended for publication) was printed as a foreword to the *Swabian Syngramma; WA 19*, 457–61.

[6] See pp. l–liii, below.

Ulrich Zwingli, by Hans Asper (reduced)

from the strife within the Protestant camp. The colloquy was held in the
Catholic stronghold of Baden in May 1526. Zwingli was afraid of arrest,
and his place was taken by Oecolampadius, who was bullied by the wily
dialectician John Eck. Many Lutherans present supported the Catholic
position, and they won perhaps only a Pyrrhic victory, for they appeared
to many to have betrayed their evangelical brethren. When Zwingli and
Oecolampadius called for another colloquy two years later, in January
1528, they were as careful as the Catholics had been to set it up on their
own terms. Bern, the city chosen for the colloquy, was on the verge of
reform and adopted it officially just after the debates were concluded.
Basel followed (to Erasmus' dismay) the next year. And the sacramentarians won considerable support in the cities of South Germany. Despite
their growing political influence, Luther continued to treat the sacramentarians like a troublesome swarm of sectarian flies, too volatile to be taken
seriously. Some theologians, like Bucer and Oecolampadius, wished for a
reconciliation. And strong pressure for Protestant unity came from Philip
of Hesse, who was afraid that the dispute would weaken the Protestant
front in the empire. Although both Zwingli and Luther were at first
unwilling, Philip arranged for a meeting between the two sides at
Marburg in October 1529. The great antagonists were paired off: Oecolampadius against the patriarch Luther; Zwingli against the subtle and
irenic Melanchthon. As the well-known story goes, Luther began the
conference by writing the words *hoc est corpus meum* in chalk on the table in
front of him. And as might be expected, the two sides reached agreement
upon every doctrinal issue except the eucharist. Zwingli and Oecolampadius were willing to concede that the real body of Christ was present *per
fidem*; Luther, that Christ's body need not be present *localiter* (in any one
particular place). Both sides rejected transubstantiation, communion in
one kind only, and the sacrifice of the mass. But on the real presence they
could not resolve their differences. The best they could do was agree to
put the quarrel aside and part in peace: "Although we have not agreed
at this moment whether the true body and blood of Christ be corporeally
present in the bread and wine of the lord's supper, none the less each side
will declare their Christian love for the other, as far as the conscience of
each will allow, and both sides will fervently pray to Almighty God that
by his Spirit he will confirm us in a true opinion."[1] The Marburg Collo-

---

[1] "Etsi autem an verum corpus et sanguis Christi corporaliter in pane et vino Coenae
Domini praesens sit hoc tempore non concordavimus, tamen una pars alteri Christianam
dilectionem, quantum cuiusque conscientia feret, declarabit, et utraque pars Deum omni-
potentem diligenter orabit ut nos Spiritu suo in vera sententia confirmet" (Beresford J.
Kidd, *Documents Illustrative of the Continental Reformation* [Oxford, 1911], pp. 254–55).

quy temporarily dampened the sacramentarian controversy in Germany and Switzerland. There was nothing more for the two sides to say to one another. Zwingli and Oecolampadius were not invited to the Diet of Augsburg in June 1530; the Lutherans at Augsburg were more concerned with bending their eucharistic doctrine toward the Catholic side than with reaching an accord with the sacramentarians.[1] And soon afterward both Zwingli and Oecolampadius died suddenly: Oecolampadius, of a fever in November 1531; Zwingli, in battle against the Catholic cantons in October. To Thomas More, Zwingli's death in the "sedycyon, stryfe, debate, and warre" that the Protestants had raised seemed like an act of providence: "And Suinglius theyr chyefe capytayne vnto whome Tyndale swarued from Luther, bycause his heresye ferther blasphemeth the blessed sacrament / was taken, slayne, and burned / and many by that meane returned from theyr heresyes vnto the trewe fayth agayne."[2]

Through the works of John Frith and *The Souper of the Lorde*, the sacramentarianism of Oecolampadius and Zwingli found its first serious expression in English. But resistance to received doctrine on the eucharist began long before these specifically eucharistic works were published. From the start the English Protestants had attacked the sacramental system, emphasis on good works, and such practices as the adoration of the sacrament. Attacks upon abuses of the mass frequently found a place in the anticlerical rhetoric of the reformers. To some extent the sixteenth-century reformers may have found the eucharist a ready subject, for Wyclif had quarreled with the scholastic definition of transubstantiation,[3] and the heretical belief that the host was mere bread was a charge commonly made against Lollards throughout the fifteenth century down to More's own time.[4] More claims in *A Dialogue Concerning Heresies*, for example, that a "mysbyleue towarde the holy sacrament of the awter" was one of the heretical beliefs held by Richard Hunne in 1514. More says of a Bible of Hunne's:

> But this I remember well that besydys other thyngys framed for the fauoure of dyuers other heresyes / there were in the prologue of that byble suche wordys touchynge the blyssed sacrament / as good crysten men dyd moche abhorre to here / and whyche gaue the

[1] See article 10 of the Augsburg Confession (Kidd, *Documents*, p. 264).

[2] *The Confutation of Tyndale's Answer*, ed. L. A. Shuster et al., vol. 8 of The Yale Edition of the Complete Works of St. Thomas More, p. 608. For the volumes of the Yale Edition, which are cited hereafter as *CW* followed by the volume number, see the bibliography.

[3] See the Commentary at 136/18.

[4] See John A. F. Thomson, *The Later Lollards, 1414–1520* (Oxford, 1965), pp. 246–47. See also More's *Apology*, *CW 9*, Commentary at 125/11.

reders vndouted occasyon to thynke that the boke was wryten after wyclyffs copy / and by hym translated into our tonge.[1]

And the messenger in *A Dialogue* provides an example of the resentment felt by the laity toward the cult of the host and the priestly "hocus-pocus" of the altar. One of the episodes in the messenger's tale of a prior's mistress, Holy Maiden Elizabeth, concerns a mechanical miracle of the eucharist: "And dyuers tymes she was houseled in sight of the people with an hoste vnconsecrate / & all the people lokyng vpon / there was a deuyce with a small here y^t conueyed the hoste from the paten of the chaylce / out of ye pryours handes in to her mouth / as though it came alone. . . ."[2]

Even More, then, could smile at abuses of the eucharist, but he had long recognized that any Protestant attack upon any aspect of the sacraments would cast doubt on the whole sacramental system. Even Luther's belief that the bread and wine remain along with the body and blood of Christ militates against the reality of the sacrament, as More suggests in his *Responsio*:

> Moreover, as for what you say in these words: that we, having long ago lost the substance of the sacrament, now fight for the sign in opposition to the most important thing, the substance, you say that "we" correctly indeed and truly. For catholics, content with the substance itself, have not been anxious about the sign, but you schismatics and heretics, fighting against the truly most important reality, that is, the will of God, have for the sake of the sign alone destroyed the whole substance of the sacrament and all its fruit.[3]

Luther himself, More says several times, would have gone on to deny the real presence, had not the young upstarts Karlstadt and Zwingli beaten him to it; Luther's defense of the real presence sprang from envy, not from theological scruple.[4]

When Zwingli's and Oecolampadius' eucharistic works were published in 1525, they found a receptive audience in England. Theirs were among the books circulated by Thomas Garret in the Protestant circle at Oxford.[5] More knew of the books by at least 1526, when he urged

---

[1] *CW 6*, 327/26–27, 330/16–22.

[2] *CW 6*, 87/16–20.

[3] For the Latin see *CW 5*, 383/7–15.

[4] *Doctissima D. Thomae Mori Clarissimi ac Disertiss. Viri Epistola, in qua . . . respondet Literis Ioannis Pomerani* (Louvain, J. Fowler, 1568), sigs. G$_2$v–G$_3$ (Rogers, pp. 361–62, lines 1351–63; cited hereafter as "*Letter to Bugenhagen*"). See also *CW 6*, 353/24–354/18.

[5] William A. Clebsch, *England's Earliest Protestants, 1520–1535* (New Haven, 1964), p. 80 (cited hereafter as "Clebsch").

Erasmus to reply to them,[1] and when he described the sacramentarian heresy in his reply to John Bugenhagen: "And now Karlstadt, Zwingli, and Oecolampadius, who finally joined the rest, have completely removed Christ's flesh from the host and left only bread."[2] In February 1527, a year and a half after Oecolampadius had published *De genuina . . . expositione*, John Fisher published his compendious reply, which runs to more than 350 folio pages.

The first and most violent sacramentarian works in English came from two English exiles in Strassburg, William Roye and Jerome Barlowe. The place of publication is not surprising, for Strassburg, a key city in the struggle for religious dominion of southern Germany, was the home of influential preachers who held various sacramentarian positions, Martin Bucer and Wolfgang Capito. In 1527 Roye's *A Brefe Dialoge bitwene a Christen Father and his stobborne Sonne*[3] (the first Protestant theological tract in English) launched an anticlerical attack on the understanding of the sacraments as good works valid by their mere performance, explaining that baptism and the eucharist were outward means of effecting an inward spiritual process. Christ's body and blood are not materially present in the eucharistic elements, for when he spoke to his apostles at the Last Supper, "he remayned bodily sittynge before their eyes."[4] Barlowe's *Rede me and be nott wrothe* (1528) is a virulent piece of anticlerical satire directed primarily against Wolsey and the Observant Franciscans, whose order Roye and Barlowe had recently deserted. The fictional premise of the poem (and the source of its popular title, *The Burying of the Mass*) is that the mass, which provided the income to support priestly self-indulgence, had died in Strassburg, slain by the two-edged sword of scripture that Bucer, Capito, and others wielded in the debates that con-

---

[1] *Opus Epistolarum Des. Erasmi Roterodami*, ed. P. S. Allen, H. M. Allen, et al. 11 vols. (Oxford, 1906–58), *6*, no. *1770* (cited hereafter as "Allen").

[2] For the Latin, see Rogers, 361/1354–362/1356; the translation is from Frank Manley's forthcoming edition of the *Letter to Bugenhagen*. On the dating of the *Letter to Bugenhagen*, see Elizabeth F. Rogers, "Sir Thomas More's Letter to Bugenhagen," *Modern Churchman*, *35* (1946), 350–60, reprinted in R. S. Sylvester and G. Marc'hadour, eds., *Essential Articles for the Study of Thomas More* (Hamden, Conn., 1977), pp. 447–54 (cited hereafter as "*Essential Articles*").

[3] Strassburg, Johann Schott, 1527; *STC*² 24223.3; Anthea Hume, "English Protestant Books Printed Abroad, 1525–1535: An Annotated Bibliography," *CW 8*, Appendix B, pp. 1065–91, no. 4 (cited hereafter as "Hume"). The book was drawn from a catechism by Wolfgang Capito; see Anthea Hume, "William Roye's 'Brefe Dialoge' (1527): An English Version of a Strassburg Catechism," *Harvard Theological Review*, *60* (1967), 307–21. See also *CW 8*, 1171–72, and Clebsch, pp. 233–34.

[4] *Brefe Dialoge*, sig. d₁v.

tinued through 1528 and led the city to adopt reform in January 1529. A
priestly choric figure laments the death of his dear friend:

> Whatt avayleth nowe to have a shaven hedde /
>   Or to be aparelled with a longe gowne.
> Oure anoynted hondes do vs lytle stedde /
>   Wher as the masse is thus plucked downe
> Vnto our dishonowre all doeth rebowne.
>   Seynge that gone is the masse /
>   Nowe deceased / alas alas.[1]

In a dialogue, the priest's two servants, now out of work because of their
master's recent impoverishment, discuss the death and forthcoming burial
of the mass, settling upon the shrine of Saint Thomas at Canterbury as
the most appropriate place for interment. The heroic slayers of the mass
are praised for their "lyuynge . . . so inculpable"[2] and the defenders are
subjected to scurrilous abuse, especially prominent Catholics like Emser,
Faber, and Cochlaeus, who were said to have been too busy elsewhere to
be in Strassburg. Erasmus, for example, is supposed (as indeed he was) to
have been occupied with writing *De libero arbitrio*:

> He was busy to make will free /
> A thynge nott possible to be /
>   After wyse clarckis estimacion.
> Wherfore he intermitted lytle /
>   As concernynge the massis tytle /
> With eny maner assercion.
>   He feareth greatly some men saye /
> Yf masse shulde vtterly decaye /
>   Least he shulde lose his pension.
> Notwithstondynge he hath in his hedde /
> Soche an opinion of the god of bredde /
>   That he wolde lever dye a marter
> Than ever he wolde be of this consent /
> That christ is not theare corporally present /
>   In bredde wyne and water.[3]

While *The Burying of the Mass* contains some incidental information about
the sacramentarian controversy and occasionally speaks (about Erasmus,

---

[1] Strassburg, Johann Schott, 1528; *STC* 21427; Hume, no. 5; ed. Edward Arber
(Westminster, 1895), p. 36.

[2] *Rede me*, p. 40.

[3] *Rede me*, pp. 42–43.

for instance) with at least poetic justice, it does not constitute a serious presentation of sacramentarian theology. Even Tyndale disliked Barlowe's "raylinge rymes"; he thought that the Word of God would be a more suitable vehicle for the Lord's ministers.[1] To More it was "a folysshe raylynge boke agaynst the clergy and moche parte made in ryme / but the effecte therof was all agaynst ye masse / & the holy sacramentes."[2]

Tyndale touches ambiguously upon some sacramentarian themes in several of his works, although he chose, in the interest of evangelical unity, not to make an issue of the real presence, so that his statements on the eucharist hover with calculated vagueness between Lutheran and sacramentarian views. In his *Obedience of a Christen Man*, he admits only baptism and the eucharist as sacraments and he defines a sacrament as a sign or promise: "This worde sacramente is as moch to saye as an holy signe / and representeth allwaye some promise of God. As in the olde testamente God ordeyned y^t the raynebowe shulde represent and signifie vnto all men an othe that God sware to Noe and to all men after him / that he wolde no more drownd the worlde thorow water."[3] Tyndale calls the eucharist the "sacrament of the body and bloud of Christe," but his stress falls upon the active faith of the individual Christian:

> Yf when thou seist the sacrament or eatest his body or drinkest his bloude / thou have this promyse fast in thine herte (that his body was slayne and his bloud shed for thy synnes) and belevest it / so art thou saved and iustified therby. Yf not / so helpeth it the not / though thou hearest a thousande masses in a daye or though thou doist no thinge else all thy lyfe longe / then eate his body or drinke his bloude: no moare then it shulde helpe the in a deed thurst / to beholde a bussh at a taverne dore if thou knewest not therby y^t there were wine within to be solde.[4]

Tyndale's theology in the beginning of this statement is not strictly inconsistent with Lutheran or with Catholic doctrine, but his irreverent analogy of the tavern sign betrays at least a sacramentarian inclination, stressing the bread and wine as mere signs dependent upon the understanding of the beholder. In his *Supplication of Souls*, More links together Roye's *Brefe Dialoge*, Barlowe's *Rede me*, and Tyndale's *Parable of the Wicked Mammon* and *Obedience* as a vile succesion of books against the

---

[1] *The Parable of the Wicked Mammon* (Antwerp, 1528; *STC* 24454; Hume, no. 6), sig. A₃.

[2] *A Dialogue Concerning Heresies, CW 6*, 291/9–11.

[3] Marburg [Antwerp], 1528; *STC*² 24446; Hume, no. 7. sig M₁; cited hereafter as "*Obedience*."

[4] *Obedience*, sig. M₁v. On the source of this analogy in Oecolampadius, see the Commentary at 223/11.

eucharist: " In whych bokys afore specyfyed they go forth playnly agaynst the fayth and holy sacramentis of Crystys church / and most especyally agaynst the blyssed sacrament of ye aulter / with as vylanous wordes as the wreches coud deuyse."[1] More claims in his *Confutation of Tyndale's Answer* that he had learned from a repentant heretic that while abroad Tyndale had spoken about the eucharist with Barnes, whom More thought to be a Zwinglian, and that Tyndale was unhappy with Barnes, for Tyndale had not yet fully fallen into that heresy. But soon " the frere made the fole mad out ryght, and brought hym blyndefelde downe into the depeste dongeon of that deuylysshe heresye."[2] More was wrong about Barnes, for, as Barnes protested to More, he was a strict Lutheran; the important issue to him was utraquism—a subject on which More planned to answer him after completing *The Answer to a Poisoned Book*.[3] More seems to have been right about Tyndale, however, and he recognizes the shrewd ambiguity of Tyndale's eucharistic statements:

> I haue in his boke of obedyence consydered his wordes of this holy sacrament / & I haue aduysed them ye better for certayne wordes y^t I haue herd of hym: & I se not one worde by whych he may be bounden to saye that euer he confessed yt to be the very body and blood of Cryste. How be yt yf he had / yt wer not yet wyth that sorte mych ye surer. For they maye do as theyr mayster hath, saye the contrarye after / and when they say worse, then tell vs that they haue sene more synnys and lerned better.[4]

The sacramentarian denial of the real presence became a major polemical issue in England when Tyndale's winning young associate John Frith was arrested and imprisoned in late 1532. Frith had returned to England from Antwerp in July of that year.[5] By October he was confined to the Tower, where he composed a short treatise on the eucharist at the request of a friend who was curious about Frith's views.[6] The treatise was not printed until about 1548, when it appeared anonymously as *A christen*

---

[1] *The supplycacyon of soulys* . . . (London, 1529; *STC*² 18093), sigs. E₃v–E₄. This passage appears in *The workes of Sir Thomas More Knyght, . . . wrytten by him in the Englysh tonge* (London, 1557), *STC*² 18076, sig. v₇v (cited hereafter as "*EW*").

[2] *CW 8*, 302/15–17.

[3] See p. lix, n. 5, below. Utraquism demands the reception of the eucharist under the forms of both bread and wine and prohibits the reception under one form alone.

[4] *CW 8*, 116/2–11. See also pp. 356–58, below.

[5] See *CW 9*, Commentary at 89/20.

[6] Frith tells the story of the treatise in the prefatory note to his *Boke . . . answeringe vnto M mores lettur* (Münster [Antwerp], 1533; *STC* 11381; Hume, no. 30), sigs. A₂–A₃. More tells the story in his *Apology, CW 9*, 122–24.

sentence . . . of the most honorable Sacrament. . . .[1] But the treatise was circulated, and More obtained a manuscript copy, probably through the treachery of William Holt, a London tailor who had ingratiated himself with Frith.[2] More answered the treatise in his *Letter against Frith*, which he completed on December 7, 1532, and which was soon in print[3] but which he withheld from publication until late 1533, hoping to avoid making the issue public until the Protestants forced his hand. But while Frith was being examined at the house of Stephen Gardiner, bishop of Winchester—Gardiner hoped to reconvert Frith, who had been his pupil—Frith saw a printed copy of More's *Letter*, and he later read a hastily drawn up manuscript copy. Frith then composed a reply, not published until after he was burned as a heretic at Smithfield on July 4, 1533. More released his own *Letter* only when he knew of the impending publication of this reply, *A boke made by Iohn Frith prisoner in the tower of London answeringe vnto M mores lettur which he wrote agenst the first litle treatyse that Iohnan Frith made concerninge the sacramente.*

Tyndale and Frith were essentially in agreement that the real presence was best treated as an indifferent matter, although Tyndale wished Frith to avoid the subject in the interest of Protestant unity and in order to save Frith from certain execution for heresy. When Frith was preparing his *Boke . . . answeringe vnto M mores lettur*, Tyndale wrote to him in the Tower, cautioning about the possible dangers of the controversy: "Of the presence of Christes body in the Sacrament, medle as litle as you can, that there appeare no diuision among us. . . . My mind is, that nothyng be put forth till we heare how you shal haue spede."[4] But Frith had already committed himself to the course of action that led to his death at Smithfield. As he explains in the preface to his *Boke*, "And albeit I was loth to take the mater in hande / yet to fullfyll [my friend's] instant intercession / I toke vppon me to touche this terrible tragedie / and wrote a treatise whyche beside my paynfull impresenment / ys like to purchase me moste cruell deth."[5] Like Erasmus, then, Frith found tragedy an apt metaphor

---

[1] *A christen sentence and true iudgement of the moste honorable Sacrament of Christes body & bloude declared both by the auctorite of the holy Scriptures and the auncient Doctores* (London, R. Wyer, 1548; *STC* 5190) (cited hereafter as "*A Christian Sentence*"). The identification was first made by Germain Marc'hadour, *Thomas More et la Bible* (Paris, 1969), p. 298.

[2] See the account in Foxe, *The Acts and Monuments of the English Church*, 8 vols. (London, 1853–70), 5, 6; on the unreliability of much of Foxe's account, see *CW 9*, Commentary at 89/20.

[3] *CW 9*, text and Commentary at 125/8.

[4] *The Whole workes of W. Tyndale, Iohn Frith, and Doct. Barnes*, ed. John Foxe (London, 1573; *STC* 24436), sig. CC₄ (cited hereafter as *WW*).

[5] *A Christian Sentence*, sig. A₂v.

for the sacramentarian controversy, and his script seemed already to have been written: he must speak his mind, as he did in his books and at his examination. In both of Frith's eucharistic works one hears the strong voice of conscience. Though Frith and Tyndale are in accord, Frith's approach to the eucharist is richer, less strident, and less calculated than Tyndale's.

Frith's first short treatise on the real presence begins by announcing his hope for reconciliation between the sacramentarians on the one side, and the Catholics and Lutherans on the other. He hopes that his "shorte instruction" will "so pacyfye both the parties that without contencion they shall admytte eche other into brotherly loue. . . ."[1] Frith proposes that belief in the real presence is a matter of indifference; neither belief nor disbelief will save or damn the Christian, so long as he feels Christ's presence in his heart through faith. This formula of *adiaphora*, which proved so useful in promoting Anglican compromise later in the century,[2] seems to have been more than mere gesture, even if Frith was perhaps more hopeful of Protestant unity than of the brotherhood of all English Christians. With moving sincerity Frith invites his opponents to debate. He hopes to make his case on the grounds of scripture, reason, and patristic evidence, and he wishes his opponents to do the same: "And so ought nether parte to dispise the other, for eche seketh the glory of God, & the true vnderstandynge of the scripture."[3] Frith attempts to demonstrate that neither Christ's natural body nor his glorified body can be in more than one place, arguing first from reason and then supporting his argument with such authorities as the words of the angel at the tomb, "Non est hic: surrexit enim" (Matt. 28 : 6) and a phrase from Augustine, "Corpus in quo resurrexit in uno loco esse oportet."[4] In interpreting figuratively the words *hoc est corpus meum*, Frith draws upon familiar examples of allegorical language in scripture: "I am the true vine" and "I am the door" (John 15:1; 10:9). He draws the parallel of the bridegroom's ring to show that Christ meant the eucharistic bread as a pledge. Finally, arguing that the benefits of the sacrament depend upon the faith of the believer, not upon the mere fact of consecration, he closes his treatise, which runs to less than three thousand words, with a prayer intended to instruct the Christian how to receive the sacrament faithfully and joyfully:

---

[1] *A Christian Sentence*, sig. A₁v.

[2] On Frith's importance to Cranmer, see Peter Brooks, *Thomas Cranmer's Doctrine of the Eucharist: An Essay in Historical Development* (New York, 1965), p. 3.

[3] *A Christian Sentence*, sig. A₃v.

[4] *Corpus Christianorum: Series Latina*, 70 vols. (Turnholt, 1954–), *36*, 289 (cited hereafter as *CCSL*). See the Commentary at 194/1–195/5.

Blyssed be thou most dere and mercyfull father, which of thy tender
fauour and benignitie (not withstandyng our greuous enormyties
commytted against y^e) vouchsauedest to send thyne owne dere and
onely sone to suffre most vyle death for my redemption. Blessed be
thou Christe Iesu my lorde and sauyour, which of thyne abundaunt
pytie consyderynge oure myserable estate wyllyngly toke it vpon the
to haue thy moste innocent body broken and bloud shede to purge
and washe me whiche am laden with iniquite. And to certyfie vs
therof haste lefte vs not onely thy worde, whiche may instructe oure
hartes but also a visible token to certyfie euen our outwarde senses of
this great beneficte that we shuld not doubt but that thy body and
frute of thy passion are oures as surely as the bread whiche by our
senses we know that we haue within vs. Blessed be also that spirit of
veritie, whiche is sent from God oure father thorowe our sauyour
christ Iesu to lyghten our darke ignoraunces and led vs thorowe
fayth into the knowledg of hym which is all veritie, strength we
besech the our fraile nature & encrease oure fayth that we may
prayse God our most mercyfull Father, and Christe his sone our
sauyoure and redemer, & the (with them) which arte our comforter
to whom be all honour and prayse Amen.[1]

In his *Letter against Frith*, More quickly dismisses Frith's scriptural exegesis, arguing that allegorical senses of scripture must not be accepted
instead of the literal sense but along with it; without this firm foundation
in the literal sense as established historically in the church, scripture
becomes a mere plaything for the fantasy of the individual. The longest
section of More's *Letter* is a point-by-point refutation of Frith's arguments
that Christ's body cannot be in more than one place at once. All things
are possible to God, More insists. And as to the passage Frith alleges from
Augustine, More wonders about its origin and questions its meaning:
saying that Christ's body must be in one place does not mean that it
cannot be in many places. More reserves special contempt for Frith's
professedly irenic motives and for his attitude of piety. To More these are
fraudulent and blasphemous when coupled with an attempt to subvert
the greatest of the sacraments. But More was perhaps moved by Frith's
youthfulness and personal appeal, and he beseeches the Lord to "gyue
thys yonge man the grace, agaynste hys owne frowarde fantasyes to
byleue, and to the same lyfe brynge hym and vs both, where we shall
wythout the vayle or coueryng of any maner sacrament, behold our
blessed Sauyour face to face"; then Frith will see in the three persons of

---

[1] *A Christian Sentence*, sigs. B_3–B_4.

the Trinity "that Cristes one body may be in many places at onys."[1] In spite of More's sympathy for Frith as a wayward young man—or perhaps because of it—More's final ironic dismissal of Frith as a heretic is especially cutting, as is his defense of his treatment of Frith in *The Apology*.[2] More's closing gesture is a prayer that he imagines every good Christian woman makes when receiving communion, thanking God for giving her, simple and unworthy, the gift of his body in the likeness of bread and looking forward to incorporation into his mystical body. Frith's final prayer, More suggests, looks shabby in comparison:

> Thys lo in effecte though not in wordes, can Chrysten women praye, and some of them peraduenture expresse it mych better to. For God can as the prophete sayth, make not onely women that haue age, faith, and wit, but the mouthes also of infauntes & yong soukyng chyldren, to pronunce his laude and prayse, so that we nede not this yong man now to come teche vs how and what we shall pray. . . . Fryth is an vnmete mayster to teche vs what we shold praye at the receyuynge of the blessed sacrament, whan he wyll not knowlege it as it is. . . . I praye God blesse these poysened errours out of hys blynd harte, and make hym hys faythfull seruaunt. . . .[3]

In the final prayers of Frith's treatise and More's *Letter* one sees two good men locked in conflict like ignorant armies upon a darkling polemical plain. More's historical, dynamic sense of the institutional authority of the church and Frith's clear, pious urgency prevented the two from seeing what might in other circumstances have provided clearer common ground. In his *Boke . . . answeringe vnto M mores lettur*, Frith ably defends himself against More's scriptural and patristic attack, and More would no doubt have been capable of launching a sharp polemical work in reply. Yet Frith wishes not merely to argue the theological issue of the real presence, but to stress the joyful gratitude man should feel for the gift of Christ's spiritual presence for the believer. For Frith, as for More in *The Answer to a Poisoned Book*, the sacrament of the altar must be seen in all its greatness and goodness, not merely as the rope in a theological tug-of-war. His long exposition of 1 Cor. 10 and 11, like More's initial exegesis of John 6 in *The Answer*, is an attempt to restore to the sacrament some of the richness of signification that it may have lost in its polemical context:

> And . . . in the sacrament / the brede and the eatinge of yt in the place and fellowshyp where yt ys receyued / ys more then comen

---

[1] Rogers, p. 462, lines 812–21.

[2] *CW 9*, 42.

[3] Rogers, pp. 463–64, lines 872–85.

bred. What ys yt more? Verelye yt ys brede which by the eatinge of yt in that place and fellowship doth testyfye openlye vnto allmen / that he ys oure verye God whose cup we drinke & before whom we eate in that fellowship / and that we put all our fyaunce in hym & in the bloude of hys sonne Christe Jesu / geuinge god all honoure & infinite thankes for his great loue wherwith he loued vs / as yt ys testifyed in the bloude of his sonne / which was shed for oure synnes.[1]

When More wrote *The Answer to a Poisoned Book* in the fall of 1533, he was committed, like Frith, to a widening dispute which he had hoped he—and all England—would be spared. Shortly after Frith's death Germain Gardiner, a nephew of the bishop, wrote *A letter of a yonge gentylman . . . wryten to a frend wherin men may se the demeanour & heresy of Iohn Fryth late burned. . . .*[2] More's own son John also contributed a work to the controversy, *A sermon of the sacrament of the aulter*, a translation of a gentle work by Frederick Nausea that celebrates the gift of Christ's body by expounding the words "Do this in remembrance of me."[3] And finally a new "poisoned book," *The Souper of the Lorde*, printed in April 1533,[4] drew More deeper into controversy.

The Souper of the Lorde was almost certainly written by George Joye.[5] Tyndale alludes disparagingly to such a book by Joye in his cautionary letter to Frith in the Tower: "George Ioye would haue put foorth a treatise of the matter, but I haue stopt hym as yet, what he will doe if he get money, I wotte not. I beleue he wold make many reasons litle seruyng to the purpose."[6] And indeed *The Souper of the Lorde* is a flimsy little tract in comparison with the sacramental works of Frith and Tyndale. *The Souper* falls roughly into two parts: first, a sacramentarian exposition of John 6, translated almost entirely from Zwingli's *De vera et falsa religione commenatarius* and interrupted by a digression on More's statements about multilocation in the *Letter against Frith*; second, a discussion of the institution narratives and of the definition of the sacrament, followed by a brief description of an evangelical communion service. More chose to put off answering the second part. The institution narratives, with their key phrases *hoc est corpus meum* and *hic est calix sanguinis mei*, deserved special and separate consideration. And the sketch of an evangelical liturgy was

---

[1] *Boke . . . answeringe vnto M. mores lettur*, sig. J₈.

[2] London, William Rastell, 1534; *STC* 11594.

[3] London, William Rastell, 1533; *STC*² 18414.

[4] Antwerp, 1533; *STC*² 24468; Hume, no. 28; reprinted in Appendix A. below; cited hereafter as *The Souper*.

[5] See Appendix B, below.

[6] *WW*, sig. CC₄.

(not surprisingly) the most lucid and moving section of *The Souper*. Joye was the author of the first primer in English and had some talent for devising simple and dignified public worship. The first part of *The Souper*, however, drew More's full and immediate attention: he would rescue John 6 from sacramentarian misreading. The reading of John 6 presented in *The Souper* tirelessly explains the references in the chapter to food or bread as figurative: "Faith in him is therefore the meat whiche Cryste prepareth & dresseth so purely powldering & spycyng it with spiritual allegoryes in al this chapiter folowinge to geue vs euerlasting lyfe thorow it."[1] When Christ says, "And the bread that I will give is my flesh, which I will give for the life of the world" (6 : 51), he refers to the gift of his body only on the cross, not in the sacrament. John 6 : 63 provides a catchphrase: "It is the spirit that gives life; the flesh is of no avail." In his *Answer*, then, More chose to address only this sacramentarian reading of John and the incidental defense of Frith, giving his book the full title *The answere to the fyrst parte of the poysened booke, whych a namelesse heretyke hath named the souper of the lorde.*

Erasmus and the Sacramentarians

IN the first edition of *The Praise of Folly* (1511) Erasmus scorns the extremes of pettiness reached by scholastic theologians in their discussions of the mode of the real presence in the eucharist: "With what fine spun and interminable persistence they strive to solve such riddles as what would Peter have consecrated during the time Christ was hanging on the cross."[2] Erasmus expands his mockery of eucharistic physics in the revisions of 1514:

> Certainly the apostles consecrated the eucharist very piously, but still if they had been asked about the "terminus a quo" and the "terminus ad quem," about transubstantiation, about how the same body can be in different places, about the difference between the body of Christ as it is in heaven, as it was on the cross, and as it is in the eucharist, about the exact point at which transubstantiation takes place . . . I don't think they would have responded with a subtlety equal to that of the Scotists when they discuss and define these points.[3]

---

[1] Appendix A, pp. 305/26-29.

[2] *The Praise of Folly*, trans. Clarence H. Miller (New Haven, 1979), p. 89. For the Latin, see Clarence H. Miller, ed., *Moriae encomium*, in *Opera omnia Desiderii Erasmi Roterodami*, 11 vols. (Amsterdam, 1969-) 4/3, 148 (cited hereafter as *ASD*). Translations of Erasmus not otherwise identified are my own.

[3] *The Praise of Folly*, p. 91; *ASD* 4/3, 150.

These are the same quibbles and quillets that More puts aside twenty years later in *The Answer to a Poisoned Book*: "these thinges and suche other in whiche lerned men maye moderately and reuerently dyspute and exercyse theyr witte and lernynge, the catholyque chyrche in suche wyse leueth at large, that yt byndeth not the people to any suche strayghtes in the mater. . . ."[1]

Erasmus' tone toward the scholastics is, as one might expect it to be in 1514, far less respectful than More's in 1533. More's concern in *The Answer to a Poisoned Book* was to defend unequivocally the traditional doctrine of the real presence against its English challengers, and as an apologist he suppressed the scorn he may have felt for the excessive subtleties of the schoolmen, though a prodding irony lurks in his faint praise of those who "moderately and reuerently dyspute and exercyse theyr witte and lernynge." More himself had engaged in some moderate and reverent theological disputation when for instance, he attacked the Lutheran doctrine of consubstantiation and the mass in the *Responsio* (1522).[2] But the Zwinglian denial of the real presence called for a fundamental appeal to truth, and in *The Answer to a Poisoned Book* More not only cast aside the quarrels of the schoolmen as indifferent matters of theological opinion but also excused himself from reaching toward any refinement of eucharistic doctrine. Only in the first of his Tower works did More find the freedom to give subtler consideration to the theology of the eucharist: his penetrating discussion of the symbol and reality of the sacrament in *A Treatise on the Passion*.[3]

Like More, Erasmus refrained from any lengthy, systematic consideration of eucharistic theology.[4] Publishing any such work would perhaps have been dangerous for Erasmus, and writing one was surely not to his taste. Erasmus was closer to the sacramentarians—both geographically and intellectually—than was More, and Erasmus' scattered remarks on the eucharist do not have the single-mindedness of *The Answer*. His abiding concern—even after the spread of the Zwinglian position—was to explore ways in which the traditional doctrine of the eucharist could be understood and even reformulated in the light of sound humanist scholar-

---

[1] 169/22–26 An example of immoderate disputation was the offer by Pico to defend 900 theses in Rome. Three of the thirteen points condemned as erroneous or heretical and then strenuously defended by Pico in his *Apologia* concerned refinements about the eucharist; see the reprint of Giovanni Pico's *Opera omnia* (Basel, 1572) edited by Eugenio Garin (Turin, 1971), *1*, 62, 181–98, 229–32. The chapter devoted to this episode in More's *Life of Pico* is entitled "Of his mynde and vaingloriouse dispicions at Rome" (*EW*, sigs. a₂-a₂v).

[2] See *CW 5*, 440–578.

[3] *CW 13*, 136–74.

[4] I am indebted to John B. Payne, *Erasmus: His Theology of the Sacraments* ([Richmond, Va.], 1970), pp. 126–54 (cited hereafter as "Payne").

ship.[1] Throughout his life Erasmus was more interested in the spiritual fruits of the eucharist than in the physical fact of the real presence. Although he accepted the real presence as *de fide*, he continued to consider some of the matters of theological opinion that More, as an apologist, felt obliged to pass over in the interest of polemical thrust. From 1525 on, Erasmus danced a theological ballet on the theme of the real presence. When pressed, he always returned to rest on the authority of the church, but this submission to authority gave him the freedom to dart into speculations that were far from the more rigid norms of sixteenth-century orthodoxy.

Erasmus' lifelong stress on the spiritual meaning of the eucharist may be seen clearly in the brief discussion of the sacrament that occurs in his *Enchiridion* (1503). In the fifth rule of the handbook, Erasmus exhorts his Christian readers to move from the world of physical appearances to the spiritual world of divine truth. The eucharist provides a key example:

> He has even scorned the eating of His flesh and the drinking of His blood unless they are taken in a spiritual sense. Whom do you think He was talking to when He said that the flesh accomplishes nothing, that it is the spirit which quickens? Certainly not to those people who think that if they have a copy of the Gospel or a copper cross hanging from their necks they are immune to every evil and that this is the perfect form of worship, but to those to whom He had disclosed the deepest significance of the eating of His body. If so great a ritual is nothing—what is more, even dangerous—why should we put our confidence in any other carnal ceremony unless the spirit is present there?[2]

Erasmus clearly accepts some sort of real presence, but he attacks the unthinking ingestion of the host as impious folly. He does not speak with awe of the miracle of the bread and the wine but demands the spiritual participation of the communicant. More important to Erasmus than the physical reality of the sacrament was its spiritual reality, which must itself be revealed in the life of the individual *miles Christianus*.

Erasmus proposes here not an outright rejection of received doctrine but a realignment of emphasis from institutional forms to personal piety.

---

[1] Some Italian humanists of the late fifteenth century, most notably Valla, wrote rhetorical or devotional treatises on the eucharist; see Charles Trinkhaus, *In Our Image and Likeness: Humanity and Divinity in Italian Humanist Thought*, 2 vols. (Chicago, 1970), *2*, 633–50.

[2] *The Enchiridion of Erasmus*, trans. Raymond Himelick (Bloomington, Ind., 1963), p. 109; cited hereafter as "Himelick." For the Latin, see Erasmus' *Opera omnia*, ed. J. Clericus (Leclerc), 10 vols. (Leiden, 1703–06; reprint, Hildesheim, 1961), *5*, 30 (cited hereafter as "*Opera omnia*"); and Erasmus' *Ausgewählte Werke*, ed. Annemarie Holborn and Hajo Holborn (Munich, 1933), p. 73 (cited hereafter as "Holborn").

No longer, according to Erasmus, would the believer be able to rely upon the outward ceremony of the mass. But Erasmus' shift in emphasis seems to give a radical dimension to traditional eucharistic doctrine. Thus while the eucharist is surely a representation of the sacrifice of Christ for the sins of man, man may understand this example in its true spiritual fullness only by imitating Christ's sacrifice:

> Let the thing visually represented—the death of your Lord—be experienced within yourself. Examine yourself and, as the saying goes, look into your heart; see how close you are to being dead to the world. For if you are still wholly possessed by wrath, ambition, greed, lust, envy—then even if you are touching the very altar, you are still far from the sacrament. Christ died for you; you, then, should kill your own beastliness. Sacrifice yourself to Him who offered Himself to the Father for your sake. If you do not think of these things and put your faith in Him, God despises your smug and gross religion.[1]

The representation of Christ's sacrifice becomes spiritually meaningful only when it takes effect in the life of the communicant. The sacrament is not complete unless the believer experiences it fully by making a continuing sacrifice of his own sinful nature.

Like the doctrine of the sacrifice of the mass, the doctrine of communion or of incorporation takes new shape in Erasmus' hands. He shifts attention from the union of the members of the mystical body with Christ, the head, in the sacrament, to the living communion among the members themselves:

> Is is possible that you attend mass every day but live selfishly, untouched by the misfortunes of your neighbors. As yet you are still in the fleshly stage of the sacrament. But if, when you attend mass, you take to heart what receiving the sacrament really means, that is, being one spirit with the spirit of Christ, one body with the body of Christ, a living member of the Church; if you love nothing except in Christ; if you think all your property belongs equally to all men; if the trials of other people grieve you as much as your own—in that case you are at last attending mass with real profit, because you are doing it in a spiritual sense.[2]

---

[1] Himelick, p. 110; *Opera omnia*, 5, 31; Holborn, p. 74.

[2] Himelick, pp. 109–10; I have changed Himelick's translation in a few places. Cf. *Opera omnia*, 5, 30–31, and Holborn, p. 73: "Tu forte cotidie sacrificas et tibi vivis, neque ad te pertinent incommoda proximi tui. Adhuc in carne es sacramenti. Verum si sacrificans das operam id esse, quod illa sumptio significat, puta idem spiritus cum spiritu Christi, idem corpus cum corpore Christi, vivum membrum ecclesiae. Si nihil amas nisi in Christo, si omnia tua bona putas omnibus esse communia, si omnium incommoda tibi perinde ut tua dolent, ita demum magno fructu sacrificas, nempe quia spiritaliter."

For Erasmus, the true spiritual observation of the sacrament links the love of Christ and the love of man, objective incorporation in the body of Christ and loving service in the community of men.

Erasmus' eucharistic theology thus moves away from eucharistic realism without ever denying it, stressing instead the Augustinian tradition of *crede et manducasti* ("believe and you have eaten"). To orthodox theologians Erasmus was suspect, and to the sacramentarians he seemed a likely source of support for their denial of the real presence and the sacrifice of the mass. Erasmus was in fact drawn into eucharistic controversy long before the fulminations of Karlstadt and Zwingli in 1524 and 1525, for in his 1516 *New Testament*[1] he had called into question the precise meaning of the wording of the consecration "hoc est corpus meum." According to Erasmus, the Greek εὐλογήσας ἔκλασεν should not be translated (as it is in the Vulgate) "benedicens fregit" ("blessing he broke it") but "cum benedixisset fregit" ("when he had blessed it, he broke it"). Erasmus suggests that Christ had *already* blessed the bread when he broke it; he did not necessarily bless it saying "hoc est corpus meum." He cast further doubt on the words of the consecration in his reading of 1 Cor. 11 : 24.[2] According to him, the verse ought to be read without the copula ἔστιν (is), which he considers a spurious addition: "τοῦτο μου σῶμα, id est hoc meum corpus, absque verbo substantivo est: quanquam in quibusdam additum reperio" ("τοῦτο μου σῶμα that is, this my body, without the substantiating verb 'is,' although I have found this added in some copies"). To many conservative theologians like Vincent Dirkx (Theodorici) of Louvain, this reading represented a denial of the real presence, but Erasmus defended it vigorously, both in letters[3] and in subsequent editions of the *New Testament*. Even after Zwingli's redefinition of "est" as "significat" in the consecration had made the words "hoc est corpus meum" a virtual battle cry, Erasmus was unwilling to let the argument pass.[4] In his 1527 edition of the *New Testament* he broadens the question, stating that it is not clear from the commentaries of the fathers whether or not Paul describes a sacramental consecration of the body and the blood of the Lord.[5] The fellowship meal celebrated by the apostles was a commemoration of the passion and a symbol of Christian community. Consecration in the precise words now used was not ordained by Christ and presented to the apostles, but a practice that developed historically in the church.

---

[1] Payne, p. 127.

[2] Payne, pp. 127–28.

[3] See Allen, *4*, 315, 317, 465; and Payne, pp. 127–28.

[4] See, for example, Allen, *8*, 190, 345; *Opera omnia*, *7*, 850; *9*, 677, 850, 878, 1064; *10*, 1564–66.

[5] Payne, pp. 128, 131.

Controversial biblical scholarship like these readings of passages dealing with the consecration, as well as the unsettling Augustinian cast of Erasmus' eucharistic theology, made him an instant (though unwilling) party to the sacramentarian controversy when it burst out in the mid-1520s. He knew, or at least knew of, all the principals; indeed his work had exerted a considerable influence on the thought of these younger reformers. Erasmus had known of Karlstadt's activities in Wittenberg from early 1519,[1] and throughout the early 1520s he carried on a running argument with Zwingli, who had been drawn to biblical scholarship by Erasmus' example and who wished his mentor to join the cause of reform.[2] "You call me a delayer," Erasmus wrote to Zwingli in August 1523—"I beg you, what would you have me do?"[3] Oecolampadius had served as one of Erasmus' assistants in the hurried preparation of the 1516 *New Testament*. Many of the Hebrew annotations are the work of Oecolampadius, and Erasmus discovered to his dismay that Oecolampadius and his fellow assistant had not measured up to his standards in reading the proofs. Erasmus had to correct many readings, and he complained about it mightily, but he forgave Oecolampadius and praised him in a letter accompanying the 1519 *New Testament* as a "true theologian."[4] Erasmus liked him and admired his talent as a humanist. He felt betrayed when he was swept away in the sacramentarian cause.[5]

By at least November 1524 Erasmus had learned of Karlstadt's teaching on the eucharist, and by December he knew of Karlstadt's pamphlets expounding the new doctrine.[6] From the very first, Erasmus saw the sacramentarian position as another worry in an already worrisome world. He was angry that the community of believers was torn apart by yet another controversy:

> Karlstadt was here but was scarcely greeted by Oecolampadius. He has published six pamphlets—the two men who printed them were

---

[1] Allen, *3*, 469–70.

[2] See Allen, nos. 401, 404, 1314, 1315, 1327, 1378, 1384, 1936. For a discussion of the relation of Zwingli to Erasmus, see Gottfried Locker, "Zwingli and Erasmus," *Erasmus in English*, *10* (1979), 2–11.

[3] Allen, *5*, 327.

[4] Allen, *2*, 168.

[5] Allen, *5*, 596 and 546, line 74 and note.

[6] Allen, *5*, 586, 591. The most judicious and well documented discussion of Erasmus' beliefs and statements about the eucharist between 1525 and his death in 1536 is by Karl Heinz Oelrich, *Der späte Erasmus und die Reformation*, Reformationsgeschichtliche Studien und Texte 86 (Münster, 1961), pp. 134–58. According to Oelrich, though Erasmus always rejected the teaching of the sacramentarians because of the authority of the church, he felt attracted to Oecolampadius' eucharistic teaching before 1529. After that time he rejected the sacramentarians unequivocally both in public and in private and placed even more stress on the eucharist as the sacrament of the church's unity and peace.

thrown in jail the day before yesterday by order of the council, most probably (I hear) because he teaches that the real body of Christ is not present in the eucharist. This no one will stand for. The lay people are angry that their god has been snatched away from them—as if God were never present except under that sign. The learned are stirred to action by the words of holy scripture and the decrees of the Church. This business will give rise to a great tragedy, when there are already more than enough tragedies.[1]

Erasmus' response is typical of his position throughout the eucharistic controversy. The metaphor of tragedy, which he often applied to the controversy, was not chosen lightly.[2] Erasmus saw clearly that ignorance, misunderstanding, and missed opportunities for reconciliation were leading Christian Europe toward division and destruction. He was unwilling, however, to give up his humanist ideals. Like the spectator at a tragedy, he cherished the hope against all odds that the crisis might yet be averted. He was still contemptuous of superstitious ignorance and still hopeful that the learned would not merely reject the new doctrine but use scholarship to prove the case against the sacramentarians on sound scriptural and historical grounds.

In Basel Erasmus found himself in the thick of the struggle, though he tried hard to stay out of it. Both sides put considerable pressure on him to join the battle. Oecolampadius and Pellicanus may even have used threats, and Allen believes that they may have secured his partial compliance—he would not oppose them publicly if they would refrain from quoting him in support of their views.[3] On the Catholic side Claude Chansonnette urged Erasmus to issue a rebuttal of the sacramentarians.[4] And at the same time Erasmus' own scattered opinions on the consecration were still being subjected to frequent and bitter criticism. His protracted quarrel with Noel Bédier of the theological faculty at Paris raged throughout 1525.[5] Continued suspicion made it all the more necessary for Erasmus to dissociate himself clearly from the sacramentarians.

In the fall of 1525, Erasmus produced a flurry of letters about the beginnings of the eucharistic controversy,[6] including a learned exchange with Conrad Pellicanus,[7] who Erasmus thought was falsely claiming him for the sacramentarian side. The letters demonstrate his political and

---

[1] Allen, *5*, 591.

[2] Allen, *6*, 182, 280.

[3] Allen, *6*, 177, note to line 17.

[4] Allen, *6*, 176–78.

[5] Allen, *6*, 65–66.

[6] Allen, *6*, 179, 182–84, 187–88.

[7] Allen, *6*, 206–21; see also *Opera omnia*, *10*, 1580–1600.

theological agility in finding his own way through the controversy, but they also reflect his intellectual restlessness, his reluctance to be satisfied with the limited choices that the time seemed to offer him. In late September 1525, for example, Erasmus wrote to Claude Chansonnette, explaining why he would not accede to Chansonnette's request that Erasmus take up the cause of eucharistic orthodoxy:

> Can I do by myself what neither emperor nor pope nor so many theological disputations have been able to do? Will the whole world yield to my theological authority by itself?—why, even the dogs of the theologians piss on me. Yet you thus call upon me to prevent schism, as if the fire were not already burning out of control. You accuse me of silence, as if I had not already dared to raise my whispering voice against this world-wide tragedy, or as if I had not already tried to settle this war on just terms. I did so without success, but not without danger to myself. . . . You seem to demand that I take upon myself the authority of making a general judgment, when each side attacks the other with gladiatorial ferocity, and when each side is afflicted with internal quarrels. Suppose I had time, suppose I did not lack the learning required for such an argument: what kind of hope can you offer for the outcome? Shall I decide by the judgment of the theologians? Cisalpine or Transalpine? Shall I decide according to the other side? For the Lutherans or for the Zwinglians? (Karlstadt, I hear, has issued a retraction.)[1]

Just a year earlier, Erasmus had made his opposition to Luther clear in De libero arbitrio, abandoning gentler forms of persuasion for a resounding polemic. Even this clear statement had failed to clear Erasmus of suspicion. It was unlikely that anything he could say about the eucharist would do so either. And in Basel it was likely to cause him trouble. He tells Chansonnette that he had begun something on the eucharist—"de Eucharistia coeperam nonnihil"—but whatever it was, Erasmus seems never to have pursued it.[2] The book would only cause trouble (he later explained to Pirckheimer); Oecolampadius had won large popular support, and Fisher was already preparing a response.[3]

When Erasmus read Oecolampadius' De genuina . . . expositione in October 1525, he found the book so full of scriptural and historical arguments for the sacramentarian side that "even the elect could be seduced," and he realized that he would have to formulate a reaction of some kind

---

[1] Allen, 6, 177–78.
[2] Allen, 6, 177; see also 288, 341.
[3] Allen, 7, 217.

to it: "I must put down my lute for a pruning hook."[1] He was soon forced to do so. The town council of Basel asked Erasmus, Ber, Amerbach, and Chansonnette to present opinions on the book.[2] Erasmus' response, or perhaps only the beginning of it, is preserved in the *Detectio praestigiarum* of 1526: ". . . I have read through the book by Johannes Oecolampadius, *On the words of the Lord's Supper*; in my opinion it is learned, fluent, and elaborate, and I would also add pious, if anything could be pious that contradicts the opinion and consensus of the church, with which I judge it dangerous to disagree."[3] Erasmus' irony cuts two ways. On the one hand he praises the style and method of the book while exposing the theological danger of its contents. On the other hand he may seem to stop short of full praise for Oecolampadius only because he knew all too well the terrible danger that dissenting from the established church could produce.

Erasmus does not merely straddle the fence on the question of the eucharist. Indeed he stands on the fence flinging down stones on his opponents in every direction. He could see some advantages in Oecolampadius' interpretation, since it would avoid some perplexing difficulties,[4] but he consistently refused to deny the received doctrine. To Tunstall he vehemently defended his view of the consecration and the spiritual emphasis of his eucharistic theology: "There is no use in eating the sacrament if faith is not present. Nor is it impious to call the true body a type or symbol since the invisible body lies hidden under types, and this same true body which is eaten is a symbol of the unity of the body with the head and the members among themselves."[5]

In contending against the sacramentarians he consistently took refuge in the authority of the church.[6] He advised a young friend who was in danger of being interrogated by the Zwinglians that he should behave like a man about to die, who evades the devil by lawyerly subterfuge: "The devil asks what he believes; he replies, 'What the church believes.' Then the devil says, 'What does the church believe?' 'What I believe.' 'What do you believe?' 'What the church believes.'"[7] When Thomas More wrote to Erasmus in December 1526, congratulating him for the pub-

---

[1] Allen, *6*, 179; see also 183, 186–87.

[2] Allen, *6*, 206.

[3] Allen, *6*, 206. For the Latin see p. l, n. 1, below.

[4] Allen, *6*, 209, 351–52.

[5] Allen, *8*, 345. Erasmus' statement is in substantial agreement with More's view of the unity of the reality and symbolism of the sacrament in *A Treatise on the Passion* (*CW 13*, 144–48).

[6] Allen, *8*, 190.

[7] Allen, *10*, 316; repeated in *De preparatione ad mortem*, *ASD 5/1*, 384–85.

lication of *Detectio praestigiarum,* a small pamphlet in which Erasmus protested against sacramentarians' attempts to adopt him as their supporter, More expressed the hope that Erasmus would produce a longer work on the eucharist: ". . . if God ever grants you the free time, I would like eventually to see a treatise in support of our belief flow from that heart of yours, so perfect an instrument for defending the truth. . . ."[1] Erasmus would never write the work More called for, and the reason was probably not lack of time. The real presence was a doctrine that Erasmus came to defend only with the greatest reluctance.

Even if Erasmus had wished to write a full and detailed disquisition on the real presence of Christ in the eucharist, there would not have been much he could have added to the long and learned refutations of Oecolampadius' *De genuina . . . expositione,* published in 1526 and 1527 by Josse Clichtove and John Fisher, except perhaps some nuances and qualifications which would probably not have been acceptable either to the orthodox or to the sacramentarians. But in 1530 Erasmus did give a fuller opinion by proxy, as it were, by publishing at Freiburg a twelfth-century treatise on the eucharist by Alger of Liège[2] entitled *De sacramentis corporis et sanguinis Dominici libri tres.* In a prefatory letter to Bishop Balthasar Mercklin, a trusted councillor of Charles V, Erasmus reasserted the futility of quibbling about thorny questions and stressed the eucharist as a source of unity and spiritual regeneration.[3] Though Alger did not entirely avoid such exotic difficulties as the Stercoranist heresy, Erasmus praised him for his learning, restraint, and devotional fervor. And there were many features of his treatise, especially in the first book, that Erasmus or More might have admired. Although he clearly asserts that the bread and wine of the eucharist are substantially changed into the body and blood of Christ, Alger does not use the word *transubstantiation.* His aim is positive, pastoral instruction. He rarely indulges in polemical dialectics. His arguments are regularly based on a wide range of patristic writings, especially those of Augustine, which he interprets with considerable sensitivity and awareness of their context. His mind is imbued with *consensus fidelium* as the bedrock of belief. Like More he carefully distinguishes the kinds of symbolism and reality in the eucharist. Like Erasmus he emphasizes the eucharist as a sacrament of unity and peace; sincere communicants become " per unitatem spiritualem . . . concorporales et consacramentales

---

[1] Allen, *6,* 443.

[2] A teacher and diocesan administrator at Liège, later an ordained monk at Cluny, Alger died about 1130. For his life and eucharistic doctrine, see Louis Brigué, *Alger de Liège: un théologien de l'eucharistie au début du XII⁰ siècle* (Paris, 1936), pp. 1–112.

[3] Allen, *8,* 377–82.

... Christo."[1] Erasmus had good reason to choose Alger as a useful model of how to present doctrines about the eucharist, though he was doubtless aware that Alger's book would not do much to calm the storms of eucharistic controversy, storms which drove Erasmus himself from Basel in December 1529 and which would rage long after his death.

More's Use of Patristic Evidence in the Eucharistic Controversy

More's polemical writings defending the real presence in the eucharist tend to reflect a more general pattern: eucharistic controversy stimulated and was stimulated by more and more intensive study of the church fathers.[2] At first patristic evidence seemed to be of no special importance in the controversy. In the five German pamphlets that Karlstadt published at Basel during the fall of 1524,[3] he relied on the fathers hardly at all. But then almost no one took his arguments seriously anyway. Melanchthon was not far from the general view of Karlstadt when he said: "Karlstadt was the first one to stir up this storm—a beastly man, without intelligence, without learning, without common sense ...."[4]

Zwingli's first treatise denying the real presence, his letter to Alber (March 1525),[5] and the five learned sacramentarian tracts that he published over the next two years attempt to make sacramentarianism tenable and respectable. But his arguments are primarily biblical and dialectical, not patristic. He insists that *est* in the biblical accounts means *significat* and that *edere* means *credere*, citing analogies from texts about the paschal lamb, manna, circumcision, or Christ as the rock or door or vine. He argues that Christ's physical presence in the eucharist would contradict the truth of his ascension and the union of the divine and human natures in his person. Only in his second eucharistic treatise, the long section of *De vera et falsa religione commentarius* that became the source of *The Souper*, does he give a catena of passages from Tertullian, Augustine,

---

[1] *PL 180*, 750.

[2] An earlier phase of eucharistic controversy between about 800 and 1100 had stimulated a similarly renewed interest in the fathers; see Pelikan, *The Christian Tradition, 3*, 216–23.

[3] See Ronald J. Sider, *Andreas Bodenstein von Karlstadt: The Development of His Thought, 1517–1525*, Studies in Medieval and Reformation Thought 11 (Leiden, 1974), pp. 293–98, and Rupp, pp. 141–48. On Karlstadt's eucharistic tracts and their dates see p. xxii, n. 2, above.

[4] *Philippi Melanthonis opera*, ed. Karl G. Bretschneider and Heinrich E. Bindseil, 28 vols., Corpus Reformatorum 1–28 (Halle/Saale and Braunschweig, 1834–60), *2*, 31 (cited hereafter as *CRM*). Melanchthon's Latin is as follows: "Carolostadius primum excitavit hunc tumultum, homo ferus, sine ingenio, sine doctrina, sine sensu communi. ..."

[5] *Ad Matthaeum Alberum de coena dominica epistola*, in *CRZ 3*, 322–54.

Hilary, Jerome, and Origen.[1] His patristic evidence is not very strong. He himself admits that one passage from Jerome is hardly relevant, and in his next eucharistic treatise five months later he remarks that he had intended to appeal once more to the testimony of the fathers but found it no longer necessary because Oecolampadius had already provided an ample stream of patristic evidence against the real presence.[2]

Oecolampadius was indeed in a better position than Zwingli to bring the fathers fully into the fray[3] and had done so by August 1525 in his famous or notorious *De genuina verborum domini, Hoc est corpus meum, iuxta vetustissimos authores, expositione liber.*[4] In the 1520s Oecolampadius had few rivals in knowledge of the fathers—especially the Greek fathers—perhaps only Melanchthon and Erasmus himself. He had made a compendious index (1520) of Erasmus' great edition of Jerome; before 1525 he had published translations of large parts of Chrysostom, Cyril of Alexandria, and Gregory of Nazianzus. His translation of Theophylactus' commentaries on the four gospels had appeared in 1524.[5] Hence it is not surprising that he relied heavily on copious and wide-ranging quotations from the fathers, attempting to show that the sacramental signs of the eucharist must be distinct from the things they symbolize and have no efficacy in themselves except as occasions for the communicant to increase and demonstrate his faith in Christ's redemptive death. His arguments based on logic and scripture do not go much beyond Zwingli. His insistence that such a miracle as the eucharist is unprecedented in scripture and that later eucharistic miracles are the work of the devil, his rules for deciding when scriptural texts must be taken in a tropological sense, his basic premise that the real presence is impossible, absurd, useless, destructive of belief in Christ's redemptive death and hence incompatible with the wisdom and benevolence of God, none of these had much strength against either Lutheran or Catholic opponents. Moreover, though his style is elegant and suave, the ideational structure of his book is somewhat loose and digressive, for long stretches hardly more than a row of pegs on which to hang a chain of patristic passages. But his patristic evidence and analysis was new, sophisticated, and formidable. At one stroke he had applied the first fruits of Renaissance philology, however embryonic and primitive by modern standards, to a central dispute of the Reformation.

---

[1] *CRZ* 3, 809–15.

[2] *CRZ* 4, 502.

[3] On the patristic knowledge of both Zwingli and Oecolampadius, see Hughes O. Old, *The Patristic Roots of Reformed Worship*, Zürcher Beiträge zur Reformationsgeschichte 5 (Zürich, 1975), pp. 101–08, 111–18.

[4] Staehelin, " Oekolampad-Bibliographie," no. 113.

[5] Old, *Patristic Roots*, pp. 113–18.

Johannes Oecolampadius, by Hans Asper (reduced)

He insisted that spurious works such as pseudo-Cyprian's *De cardinalibus operibus* be pruned away from the writings of the fathers.[1] He denied that two eucharistic works which were assigned to Ambrose and which pretty clearly supported the real presence, were genuinely Ambrose's.[2] In this he was wrong but understandably so, since their authenticity was never firmly established until this century.[3] He berated Peter Lombard and Gratian for not citing more complete and correct texts of the fathers in their catenas on the real presence,[4] though Oecolampadius himself (as his opponents were quick to point out) did not always follow his own good advice. He gave many patristic passages on the proper reception and effects of the eucharist which have little bearing on the real presence.[5] But he was also aware of passages not in Lombard or Gratian which seem to be strongly against him, particularly passages from Tertullian, Irenaeus, Hilary, Cyril, and Chrysostom.[6] To his credit, he quoted these passages, usually fully and fairly, and tried mightily, though often unsuccessfully, to turn them to his side by applying them to the incarnation rather than the real presence or by insisting that the language is hyperbolic or metaphorical. With hindsight we can see that from the beginning the patristic evidence offered considerable holds to both sides so that it was not likely to resolve the dispute. As late as 1913 G. Bareille, in his article on the fathers and the eucharist in the *Dictionnaire de théologie catholique*,[7] was still lining up the passages on both sides and explaining away difficulties and ambiguities, but Bareille's article also shows the enormous advance in patrology which was stimulated to a great extent by eucharistic controversy.

One reason patristic evidence became important so early in the eucharistic controversies is that there are few scriptural texts on the point. The only directly relevant passages are accounts of the Last Supper in the synoptic gospels, the sixth chapter of John's gospel, and some texts in chapters 10 and 11 of Paul's first letter to the Corinthians. Disputes about faith and works or free will and grace could be based primarily on biblical evidence, though patristic interpretation of scripture could hardly be completely ignored. Except for a long passage from Chrysostom,[8]

---

[1] *De genuina ... expositione*, sigs. C_4v, K_1v.

[2] Sigs. B_1, K_1v.

[3] See Dom Bernard Botte's introduction to his edition of Ambrose's *De sacramentis* and *De mysteriis*, Sources chrétiennes 25/2 (Paris, 1961), pp. 7–21.

[4] *De genuina ... expositione*, sigs. K_1–K_2v.

[5] Sigs. F_6–G_3.

[6] Sigs. B_5v, G_3–H_8.

[7] 15 vols. (Paris, 1908–50), 5/1, 1121–83 (cited hereafter as *DTC*).

[8] *Opera omnia, 10*, 1430–35.

Erasmus' *Hyperaspistes diatribae libri duo* defending free will against Luther relies almost entirely on biblical evidence, though there are frequent allusions to the fathers. In fact, Erasmus may have realized very soon that patristic disputation was not likely to settle very much in the eucharistic controversy. In his very pithy and carefully worded opinion of Oecolampadius' *De genuina ... expositione*,[1] he finds the work "doctum": no one could deny it; Oecolampadius brought streams of new patristic evidence to bear on the question. "Disertum": Oecolampadius' style is suave, unctuous, sometimes a bit lubricious. "Elaboratum": certainly, sometimes even excessively, as he works or overworks his texts for all (and sometimes more than) they are worth. But not "pium," because he propounds a dogma against the *consensus fidelium*—a consensus which perhaps cannot be established even by learned patrology, a consensus with which it is dangerous but possible to disagree, at the right time and in the right way and on the right questions—for example, about *how* Christ is physically present in the eucharist.[2] Erasmus consistently refused to answer Oecolampadius, not because he secretly agreed with him in denying the real presence but probably because he believed that neither logical, nor scriptural nor patristic polemics was likely to resolve the issue.[3]

As other opponents, Catholic and Lutheran, plunged boldly and copiously into the melee, the patristic battle grew more intense. In 1525 the theological faculty of the University of Paris condemned Oecolampadius' book, and in 1526 Josse Clichtove, a member of that theological faculty, published an elaborate answer to Oecolampadius entitled *De sacramento eucharistiae, contra Oecolampadium, opusculum* (Paris, 1526).[4] That

---

[1] "... perlegi librum Ioannis Oecolampadii De Verbis coenae Domini, mea sententia doctum, disertum et elaboratum; adderem etiam pium, si quid pium esse posset quod pugnet cum sententia consensuque Ecclesiae: a qua dissentire periculosum esse judico" (Allen, *6*, 206). See p. xlv, above.

[2] See, for example, his prefatory letter to Alger of Liège's *De sacramentis corporis et sanguinis Dominici*, in Allen, *8*, 379–80; and *Moriae encomium*, *ASD 4/3*, 148/403–06, 150/427–32.

[3] For a penetrating analysis of Erasmus' view of the meaning and value of *consensus fidelium*, in regard to doctrine and ecclesiology, see James McConica, "Erasmus and the Grammar of Consent," in *Scrinium Erasmianum*, ed. J. Coppens, 2 vols. (Leiden, 1969), *2*, 77–99.

[4] For a full discussion of Clichtove's pastoral works, his combination of humanism and scholastic theology, and a brief analysis of his eucharistic teaching, see Jean-Pierre Massaut, *Josse Clichtove: l'Humanisme et la reform du clergé*, 2 vols. (Paris, 1968), especially *2*, 313–18. Clichtove mentions the condemnation of Oecolampadius by the Paris faculty of theology on sig. x₅. During the convocation of the diocese of Canterbury held at London between 5 November 1529 and 29 April 1530 a list of heretical books was condemned. Among works by Luther, Zwingli, Melanchthon and others, it included *De genuina ... expositione* and other works by Oecolampadius. (*Concilia Magnae Britanniae et Hiberniae ab anno MCCCL ad annum MDXLV*, ed. David Wilkins, 4 vols. (London, 1737; reprint Brussels, 1964), *3*, 720.

DE SACRAMENTO

EVCHARISTIAE, CONTRA OECO
lampadium, opufculū:per Iudocum Clich
toueum Neoportuenfem, doctorem theo‑
logum Parifiensem, elaboratum: duos li‑
bros complectens.

¶Primus, multiplici authoritate & ratione
comprobat: fub forma panis & vini in eu‑
chariftia, verum Chrifti corpus & fangui‑
nem, re ipfa contineri.

¶Secundus, rationes Oecolampadij, conten‑
dentes in pane & vino confecrato figuram
tantum effe & repræfentationem corporis
& fanguinis Chrifti: diffoluit.

Conuentus Graánopolitani VdJ4 Prædicatox

Lum Priuilegio.

PARISIIS
Ex officina Simonis Colinæi.
1 5 2 6

Title page of Josse Clichtove, *De sacramento eucharistiae*, Paris, 1526 (reduced)

John Fisher, by Holbein (reduced)

the *opusculum* or "little work" consists of 330 packed pages followed by a
25-page index gives an idea of the grand scale on which theological
learning was executed in those days. But Clichtove is not wordy, much
less so than Oecolampadius. And his plan is orderly: one book devoted to
propounding and establishing the real presence by scripture, canon law,
the fathers, and the liturgy; and a second book refuting thirty-five specific
points asserted by Oecolampadius. His refutations show that many of
Oecolampadius' arguments were hardly new and that some were merely
frivolous. But he relies on many authorities whom Oecolampadius would
hardly accept, such as Anselm of Canterbury, Hugh of St. Victor, and
Thomas Aquinas. For the fathers, he relies partly, but not exclusively, on
Gratian's collection.[1] On the other hand, his evidence from the history
and texts of the liturgy was important and too often neglected.[2] And his
plan of positive exposition followed by negative refutation was successful;
More did the same in *The Answer to a Poisoned Book*.[3]

The next Catholic reply to Oecolampadius, John Fisher's exhaustive
and exhausting *De veritate corporis et sanguinis Christi in eucharistia*
(completed in 1526 and published at Cologne the following year), probes
more deeply into the fathers. Apart from the long prologues to each of the
five books, Fisher quoted Oecolampadius piece by piece, answering each
piece as he went—the same method More himself used in such works as
Responsio ad Lutherum and *The Confutation of Tyndale's Answer*. The method
has the appearance of dialogue, since the passages are labeled alternately
"OECOLAMPADIVS" and "ROFFENSIS" (or Rochester, of which
Fisher was the bishop). (Oecolampadius, by the way, is printed in black-
letter and Fisher in a sleeker roman typeface.) And Fisher does usually
address himself to his opponent in the second person. But this method can
be almost as devastating to the reader as to the victim, especially without
any relief through banter or merry tales.

Fisher's knowledge of the fathers, Latin and Greek, was wide and
deep,[4] and he had apparently made a special search for books and manuscripts on the eucharist among his fellow bishops, since he mentions that
Warham had given him Lanfranc's book against Berengarius and that
Tunstall had sent him the Greek liturgy of the mass by Basil.[5] He relent-

---

[1] For example, sigs. e_6v–f_5.

[2] On this point see Jaroslav Pelikan, *Development of Christian Doctrine: Some Historical Prole-
gomena* (New Haven and London, 1969), p. 50.

[3] Clichtove, like More, also describes sacramentarianism as poison; see *De sacramento
eucharistiae*, sigs. a_3, a_4, a_7v, a_8v, g_5, g_7, q_2.

[4] See Edward Surtz, S.J., *The Works and Days of John Fisher* (Cambridge, Mass., 1967),
pp. 111–13.

[5] Sigs. P_4v, Q_1. Fisher also mentions (sig. a_3v) that Cochlaeus had pointed out to him an
argument propounded by Abbot Rupert of Deutz.

lessly and sometimes repetitively exposes every deficiency of Oecolampadius in presenting or interpreting patristic texts—for the reader who has
the energy or the patience to hold out to the end.[1]

More interesting and more readable than the polemical dialogue are
the prefaces to the five books, which are lengthy essays addressed to the
reader. The first argues that immorality and dissension among the heretics expose their errors—a standard argument against the reformers but
one with a special relevance to the eucharist, since the bitter dispute
between the Lutherans and the Zwinglians about the real presence had
already begun in 1525 and would grow more and more bitter until it
became clear at the Marburg Colloquy of 1529 that no agreement could
be reached.[2] Fisher's second preface on the implications of the various
names of the eucharist is paralleled by More's treatment of the same
subject in his *Treatise on the Passion*.[3] The third preface consists of fourteen
proofs of the real presence, the third of which is the *consensus patrum*. Here
Fisher chooses only three prime examples, since he intended to give more
complete and detailed evidence from the fathers in the fourth preface. Of
the three—Chrysostom, Cyril of Alexandria, and Cyprian—the first two
are also the fathers on whom More relies most heavily in his *Answer to a
Poisoned Book*. The fourth preface, devoted entirely to past witnesses to the
real presence, is divided into five periods of 300 years each, extending
from 1500 back to the birth of Christ. The three periods from 600 to 1500
are comparatively brief, and Oecolampadius would hardly accept the
testimony of scholastic theologians like Aquinas, Bonaventure, Scotus, or
Ockham. But Fisher's strategy is to stress the continuity of church teaching right up to his times and to reject the unhistorical idea, propounded
by some of the reformers, that in 700 or 900 or 1100 the institutional
church became completely corrupt and remained so until the Reformation. Certainly the survey shows the naiveté of Oecolampadius' assertion that Peter Lombard in the middle of the twelfth century plunged the
church into the abysm of error about the real presence.[4] For the period
between the birth of Christ and the year 600, Fisher gave many passages
from Greek and Latin fathers, including again Cyril and Chrysostom, but
many of these passages do not clearly and unambiguously assert the real
presence, so that Oecolampadius might have interpreted some of them as
consonant with his own position. The fifth preface is devoted to showing
that the sixth chapter of John predicts the institution of the eucharist, a

---

[1] See Surtz, *Works and Days of Fisher*, pp. 341–45.

[2] See p. xxv, above.

[3] *CW 13*, 152–56.

[4] "Is [Petrus Lombardus] enim est, qui nos simul in barathrum erroris praecipitauit"
(*De genuina . . . expositione*, sig. A$_2$v).

point that was strenuously and repeatedly denied by Luther and Zwingli as well as Oecolampadius and which was to be the main subject of More's *Answer to a Poisoned Book*. Fisher, like More, quotes several fathers but relies most heavily on the clear testimony of Cyril and Chrysostom.

Oecolampadius never answered the replies of Clichtove or Fisher, though he did exchange a series of volleys and countervolleys with Willibald Pirckheimer in 1526 and 1527. He was busy between 1526 and 1529 trying to placate the Lutherans.[1] The failure of the Marburg Colloquy between Zwingli and Oecolampadius on the one side and Luther and Melanchthon on the other led Melanchthon to break his public silence by publishing a short letter to Oecolampadius in April 1529[2] admonishing him in a friendly spirit that much of his patristic evidence on the real presence was ambiguous and that Oecolampadius had cleverly twisted some of it to his own advantage. Melanchthon added that only clear passages should be cited and that, if they were, it would become clear that the preponderance of patristic testimony favored the real presence. In 1530 Melanchthon followed his own suggestion by publishing a catena of twelve substantial passages from the fathers clearly in favor of the real presence.[3] Two of these are from Cyril, three from Chrysostom, and two from Theophylactus[4]—the very fathers More stressed in his *Answer to a Poisoned Book*.

In the same year Oecolampadius replied to Melanchthon's brief treatise with a long patristic dialogue entitled *Dialogus ... Quid de eucharistia veteres. ... tum Graeci, tum Latini senserint ....*[5] Nathaniel, the straight man of the piece, meets Oecolampadius and expresses his concern that not merely papists like Clichtove, Faber, and Fisher have attacked Oecolampadius' doctrine on the eucharist, but also Erasmus and Melanchthon. Nathaniel reads Melanchthon's printed letter aloud while Oecolampadius checks it against the original, and then Oecolampadius reads his reply to Nathaniel, who duly gives its main points afterwards. Then Nathaniel is instructed to read Melanchthon's catena, which is completely reprinted, while Oecolampadius goes off to get his collection of patristic passages on the eucharist. When he returns he recites and explains to Nathaniel many new passages and attempts to refute those of Melanchthon. He concludes by instructing the long-suffering Nathaniel on a point raised by Melanch-

---

[1] Ernst Staehelin, *Das theologische Lebenswerk Johannes Oekolampads*, Quellen und Forschungen zur Reformationsgeschichte 21 (Leipzig, 1939), pp. 287–300, 308–27, 598–611.

[2] *CRM 1*, 1048–50.

[3] *Sententiae veterum aliquot scriptorum de coena Domini* (Wittenberg, 1530; *CRM 23*, 734–52).

[4] *CRM 23*, 734–39.

[5] Staehelin, "Oekolampad-Bibliographie," no. 164. I cite the Heidelberg edition of 1572 (Staehelin, no. 218).

thon about a passage from Augustine given by Gratian on the necessity of Christ's body being in only one place. Melanchthon had made it clear that in its original context it did not refer to Christ's presence in the eucharist at all, but rather to Christ's visible presence on earth as a preacher.[1] Oecolampadius worries the point at length, insisting that the multilocality of Christ's body would attribute divinity to a creature or undermine the true physical humanity of Christ.[2] Oecolampadius' new patristic evidence does not really advance the argument and he hardly succeeds in reinterpreting the passages Melanchthon had quoted. But four years of disputation have caused him to temper and refine his eucharistic theology far beyond the simpler views of his first sacramentarian treatise, *De genuina ... expositione*. He now admits that Christ is more fully present in New Testament figures than in the figures of the Old Testament, that Christ is truly present in the sacrament in the sense that he is truly present in the believing mind of the recipient through the operation of the Holy Spirit, that the sacrament can be reserved and taken to the sick, and that both the worthy and the unworthy receive the sacrament.[3] It was through this book rather than through his *De genuina ... expositione* that Oecolampadius influenced the eucharistic theology of Frith and Cranmer.[4]

Keeping in mind these major eruptions of patristic argumentation, we can now turn our attention to Thomas More's use of the fathers in the eucharistic controversy. More first treated the subject in 1523 in *Responsio ad Lutherum*, his answer to Luther's attack on Henry VIII's *Assertio septem sacramentorum*. To support transubstantiation Henry had quoted brief passages from Hugh of St. Victor and six earlier authorities, including Ambrose, Augustine, Cyril, and Gregory of Nyssa.[5] With the exception of Hugh, however, all of Henry's passages can be found in Gratian's *Decretum* or Aquinas' *Catena aurea*; Henry, or whoever helped gather his evidence, had no direct recourse to the fathers themselves. In his reply to Henry, Luther rejected the passage from Ambrose out of hand and

---

[1] *CRM 23*, 744–48.

[2] *Quid veteres senserint*, sigs. P₃-Q₃.

[3] *Quid veteres senserint*, sigs. I₅-I₇, O₇-O₈, Q₄, Q₅(missigned P₅), Q₆v.

[4] Peter Brooks, *Thomas Cranmer's Doctrine of the Eucharist: An Essay in Historical Development* (New York, 1965), pp. 90–91.

[5] *Assertio septem sacramentorum* (London, 1521; *STC* 13078), sigs. c₂, e₂v–e₃v. The passages from Ambrose, Eusebius, Emiscenus, and Augustine can be found in Gratian's *Decretum* De consecratione 2.74; 2.35; and 2.41; *CIC I*, 1325, 1328, 1344. The passages from Gregory of Nyssa and Cyril are in Aquinas' *Catena aurea* on Luke 22, *Opera omnia*, vols. 11–12 (Parma, 1861–62), pp. 227–28 (cited hereafter as "*Catena aurea*"). The passage Henry assigns to Theophilus is ascribed to Theophylactus in the *Catena aurea* on Mark 14, p. 423.

Philip Melanchthon, by Holbein (reduced)

ignored the others entirely. More pointed this out, with the usual measure of scorn, but he himself employed no patristic evidence against Luther.[1] In the *Babylonian Captivity* of 1520 Luther had already firmly rejected the *consensus patrum* when it conflicted with the truth of scripture,[2] and he did so even more vehemently in his book against Henry in 1522: "The word of God is above all things. The majesty of God causes me not to care if a thousand Augustines, a thousand Cyprians, a thousand Henrician churches stand against me."[3] It is a measure of the vastly greater importance of patristic testimony after the disputes of the late 1520s that Luther himself defended the real presence in 1532 and 1543 by an emphatic appeal to the *consensus patrum*.[4]

Apart from various passing remarks which show More was aware of the main continental figures in the eucharistic controversy, he wrote nothing on the subject until 1532, when he composed his brief letter against John Frith's *A christen sentence and true iudgement of the moste honorable Sacrament of Christes body & bloude. ...*[5] The only patristic evidence Frith gives is a single sentence, quoted incompletely from Augustine with no specific source: "Corpus in quo resurrexit in vno loco esse oporteth [sic]."[6] More complained, and any frustrated editor can sympathize with him, that "to seke out one lyne in all hys bokes, were to go loke a nedle in a medew."[7] In fact the sentence was the last sentence in a farago of Augustinian texts combined by Gratian,[8] the same passage Melanchthon had refuted by placing it in its proper context. Being unable to locate it, More simply accepted it as possibly genuine and refuted it on the logical grounds that having to be in one place does not necessarily preclude being in many

---

[1] *CW 5*, 447, 821. More had, however, given as his fourth postulate that when the interpretation of scripture is disputed, the consistent agreement of the fathers and the faith of the church should be accepted (*CW 5*, 300/5–9).

[2] *WA 6*, 524.

[3] "Dei verbum est super omnia, Divina maiestas mecum facit, ut nihil curem, si mille Augustini, mille Cypriani, mille Ecclesiae Henricianae contra me starent" (*WA 10/2*, 215; quoted in *CW 8*, Commentary at 623/30–624/5). For a summary of Luther's view of the fathers, see Bengt Hägglund, "Verständnis und Autorität der altkirchlichen Tradition in der lutherischen Theologie der Reformationszeit bis zum Ende der 17. Jahrhunderts," in *Tradition in Lutheranism and Anglicanism*, Oecumenica 1971/72, pp. 35–39.

[4] Peter Fraenkel, "Ten Questions Concerning Melanchthon, the Fathers, and the Eucharist," in *Luther and Melanchthon in The History and Theology of the Reformation*, ed. V. Vajta (Philadelphia, 1961), p. 161.

[5] First printed in London, 1548 (*STC* 5190).

[6] *A Christian Sentence*, sig. A$_4$v.

[7] *A Letter against Frith*, sig. e$_3$v.

[8] *Decretum*, De consecratione 2.44 (*CIC 1*, 1330).

and on the philological grounds that *oportere* may denote expedience, not necessity.[1]

In 1533, while More was waiting for Frith's reply, *The Souper of the Lorde*, by "a nameless heretic" as More called him, was smuggled into England. In December of that year More published his reply to the part on John 6, entitled *The Answer to the First Part of the Poisoned Book ...*, and at the same time released for sale his *Letter against Frith*. More dubbed the author of *The Souper of the Lorde* "Master Masker" because of the shameless chicanery and juggling he allows himself under the mask of anonymity. Indeed the Masker silently cribbed his whole section on John 6 from Zwingli's *De vera et falsa religione*, translating sporadically, omitting more difficult points, interjecting here and there his own naive reflections and raucous raillery.[2] In a way, the poor quality of the Masker's book was a blessing in disguise because it made it unnecessary and undesirable to quote and refute him piece by piece as More had done with worthier opponents like Luther, Tyndale, and St. German. Instead he begins by translating the eucharistic part of John 6 in full and devotes over two-fifths of his book to a detailed, continuous exposition of this passage, bolstered by long translations from the fathers. Only then does he refute the Masker's exposition, his exegetical principles, his attempted defence of Frith, and his ludicrous (if not fraudulent) attempt to catch More in two inconsistencies. For the earlier part of his exegesis, which covers a passage in John 6 that is not primarily eucharistic, More is usually content to follow his normal method of relying on the *Glossa ordinaria* or Aquinas' *Catena aurea* for patristic evidence, often giving only a paraphrase.[3] But beginning with the verse "And the bread which I shall give you is my flesh which I shall give for the life of the world," More reinforces his exposition with long translations directly from the major patristic commentators on John 6.

Among the Latin fathers this was above all Augustine, together with Bede and Alcuin, who relied heavily on him. But Augustine was the most problematical of all the fathers on the question of the real presence.[4] Passages could be cited from him on both sides, and Melanchthon had omitted him entirely from his catena of unambiguous patristic passages

---

[1] *A Letter against Frith*, sig. e₄v. See Richard Marius, "The Pseudonymous Patristic Text in Thomas More's Confutation," *Moreana*, *15–16* (1967), 257–59; and Richard Schoeck, "The Use of St. John Chrysostom in Sixteenth-Century Controversy: Christopher St. German and Sir Thomas More in 1533," *Harvard Theological Review*, *54* (1961), 21–27.

[2] *CRZ 3*, 776–84. See Appendix A, pp. 299–300.

[3] In this part he does translate one long passage from Augustine; but he could have found it in the *Catena aurea* (see the Commentary at 39/1–16).

[4] See, for example, Pelikan, *The Christian Tradition*, *1*, 304–05.

supporting the real presence. Two passages from Augustine's commentary on John 6 had become watchwords of the sacramentarians: "Believe and you have eaten" and "To believe in him, that is to eat the living bread."[1] From Augustine's commentary on John 6 More drew the ideas that when the Jews murmured at Christ's saying he would give them his flesh to eat, they thought he meant he would give it in dead pieces like meat in a butcher shop, and that Christ's saying "The flesh profits nothing" refers only to his flesh without his spirit.[2] He also translated passages from other works of Augustine to show that the wicked, in particular Judas, also receive the body of Christ in the eucharist, though they do not receive his spirit.[3]

Because of difficulties with Augustine, More turned to the three leading Greek commentators on John's gospel, who had recently been printed in Latin translations: Cyril of Alexandria, John Chrysostom, and Theophylactus.[4] In this he was following the strategy of Melanchthon, who relied heavily on the same three.[5] More quoted only one passage from Theophylactus (52/9–33), who is so irrefragably clear about the real presence that Oecolampadius did not even attempt to reinterpret him but simply rejected him as flatly wrong.[6] But since Theophylactus was comparatively late—eleventh century—he did not have the prestige of Cyril and Chrysostom. More's translations from Cyril total about 1700 words; those from Chrysostom, about 1600. For his exposition of John 6, More relies on Cyril, translating only one passage from Chrysostom,[7] whom he keeps in reserve for the next three shorter books against the Masker.[8] In Books 2

---

[1] Pontien Polman, *L'élement historique dans la controverse religieuse de XVIe siècle* (Gembloux, 1932), pp. 60–61.

[2] 80/25–30, 82/33–83/6.

[3] 73/38–74/35, 75/17–35. More was countering a passage given by Frith, not in his *Christian Sentence* but in his *Answer to M. mores lettur*, which More must have seen in manuscript form sometime after he began his *Answer to a Poisoned Book*. Frith quoted the passage not directly from Augustine, but from Prosper, *Liber sententiarum* (see the Commentary at 73/17–22).

[4] Cyril (1528) and Chrysostom (1530) were translated by George of Trebizond, and Theophylactus (1524, 1525, 1527, 1528) was translated by Oecolampadius himself. Origen's commentary on John's gospel, which lacks the part on chapter 6, had not yet been printed (*PG 14*, 16–17).

[5] Melanchthon quoted Theophylactus on Mark and Matthew rather than on John (*CRM 23*, 739–40), but the passages are very similar to More's (52/9–33). He also gave one of the same Cyril passages (*CRM 23*, 734–35) and one of the same Chrysostom passages (*CRM 23*, 737–38) that More translated (63/32–65/21, 173/28–175/4).

[6] *Quid veteres senserint*, sigs. O₃–O₃v.

[7] 93/7–33.

[8] At the end of Book 3, More himself says he is keeping some passages in reserve (148/12–16).

and 3 More translates two striking passages from other works of Chrysostom, and in Book 4 he translates the longest passage of all, a stunningly beautiful section from Chrysostom's commentary on John 6.[1]

More's use of patristic evidence in *The Answer to a Poisoned Book* is strikingly different from what he had done in his polemical works up to this time. With one exception he had usually contented himself with giving lists of fathers supporting a position, without citing specific works or translating passages.[2] The single exception is his long *Confutation of Tyndale's Answer* (1532–1533), where, taking his cue from Fisher, he translated a long series of passages from the fathers to defend the doctrine that tradition apart from scripture has binding authority.[3] It is easy to see why this issue, like the eucharist, would call forth detailed patristic evidence, but in *The Confutation* More is far less careful in his use of the fathers than he is in *The Answer to a Poisoned Book*.[4] In *The Confutation* the passages he translated are usually short,[5] and he was willing to excerpt a passage from a work falsely attributed to Augustine which had been branded as pseudonymous by both Luther and Erasmus.[6] He cited Jerome from Gratian rather than from the original text,[7] whereas in *The Answer to a Poisoned Book* he always translates from the latest editions.[8] Of the eleven passages More translates from Cyril and Chrysostom, two could have been taken from Fisher;[9] two could have come from Oecolampadius;[10] one could have come from Fisher or Oecolampadius;[11] and one, from Fisher, Oecolampadius, or Clichtove.[12] But five of them do not appear in

---

[1] 172/28–175/9.

[2] See the Introduction to *CW 6*, 526–30.

[3] *CW 8*, 368–75. See also patristic translations on the same point in *CW 8*, 354, 736–38, 867–68, 933–35, 960–61, 975–78.

[4] See Richard Marius, "Thomas More and the Early Church Fathers," *Traditio, 24* (1968), 379–407; reprinted in *Essential Articles*, pp. 402–20.

[5] The single exception is a long passage from Augustine's *Confessions* (*CW 8*, 372–74).

[6] Marius, "The Pseudonymous Patristic Text in More's *Confutation*," *Moreana, 15–16* (1967), 254–56.

[7] *CW 8*, 917–18.

[8] More translated a passage from Chrysostom on the Epistles to the Hebrews directly from the recent editions (see the Commentary at 116/8–25 and 117/13–15), but he notes that it is substantially repeated in Gratian, who assigned it to Ambrose.

[9] 71/10–31, 172/28–175/4 (Fisher, *De veritate*, sigs. S_6, F_3v, X_3–X_3v).

[10] 63/32–65/21, 66/22–67/13 (Oecolampadius, *Quid veteres senserint*, sigs. C_5v–C_7, C_7–C_7v).

[11] 72/14–18 (Fisher, *De veritate*, sig. R_3v; Oecolampadius, *Quid veteres senserint*, sig. C_5).

[12] 116/8–25 (Fisher, *De veritate*, sig. H_3v; Oecolampadius, *De genuina ... expositione*, sig. C_4v; Clichtove, sig. n_8). But all three lack the opening question "Quid ergo nos?" which is translated by More.

any of the three.[1] The precision and profusion of patristic evidence on the eucharist made it unwise to rely on secondary sources (though some continued to do so),[2] and More clearly returned *ad fontes*.

The same cannot be said for the Masker. He gives no patristic evidence whatever in his exposition of John 6, presumably because he found none in Zwingli, but in the second part of his book he accuses More of attacking Oecolampadius' use of the fathers in a book which in fact More had not written. More was supposed to have accused Oecolampadius of adding to and subtracting from the language of the fathers. To defend Oecolampadius, the Masker quoted and translated three short passages from Tertullian, Augustine and Chrysostom.[3] The passage from Tertullian appears in Oecolampadius' *De genuina ... expositione*, though the Masker omits a genuine seven-word clause given by Oecolampadius. The passage from Augustine was given by Oecolampadius in his dialogue against Melanchthon, but the Masker, like Oecolampadius, makes his point by bringing together sentences separated by over 700 words in their original context. The Masker's passage supposedly from Chrysostom had appeared in Oecolampadius' dialogue, but what the Masker gives is four words by Chrysostom followed by Oecolampadius' explanation, which the Masker sets forth as if it were Chrysostom's own words.[4] More was surely right when he said: "And where he bringeth forth for hym in his seconde parte, Austayne, Tertullyan, and saynte Chrysostom (For in all this his fyrst course he bryngeth forth neuer one) those thre dysshes I warraunt you shall whan I come to them, but barely furnysshe hys borde" (136/33–137/2).

More intended to answer not only the second half of the Masker's book, but also Barnes on utraquism and Frith's answer to More's *Letter against Frith*.[5] Frith's answer to More is a long work filled with quotations from the fathers, mostly but not entirely borrowed from Oecolampadius,[6] and More's answer to it would probably have been lengthy and laborious. But in April 1534, about four months after the publication of *The Answer to a Poisoned Book*, More himself was imprisoned and none of the projected answers to the Masker, Barnes, or Frith was ever written. Instead More incorporated his last discussion of the eucharist in his theological *Treatise*

---

[1] 83/16–35, 92/18–93/4, 93/7–33, 94/12–15, 140/15–33.
[2] See S. L. Greenslade, *The English Reformers and the Fathers of the Church* (Oxford, 1960), pp. 13–16.
[3] Appendix A, pp. 332–34.
[4] See the Commentary at 136/33–137/2.
[5] 73/1–5, 135/19–21, 221/26–222/5.
[6] See the Commentary at 221/26–222/5.

on the Passion,[1] which he began before he was imprisoned but continued working on in the Tower.[2] Here, as in *A Dialogue of Comfort*, More renounced polemical refutation. Instead, he presented three general principles of eucharistic interpretation and analyzed the *sacramentum et res* of the eucharist, interweaving the main scriptural texts but translating only one patristic passage from Augustine's commentary on John 6. He also discussed the implications of the many names given to the sacrament by the fathers. Twenty-four pages long in the Yale edition, it is a brilliant piece of technical exposition in English, remarkably compact and subtle, partly because More was aware of the multifarious difficulties and objections and constructed it in such a way as to counter them without explicitly refuting them, usually without even mentioning them. *A Treatise on the Passion*, which is unfinished,[3] ends with a catena of twenty passages from the fathers, in Latin and English, supporting the real presence.[4] The catena exists in two forms: one in the 1557 *English Works* and one in a British Library manuscript.[5] And More was not responsible for its final form, perhaps not even for all the English translations, for there is a Latin note in the British Library manuscript from More to some assistant, probably his secretary John Harris, which may be translated:

> Insert here the words of the saints which seem suitable and first take those which seem suitable from the *Catena aurea* on the Lord's supper in Matthew 26, Mark 14, and Luke 22. Insert them in Latin and translate them. Then put in whatever it seems should be added from those places which we collected a while ago, those which are clear and which have not been published in the book which we published before on the Lord's Supper.[6]

The book More refers to on the Lord's Supper is *The Answer to a Poisoned*

---

[1] *CW 13*, 137–60. Germain Marc'hadour (*Thomas More et la Bible*, Paris, 1969, pp. 311–12) suggests that this treatise was in effect an unpolemical answer to the second half of *The Souper of the Lorde*. On the importance of the eucharist for More as a juncture of the flesh and spirit, see Louis L. Martz, "Thomas More: The Sacramental Life," *Thought*, 52 (1977), 300–18.

[2] See *CW 13*, xxxix–xl.

[3] On the link between *A Treatise on the Passion* and *A Treatise to Receive the Blessed Body*, see Louis L. Martz, "Thomas More: The Tower Works," in *St. Thomas More: Action and Contemplation*, ed. Richard S. Sylvester (New Haven and London, 1972), pp. 69–75.

[4] *CW 13*, 160–77. Of all the passages as they are given in the 1557 *English Works*, only two appear in the *Catena aurea* and those two only in redactions which are shorter than More's or different from his. Only six of More's patristic passages appear in Gratian; of the six, all but one of Gratian's redactions are briefer than More's or inferior to his.

[5] *CW 13*, 178–88.

[6] For the Latin, see *CW 13*, 160.

Book, and the note shows that he had selected the patristic evidence for that book from a larger catena that he had prepared.

Thus More's example reveals how eucharistic controversy encouraged a wider, more detailed, and more accurate use of patristic texts. But it also shows that Reformation polemics did not always advance the understanding of the fathers through the best of Renaissance philology, represented, for example, by Erasmus' *New Testament* and Saint Jerome, Vives's *City of God*, and the work done on many classical authors. For the controversialists rifled the fathers to gather catenas or armories of excerpts. Zwingli,[1] Melanchthon,[2] and Oecolampadius as well as More had constructed such catenas, and later apologists such as Jewel would do the same.[3] One manuscript catena of patristic passages on the eucharist, compiled in England in the late sixteenth century and now preserved at Concordia Seminary in St. Louis, grew to mammoth proportions, 1,680 folio pages.[4] The use of such *loci communes* was what would now be called a retrieval system, useful and probably necessary, not to be scorned. But it was often a hindrance to seeing the fathers steady and seeing them whole. Nevertheless, religious controversy about the eucharist caused More to translate into English for the first time and from the latest Renaissance editions, long passages from Cyril and Chrysostom. And eucharistic polemics, in spite of all their wearisome repetition and rancor, helped to recover and restore the great and varied treasure of patristic thought and eloquence.

II. THE ARGUMENT OF THE BOOK

Exposition and Theology in Book I

T
He Answer to a Poisoned Book is the last of the swift and steady stream of polemical works that More wrote after resigning the chancellorship in

---

[1] Rudolf Staehelin, *Huldreich Zwingli: Sein Leben und Werken*, 2 vols. (Basel, 1895–97), 2, 223.

[2] Peter Fraenkel, *Testimonia Patrum: The Function of the Patristic Argument in the Theology of Philip Melanchthon*, Travaux d'Humanisme et Renaissance 46 (Geneva, 1961), pp. 44, 47. Melanchthon had made such a collection as early as January 28, 1525; *Supplementa Melanchthoniana*, ed. Otto Clemen, 6 vols. (Leipzig, 1910–26), 6/1, 277–78.

[3] William P. Haugaard, "Renaissance Patristic Scholarship and Theology in Sixteenth-century England," *Sixteenth-Century Journal*, 10/3 (1979), 54–55. See also p. lix, n. 2, above.

[4] J. R. Brink, "'Fortres of Fathers': An Unpublished Sixteenth-century Manuscript Relating to Patristic Writing on the Eucharist," *Sixteenth-Century Journal*, 10/1 (1979), 83–87.

1532. By spring 1533 he had completed *A Letter against Frith*, *The Apology*, and the second half of *The Confutation*. That summer he dashed off *The Debellation of Salem and Bizance*, and More tells us that he had plans for two other works: a reply to Barnes on the question of utraquism and a rebuttal of Frith's *Answer*. But as an increasing number of Protestant books slipped into England and as More's own relations with the crown grew strained, he had to focus his efforts more narrowly. In the late summer of 1533 the task of answering *The Souper of the Lorde* clearly took priority over any other polemical engagements. Answering the first half of *The Souper* took priority over answering the second. And the "books" of *The Answer to a Poisoned Book* are themselves laid out by priority—a plan that More follows in no other polemical work. First and most important, More sets forth the correct interpretation of John 6, presenting his own exposition in Book 1, criticizing the Masker's exposition in Book 2, and examining the Masker's general arguments against the received interpretation in Book 3. In Book 4 More replies to the Masker's objections to *A Letter against Frith*; in the fifth and final book, he quickly considers two places where the Masker had accused him of contradicting himself. The argument of *The Answer to a Poisoned Book* thus proceeds from revelation to quarrel, from the all-important work of showing the truth of the received interpretation of John 6 to the settling of a personal disagreement. Before defending himself, More must show how John 6 clearly presents the doctrine of the real presence of Christ in the Lord's Supper, the essential Christian nourishment that the Masker's poisonous exposition would take away.

The "whole somme" (16/2, 33) of the Masker's exposition, More claims, is that Christ's words in John 6 about the giving of his flesh and the eating of his flesh may be applied *only* to the gift of his body in the passion and to the faith of his believers, which they consume as the spiritual food of their souls (16/2–17/6). More's disagreement with the Masker centers upon the "only," for in John 6 Christ does not merely allude to the passion and the fruits of faith, but describes "the very bodyly eatyng & drinkyng of his very fleshe and bloude in dede" (20/29–30). The Masker's exposition, "all though there were not one false word therin / yet were it in dyssemblynge of the trouth, very lewd and falsely handelyd" (20/33–34). The Masker limits John 6 to a single, secondary, allegorical sense. He discards the literal foundation of the text. He presents his own reading as the sole truth, excluding the wealth of interpretation handed down in the church. The Masker's exposition is thus a mere "pageaunt" (18/8), the empty form of biblical exposition. He diminishes and perverts the richness of scripture. More's first order of business, then, is to provide an exposition that will restore to John 6 the full richness of significance that centuries of careful expositors have found in it. Here alone in his polemical works More uses exposition as his weapon of choice. He sets forth traditional eucharistic theology through sound and thorough biblical exegesis, confronting the sacramentarians on the ground that reformers wished to expropriate as theirs alone—scripture.

More prefaces his exposition with a reminder of the richness of scripture. The Masker sees only one sense, but to More scripture presents a profusion of significance through which God enriches man's spiritual knowledge.[1] More describes the four traditional levels of biblical interpretation not so much in order to lay out a rigid hermeneutical scheme as to suggest how the manifold senses of scripture are a reflection of the immensity of God and the unity of his revelation:

> It is I trow good readers to no man almost vnknowen, that the holy scrypture of god is in suche meruelous maner, by the profound wysedome of his holy spyryte, for ye more plentuouse profyte of his chyrche, deuised, indyghted, and wryten, that it hath not onely that one sense trewe which we call the litterall sence (that is to wytte that sence whiche for the fyrst lesson therof, god wold we shold perceiue and lerne) but also diuerse other sensys spirytuall, pertaynynge to the profyte of our maners, and instruccions in sundry vertues, by meane of allegoryes, openyng of misteries, and lyftynge vppe of the soule into ye lyuely lyght and inward hygh sighte of god. And all those manyfold senses (diuers in the waye and all tendynge to one ende) maye be conuenient and trew, and all by one spyryte prouyded, and in to diuerse spyrites by the same one spyrite inspyred, for spyrituall profite to be by many meanes multyplyed and encreaced in hys chyrche. [17/27–18/6]

More's stress in his exposition falls upon the literal sense of John 6. In order to rebut the Masker, he shows that Christ referred literally to the eating of his flesh in the eucharist and that all secondary readings must proceed from the literal. But he does not lose sight of the richness of scripture or of its unity of purpose, "all tendynge to one ende." After presenting the passage in a straightforward translation, More examines it piece by piece, showing in considerable detail how it concerns such complex and diverse doctrines as *fides formata* and free will. He seems particularly interested—and particularly skilled—in explaining the motivations of the words spoken by Christ and the incredulous apostles. He does not harp upon the single string of the literal exposition of the real presence in John 6. Indeed he begins, with a touch of irony, by suggesting an "allegorical" meaning for the ships in John 6 : 17–23 (21/8–19).

---

[1] More often remarked that difficulties in scripture were a healthy challenge to men of intelligence; see *De Tristitia, CW 14*, text and Commentary at 13/7–15/1.

More is concerned not with the literal sense alone but with the full coherence of figure and reality in the eucharist and in the scripture concerning it. And in the richness of John 6, More sees a structural unity that reflects the unity of its theological truth. In chapter 13 of Book 1 (the center of his own exposition) More presents what he sees as the cardinal feature of John 6: the chapter turns upon the manifold significance of the "bread" that Christ promised his apostles. In John 6 : 27–50 Jesus explains to the apostles the "bread of his godhead," that is, the spiritual knowledge of God that they will possess in the beatific vision and that God gives them now in the incarnation, feeding them through faith with spiritual doctrine. In the rest of John 6, Christ tells his apostles that he will give his own body to be eaten in the form of bread:

> . . . he telleth them now that he wyll not onely geue them that brede to fede vppon, by fruycyon of the byholdynge face to face whan the tyme shall come, as he hath also gyuen yt theym in one maner all redy by his incarnacyon to fede them spyrytually in the meane whyle by spyrytuall doctryne / but that the brede that he wyll geue them to fede vppon, shall besyde that be his owne flesshe, euyn the very same that he wyll geue for the lyfe of the worlde / menynge that he wolde veryly geue men the same very flesshe to eate and fede vppon, bothe bodyly and spyritually in remembraunce of his deth, that he wold for mannys redempcyon veryly geue to deth, and veryly for a sacryfyce offre vp to god by deth. [50/32–51/8]

In the bread of John 6, then, More finds a dynamic coherence: the bread of godhead and the bread of Christ's flesh, the figure of his sacrifice and the reality of his presence, spiritual food and bodily eating all coincide. In the multiplication of loaves and fishes at the beginning of John 6, Christ merely "towched" (49/36) upon the full meaning of this bread; in the following sections of John 6 he presents it explicitly; and in the eucharistic miracle of incorporation—which emerges in the course of Book 1 as the most important aspect of the eucharist—the spirit and the body, the faithful and God, the sign and the reality become one.

Recognizing the theological underpinnings that More sees in John 6 makes the task of reading his sometimes diffuse exposition somewhat easier. In chapters 6 through 12 More shows how Christ declares his godhead to his disciples by promising living bread and how the individual Christian must work for this living bread through a faith fully formed in charity. In chapters 14 through 25 More demonstrates that Christ refers to the sacrament in both figure and reality and shows how faith makes it possible for the eucharist to work both sacramentally and effectually. Chapters 17 through 19 in the section on the bread of the eucharist, like chapter 11 in the section on the bread of godhead, stress the miracle of incorporation. And chapters 20 to 25, like chapter 12, focus on the running theme of the deficiencies of human faith, bringing home to the reader's own spiritual life the problem of belief in scripture. Will the reader, like the incredulous apostles, like Judas, like the Masker, doubt Christ's words about the living bread?

When More first introduces the theme of the " breade of Godhead," the connection drawn between this bread and the bread of the eucharist is straightforward:

> Our sauyour also to enduce them the better to the bylyefe of his great kyndnes, in that he wold vouchsaufe to gyue them his owne body to be receyued and eaten in to theyrs, he dyd tell them two other thynges / the tone y^t he was very god, the tother that he wold dye for theyr sakes. Of these two poyntes / the tone myght make them sure that he wold do it, and the tother that he coulde do it. For what coulde he not do that was god almyghty? or what wolde he dysdayne to do for vs, that wolde not dysdayn to dye for vs. [25/28–35]

As More's exposition continues, the relation he sees between the two kinds of bread emerges as more complex. More comments on the chapter verse by verse, and his remarks seem at first ad hoc and disjointed. But a sense of remarkable consistency slowly emerges from them. As More comments at length on the Trinity, on the incarnation, on prevenient grace, on the cooperation of faith, hope, and charity, these doctrines emerge as elements of a single theology that shows how man is led to consume both the bread of Christ's godhead and the bread of his body. In "sealing" God the Son, God the Father "dyd . . . gyue hym all that euer was in hym selfe . . . and yet kepe neuer the lesse all the same styll hym selfe" (30/28–33). Not only is Christ the Son capable of giving men " euerlastynge lyuely meate " (31/11); he was sent into the world for that express purpose. Through the incarnation, and through the continuing grace of God the Father, man's will can be moved to consume the bread of Christ's godhead, to do the hard work of faith, joining to it hope and charity. When the believer does this, when he dwells in Christ through faith, then Christ will dwell in him, making the gift of his own eucharistic body work in the believer, incorporating the believer in himself.

Once More has established this essential relation between eating the bread of Christ's godhead through belief and eating his eucharistic body, he goes on to an exposition of those verses in John 6 that he believes deal specifically with the real presence. Again and again he supports his views with passages from the fathers. In the sacrament we see both figure and reality; Christ gave us his body on the cross and again and again in the sacrament. In order for the eucharist to work sacramentally and effectually, in order for the communicant to be truly incorporated in God, he must believe. If he does not believe, he will eat the eucharistic body to his damnation—like Judas.

More's exposition insists upon the rich unity of all God's works. Eating the bread of Christ's godhead through faith and eating his eucharistic body in the host are the equally important constituents of the effectual working of the sacrament and the miracle of incorporation. Incorporation looks forward to the beatific vision—the *cibus angelicus*—of the next life. Everything agrees; in everything is found the just proportion and harmony of divine providence. Even to the smallest details More seems absorbed by the congruity he perceives in God and his works. He lingers lovingly, for example, on the unity of persons in the Trinity, using language that looks forward to his discussion of the unity of figure and reality in the sacrament: "And thus the sone of god so sealed by his father and not onely expressely representynge, but also veryly beynge one equale god, . . . beynge sent in to the worlde by hys father and hym selfe, and theyre bothe holy spyryte equale god wyth theym bothe, toke vppon hym the manhode, the very flesshe, and the very soule of our sauyour Chryste. . ." (30/34–31/5). Just as in sealing something, More explains, the one thing

> leueth in the tother the very whole expresse thynge that it is it selfe, not as it is iron, stele, or coper, syluer, brasse, or golde, but as yt is a seale, that ys to wytte thys fasshyoned fygure or y^t, and yet kepeth it whole styll neuer the lesse it selfe, so dyd god the father in the sealyng of god the sone, that is to wytte in hys eternall bygettynge, gyue hym all that euer was in hym selfe . . . and yet kepe neuer the lesse all the same styll hym selfe. [30/24–33]

Nowhere is More's emphasis on divine wholeness and harmony more pronounced than in the passages dealing with incorporation. In chapter 11, which brings the section on the bread of godhead toward a close, and in chapters 17 through 19, More shows how everything that Christ treats in John 6 is tied together in the miracle of our incorporation into his living body and the promise of our incorporation into his mystical body, the society of saints. Those who faithfully receive his body are incorporated into Christ's body like wax melting into wax. His everlasting life becomes part of them: "For as the godhead is of his owne nature euerlastyng lyfe: so is the flesshe ioyned in vnyte of person to the godhed, by that immedyate coniunccyon and vnyte, made bothe euerlastyng & lyuely in it selfe, and also euerlasting lyfe to the geuyng of life euerlastyngly to all other, that well and wurthely receyue hym, and wyll perseuer and abyde wyth hym" (70/35–71/4). The circularity of the phrase "also euerlasting lyfe to the geuyng of life euerlastyngly" suggests More's idea of incorporation, which he develops at greater length in subsequent passages. The sacramental reality of our incorporation into Christ's living body is also a sacramental sign for our incorporation into his mystical body: those who receive the sacrament effectually as well as sacramentally "be made therby very lyuely membres of that thyng that the blessed sacrament signifyeth & betokeneth, y^t is to wyt of the mystycall body of Cryst, the chyrche and congregacyon of sayntes" (72/33–36). The sacramental sign of Christ's living body, then, is a special kind of sign indeed, for it is itself a foretaste of a future fulfillment. More's phrase for this sign—taken from Paul's "pignus" (2 Cor. 1 : 22; 5 : 5)—is "an ernest peny" (44/36) or "a sample" (45/7). Eucharistic incorporation tells the faithful what incorporation into the heavenly mystical body will be—but only through perseverance in faith can they hope to receive that knowledge in its fullness. And those who receive the body of Christ unworthily, More stresses repeatedly, do not receive the effect of the sacrament:

> And veryly to be a quycke lyuely member of that body doth no man attayne that receyueth the sacrament without fayth and purpose of good lyfe / but waxeth a more weke membre & a more lame, more astonied, and more losely hangynge theron than he dyd before / and by suche often receyuynge so rotteth more and more, that finally it falleth quyte of, and is cast out into the dunghyll of hell, and shal neuer be resuscytate & reysed agayne to be made a membre of that body in glory. [76/32–77/3]

More finds in incorporation the central image of the wholeness of God's grace. The function of his entire exposition in Book 1 is to show the full significance of John 6 by placing this scriptural text in relation to the whole body of scripture and to the rich interpretation that scripture finds in the church. Thus he begins by translating the whole passage, and by discussing the importance of the initial episode of the loaves and fishes, and thus throughout Book 1 he brings to bear on John 6 a profusion of biblical parallels and contrasts from both the Old Testament and the New. The allegories found in the description of the four rivers of paradise in Genesis 2 : 4–10 or of Samson tying the foxes together by their tails provide a parallel to the secondary senses one finds in John 6. These allegories are useful and true, but only if one also accepts the literal sense. If anyone, like the Masker, would "make vs byleue that those wordes were to be none otherwyse vnderstanden bysyde, but that there were no

such floodes flowynge forth of paradyse, nor no such paradyse at all / I
wold wene verely that he were a very heretyke" (19/9–13). Other parallels are woven throughout More's exposition. He shows, for example, that
the other principal sacrament, baptism, like most things hard to believe,
was introduced in words before it was instituted in deeds. Christ suggested
the function of baptism to Nicodemus just as he suggests the eucharist to
his apostles in John 6, teaching them the "thynge" but not the "forme"
(24/28). The manna that fell from heaven was a clear figure of the
eucharist (78/33–36), as were Aaron's rod turned into a serpent (Exod.
4 : 3) and the brazen serpent erected by Moses in the desert (Num.
21 : 8–9; see 68/7–18). Elsewhere More compares the faithless incredulity
of the Jews in John 6 to the unobjectionable puzzlement of Mary at the
Annunciation—"how shall that be?" (58/23)—to Zachary's craven
demand for a token of Elizabeth's miraculous pregnancy (61/30–37), and
to the honest confusion of Nicodemus when Christ told him that he would
be reborn—"how may a man be borne agayn whan he is olde" (62/7).
Even matters of linguistic usage may be explained by the scrutiny of
comparable texts. More explains, for example, Christ's reference to his
flesh as bread by suggesting a similar use of the phrase "son of man":
"And therfore as he sayde vnto Nichodemus, the sone of man descended
from heuyn: so sayth he here of hys flesshe, this is the brede that is
descended from heuyn" (78/11–14). Few, if any, of these parallels are
original with More. Some of them the sacramentarians themselves had
used to deny the real presence. But instead of rejecting or ignoring them
as argumentatively frail or subject to misinterpretation, More embraces
them and tries to place them in the full and unfathomable harmony of
scriptural revelation.

   More finds that the diverse threads of scripture are woven into the
single fabric of revelation, a fabric formed not only by the scripture but
by the tradition of the church. As he says repeatedly here and elsewhere,
only the church can tell us what is scripture, and only through the contin-
ual resifting of doctrine in the church can the truth of scripture be recognized. As he proceeds with his exposition of John 6, More relies heavily
on the works of the fathers. In the central chapter (13) of Book 1, he calls
upon Theophylactus to demonstrate the coherence of figure and reality in
the eucharist; on Bede to show how the gift of Christ's body in the
sacrament is a memorial of the gift of his body on the cross; on Augustine
and Cyril to gloss John 6 : 64 ("It is the spirit that gives life"). Again
and again More recalls that all the old holy doctors and expositors
affirmed the doctrine of the real presence and believed it to be expressed
in John 6. He speaks "not of myne own mynde, but of ye mynde of
dyuerse holy doctours, Alcuinus, saynte Thomas, Theophylactus, and
saynte Cyrill" (50/5–7).

In his exposition of scripture in its wholeness, More also strives to show the theological consistency of individual scriptural texts. He delights in erecting complex theological and moral distinctions upon the formulas provided by John 6: "the meate that peryssheth" and "the meate that abydeth into euerlastynge lyfe" (27/12–34/12); "manna . . . from heuyn" and "the very brede from heuyn" (35/12–41/3); "my wyll" and "the wyll of hym that hath sent me" (41/5–45/29); "dwelleth in me and I in hym" (72/11–77/16). He even adds a refinement to "the meate that peryssheth," noting that material meat perishes in two ways: by being converted into man's own body through healthful digestion or by rotting uselessly, even destructively, when consumed through gluttony (27/21–29/12). Similarly, in looking at a variant reading of John 6 : 51, More relishes a possible congruity between the wording of scripture and the structure of theology. The Vulgate, More says, presents "Et panis quem ego dabo caro mea est pro mundi vita" ("And the bread that I shall give is my flesh for the life of the world"). But the Masker, the Septuagint, and many Greek and Latin expositors have the reading "Et panis quem ego dabo caro mea est, quam ego dabo pro mundi vita" ("And the bread that I shall give is my flesh, which I shall give for the life of the world"). More slyly claims that the Vulgate would be "more for my purpose"—it does not suggest the sacrifice of the cross as strongly as does the other. But in accepting the text as the Masker and the Greek version have it, More finds an even nicer precision in the repeated "dabo," which thus points specifically to both the sacrifice of the cross and the eucharist: "And loke now whyther the very wordes of Chryst agre wyth this exposycyon or not / the wordes ye wote well be these: and the brede that I shall geue you is my flesshe. Here is lo the tone geuyng. . . . Than sayth he ferther, whyche I shall gyue for the lyfe of the world. Lo here he telleth them of the tother gyuynge, by whyche he sholde geue it for them" (55/28–34). More goes on to explain that the eucharistic gift of Christ's body is a memorial of the gift of his body on the cross. Since Christ's principal purpose in John 6 was to speak of the sacramental giving, that thought is couched in a "very playne and expresse declaracyon in many playne open wordes" (56/3–4). But of the other giving, the giving for them on the cross, "he spake but a lytell, and as it were but for a declaracyon of the tother geuynge" (56/4–5).

More's desire to find the theological wholeness and consistency of John 6 even leads him, in chapter 11, to skip ahead in his exegesis in order to stress our heavenly incorporation with Christ, which follows in More's theological argument, though not in his text. More is discussing John 6 : 37–39: "All that my father gyueth me shall come to me. . . . For hym that commeth to me wyll I not caste out. . . . I am descended from heuyn, not to do my wyll but to do the wyll of hym that hath sent me.

And thys ys veryly the wyll of the father that sent me, that all that he hath gyuen me I sholde lese nothynge therof, but that I sholde reyse vppe that agayne in the laste daye" (40/7–41/9). Here More sees coming together in man's redemption the hard-working faith of man, the sacrifice of Christ, and the will of God. The perfect fulfillment of this coming together is our incorporation into Christ's glorious body in heaven, of which the sacrament of the body and blood of Christ is "an ernest peny" (44/35–36). More thus reads eucharistic incorporation into the verse "hym that commeth to me wyll I not cast out." In More's paraphrase, "commeth to me" means the effectual receiving of Christ's body and blood by the faithful Christian:

> . . . so shall you wurkyng with him by your own good wyll, in subdueng of your reason to yᵉ obedyence of fayth, by bylief come to me, and with good wyll of well wurkynge also with the bylief / shall not onely byleue me, but also byleue in me, and go into me, by beynge a membre of myne, and incorporatynge your self in me / and I shall by the gyfte of myne owne body to be eaten and receyued of yours, incorporate my selfe in you, and I wyll not cast you out fro me but be styll incorporated wyth you, but yf you cast me out frome you. . . . [44/1–10]

More confesses at the end of the chapter that he has "inserted the incorporacyon" in the interest of ultimate theological unity and truth:

> Where as I haue good reader in thexposycyon of these wordes of our sauyour, inserted the incorporacyon of hym and vs togyther, by the receyuynge and eatynge of his owne body into ours: I haue not done it to make any man wene that that poynt appered and were proued by any parte of those wordes, but bycause yt ys a very trouth in dede / and not onely towched and signyfyed in other wordes of hys before, but also playnely expressed and declared by other wordes of hys owne after, as you shall hereafter se. Therfore so playne a trouth, and so necessary, and so necessaryly parteynynge to that place of yᵉ mater, me thought it not metely for to be lefte out. [45/30–46/4]

Here, more than elsewhere, one senses the yielding of More's exegetical rigor to his desire for theological synthesis and clarity.

As More winds towards the end of his exposition of John 6, he focuses on the decision to believe or not to believe, discussing the murmuring Jews, the disciples who "went backe, & now walked no more with hym," and the devil he had chosen among the twelve, Judas Iscariot. More thus points chillingly to the ethical problem sacramentarianism posed for his own English readers in 1534. They, like those present at Capernaum, will

stand firm in belief or fall away like diseased members from the body of
Christ's church. The Jews and the unbelieving disciples did not understand what Christ meant by giving them his flesh to eat, imagining his
body cut up like meat at a butcher's. Yet how much worse is the disbelief
of modern heretics, "For I wene veryly that there were neyther of those
disciples nor of those Iewes neyther, any one so euyll as now be mayster
Masker, & Fryth, & hys felowes, that seynge the receyuyng nothynge
lothesome, and byleuynge that Cryst was god (yf they byleue it) wyll not
yet byleue he can do it / but murmur & grudg agaynst it styll" (80/38–
81/5). The modern Christian knows more than these Jews did—he suffers
from a deficiency of faith rather than of knowledge, and he is perhaps
closer to the apostle Judas than to the Jews. More establishes that Judas
made a free choice of the wrong way by contrasting him with Peter, who
when asked with the other apostles "wyll you be gone to?" responded,
"Lord to whom shall we go. Thou hast the wordes of euerlastynge lyfe.
And we byleue and know that thou arte Chryst the sone of god" (87/28–
88/2). The choice is ours, More tells us, to stay with Peter or to depart
with Judas to our damnation:

> Lo good reders . . . our sauyour gaue that secrete warnyng of Iudas
> falshed, and sayed that one of the twelue was a deuyll, to the entent
> that all folke of what holynesse so euer they were, shulde stand euer
> in drede and fere / and not do as these heretykes teche, vpon boldnes
> of any felynge fayth or fynall eleccyon, presume them selfe so sure of
> saluacyon. . . . [93/34–94/4]

Those who receive the sacrament without believing in it do so to their
damnation, like Judas.

Thus Book I of *The Answer to a Poisoned Book* is More's first detailed
exegesis—theological, moral, and even philological—of an extended
passage from scripture. *The Answer* arose from the same sort of bitter
controversy as his other polemical works, but the first book of *The Answer*
also tends to rise further above the dust and heat of the battlefield. It
foreshadows the exegetical plan and the loftier, calmer tone of *A Treatise
on the Passion* and *De Tristitia Christi*.

Return to Battle: Books II–V

After the riches of positive biblical exposition in Book I, the return to
the hurly-burly of the polemical style in the final four books seems like a
fall from grace. Having set forth the positive case for the real presence,
More gets down to the grimy struggle of wrestling his opponent to
the ground. The exposition alone would suffice: "now I say by thys

exposycyon of myne ye se his exposycyon auoyded clerely for nought, and all the mater clere vpon our parte, though no man wrote one worde more" (96/29–31). More wishes, however, not merely to correct, but to humiliate and expose the Masker in all his shallowness and trickery: "And yet wyll I for all that, for ye ferther declaracyon of mayster Maskers handelynge, shewe you some peices of hys exposycyon in specyall, by whych ye maye clerely se what credence may be geuen to the man, eyther for honesty, or lernynge, vertue, wyt or trouth" (96/32–97/2). More sticks to his original plan, answering the Masker's false glosses on John 6 in Book 2, his general arguments in Book 3, his attack on the *Letter against Frith* in 4, and his exposure of More's supposed contradictions in 5. But More's aim here is not to present a single coherent chain of reasoning, and as he passes judgment on passage after passage in *The Souper*, the topics of debate change quickly and sometimes arbitrarily. To some degree, too, More repeats himself, attacking the same issue as it occurs in several places of *The Souper*. Point by point, More considers the Masker's denial of the real presence, and familiar topics of the controversy pass by in a tireless parade.

In Book 2, More seizes upon some eight passages of *The Souper* which can be quickly exposed as foolish and fallacious. Most of these passages concern the Masker's assertion that faith is the food Christ spoke of in John 6, and the unifying theme of the discussion is the conflict between the doctrine of good works and the doctrine of justification by faith alone, although other doctrinal issues, like the sacrifice of the mass, come up along the way. When the Masker applies Habakkuk 2 : 4 ("the just shall live by faith") to John 6 : 27 ("Worke you, not the meate that perisheth, but that abydeth into euerlastyng lyfe"), defining "meate" as "faith," More argues that this exegesis confuses means (faith) with ends (incorporation into everlasting life in Christ's body). Christ clearly says that *he* is the meat (John 6 : 35, 51, 56). More takes special glee in picking apart the Masker's exposition of John 6 : 35: "he that cometh to me shall not hungre, and he that byleueth in me shal neuer thyrst." The Masker again claims that Christ refers to faith alone: "Fayth it is therfore in Cryst that fylleth our hungry hartes, so that we can desyre no nother yf we ones thus eate and drynk hym by fayth . . . for than are our sowles satysfyed and we be iustyfyed" (100/22–26)[1]. Do the faithful not feel physical thirst and hunger? And is not hope a kind of thirsting after heaven? Does not a man who has drunk one glass of ale thirst for another? Ecclesiasticus 24 : 29 says: ". . . He that drynketh me shall yet thyrst styll." And yet the Masker argues that if we "ones" come to Christ

---

[1] Appendix A, 306/9–13.

by faith we shall be satisfied—as if we could not fall from a faith once held. The Masker ridicules the Roman program of works, telling us to desire none other than faith alone, and to be satisfied with it. But are the reformers themselves satisfied, More archly asks. Has not one after the other desired a wife? And merely believing in the redemptive power of the crucifixion is a kind of empty faith, for when we say, with Saint Paul (1 Cor. 2 : 2), that we know nothing else " then Iesus Cryste, and that he was crucyfyed," that belief in Jesus stands for the whole of revelation, written and unwritten. Though the Masker tries to reconcile justification by faith with the contradictory text 1 John 4 : 16 ("By loue we abyde in god & he in vs"), attempting to demonstrate the priority of faith to love in " the order of our vnderstandyng," he plays right into More's hands. More makes short work of this scholastic chicanery, for faith is fully formed only when " he hath his two felowes with hym " (121/29–30).

The chief of the general principles that More attacks in Book 3 is the Masker's repeated statement that if Christ had meant to refer to the presence of his real body and blood in John 6, he would have spoken more clearly. To More, this argument is absurd, for Christ *did* speak clearly: " the brede whych I shall gyue is my bodye, whiche I shall geue for the lyfe of the worlde" (John 6 : 51). And there are many other passages of scripture that are similarly " unclear " in that explanations are not given in full: the discussion of baptism with Nicodemus (John 3 : 1–20); the restitution of the kingdom (Acts 1 : 6); or the proclamation of Jesus as Messiah (Matt. 12 : 16 and 16 : 20). The Masker's other principal argument is equally absurd—his use of John 6 : 63 ("The spirit is it that geueth lyfe / the flesshe auayleth nothyng") as an exegetical principle. Here, according to the Masker, Christ states that he meant the chapter to be taken allegorically, that is, according to the spirit. But as Augustine and Cyril clearly show (More replies), these words refer to Christ's body living with his spirit; the passage distinguishes his everlasting body from a body dead and cut up into pieces. Other arguments are also dismissed. The question of bilocation, of how Christ's body can be in heaven after the ascension, is touched upon, to be taken up more fully in Book 4. More considers at greater length the Masker's facile argument that if John 6 : 55 (" but yf you eate the flesh of ye sone of man & drink his bloude ye shall not haue lyfe in you") is taken literally, then children who have never been communicants of the eucharist, and even laymen, who never receive the consecrated wine, will be damned. The second charge is really a matter of utraquism, which More promises to answer in his book against Barnes. And as to the children, this passage, like John 3 : 5, contains one of those hard sayings that we must depend upon the presence of Christ in the church to lead us to understand.

In Book 4, More seems to relish the chance to draw from the arsenal of scholastic logic enough polemical firepower to flatten, crumble, and pulverize the Masker's pretentious analysis of two passages from *A Letter against Frith*. From five leaves of *The Souper of the Lorde* come eighty-five of *The Answer to a Poisoned Book*. Book 4 swells out of proportion to its penultimate position—all the other books decrease successively in size. More fears that in at least one place in *A Letter* he had not made his cause as strong as he might have, and he proceeds with a massive counterattack. He also believes that the Masker has ignored the first argument he had advanced, and he promises to set his argument before the Masker with a schoolmaster's pointer, but defers this until Book 5, dealing first with the arguments the Masker did attack, and renumbering them to take the neglected first argument into account. More's renumbering of the arguments in the opening pages of Book 4 is an index of the fine scholastic resifting that is to follow.

More's second argument in *A Letter against Frith* deals with the comparison of John 6 with the two familiar passages "I am the dore" (John 10 : 9) and "I am the very vyne" (John 15 : 1). More had claimed that the Jews "meruayled" when he promised them his flesh to eat, for they knew that he meant his words literally, but they did not know that he spoke of his everlasting body and spirit, not of his dead flesh. When he said that he was the door and he was the vine, on the other hand, no one marveled at all, for these statements were clearly intended as allegory. First, More deftly defends himself against the Masker's criticism of his use of the word *marvel* instead of the *murmur* of the text. His concern is the meaning rather than the word, and must not the Jews have marveled before they murmured? More then goes on to discuss two questions the Masker has posed about the passages: whether or not the apostles and disciples heard and understood Jesus, and whether, if they understood, they marveled. In the first question, More distinguishes four separate questions: Did the apostles hear? Did the apostles understand? Did the disciples hear? Did the disciples understand? And these four questions are to be applied to three passages: "I am the very vyne," "I am the door," and "I am the bread." Out of the Masker's one question come twelve, More crows. When this line of attack has been exhausted, More examines whether or not those who did hear and understand marveled when Jesus said "I am the bread." The Masker claims that those apostles who remained behind did not. But according to More, the Masker thus argues in a circle:

> And vppon that that hym selfe sayeth, that the cause wherfore the disciples and apostles meruayled not, nor murmured not at these wordes of Christ, *The brede y^t I shall geue you is my flesh &c.* was

bycause they perceyued that Chryste spake yt in a parable (as I say
of his other wordes, I am the dore, and I am the very vyne) vppon
these wordes of mayster Maskers owne, mayster Maskar concludeth
for his purpose, the selfe same thynge that he fyrste presupposeth, the
thyng that he shold not presuppose but preue, that is to wyt that
Chryst spake yt but by way of a parable. [167/14–23]

More then quickly dismisses as an ill-conceived syllogism the Masker's
contention that the doctrine of transubstantiation, if expressed in John 6,
would surely have made the apostles wonder. The Masker's " major " and
" minor " are nonsense formally, and the church by no means demands
that we believe in any one particular mode of presence, as long as we
believe that Christ's body and blood are indeed truly present in the
eucharistic elements. A long and moving passage from Chrysostom provides More with a means of setting this argument finally to rest. Chrysostom comments upon John 6, noting that the Jews' incredulity must not
be continued by us. We must acknowledge and be thankful for the
miracle of Christ's loving sacrifice for us:

> *From goddes borde therfore let vs ryse like lions that blew out fyre at the mouth*
> *suche as the deuyll maye be aferde to beholde vs / & let vs consyder Chryst our*
> *hed, & what a loue he hath shewed vs. The fathers and mothers oftentymes put*
> *out theyr chyldren to other folke to nurse. But I (may our sauyour say) nuryshe*
> *& fede my chyldren with myne owne flesshe. I geue them here myne own selfe /*
> *so fauour I them all.* [174/15–21]

More himself continues to fight like a Christian dragon, breathing
learned fire as he defends himself against the Masker's attack upon the
next section of *A Letter against Frith*. In this discussion of the " third "
argument (the second in the Masker's numbering), More again submits
the Masker's words to debilitating logical scrutiny. More picks so closely
at every word—breaking the Masker's argument into points and separat-
ing major and minor—that he is sometimes diffuse and often repetitive.
But the principal topic of debate is the problem of multilocation—of how
Christ's body can be in many places at once—and More's response seems
to follow three main lines of reasoning.[1]

First, the Masker claims that More has argued *a posse ad esse*—that since
God could allow multilocation, therefore he did—and the Masker thus
demands better proof, by express words of scripture interpreted in a
credible manner. More here becomes humorously exacting. Will the

---

[1] On More's arguments for multilocation, see Walter M. Gordon, "A Scholastic Problem
in Thomas More's Controversy with John Frith," *Harvard Theological Review*, 69 (1976),
131–49.

Masker believe nothing, not even the existence of God, unless it is proven to him by More in express words of scripture? But more important is the question of the relative authority of church and scripture. More, of course, can find ample scriptural evidence for his case—and he doubts that the Masker can for his. But scripture is validated and validly interpreted by the church, as More has argued again and again, and all believers must depend upon Christ's spirit operating in the church to provide the right interpretation of scripture—as it does, for example, about hell-fire, to which the Masker and all others who wish to allegorize away the truths of scripture will be confined for ever and ever.

More's second line of reasoning is concerned with a distinction the Masker attempts to draw between Christ's humanity and his divinity. The doctrine of multilocation, according to the Masker, ascribes infinity to a mere creature—only God is everywhere. To More, this whole argument is irrelevant, since he never claimed that Christ's body was everywhere, or in all places, only that it is in heaven and wherever the eucharist is celebrated. And the argument itself is also absurd. The Masker attempts to limit God's power, as if God could not put Christ's body in all places. And being in all places is not the same as being infinite, for God's infinity goes beyond the places of creation.

After a brief digression on the meaning of *oportet* in a passage from Augustine cited in *A Letter*, More settles down to the third and final problem posed by the Masker, the repugnance of multilocation to reason and the senses. Unless God clearly tells us otherwise, the Masker claims, we must believe what we see. More returns to the argument that the truth of multilocation has been demonstrated in scripture and continually confirmed in the church by Christ's guiding spirit. He closes the book by defending the image of one face appearing in the many fragments of a broken mirror as an analogy to the presence of Christ in many places through the conversion of bread and wine. The Masker, More points out, wishes to argue that, since the physical substance of the face does not appear in the glass, Christ's body does not appear in the sacrament—a fallacious argument from a mere similitude. As a similitude, however, the broken glass is useful. Common people can easily understand it. Little would the fathers who first used such simple analogies from nature ever have dreamed that learned men would stoop so low as to make the real presence subject to doubt.

In Book 5, as he had promised, More addresses the last and least important of the matters at hand: the contradictions the Masker has charged him with. The second and lesser More treats first. In *A Dialogue concerning Heresies*, the Masker alleges, More claimed that the doctrine of the perpetual virginity of Mary was an unwritten verity, but if More looked "narowly" in his own *Letter against Frith*, he would find that he there claims it for a written truth, expounding "virum non cognosco" (I do not know a man) in Luke 1 : 34 as "virum non cognoscam" (I shall not know a man). More does not deny that he has made a case for scriptural proof of the doctrine, and a good proof indeed, which he has been proud to advance again in *The Answer*. But he does not presume that his exposition is entirely sure, since others, like Jerome, have hesitated to advance scriptural proof. As the Masker's own words suggest, such exposition demands that one interpret scripture too "narrowly." And besides there is no need at all of scripture to prove a doctrine so faithfully passed on in the church. Even Tyndale is willing to accept the perpetual virginity of Mary as an indifferent matter. Perhaps the heretics' objection to the scriptural proof, More concludes, lies in the failure of these marrying friars and nuns to understand the true value of a vow. With this redoubtable charge, hauled out again and again in More's polemical works, he moves on to the second and more serious of the alleged contradictions. The Masker claims that on folio 249 of the *Confutation* More had said that "Iohan spake nothynge at all of" the eucharist. With the help of a friendly gentlewoman, More finally finds the reference—the Masker had cited a misnumbered folio—and exposes the Masker's blatant misquotation. More had said not that John 6 did not concern the eucharist, but that Tyndale, given the Lutheran denial of the eucharistic application of the chapter, could hardly use that text to dispute the sacrament. The Masker's visor should blush red indeed.

Before taking his leave, More fulfills the promise he had made the reader in Book 4, to set before the Masker with a schoolmaster's pointer More's first argument against Frith. The argument turns out to be a patristic one: none of the fathers ever interpreted the places where Christ is called the vine or the door literally, just as none ever failed to find the literal sense in John 6. If the Masker believes otherwise he is "myche more fole than a naturall fole in dede" (221/18-19).

The Masker's folly in handling the fathers leads More into a brief glimpse of the works he has projected. In his answer to the second part of *The Souper*, he will treat the Masker's three places of Augustine, Tertullian, and Chrysostom, paring down these insubstantial references like so many pears. This will be an easy task. But first, More plans to take on the patristic arguments Frith had borrowed from Oecolampadius and used in his *Answer to More*. This task he will undertake as soon as he can get a copy of the book. Soon too, he will release his *Letter against Frith*. The eucharistic controversy has begun in earnest, and More will not rest until he has the last word, promising that he will return to his answer against the second part of the poisoned book, "whyche yet I wyll after all thys (god wyllyng) not leue nor let go so" (222/23–24). The forsaking of our saviour in the blessed sacrament is the "end and conclusyon" of all the other vile abuses the heretics have endorsed, to their damnation. May God give them the grace to turn from this infidelity, More says in his moving final prayer, so that all Christians may be incorporated here in one catholic church through faith, hope and charity, and through the gift of the blessed sacrament, and so that "after the shorte course of this transytorye lyfe, wyth hys tender pytye powred vppon vs in purgatorye, at the prayour of good people, and intercessyon of holy sayntes, we may be wyth them in theyr holy felyshyppe, incorporate in Chryste in hys eternall glorye" (223/29–33).

Masks and Reality

More begins *The Answer to a Poisoned Book* by discussing the abuse of language, for the sacramentarian heresy, like all others, is spread and strengthened by careless or vicious conversations and books. More wishes that all good Christians were as zealous as the heretics, and that they were "as loth to here any worde spoken wronge agaynste fayth, as they wolde be to speke it them selfe" (3/16–18). Once men were wiser and followed Saint Paul: "let not fornycacyon or any vnclennesse be so mych as named amonge you" (3/28–29). But after these golden apostolic times, men "fell vnto more lybertye / and suche as wolde forbere the doynge, wolde yet be wel content to fall in the feleshyp of foule and fylthy talk-ynge: than beganne clennesse greatly to dekaye. For as thapostle also reherseth, euyll communicacyon marreth and corrupteth good maners" (3/32–4/5). Now the corruption has spread so far that men will suffer even heresy to be spoken at their tables. Paul had advised that twice-warned heretics should be shunned, but now men everywhere tolerate heretics, even converse with them and entertain them, either from negligence or from fear, or from what More calls "synful ciuilyte" (5/25–26), a poign-ant phrase from one so attached as he to the cultivation of civility. Men buy the heretics' books and proudly babble about them, spreading the pernicious doctrine abroad. "Dyssymylyng sufferaunce" (5/35) has made many more heretics than there would otherwise have been.

The abuse of language is also touched upon in the full title that More gave to his book: *The answere to the fyrst parte of the poysened booke, whych a namelesse heretyke hath named the souper of the lorde. By syr Thomas More knyght.* This "namelesse heretyke" thinks that he can hide his shame merely by remaining anonymous. And by giving his book the title *The Souper of the Lorde*, he is again distorting reality through the abuse of a name, for the book itself denies the real presence of Christ in his supper, and no name of the many for the eucharist could ever be adequate to the reality of that miraculous supper. As More points out in *A Treatise on the Passion*, this sacrament contains and signifies so many mysteries that "the holye cunninge fathers afore oure dayes, haue hadde muche a doe to fynde names ynoughe and conuenient, with whyche they myghte in anye wyse insynuate and shewe, so manye suche manner thinges of this blessed sacrament, as are partly conteined therein, & partlye signified thereby."[1] And later in *A Treatise* More analyzes the reality reflected by ten different names of the sacrament, including "*Cena dominica*, the supper of our lorde," which signifies the superiority of Christ's body over the paschal lamb and indicates the reality of Christ's body in the sacrament: "And therfore is it called the supper of our lord, to let vs as I say, perceiue, that the thing that we receue at Goddes borde nowe, is the very self same thyng, that the apostles receyued than: and that is not the same bread and the same wyne that wer than tourned, but the very self same body & bloud into which they wer than turned."[2]

John 6 itself evokes the problem of language and interpretation, for some who hear Jesus' words fail to understand him fully. Judas, the Jews who murmur in disbelief, and the unfaithful disciples all make errors in interpretation. Others, like Peter, labor to understand what Jesus has been saying. The interpretation of scripture in the church presents another layer of language that must be studied and understood. As More sifts through the language of John 6 and its expositors, attempting to come as close as he can to the full truth, the words of scripture and of the fathers are subjected to close scrutiny. Because More once slipped and said the Jews marveled (rather than murmured), for example, he devotes many pages to a discussion of the meaning of the two words. In another place he debates at length the meaning of *oportet* in a passage from Augustine. And the language of the Masker and of other heretics becomes a parallel concern. More carefully examines the structure, diction, and logic of his opponents' language, looking for abuses of the truth in the shifting surface of words. He often accuses the Masker of using the colors of

---

[1] *CW 13*, 140/8–12.

[2] *CW 13*, 155/32–156/3. In *Responsio ad Lutherum* More refers playfully to the opposing positions of Plato and Aristotle on the relation between names and things: Aristotle held that names were assigned to things arbitrarily; Plato, that there is a direct correspondence between names and things (*CW 5*, text and Commentary at 584/11–19). He also alludes to Plato's stance (*Cratylus* 435–36, 438) in a jesting Latin poem, no. 96 in *CW 3/2, Latin Poems*, ed. Clarence H. Miller et al. (New Haven and London, 1984). In neither place does More himself defend either position. The eucharist is a special case: it has many names but each does correspond directly to some facet of the reality of the sacrament. On the divinely ordained correspondence between names and things in scripture, see *CW 14*, 13–15.

rhetoric, lofty language, false constructions, and captious questions.[1]
Several times he breaks the Masker's statements down into logical terms
in order to expose his fallacious reasoning.

More's fundamental charge against the Masker (and the Masker's
against him) is misinterpretation. The Masker misunderstands John 6; he
misquotes and misunderstands More's *Letter against Frith*. As More says,
"Why sholde we thynke that your wyt wyll perse into the perceyuynge of
harde wordes in the holy scripture of god, whan yt wyll not serue you to
perceyue suche pore playne wordes of myne" (219/16–19). Because of this
fundamental sloppiness with words, no fault in the Masker's language—
not even a trivial error in usage— is too small to escape More's censure.
He picks upon the Masker's use of "yes" and "yea," "no" and "nay,"
for example, recalling how he had rebuked Tyndale for the same error in
The Confutation.[2] He comments uncannily (since he presumably did not
know that *The Souper* was a translation) upon the Masker's unidiomatic
usage: "he speketh englyshe as congrewe as a man myghte that hadde
lerned his englishe in a nother lande" (159/6–7). In another passage he
rebukes the Masker for the improper use of *dissemble*, a word that, when
used correctly, accurately describes the Masker's behavior: "Now where
he sayth, or else they dyssemble theyr bylyefe: I wyll not dyssemble with hym,
but tell hym very playne, that as great a dyssembler as he is, he woteth
not as it semeth what this worde dyssemblyng meneth, or ellys wote I
nere what he meneth therby" (126/4–8). The verb *dissemble* (and its
Latinate cousin *dissimule*) and the noun *dissimulation* are applied by More
again and again to the Masker, who wears, for example, "a visour of
dyssimulacyon" (13/5).[3] Another error of the Masker's that More criti-
cizes is pleonasm. The Masker says that God is "present, and fyllynge all
places at ones, essencyally, presently, wyth his almyghtye power" (191/
10–12), and More objects to the unnecessary "presently": "I let passe
here his word presently, whose presence nedeth not in that place for
ought that I can se. For whan he sayd byfore, present and fyllynge all
places at ones essentyally: his other worde presently may take his leue and
be absent wel ynough. For howe can he be present & essentyally fyll the
place, and not presently?" (191/13–18).

The Masker not only abuses language to dissemble the real presence of
Christ in the eucharist; he also hides his real self behind the false mask of
flamboyant and impudent anonymity. More had already found it necess-

---

[1] See, for example, 98/3–13, 151/14–19, 175/24–25.
[2] See the Commentary at 158/35–159/7.
[3] See also 52/3–5 and 148/9.

ary or convenient to invent labels for anonymous opponents. In *A Suppli-cation of Souls* More answered " the beggars' proctor." In *The Apology*, his anonymous adversary was ironically called " the pacifier" because he pretended to establish peace between the clergy and the laity. In *A Letter against Frith*, More often called his opponent " the young man" because of the youthful enthusiasm in Frith that More sought to overcome. In *The Souper of the Lorde*, More in turn is called " Master Mock." And since the author of *The Souper* chose to conceal his name, More takes a measure of glee in making one up for him: " Master Masker." More's name calls to mind the fashionable Italianate entertainments popular at court early in the sixteenth century.[1] Masked courtiers preened themselves in a glit-tering spectacle of music and dance. More knew these entertainments well. He mentions having seen them, and he knows the failings that splendid disguises often conceal: "As some haue I sene ere thys, full boldely come daunce in a maske, whose dauncynge bycame them so well, that yf theyr visours hadde ben of theyr facys, shame wolde not haue suffred theym to sette forthe a fote" (12/33–36). Later More recalls one whose dancing was so bad that he felt himself blushing through his mask—as Master Masker should when he is caught in an outright lie: " I wyste ones a good felow, whyche whyle he daunsed in a maske, vppon boldenesse that no man coulde haue knowen hym, whan he perceyued that he was well espyed by hys euyll fauored daunsynge: he waxed so ashamed sodaynly, y' he softly said vnto his felowe, I pray you tell me doth not my visour blosh rede?" (219/26–30).

More's images of masks and maskers mock the pretentiousness of *The Souper*, but they also recall a side of life somewhat seamier than the Italianate masque. He refers to " mummings," courtly entertainments distinguished from the masque by the dicing or " mumchance" often introduced at them: "And mayster Mummer vnder his maskers face forceth not myche to shyfte a false caste amonge, wyth a payre of false dyce" (13/1–3). More chooses not to call him " mayster Mummer," because he " speketh to mych" (13/6–7). But More's imagery of the mask gravitates toward the streets rather than the court, toward the Christmas and Easter mummings from which the courtly mummings stemmed.[2] Indeed, More sarcastically reminds his opponent that a great man who dons a mask and goes down a-mumming in the streets no longer has a right to the respect he would otherwise be entitled to:

---

[1] See the Commentary at 13/1–10.
[2] See the Commentary at 13/1–10.

But yet lyke as yf a ryght greate man wolde wantonly walke a
mummynge, and dysguyse hym selfe, and with nyce appareyle dyssemble hys personage, and with a fonde visour hydde and couer his
visage, he muste be content to be taunted of euery good felow that he
meteth, as merely as hym self lyste to ieste wyth them: so tyll mayster
Masker here put of his maskers visour, and shewe forth his owne
venerable visage, that I may se hym such an honorable personage, as
it may become hym to saye to me what he lyste, and me to requyte
hys mockes with no mery worde in this world, but stande styll
demurely and make hym lowe curtesy agayne, I wyll not let in y^e
meane tyme . . . to laugh yet & make mery wyth hym where I se
hym playe the fole. [99/27–100/5]

Master Masker becomes a fool, a jester, a cheating dicer, a street
magician. His rhetorical and theological trickery is a version of the street
entertainer's sleight-of-hand. When he presents More's words, he uses
"interlacynge, ruffle, & confusyon" (119/8–9). To entrap More, he sets
up "gynnys and his grinnes and all his trymtrams" (175/26–27)—to no
avail. One must always look closely at his hands: "But yet in these
wordes he iugleth with vs, and may with his wylynes begile them that wyl
take none hede. But who so loke well to his handes shall perceyue where
his galles goo well inough" (121/21–23). In the Masker's hands, *sola fides*
becomes a magic wand, scripture a trick box:

Here is mayster Masker fall to iuglynge lo / and as a iugler layeth
forth hys trynclettes vpon the table . . . so fareth maister Masker
here / that maketh Christes holy wordes serue hym for his iugling
boxes and layeth them forth vppon the borde afore vs / and byddeth
vs lo loke on this texte / and than loke lo vpon this / and whan he
hath shewed forth thus two or thre textes and byd vs loke vpon them
he telleth vs not wherfore / nor what we shall fynde in them. But
bycause they be so playne agaynste hym he letteth them slynke
awaye / and than to blere our eyen / and call our mynde fro the
mater / vp he taketh his iuglynge stycke the commendacyon of
fayth / and whyrleth that about hys fyngers and sayeth, Let it neuer fall
fro thy mynde chrysten reader that fayth is the lyfe of the ryghtuouse, and that Chryst
is thys lyuynge brede whom thou eatest, that is to saye in whom thou byleuest.
[133/21–134/3]

Thus More never really allows the Masker to remain in the world of
the courtly entertainment. Men like More's masker could be not only
vulgar but also criminal: In the parliament of 1512 an act was passed

"agaynst disguysed persons and Wearing of Visours."[1] More's masker is
always more like a man who makes his living in the gutter than like a
courtier in disguise: he is like "some bestely body, y^t wolde not care to
sytte downe wyth his face to the walwarde, and ease hym selfe in the open
strete / and though all the towne at onys tote in his tayle, take it for no
shame at all, bycause they se not hys face" (12/23–26). The Masker
merely puts plasters over the cancers and marmols of his foolish argument, and he does not even bother to disguise his heretical beliefs, but
displays them like a true creature of the street: "But as for ye boch of hys
cancred heresyes without any clowt or plaster he laieth out abrode to
shewe, to begge withall amonge the blessed bretherne as beggers laye
theyr sore legges out in syght that lye a beggynge a frydays aboute saynt
sauyour and at ye Sauygate" (99/11–15). Finally the Masker is deprived
even of his humanity. When the Masker attempts to refute More's use of
the analogy of the mirror, More comments: "mayster Maskar hath
caughte that glasse in hand and mocketh and moweth in that glasse, and
maketh as many straunge faces and as many pretye pottes therin, as yt
were an olde ryueled ape" (206/17–20). Lacking a real identity, the
Masker wears a series of sordid false faces that change from one moment
to the next. When he accuses More of wearing two faces in one hood,
More turns the proverb around, for the many faces of the truth will surely
outface the shameless falsehoods of the heretics: "I haue brought agaynst
you to your face, saint Bede and Theophilactus, saynt Austayne, and
saynt Hylary, saynt Hyreneus, saynt Cyryll, and saynt Chrysostome, so
many suche good facys into this one hode, that al the shameful lyes y^t
your shamelesse face can make, shall neuer agaynste these facys be able to
face out the trouth" (211/26–31).

---

[1] *The Statutes of the Realm*, 11 vols. (London, 1810–28), 5, 30. It provided: "Forasmoche as
lately wythin this realme dyvers persones have disgysed and appareld theym, and covert
theyr fayces with Vysours and other thynges in suche manner that they sholde nott be
knowen and divers of theym in a Companye togeder namyng them selfe Mummers have
commyn to the dwellyng place of divers men of honor and other substantial persons; and so
departed unknowen; Wheruppon Murthres felonye Rape & oder greate hurtes & inconven-
iences have afore tyme growen & hereafter by lyke to come by the colour therof, . . . be it
ordeyned and enacted. . . . That yf eny persone hereafter dysgyse or apparell them wyth
Vysoures or other wyse uppon theyr faces, and so disgysed or apparelde as Mommers . . .
attempte to entre or entre into the house of eny persone or persones, or assaute or affraye
make uppon eny persone in the Kinges hye waye, . . . That then the seid Mommers or
disgysed persones . . . shalbe arrested . . . as Suspectes or Vacabundes and . . . imprisoned
by the space of thre monthes wythoute bayle. . . . And also it is ordined & enacted . . . that
yf eny persone . . . sell or kepe any Vysoures . . . the seid persone . . . shall forfeyte . . . for
every Vysoure xx^{ti} shillynges." . . .

Among the mean and diseased images of the Masker is the Chaucerian "scald Colyn coke" that More evokes at the end of *The Answer*. This "rude ruffyn" has falsely called his dish the "last souper of the lorde," but he has poisoned it and "made yt the souper of the devyl," and the food is so bad that even the devil disdains to eat it (219/35–220/7). Here as throughout *The Answer*, More mockingly makes literal the title *The Souper of the Lorde*, turning the Masker's words into the dishes served at a supper. As More says in his preface: "This boke is intytled, The souper of our lord. But I beshrew suche a shewer, as so serueth in the souper, that he conuayth awaye the best dyshe, and bryngeth yt not to the borde / as this man wold yf he could, conuey fro the blessed sacrament Cristes owne blessed fleshe and bloode, and leue vs nothynge therin, but for a memory-all onely bare brede and wyne" (7/6–13). More's metaphor of the supper establishes a sharp contrast between the true sacrament and the insubstantial sustenance that the Masker provides the faithful. Taking away Christ's real presence in the eucharist would make that sacrament no different from the meal served at any alehouse. "Poison," then, is somewhat more than metaphor, for whatever the Masker offers in place of the edifying spiritual food of Christ's real presence in the eucharist, it can be only poison to the soul.[1]

The way More makes literal the Masker's title suggests one of his most successful polemical techniques: reducing the Masker's often high-flown arguments to the level of common sense—where they fall apart. "Folosopher" that he is (179/31), the Masker likes to parade the jargon and chop-logic of the schools.[2] But again and again More translates the Masker's pretentious and confusing theological argument into everyday language, using images often drawn literally from the London streets:

> But mayster Masker bycause yᵉ bylyefe is the waye to this meate, therfore he calleth the bylyefe the meate / as wysely as though he wold call the kynges strete Westmynster chyrche, bycause it is the way thytherward yf he come from charing crosse. And bycause men must spyrytually eate thys meate with fayth: therfore he calleth the fayth the meate as wysely as yf he wold, bycause he eateth his meate wyth his mowth, therfore call his mowth his meate. What wyt hath thys man? [98/20–27]

A *reductio ad absurdum* often allows More to sidestep a prolonged and tedious debate. When the Masker suggests, for example, that all Chris-

---

[1] On More's principal metaphors for heresy—fire, poison, and disease—see Marc'hadour, *Thomas More et la Bible*, p. 305.

[2] As More pointed out (121/16–19).

tians need to believe is Christ and Christ crucified, More tersely remarks, "Maister masker maketh vs a pretty short crede now" (109/18–19). And when the Masker claims that we need to believe in nothing except what is written in scripture, More asks: "dothe not he good readers say and afferme therby, that it was all together vnperfyte & vnsufficyent, all the whyle that god taughte it hym selfe by his own reuelacyon of spyryte, and that our sauyour taught it hym selfe by his own blessed mouth, tyll Moyses and the prophetes & thapostles wrote it wyth the penne?" (110/24–28). The mundane image of the pen, like the casual reference to the layman's *credo*, gives More's argument a firm grounding in the reader's world.

In one passage, More manages to state a sophisticated rebuttal of the Masker's notions of the priority of faith, hope, and charity in terms that savor more of the patient schoolmaster[1] or nurse than of the niggling theologian:

> For trewe it is that whan so euer god infoundeth eyther thabyt of fayth, or ye full perfite quycke lyuely faith that is called fides formata: he infoundeth in lyke wyse hope and cheryte bothe. But this is not the fayth alone. For fayth is neuer such fayth, but whyle he hath his two felowes with hym. But fayth maye begyn & tary to, before his two felowes come to hym. As a man maye beleue well longe ere he wull do well. And fayth may tary also whan both his felowes be gone from hym. . . . [121/24–33]

This explanation sounds like a fable, and elsewhere in *The Answer* More draws on his rich store of popular lore to give the ring of conviction to his arguments. The Masker's ineffectual polemical technique is like trying to catch a bird by putting salt on her tail (163/21–25); taunting and scoffing suit the Masker "as it becometh a camell or a bere to daunce" (178/3–4); the Masker's summary of More's argument is nothing but a child's castle of tile shards, erected only in order to be knocked down (208/19–21). More, on the other hand, has so soundly beaten the Masker "that if this great clerke had so many gret fallys geuen hym at Clerkenwell at a wrestelynge, he wolde haue had I wene neyther rybbe, nor arme, nor legge lefte hym hole longe ago, nor at thys laste lyfte, his necke vnbroken neither" (177/6–10).

More's common sense brings his points home to his lay audience with sureness and force. He frequently appeals directly to them: "good readers" and "good Christian readers."[2] Reason and truth are so clearly

---

[1] See the Commentary at 13/1–10.
[2] For example, at 176/12–14; 177/1, 14, 29, 33; 185/28; 188/14.

on More's side that "euery chylde" knows he is right (170/21–22). More's argument about God's omnipotence is so basic that "the symplest man or woman in a towne" (189/26) could have advanced it. The pretentious Masker is out of place in this honest company, as More sarcastically suggests when he says, "I must nedes take better hede what I answere him, than I shold nede, yf I were to answere a good plain man of the countrey" (159/14–16). A good gentlewoman saves More from thinking the Masker is right in accusing him of contradicting himself: she very commonsensically advises him to take a look at the suspect pages and therewith sends for the book (216/28–217/10).

More's homely sensibility is thus suited to his intended audience. But there is more than rhetorical opportunism here. For the truth of the real presence is not a matter of theological erudition, reserved for the schools. It is a truth cherished and passed down among good Christian people for fifteen hundred years. There is a "doctrine" of the real presence, to be sure, and scholars are free to debate its definition, but the body and blood of Christ in the eucharist are so vital and so real that no faithful man, woman, or child would ever doubt or challenge them. In Book 1, More strove to show the unity of revelation in John 6, the whole scripture, and the church. That same unity can be known in a different way to the everyday Londoner. Through the eucharist all good Christians are incorporated into Christ's body. His body and blood are as real to them as the streets they walk on when they leave their churches and stroll past the wrestlers at Clerkenwell or pause to give a penny to a lame beggar at the Savygate.

III. THE TEXT

The Editions

By comparison with some of More's other works, the textual history of *The Answer to a Poisoned Book* is simple and straightforward. No manuscript copies of it are known, and our text is based on the first edition of December 1533 (STC^2 18077; Gibson, no. 45; hereafter designated *1533*), which was reprinted in the *English Workes* of 1557 (sigs. V_2–CC_5v; Gibson, no 73; hereafter designated *1557*). It has never been reprinted or edited since 1557. Fortunately the two sixteenth-century editions were rather carefully printed.

Though William Rastell, the printer of the first edition, dated it 1534
in the colophon (sig. N_1), More himself wrote Thomas Cromwell on
February 1, 1534 that it had been printed, and many copies of it sold,
before Christmas 1533.[1] Since the book it answers, *The Souper of the Lorde*,
is dated April 5, 1533,[2] it must have been written later than that date. It
was probably written in the last three or four months of 1533. In the late
summer More was occupied for a short while with *The Debellation of Salem
and Bizance*,[3] and in the preface to *The Answer* he mentions that printed
copies of Frith's reply to More[4] were expected in England "thys bartlemew tyde laste passed" (6/34), that is, August 24, 1533.[5] The work to
which Frith was replying, More's *Letter against Frith* (Gibson, no. 66), was
published (that is, offered for sale) at the same time as *The Answer to a
Poisoned Book*, though it had been written and printed more than a year
earlier, late in 1532 (222/6–18).[6] Thus More's first two works devoted to
the eucharist were offered to the public together late in 1533.

---

[1] Rogers, p. 468. See the Commentary at 222/17–18. In *Early Tudor Drama* (London,
1926), Arthur W. Reed expressed the opinion that William Rastell "rather perversely dated
the New Year from Christmas or 1st January, because it had a bearing on the important
question whether the Papal Brief conveying the dispensation for the marriage of Henry VIII
to Katherine was a forgery or not. Since the Papal Briefs dated the New Year from the Feast
of the Incarnation, i.e. Christmas Day, the friends of Katherine claimed that the dispensation was good" (p. 81).

[2] Hume, no. 29.

[3] *CW* 9, xxxiii. *The Answer to a Poisoned Book* had to have been printed later than *The
Debellation of Salem and Bizance* because *The Answer* reprints four pages entitled "Syr Thomas
More knyght to the chrysten reader" added at the end of *The Debellation* on an extra pair of
conjugate leaves (the first of which is signed "♃") to correct an error on sig. h_5 of *The
Debellation* by cancelling nine lines. The same four pages were partly reset (with a few
changes in the opening lines to refer back to *The Debellation*) and printed as the last part of
the last gathering of *The Answer* (sigs. N_4–N_6), preceded by the errata and followed by the
colophon (sig. N_6).

[4] *A Boke . . . answeringe vnto M mores lettur . . .* , Monster ([Antwerp?], 1533; Hume, no.
30; *STC* 11381.

[5] The signatures of the preface are independent of those of the main body of *The Answer*,
but that means only that the setting of Book 1 began before the preface was available, not
that the preface was written after the main body was completed. When More wrote the
preface he still did not know whether printed copies of Frith's reply had arrived in England
(6/33–35), and later in the work (73/2–3) he still did not know, but when he wrote the last
pages he knew for certain that it had arrived (221/26–29). It is true that at 51/21–24 More
gives specific details from Frith's reply, but he may have learned them from a manuscript
copy or from someone who had seen one. The running head on the last page (sig. Bb_7v) of
the preface is "The fyfth boke," which suggests that the setting of the fifth book had begun
when the preface was set, but this does not help to pinpoint exactly when the preface was
written.

[6] The colophon of *A Letter to Frith* gives the year 1533. Rastell must have postdated it, as
he did *The Answer*.

A mistake in *1533* caused by a succession of minims ("insumate" for "insinuate," 27/22) suggests that it was set from manuscript copy, perhaps from More's autograph.[1] It was proofread rather carefully, as the three pages of errata (sigs. N_2v–N_3v) show, though all of the corrections could have been made by a proofreader at the press and would not have required any intervention by More himself.[2] The proofreader missed only eight substantive errors,[3] but his attempt to correct the misnumbered chapters in the second book only made matters worse. The following list shows the correct sequence in the first column and the roman numerals of *1533*, followed by the "corrections" of the *1533* errata in parentheses:

1	i
2	ii
3	iii
4	iv
5	v
6	v
7	vii (vi)
8	vii
9	ix (viii)
10	x (ix)
11	xi (x)
12	xii (xi)
13	xiii (xii)

The compositor set chapter 6 as chapter .v. and chapter 8 as chapter .vii. merely through inadvertence, retaining More's numbers in the other chapters.[4] Partly because chapter 5 is exceptionally long, the corrector failed to notice that the second chapter .v. was incorrect and adjusted the remaining numbers to make them follow in sequence the erroneous chapter .v. I have also supplied the missing chapter heading between chapters 20 and 22 of book 4. It is fairly easy to see where the chapter heading should have been placed. At the end of chapter 18 More quoted

---

[1] See *CW 6*, Commentary at 146/22.

[2] The errata pages have not been reprinted in this edition, but the charges they make have been recorded in the variants.

[3] See the variants at 44/29, 64/31, 71/26, 129/10, 154/6, 154/20, 167/12, 206/33.

[4] If More had made these errors, it is hard to see how he could have numbered chapters ix through xiii correctly. The first full gathering in the second book, gathering p, contains six erroneous running headlines retained from the first book: The fyrst boke (p_1v); The fyrste boke (p_2, p_4, p_6); and The fyrste boke. (p_3v, p_5v). The leaf b_3 is missigned "bii."

The.xvi.chappter.

BUt yet shall ye se that vpon the wordes of Cryste folowynge, How saynte Cyryll all waye more and more declareth that Christ spake there of his very body, that he wold geue men to eate in the blessed sacrament. for it foloweth in the text of the gospell.

¶ Than sayd Jesus vnto the Je-
,, wes, Veryly veryly I say vnto you,
,, but yf ye eate the flesshe of the sone of
,, man ye shall not haue lyfe in you. He
,, that eateth my flesshe and drynketh
,, my bloude, hath euerlastynge lyfe.

Cyrillus
li.4.ca.14
in eud. Jo.

Vppon those wordes thus sayth saynt Cyrill.

¶ Cryst is very mercyfull and mylde
,, as the thynge it selfe sheweth. For he
,, answereth not here sharpely to theyr
,, hote wordes, nor falleth at no conten-
,, cyon wyth them/but goeth about to
,, inprente in theyr myndes the lyuely
knowe

Whych hym selfe calleth my second,
bycause he wold haue þ fryst forgote

The.xi.chappter.

SO thus good readers goeth
mayster Masker forth.
The secunde argument of More.
After thys texte thus wysely proued to be vnderstan
den in the lyterall sense wyth the carnall Jewes, τ
not in the allegozyke oz spyzytuall sense with Cryst
and hys apostles : The whole somme of Morys cō
futacyon of the yonge man, standeth vppon this argument, a posse ad esse/that is to wytte, God maye
do it, ergo it is done. God may make thys body in
many oz in all places at onys, ergo it is in many oz
in all places at onys. Whyche maner of argumentacyon how false and naught it is, euery Sophyster τ
euery man that hath wytte, percepueth. A lyke argument. God may shew More the treuth and call
hym to repentaūce as he dyd Paule foz persecutyng
hys chyzche, ergo More is conuerted to god. Oz
god maye lette hym runne of an indurate harte with
Pharo, and at last take an open and sodapne vengeaunce vppon hym foz persecutynge hys wozde, τ
burnyng hys poze mēbzes : ergo it is done all redy.

In all thys tale good reders pou
se, that mayster Masker is yet at the
leste wyse constant τ nothynge chaū-
geth

The Answer to a Poisoned Book, sig. E₃

a long paragraph by the Masker. He discussed the first two parts of it in chapters 19 and 20. His discussion of the third part should have been set off as chapter 21. Book 4 is also the only book which has no heading for the first chapter; I have not supplied it because its absence causes no confusion. More himself added four and a half pages after the errata (sigs. N_4–N_6) to make a correction in *The Debellation of Salem and Bizance*.[1]

Certain typographical features of *1533* are ordinary enough: larger type in the first two lines of the title page, large block letters at the beginning of the preface and each of the five books, larger type for the first two letters of each chapter, smaller type for the sidenotes,[2] and contrasting typeface[3] for the running heads, the headings of the errata, and More's last pages correcting *The Debellation*. But the size and variation of typeface within the body of the text and the use of double quotation marks in the outer margins are distinctive and probably due to More himself. The usual typeface is Bastard 102. Quotations from the Masker are set in a smaller form of the same type, Bastard 68,[4] without marginal quotation marks.[5] Quotations from scripture and the fathers are regularly set in Textura 92, which contrasts in appearance but not in size with the Bastard 102 of the main text. Such quotations are also set off by a vertical line of double quotation marks in the outer margin.[6] This is close to More's own procedure in the Valencia autograph, where More uses mar-

---

[1] These pages will be included in the Yale edition of *The Debellation of Salem and Bizance*. In *1557* this passage occupies the recto of a leaf inserted in some copies after the fifth leaf of gathering CC. It appears in the Larned Fund copy at Yale, but not in Yale's Klein copy. More had printed errata for the second part of *The Confutation* at the end of *The Apology* (see *CW 8*, 1421, 1431; and *CW 9*, xc).

[2] The typefaces used by William Rastell in *1533* are identified and reproduced by Frank Isaac in *English & Scottish Printing Types 1501–35*1508–41* (Oxford, 1930). The larger type on the title page is Textura 220. The first letter of each chapter (except the opening chapter of each book) is also Textura 220 and the second letter is the uppercase form of the predominant typeface of the book, Bastard 102. The sidenotes are set in Bastard 68. See Isaac, *Printing Types*, figs. 74–75. Chapter 4 of Book 1, which consists entirely of More's translation of John 6 : 26–72, is set in Textura 92 and has no large initial letters.

[3] Textura 92.

[4] Quotations from More's opponents in *The Confutation* are set in an italic typeface smaller than the Textura which is the normal typeface of the book (*CW 8*, 1420 and Appendix D).

[5] The first four quotations from the Masker in chapters 3 and 4 of Book 2 do have marginal quotation marks, but after that they are never used for the Masker. It looks as if it took a little while to get the convention established.

[6] Luther's words are also distinguished once in this way (118/3–18), but only when he is citing the fathers and the canon of the mass against his own position.

ginal quotation marks (normally double) exclusively to set off passages from scripture or the fathers.[1] Quotations from More's own works, *A Letter against Frith* and *The Confutation*, are also set in contrasting Textura 92, but without marginal quotation marks.[2] Thus typography becomes a way of expressing More's superiority to his opponent and the venerable authority of scripture and the fathers. These typographical distinctions disappear in *1557*, the text of which is printed entirely in Textura 72, except for the few Latin phrases, which are set in Italic 72.[3] Quotations from the Masker are placed between a pair of hands with index fingers pointing toward the opening and closing words. All other quotations are placed between marks consisting of a vertical line with two crossbars.

Several variants show that *1557* was set from *1533*.[4] Nor is there any reason to believe that a manuscript was used to alter the text. All but two of the corrections in the errata of *1533* appear in *1557*.[5] The compositor of *1557* introduced about seventy-five minor misprints, usually by adding or omitting small words like *as*, *the*, or *so*. His occasional interchanging of *the* and *that* is understandable because the superscript letters of y^e and y^t in *1533* are often smudged and difficult to distinguish. Twice he interchanged "maner" and "matter" (69/8, 108/32) and twice he fell into a *facilior lectio* ("wisely" for "wyshly," 219/21, 219/23). But he occasionally improved the punctuation of *1533* and he corrected about as many misprints as he himself introduced. Most of these are easy corrections, but he (or a corrector) had to be paying attention to correct "insumate" to "insinuate" (27/22), "found" to "fond" (179/36), and "boldely" to "bodely" (206/33). *1557* adds a considerable number of sidenotes but it also omits eight sidenotes found in *1533*.[6] Among those added in *1557* is "Transsubstanciacion" (53/22–23), a technical term in keeping with the theological conservatism of Mary's reign. But More himself does not use it in *The Answer*, though Joye had employed it more than once in *The Souper*.[7]

---

[1] See *CW 14*, 714–15.

[2] 150/9–32, 217/19–28, 218/35–219/2, 220/14–30.

[3] Isaac, *Printing Types*, figs. 139, 142.

[4] See variants at 44/29, 97/6, 113/8, 114/1, 119/12, 189/39, 203/2.

[5] The corrections at 55/7 and 186/5 were overlooked. William Rastell was not consistent in his use of errata in his copytexts. He used them for *A Dialogue Concerning Heresies* (*CW 6*, 576), but not for *The Confutation* and *The Apology* (*CW 8*, 1434–35; *CW 9*, xc).

[6] See the variants at 5/21–23, 6/8–9, 57/20–21, 73/14–15, 112/23–24, 124/33–34, 169/35–36, 175/33–34.

[7] 129/12–13, 129/25 and Appendix A, 309/37, 319/8, 334/19.

A Note on the Text

T HE copytext of this edition is *1533*, of which four copies[1] have been completely collated and three others[2] consulted where there seemed to be a difficulty. Collation of the four copies revealed no stop-press corrections, but some of the sidenotes seem to have been damaged during printing.[3] The Klein copy of *1557* at Yale has been completely collated and the substantive variants from it recorded in the textual apparatus according to the norms given in *CW 8*, 1447–50.[4] Sidenotes present only in *1557* are marked with an asterisk.[5] I have silently expanded most abbreviations and made certain typographical adjustments in accordance with the norms presented in *CW 8*, 1447–50. The abbreviated form "Iohñ" in *1533*, which appears as "Iohn" in *1557*, has been expanded to "Iohan," for that is the form given in the two places (18/15, 53/14) where the name is spelled in full.[6] Paragraphs in *1533* are indicated by a pilcrow,[7] for

---

[1] Microfilms of the copies at the Bodleian Library, Oscott College, (Sutton Coldfield, Warwickshire), Lincoln Cathedral Library, and the Huntington Library.

[2] Microfilms of the copies at the British Library, the John Rylands Library (Manchester University), and Trinity College (Dublin). I have not seen the copies at the Folger Shakespeare Library, the Vatican Library, and Stonyhurst College (Lancashire), or the imperfect copy at the British Library. For the known locations see Constance Smith, *An Updating of R. W. Gibson's St. Thomas More: A Preliminary Bibliography* (St. Louis, 1981), p. 29. The Lincoln Cathedral copy lacks the title page; many of its sidenotes have been partially trimmed away and a few words have been torn off the lower right corner of sig. Aa$_2$. All the copies I have seen except that at the Bodleian contain the blank leaf between sig. Bb$_7$ and sig. a$_1$. All the copies I have seen, except for that at Lincoln Cathedral, contain More's address to the reader correcting a passage in *The Debellation of Salem and Bizance* (sigs. N$_4$–N$_6$), The Lincoln Cathedral copy lacks the last four leaves of the last gathering (N$_3$–N$_6$).

[3] The sidenote at 93/8–10 is complete only in the copy at the John Rylands Library. The other copies I have seen lack "Chriso." and all but the "h" of "hom. 46" except the Lincoln Cathedral copy, which has "Ch" "ho" and "in I" at the beginning of each line. The sidenote at 6/8–9 appears only in the Huntington copy of *1533*. It is incorrect and was perhaps removed early in the printing. But the other sidenotes omitted by *1557* do appear in all the copies of *1533* I have seen. The British Library copy of *1533* lacks the two sidenotes at 155/1–2 and 155/5–6, which are present in the other copies I have seen.

[4] I have also consulted the other two copies of *1557* at Yale. The sidenotes at 49/15–17 and 94/33–34 are complete only in the Roper copy at Yale.

[5] In the glosses a few hyphens have been silently added to words broken at the ends of lines.

[6] The line above *n* is not intended to represent a second *n* but is the printer's equivalent of "Iohn" with a horizontal line through the ascender of *h* and extending over the *n*. In the Valencia autograph of *De Tristitia Christi*, More normally writes the name in full ("Ioannes") but once he abbreviates it with a line through the *h* (*CW 14*, 41/3).

[7] See the illustrations facing pp. lxxxviii–lxxxix.

which I have substituted indentation (as in *1557*). I have not reproduced the running heads of *1533*, which identify the preface and each of the five books. Passages marked off by double quotation marks in the outer margins of *1533* are here enclosed within pairs of double quotation marks. The typeface Bastard 102 in *1533* appears here as roman; Bastard 68, as smaller roman; and Textura 92, as italic corresponding to the larger roman. In the variants both text and sidenotes are uniformly printed in roman typeface to distinguish them from the editorial information in italic.

I have not reprinted sigs. N₄-N₆ which contain "Syr Thomas More knyght to the chrysten reader." These pages are a reprint (with a few modifications) of two leaves which had been added to *The Debellation of Salem and Bizance* to correct an error in that book.[1] They will be taken into account in the Yale edition of *The Debellation*.

---

[1] See p. lxxxvii, footnote 3, above. In some copies of *1557* these pages are reprinted (with changed page and line numbers) from *1533* on the recto of an extra leaf tipped in after CC₅, right after *The Answer*. They do not appear after *The Debellation* in *1557*.

THE ANSWER
TO A
POISONED BOOK

The answere to the fyrst parte
of the poysened booke,
whych a namelesse
heretyke hath
named
the souper of the lorde.

By syr Thomas More knyght.

---

7 knyght.] knight. Anno. 1533. after he had geuen ouer the offyce of Lorde Chauncellour of
Englande. *1557*

The preface.
Syr Thomas More knyght
to the chrysten reader.

Wolde god good christen readers as I haue often sayde, yᵗ
euery good chrysten man, ye man & woman both, which are of 5
that inwarde good and graciouse mynde, that they wolde not for
all thys world forsake the trewe fayth them selfe, hadde as mych
burnynge zele and feruour in theyr hartes, to se it outwardly kepte
and preserued amonge all other, as these that are fallen in false

A godly wysh* heresyes and haue forsaken the fayth, 10
haue an hote fyre of hell in theyr hartes,
that neuer can suffre them to reste or ceace, but maketh them
bothe day & nyght, [Aa₂v] bysily labour and worke, to subuerte
and destroye the catholyke chrysten fayth, wyth all the meanes
that euer they can deuise. 15

For surely yf all suche as byleue well them selfe, were as loth to
here any worde spoken wronge agaynste the fayth, as they wolde
be to speke it them selfe: there sholde neyther felesshyppe of theyr
matchys, nor fere of any suche as are after the worldly compte
accompted for theyr betters, any thynge lette or wythstande them 20
bothe by worde and countenaunce to shewe them selfe playnely, to
hate & deteste and abhorre vtterly, the pestylent contagyon of all
suche smoky communycacyon.

The tyme hathe bene ere thys, whan honest chrysten people
wolde walke so farre of from al lecherouse lyuynge, that they wolde 25
not come so [Aa₃] mych towarde it as to abyde the talkynge but

Ephes. 5 folowed thapostles precepte that sayth,
let not fornycacyon or any vnclennesse
be so mych as named amonge you.

In that whyle was there myche honest clennesse, & by shame- 30
fastnesse mych was chastyte conserued. But after tyme yᵗ in wordes,
folke fell vnto more lybertye / and suche as wolde forbere the

---

25 from al] from *1557*

doynge, wolde yet be wel content to fall in the feleshyp of foule and
fylthy talkynge: than beganne clennesse
greately to dekaye. For as thapostle also
reherseth, euyll communicacyon marreth
and corrupteth good maners.

1. Corin. 15

*Euil communicacion**

5

But this dekaye from chastite by declynacyon into foule and
fylthy talkynge, hath bygonne a great whyle agoo, and is very farre
growen on. But the tyme hath ben euyn vntyll [Aa₃v] now very
late, that albe it of fleshly wantonesse men haue not letted to vse
10 them selfe in wordes bothe lewd and very large: yet of one thynge
euer wold euery good man be well ware, that heresye wolde he no
man suffre to talke at his table, but
wolde bothe rebuke it and detecte it to,
all though the thynge touched hys owne
15 borne brother. Such hath ben tyll of late ye comen chrysten zele
towarde the catholyke fayth.

And woulde
*God it wer so nowe**

And albe it that I dowte not, but that (god be thanked) the
fayth is it selfe as faste roted in thys realme styll as euer it was
before (excepte some very few places, & yet euyn in those few, the
20 very faythfull folke many mo than are the faythlesse to) yet syth
good men haue of late not letted to here the euyll talke, and
vncontrolled to speke blasphemouse wordes in theyr company, the
cowrage [Aa₄] therof hath out of all questyon mych geuyn
occasion y^t heretikes haue spred theyr errours mych ye more
25 abrode. For it is not only lechery y^t thapostles wordes are verified
of, where he saith y^t euyll com-
municacyon corrupteth good maners
(albe it therof be they veryfyed to) but specyally be they veryfyed
of heresye. And agaynst the communicacyon of heretikes dyd
30 saynte Poule specyally speke them in hys fyrst pystle to y^e
Corynthyes / among whom some began homely than to talke
agaynst ye generall resurreccion, as some begynne among vs now,
to talke agaynst the blessed sacramentes.

1. Corin. 15

And such communicacion it is therfore that thapostle speketh
35 agaynst / of which he sayth also y^t the
contagion crepeth forth and corrupteth
ferther, after ye maner of a corrupt cankar.

2. Timo. 2

---

24 errours] *1557*, errous *1533*

And therfore he byddeth vs that we sholde haue none other communyca[Aa₄v]cyon with heretykes, but onely of reprouyng theyr heresye & geuyng them warnyng to leue. And yet not euery man be bold, to talke to long with them not euyn therof neyther,

Be not bolde
to talke longe
*with an heretyke**

nor ouer often to medle with them / lest as the pestylence catcheth somtyme the leche that fastynge cometh very nere and longe sytteth by the syke man bysy about to cure hym: so some folke faynt and feble in the fayth matched with a felow stoburne & stronge in heresye, may soner hym selfe take hurte than do the tother good.

Saynt Poule therfore inspyred with the spiryt of god, compendiousely toucheth in very few wordes, bothe these two poyntes at onys, where he wryteth vnto Titus: That man yᵗ is an heretyke

Titi .3.

after onys or twyse warnynge (Lo here the communicacyon that he wolde we sholde haue wyth [Aa₅] hym) voide & escewe hym. So here ye se lo that after onys or twyse warnynge of them, the byshop sholde as folke incorrigible expell them / & we sholde yf we well dyd, kepe no more company nor no more communycacyon with them / no

2. Iohan.
epist.

sayth saynt Iohan, not so mych as byd theym good spede or good morow whan we mete them.

These byddynges of these blessed appostles, yf all catholyke folke wolde folowe (whych eyther of neclygence or fere, or for synful ciuilyte, whyle we folow not, we neuer dyscharge well our conscy-

*Note**

ence towarde god), there wolde withoute any great suyt or trouble be shortly farre fewer heretyques than there be. And they yᵗ are, shold shortly perceyue in euery place where they wene them self many, how very few they be / whych as [Aa₅v] few as they be, wolde god yet they were yet farre fewer than they be. For all be yt there are of heretyques farre fewer than those that are wold haue it seme there

Dissimulyng
*sufferaunce**

were: yet are there vndoutedly by suche dyssymylyng sufferaunce, many mo than elles there sholde haue ben.

21–23 *gloss* 2 Iohan. epist.] *om. 1557*   24 byddynges] byddinges *1557*, bydddynges *1533*
27 god), there] god). There *1533*, God:) There *1557*   34 vndoutedly] *1557*, vndoutely *1533*

And this is also the cause, that of these heretyques bookes there
be so many now brought in as there be. For whyle men may so
boldely speke out theyre heresyes, euen amonge theym whome
they knowe none heretykes: this maketh many folke y^t elles durst
5 not medle wyth suche bokes, to bye theym and loke on theym, and
longe to se what they saye.

But some there are that fyrst begynne but of suche a vayne

Titi .3.

curyouse mynde, whome the deuyll
dryueth after forwarde, and fyrst maketh
10 them doute of the trouthe. And after bryn[Aa$_6$]geth theym oute of
doute to a full belyefe of heresye.

And thus of suche bokes, as sore as they be forboden: yet are
there many bought. Nor the parel refrayneth not myche people
from the byenge, syth there is none house lyghtly that hathe so
15 lytle rome, that lacketh the rome to hyde a boke therin.

But when they hadde the bokes, yf men wolde abhorre theyr
talkyng gone were all the pleasure that they take therin. But now
while men controlle theym not, but laugh and lette theym bable,
pryde maketh theym procede, and they procure mo, and sprede
20 the bokes more abrode, and drawe mo bretherne to theym.

There ys no small nomber of suche erronyouse englyshe bookes
prented of whyche yf fewe were boughte, there wolde not of
lykelyhed so many be putte in prente / [Aa$_6$v] sauynge that some
brethern there are in this realme, that of theyr zele to theyr sectes,
25 beyng of such substaunce that they may forbere yt, geue some

*And yet there
are mani such
brethren**

money therto before hande, content to
abyde thaduenture of the sale, or geue
the bokes aboute for nought to brynge
men to the deuyl.

30 And in this wise is there sent ouer to be prented, the boke y^t
Fryth made laste agaynste the blessed sacrament, answerynge to
my letter, wherwyth I confuted the pestylent treatyce that he
hadde made agaynste yt byfore. And the bretherne loked for yt
nowe at thys bartlemew tyde laste passed and yet loke euery daye,
35 except yt be come allredye, and secretely runne amonge theym.

But in the meane whyle, there is come ouer a nother boke

8–9 *gloss* Titi .3.] *om. 1557*

agaynst the blessed sacrament / a boke of that sort, [Aa₇] that
Frythes boke the bretherne may nowe forbere. For more blasphemouse, and more bedelem rype than this boke is, were that
boke harde to be / which is yet madde inough as men say that
haue sene yt.

This boke is intytled, The souper of our lord. But I beshrew
suche a shewer, as so serueth in the souper, that he conuayth
Are there not awaye the best dyshe, and bryngeth yt
manye suche not to the borde / as this man wold yf he
shewers* could, conuey fro the blessed sacrament
Cristes owne blessed fleshe and bloode,
and leue vs nothynge therin, but for a memoryall onely bare brede
and wyne.

But his handes are to lumpyshe and this messe also to great for
hym to conuey clene / specyally syth yᵉ dishe is so dere and so
dayntye, that euery chrysten man hath his hart bent therto [Aa₇v]
and therfore his yie set theron to se where yt bycometh.

The man hath not set his name vnto his boke / nor whose yt is I
can not surely say. But some reken yt to be made by Wyllyam
Tyndale / for that in a pystle of his vnto Fryth, he wryteth that in
any thynge that he can do, he wolde not fayle to helpe hym forthe.

Howe be yt some of the brethern reporte that the booke was
made by George Iay. And of trouth Tyndale wrote vnto Frith, that
George Iay hadde made a boke agaynste the sacrament, whych
was as yet partly by his meanes partly for lacke of money,
reteyned and kepte fro the prent. Howe be yt what George Ioy
wolde do therin afterward whan hys money were come / that
coulde he not (he sayth) assure hym. [Aa₈]

Nowe of trouthe George Ioye hath longe hadde in hande and
redy lyenge by hym, his boke agaynst the sacrament. And nowe yf
this be yt / he hathe somwhat enlengthed yt of late, by a pyece that
he hath patched in agaynst me, wherin he wolde seme to soyle
myne argumentes, whyche in my letter I made in that mater
agaynste the deuelyshe treatyce of Fryth.

And in very dede, dyuerse that are lerned and haue redde the
booke, reken yt veryly to be the booke of George Iaye, whereof

---

1 agaynst] againste *1557*, aguynst *1533*   28 sayth)] sayth *1533*, saith) *1557*

Tyndale wrote vnto Fryth / specyally by certayn wordes that were
in that letter. For therin wryteth Tyndale, that yf George Iay dyd
put forth his boke, there shold be founden in it many reasons &
very few to the purpose.

5   Howe be yt me thynketh by that [Aa₈v] marke, that this boke
sholde not be that. For in this boke be there very fewe reasons, and
of them all neuer one to the purpose.

    The maker of the boke in yᵉ ende of his boke, for one cause why
he putteth not his name therto, wryteth in thys wyse, Mayster
10   mocke whom the veryte moost offendeth, and doth but mocke it out whan
he can not soyle it, he knoweth me well inough.

    Thys sadde and sage ernest man that mockyng at myne name
calleth me mayster Mocke, dothe in these wyse wordes nothynge
but mocke the readers of his boke / saue that his reason is so rude
15   and folysh, that the mocke returneth to hym selfe.

    For syth he wryteth not his booke to me, nor sendeth me none of
theym, but the bretherne kepe theym fro me as closely as they can:
what if I wyst neuer so wel who he were that wrote [Bb₁] yt, what
were this to the bretherne that reade yt? know they therby who yt
20   is to?

    Now for my selfe also, though I knowe Tyndale by name, &
George Iay or George Ioy by name also, and twenty such other
fond felowes of the same secte mo: yet yf tenne of those wolde
make tenne suche folysh treatyses and sette theyre names to none,
25   coulde I know therby whych of those madde foles, made whyche
folyshe boke?

    Dyuerse there are in dede, of those that are lerned and haue
redde the boke, that thynke for the lacke of lernynge and of wytte
also, that they fynde euery where therin, the booke sholde neyther
30   be made by Tyndale nor by George Iay neyther / but rather by
some yonge vnlerned fole. [Bb₁v]

    Howe be it as for me, I thynke the boke myghte be for all that
made by Tyndale or by George Iaye eyther. For the mater beynge
dyuysed agaynst the blessed sacrament, the wysest or the moste
35   fole, the moste lerned or the leste, is all in maner one, and in that
mater maketh lytle dyfference. For I neuer founde yet any man so

---

2 letter.] *1557*, letter, *1533*   3 founden] founded *1557*   11 knoweth] *1557*, koweth *1533*
12 ernest] *1557*, ernest, *1533*   35 maner] a maner *1557*

*Beware of
the defendyng
of heresye**

wel lerned, and so naturally well wytted wythall, but after that he fell ones to ye defense of heresies, & specyally of this abomynable heresye agaynst the blessed sacrament: neyther lernyng, nor wyt, neuer wel serued hym after.

For as for Tyndale the captayne of our Englyshe heretyques (who byfore he fel to these fransyes, men had went had had some wyt, and was taken for full pretyly lerned to) ye se [Bb₂] good chrysten readers playnly tryed by his bokes, that an vnlettered man myghte be ashamed to write so vnlernedly / and a madde man wolde allmost wax rede for shame, to wryte in some thynges so frantykely.

As touchynge frere Barons and George Iay, the bretherne & systern them selfe se theyr wyttes so wasted and theyr lernyng waxen so slender, that the bretherhed hath lytle lyste to reade them.

And some of the bretherne that say this new worke was made by George Iay, thynke that the cause why he sette not his name therto, was bycause he wyst well the brethern dyd not regarde hym. And Tyndale had in his letter also declared him for a fole, by reason wherof he thought y^t if yt came vnder his name, thestimacyon therof were but loste. [Bb₂v]

Fryth was lo a proper yonge man and a towarde, tyll he fell vnto these folyes. After whyche to what dekay both his wyt and his lernynge came, euery wyse man myche meruayled, that in his open examenacyon herd and consydered his answeres.

For all be yt that in the booke that the bretherne that are here haue sent ouer to prent, Tyndale and hys felowes to bygyle the worlde wythall, purpose to make many chaunges, and amende and aduaunce hys parte, vnderpropyng yt wyth theyre own proper lyes: yet shal ye meanes be metely well founden to controll theyre falshed I truste, and to take awaye theyr clokes, and leue hys foly bare. And than shall men playnely se, that of one whome the bretherne boste for so wyse, there neuer [Bb₃] dyed in Englande byfore, any false heretyque so folyshe.

But now as touchynge this new come ouer boke, whyche the

---

15 bretherhed] brotherhead *1557*   26 answeres] answer *1557*   28 bygyle] *1557*, bygylde *1533*   34 Englande] *1577*, Englange *1533*

maker hath entitled The super of the lord: though the man haue
named yt the souper of our sauyour Chryste, yet hathe the man
made yt the souper of the deuyll.

The specyall effecte of all hys whole purpose is to fede vs wyth
5   the moste poysoned heresye that laboreth to kyll the catholyque
christen fayth, concernynge the blessed sacrament of the autare /
all be yt by the waye he putteth forthe dyuerse other heresye
besyde.

Thys vnsauerye souper of his, withoute any corne of salte, and
10 spyced all wyth poyson, he dyuydeth as yt were into two courses /
that ys to [Bb₃v] wytte into the treatynge and declarynge of two
specyall thynges specyfyed in the gospell of Chryste, wherby chrysten people playnely perceyue, that in the blessed sacrament of
thaulter, is the very blessed bodye of Chryste, his very fleshe and
15 hys bloude.

In the fyrste parte whych I call here his fyrst course, occupyenge
the tone halfe of his boke, he treateth the wordes of Chryste spoken
in the syxte chapyter of saynte Iohan / whyche wordes our sauyour
speketh, of the eatyng of his flesh and drynkyng of hys bloude.

20 In his secunde parte, whyche I call hys secund course, he treateth yᵉ maundye of Chryste wyth hys apostles vpon shere thursday,
wherin our sauyour actually dyd instytute yᵉ blessed sacrament, &
therin veryly [Bb₄] gaue his awne very fleshe and blood to his
twelue apostles hym selfe.

25 I shal therfore diuyde this worke of myne into two partes in lyke
wise, of whyche twayne this shall be the fyrste, wherin I shall
detect & make euery man perceyue thys mannys euyll coquery in
hys fyrste course, concernynge the treatynge of Chrystes wordes in
the syxt chapyter of saynte Iohan.

30 And all be yt yᵗ I shall afterward send you forth my secunde
parte also agaynst his secunde course: yet shall I so handle thys
mannes myscheuouse heresye in this fyrst part, that though I neuer
wrote worde mᵥre herafter of the mater, yet to the perceyuynge of
the trouth, and deteccyon of his falsed, this fyrst part might suffyse
35 for all the whole mater.

---

9 vnsauerye] vnsauery *1557*, vsauerye *1533*   23 awne] owne *1557*   24 twelue] *1557*,
twelne *1533*

In hys fyrste parte, he fyrste ex[Bb₄v]powneth the later parte of the syxte chapyter of saynte Iohan / and by hys declaracyon laboreth to drawe men from the perceyuynge of the trouth, and setteth forth also both his pryncypall heresye, and ouer that dyuerse other.

Also in the same parte he argueth agaynste all men in generall that expowne any of those wordes of Crist there spoken, to be ment by Chryste of the very eatynge of hys fleshe (as the catholyque chyrch byleueth) in the blessed sacrament.

In that fyrste parte also he argueth agaynste me by name in specyall / and pretendeth to soyle such argumentes as I made in my letter agaynste the poysoned treatyse, that Iohan Fryth had before made in that mater agaynst the blessed sacrament. [Bb₅]

In that parte also the man bryngeth in two placys all in great, which he hath pyked out by longe leysoure amonge all my bokes / in eyther of whyche two places, he sheweth that I haue notably contraryed myn own wrytynge, that I haue wryten my self in other places before & sheweth also the places where.

I shall therfore good readers in thys fyrste parte of myne gyue you fyue bokes / and some of them very shorte.

In the fyrst wyll I geue you the exposycion of the selfe same wordes of Chryste, mencyoned in the syxte chapyter of saynt Iohan / by whyche who so conferre them and consyder them togyther, shall I trust perceiue well the falshed of his exposycyon, & not be deceiued therby. And for myne [Bb₅v] exposycyon ye shall not geue me the thanke. For I haue but pyked it out here and there out of the wrytynges of dyuers olde holy menne.

The seconde shall shew you for a sample, some of the fawtes both in folies and errours, that the man hath made vs in his exposycyon.

The thyrde shal answere & soyle hys wyse reasons, wyth whyche he wolde make all men folys, that haue expowned that place before, contrary to hys heresye now / that is to wytte, all the olde holy doctours and sayntes frome thapostles dayes vnto oure owne tyme.

---

1 he fyrste] *1557*, he forste *1533*   2 the syxte] *1533 corr. err.*, the sixt *1557*, his syxte *1533*   24 falshed] *1533 corr. err.*, falsehood *1557*, fashed *1533*   32 expowned] expounded *1557*

In ye fourth shall ye se what wyt and what lernyng he sheweth, in soylynge of myne argumentes made before in that mater agaynst his felow Iohan Fryth. [Bb₆]

5 The fyfth shall declare you the dylygence that the man hath done, in sekyng out my neglygence, leuynge some places in my wrytynge, repugnaunt & contrary the tone place to the tother. And of such places ye shall (as I sayd) se hym with dylygent serche of thre yere, at laste brynge you forth twayne. And there shall you se good chrysten reders, that in those twayn, my neglygence shall

10 for all his dylygence proue hym twyse a fole.

But in the treatyng of this mater with hym, I shall lacke somwhat of the commodyte that the man hath in dysputynge wyth me. For he hath a greate pleasure oftetymes, nowe in one maner, now in another, now to talke of me, and nowe to speke to me by

15 name, wyth, thus sayth More, and, lo mayster More, and sometyme, mayster Mocke, and, let More mocke on and lye to / and [Bb₆v] many such goodly garnyshynges mo. But he wyll be for hys owne parte sure that I shall not dyspute wyth hym by name, and therfore he kepeth it awaye.

20 And therfore what foly and what falsed be founden in his boke, he forceth very lytell. For shame he thynketh he can none take therby, whyle folke knowe not hys name.

Wherin he fareth myche lyke to some bestely body, y^t wolde not care to sytte downe wyth hys face to the walwarde, and ease hym

25 selfe in the open strete / and though all the towne at onys tote in his tayle, take it for no shame at all, bycause they se not hys face.

And veryly as we se somtyme, that suche as walke in visours, haue mych the lesse fere and shame, bothe [Bb₇] what they do and what they saye, bycause they thynke theym selfe vnknowen: so

30 do these folke oftentymes lytell force what they wryte, that vse to putte out theyr bookes, and set not theyr names vnto theym. They thynke theym selfe vnsene whyle theyr name is vnknowen / and therfore they fere not the shame of theyr foly. As some haue I sene ere thys, full boldely come daunce in a maske, whose dauncynge

35 bycame them so well, that yf theyr visours hadde ben of theyr facys, shame wolde not haue suffred theym to sette forthe a fote.

---

31 out theyr] theyr *1557*

And mayster Mummer vnder his maskers face forceth not myche
*And that is most true**   to shyfte a false caste amonge, wyth a
payre of false dyce.

And therfore syth thys man by [Bb₇v] wythdrawynge his name
from hys booke, hath done on a visour of dyssimulacyon, dys-   5
simulynge his person to voide the shame of his falshed, and speketh
to mych to be called mayster Mummer, whyche name he were els
well worthy for hys false dyce: I shall in this dyspicyon bytwene
hym and me, be content for thys onys (syth by some name muste I
call hym) for lacke of hys other name to call hym mayster Masker.   10
And thus finishynge this preface, we shall begynne the mater.

---

6 falshed] *1533 corr. err.*, fashed *1533*, falshode *1557*

The fyrst booke.

The .i. chapyter.

Mayster Maskar hath in thys hys poysened treatice agaynst
Crystes holesome sowper xxxii. leuys. In yᵉ first .xiiii. wherof he
expowneth vs the later parte of the syxte chapyter of saynt Iohan.
And incidently by the way, the man maketh as though he
answered the reasons whiche I made in my letter, agaynste the
pestylent treatice that Fryth made fyrst agaynst the blessed sacrament. And in the same .xiiii. leuys also, he bryngeth forth two
thynges for specyall notable, wherin he sayth I haue openly contraryed myn owne wrytynge.

I wyll good reader peruse the remanaunt of hys booke after this
fyrst [a₁v] part answered. In whyche conteynyng these thre
thynges that I haue rehersed you / the fyrst hath he so handeled, yᵗ
all were there not (as there are in dede) dyuerse false heresyes
interlaced therin, yet it were for the mater of very sleyght effecte.
For in his exposicion he nothyng toucheth nor cometh nere to the
thyng wherin the poynt of all the mater standeth.

The secund point hath he so well treated in hys argumentacyon,
that the reasons whyche I laye agaynste Frith, mayster Masker
fyrst falsely reherseth, and after so folyshely soyleth, that he leueth
them more stronger agaynst hym whan he hath done, than he
fownde them whan he bygan.

And as for the thyrde poynt concernynge hys notable notys of
suche thynges as he layeth to myne ouersyghte, them he so garnessheth & set[a₂]teth out so semely to the show, that I wolde no
man sholde euer after this daye truste any worde that I shall wryte,
but yf ye se mayster Masker playnely proued therin, eyther so
folyshe as no man shold trust his wyt, or so false that no man shold
trust his trouth. Let vs therfore now come to the fyrste point, that
is to wytte hys exposicyon.

---

5 expowneth] expoundeth *1557*

The .ii. chapyter.

THE whole summe of his exposicion is, that our sauyour in all
those wordes takynge occasion of the myracle that he so late before
had wrought among them, in fedyng fyue thousand of them with
                        fyue barly louys and two fysshes, dyd in
5   *Iohan. 6*   those wordes vppon theyr new resort
vnto hym whan they folowed hym to Capharnaum, fyrst rebuke &
blame them bycause they soughte hym not [a₂v] for the miracles
that they had sene hym wurke, but bicause they had ben fedde by
hym & fylled theyr belyes / and that therfore our sauyour exhorted
them to labour rather to gete that meat that neuer sholde perysshe.
Vppon whiche exhortacyon whan the Iewes asked hym what they
sholde do wherby they sholde wurke yᵉ wurkes of god / Chryst sayd
vnto them, that the wurke of god was, to byleue and trust in hym
whom the father had sent.

Than goeth he ferther & sheweth, that vpon the wordes of the
Iewis askyng our lord what token he shewed for whiche they shold
byleue in hym, syth theyr forefathers had gyuen them the brede of
                        Manna in deserte, of whiche it was
            Exodi. 16   writen, he gaue them bred from aboue /
our lorde shewed them that Moses gaue them not that bred [a₃]
from heuen, but his owne father had geuen them the very brede
that was descended from heuen, and that oure lorde there by all
the remanaunt of those wordes in the sayd syxte chapiter of saint
Iohan, declareth that hym selfe is that very bred, & is to be eaten
by the fayth and the byliefe yᵗ Chrystes flesshe and body was
broken and his bloude shed for our synnes. And so expowneth he
forth all these wordes of Chryst, applyeng them onely to the
declaracyon of his passyon to be suffred for our redempcion / and
that our sauyour wold haue them byleue that point, & that the
byliefe of yᵗ point was ment by the eatynge, and that that fayth
and byliefe is yᵉ mete of our soules.

The Whole somme of his exposicyon is this in al his sayd .xiiii.
leuys. I mene not that this is all that euer [a₃v] he sayth therin /
for I leue out his circumstaunces, his garnysshynges, his notes, his
argumentacions, his contencyons with me, his mokkes, his tauntys

---

7 Capharnaum] Capernaum *1557*   21 Moses] Moyses *1557*   27 synnes] synne
1557; expowneth] expoundeth *1557*

agaynst all catholyke folke, & his manyfolde heresyes also, with all whiche here and there he furnyssheth all the progresse of his paynted processe / all whiche thynges I shall after touche by them selfe. But the somme, the substaunce, and the ende wherto all the whole processe of his exposicyon cometh, is this that I haue rehersed you. 5

The .iii. chapyter.

But now good chrysten readers all this exposicyon, were it neuer so trew, neuer so comely, nor neuer so cunnyngly handeled / yet were it (as I tolde you before) very farre from the purpose. For this exposicyon myghte be good ynough, & yet myght [a₄] Chryste in those wordes teache the thynge that we speke of besyde, that is to

John. 6* wytte besyde the teachyng them that hym selfe was the very brede y^t was descended from heuyn to gyue lyfe to the world, and that he sholde suffre deth for the synnes of ye world and that they shold byleue these thynges, and so eate hym here by fayth / he myghte I saye teche in those wordes also, that he wolde gyue vnto men his very body & his very flesshe to eate, and his very bloud to drinke, and that he wolde that they shold byleue that lesson also. And wyth ye spyrituall eatynge therof, by fayth receyue and eate also his very blessed body flesshe and bloude by the mouth, not in his owne flesshely forme as ye flesshely Iewes mysse toke it, but (as hym selfe than ment it and parte there expowned it, and by his institu[a₄v]cion dyd after more clerely declare it) in forme of brede and wyne in ye blessed sacrament of the aulter. 25

It is I trow good readers to no man almost vnknowen, that the holy scrypture of god is in suche meruelous maner, by the profound wysedome of his holy spyryte, for ye more plentuouse profyte of his

The scriptur hath many-fold censes* chyrche, deuised, indyghted, and wryten, that it hath not onely that one sense trewe which we call the litterall sence (that is to wytte that sence whiche for the fyrst lesson therof, god wold we shold perceiue and lerne) but also diuerse other sensys spyrytuall, pertaynynge to the profyte of our maners, and instruccions in sundry vertues, by meane of allegoryes, openyng of mis- 35

10

15

20

30

---

22 mouth,] *1557*, mouth *1533*

teries, and lyftynge vppe of the soule into yᵉ lyuely lyght and
inward hygh sighte of god. And all those manyfold sen[a₅]ses
(diuers in the waye and all tendynge to one ende) maye be conuenient and trew, and all by one spyryte prouyded, and in to diuerse
5 spyrites by the same one spyrite inspyred, for spyrituall profite to
be by many meanes multyplyed and encreaced in hys chyrche.

But neuer hath any good man ben accustumed to playe the
pageaunt yᵗ mayster Maskar playeth vs here, with a spyrytuall
exposicyon of allegoryes or parables, to take awaye yᵉ very fyrste
10 sense that god wolde we shold lerne of the letter / and bycause of
some allegories, turne all yᵉ playn wordes fro yᵉ first right vnderstanding, into a secundary sense of allegoryes.

Of this maner handelyng of scripture I make mencyon in my
letter agaynst Frythes false handelynge of this same place of saynt
15 Iohan. And [a₅v] there I shewed in what wyse yᵉ false heretikes yᵉ
Arrianys vsed by yᵉ same meanys, to take yᵉ godhed from Crystes
persone / as Fryth and these felowes by the selfe same maner of
expownynge the scrypture, do take awaye Chrystes manhed from
Chrystes blessed sacrament.

20 In that pistle I shewed also that I wold in allegoricall exposycyons fynde no faute, but be well content with them, so that men
mysse vse them not, to the takynge away of the trew litterall sense
bysyde.

This thynge I there shewed good readers in the self same pystle,
25 that mayster Masker maketh here as though he could & wold
answere. And yet as though he had neuer herd my wordes but
slepte while he redde them, he playeth here the selfe same
pageaunt hym selfe, whyle with his [a₆] allegorycall exposycyon of
spyrytuall eatynge of Chrystes godhed and of his body by byliefe of
30 his passyon, he goth about to take awaye from vs yᵉ very lytterall
trewth, of the very eatynge and bodely receyuynge of Chrystes
owne very flesshe & bloud.

Now wyll I not lay any maner blame at all, to any man that
wyll expowne all the whole processe of
Allegoryes are to be   Genesis, by allegories / and teche vs cer-
35   *suffered & accepted**   teyne conuenyent vertues, vnderstanden

---

11 fro] *1533 corr. err.*, for *1533 1557*   18 expownynge] expoundyng *1557*
35 allegories] all allegories *1557*

by the four floodes of paradys, and tell vs that paradyse is grace,
out of whyche all the flodys of all vertues flowe, and water the erth,
callynge the erth mankynd, that was made therof, beynge barayne
& frutelesse but yf it be watered with y^e floodes of vertue / and so
forth in some suche maner expowne vs all the remanaunt. He lo 5
that thus doth, doth [a$_6$v] in my mynde ryght well. But mary yf he
wolde do it in the maner & with the mynde, that mayster Masker
expowneth vs Christes wordes, all in allegoryes here, and wold
teche vs suche a spyrytuall sense, to make vs byleue that those
wordes were to be none otherwyse vnderstanden bysyde, but that 10
there were no such floodes flowynge forth of paradyse, nor no
suche paradyse at all / I wold wene verely that he were a very
heretyke.

    I fynde no fawte also with them, that expowne the story of
Iudicum. 15 Sampson tayenge the foxes togyther by 15
y^e taylys, and settynge a fyre in them,
and sendynge them so in to the felde of y^e Phylistyes to burne vp
the corne / in those I saye that expowne that story by the deuyll,
sendyng his heretykes in to the corne felde of god the catholyke
chyrche of Chryste, wyth y^e fyre [a$_7$] of false wordes to destroye y^e 20
*Note this allegory** corne, bothe of trewe fayth and good
wurkys, tayed togyder by the tayles, in
token that all theyr heresies be theyr hedes neuer so farre a sunder,
yet are theyr tayles tayed togyther in that y^t all tende towarde one
ende, that is to wytte to the destruccion of all maner grace and 25
goodnes / & that the tayeng of the fyre and theyr tayles togyther
signifieth also y^t for theyr foxly falsehed, finally in the ende the
hote fyre of hell shalbe so fast tayed in all theyr tayles wrabelynge
there together, y^t neuer shall they gete y^e fyre fro theyr taylys, nor
fro the bandes of hell be seuered or breke asundre: with this alle- 30
gorye of those good men that thus expowne y^t story, I fynd no
faute at all. But on the tother syde if any man wold expowne it so
by that spirituall allegorye agaynst these heretykes, y^t [a$_7$v] he
wold therwith enforce hym selfe to take away the lytterall sense,
and say the text signifyed nothyng ellys, and that there was no 35
suche thynge done in dede / hym wold I reken for an heretyke to.

---

22 tayed] tyed *1557*   26 tayeng] tieng *1557*   27 signifieth] signiifeth *1533*, sygnyfyeth
1557.   28 tayed] tyed *1557*   31 y^t] the *1557*

And in lyke wyse good readers yf mayster Masker here dyd
onely expowne all those wordes of Chryste, as thynges spoken of
spyrytuall eatyng by waye of allegory / that waye wold I well allow /
for so doth not onely suche as he is, but also good faythfull folke to.

5   But now whan he draweth all Christes wordes to those allegoryes of
a false wyly purpose, to make men wene (& so sayth hym self for
his part) y^t they signifye none other thyng: this is the poynt y^t
proueth mayster Masker an heretyke.

And therfore as I sayd, all his exposicyon is farre of fro the
10 purpose, & [a$_8$] approcheth not to the poynt. For the questyon is
not whither those wordes may be well veryfyed & expowned of
spyrituall eatyng by way of an allegory / but whyther it may
bysyde al y^t, be trewly expowned of the very bodyly eatyng of
Crystes blessed body in dede. For yf it so may / than is there no
15 man of so slendre wytte, but he may well se, y^t all mayster Maskers
allegorycall exposicyon of his onely spirituall eatyng, flitteth fro the
purpose quite, & dare not come nere ye point.

Wherfore to thentent y^t ye may clerely se, y^t in this exposicyon of
his (as holy as he wold haue it seme) he doth but clerely mokke
20 (sauynge that it is myche worse thanne mockynge, to make men
fall fro the fayth) I shall geue you of the same wordes of Chryst
wryten in the syxt chapyter of saynt Iohan, another exposycyon
[a$_8$v] my selfe / in which I shall bysyde all suche spyrytuall exposi-
cyons, as this man vseth therin by waye of allegoryes or parables,
25   declare you y^e very lytterall sense of
       *Iohn. 6**   those wordes: My flesshe is veryly meate
& my bloude veryly drynke. So that ye maye se therby, y^t our
sauyour veryly spake & ment, not onely suche a spyrytuall eatyng
as mayster Masker sayth he onely ment / but also the very bodyly
30 eatyng & drinkyng of his very fleshe and bloude in dede. Whiche
exposicyon of myne, yf it be in that poynt trewe / than must it
nedes folow (ye se wel) that his exposicyon is farre fro the purpose.
For all though there were not one false word therin / yet were it in
dyssemblynge of the trouth, very lewd and falsely handelyd.

35 And now that myne exposycyon shalbe trew indede, that shall
you ere [b$_1$] I leue you, so clerely perceyue and see, that I trust
there shall neuer any suche heretyke as thys is, be able to blynde

---

17 y^e] that *1557*;   point.] *1557*, point *1533*   36 you,] *1557*, you *1533*

any man after that redeth it / except some such as wyllyngly lyste
to wynke, or whyle he put out theyr eyen, wyll hold theyr heddes
to hym them selfe.

Now to the entent ye may the better perceyue & marke,
whyther myne exposycyon agre with the texte, and whyther I leue
any thyng vntowched: I shall fyrst gyue you the wordes of the
texte it selfe in englysshe all to gyther, and than expoune it you
piece by pyece after. And yet hadde it not bene euyll to begyn
somwhat before at Chrystes dyscyples goynge in to the shyppe in
the euenynge, and Chrystes owne walkynge after vppon the see,
and after y^t on the morow the people comyng after to seke hym
[b$_1$v] in other shippes / which piece maister Masker left out and
wold not medle with, bycause it hath an hard allegory declared by
holy doctours, whyche shewe that the shyppe in whiche the discyples went, bytokened the chyrch which was but one / and the
other diuerse shyppes that came after, betokened the dyuerse
chyrches of heretykes. And yet in that one shyppe that sygnyfyed
the chyrch, there were as appered after, both good & badde to
gyther. But lette this piece passe for this onys / I wyll begyn y^e
texte but there as mayster Masker begynneth hym selfe. Lo good
chrysten readers these be the wordes.

The .iiii. chapyter.

" *Veryly veryly I saye to you, you seke me, not bycause ye haue sene*
myracles, but bycause ye haue eatyn of the loues and are fylled. Worke you,
not the meate that perisheth, but that [b$_2$] *abydeth into euerlastyng lyfe,*
which the sone of man shall gyue you / for hym hath god y^e father sealed.
They sayde therfore vnto hym, what shall we do that we maye worke the
workes of god? Iesus answered & sayde vnto them. This is the worke of god
that ye byleue in hym whom he hath sent. Than they said vnto hym, what
token shewest thou, therfore that we may se and byleue the? what workest
thou? Our fathers haue eaten manna in the deserte as it is wryten / he gaue
them brede from heuyn to eate. Than sayd Iesus to them, veryly veryly I say to
you Moyses hath not gyuen you the brede from the heuyn, but my father
gyueth you the very brede from the heuyn. For the very brede is that that is
descended from heuyn, and gyueth lyfe to the worlde. Than sayde they to hym,

5

10

15

20

25

30

35

23 to] vnto *1557*; you, you] *1557*, you you *1533*   26 god] good *1533*, God *1557*
30 thou, therefore] thou therefore, *1557*

lorde gyue vs all waye this brede. Than sayd Iesus to them, I am the brede of
life / he that cometh [b₂v] *to me shall not hungre, and he that byleueth in me*
shal neuer thyrst. But I haue sayd vnto you, that ye haue bothe sene me and
haue not byleued. All that my father gyueth me shall come to me / and he that
5 *cometh to me I shall not caste hym out. For I am descended from heuyn, not to*
do myne owne wyll, but the wyll of hym that hath sent me. This is veryly the
wyll of hym that hath sent me, that is to wytte the father, that all that he
hath gyuen me I shold not lese any thyng therof, but sholde reyse it agayne in
the last daye. This is veryly the wyll of my father that hath sent me, that
10 *euery man that seeth the sone and byleueth in hym, shold haue euerlasting*
lyfe, & shall reyse hym agayne in the last day. The Iewes murmured therfore
of that that he had sayde, I am the lyuely brede that am descended from
heuyn. And they sayde, Is not this man the sone of Ioseph, whose [b₃] *father*
and mother we haue knowen. How sayth he therfore I am descended from
15 *heuyn? Iesus therfor answered & sayd vnto theym, murmure not amonge your*
selfe. There can no man come to me but if the father that sent me draw hym,
and I shall reyse hym agayne in the last day. It is wryten in the prophetes:
And they shalbe all taught of god. Euery man that hath herd of the father
and hath lerned cometh to me / not bycause any man hath sene the father, but
20 *he that is of god hath sene the father. Veryly veryly I tell you, he that byleueth*
in me hath lyfe euerlastynge. I am the brede of the lyfe. Your fathers haue
eaten manna in the desert and be dede. This is the brede descendynge from the
heuyn, that yf any man eate therof, he sholde not dye. I am the lyuynge brede
that am descended from the heuyn. If a man eate of thys brede he shall lyue
25 *for euer, & the brede whiche* [b₃v] *I shall gyue is my fleshe, whyche I shall*
geue for the lyfe of the worlde. The Iewes therfore stroue amonge them selfe
sayeng, how can this man geue vs his fleshe to eate. Than sayd Iesus to them.
Veryly veryly I saye to you, but yf ye eate the fleshe of the sone of man and
drynke his bloude, ye shall not haue lyfe in you. He that eateth my flesshe and
30 *drynketh my bloude, hath lyfe euerlastyng, and I shall reyse hym in the last*
daye. My flesshe is veryly meate and my bloud is veryly drynke. He that
eateth my flesshe and drynketh my bloude, dwelleth in me & I in hym. As the
lyuyng father sent me, I also lyue for the father. And he that eateth me, he
shall also lyue for me. This is the brede yᵗ hath descended from heuyn / not as
35 *your fathers haue eaten manna and are dede. He that eateth this brede shall*
lyue for euer. These thynges sayd he in the synagoge, teachyng in [b₄]
Capharnaum. Many therfore of hys dyscyples herynge, sayde, This is a hard

---

5 descended] descenden *1557*   37 Capharnaum] Capernaum *1557*

sayeng, and who may here hym. Iesus therfore knowyng in hym self that his
disciples murmured at this, sayd vnto them, doth this offend you: yf ye shall
than se the sone of man ascendynge vppe where he was before. The spyryte it
is that gyueth lyfe / the flesh auayleth nothyng. The wordes which I haue
spoken to you, be spyrite & lyfe. But there be some of you y byleue not. For* 5
Iesus knew from ye begynnyng who shold be ye byleuers & who shold bytraye
hym / and he sayd, Therfore I haue sayd vnto you y no man can come to me*
but yf it be gyuen him of my father. From y time many of his discyples went*
backe, & now walked no more with hym. Than sayd Iesus to the .xii. wyll
you go your wayes to. Than answered vnto hym Symon Peter, lord to whom 10
shal we go. Thou hast the wordes of euerlastyng lyfe, & we byleue & haue
knowen [b₄v] that thou art Chryst the sone of god. Iesus answered vnto hym:
Haue not I chosen you .xii. & one of you is a deuyll. He sayd y by Iudas*
Iscaryotte ye sone of Symon. For he it was that shold betray hym, beyng one
of y^e .xii." 15

The exposycyon of the sayd texte.

The .v. chapyter.

Wᴴᴼ so rede & consyder well good crysten reders, the doctryne
and ye doynges of our sauyour Crist, shall by sundry places of holy
scrypture perceyue, y* of his heuynly wysedome his holsome vsage 20
was, in many great thynges y* he purposed to do, byfore the doyng
of the same (besyde the fygures of the old testament fore fygurynge
the same / & besyde the prophecyes of the old prophetes fore
prophecyeng the same) for mennes more redynesse toward y^e
thinges whan he wolde execute theym by his dede, to geue them 25
some warnyng & informa[b₅]cyon therof before by his wordes.

Thus before he made saynt Peter his chyefe shepeherd ouer hys
Iohn. 21* flocke, iii. times at ones, specially
byddynge hym to fede his shepe, he
fyrste sayd vnto hym, thou shalt be called stone / & after sayd also 30
to hym, whan he confessed hym to be Christ: Thou art stone / &
Math. 16* vpon the same stone shal I byeld my
chyrche, and the gates of hell shall not
preuayle agaynste yt.

---

1 hym.] hym *1533*, him. *1557*   2 you:] *1557*, you *1533*   3–4 it is] is it *1557*
23 besyde] besides *1557*   29 fede] *1557*, fed *1533*

Thus before he made him his generall vicare, he gaue hym
the name of stone / which stone he
Iohan. 1
sayd after he wold byelde hys chyrche
Matt. 16
vppon.

5   Thus he gaue his apostles & dyscyples warnyng of his betrayeng, of his takyng, of his deth, of his
Luce. 9
resurreccion, of his ascensyon, by his
word before the thinges were done in dede. And of his comynge
agayne to the dome also at yᵉ general resurreccyon, whyche thynges
10 surely shalbe & are [b₅v] not yet done in dede. And alwaye the
more straunge the thynges were / the more he opened them wyth
wordes. And yet hadde he for all that, some of those thynges for
that whyle not very wel byleued, not euyn of some of his owne
dyscyples. But yet neyther were his wordes fully frutelesse at the
15 time, but that they toke some hold in some folke, and wrought in
some sowles, though not a full fayth, yet an inclynacyon and a
disposycyon towarde yt / and nowe serue, and euer synnes haue
serued, and euer whyle the worlde lasteth shall serue, to the plant-
ynge, rotynge, and waterynge of the fayth, in al chrysten nacyons
20 all the worlde about.

Nowe as our lorde dyd in many thynges / so dyd he specyally in
the two great sacramentes / the sacrament of baptysme, and in this
hygh blessed sacrament of the aulter. [b₆]

Of the tone he talked with Nichodemus that came to hym
25   by nyght, and durst not be sene with
Iohan. 3
him by day for drede of the Iewes.

And of the tother, that is to wytte of the sacrament of the awtre,
he talked here, and taught the very thynge but not the very forme
therof vnto the Iewes & hys dyscyples amonge theym.

30 And as he founde Nichodemus farre of fro the perceyuynge of
the spyrytuall frute that ryseth in the sensyble ablucyon & faythfull
wasshyng of baptysme / so founde he the substaunce of these folke
very farre fro the perceyuynge of the spyrytuall fruyt, that groweth
of the bodyly receyuynge of Chrystes owne blessed body, to them
35 that faithfully receyue it in the blessed sacrament vnder the sensyble forme of brede. [b₆v]

27 awtre] aulter *1557*

Our sauyour also good reder bycause the thynge that he nowe
wente about to tell them, was a meruelous hygh thynge and a
straunge, vsed in the proponynge therof vnto them, diuers wayes
deuysed of hys diuyne wysedome.

Fyrst to make them the more mete to receyue the doctryne of 5
that poynt and to perceyue it / he dyd two myracles before he
Iohan. 6 began to speke therof. One (which
though they were not at it, yet they per-
ceyued well as the gospell sheweth) in goyng ouer ye water without
a vessell / and another that he dyd not onely in theyr presence, but 10
also made them all parteners of the profyte, that is to wyt
Matt. 14 whan he fedde them all beynge fyue thousande in nombre, of two fysshes and fyue
louys / and yet whan all theyr belyes were full, gathered & fylled
twelue [b7] baskettes of the fragmentes. 15

Vppon the occasyon of this myracle good reader of these fyue
louys by suche a myracle so multyplyed as a thynge very conuenient, he toke his begynnynge to induce theruppon the feste that
he wold in this world leue perpetually with his chirche, by fedynge
of innumerable thousandes with that one lofe that is his blessed 20
body in the forme of brede. Not for y^t ye myracle of y^t fedyng of the
Iewes and this fedyng of Chrystes chyrch, is in euery thynge lyke /
(bytwene whiche twayne there are incomparable differences) but
bycause the lesse miracle and in some part lyke, is a conuenient
thynge for an entre and a begynnynge wherwyth to drawe them 25
ferther. And vnto his apostles at y^t tyme so was it and yet vnto this
time vnto all good chrysten peple so is it. [b7v]

Our sauyour also to enduce them the better to the bylyefe of his
great kyndnes, in that he wold vouchsaufe to gyue them his owne
body to be receyued and eaten in to theyrs, he dyd tell them two 30
other thynges / the tone y^t he was very god, the tother that he wold
dye for theyr sakes. Of these two poyntes / the tone myght make
them sure that he wold do it, and the tother that he coulde do it.
For what coulde he not do that was god almyghty? or what wolde
he dysdayne to do for vs, that wolde not dysdayn to dye for vs. 35

7–8 *gloss* Iohan. 6] Iohn. 8 *1557*   21 y^t fedyng] the feeding *1557*   35 dye for vs.] dye for
vs? *1557*

Now good readers remembryng well these thynges, marke what our sauiour hath sayd in this gospell, and consyder well what he ment. [b₈]

The .vi. chapyter.

5　Wʜᴀɴ that after the myracle of the fedyng so many people with so fewe louys, our lord had (as it foloweth in the gospel)

Iohn. 6*　withdrawen hym selfe asyde into the hyll, bycause he sawe the people were mynded to make hym theyre kynge, the dyscyples hadde entred in

10　the euenynge after into a shyppe, and Chryste apperynge to theym walkynge vppon the see, and calmynge the tempest, whan they wolde haue taken hym in to theyr shyppe, the shyppe was sodaynly comen to the land. The people on the morowe longyng to fynde oure lorde agayne, toke other lytell shyppes that came thyther

15　after, and folowed hys dyscyples, from whom they thought he wolde not longe be, all though they knewe that Chryste wente not in the shyppe with theym. [b₈v] And whan they came on the tother syde of the se to Capharnaum, & founde not onely them there but hym to / than merueylynge mych therof, they sayd vnto

20　hym, Mayster whan camest yᵘ hyther? Our lord answered agayne & sayd vnto them: syrs I tell you very trewth, the cause that you seke me now, is not the myracles that you haue sene, but it is bycause that of the louys yᵗ I gaue you you haue well eaten and well fylled your belyes.

25　In these wordes our sauyour well declared his godhed, in that he tolde them theyr myndes & thoughtes,

A property of the Godhead*　whiche is a property belongynge onely to god. For as the scripture sayth: our

Regum. 2　lord beholdeth the harte. And specyally

30　syth he told them theyr myndes beynge suche as reason wolde haue went theyr myndes had ben the contrary. For syth that after that god [c₁] had so fedde and fylled them of that brede, and that they had sene so mych lefte yet besyde, they dyd vppon the syghte of that myracle saye, " *Thys is*

35　*the very prophete that shall come in to the worlde* " / and by those wordes

---

18 Capharnaum] Capernaum *1557*

declared clerely y^t they thoughte he was Chryste, that is to wytte

Deutero. 18* Messyas, whom they loked for by the prophecye of Moyses and other prophetes, that shold come to saue ye world, and that theruppon they
wold haue made hym kynge: who could haue went that they could   5
haue hadde so soone vppon the morowe so colde a mynde toward
hym, as to go sayle & seke hym for none other deuocyon but for
the fedynge of theyr belyes. But our sauyour (whose depe syghte
entred into theyr hartes, & labored not vppon any fallible
coniecturys) both saw the sykenesse of theyr vnperfait [c$_1$v]   10
myndes, and as a perfyt phisicyon agaynst theyr dysease, diuised
them a good and perfyte medecyn, sayenge vnto them thus, *"wurke*
syrs and labour for the meat, not the meate that peryssheth, but for the meate
that abydeth into euerlastynge lyfe / whyche meate the sone of man shall gyue
you / for hym hath god ye father sealed." As though he wold say, ye   15
labour hither & seke me for such meate as I fedde you with y^e
tother daye / but y^t meat is soone gone and perysheth. Labour &
wurke, and make you mete that you maye eate the meat y^t shall
neuer be gone nor neuer perysh, but shall last with you for euer in
euerlasting lyfe.   20

By these wordes of the meate euerlastynge our sauyour dyd as
the olde holy doctours declare, insinuate and secretely sygnifye to
theym the meat of his own blessed person, both [c$_2$] the spiritual
eatyng of his godhed by fruicyon in heuyn, & the bodyly eatyng of
his very body here in erth / of which both meates he more de-   25
clareth after.

For the better perceyuing wherof ye shall vnderstand that y^e

Materyall meat materyall meate that men eate here,
perishith two wayes* hath two maner of peryshynges. One by
which thorow the naturall operacyon of   30
the body that receyueth yt, it is altered and chaunged, and leseth
his own forme, shape, nature, and substaunce, and is tourned into
the nature & substaunce of the body which it norisheth. And in
this maner of peryshynge perysheth all the meate that euery man
eateth, or els it nothyng nurysheth.   35

The tother maner of perysshyng by which the meate perysheth,

---

18 mete] *1533 corr. err.*, meat *1533*, meete *1557*; eate] eare *1557*   22 insinuate] *1557*,
insumate *1533*

is that peryshynge, by which the meate that is taken thorough
glotony, is for the inordynate appetyte and vse therof / [c₂v]
destroyed and punyshed by god, and the glotonous bely to. Of
whyche maner of peryshynge saynte

1. Corin. 6

5   Poule sayth, The meate for the bely, &
the bely for the meate / and god shall destroye both the tone and
the tother. This is spoken agaynste those that eate not for the
conseruacion of theyr lyfe and theyr helth, to preserue them selfe to
the seruyce of god, but eate & drynke onely for the voluptuouse
10 pleasure of theyr body.

Now taught our lord the Iewes in these few wordes a doctryne
short and compendyouse, that they

*A shorte doctryne**

sholde neyther be glotons in laborynge
for the meate that perysheth of that secunde fashyon, nor so very
15 hyghly esteme the meate that perysheth of the fyrst fasshyon, that
is to wyt any maner of meate that onely nurisheth the body / but
that they sholde labour [c₃] and wurke and endeuour them selfe,
that they myght be mete to receyue and eate that meate that shall
abyde & endure with them in euerlastinge lyfe / that is to saye that
20 as theym selues were bothe bodyes and soules, so spirytually to
receyue and eate of hys own godhed, with the fruicyon wherof they
shold after this lyfe be euerlastyngly fedde among his angellys in
heuyn / and for the meane whyle in thys world bodyly to receyue
& eate his owne blessed body into theyrs, as an ernest peny of
25 theyr perpetuall coniunccyon and incorporacyon with hym afterwarde in the kyngdome of hys eternall glory / where our bodies
shal also be fedde for euer, wyth the farpassynge pleasure of the
bodyly beholdynge of his gloryous body there in his owne bewtyfull
forme, whiche we now veryly receyue here, hydde [c₃v] in the
30 blessed sacrament in lykenesse and forme of brede.

This is the meat that Cryste in those wordes ment, & wold they
shold labour to make them selfe mete for. For this meat wyll in no
wyse perish. But where as the bodyly meate that the man eateth of
the shepe in the nuryshynge of the man, perysheth and leseth his
35 owne nature, not turnynge the flesh of the man in to the flesh of
the shepe / but beynge turned from the owne proper nature of

---

14 very] veryly *1557*   18 mete] *1533 corr. err.*, meate *1533*, meete *1557*   27 farpassynge]
far passing *1557*

shepys fleshe, in to the naturall fleshe of the man / this meate is of
suche vigour & strength, that in the nuryshyng of the man it
abydeth whole and vnchaunged / not beynge turned into the flesh
of the man, but alterynge, turnyng, & transformyng, as holy saynt
Note* Austayn sayth the fleshely man from his
groce fleshelynes into a certayn maner of
[c$_4$] the pure nature of it selfe, by particypacyon of that holy
blessed flesh and immortall, that is with his liuely spyryte immedyately ioyned and vnseparably knitte vnto y^e eternall flowyng foun-
tayn of all lyfe, y^e godhed. This meat therfore Cryste byddeth them
labour & wurke for in those wordes: *"wurke you not the meat y^t
peryssheth but that abideth into euerlasting lyfe."*

But yet though Cryst commaunded them that they shold not be
idle slougardes & slouthfull of them self, but that they sholde
wurke & labour for theyr owne parte to gete this meate, and make
them selfe mete therfore: yet he let them knowe that no man could
by hys owne onely power attayne it. And therfore he added these
wordes, *"whych meate the sone of man shall gyue you"* / tellyng them
therby that hym selfe which had fedde them [c$_4$v] before wyth that
other meate whiche was peryshable, wold also (yf them selfe wold
wurke and labour for it) geue theym the tother meate, that is
permanent in to lyfe euerlastyng to.

And therfore (as dyuerse holy doctours say) whan the preste
minystreth vs this mete, let vs not thinke
The prieste doth not that it is he that gyueth it vs / not the
giue vs the sacrament, preste I saye whome we se, but the sone
but doth deliuer it vs* of man Chryst hym self, whose own
fleshe not ye preste there geueth vs, but as Chrystes mynystre
delyuereth vs. But ye very geuer therof is our blessed sauyour hym
selfe, as hym selfe in these wordes wytnesseth, where he sayth,
" quem filius hominis dabit vobis," whyche meate the sone of man shall
gyue you.

Now lest the Iewes myght haue cause to mystruste, that he y^t
were the sone of man coulde not gyue them y^t meate, [c$_5$] that
were fre from all peryshynge & permanent into euerlastynge lyfe:
he taketh awaye that obieccion, and sheweth them that he is not

---

11 not] not for *1557*   12 lyfe.] *1557*, lyfe *1533*   13 commaunded] *1557*, tommaunded
1533   34 coulde not] *1533 corr. err.*, could *1533*, could not *1557*

The sonne of man* onely ye sone of man but also the sone of god / and no more verily man by that that he is the sone of man (that is to wyt not of Ioseph but of our forefather Adam the fyrst man) than he is veryly god in that he is

5   *The sonne of God** the sone of god, as veryly and as naturally begotten of god the father by generacyon, as he was veryly and naturally descended of our forefather Adam by liniall dyscent and propagacyon. Which thynge our sauyour shewed theym in these wordes: "*Hunc enim pater signauit*

10 *deus.*" For hym hath god the father sealed. This is to say, that hym hath god the father specyally sequestred and seuered and set asyde out of the nomber of all creaturs, and hath sent [c₅v] hym in to ye world, anoynted, sygned, and marked with the very prent of his owne seale. For (as the olde holy doctours declare, and amonge

15 *The seale of god the father** other saynt Cyrill and saynt Hilary) the seale of the father with which he sealed his sone is nothynge els but hym self his own very nature & substaunce. And therfore hath god caused these wordes to be writen in holy scrypture, that god the father hath

20 sealed hys sone, as our sauyour sayd here to the Iewes / and that

Collossi. 1* Crist is the image, prent, and character of the father, as saith saint Poule, bycause we therby sholde lerne and vnderstand, that as a trewe seale trewly prented, leueth in the tother the very whole expresse

25 thynge that it is it selfe, not as it is iron, stele, or coper, syluer, brasse, or golde, but as yt is a seale, that ys to wytte thys fasshyoned fygure or y^t, [c₆] and yet kepeth it whole styll neuer the lesse it selfe, so dyd god the father in the sealyng of god the sone, that is to wytte in hys eternall bygettynge, gyue hym all that euer

30 was in hym selfe, all hys whole wyll, all his hole wysedome, all hys whole myghte and power, and fynally all his whole nature substaunce and godhed, and yet kepe neuer the lesse all the same styll hym selfe.

And thus the sone of god so sealed by his father and not onely

35 expressely representynge, but also veryly beynge one equale god, in nature, substaunce, wysedome, wyll, myghte, & power, with

---

almyghty god hys father, beynge sent in to the worlde by hys father and hym selfe, and theyre bothe holy spyryte equale god wyth theym bothe, toke vppon hym the manhode, the very flesshe, and the [c₆v] very soule of our sauyour Chryste, anoynted aboue all other crea- 5 turys with fulnesse of all graces, by the coniunccion of his manhed in wonderful vnite with hys omnipotent godhed, meruelousely makynge one perfyt persone and one farpassynge perfyte person of god and man togyther.

Psal. 44

Thus hath our sauiour not onely shewed them the great gyfte of 10 euerlastynge lyuely meate, that yf they wold wurke for it he wold gyue them / but hath also shewed them that hym self is equale god with his almighty father, and therby well able to gyue it them, and also sent into the worlde for the nonys, bycause he sholde to such folke as wold be well wyllyng to labour and wurke therfore, wurke 15 with theyre good wyl and wyllyngly gyue it them. [c₇]

The .vii. chapyter.

Whan that the Iewes had herd oure sauyour speke of suche a meate that wolde not perysshe, but sholde abyde & endure with them into euerlasting lyfe / glad men were they. For yet they 20 hoped to haue som meate that so shold fyll theyr belyes and so satysfye them, that they shold neuer nede to labour for any more.

Now were those iewes yet somwhat lesse glotons than are many chrysten people now a dayes. For they coulde haue ben content so that they sholde neuer haue felt hunger more, to haue forborne 25 eatyng for euer. As the woman of Samary, so that she myghte haue had of our sauyour one draught of suche water as myghte haue quenched her thyrste for euer, was well contented in her own minde to haue forborne drynke for euer. [c₇v] But many chrysten men there are, 30 yᵗ wold not I wene be content to take eyther suche meate or suche drynke, though god wold offer it theym. For many men haue suche a pleasure in eatynge and drynkynge, that they wolde not gladly lyue but euyn to eate and drynke. And for the pleasure therof, they loue better 35 hunger and thurst than the harmelesse

Iohn. 4*

Mani men liue to eate*

---

1 father, beynge] father beynge *1533*, father, being *1557*   6 manhed] manhoode *1557*

lacke of them bothe though god wold gyue it them. For we se that
they seke meanes to make theyre appetyte gredy. And some wyll
eate salt meate, purposely to gyue theym a corage to the cuppe.
These folke do not longe to eate & drynke to lyue the lenger, but
longe to lyue to eate and drynke the lenger. These be those therfore of whom ye apostle sayth, " *Esca ventri et venter escis, deus et hunc*

1. Corin. 8

et illam destruet." The meat for the bely &
the bely for [c8] the meat, god shall
destroye bothe the tone and the tother.

And surely besyd the punyshement of god in another world, &

*Siknes doth spring
of glotony**

besyde all the paynes that euyn in this
worlde thorough sykenesse & sorys aryse
and sprynge of suche glotonye / they that
gladly wold endure a gryefe perpetually, to haue the pleasure of
the continuall swagyng, haue in theyr beste welth but a dysplesaunt pleasure / except men be so mad as to thynke that he
were well at ease that myghte be euer a hungred & euer eatyng,
euer a thurst & euer drynkyng, euer lowsy & euer clawing, euer
skoruy & euer scratchyng.

These iewes I saye therfore & the woman of Samary, were

Iohan. 6

not of this mynd / but so y^t they might
haue lacked ye grief of hunger & thurst
they wold haue ben content as it semeth to haue forborne meat &
drynke. [c8v]

How be it to say the treuth, theyr wordes well wayed, it semeth
y^t theyr affeccions were wurse than they seme at ye fyrst syghte.
For as me thynketh they were not so gladde to put away theyr
fawte, as to make a chaunge of one fawte for an other / not so glad
to lese the pleasure of ye meate that is ye mayntenaunce of

*Rest the maintenance
of sloth**

glotony, as to gete them to reste and idle-
nesse that is the mayntenaunce of slowth.
And oure lorde towched thappetyte of
slouth in these Iewes, whan he bad them, " *Operamini non cibum qui
perit &c."* Worke you for the meate, not y^t that peryssheth but that
that abydeth into euerlastynge lyfe / notynge therein as sayth saynt
Chrysostom ye slouthfull appetyte by whiche they wolde fayne

---

2 appetyte] apppetyte *1533*, appetite *1557*   14 gryefe] gryete *1557*   36 y^e] that *1557*

Iohan. 4

haue had hym fede them stylle by
myracle, wythout any labour of theyr
owne. And the woman of Sa[d₁]mary sayd vnto hym: Lord gyue
me of yᵗ water that I nede no more to laboure hyther, and draw
vppe water here at thys depe welle.   5

But surely who so put not away his vyce but make a chaunge,
maye soone happe to take as euyll as he leueth, and not a wurse

Sloth is veri noius
*vnto mankynde**

Gene. 2

lyghtely than slouth. Whiche vyce god
saw so noyouse vnto mankynde, that
euyn whan he sette hym in paradyse, he   10
bad hym be occupyed in the kepynge of
that pleasaunt gardayn. And afterwarde

whan he sholde be dreuyn thense into the erth, he gaue hym a
necessyte to labour / makyng the erth to be suche as without
mannys labour shold not brynge hym forth hys lyuynge.   15

And therfore an euyll and a perylouse lyfe lyue they, that wyll in
this worlde not labour & wurke, but lyue eyther in idelnesse or in

Againste ydle
*gamsters**

idle bysinesse, [d₁v] dryuynge forth all
theyr dayes in gamyng for theyr passe
time, as though that els theyr tyme could   20

neuer passe but the sone wold euer stande euyn styll ouer theyr
hedes & neuer draw to nyght, but yf they draue away the daye
with dauncynge or some suche other goodly gamynge.

God sent men hyther to wake and wurke / and as for slepe and
gamynge (yf any gamynge be good in thys vale of myserye in thys   25

Wherto gaming
*must serue**

tyme of terys) it muste serue but for a
refresshynge of the wery and forewatched
body, to renewe yt vn to watche and

laboure agayne, not all men in bodyly labour, but as the cyrcumstaunces of the persons be, so to be bysyed in one good bysines or   30

*Sawce**

other. For rest & recreacyon shold be but
as a sawse. And sawce shold ye wote wel

serue for a faynt and weke stomake, [d₂] to gette yt the more
appetyte to the meate, and not for encreace of voluptuouse pleasure in euery gredy gloton that hath in hym selfe sawce malapert   35
all redy inough. And therfore lyke wyse as it were a fond fest yᵗ had

---

11 *gloss* Gene. 2] *placed opposite lines 12–13 1533*   29 agayne,] *1557,* agayne *1533*

all the table full of sawce, and so lytle meate therwyth that the
gestes sholde go thense as emptye as they came thyther: so is it
surely a very madde ordered lyfe that hath but lytle tyme bestowed
in any frute full bysynesse, and all the substaunce idely spent in
5 playe.

And therfore to thende that the Iewes shold know that he wold
not nurysshe them in theyr slouth & idelnesse, he bode them
wurke. And yet leste they myght wene that he wold haue all theyr
wurke aboute worldly bysynes, he bode them wurke, not for yᵉ
10 [d₂v] meate yᵗ peryssheth, but for the meate that abydeth into
euerlastynge lyfe. Wherby he ment not to forbede them to labour
for the tone, but to teche them to labour mych more for the tother.

The .viii. chapyter.

Bᵤₜ they as I tolde you (theyr mynde set vppon theyr bely ioy,
15 and therfore not vnderstandyng his wordes) hoped by that worde
to haue theyr belies so wel fylled ones, that they shold neuer nede
more to laboure for theyr lyuynge after. And therfore they sayd
agayn vnto hym: *"what shall we do that we may wurke the wurkes of
god?"* For they thought (as it semeth) that some thynges there
20 were that Chryste wolde haue them do / after which ones done,
than shold they haue that mery feste of yᵗ meate that he spake of /
and therfore wolde [d₃] they fayne wytte what wurke that were
that they myght shortely rydde it out of hande that they were at
dyner, for they waxed a hungered. Our sauyour than vppon that
25 questyon of theyrs, shewed theym what worke it was that he wolde
haue them do for that meate, & sayd vnto them: *" This is the wurke
of god, that you sholde byleue in hym whom he hath sent."* As though he
wolde say, This is the worke that god wyll ye shall worke, before he
wyll I shall geue you thys lyuely meate that I tolde you of / he wyll
30 ye shall fyrst byleue in me whom he hath sent vnto you.

Cryste here for the gettynge of that spyrituall meate, setteth

*To beleue wel is
no little worke**

theym about a spyrituall wurke / byddynge them labour to byleue. Why is
it any labour to byleue? ye veryly good
35 readers to byleue wel is no litell wurk / [d₃v] and so great a

---

9 worldly] *1557*, worldy *1533*   21 yᵗ meate] the meate *1557*   32-33 byddynge them]
1533 corr. err., byddynge *1533*, bidding them *1557*

wurke, that no man can do it of hys owne strength without the
specyall helpe of god.

But here shall you se clerely that Cryst truely told them theyr
thought, when he sayde vnto them / that they sought hym not for
his myracles but for theyr belyes. For whan our sauiour here had
shewedde them, that yf they wold haue y^t lyuely meate, they must
fyrste byleue in hym / theyr myndes were so sette vpon theyr
belyes that they thought they wolde make hym by craft come of
and geue them some meate a pace for theyr dyner. And therfore
they sayde vnto hym: "*what myracle than shewest thou that we maye se*

Psalm. 77 *

*it and therby byleue the? what thynge wurkest
thou? Our fathers dyd eate manna in deserte as
it is wryte / he gaue them brede from heuyn to eate.*" [d₄]

Here you maye se that where as Cryst told them they must
byleue in hym before they shold haue y^t lyuely meate y^t he told
them of, they thought they wold by craft before they wold wurke
toward ye bylief, cause hym to geue theym some other meate in the
meane while / & therfore they not onely sayd y^t it were reason he
shold wurk some myracle before them ere he shold loke y^t they
shold byleue him, but also they assigned him in maner / what
maner a miracle they wold haue him do, y^t is to wyt geue them
some meate by miracle by & by one or other without any worke or
labour of theyrs. And therfore they put hym in mynd of the meat
of manna y^t theyr fore fathers had from heuen whyle they were in
wyldernesse & wurked nothyng therfore.

But agaynst thys our lorde tolde them agayne, that the brede
that they [d₄v] dyd eate in deserte was not geuen them by Moyses,
nor geuen theym veryly from heuyn neyther. For though that
Moyses was theyre prophete and theyr guyde / yet was that brede
of Manna geuen them by god. And it came not also veryly downe
from heuyn, but from a farre lower place of the eyer. But he
shewed theym that god his owne father that gaue them that brede
than out of the ayer, geueth them now verily downe from heuyn
that brede, that is for spyrituall sustinaunce and lyuely nuryssh-
ynge such maner of very brede, that in comparyson and respecte
therof, the tother brede of manna myght seme no brede at all. For

---

10–13 "what . . . eate."] *Marginal quotation marks begin at* what thynge *1533*   13 wryte]
wrytten *1557*   24 fore fathers] forefathers *1557*

" verily veryly said our lord vnto theym, not Moyses gaue you that brede from heuyn / but my father gyueth you the very brede from heuyn. For the very brede is that that [d₅] *cometh downe from heuyn, and gyueth lyfe to the worlde."*

5   Now whan they herde this, wenynge yet that Cryste spake of some suche brede as manna was, that god wold at hys request geue them downe from heuyn, as manna was geuyn downe in Moyses dayes, & that thys brede sholde fede the body as manna dyd, and yet be farre better to / they prayed hym and sayd, *"Lorde gyue vs*
10 *this brede alwaye"* / as though they wold saye, Good lord gyue vs thys very brede that thou spekest of that thy father sendeth downe from heuyn, that we nede not to labour and toyle for brede in tyllynge of the erth / and gyue it vs good lorde alway, not for a season as our fathers had the tother in desert, but gyue it vs for
15 euer, and let vs neuer lacke it, nor nede no more to wurke and labour for it. [d₅v]

The .ix. chapyter.

T̲han was our lord playne with them and sayed, *" I am the brede of life / he yᵗ cometh to me shal not hunger, and he that beleueth in me shall*
20 *neuer thyrste."*

Lo sayth our lord the brede of life that I speke of is my self whom my father gyueth downe from heuyn, to geue not onely nuryshynge, but also lyfe to the worlde.

The comen brede doth but helpe to kepe and conserue the lyfe
25 that the man hath all redy. But my father hath sent me down / me I say the very brede wherof angelles fede, not onely to conserue and kepe the life of the body / (all be it that do I to, & hele of your syke folkes full many) but also to quycken them that are dede, many in body and al the whole world in soule / wherof none can
30 haue lyfe [d₆] but by me.

And therfore he yᵗ cometh to me, that is to wytte, who so wyll wurke the wurke of god that I tolde you, yᵗ is to wytte come by fayth vn to me, and byleue in hym whom the father hath sent, that is to wytte in my self, hys hunger and thyrste shall I take awaye for
35 euer.

Good is it good readers to consyder well these wordes, leste by these wordes wronge vnderstanden, some men myghte wene (as these heretyques teche, that now a dayes renew that olde heresye

Iacobi. 2
Gala. 5

that bothe saynte Iamys and saynte Poule by playne expresse wordes reproue) that oure lorde wolde aske no more of any christen man but onely bare faythe alone. Whyche

*Fayth alone**

heresye / (wherof they so myche bosted a whyle) these heretykes now fele so fully confuted, that [d₆v] though they lyue styll lyke those that byleue it, yet in theyr wordes & wrytynge they be fayne to retrete for shame, & to seke suche gloses to saue theyr olde wrytynge, as myght make vnwyse men wene that they neuer ment otherwyse than the whole catholyke chyrche comenly techeth and precheth. Whiche yf they had ment none other in dede (as in dede they ment and yet mene farre other styll) than hadde they ye wote well made myche bysynes about nought.

But lettynge these heretyques passe / ye shall good chrysten readers vnderstande, that lyke as yf a man wold teche a chyld to rede, he muste fyrst begynne at his A b c (for without the knowlege of hys letters he can neuer go forward) so for as mich as no man can come vnto Cryst without fayth, but faith must nedes be

*Faythe is the fyrst entrie to vertue**

the [d₇] fyrst entre toward all chrysten vertues, syth no man can eyther hope in hym or loue hym whom he knoweth not, and Chryst can no man chrystenly know, but by fayth (for as

Hebre. 11

saynte Poule sayth he that commeth vnto god he must nedes byleue) so dyd our sauyour therfore as a good & a wyse mayster of his chrysten scole, bygyn ther with yᵉ Iewys that there offred them self as his scolers, he began I say with fayth. But yet he ment not that to saluacyon they shold nede no thynge elles but onely bare fayth / so that yf they wold byleue all thynges that he sholde tell them, they sholde therby be surely saued, though they wolde do nothynge that he wold byd theym.

But than what saye we to these wordes of our sauyour? *" He that byleueth in me shall neuer thyrste."* By [d₇v] thys worde of neuer thyrstynge, he meneth euerlastyng saluacyon, which he promyseth here to all those that byleue in hym / wherfore it may seme yᵗ who

5

10

15

20

25

30

35

---

30 no thynge] nothing *1557*

so euer byleue though he do no thynge els, shall by this promyse of
our sauyour be saued.

Saynt Iohan the baptyst at suche tyme as people came to hym,
Luce. 3   & asked what they sholde do whereby
5   they myght auoyde dampnacion he
bode them geue almoyse. And whan the Publicanys asked hym
what they shold do to auoyde dampnacyon, he bode theym forbere
brybys, and take no more than the dew custumes & toll. And to
the souldyours askynge hym the same questyon for theyr part, he
10 answered that they sholde pyke no querellys, nor do no man no
violence, nor take nothynge by force, but holde theym selfe content
wyth theyr wagys. [d₈] Yet dyd he not mene that any of all these
lessons was inough to saue them wythout any more / but he tolde
them for the whyle, eche of them the thyng that sholde be most
15 metely for them / and moste proprely pertayne to theyr persons,
and therfore moste metely for them to lerne fyrste / and the remanaunt shold ech of them after lerne, lytell and lytell at length, so
that at laste they sholde eche of them do that one thynge wyth all
other thynges necessary also, and wythout whych that one thyng
20 could not saue them.

Thus dyd our sauyoure also, bycause the Iewys were full of
infydelyte and full of incredulyte / which vnbylyefe endurynge,
they coulde not entre into the way of saluacyon. He therfore fyrste
taughte theym the lesson of bylyefe and fayth / whyche onys
25 hadde, they shoulde [d₈v] be mete to lerne on the remanaunt, &
encreace both in hope & in well wurkyng cheryte / so that fayth
ones had, he tolde them they shold not peryshe. For yf they onys
byleued his worde / it was a meane to make them hope in hym and
loue hym both, & those thre thynges wold make them obay hym
30 and wurke in suche other vertuouse, as he wolde for theyr owne
weale commande them.

There are also good readers dyuerse holy doctours, that saye
that in these wordes by whych our sauyour sayde vnto the Iewes,
he that byleueth in me shall neuer thyrst / he ment not hym that
35   *Iacobi. 1*   had a bare fayth alone (which is as saynt
Iamys sayth but a dede fayth) but hym
that had fayth well formed wyth hope & cheryte.

---

1 no thynge] nothinge *1557*   5 dampnacion] damnacion: *1557*   6 almoyse] almes
1557   12 these] *1557*, thesse *1533*   24 the] *1533 corr. err.*, *1557*, fyrst the *1533*

And therfore sayth holy saynt Austayne thus: *" Chryst sayth not byleue* [e₁] *hym, but byleue in hym. For it foloweth not by and by that who*

*Belieue Christ and in Christ***

so byleue hym, byleueth in hym. For the deuyls byleued hym, but they byleued not in hym. And we byleue saint Poule, but we byleue not in 5 *saynt Poule. To byleue therfore in hym, is wyth byleuynge to go into hym, and to be incorporate in hys membrys. This is the fayth that god requireth and exacteth of vs / that is to wytte the fayth that by loue wyll wurke well. Yet ys fayth dyscerned and seuered from workys / as the apostle sayth a man is iustifyed by fayth without the wurkes of the lawe. And there are wurkes* 10 *that seme good without the fayth of Chryste, but they be not / for they be not referred vnto that ende of whiche all good thynges come. For the ende of the law is Christ vnto iustice vnto all that byleue. And therfore our sauyour wold not dyscerne and deuyde fayth from the worke / but sayth that* [e₁v] *the fayth it selfe was* yᵉ *worke of god / that is to wytte the fayth that by loue* 15 *wurketh."*

Here ye perceyue good readers, that to byleue meritoriousely, so as it shalbe rewarded with saluacion, may not be fayth alone, but fayth wyth a wurkynge loue. Nor it may not be a bare byleuynge of Cryst, but it must be a byleuynge in Cryste / that is as saynt 20 Austayn sayth, not an idle dede standynge bylyefe, but a bylyefe lyuely, quycke, & styrynge, & by cheryte and good wurkes euer walkyng and goyng into Cryst. And than they that so byleue in hym, not wyth the bare onely fayth that these heretykes preche, but with the well wurkyng faith yᵗ the catholyke chyrche techeth / 25 they shalbe saued sayth our sauyour from eternall hunger & thyrst. [e₂]

The .x. chapyter.

Bᵁᵗ than goth Crist ferther, and sheweth them yᵗ they lacke thys meat though it stand before them. And sheweth them also by what 30 mene they may gete it. Lo thus he sayd vnto them. *" But I haue tolde you* yᵗ *both you haue sene me and you haue not byleued"* / as though he wold say, you haue sene me done myracles, and yet it hath not made you byleue.

He bode them before yᵗ they sholde wurke to gete the lyuely 35 meate / and he told them after yᵗ the wurke which they shold

---

9 Yet] *1557,* yet *1533*   29 goth] goeth *1557*

wurke to gete it with was fayth & bylief. And he wrought myracles whiche they saw, to make them byleue. And now he sheweth them y^t for all this they haue not y^e bylief yet, but yet muste wurke & labour to haue it.

5   Than myghte they haue asked hym, whych way may we come to it? [e$_2$v] But bycause they asked hym not / he of his hygh goodnesse tolde them the meane vnasked and sayd, *" All that my father gyueth me shall come to me."* As though he wold saye, Though my father haue sent me downe to call you to me, and though I preche

10 to you and tell you the trouth at your eare, & worke myracles before you that you may se them at your eyen, ye and fede you by myracles, & putte them euyn in your bely: yet can you neuer come to me by fayth, but yf my father brynge you. Neuer can you be myne by fayth, but yf my father gyue you me. Now yf ye knowe of

15 any good guyde that could brynge you to the place whyther ye wold fayne go, where you sholde fynde the thynge that ye wolde fayne haue: what wold you do / wold you not labour to hym / wolde you not pray and entreat hym [e$_3$] to go with you & guyde you thyther? Now haue I told you who can bryng you to me by

20 fayth, that is to wytte god my father / and therfore labour to hym to guyde you to me, pray hym to geue you to me, wythout whose helpe ye can neuer come to me. It is I tell you no smale thynge to byleue in me. For but yf the grace of my

*A preuenting grace**   father fyrst preuent you, ye can neuer

25 begynne to thynke thereon. But he hath now preuented you by sendynge me to call vppon you. How be it yet for all that, but yf he go forth wyth you and helpe to lede you forwarde, you maye faynte & fall and lye stylle by the waye, & come no ferther forth toward me. But now he helpeth you forwarde by myne outwarde

30 myracles whyche hym selfe worketh with me. But yet except he wurke wyth you inwardly / with his inward helpe [e$_3$v] to draw you, you can for al this neuer come at me. Call well vpon hym therfore, & pray hym to draw you & bryng you & geue you to me. Which if you do & endeuour your selfe for your own parte, as I

35 bode you before to wurke and walke wyth hym toward me, he shall surely brynge you in to faith, and by fayth in to hope and in

---

3 y^e] that *1557*   9 haue] *1557*, haue haue *1533*   17 do/] doe? *1557*   31–32 draw you]
draw yon *1557*   34 Which] which *1533 1557*

to cheryte bothe, and so gyue you gracyousely to me. And than
shall I geue you the lyuely meat that I spake of, yf ye wyll abyde
with me. *" For hym that commeth to me wyll I not caste out."* Let hym
loke that he caste not hym selfe out / For surely I wyll not yf hym
selfe wyll abyde. For it is my fathers wyll that I sholde not, *" and I* 5
am descended from heuyn, not to do my wyll but to do the wyll of hym that
hath sent me. And thys ys veryly the wyll of the father that sent [e₄] *me, that*
all that he hath gyuen me I sholde lese nothynge therof, but that I sholde reyse
vppe that agayne in the laste daye."

The .xi. chapyter 10

Tʜᴇsᴇ wordes myghte good readers seme to an vnchrysten man
or to a false christened Arryane, to sygnyfye that our sauyour were
not equale god with his father, in that he speketh so often (as in
many mo placys of scrypture he speketh more often) that he is
obedyent to hys father, and that his father sent hym, and that he is 15
lesse than hys father / and many suche other placys, by whyche the
olde Arriane heretyques defended theyr heresye agaynste the
godhed of Chryste in hys person / as these Lutherane heretyques /
and these Huyskyns, [e₄v] zuynglians, and Tyndalyns, draw now
diuerse other textes to yᵉ mayntenaunce of theyr false heresyes, 20
agaynst the precyous body and bloud of Cryst in his blessed sacrament.

But as good chrysten men well know that these newe heretykes
are falsely now deceyued in the tone / so know they to, that those
olde heretykes were falsely than deceyued in yᵉ tother. 25

For all the minorite and the obedience that the scrypture
speketh of in Chryste, is all ment of his manhed (whyche was lesse
in dede) and not of his godhed, for they were bothe equale.

For how coulde they be in godhed vnequale, whan that in
godhed they were bothe one, though in persons diuerse. And ther- 30
fore our sauyour by his godhed hath the
What the godhead of selfe same wyll [e₅] that hys father hath
the sonne hath equall and none other / as he hath the same
with the father* wytte, & the same myght, the same
nature, the same substaunce, and finally the same godhed and 35

---

27 manhed] manhod *1557*   28 godhed] goodhed *1533*, godhead *1557*

none other. And therfore what so euer the tone doth the tother
dothe / & as the sone was sent by the father, so was he also sent
bothe by hym selfe and by the holy goost to. And whan ye holy
goost was sent, he was sent bothe by the father and ye sone & by
himselfe also. But incarnate was there no mo but the sone alone /
who as he had by hys godhed none other wyll but the very selfe
same that hys father had and the holy goost, so had he by his
manhed another seuerall wyll and propre vnto the persone of his
manhede it selfe as euery man hath his owne. And of that wyll is it

Iohan. 6   that he sayth, I am descended from
                       heuyn, not to do my wyll but y^e wyll of
hym [e$_5$v] that sent me / for in the wyll of hys manhed he obayed
the godhed.

But nowe yf thys obedyence be vnderstanden of hys manhed,
how can it stande wyth these wordes of his, I am descended from
heuyn not to do my wyll but the wyll of hym that sent me. With
that poynt good reader shall no man nede to be moued. For syth
bothe the godhed and manhed were ioyned and vned together
bothe, in the one person of Chryste, that whole person myghte saye
of it selfe suche thynges as were veryfyed and trewe in any of the
bothe naturys. For lyke as a man maye saye of hym selfe, I shall
dye and retorne into the erthe, and yet that shall not hys soule do
but his body onely / and I shall after my dethe go forthwith to ioy
or to payne, and yet that shall not hys body do by and by but his
[e$_6$] soule: so myghte Chryste saye of hym selfe, I am descended
from heuyn, bycause hys godhed descended frome thense though
hys body dyd not / and he myghte saye I shall suffre and dye
bycause hys manhed so sholde, and yet was hys godhed neyther
mortall nor passyble. And for all that, myghte it be sayde of Cryst,

God dyed for vs*   God dyed for vs, bycause he dyed that
                         than was god. And of Chryste myghte it
well be sayed, Thys man made heuyn and erthe, and yet hys
manhed made it not, but was made by hys godhed as other crea-
turys were. But those wordes are well veryfyed by the reason that

---

1 doth] doeth *1557*   2 dothe] doeth *1557*   8 manhed] manhod *1557*   9 manhede]
manhod *1557*   12 manhed] manhod *1557*   14 manhed] manhod *1557*   18 manhed]
manhod *1557*   28 manhed] manhod *1557*   32 sayed] layed *1533*, sayde *1557*
33 manhed] manhod *1557*

he, whyche of the person of Chryste sayth thys man, sygnyfyeth and meaneth not hys onely manhed but his whole person, whiche is not onely man but very god also. [e₆v]

Thys thynge and this maner of spekynge expressed our sauiour very playne hym selfe, whan he sayd vnto Nichodemus in talkynge 5 with hym of the sacrament of baptisme, " *No man hath ascended into heuyn but he that descended frome heuyn, the*

Iohn. 3* *sone of man that is in heuyn."* In these wordes he sheweth vnto Nichodemus, that there was more credence to be geuyn vnto hym selfe alone, than vnto all the proph- 10 etes that euer were before. For hym selfe more perfytely knewe all thynge than all they dyd. For neuer man had there ben in heuen but he. For neuer man sayd our lorde hath ascended into heuyn, but he that descended frome heuyn, the sone of man that is to wytte I my selfe that am in heuyn. 15

Here he sayed that yᵉ sone of man had bene in heuen, and had descended [e₇] from heuyn, & was yet in heuyn styll. Now was not his godhed the sone of man but the sone of god, nor his manhed the sone of god but the sone of man. But now though the godhed & the manhed were not bothe one, but two distincte naturs styll / yet 20 syth the sone of god and the sone of man were bothe one, that is to wyt both twayne one person Cryste / Cryste therfore myght well say than of hym selfe, I the sone of god am the sone of man, & I the sone of man am yᵉ sone of god, and I the sone of god am walkynge amonge men on erth, and I the sone of man am syttynge 25 wyth my father in heuyn.

Now that ye maye good readers the better conceyue thys mater, and more easely perceyue the sentence of these wordes of Cryst, *All that my father gyueth me &c.* I shal expoune [e₇v] you these wordes of his in order, as it were in hys owne person, spekynge the wordes of 30 thys exposycyon hym selfe.

No man can come to me by hys owne labour alone. But all that my father geueth me shall come to me. Labour therfore to my father & pray hym to geue you to me, geuynge you occasyon and helpynge you & (wyth your own wyll wurkyng with hym) makyng 35

---

1 sayth] saith, *1557*   2 manhed] manhod *1557*   14–15 man that is to wytte] man, that is to witte, *1557*   18 manhed] manhod *1557*   20 manhed] manhod *1557*

you byleue me, and so shall you wurkyng with him by your own
good wyll, in subdueng of your reason to

Subdue reason
*to fayth**

y^e obedyence of fayth, by bylief come to
me, and with good wyll of well wurkynge

5   also with the bylief / shall not onely byleue me, but also byleue in
me, and go into me, by beynge a membre of myne, and incorporatynge your self in me / and I shall by [e_8] the gyfte of myne
owne body to be eaten and receyued of yours, incorporate my selfe
in you, and I wyll not cast you out fro me but be styll incorporated

10   wyth you, but yf you cast me out frome you, and so by synne caste
your selfe awaye fro me / els of all that commeth to me by my
fathers bryngynge, I wyll caste none oute. For yf ye came to me by
my father thorow fayth, and that I wolde not than suffre deth for
your saluacyon, than dyd I caste you oute. For none can come in

15   to my blisse of heuyn, but by hys rawnson payed by my dethe and
passyon. But I wyll not refuse that, but I wyll suffre and dye for
the worlde, to gyue the dede worlde lyfe by my deth. For I am
descended from heuyn sent by my father not to do myne owne
wyll, but the wyll of [e_8v] hym that hath sent me. But I mene not

20   by these wordes that I wyll dye agaynst myne owne wyll, but that
al be it the sensuall part of my manhed wolde of the nature of man
abhorre, shrinke and withdrawe from the

The nature of man
*abhorreth death**

greuouse payne of suche an intollerable
passyon: yet shall my wyll bothe of my

25   godhed be all one with the wyll of my father, and therby in suche
maner obedyent vnto his father, as we say a man is obedyent vnto
his owne reason, and yet is not his owne reason another power
superiour aboue hym selfe. And my wyll of my manhed shall also
be so conformable to y^e wyll of my father, y^e wyl of the holy goost

30   and the wyll of myne owne godhed (all whiche thre wylles are in
dede one wyll as all our thre persons are in godhed one god) that I
wyll wyllyngly dye for them all that so come [f_1] to me by my
fathers bryngynge thorough the well wurkynge fayth, and wyll
abyde and perseuer. And like wyse as I wyll by myne owne body

35   gyuen vnto theym by eatynge in to theyre owne, gyue them an
ernest peny of our incorporacyon togyther, and a memoryall of

---

21 manhed] manhod *1557*   28 manhed] manhod *1557*   29 conformable] confortable *1533*
1557

that deth and passyon, by whiche I wyll wyllyngly geue my selfe
for them, by beynge slayne and sacryfysed for theyr synne, and
made the raunsom of theyr redempcion: whan god shall for this

Philip. 2* obedyence of my manhode vnto the deth
the vyle deth of the crosse, lyfte me vp   5
and exalte me, and gyue me the name that is aboue all names,
than shall I by my resurreccion agayne to lyfe, geue them a sample
and make them sure, that I shall in lyke wyse at the laste day leue
none of them to be loste, no more in body than in soule / but shall
[f₁v] so resuscitate and rayse agayne theyr bodyes, that lyke as I   10
shall my selfe ascende into heuyn agayn from whense I came, so
shall they as membres of my body ascend thyther with me, and

Euerlasting lyuely
bread* there be fedde of thys euerlastynge lyuely
brede that I tell you of, that is to wytte of
the fruycion of my godhed and   15
byholdynge also of my gloryouse manhed for euer, eche of you that
haue vse of reason after thanalogye and proporcyon of the well
formed fayth, with hope & well wurkynge cherite that you shall
haue had in thys lyfe here before. For thys ys as I byfore told you,
the wyll of my father that sent me, that euery man that sethe hys   20
sone as you do, and not onely seeth him as you do, but also
byleueth in hym as you do not, shall haue (yf he perseuer in that
well wurkynge bylyef) the meat that I speke [f₂] of that shall not
peryshe but abyde in to euerlastynge lyfe. For though ye se euery
man dye here for the whyle / yet I shall (as I tolde you) beynge of   25
egall power with my father, reyse them all vppe agayne my selfe at
the laste daye, & than shall my faythfull folke be fedde wyth this
euerlastyng lyuely brede of myne owne person bothe god and man
for euer. And lo now haue I playnely told you what brede I mene.

Where as I haue good reader in thexposycyon of these wordes of   30
our sauyour, inserted the incorporacyon of hym and vs togyther,
by the receyuynge and eatynge of his owne body into ours: I haue
not done it to make any man wene that that poynt appered and
were proued by any parte of those wordes, but bycause yt ys a very
trouth in dede / and not onely [f₂v] towched and signyfyed in   35
other wordes of hys before, but also playnely expressed and

---

16 manhed] manhod *1557*   20 sethe] seeth *1557*   26 egall] equall *1557*   36 of hys]
om. *1557*

declared by other wordes of hys owne after, as you shall hereafter
se. Therfore so playne a trouth, and so necessary, and so necessaryly parteynynge to that place of ye mater, me thought it not
metely for to be lefte out.

5

The .xii. chapyter.

But nowe shall you here howe Chrystes audyence that came to
seke hym, were affeccyonate to thys euerlastynge lyuely brede,
whan they had herde hym declare it.

All the whyle that he spake those other wordes before / they
were yet in good hope, y^t what so euer he ment besyde, he wolde
gyue them some meat for theyr belyes. And as they were groce / so
had they at the fyrste went. [f$_3$] And so had they leuer that he
wolde haue gyuen theym some suche groce brede made of erthely
corne for theyr erthely belyes, such as he gaue them and multi-
plyed for them byfore, than any manna that came downe from y^e
eyre. But afterwarde whan they herde hym tell them of farre better
brede that sholde come from heuyn, than manna was which theyr
fathers dyd eate in desert / than were they better a payed / and
prayed him that they myght haue of that. But than whan they
perceyued in conclusyon, that he ment all of suche brede as sholde
fede theyr soules, and gaue them no good comfort after theyr groce
mindes, of any groce fedynge for theyr groce bodyes than lyke as
some of theyr fore fathers murmured in desert agaynst Moyses for

Nume. 21

manna, and sayed that theyr stomake
wambled agaynst that [f$_3$v] lyght meate,
and wyshed theyr olde boundage agayn, of which they were before
so wery whyle they were in Egypte / yet thought they now that
they were well than, bycause they myght than syt ouer the pottes
y^t had the sodden fleshe in them, of such flesh yet some of suche
bond slauys hadde happely than but the sauour. Whan these had
herd hym now speke all of such spyrytuall fode / theyr hartys so
sore arose agaynst hym, that theyr affeccyons were clene fallen
from him sodaynly. For a daye before they had hym in hygh
estymacyon, & called hym the prophete that shold come and

---

9 other] *om. 1557*   18 a payed] apayde *1557*   22 bodyes] bodyes, 1557   28 syt] set
1557

*Iohn. 6**   redeme ye world / & wold haue made
                            him kynge, bycause they thought he
wold fede them by myracle without theyr labour / where theyr
*The vsage of kynges**   other kinges vsed to pyll them & poll
                            them & kepe them vnder trybute so   5
bare, y^t with great [f₄] labour they could scant fynd them self
meate. And therfore wold they as I saye after that fedynge that he
fedde theym so by myracle, so fayne haue made hym kyng, that he
was fayne to withdraue hym selfe a syde & fle from them, tyll that
mynde of theyrs were gone. And that was not longe as ye se. For   10
now y^t after theyr great hope of such another fest for theyr bodyes,
they herde hym turne all to the fedyng of theyr soules / and that
for ye fedyng of theyr belyes, he went not about to geue them so
mych as one lofe among them all to theyr breke fast / they murmured agaynst y^t that he had said of hym self, " *I am the quycke brede*   15
y^t am descended from heuyn. And than they sayd: Is not thys Iosephes sone?
Know not we his father and his mother both? How sayth he than of hym selfe
I am descended from heuyn." [f₄v]

Lo here they called hym a carpenters sone, and therin they
bylyed hym vnware / but farre were they nowe fallen fro the   20
makynge hym a kyng.

Then sayed our sauiour to them: " *Murmur not amonge your selfe,*
no man cometh to me, but yf my father drawe hym." As though he wolde
say: leue your murmurynge and fall to prayour, and wurke and
walke with my father in comyng to me by fayth. Men are so weyke   25
of them selfe in ye walkynge of this way, that there can no man
come to me but yf my father not onely come to hym and take hym
by the hande and lede hym, but also drawe hym to. And therfore
syth he muste do so myche for you or els you can not come / so
myche haue you the more nede to leue your murmuryng, and   30
applye your self to pray hym (yf he draw you not) to draw you,
Psal. 31   and as [f₅] the prophete saith to pray
                            him strayn your iawys with a bytte and
a brydle and draw you by the chekys, magry your teth, and make
you turne your wylles from your bely ioy, to come to the soule fode   35
with me. For where as your bely meat shall peryshe bely and all /
he that thus shall come to my feste, he shall not perysshe. For I

---

9 withdraue] withdraw *1557*

shall rayse hym vp agayn in the last day vnto euerlastynge lyfe.
And if ye merueyle at this that I saye,
My father must
*draw you**
that my father muste brynge you &
drawe you, that is that he muste besyde
5 all outwarde techynge teche you within by ledynge and drawynge
you into ye trewth of fayth, by hys inwarde operacion ioyned with
the towardnesse of your wylles preuented moued and sette a wurke
with occasions of his formare grace / yf ye merueyle of this maner
of drawynge and of my [f₅v] fathers inward techynge, remembre
10   that your own prophetes saye, that "all
Esaie. 54
folke shalbe taught of god." And now
god techeth you / for I tech you, whiche am as I told you ye brede
of lyfe that am descended from heuyn. And surely there shall no
man be taught ye fayth but yf god tech hym. Nor euery man is not
15 full taught that hereth it, but he that hereth it and lerneth it /
whyche no man can do by any outwarde voyce, without god
wurkyng within. And he wyll not wurke, nor his wysdome wyll not
entre into an euyl wylled harte. And
Sapien. 10
therfore leue your murmurynge, and
20 pray my father to tech you / not onely outwardly as he techeth you
nowe by me, but inwardly also, that you maye be lerned by his
wurkynge to fayth, wyth you and within you. But why do I tell
you so often that you can not come [f₆] to his gyfte of fayth
(wythout which you can not come at me) but yf my father geue it
25 you. Veryly bycause I wolde you sholde praye hym for it. For
though he preuent you and gyue you occasyons toward the gettyng
of that gyfte: yet setteth he not so lytell by this great gyfte of
lernyng & fayth that he lyste to caste it awaye vppon them, that
whan it is shewed them set not so myche therby as to desyre it &
30 praye therfore.
And therfore I wolde haue you desyre it of hym that may geue it
you. And yet ys not that my father onely but my selfe also. How be
it yf I shold byd you aske it of me, and pray me geue you thys
grace: you be so farre frome the bylyefe in me that ye wolde not do
35 it.
And therfore not spekynge of myne [f₆v] owne power / I tell you
all of the power of the father, y^t without hym ye can not come to
me / bycause I wold haue you praye to hym, that he wold geue

---

you the grace, that as ye know by faith and knowlege hym all redy for god, so ye maye knowe by fayth and knowlege hym for my father to / and than shal you by the same fayth, knowe and know-lege me also for his sone. And than shall you not murmur at my wordes, but humbly come to me, as to the sone, not of Ioseph but of god / & knowlege me for the quycke brede y^t is descended from heuyn. *" For euery man that hath herd this lesson of my father, and hath not onely herd it but also lerned it / he cometh (as I haue told you) to me. But yet thys wyll I tell you, that neuer man saw my father yet. But he that is of god (that is to wytte my selfe y^t* [f$_7$] *am hys owne sone) he hath sene the father, and so hath no man ellys."* And therfore the lesson that any man hereth and lerneth of my father, he muste here of hym by me, and lerne it by the inward wurke of my father with whose wurke I wurke also. And so shall he come to me / thorowe perfyt well

*Note how to come to Christ** wurkynge faith in me. And I tell you very trouth, he that so byleueth in me, and perseuereth at his deth in that perfite bylief, is sure of eternall lyfe. For I am (as I dyuerse tymes now haue told you) the very brede of life. *" Your fathers that mur-mured as you do now, dyd eate the brede of manna in desert, and they be dede and perysshed."* Leue therfore that wronge waye of your fore fathers, leue your grudge & your murmur, and labour to my father that he may brynge you to me by suche faith [f$_7$v] as ye maye eate this brede that is my selfe. For thys brede is brede descendyng from heuyn for the nonys, that who so maye eate & be fedde of that, shal not peryshe by euerlastyng deth. For I tell you yet agayn y^t " I am the quycke brede that am descended from heuyn." Who so euer come to me by my fathers bryngyng, so that by perfyt per-seueraunce and well wurkyng fayth, he may eate & be fedde of thys brede, that ys to wytte attayne the fruicyon of my gloryouse godhed, with the gloryouse syght wherof the angels are fedde in heuyn: he shalbe sure of euerlastynge lyfe.

The .xiii. chapyter.

Where as our sauyour good readers in the begynnynge vppon accasyon of his miracle wrought vpon the multyplicacion of the brede, [f$_8$] towched bothe the brede of hys godhed and also of the

---

26 deth.] deth *1533*, death. *1557*   26-27 "I . . . heuyn."] *Marginal quotation marks two lines too low in 1533*   35 accasyon] occasion *1557*

geuynge them of his owne body to be eaten in forme of bred, &
that he somwhat dyd insinuate & set forth the same in those
wordes, *"wurke you not the bred y^t peryssheth, but ye bred y^t abideth into
euerlasting life, which ye sone of man shal geue you"* as I somwhat tolde
5   you before, not of myne own mynde, but of ye mynde of dyuerse
holy doctours, Alcuinus, saynte Thomas, Theophylactus, and
saynte Cyrill: Ye se that our sauyour in many wordes whych I
haue now declared you, hath opened & shewed vnto theym the
brede of hys godhed.
10   And now good readers take hede how in those wordes that now
folow he declareth vnto them the brede of his own very body,
which he gyueth vs verily to eate in the blessed sacrament. [f₈v]

And moste truelye   Wherin that exposicyon that I shall geue
spoken*   you shall be none inuencyon of myne,
15   but the clere fayth and sentence of all the
holy doctours of Chrystes chirch olde and new both, from Christes
deth to this daye. Of whome I shall for a somple geue you ere I
make an ende, the names and the sentences of some such as your
self shall well se and perceyue for other maner men than I am or
20 mayster Masker eyther / & that yf they were good men and trewe,
ye shall than your selfe saye, that mayster Masker is nought and
false, and that his exposicion (though it were trewe as it is bothe
folysshe and false) yet syth it cometh not nere the purpose, is (as I
tolde you before) very falsely handeled.
25   Let vs here now therfore of the gyuynge of Chrystes owne blessed
[g₁] body verily to vs to eate in the blessed sacrament, what
Chryste hym selfe sayth.
        After his declaracion of the brede of his glorious godhed, these
are his wordes. *" And the brede that I shall geue you, is my fleshe whych I
30 shall geue for the lyfe of the world."*
        Where as before they murmured at the lyght spyrytuall brede of
hys godhed / he telleth them now that he wyll not onely geue them
that brede to fede vppon, by fruycyon of the byholdynge face to
face whan the tyme shall come, as he hath also gyuen yt theym in
35 one maner all redy by his incarnacyon to fede them spyrytually in

7 whych] *1533 corr. err.*, wpych *1533*, whiche *1557*   15 fayth] *1533 corr. err.*, *1557*, faytk
1533   18 some such] *1533 corr. err.*, *1557*, some, as suche *1533*   22 it is] *1533 corr. err.*,
1557, is *1533*   25 gyuynge] *1533 corr. err.*, hyuynge *1533*, geuing *1557*

the meane whyle by spyrytuall doctryne / but that the brede that
he wyll geue them to fede vppon, shall besyde that be his owne
flesshe, euyn the very same that he wyll geue for [g₁v] the lyfe of

*1. Cor. 11** the worlde / menynge that he wolde
veryly geue men the same very flesshe to   5
eate and fede vppon, bothe bodyly and spyritually in remembraunce of his deth, that he wold for mannys redempcyon veryly
geue to deth, and veryly for a sacryfyce offre vp to god by deth.

But now sayth mayster Masker the aduersary of the blessed
sacrament yᵗ our sauyour ment no more in those wordes, " *And the*   10
brede yᵗ I shal geue you is my flesshe whych I shall geue for the lyfe of the
worlde," but that he wold geue it for the lyfe of the world by hys
deth / and ment no thynge at all of the geuynge of his flesshe
before his deth, or after hys deth / nor nothynge in these wordes or
any that in the same chapyter folowe, entended to speke of any   15
suche maner of geuynge his body to eate, as he is re[g₂]ceyued and
eaten in the blessed sacrament, nor nothynge ment in thys chapyter any thynge to speke of that mater.

Thus wolde mayster Masker that all men sholde wene, as it
appereth playnely by his exposicion. And thus also sayth Luther,   20
& thus sayth Fryth also / & affermeth this sayenge so boldely, that
he saith it twyse in his one booke wherin he answereth me. There
in sayth he twyse, that all lerned men are full and whole agreed in
that poynt.

And therfore wyll these aduersaryes of the sacrament say, that in   25
this exposicyon of myne, all that euer I saye wherby it maye
appere that our sauyour in these wordes writen in this vi. chapiter
of saynt Iohan, any thyng spake or ment of yᵉ geuyng of his body
to be eaten in the blessed sacrament, [g₂v] is an imaginacion of
myn own hed / as mayster Masker argueth & speketh all way of   30
mayster More his fayth, as though it were no mannes ellys but
myne.

But to the entent good readers that ye may clerely perceiue
mayster Maskers malycyouse falsed therin, I shall in dyuers places
of thys exposycyon, concernyng specyally this poynt of Chrystes   35
spekyng and menynge of the gyuynge of his owne very body in the
blessed sacrament, reherse you the namys of some of those whom I

---

13 no thynge] nothyng *1557*   31 though] thought *1557*

folow therin, & some of theyr wordes to / by whych ye shal se that
I deceyue you not as maister Masker doth, that thorow all his
exposycyon flytteth all fro the poynte, and dysimuleth all ye wordes
of those olde holy men y^t expowned it in suche wyse as he wolde
we sholde wene [g₃] that no good man euer dyd.

Vppon these wordes therfore of our sauyour: And the brede that
I shall gyue you is my flesshe, that I shall geue for the lyfe of the
worlde: thus sayth Theophylactus.

Consyder that that brede that we eate in the sacrament, is not
onely a fygure of the fleshe of our lorde /
Theophylactus vppon
the .6. chapiter of
saint Iohan
but it is also the fleshe of our lord it self.
For he sayd not: ye brede that I shall
geue is a fygure of my flesshe, but he
sayd it is my flesshe. For the same breade by secrete wordes,
thorow the mysticall benedyccyon, & by the cummyng also of the
holy spyryte therevnto, is transfourmed and chaunged into the
flesshe of our lorde. And lest that any
*Note these woordes**
man sholde be trowbeled in his mynde,
wenynge that it were not to be byleued y^t brede sholde be flesh /
this is well knowen that whyle our [g₃v] lorde walked in his flesshe,
& of brede receyued his noryshynge, that brede whyche he than
eate was than chaunged into hys body, & was made suche as his
holy flesshe was, and dyd susteyne and increace his flesshe after y^e
comen maner of men. And therfore now also is the brede chaunged into the flesshe of our lorde. And how is it than (wyll some
man say) that it appereth not to vs flesshe but brede. That hath
Chryste prouyded, to the entent we shold
Note the prouision
*of god**
not abhorre from the eatynge of it. For yf
it were geuen vs in lykenesse of flesshe,
we sholde be dysplesauntly dysposed towarde the receyuyng of our
howsle. But now by the goodnesse of god condescendynge to our
infyrmytye, this sacramentall meat appereth vnto vs such as we
haue at other tymes bene accustomed wyth. [g₄] These are not my
wordes lo good christen reader, but the wordes of that old holy
cunnyng doctour Theophilactus, whyche was also no latyn man
but a greke / bycause mayster Masker speketh so mych of papystes
as though ye catholyke fayth wherby the catholike chyrch
byleueth, y^t in the blessed sacrament is the very blessed body of
Crist, were a thing but made & imagyned by some pope of rome.

Now yf mayster Masker wyll say y^t myne exposicion is in this poynt false: here you se good readers that myne exposicyon is not myne, but the exposicion of Theophilactus. And therfore let hym leue dauncynge with me, & daunce another while with hym.

But marke well two thinges now good reader in these wordes / 5 one y^t this good holy doctour calleth y^e blessed sacrament brede as

1. Corin. 11

saint Poule doth, [g$_4$v] and oure sauyour hym selfe also, in these wordes of his in this syxte chapyter of saynt Iohan, and so doth also euery doctour of the chyrche almost. Vppon whyche callynge of it brede, frere 10 Luther and Melancton & theyr felowes, take theyr holde to saye and afferme that it is very brede styll, as well after the consecra- cyon as afore. And frere Huskyn, with zuynglius, George Ioye, Iohan Fryth, & Tindale, turne forth ferther to the deuyll and not onely say that it is very bred styll, but also that it is no thynge els. 15

But now consyder therfore as I say, that Theophilactus here calleth it brede as well as they / sayenge, the brede that we receiue in the misteries or sacrament, is not onely a certayne fygure of the fleshe of our lorde, but it is also the fleshe of our lord it self. But than expresseth he plainely that [g$_5$] though he calleth it brede, he 20 meneth not that it is very materyall brede styll as it was / but that the brede ys transformed, gone, and changed into the very fleshe of

*Transsubstanciacion**

Chryste. And he setteth it out also with an ensample of the brede that is eaten and turned in to the flesshe of the man whom it nurysseth, whyche 25 euery man well woteth that any wytte hath that it is no lenger brede than.

And therfore Theophilactus calleth it brede, bycause it was brede / as in the scrypture the serpent in to which Aarons rodde was turned is called a rodde styll, whyle it was no rodde but a 30

Exodi. 7

serpent. For there is it thus writen. " *The rodde of Aron dyd deuour the roddes of the magycianis.*" And as the scrypture calleth the serpent there a rodde: so calleth it the sacrament brede. And as Theophilactus [g$_5$v]

---

3 therfore] *1557,* the fore *1533*   4 me,] *1557, comma displaced upward 1533. See n.*
6 doctour] *1533 corr. err.,* doctours *1533,* doctor *1557*   10–12 frere . . . styll] *Emphasized by 3 double quotation marks in margin 1533*   12 well] *1557,* vell *1533*   15 no thynge] nothing *1557*   33 rodde] 1557, oodde *1533*

calleth here the blessed sacrament by the name of brede, and yet
declareth that it is no brede: euyn so do all holy doctours that call
it by that name of brede bothe mene in dede, and also do clerely
declare, that though they call it brede, they know well it is no
5   brede but in lykenesse and forme of brede vnder the sacramentall
*Note**   signe, ye very blessed body of Cryst, flesh,
                          bloude,   bonys   and   all,   &   neyther
wythout the soule nor the godhed neyther.

Marke also good reader, y^t Theophylactus sayth, The brede
10 whyche we eate in the misteryes or sacrament, is not onely a fygure
of the flesshe of our lorde, but it is also the flesshe of our lorde it
selfe.

In these wordes good readers marke wel that he sayth it is a
figure and yet for all that the very fleshe of Chryste. [g$_6$]

15 Thys thynge I specyally desyre you to note, bycause that by the
markynge of thys one poynt / ye maye voyde almoste all the crafte,
wyth whiche mayster Masker, Fryth, and Tyndale, and all these
heretykes labour to deceyue you in the wrytynges of all the olde
holy doctours.

20 For where so euer any of them call the blessed sacrament a
fygure, there wolde these felowes make vs wene that he ment it
were nothynge ellys. But here you se that Theophylactus saith it is
a figure as it is in dede / but he telleth vs that it is also (as in dede
it is) the very flesshe of oure lorde.

25 And therfore marke well these .ii. poyntes in this one place,
Two poyntes to   y^t whan these heretikes proue that the
*be marked**   blessed sacrament is called bred, they
                          proue nothing [g$_6$v] agaynst vs. For they
that call it brede declare yet that in dede it is not brede but the
30 body of Chryste. And whan they proue that it is called a fygure /
they proue no thynge agaynste vs. For they that saye it is a fygure,
saye it is not onely a fygure, but also the flesshe of Chryste. But
whan we proue that the blessed sacrament is not onely called the
body and bloude of Chryst, but also y^t the olde holy doctours and
35 the exposytours of holy scrypture do playnely declare that it is so /
than proue we playne agaynst them. For we denye none of y^e
tother two poyntes / but thys poynt do they denye.

---

31 no thynge] nothyng *1557*

The .xiiii. chapyter.

Yet to thentent that ye may se that mayster Masker in his exposicyon, doth but playnely mocke you: consider yet agayne these wordes well, [g₇] " *Et panis quem ego dabo caro mea est, quam ego dabo pro mundi vita.*" Whyche texte, albe it that in the latyn it be somwhat otherwyse, that is to wytte. " *Et panis quem ego dabo caro mea est pro mundi uita,*" without these wordes, *quam ego dabo,* in the secund place / whiche laten texte were yet more for my purpose, yet syth not onely the greke texte is as I rehersed you fyrst, whyche was the language wherin theuangelyst wrote, but that also bothe the greke exposytours and many of the laten exposytours to, do so expowne it / and that though those wordes were out, yet they be such as the sentence wolde well requyre to repete and vnderstande / and finally bycause I fynde that mayster Masker hym selfe doth in his exposycion take that texte in the fyrste fasshyon, onely chaungynge one worde in the [g₇v] secund place, yᵗ is to wytte this word (geue) into thys word (paye) whiche chaunge he maketh as for an exposicyon: I am content to take the texte as hym selfe doth, that is to wytte after the fyrst maner thus, And the brede that I shall geue you is my flesshe, which I shall geue for yᵉ lyfe of the world.

Consyder now good reader that in these wordes, our sauiour here speketh of geuynge his flesshe twyse, by whyche he meneth, that in the tone geuyng he wold geue it to them / and in the tother geuynge he wolde geue it for them. The tone geuynge was in the blessed sacrament / the tother was on the crosse.

*Christ gaue his fleshe twise**

And loke now whyther the very wordes of Chryst agre wyth this exposycyon or not / the wordes ye wote well be these: and the brede that I [g₈] shall geue you is my flesshe. Here is lo the tone geuyng, by which he shall sayth he geue his flesshe to theym. Than sayth he ferther, whyche I shall gyue for the lyfe of the world. Lo here he telleth them of the tother gyuynge, by whyche he sholde geue it for them. And bycause hys geuyng to them sholde be a memoryall of his geuynge for them, therfore he spake of them both to gether. But yet bycause his princypall purpose was to speke in

---

1 chapyter.] chapyter, *1533*   4 wordes] vordes *1533*, woordes *1557*; quem] *1557*, qnem *1533*   7 quam] *1533 corr. err.*, quem *1533 1557*

that place, not of his geuyng of hys flesshe for them, but of his
geuynge it vnto them: therfor of hys geuynge it to them he
maketh after a very playne and expresse declaracyon in many
playne open wordes / but of hys geuynge it for theym, he spake but
5   a lytell, and as it were but for a declaracyon of the tother geuynge.
[g₈v] For whan he had sayd, and the brede whyche I shall gyue
you shalbe my flesshe / than to declare that he ment to geue them
hys very fleshe, he added therto these wordes / whiche I shall gyue
for the lyfe of the worlde. As though he wolde saye, wyll you wytte
10 what flesshe this brede is that I wyll gyue to you: veryly the selfe
same that I wyll geue for you / and not onely for you, but for the
lyfe of the whole worlde to, that is to wytte for as many of the
worlde as whan they here it preched, wyll not refuse to take it.
And therfore whan ye know hereafter whiche flesshe of myne I
15 shall haue gyuen for you vppon the crosse / than shal you not nede
to dowte whiche flesshe of myne I shall geue you in the brede of
the sacrament, excepte you lyste not to byleue me. For now I tell
you as playne as I can, [h₁] that it shalbe the same flesshe.

      This exposycyon good readers ye se is euydent open and playne.
20 But now se good readers for goddes sake the falsehed of mayster
Masker in hys exposycyon vppon yᵉ same wordes. Where as our
sauyour as you se speketh in these few wordes of these two
geuynges, the geuynge to eate and the geuynge to dye, the geuynge
in the sacrament & the geuyng on the crosse / cometh me now
25 maister Masker, and expowneth Chrystes wordes all to gether of
the tone geuynge, that is to wytte the geuynge by deth on the
crosse / and letteth the tother geuynge go by, as though he saw it
not, albe it that Chryst speketh of that gyuynge both fyrst and
most.

30   Now yf mayster Masker wyll say that I do but fayne these two
geuynges, and saye as he sayth often [h₁v] that Chryste ment there
but one geuynge, that is to wytte by hys deth, and wyll saye that
Cryste speketh there no worde of the sacrament / I shall tell hym
agayne that so myghte mayster Masker marre all his owne
35 exposycyon vtterly. For Cryst whan he sayth, whiche I shall gyue
for the lyfe of the worlde, speketh no word in the world neyther of
his crosse nor of his deth. If he say that they be vnderstanden, than

---

5 as it] 1557, as is 1533   19 euydent] euident, 1557   28 of that] of the 1557

must he geue me leue to say the lyke for my parte, that as deth &
the crosse are vnderstonden in ye tone geuing, so eatyng & the
sacrament is vnderstonden in ye tother geuynge. How be it for my
part yet touchyng the fyrst geuyng, I may say y^t Cryst speketh of
the sacrament, & signyfyeth his menyng in this word, brede, whan
he sayth the brede that I shall geue you is my fleshe. And of the
eatynge [h₂] therof he speketh expressely after. And therfore shall
mayster Masker neuer wade out therof, but that I haue the wordes
of the scrypture mych more clere for the fyrst geuyng, than he for
the secund. And ye may se that of the two geuynges mayster
Masker to mocke vs with, hath in hys exposycion of a folysh wyly-
nesse wynked and dyssembled the tone.

But yet if maister Masker striue with me styll vpon this point,
whither our sauyour speke of two geuynges of hys fleshe, or but of
one / albe it y^t I haue proued my part therin metely playne my
selfe, yet am I content that a better than we both shall breke y^e
stryfe bytwen vs. I shall therfore name you y^t holy cunnyng
doctour saint Bede, whose wordes I trust euery wyse man wyll
byleue a lytell better than eyther maister Maskers or myn. [h₂v]

S. Bede   Lo thus sayth saint Bede vpon these
wordes of Chryste, " *And the brede whych I*
shall gyue is my body, whiche I shall geue for the lyfe of the worlde." Thys
brede (sayth saynte Bede) dyd our lorde gyue whan he gaue the
sacrament of hys body and hys bloude vnto his dyscyples, and
whan he offred vp hym selfe to god hys father vppon the awtre of
the crosse.

Here you se good readers that saynte Bede telleth you playne the
same tale that I tell you, that is to wytte that our sauyour in those
wordes speketh of two geuynges of him selfe, the tone to his dyscyples in the sacrament, the tother to deth for hys dyscyples on the
crosse. And therfore whyle mayster Masker with his heresye doth
vtterly denye the tone, & by his exposicion affermeth that Crist
[h₃] in thys place dyd speke but of the tother / saynt Bede bereth
me recorde that maister Masker lyeth, and hath made his exposicyon false. And the ferther ye go in the wordes of thys gospell, the
more shall mayster Maskers false dyce appere.

20–21 *gloss* S. Bede] *om. 1557*   25 awtre] aultare *1557*

The .xv. chapyter.

Whan the Iewes harde our lord saye, that bysyde the spyrytuall meat of the brede of his godhed, the brede that he wolde gyue theym sholde be hys owne flesshe / than began they to contende
5 and dyspute amonge them vpon that worde, as one of the moste meruelouse and straunge wordes that euer they had herde before. And therfore they sayd how can this man geue vs his flesshe to eate?

Saynt Bede sayth here, and so sayth saynt Austayne both, that
10 they [h₃v] had conceyued a false
August. in
Enarratione
in psal. 98
opinyon, that our lorde wold cut out hys own body in gobettes, and make them eate it so, in such maner of dede peces, as men bye byefe or moten out of yᵉ bouchers shoppys. Thys thyng
15 they thought that he neyther coulde do / and also that though he could, yet wolde they not eate it as a thynge fowle and lothsome.

We fynde good readers of one or two mo bysyde these Iewes
here, yᵗ at the worde of god asked how.
Iohan. 3
Of this word howe*
For bothe our lady asked how, and
20 Nichodemus also asked how.

Our blessed lady whan thangell told her that she shold conceyue and brynge forth a chyld, asked
Luce. 1
this questyon, how shall that be? For man
I know none / not for that she any thing dowted of the trewth
25 of goddes word sent her by goddes messenger, but by[h₄]cause
she wold know the meanis, for as mych as
Mary vowed
perpetuall virginitie*
she had determyned her selfe vpon
perpetuall virginite / and therof a pro-
myse had passed & a vow was made, and Ioseph well agreed
30 therwith, as it maye welbe gathered vppon the gospell.

For thangell sayd not yᵘ hast conceyued, but thou shalt con-
ceyue. And therfore whan she answered, how shall yᵗ be syth I know no man, this answer had not ben to the purpose, yf she had ment no more but yᵗ she knewe none yet / for he sayd not yᵗ she
35 was conceyued yet but shold conceiue after. Which she myght after do by yᵉ knowlege of her husband after, though she knewe no man yet. And therfore we may wel gather of his wordes & hers togyther

---

10–11 *gloss* August.] *1557,* Angust. *1533*   27–28 *gloss* virginitie] virgintie *1557*

as I haue shewed in my dialoge, y^t whan she sayd how shall this be
for I knowe no man, she ment therin [h$_4$v] not onely that she knew
none al redy, but also that she hadde promysed and vowed that
she neuer wolde knowe man afterwarde / vsynge therin such a
maner of spekynge, as a mayed myghte saye by one whom she   5
wold neuer haue, we may well talke togyther but we wedde not
togyther.

Now that her determinacyon was not with her selfe onely, but
conformed also with ye consent of her spouse, it maye well appere.
For without his agrement she coulde not reken her selfe to be sure   10
to kepe it.

And that her determynacyon of perpetuall vyrginite, was a
promyse and a vow to god, it may well appere by this, that els
whan she had worde from god by the angell that she shold conceyue and beare a chylde, she had had no cause to aske y^e ques-   15
tyon how. For if she were at lyberty to lye with [h$_5$] a man, than
had that reuelacion ben a commaundement vnto her to labour for
the concepcyon, whyle there were vppon her part no let or impedi-
ment, neyther of nature nor conscience.

And very lyke it is that yf she had ben in that poynt at her   20
libertye / than though she had mynded perpetuall virgynite, yet
syth she had entended it neyther for auoydyng of the bodyly payne
of the byrth, nor for any abominacyon of goddes naturall ordynaunce for procreacyon (for suche respectes be bothe vnnaturall
and synfull) but onely for goddes pleasure & of deuocyon, it is well   25
lykely that herynge by the messenger of god, what maner of chyld
that was y^t god wold she shold haue, she wolde haue made no
questyon of the mater, but gladly gone about the gettynge.

But here may some man happely [h$_5$v] say, that this reason by
which I proue her vow, wyll serue well inough to soyle it selfe, and   30
proue that it appereth not that she had made any vow at all, but
had onely some mynde and desyre of perpetuall virginyte, but yet
styll at her lybertye / without any promyse or bonde. For syth she
hadde now by reuelacyon from god, that his pleasure was she
sholde haue a chylde / a bare purpose of virgynyte & a vow of   35
virginyte were all of one weyght. For god was able as well to
dispence with her vow, as to byd her leue of her vnuowed purpose.

---

32 virginyte] virginyre *1533*, virginitie *1557*

Of trouth yf our lady had wayed her vow as lyght as happely
some lyght vowesse wold / thys mynd she myght haue had. Ye &
some vowesses peraduenture there are, which as yet neuer entend
to breke theyr vow but thynke they wolde not with the bre[h₆]-
5 kyng of theyr vow fall in yᵉ dyspleasure of god, though they wist to
wyn therwith al this hole wretched world, whiche yet wold be
peraduenture well content, yᵗ god wold sende them word & byd
them go wedde & gete chyldren.

And those vowesses lo that hapen to haue any suche mynde / let
10 them at the fyrste thought make a crosse on theyr brest and blesse
it a waye. For though it be no breking of theyr vow yet is it a waye
well towarde it, and draueth (yf it be not synne) very nere the
pyttys brynke of synne, whan they wolde be gladde that god wold
sende them theyr pleasure without any sinne.

15 And surely yf vpon yᵉ delite in such a noughty mynde, god wold
suffre yᵉ deuyl to illude such a vowesse, & transfygure hym self into
the lykenesse of an angel of light, & call hym self Gabriel, & tell
her yᵗ god greteth her well [h₆v] and sendeth her worde that she
shall haue a chyld: though he therewyth went his way & neuer
20 tolde her more whyther it shold be good or bad, her secrete inward
affeccyon toward her flesshely luste lurkynge in her harte vnknowen vnto her selfe, couered & hyd vnder the cloke of that
mynde, that she wold not for all the worlde take her own pleasure
without goddes wyll, wold make her vnderstand this message for a
25 dyspensacyon of her vow, and for a commaundement to breke it /
and so go forth and folow it wythout any ferther questyon, and go
gete a chylde, and make the deuyll a prophete.

But thys blessed virgyn Mary, was so surely sette vpon the
kepyng of her vowed virginyte, that she neuer neyther longed nor
30 loked for any messenger from god, that sholde byd [h₇] her breke
it. And therfore was she so dyscrete and cyrcumspecte, that she
wolde not onely consyder who spake to
*The which thinges
are to be wayde** her to dyscerne whyther it were man or
spyrite, and also whyther it were a good
35 spyryte or an euyll / but she wolde also way well the wordes were
the spyryte neuer so good, leste her own mysse takyng by neglygence, myght marre the reuelacyon. And therfore at Gabrielys
fyrste apperaunce, bycause he was goodly, & hys wordes were faire

---

6 world,] *1557*, world *1533*   12 draueth] draweth *1557*

and plesauntly set and spoken somwhat lyke a woer / she was
somwhat abasshed and troubled in her mynde at the maner of his
salutacyon. But after vpon his ferther wordes whan she aduysed
hym and hys message well / than perceyuynge hym to be, not a
man but an angell, not an euyl angell but a good, [h₇v] and
specyally sent from god, and hys mater no worldly wowyng but an
heuynly message: she was not a lytell ioyful in her hart. And as I
sayd had she not vowed virgynyte, but hadde ben at her lybertye,
she had as me semeth had no cause to dowte what god wolde haue
her do / namely hauynge an husband all redy. Nor neuer wold she
haue thought that it had ben better for her to lyue styll in
virgynyte, than to go about yᵗ generacyon wherof god had sent her
word. But now for as mych as she was by her vow bounden to
virginite, wherof she wist wel she myght not dispence with her self /
and the angell bode not her go about to conceyue, but onely tolde
her as by way of prophecye, that she shold conceyue / & wel she
wyst god from whom the message came, could make her conceyue
without man yf he wold: ther[h₈]fore she neyther wold tempte god
in desyryng hym to do that myracle, nor by mysse takynge of his
message for hast & ouersyght, offend his mayster by the brekyng of
her vow / but dyscretely dyd aske the messenger, how & in what
wyse she shold conceiue. Wherupon he shewed her that she shold
be conceyued by the holy goost.

Here you se good reders that the cause of her question in her
askynge how, rose of no diffidence, but of veri sure faith / bicause
she surely byleued yᵗ he could make her conceyue & her virginite
saued. For els had she not had fermely yᵗ faith, she had had no
cause to aske the questyon, but myght haue rekened clerely / that
he wolde haue her conceyued by her husband.

And therfore was her questyon farre fro the question of zachary,
Luce. 1   the father of saynt Iohan, whiche asked
[h₈v] not the angell how, but what
token he sholde haue that he sayd trew / for ellys it semed that for
all his worde, bycause of theyr bothe agys, he was mynded no more
to medle with hys wyfe, syth he thought possybylite of generacyon
passed. And for that dyffydens was he punyshed by losse of hys
speche tyll the byrth of yᵉ chyld.

And her questyon was also very farre fro this questyon of the

---

36 losse] yᵉ losse *1557*

Iewys here, and from theyr askynge how / whyle the cause of her
questyon was fayth, and the cause of theyr questyon dyffydens.

Nichodemus also whan our lord bygan to tell hym of the sacrament of baptysme, and sayd vnto hym,

Iohan. 3

5   *" verily veryly I tell the, but if a man be born*
agayne he can not se the kyngdome of god / answered our sauyour & sayd
how may a man be borne agayn whan [i₁] *he is olde: maye he entre agayne*
into hys mothers bely & be born agayne?"

Lo here the man was deceyued in that he thoughte vpon a
10 bodyly byrth, where as our sauyour ment of a spyrytuall byrth, by
fayth and by the sacrament of baptysme. And therfore our lorde
tolde hym forthwyth, that he ment not that a man sholde be
bodyly borne agayne of his mother, but ment of a spyrytuall regen-
eracyon in soule, by the water and yᵉ holy goost.

15 How be it he told hym not for all that all the forme and maner
of that sacrament, but what the substaunce sholde be, and by
whose power, and wherof it shold take effecte.

Now these iewes here, to whome, Cryste preched of the geuyng of
his body to them for meat, were not fully in the case of Nicho-
20 demus, but in some point they were nerer yᵉ trewth [i₁v] than he
was at the begynnynge. For they toke our sauyours wordes ryght in
that they vnderstode that he spake of his owne very fleshe, and that
he wold geue it them to eate / where as Nichodemus vnderstode no
part of the generacyon and byrth that Cryst spake of. But they
25 myssetoke the maner how he wolde geue it them, & ran forth in
the deuyce and imagynacyon of theyr owne fantasy. But in dyffydence & dystrust they were lyke Nichodemus which sayd, *"how*
maye a man be borne agayn whan he is old?" And peraduenture the
farther of from endeuour towarde byleuynge. For in Nichodemus
30 though I fynd no consent of faith in conclusyon / yet yᵉ gospell
speketh not of any finall contradyccyon in hym, nor of any desperate departynge, as these Iewes & these disciples dyd. And Nichodemus spake in his cause after, but these discyples [i₂] neuer
walked after with hym.

35 Now Cryste there vnto Nichodemus, bycause he was clene fro
the mater, told him yᵗ it shold be no bodyly byrth but a spiritual /

4–5 *gloss* Iohan. 3] Iohn. 2 *1557*

and bode hym meruayle not therof no more than of ye spiryng or mouyng of the spiryt or of ye wynd (for y^t word diuerse doctours take diuersely) whose voice though he herd, he neither wyst from whens it came nor whyther he wold go. But now whan y^t Nichodemus perceyuynge what ye thyng was, dyd yet wonder on styl & sayd: how may these thinges be. Than our lord dyd no more but leue hym with y^e same tale styll, & byd him byleue, & tell hym why he so sholde, syth hym self y^t so told hym came from heuyn, and therfore could tell it / and gaue hym a sinificacyon of hys deth, wherby that sacrament shold take the strength. But as for hys questyon how this myght be, otherwyse than y^t [i$_2$v] it was by the power of god, that questyon Cryst lefte vnsoyled.

Now dyd he lykewyse with these iewys here. Syth it was so that they perceyued allredy that he spake of his very flesshe, and yet for all that wold not byleue he could geue it them / but thoughte the thynge so straunge and wonderfull, that they thought he could not do it, & therfore asked how he could do it: he dyd no more but styl tell them that he wolde do it, and that he veryly wold gyue them his fleshe to eate and his very bloud to drynke / and tolde them the profyte that they shold haue, yf they byleued hym and dyd it, and what losse they shold haue yf for lacke of bylyef they wold leue it vndone / and that he was come from heuyn, and therfore they ought neyther to myssetruste hys word nor his power to performe hys worde. And [i$_3$] as for otherwyse how and in what maner he could or wold do it, he lefte theyr questyon and theyr how vnsoyled.

But now lest mayster Masker myght make men wene, that I make all thys mater of myne own hede, ye shall here good readers vppon thys questyon of the Iewys what saynte Cyryll sayth.

S. Cyrillus
lib. 4. cap. 13.
in euang. Io.

" *The Iewes (sayth he) wyth greate wyckednes cry out and saye agaynst god: How may he gyue vs his flesh? & they forgete that there is nothynge impossyble to god. For whyle they were fleshely, they could not (as saint Poule sayth) vnderstande spyrytuall thynges / but thys great sacrament & mystery semed vnto*

1. Co. 2

---

9 sinificacyon] significacion *1557*

theym but foly. But lette vs I beseche you take profyte of theyr synnes, and let
vs geue ferme fayth vnto the sacramentes, & lette vs neuer in suche hygh
thynges [i₃v] *eyther speake or thynke that same*

Beware of this
woord howe*

how. For it is a Iewes worde that same, and a
5 *cause of extreme ponysshement. And Nicodemus*
therfore when he sayd: How may these thynges be, was answered as he wel
was worthy, Art thou the mayster in Israell and knowest not these thynges.

Let vs therfore (as I sayd) be taught by other

Ask not how in
Goddes woorkes*

folkes fawtes, in goddes worke not to aske:
10 *How: but leue vnto hym selfe the science and*
the way of hys owne worke. For lyke wyse as though no man knoweth what
thing god is in hys owne nature and substaunce, yet a man is iustified by
fayth when he byleueth that they that seke hym shalbe ryally rewarded by
hym: so thowgh a man know not the reason of goddys workys yet when
15 *thorow fayth he dowteth not but that god is able to do all thyng, he shall haue*
for thys good mynde great rewarde. [i₄] *And that we shold be of thys mynde,*

Esai. 55

our lorde hym selfe exhorteth vs by the prophete
Esaye, where he sayth thus vnto men.

My deuyces be not as your deuyces be nor my wayes suche as your wayes be
20 *sayth our lorde: but as the heuyn is exalted from the erth, so be my wayes*
exalted aboue yours, and my deuyces aboue your deuyces. Chryste therfore
whyche excelleth in wysedome and power by his godhed how can it be but that
he shall worke so wonderfully, that the reason and cause of hys workes shall
so farre passe and excelle the capacyte of mannes wytte, that our mynde shall
25 *neuer be possyble to perceyue it. Doste thou not se oftentyme what thynge men*
of hande crafte do. They tell vs somtyme that they can do some thinges wherin
theyr wordes seme of them self incredyble. But yet bycause we [i₄v] *haue sene*
them somtyme done suche other thynges lyke, we therby byleue them that they
can do those thynges to. How can it be therfore but yᵗ they be worthy extreme
30 *torment, that so contempne almyghty god the worker of all thynges, that they*
dare be so bolde as in hys workes to speke of how, while he is he, whom they
knowe to be the geuer of all wysedome, and whyche (as the scrypture techeth
vs) is able to do all thynge. But now thou Iewe yf thou wylte yet cry out and
aske how, than wyll I be content to playe the fole as thou doest, and aske how

---

3 thynke] *1557*, thynge *1533*   5 extreme] *1557*, exterme *1533*   16 great rewarde.] great.
rewarde *1533*, great reward. *1557*   22 godhed] godhed, *1557*   31 workes] wordes *1533*
1557

Exod. 4*

Exod. 4*

Exod. 7*

Exod. 14*

Exod. 15*

Exod. 17*

Iosua. 3*

Iosua. 6*

to. *Than wyll I gladly axe y^e, how thou camest out of Egipt, how Moyses rodde was turned into the serpent, how the hand strykken wyth lepry, was in a moment restored to hys formare state agayne / how the waters turned into* 5 *bloude / how thy fore fathers went thorow the mydde sees as though they had walked on* [i₅] *drye grounde / how the bytter waters were chaunged swete by the tree / how the fountayne of water flowed out of the stone / how the* 10 *runnyng ryuer of Iordane stode styll / how the inexpugnable walles of Ieryco were ouerthrowen with the bare noyse and clamour of the trum-pettes. Innumerable thynges there are in whyche yf thou aske how, thou must nedes subuerte and set at nought all the whole scrypture, the doctryne of the* 15 *prophetes, and Moyses owne wrytynge to / wherupon you Iewes ye shold haue byleued Cryste / & yf there semed you than any hard thynge in his wordes, humbly than haue asked hym. Thus sholde ye rather haue done, than lyke dronken folke to crye out: How can he gyue vs hys flesshe? do ye not perceyue that when ye say such thynges there appereth anone a great arrogaunce in your* 20 *wordes.*" [i₅v]

Here you se good readers, that S. Cyrill in these wordes playnely shewed y^t Crist here in these wordes, The brede that I shall geue you is my flesh whych I shall geue for the lyfe of the worlde, ment of ye geuyng of hys flesshe in the sacrament. And that the Iewes 25 wondered that he sayd he wolde geue them his flesshe, and asked how he could do it, bycause they thought it impossyble. And in reprofe of theyr incredulyte and that folyshe mynde of theyrs (by whiche they could not byleue that god could geue them his owne fleshe to eate) S. Cyrill both sheweth that many hand crafted men 30 do thynges such as those that neuer sawe the lyke wolde wene

*It is a madnes to aske how god can doe thys**

impossyble, and also that in any worke of god it is a madnes to putte any dowt and aske how he can do it, syth he is almyghty and able to do all [i₆] thynge. 35

---

1 y^e] thee *1557*   4 moment] *1557*, momet *1533*   19 flesshe?] flesshe, *1533*, flesh?
1557   30 hand crafted] handycraft *1557*

And to the entent that no chrysten man sholde dowt of the
chaunge and conuersyon of the bred in to Crystes blessed body in
the sacrament, Saynt Cyrill here by waye of obieccyon agaynste
the Iewes, putteth vs in remembraunce (for vs he teacheth though
5   he spake to them) among other myracles he putteth vs I say in
remembraunce of dyuerse conuersyons and chaunges out of one
nature into another, that god wrought in the olde lawe. As how the
hande was turned from hole to sore, and from sore to hole agayne
sodaynly. How the waters were sodaynly turned from bytter into
10 swete / and how the waters were turned from water to bloude /
and how the dede rodde of Moyses was turned into a quycke
serpent. [i₆v]

B

The .xvi. chapyter.

But yet shall ye se that vpon the wordes of Cryste folowynge,
15 saynt Cyryll all waye more and more declareth that Christ spake
there of his very body, that he wold geue men to eate in the blessed
sacrament. For it foloweth in the text of the gospell.
     Than sayd Iesus vnto the Iewes, " *Veryly veryly I say vnto you, but yf*
ye eate the flesshe of the sone of man ye shall not haue lyfe in you. He that
20 *eateth my flesshe and drynketh my bloude, hath euerlastynge lyfe.*"
     Vppon those wordes thus sayth saynt Cyrill.
     " *Cryst is very mercyfull and mylde as the thynge it selfe sheweth. For*
                              he answereth not here sharpely to theyr hote
            Cyrillus   *wordes, nor falleth at no contencyon wyth them /*
            li. 4. ca. 14   *but goeth about to inprente in theyr myndes the*
25   *in euan. Io.*   *lyuely* [i₇] *knowlege of thys sacrament or*
mystery. And as for how (that is to wyt in what maner) he shall geue them
hys flesshe to eate, he teacheth them not. For they coulde not vnderstande yt.
But how greate good they shold get by the eating if they eate it with faith that
30 *thynge agayne and agayne he declareth them to dreue them to faith by the*
desyre of eternall lyfe / & fayth fyrst onys had, they shold be than the more
easy to be tawght. For the prophete Esay sayth, But yf ye byleue
                              ye shall not vnderstande. Therfore it was of
            Esai. 7   *necessyte requysyte / that they sholde fyrst*

---

10 to] into *1557*   15 saynt] *1533 corr. err.*, *1557* How saynte *1533*   29 faith] fayth,
1557   30 dreue] driue *1557*   33 vnderstande] vnderstaude *1533*, vnderstand *1557*

fasten the rotes of fayth in theyr mynde, and than aske suche thynges as were
metely for a man to aske. But they before they wolde byleue, wolde out of
season aske theyr importune questyons fyrste. And for thys cause our sauyour
declared not vnto them how it myght be done / but exhorteth them to seke the
thynge by [i₇v] fayth. So on the tother syde, to his dyscyples that byleued, he 5
gaue the peces of the brede sayeng : Take you and eate this is my body. And

Math. 26* *in like wyse he gaue them the cuppe about*
sayenge, drynke you of this all, thys is the cuppe
of my bloude, whyche shall be shed for many, for remyssyon of synnes. Here
thou seest that to them that asked wythout fayth, he opened not the maner of 10
thys mystery or sacrament. But to them that byleued, he expouned it though
they asked not. Therfore let theym heare thys, those folke I saye that of
arrogaunce and pryde wyll not byleue the faythe of Chryste."

Here ye se good readers that saynt Cyrill playnely declareth you,
that our sauyour wolde not teache theym at that tyme the maner 15
of the eatynge, bycause of theyr infydelyte for all theyr askynge /
but afterward [i₈] he tolde and taught it hys faythfull dyscyples at
hys laste souper and maundye, whan he toke them the bred and
bode them eate it, and tolde them that the same was hys body /
and the cuppe and bode them drynke therof, and shewed theym 20
that that was his bloud. And thus you se well by saynt Cyrill that
mayster Masker here, whych by hys exposycyon wold make vs
wene that our sauyour in all hys wordes here to the iewes, ment
onely to tell them of yᵉ geuyng of hys flesh to the deth, & that he
ment nothyng of the geuynge of hys fleshe to eate in the blessed 25
sacrament, doth in all hys exposycyon but play with false dyce to
deceyue you.

Now as for that saynt Cyril here calleth it by the name of brede,
that is I trow the thynge that can nothynge trouble you. For I
Why the sacrament haue shewed you [i₈v] before by the 30
*is called bread** wordes of that greate holy doctour Theophylactus, that it is called bred, bycause
it was bred, and bycause of the forme of brede yᵗ remayneth / &
yet is no brede in dede, but is the very blessed body of Crist his
very flesshe and hys bloude. As you se also by saynt Cyrill here, 35
whiche of thys blessed sacrament so often reherseth and inculketh

---

5 on] *1557*, vn *1533 corr. err.*, vnto *1533*   14 ye] you 1557   29 you. For] *1557*, you, For
1533

the myracle, exhortynge all folke that no man be moued to mystruste it, though the thynge be meruelouse, nor aske as ye Iewes
dyd how such a wunderfull wurke can be wrought / but mekely
byleue it, syth he is god that sayth it / & therfore as he sayth it, so
5   dowt not but he can do it / as he doth other lyke thynges, and dyd
ere he were born into thys world / of whyche thynges saint Cyrill
hath here rehersed some. As the turnynge of the water into [k₁]
bloude, as he turneth in the sacrament the wyne into bloud / and
the turnyng of Aarons rod into a serpent /

Exodi. 7

10 and that into such a serpent as deuowred
vp all the serpentes of the Egypcyane wytches. Lyke as our
sauyour in the blessed sacrament turneth the brede into hys
owne body, y^t holy holesome serpent that deuowreth all the poysened serpentes of hell / and was therfore figured by the brasyn
15 serpent that Moyses dyd sette vp in the

Nume. 21

maner of a crosse in the desert / the
byholdyng wherof deuowred & destroyed the venym of all the
poysen serpentes that had stongen any man there.

The .xvii. chapyter.

20 And all be it that I shewe you good chrysten readers, saint
Cyrilles wordes and hys exposycyon vpon the place, bycause
maister [k₁v] Masker shall not make men wene y^t I make all the
mater of myn owne hed: yet semeth me that our sauyour declareth
thys mater wyth playne wordes hym selfe. For what can be playner
25 wordes than are hys owne, whan that vppon theyr wunderynge
and theyr murmuryng question, how can he gyue vs his flesshe to
eate, he said vnto them, " *Veryly veryly I say to you, but yf you eate the
flesh of ye sone of man & drink his bloud ye shall not haue lyfe in you. He y^t
eateth my flesh & drynketh my bloude, hath lyfe euerlastynge / and I shall
30 rayse hym vppe agayne in the laste daye. For my flesshe is veryly meate, and
my bloud is veryly drynke. He that eateth my flesh and drynketh my bloude,
dwelleth in me and I in hym.*"
In these wordes ye se good readers howe playnely that our lorde
sheweth theym, bothe the profyte of [k₂] the receyuynge, and the
35 peryll of the refusynge / and also bothe that he not onely speketh of

---

23 yet] it *1557*

his very body and bloud (whyche thyng mayster Masker agreeth) but ouer that also that he more playnely and more precysely sayth, that they shold veryly eate it and drynke it (whyche thyng mayster Masker denyeth) and yet is that the thynge that our sauyour in these wordes most specyally laboreth to make theym byleue. For that he spake of hys very flessh, they perceyued well inough. But that he wold haue them verily eate it / that they thoughte such a maner thynge that they neyther wolde do nor could byleue, bycause they myssetoke the maner thereof, wenynge that they sholde eate it in dede peces cutte out as the bochers cutte the bestes in the shammellys. [k₂v]

And Cryst therfore wold at thys tyme for theyr arrogaunt infy-delyte (as saynte Cyrill hath told you) no thynge declare them of the maner of hys geuynge it to be veryly eaten, not in the proper forme of flesshe (as they flesshely imagyned) but in the forme of bred in the blessed sacrament bycause (as Theophilactus declared you) men sholde not abhorre to eate it. But leuynge that vntaught tyll the tyme of hys maundy souper (where as saynte Cyrill hath also shewed you he taught it his faithfull dyscyples at the instytu-cyon of that blessed sacrament) he laboreth as I say in these wordes here most speciall, wyth as playne wordes as can be deuysed, to tell them and make them byleue that they shall veryly eate hys flesshe. Whyche thyng for any thyng that he could say to them, they were [k₃] so hard harted that they wolde not byleue hym.

And yet is mayster Masker here mych more obdurate now, and mych more faythlesse to, than all they were than. For he, bothe hauyng herd what Criste sayd to those infydeles than, & also what he taught his faythfull dyscyples at hys maundy after, and what all holy doctours and sayntes haue sayde theron and byleued euer synnys: yet wyll he with a few fond heretykes, take a folysshe frowarde waye, and byleue the contrary / or at the leste wyse saye that he byleueth yᵉ contrary. But in good fayth yᵗ they veryly byleue as they say that can I not byleue, except that of yᵉ scrypture and the chrysten fayth these folke byleue nothyng at all. And so

5

10

15

20

25

30

35

---

9 maner] matter *1557*   10 dede] ded, *1557*   13 no thynge] nothing *1557*
16 declared] declareth *1557*   18 where as] wheras *1557*   27 he, bothe] *1533 corr. err.*,
bothe he *1533*, he both *1557*

vpon my fayth I fere me that you shall se it proue at laste / as appereth by some [k₃v] of them that so begynne all redy, and haue in some places put forth suche poysen in wrytynge.

But surely though neyther any man had euer wryten vppon
5 these wordes of Cryste, nor our sauyour hym selfe neuer spoken word therof after, that euer had in wrytyng comen into mennys handes: yet are these wordes here spoken so playne & so ful, that they must nedes make any man that were wyllyng to byleue hym, clerly perceyue and knowe that in one maner or other, he wolde
10 gyue vs hys awne very flesshe verely to be receyued and eaten. For whan the Iewys sayd, how can he geue vs his flesshe to eate? He answered them with no sophims, but with a very playn open tale tolde them, they sholde neyther dystruste that he could on hys parte geue them his flesshe to eate, nor yet [k₄] refuse vppon theyr
15 parte to eate it, if euer they wolde be saued. As though he wold say: Maruayle you and mystruste you my word? and aske how I can geue you mine own flesh to eate? I wyll not tell you how I can geue it, nor in what forme or fasshyon ye shall eate it / but this I wyll tell you, neyther in tropis, allegories, nor parables, but euyn
20   *And verely* for a very playne trouth, y^t eate ye shall
         *so we doe** my very flessh in dede, yf euer ye
purpose to be saued, ye and drynke my
very bloude to. For but yf you be content to eate, and wyth a trewe fayth to eate, the flessh of the sone of man, and drynke hys
25 bloude: ye shall not haue lyfe in you. But who so wyth a trewe well wurkynge fayth, eateth my flesshe and drynketh my bloude, he hath euerlastynge lyfe. Not onely bycause he ys as sure [k₄v] to haue it whan the tyme shall come as though he had it all redy, by reason of the promyse that Chryste here maketh, where he sayth,
30   *The bodye of Christ* And I shall resuscitate and rayse hym vp
         *is very lyfe** at the last day / but also for that the very
body of Cryste that he receyueth, is very lyfe euerlastyng of it selfe / and such a lyfe, as to them that well wyll receyue it, in trew fayth, and purpose of good lyuynge, it is
35 the thynge that is able to gyue lyfe & quyknesse euerlastynge. For as the godhed is of his owne nature euerlastyng lyfe: so is the flesshe ioyned in vnyte of person to the godhed, by that immedyate

---

10 awne] own *1557*   18 or] and *1557*

coniunccyon and vnyte, made bothe euerlastyng & lyuely in it selfe, and also euerlasting lyfe to the geuyng of life euerlastyngly to all other, that well and wurthely receyue hym, and wyll perseuer and abyde wyth hym. For [k₅] though euery man here naturally dye for the whyle: yet shall Chryst as he promyseth here, reyse & resuscytate hym agayne to euerlastynge lyfe in the laste daye. 5

The .xviii. chapyter.

Aᴎd to shew more and more that he meneth playnely of very eatynge and very drynkynge: he sayth, my flesshe is veryly meate, & my bloude is veryly drynke. Vppon 10 these wordes sayth saynt Cyril thus *" Chryste here declareth the dyfference agayne, bytwene the mystycall benedyccyon, that ys to wytte the blessed sacrament and manna, and bytwene the water flowynge out of the stone, and the communion of the holy bloude. And thys he repeteth* 15 *agayne, to the entent they sholde no more merueyle of yᵉ myracle of manna / but that they sholde rather receyue hym whyche is [k₅v] the heuynly brede and the gyuer of eternall lyfe. Your fathers sayd our sauyour, dyd eate manna in the desert and they be deade. But thys brede is descended from heuyn, that a man sholde eate therof and not dye. For the meate of manna brought not* 20 *eternall lyfe, but a short remedy agaynst hunger. And therfore manna was not the very meate / that is to wytte manna was not the brede from heuen / but the holy body of Chryst that ys the meate that noryssheth to immortalyte and eternall lyfe. Ye, sayth some man: but they dranke water out of the stone. But what wanne they by that for deade they be, and therfore that was not yᵉ very* 25 *drynke / but the very drynke ys the bloude of Chryste, by whyche death ys vtterly turned vppe and destroyed. For it ys not the bloude of hym that ys onely man, but the bloude of that man, [k₆] whych beynge ioyned to the naturall lyfe (that ys to wytte the godhed) ys made also lyfe hym selfe. Therfore we be the body and the membres of Chryste. For by thys blessed sacrament we* 30 *receyue the very sone of god hym selfe."*

Here you se good readers that saynte Cyrillus playnely declareth here, yᵗ these wordes of Chryst, My flesshe is veryly meate &c. are spoken and ment of hys holy flesshe in the blessed sacrament / of whyche mayster Masker in all hys exposycyon and in all his hole 35

Cyrillus
li. 4. ca. 16
in euan. Io.

---

24 Ye,] ye *1533*, Ye *1557*   26 bloude] drynke *1533 1557*

wyse wurke, telleth vs playnely the contrary. But saynte Cyrillus is
here open and playne, bothe for that poynte & for the hole mater.
For who can more playnly declare any thyng than y^t holy doctour
declareth in these wordes, y^t in [k$_6$v] the blessed sacrament is
5   veryly eaten and dronken the very blessed body & holy bloude of
Chryst. And yet doth not saynt Cyrillus say it more openly than
doth our sauyour in hys owne wordes hym selfe.

    And now ferther to shewe that it must nedys be so, that he
whyche eateth hys flesshe & drynketh his bloud, muste nedes be
10   resuscytate & reysed agayne in body to euerlastynge lyfe: our
sauyour addeth therunto & saith, " *He that eateth my flesshe and
drynketh my bloude, dwelleth in me and I in hym.*" Vppon whyche
wordes also, thus sayth holy saynt Cyrill.

    " *Lyke as yf a man vnto molten wex put other wex, it can not be but that*
15   *he shall thorow out mengle the tone wyth the tother : so yf a man receyue the*
flesshe and the bloude of our lord worthely and as he sholde, it can not [k$_7$]
be but that he shall be so ioyned wyth Chryst, as Chryst shalbe wyth hym &
he wyth Chryst."

    Thus may you good readers se, how veryly a man eateth in the
20   sacrament the blessed body of Cryst / and by that eatynge how
eche of them is in other. And than yf he so perseuer, how can it be
that that body shall haue euerlastynge deth, in whych there is
                 Note*   dwellynge euerlastynge lyfe? For as ye
                                      haue herd, the body of Chryste is by the
25   coniunccyon wyth his godhed made euerlastynge lyfe.

    But this is ment as I saye (and all the holy doctours do declare
the same) of them that receyue the sacrament, not onely sacramen-
                                 tally, but also effectually. That is to wyt,
        What it is to receiue   of them that not onely receyue the body
          the sacrament   of our sauyour by the sacrament into
30   *effectually**   theyr bodyes, but also by trew fayth
[k$_7$v] and trew repentaunce and purpose of good lyuyng, receyue
hys holy spirit therwith into theyr soules, & be made therby very
lyuely membres of that thyng that the blessed sacrament signifyeth
35   & betokeneth, y^t is to wyt of the mystycall body of Cryst, the
chyrche and congregacyon of sayntes.

    For as you haue herd by Theophilactus before, this blessed sac-
rament is not onely the very flesh of Cryst, but is also a figure. And

---

34 blessed] *1557*, blssed *1533*

that is it in diuerse wyse, as I shall ferther declare you in my boke
agaynst Frithis answere to my pystle. With whyche boke (were hys
onys come in prente whyche is all redy sent ouer to be prented) I
shall god wyllyng well make all his englysshe bretherne se & perceyue his foly, y^t lyst not wyllyngly to contynue folys and wynke.   5

But as I was about to say, they [k$_8$] that receyue our lord by the
sacrament onely, & not by fayth & purpose of amendement:
though they receyue hym yet they receyue hym not / & though
they eate hym they eate hym not. For though his blessed body be
receyued in to theyr bodyes: yet hys holy spirit is not receyued into   10
theyr soules / & therfore he dwelleth not in them nor they in hym,
but they eate & drynke theyr iugement, & receyue hym to theyr
dampnacyon, for that they receyue hym without faith & dew

1. Cor. 11   reuerence / & therfore do not as saith
                    saint Poule, discerne ye body of our   15
lorde.

And therfore sayth saint Austayn as Prosper reherseth in lib.
sententiarum prosperi, *" He receyueth the meate of lyfe, he drynketh y^e*
draught of eternyte, y^t dwelleth in Cryst, & in whom Cryst dwelleth. For he
y^t discordeth from Cryst neyther eateth y^e fleshe of Cryst, nor drinketh his   20
bloud, though he receyue [k$_8$v] *euery daye indyfferentely the sacrament of that*
great thynge to the iudgement and dampnacyon of hys presumpcyon."

This text of saynt Austayne alledged Fryth for hys purpose in a
certayne communycacyon / wyllyng to proue therby that the very
body of Cryste was not alwaye veryly receyued and eaten in the   25
sacrament, as ye chyrch sayth. For here (sayd Fryth) saynt Austayne sayth playne y^t euyll men though they receyue the sacrament, eate not the body of Cryst.

But here Fryth eyther had not lerned or ellys had forgoten, that
saynt Austayne ment of the effectuall receyuynge, by whych a man   30
not onely receyueth Chrystes blessed body into hys own sacramentally, but also virtually and effectually so receyueth therwyth the
spyryte of god into hys [l$_1$] soule, that he is incorporate therby
with our sauyour, in suche wyse, that he is made a lyuely member
of his mystycall body that is the congregacyon of sayntes by recey-   35
uyng it wurthyly, whiche euyll folke do not, that receyue it to
theyr dampnacyon.

For that saynt Austayne ment not to deny that ye blessed body

---

14-15 *gloss* 1. Cor. 11] *om. 1557*

of Cryst is veryly receyued and eaten in the blessed sacrament,
both of euyll folke and good, it appereth playne by that that in mo
places than one, he speketh of the traytour Iudas. For all be it that
in some places he putteth it in dowte and question, whyther Iudas
5   receyued the sacrament amonge the apostles at Chrystes maundy,
or els that yᵉ morcell that he receyued were not it: yet in dyuers
places he affermeth that he dyd. And in those places he affermeth
playnely that in the sa[l₁v]crament he receyued Chrystes blessed
body, as euyll and as false as the traytour was, as in his fyfth boke
10 de baptismo he clerely declareth in these wordes.

   " Lyke as Iudas to whom our lord gaue the morsel, not by receyuynge any
   euyll thynge, but by euyll receyuynge of a good thyng, gaue the deuyll a place
   to entre into hym selfe: so euery man yᵗ vnworthyly receyueth the sacrament of
   Cryst, maketh not yᵉ sacrament euyll bycause he is euyll, nor maketh not
15   *therby that he receyueth nothyng because he*
         The euyl receiue the   *receyueth it not to his saluacyon. For it was*
           bodi of Christ*   *neuer the lesse the body of our lorde and the*
   bloud of our lord, euyn vnto them of whom the apostle sayd, he that eateth it
   & drynketh it vnworthily, he eateth & drynketh dampnacyon to hym selfe."

20 Here saint Austayn good readers expressely declareth, yᵗ not
onely good folke but euil folke also, receiue & eat [l₂] in yᵉ sacrament yᵉ very body & bloud of Cryst, though the tone to saluacyon
the tother to dampnacyon. And therfore you se yᵗ saint Austayn
here playnely reproueth Fryth.

25 And that ye may playnely se also that saint Austayn in callynge
                                  yᵉ blessed sacrament the body of Cryst,
         August. in epist. 163.   meneth not to call it onely a fygure
         Ad Eleusium Glorium   or a memoriall (besyde his other playne
             & Felicem   wordes in many sundry places) he
30 writeth in a pistle vnto Eleusius, Glorius, & Felix, declaryng the
great excellent goodnes yᵗ Cryst shewed to the false traytour
Iudas, he writeth I saye yᵗ Cryst gaue vnto Iudas at his laste
                                  souper yᵉ pryce of our redempcyon. And
         The price of our   what was the pryce of our redempcion,
           redempcion*
35   but his owne very blessed body.
   How be yt Frith was on euery syde deceyued in the perceyuynge

---

27–28 *gloss* Glorium] Gloriam *1557*   33–35 *gloss* The price of our redempcion] *Placed*
opposite line 31 in 1557

The Last Supper, artist unknown (Italian, ca. 1470) (reduced)

of saynt Austayns mynd / which mysse [l₂v] happed hym as I
suppose for lacke of redynge any ferther in saynt Austayns wurkes,
than those placys yᵗ he founde falsely drawen out into frere
Huyskyns boke.

For saynt Austayne in very many places playnely declareth, that
euery man good and badde both, receyueth and eateth in the
sacrament the very body and bloude of Cryste. And also those
wordes in whych he sayth, that euyll folke eate it not, he meaneth
Note* yᵗ they eate it not so as they receyue the
effecte therof, that is to wytte to be by
the receyuynge and eatyng therof incorporate spyrytually with
hym, as a lyuely member of hys mystycall body the socyete of
sayntes, so that he may dwell in Chryste and Chryst in hym / but
lacketh yᵗ spyrytuall effecte of hys eatynge, bycause he is euyll &
eateth not Chrystes flesshe in suche [l₃] maner as he sholde do,
that is to wyt worthyly in trew fayth and purpose of clene and
innocent lyfe, as saynte Austayne in his boke de blasphemia spiritus sancti, declareth wel in these wordes.

" *Thys also that Cryst sayth, he that eateth my flesshe and drynketh my*
bloud, dwelleth in me and I in hym. How shall we vnderstande it. Maye we
1. Co. 11 *vnderstande those folke therin to, of whom tha-*
postle sayth yᵗ they eate & drynke theyr iuge-
ment, whan they eate the same flesshe and drynke the same bloude? Dyd
Iudas the traytour and wicked seller of his mayster though he fyrst wyth the
other apostles as saynt Luke theuangelyste very clerely declareth, dyd eate and
drynke the same sacrament of hys flesshe and his bloude made with his awne
handes, dyd he abyde yet in Cryst & Cryst in hym? Finally many men
whyche with a fayned harte eate [l₃v] *that flesshe and drynke that bloud, or*
ellys whan they haue eaten and dronken it, bycome apostatas after / do they
dwell in Cryst & Cryst in them? But there is vndowtedly a certayne maner of
eatynge that flesshe and drynkynge that bloude, in whyche maner he that
eateth it and drynketh it, dwelleth in Cryste and Cryste in hym. And therfore
not who so euer eate the flesshe of Cryste and drynke hys bloude, dwelleth in
Cryste and Cryste in hym / but he that eateth it and drynketh it after a
certayne maner, whyche maner Cryste saw whan he spake the wordes."

Here you se good readers that saint Austayn sheweth, that Iudas
in the sacrament receyued & dyd eate yᵉ body of Cryst, and

---

26 awne] owne *1557*   29 apostatas] *1557*, apostataas *1533*

declareth also the very whole thyng that he meneth concernyng
the vnderstandyng of this word of Crist, He y^t eateth my flesh and
drynketh my bloude dwelleth in [l$_4$] me
He that eateth my   and I in hym / that is to wyt they y^t eate
*fleshe**   it in a certeyn maner by which he
5   meneth they y^t eat it wel & in y^e state of grace / as he playnely
declareth bothe in hys exposycyon vppon saint Iohans gospel, and
many sundry places bysyde.

And those that receyue hym other wyse with a fayned hart and
in purpose of deadely synne / they folowe Iudas and shortely shew
10 them self. For suche as they were wont to be, such wyll they be
styll, or yet rather mych wurse if they were before veri nought.
And therfore sayth saynt Austayn, y^t a man to eate y^e flesh of Crist
is to dwell in Cryst, & to haue Cryst
*Note thys declaracion**   dwellyng in hym. For he y^t dwelleth not
15 in Crist, wel declareth y^t though he haue receyued & eaten his
flesh into his body by the sacrament, yet hath he not receyued &
eaten his spirit as I sayde [l$_4$v] into hys soule / and therfore hath
not receyued and eaten his flesshe effectually, but without theffecte
of the spyryte and lyfe, whiche is the thyng wherby the flesshe
20 geuyth the lyfe, and wythout whiche as our sauyour saith, his flesh
auayleth vs nothyng. And so for lacke of the spyrytuall eatynge,
the flesshely eater of his flesh though he receyue the sacrament,
receyueth not theffecte of the sacrament the thynge that the sacrament sygnyfyeth, that is the partycypacyon of ye mystycall body of
25 Chryste, that is to wytte the chyrche and congregacyon of all
sayntes, whyche chyrch and congregacyon is gathered togyther as
many membres into one body Cryste / as the brede whyche our
lorde in the sacrament chaungeth into hys blessed body, is one lofe
made of many graynes of whete / and the wyne whyche [l$_5$] he
30 chaungeth into his bloude, is one cuppe of wine made of many
grapes as thapostle declareth.

And veryly to be a quycke lyuely member of that body doth no
man attayne that receyueth the sacrament without fayth and
purpose of good lyfe / but waxeth a more weke membre & a more
35 lame, more astonied, and more losely hangynge theron than he
dyd before / and by suche often receyuynge so rotteth more and

---

28 chaungeth] chaunged *1557*

more, that finally it falleth quyte of, and is cast out into the dung-
hyll of hell, and shal neuer be resuscytate & reysed agayne to be
made a membre of that body in glory.

But as saynt Austayne sayth, yf a man after the receyuynge of
the sacrament do dwell styll in god, that
What it is to dwel
stil in god*   is to wytte abyde and perseuer in trew   5
fayth and good wurkes: than is it a [l₅v]
good sygne and token that he hath effectually eaten the flessh of
Cryst in the blessed sacrament. And therupon muste it nedes good
crysten reader folow, yᵗ he that receyueth the blessed sacrament
well, & eateth therin yᵉ flesh of Cryst, not onely veryly, whyche   10
euery man doth good & bad, but also (which onely the good folke
do) effectually, & so dwelleth in Cryste and Cryste in hym perseuerauntly: that man or woman without dowt, it must nedes be
that they can neuer euerlastyngly dye / but Cryst dwellyng in
them, shall conserue theyr soules and resuscytate agayn theyr   15
bodyes that so dwell in hym, into euerlastynge lyfe.

The .xix. chapyter.

For the surety and vnfallyble profe wherof, our sauiour said forthwith vpon his wordes afore remembred forther vnto the Iewes, " *as*
the [l₆] *lyuynge father sent me, so also do I lyue for my father. And he that*   20
eateth me, shall lyue also for me."

The father of heuyn beynge the orygynall substaunce of lyfe,
before all begynnyng begate hys coeternall sone, and gaue vnto
hym his owne whole substaunce, & therfore his own whole lyfe, as
to hym whome he begate one equale god wyth hym selfe, in   25
nothynge dyfferent but in onely persone.

The father I saye gaue all hys owne whole lyfe to his sone, and
yet none therof from hym self. And therfore sayth our sauyour
Cryste, that hym selfe lyueth for or by his father. And so yᵗ man
saith he that eateth me, shall lyue thorow me. For syth that by the   30
very eatyng of hys very blessed body, the eater (but yf hym selfe be
the let) is ioyned wyth the flesshe [l₆v] of Chryst (as holy saynt
Cyrill hath declared) and therby with that holy spyryt of hys also
whyche from that holy flesshe is vnseparable, and so ioyned vnto

---

19 forther] ferther *1557*   30 eateth] eath *1557*

the very substaunce of lyfe, that is lyfe and geueth lyfe to: he can
not but lyue thorow Chryste.

    Vppon this our sauyour fynally for conclusyon telleth them, that
this brede also is come from heuyn sayeng, " *Thys is the brede that is*
5 *descended from heuyn.*" Not meanynge that his flesshe was fyrst in
heuen, and so sent downe from thense as some heretykes haue ere
this holden an opynyon / but that hys body was in the blessed
virgyn hys mother, by the heuynly obumbracyon of the holy goste.
And also syth hys godhed and hys manhed were ioyned and knytte
10 togyther in very vnite of person: our sauyour vsed that maner of
spekynge by the [l₇] tone, that he vsed by the tother. And therfore
as he sayde vnto Nichodemus, the sone of man descended from
heuyn: so sayth he here of hys flessh, this is the brede that is
descended from heuyn.

15   And bycause that the Iewys had in the begynnynge of this communicacyon, bosted vnto hym the brede of manna, bryngynge
Psal. 77
forth for yᵉ preyse therof the wordes of
the prophete, Thou hast geuyn them
brede from heuyn: Our lord here shewed theym that thys brede
20 that he wolde geue them to eate, that is to wyt his owne very
flesshe (as hym self very playnely declared them) is of an other
maner descended down from heuen, than the manna, whose
descendynge from heuyn they in the begynnynge bosted so. And
therfore he sayd, " *Thys is the brede that is descended from heuyn* / [l₇v]
25 *not as your fathers dyd eate manna & are dede. He that eateth thys bred,*
shall lyue for euer." As though he wold say. This is another maner of
brede, otherwyse come from heuyn than manna was that ye boste
of so. For that bred was gyuen you but for the sustenaunce of the
lyfe in thys worlde / but this brede yᵗ is myne own body, conceyued
30 by the holy goost, & in vnyte of person ioyned wyth my godhed, as
verily as it is ioyned with myne own soule, is another maner of
heuynly brede, and shalbe gyuen you to eate for another maner of
purpose. For manna that was geuen your fathers to eate for the
onely sustinaunce of theyr temporall lyfe, was but a fygure of this
35   *Manna was a figure*   brede thus geuyn you to eate, as I shal
      *of the sacrament**   begyn to geue it at my maundy souper,
the maner wherof I wyll not tell you

---

33 purpose.] *1557*, purpose *1533*

now. And therfore [l₈] as the figure or yᵉ shadow of a thyng, is
farre fro the propertye of yᵉ thyng it selfe: so was the brede of
manna farre fro the propertye of this brede yᵗ is my flesshe. For
lykewyse as bycause it was a fygure of thys brede that is very lyfe,
it serued for the sustynaunce of lyfe: so bycause it was but a fygure, 5
and not the very lyfe it selfe, it serued therfore not to geue lyfe, but
to sustayne life / not for euer but for a whyle. But this brede that is
my flesshe / (whyche I shall geue you as veryly to eate as euer your
fathers dyd eate manna) bycause it is not the fygure onely of the
thynge that is lyfe, but is also (by coniunccion with the godhed) 10
the very lyfe it self that was figured: I shall geue it you to eat in
such a maner, that it shal not onely mayntayn, fede, and sustayne
the body of the eater in thys present [l₈v] lyfe, but it shall also
gyue lyfe, ye & that euerlastynge lyfe in glory / not onely to yᵉ
soule, but also to the body to, in tyme mete and conuenyent, 15
raysynge it vp agayne from deth, and settynge it wyth the soule in
eternall lyfe of euerlastynge blysse.

The .xx. chapyter.

" *Tʜʏs communycacyon wyth the Iewys had our lorde, techynge in the*
synagoge at Caparnaum. And many therfore of hys dyscyples herynge these 20
thynges sayde, Thys word is hard, and who can here hym."

The more and more that our sauyour playnely tolde them that
he wolde geue them hys very flesshe to eate, the more and more
meruelouse harde they thought his sayenge, and rekened that it
was impossyble for any man to byleue it. And therfore for lacke of 25
bylyefe they loste the [m₁] profyt. And these that thus thought
thys mater so meruelouse harde and straunge that they wolde not
byleue, but for lacke of bylyefe lost the profyte, were not onely
such Iewes as were his enemies, but many of those also that were
his owne dyscyples. 30

But oure sauyour knowynge in hym selfe (as he that was god and
neded no man to tell hym) that hys dyscyples murmured at his
wordes, bycause he tolde them so often and so playnely that men
shold haue no life, but yf they wolde be content veryly to eate hys
owne flessh he sayd vnto them, " *Doth thys offende you? do you stumble* 35

---

19 Iewys] *1533 corr. err., 1557*, Hewys *1533*   21 thynges] *1533 corr. err., 1557*, thynger *1533*

*at thys? what than yf you shall se the sone of man ascende vppe where as he
was before? The spyryt is that that quyckeneth, the flessh auayleth nothing.
The wordes that I haue spoken to you be spirit & lyfe."* [m₁v]

In these wordes our lorde shortely towcheth all theyr obiectyons
5   growynge vpon theyr infydelyte, & also confuteth theyr infidelyte /
and in hys wordes after folowyng, putteth them yet agayne in
mynde of the medicine yᵗ might remoue theyr vnfaithfulnes & geue
them the very fast fayth.

The Iewes had byfore murmured agaynst that that he had
10 sayde, yᵗ he was descended from heuyn. Agaynst whiche they sayd,

Iohn. 6*   Is not he the sone of Ioseph whose father
                                 and mother we know? And how sayth he
than that he is descended from heuyn? And a great pyece of theyr
murmure therin arose as ye se, vppon that poynt that they had
15 mysse conceyued, wenyng yᵗ Ioseph had ben his father. For had
they byleued that his manhed had ben conceyued by yᵉ holy goste,
they wold haue murmured yᵉ lesse. And had they [m₂] byleued yᵗ
his godhed had descended in to it from heuyn, they wold not haue
murmured at all.

20   In Lyke wise they murmured at the secund poynt, in that he
shewed them so playnely yᵗ he wold geue them his very flesshe to
be theyr very mete, & sayd how can he gyue vs his flesh to eate.
And many of his dysciples sayd also, this is an hard word, & who
may here hym. And a great parte of theyr murmure was, bycause
25 they thought that they shold haue eaten his fleshe in yᵉ self fleshly
                                 forme / & bycause (as saint Austayn
August. in enarra. in   saith in sundry treatices) yᵗ they thought
psal. 168. et in serm.   they shold haue eaten his fleshe in dede
2 de verbis apostoli   gobbettes, cut out piecemele as the meat
30 is cut out in yᵉ shamelles / & also bycause they knew him not to be
god. For had thei knowen that the maner in whyche he wolde geue
them hys very flesshe to eate, [m₂v] shold not be in the self same
fleshely forme, but in the pleasaunt forme of brede: though they
wolde yet haue meruayled, bycause they wolde haue thought it
35 wonderfull, yet wold they haue murmured the lesse, bycause they
wold not haue thought it lothely. But than had they ferther
knowen that he had ben god / than wolde they not I suppose haue
murmured at the mater at all. For I wene veryly that there were

---

26–27 *gloss* August.] *1557*, Augnst. *1533*

neyther of those disciples nor of those Iewes neyther, any one so
euyll as now be mayster Masker, & Fryth, & hys felowes, that
seynge the receyuyng nothynge lothesome, and byleuynge that
Cryst was god (yf they byleue it) wyll not yet byleue he can do it /
but murmur & grudg agaynst it styll.

For though mayster Masker say that yf Cryst sayd he wold do it,
[m₃] than hym selfe wold byleue he could do it: yet it shall appere
ere we part, both that Cryst sayth it, and he wyll not byleue that
Cryst though he say it meneth it, and also that the cause why he
wyll not byleue that Cryste meneth it, is bycause he byleueth that
god can not do it.

But now sayd our sauyour vnto them in answerynge all thys
gere. *Do you stumble at thys? what yf ye se the sone of man ascende vp
where he was before? what wyl you than say?* For than could they haue
no cause to distruste that he descended downe, whan they shold se
hym ascende vp. For that thynge semeth in mennys madde eyen
suche as they were that wolde not take hym but for a man, farre
the gretter maystry of the both.

Also whan they sholde se hym ascende vp to heuyn whole / than
sholde [m₃v] they well perceyue that they mysse toke hym by a
false imagynacyon of theyr owne deuyce, whan they constrewed
the geuynge of hys fleshe to eate, as though he ment to gyue it
them in such wyse, as hym selfe shold lose all that they sholde eate.

And whan he sayde they shold se the sone of man ascend vp
there as he was byfore / he gaue them agayne a sygnyfycacyon that
hym selfe yᵉ sone of man was the sone of god also, and therby hym
selfe god also, & into the worlde comen and descended from
heuyn.

In these wordes our sauyour sheweth that his ascensyon shold be
a sufficient cause to make them knowe his power & leue theyr
murmuryng. And therfore they that leue not murmuryng at his
blessed sacrament yet, shew a great token that they byleue [m₄]
not his wonderfull ascension neyther. For yf they byleued well that
he had power of hym selfe to ascende vp in body, and syt in heuen
one equale god with his father & the holy goost: than wold they
neuer wene as they do, yᵗ god lacked power to make hys owne
body to be in dyuerse places at onys, and be both in heuen and
erth.

5

10

15

20

25

30

35

The .xxi. chapyter

But now for as mych as a greate parte of these folkes diffydence
and distrust, rose of that that the respecte of the lothsomnes made
them the lesse wyllynge to byleue, in that they thought that he
5   ment to geue them his flesshe to eate in gobbettes cutte out dede
wythout lyfe or spyryte: our sauyour answered them to that poynt.
And though he wold not at that tyme tell them the maner how
[m₄v] he wolde geue it them to eate: yet he tolde them that he
wolde not geue it them so. And therfore he sayd vnto them. *" The*
10   *spirit is it that quycketh or geueth lyfe / the flesshe auayleth nothyng. The*
wordes which I haue spoken to you be spyrit and lyfe."
As though he wold say vnto them. I tolde you before that who so
wold eate my fleshe sholde haue euerlastyng lyfe. And therfore why
be you so madde as to wene that I mene my fleshe cut out in
15   gobbettes dede wythout lyfe or spyryt? it is the spirit that geueth
lyfe. And therfore without the spirit the fleshe shold auayle you
nought. But beyng knytte with the spirite of my godhed, whyche is
the substaunce and very fountayne of lyfe / so it shal (to them that
worthyly eate it) geue euerlastynge lyfe. And therfore the wordes
20   that I speke be [m₅] not onely fleshe / for yᵗ wyll no more geue lyfe
alone, than wyll fayth alone geue life that is dede without yᵉ wyll
of good wurkes. But my wordes therfore that I haue spoken to you
of my fleshe to be eaten, be not fleshe alone, but spyryte also and
lyfe. Therfore you muste vnderstande them not so fleshely as you
25   do, that I wolde geue you my fleshe in gobbettes dede / but you
must vnderstand them spyrytually, that you shall eate it in an
It is the spirite   other maner animated wyth my soule,
*that gyueth life**   and ioyned with the spyrite of my
godhed, by whych my flessh is it self
30   made not onely lyuely but also geuynge lyfe.
Thus ment our lord in those wordes. Wherin leste mayster
masker myght make men wene that I runne all at ryotte vppon
Aug. in tractatu   myne own inuencyon, holy saynte Aus-
27. in Io.   tayne sheweth [m₅v] that in these
35   wordes, *" The spyryt it is yᵗ quyckeneth, the*
fleshe auayleth no thyng. Our sauyour meneth that his flesh dede & without

27 maner] maner, *1557*   36 no thyng] nothing *1557*

ye spirit auayleth nothyng / as cunnyng nothyng auayleth without cherite,
without whiche as saint Paule saith it doth but
Cunning doth puffe   *puffe vp a man in pride. But on ye tother side*
vp a man in pride*   *lyke as cunnyng mych edifyeth & profiteth*
1. Cor. 8   *ioyned with cheryte : so ye flesh of our sauiour*   5
mych auayleth ioyned wyth hys holy spyryte."

Saynt Cyrill also vppon ye same wordes declarynge them by a
longe processe to the purpose that I haue shewed you, saith among
many other thynges in thys maner, as it were in the person of Cryst
spekyng to those Iewes, & to those dyscyples of hys, that sayde his   10
wordes were so hard that no man could abide to here hym / which
Chrisosto. hom. 46.   they sayd as sayth saynt Chrisostom for
in Ioannem   theyr own excuse, bycause them self were
about to walke theyr way. To them ther-
fore sayth our sa[m₆]uyour thus in saynt Cyrilles exposicyon.   15
" Wene you whan I sayd that who so eate my flesh shal haue euerlasting lyfe,
that I ment therin, that this erthely body of myne doth gyue lyfe of his own
proper nature? Nay veryly. But I dyd speke to you of the spyryt and of
eternall lyfe. But it is not the nature of the flesshe that maketh the spyryt geue
lyfe / but the power of the spyryte maketh the fleshe geue lyfe. The wordes   20
therfore y^t I haue spoken to you be spirit & lyfe / that is to wytte they be
spyrituall & spoken of the spirit and lyfe / that is to wytte of y^t spirit y^t is
the natural life, y^t geueth lyfe. But yet the thyng y^t we haue all redy said, it
shal do no harme though we repete it agayn. The thing that I haue sayd is
this. The nature of the flesh can not of it self geue lyfe. For what had than   25
the nature of ye godhed more? But than on ye tother syde, there is not in Crist
onely flesh / but he hath ye sone of god ioyned with it which is ye equale
substauns of life with his fader. [m₆v] And therfore whan Cryst calleth hys
fleshe a geuer of lyfe / that power of geuynge lyfe he doth not attrybute vnto
his fleshe and vnto hys holy spirite bothe of one fashyon. For the spiryte   30
geueth lyfe by it selfe and of hys owne nature. But the fleshe ascendeth vnto
that power of geuynge lyfe, by reason of the coniunccyon and vnyte that it hath
wyth that holy spyryte. How be it how and by what meane that thynge is
done, we neyther are able with tonge to tell, nor with mynd to imagyne / but
wyth sylence & ferme fayth we receyue it."   35
Thus haue you herde good readers that the thynge that I saye,

---

5 *gloss* 1. Cor. 8] *Placed opposite line 6 in 1557*   12–14 *gloss* Chrisosto. . . . Ioannem] *Placed*
opposite lines 14–15 *in 1557*   26 godhed] *1557,* gddhed *1533*   28 fader.] fader *1533,*
father. *1557*

do not onely I say, but saynt Austayne also and saynt Cyrill both.
Whych is inough to you to perceyue that I dyuyse not myne
exposycion all of myne owne hed / and may be inough to any good
chrysten man also, to perceyue [m7] clerely that our sauyour in
5 these wordes dyd speke, not onely of a spyrytuall eatynge of his
fleshe by bylyef and remembraunce of hys deth and passyon, as
mayster Masker & Fryth and these fond felowes styffely bere vs in
hande, but spake also and ment it of the remembrynge of hys deth
and passyon, by the very eatynge of hys very blessed body as it is
10 eaten in the blessed sacrament.

The .xxii. chapyter.

Βut these heretykes are so sette vppon myschyefe and wylful-
nesse, that they wyll not in any wyse vnderstand the truth. And
how coulde they vnderstande the trouth, whan they wyll not
15   *Esaie. 7*   byleue. For (as the prophete Esaie sayth)
                              but yf you byleue you shal not vnder-
stand. And therfore these heretykes can not vn[m7v]derstand. For
they be in the case now that those dyscyples & those Iewes were,
with whom our sauyour founde that faute than, in his wordes nexte
20 ensuenge & sayd: But there be some of you that byleue not / as
though he wold say as playnely as I haue told it you and as often,
yet are there some of you y^t byleue it not. But he knewe from the
begynnynge who shold byleue, and who also sholde betraye hym.
And so knoweth he lyke wise now to, who be good and who be
25 nought, and who shall amende and who shall neuer amende. Not
      Of the foreknowledge   that hys fore knowlege forceth them to be
          of God*   nought / but for it is impossyble for them
                              to be nought, but that hys infynite fore-
syght muste nedes from the begynnynge fore se it. And yet whan
30 he forseeth that it so shall be / it shall so [m̄8] be in dede, and can
not otherwyse be but that it shall so be yf he fore se that it shall so
be. For he sholde not forese that it shall so be, yf it so were that in
dede it sholde otherwyse be. But lykewyse as yf I se one syt, it
muste nedes be that he sytteth, for ellys sholde I not se hym sytte /
35 and that therfore it well foloweth I se hym sytte: ergo it muste
nedes be that he sytteth. And yet my syghte forceth hym not to

---

21 say] say, *1557*

sytte / nor of that argument the consequent proposycyon of hys
nature necessarie but contingent / though of the tone proposycyon
inferred vppon the tother, the consequency, or consecucyon be
necessary. So beynge presupposed that god forseeth such a thyng
whych he shold not forese but yf the thyng shold be, yet hys fore   5
syghte no more forceth [m₈v] the person that doth it in the thynge
that is yet to come, than my syghte forceth hym to sytte whom I se
syt / of whom no man can say but that he must nedes syt in the
whyle in which he wyl presuppose that I se hym syt.

And therfore bycause hys prescyence and hys prouidence, forced   10
them not to contynue in theyr wylfulnes to theyr dampnacyon / he
putteth them onys agayne in remembraunce of the meanes wherby
they maye voyde y' wylfull ignoraunce and infydelyte and thus he
sayth vnto them: " *Therfore I haue tolde you all redy, that no man can
come to me but yf it be gyuen of my father.*"   15

" *Thynke not,*" sayth saint Crysostom vppon these wordes, " *that euery*
man to whom the father gyueth it, hath it
Crisost. hom 46
in Ioh.
as by waye of a specyall pryuylege / so that
they y' have not geuen them lacke it onely
therfore, bycause god [n₁] *wyll not gyue it them. God (sayth S. Chrysostom)*   20
*wyll gladly gyue it them, yf they wolde not by theyr owne delynge make them
selfe vnwurthy to receyue it.*" And therfore sayth saynte Cyryll vppon
the same wordes, " *that those that amonge the Iewys lyued well and were
of good condycyons, had the fayth geuen them and came to Cryst. But they
that were stuberne, arrogant, malycyouse, & wylfull, as were the scrybes &*   25
*the pharyseys and the styffenecked bysshoppes they letted them selfe from the
gyfte of fayth.*"

This gyfte of fayth without the helpe of god cannot be hadde /
nor no man can come to the sone but yf
Aug. in tractatu
26. in Io.
the father draw hym. And whom he   30
draweth, and whom he draweth not, and
why hym, and why not hym, let vs not seke nor serche as saynt
Austayne sayth yf we wyll not erre. [n₁v]

But yet that he reiecteth no man that wyll seke for hys soule
helthe, but rather calleth vpon to be sought vppon, that doth the   35
scrypture well wytnesse, where god sayd
Apoca. 3*
hym selfe, Lo I stande at the dore knock-
ynge, yf any man heare my voyce & open me the dore, I wyll go in

---

29 the sone] soone *1557*

to hym and suppe with hym and he with me. And the prophete
Esaie sayth, Seke you our lorde whyle he
may be founden. Call you vppon hym
whyle he is nere. Lette the wycked man leue hys way, and the
5 vnrightuouse man leue hys deuyces, and lette hym turne to our
lorde and he wyll haue pytie vppon hym. For he is great in forgeuenesse. Our sauyour sayth hym selfe
also. Aske and you shall haue. Seke and
you shall fynde. Knocke and you shall be lette in. And finally that
10 no man sholde take these wordes of [n₂] our sauyour, that no man
can come to hym but yf it be geuen hym of the father, and these
wordes of hys also, No man can come to me but yf my father draw
hym, that no man I say sholde so take these wordes in suche a
presumptuose way of eleccyon, that wenynge he were drawyn into
15 suche a felyng faith that could neuer fayle and so sholde as
Tyndale teacheth, make hym selfe so sure of hys owne saluacyon
by hys sure and infallyble eleccyon, that he sholde stande out of all
feare and wax slouthfull: yᵉ scrypture cryeth, Lette hym that
thynketh he standeth, beware lest he fall.
20 And on the tother syde, that no man
shold vppon these wordes, take that imaginacyon that these heretykes also tech, of desperate ineuitable destyny of dampnacyon,
and sytte styll and do no good hym selfe,
wenynge that his [n₂v] owne deuour
25 were in vayne, bicause he felyth not god
any thynge drawe hym: holy saint Austayn (whose wordes these
heretykes for eleccyon and destynye
agaynst the deuour of mannys fre wyll
most lay for them) byddeth euery man
30 for al theyr babeling if yᵘ be not drawen pray god to draw yᵉ.

And therfore to that entent dyd our sauyour Cryst putte them
agayne in mynde of that he had sayed before, yᵗ they coulde not
come to hym but yf it were geuen them by his father, bycause he
wold yᵗ they shold for theyr parte labour to remoue yᵉ lettes yᵗ on
35 theyr own parte, letted his father to geue them yᵗ gyft. And that is

Esaie. 55

Matth. 7

1. Cori. 10

*Beware of ineuitable
desteny**

*August. in tracta. 27
in Ioannem*

---

5 vnrightuouse] vnriteouse *1557*   14 presumptuose] presumpteouse *1557*   20 on] *1557*,
vn *1533*   30 yᵘ] yᵉ [?, *superscript blurred*] *1533*, thou *1557*; yᵉ] yᵉ [?, *superscript blurred*] *1533*,
thee *1557*

that they shold haue lesse cure & care of theyr belies / the desire of
whose fleshely fyllyng with perishable
Haue lyttle care for
the bellie*
meat, made them angri to here of ye spiritual fode of his own holy flesh / by the
wel eating wherof [n₃] they myght haue euerlastyng lyfe.   5

He taught them also by those wordes to perceyue (yf they
wolde) that Ioseph was not his father. For whan he sayd that they
could not haue that great gyft but of his fader, nor could not come
to him but if his fader drew them: they myght well wyt he ment
not Ioseph, but his father of heuyn. And therfore wold he by those   10
wordes geue them warnynge, that they shold leue theyr murmuryng, & pray his father geue them the grace to byleue hym.

The .xxiii. chapyter.

But where as they shold haue taken this way & walked forward
with hym, they toke the contrary way / not onely the other Iewes   15
but many also of hys own discyples, & went away bakward from
hym, & as ye gospel saith walked no more with him.

But though that many of hys dis[n₃v]cyples went awaye from
hym, bycause hys father brought theym not vnto hym: yet as hym
selfe sayd before, all that my father geueth me shall come to me /   20
all went not away. His apostles taried. And yet amonge those
twelue taryed one false shrew. And in the stede of those dyscyples
Luce. 10
y^t went away, which were as saint
Austayn sayth about thre score & ten /
he chose soone after other .iii. score & ten, whome he sent to   25
preche about as he had sent hys twelue apostles before.

But than seynge there were at y^t tyme so few lefte & so many
gone, he sayd vnto his .xii. apostles, wyll you be gone to? He
neyther bode them go as though he wolde be glad of theyr goynge /
nor yet bode them abyde, as though he had nede of theyr abydyng   30
but only asked theym whyther they wolde go or not / sygnifyeng
that for [n₄] all theyr eleccyon they were in the liberty of theyr
owne fre wyll, eyther to go after the tother / or to abide styll wyth
hym. Than answered Simon Peter and sayd: Lord to whom shall

---

8 fader] father *1557*   9 fader] father *1557*   17 him.] *1557*, him *1533*   25 chose] *1533*
corr. err., *1557*, hose *1533*

we go. Thou hast the wordes of euerlastynge lyfe. And we byleue
and know that thou arte Chryst the sone of god. As though he
wolde saye yf we loue lyfe, to whom sholde we go fro the? For
onely thou hast ye wordes not of lyfe onely but also of life euer-
5   lastynge / for all thy wordes and thy doctryne drawe men therto.
And we byleue, and by bylyef we know, that thou art Cryst the
very sone of god. And therby we knowe that thou arte not onely
very man, but also very god. And we perceyue well therfore that
thou arte the brede that is descended from heuen, and that thou
10 shalt ascende thyder agayne, and that ther[n₄v]fore thou arte able
and of power to geue vs that meruelouse meate of thyn owne holy
fleshe to eate. And that thou so wylt do, we byleue and wote well,
bycause thou so doste promyse. And we perceyue well y^t thou
                          wylt not geue it vs in dede gobbettes that
*Note**
15   could not auayle vs / but alyue, & with
thyne holy spyryte ye fountayne of lyfe, wherby thy fleshe shall
geue vs yf we wyll eate it euerlastynge lyfe, whan thou shalt
resuscytate our bodyes in the last day. But in what meruelouse
maner thou wylt geue it vs to eate, that haste thou not yet declared
20 vs / nor we wyll not be to boldely curyouse or inquisytyue of thy
meruelouse mistery. But therin abyde the tyme of thyne own
determynacyon, as to whose hyghe heuynly wysedome the season
mete and conuenyent is open and knowen, and vn[n₅]knowen to
mortall men. And we wyl therfore obedyently receyue it & eate it,
25 at what tyme and in what wyse y^t thy gracyouse pleasure shalbe to
commaunde vs.

Whan saynt Peter as hed vnder Cryst of that company, had
made this answere, not onely for hym selfe but also for them all,
not sayenge I but we: our lorde to lette hym se that he was
30 somwhat deceyued, & had sayed more than he coulde make good.
For one false shrew was there yet styll remaynynge amonge the
twelue / wherof .xi. were not ware / our sauyour therfore sayd.
Haue not I chosen you twelue & of you twelue yet is there one a
deuell? Thys he spake by Iudas Iskariot the sone of Simon for he it
35 was that shold bytraye hym beyng one of the twelue. [n₅v]

Our lorde here good readers shewed hym selfe not deceyued. For
though Iudas falsed was vnknowen to his felowes, yet was it not

---

13 doste] doest *1557*   31 For] (For *1557*   32 ware/] ware) *1557*   35 twelue.] *1557*,
twelue *1533*

vnknowen to hys mayster / which though he shewed hym selfe not
ignoraunt of hys seruauntes euyll mynde, & traytorouse purpose
towarde his owne persone (towarde whych purpose as it semeth
Iudas hart had at thys tyme conceyued some inclinacyon) yet had
he pacyence with hym, and continually dyd vse ye wayes to 5
reforme and amende hym / neuer castyng hym out, tyll he clerely
caste out hym self, accordynge to the sayenge of our sauiour, He

Iohan. 6   that cometh to me I wyll not caste hym
                out.

The .xxiiii. chapyter.   10

But here do many men meruaile not onely that our sauyour
wold kepe hym so longe knowynge [n$_6$] hym so false, but also that
he wolde take hym to him for his apostle in the begynnyng, fore
knowynge by hys godhed from the begynnynge that he wolde after
be false. And dyuerse holy doctours hold also, that he was neuer 15
trew nor good, but nought and false fro the begynnyng. And in this
mater wherof god hath not so fully reueled vnto men the certeynte,
that we be precysely bounden to the bylyef of eyther other parte /
euery man ys at lybertye to byleue whyther parte that hym selfe
thynketh moost lykely by naturall reason and scripture.   20

And therfore though some good holy men and sayntes haue

Whither Iudas was at   thought that Iudas was neuer good, but
any time good*   y^t our sauyour toke hym to his apostle,
                and so kepte hym in all hys malyce styll,
for thaccomplysshement of the great mystery of hys passyon, well 25
[n$_6$v] vsyng therby y^e euyll of man, as man euyll vseth the goodnes

Cyrillus li. 4. ca. 30   of god: yet thynketh me that as Theo-
in euan. Io. et Chryso.   phylactus sayth, and saynt Cyrill, &
                saint Chrisostome to, Iudas was ones
very good whan our lorde dyd chese hym for his apostle, and was 30
at that tyme geuyn vnto Cryst by his father. For profe wherof that

                godly cunnynge doctour M. Lyre, well
Lyra   bryngeth in ye wordes of our sauyour
Iohan. 17   hym selfe, sayenge to his father a lytle
                after his maundye finished: " *Them that* 35

---

18 precysely] *1533 corr. err.*, preasely *1533*, precisely *1557*   30 chese] chose *1557*   33 *gloss*
Lyra] Lyre *1557*

thou haste geuen vnto me I haue kepte, & none of them hath perysshed but the sone of perdycyon." Which he ment by Iudas beyng than yet alyue in body by nature, but dede in soule by dedely synne. Hym our lord toke vnto hym for hys apostle whyle he was good / and not of the
5   comen sorte of good men but also very specyall good as [n₇] these holy doctours do diuine & gesse.

And though Cryste foresaw the wrechednes that he wolde after fall to: yet wolde he not forbere yᵉ ryght order of iustyce, but take hym in such degre for the tyme, as hys present goodnes of good
10   congruens deserued. For beynge at that tyme more mete for thoffyce of an apostle than another man / if Cryst shold haue reiected him as vnworthy & vnmete, for the fawt yᵗ hym self knew he wold after do, toward which fawte he was at yᵗ tyme nothynge mynded: than shold he haue reproched hym at suche tyme as he
15   was not worthy to be reproched. And than were it somewhat lyke, as yf a man bycause he maketh hym selfe very sure that hys wyfe and hys chylderne wyll one tyme or other not fayle to dysplease hym afterwarde at some one tyme or other, be [n₇v] angry therfore wyth them all, & chyde them and bete them byfore. Our sauyour
20   therfore whan Iudas was very good, after suche rate of goodnesse as is in mortall men, toke hym and promoted hym to the offyce and dygnyte of hys owne apostle after that order of iustyce / by whych he rewardeth one man aboue another after the rate of theyr merytes, and yet euery man of them all farre aboue al hys
25   merytes.

Now whan he was afterwarde thorow couetyce waxed nought / yet our lorde kepte hym styll, and wolde not by takynge hys offyce from hym dysclose his secrete falsed, and putte hym to shame / but vsed many other meanes to mende hym, and kepe therwith the
30   honestye of hys name / not lettynge to procure hys amendement on hys parte though he well knewe [n₈] the wreche wolde neuer amende vppon hys parte.

But lyke wyse as though a man haue an incurable syknes, it yet becommeth the physycyon all the tyme that he lyueth therwyth, to
35   do hys parte styll toward the curynge therof: so bycame it our sauiour to do it as he dyd, and not to leue of or slake hys goodnes

---

10 deserued.] *1557*, deserued *1533*   13 toward] *1557*, to [*new line*] ward *1533*
36 sauiour] *1557*, saunour *1533*

towarde the cure and amendement of the mannys incurable
malyce.

For though Iudas was wyth all that goodnes of Cryste vsed vnto
hym, not onely nothynge the better, but also very farre the worse,
& fell farre the deper into deth and dampnacyon: yet syth there   5
came of his traytorouse delynge none harme, but vnto Crist whose
goodnes was for our well very gladde to suffre it, and vnto the
traytour hym selfe and suche [n₈v] other as wylfully wolde deserue
it: it had ben neyther ryght nor reason, that for to saue them from
hell that nedes wolde walke in to it, he sholde haue lefte any of hys   10
goodnesse and sufferaunce vndone, wherby he procured the
saluacyon of so many thousandes as sholde be saued by his bytter
passyon.

And mych more reason it was, y^t our sauyour shold haue
respecte and regard / to procure the blysse of those that sholde be   15
saued, than to care for the payne of those that shold be dampned.
For it had ben (as it semeth) not consonaunt vnto ryght, yf our
lorde sholde for auoydynge of theyr payne y^t for all his callynge
backe to the contrary wold yet wyllingly runne forth into dampnacyon: haue kept awaye the reward of blysse fro them y^t wold   20
with hys helpe deserue it. [o₁]

And therfore our lorde as I saye toke Iudas and made hym his
apostle, beynge very good / and after had longe pacyence wyth
hym whyle he was very nought, tyll that thorow his immedicable
malyce he fell of hym selfe, and so was cast out and perysshed. But   25
by his peryshynge our sauyour loste not but wan. For of hys euyll

Actorum. 1

came there mych more good, & hys
owne place of apostleshyp was afterwarde fulfylled wyth saynte Mathy.

And in lyke wyse the other dyscyples that departed now, whych   30

Crisosto. hom. 46. in Iohan

were (as saynt Chrisostom sayth and as
ye gospell semeth also to saye) all that
than were present saue onely hys .xii.
apostles, and were as saynt Austayn sayth in nomber aboue thre
score and tenne: all they loste them selfe whan they wyllyngly lost   35

Luce. 10

theyr sauyour. [o₁v] And he founde
better to succede in theyr places. For

---

7 well] weale *1557*   27–28 *gloss* Actorum. 1] Actes. 1 *1557*   29 Mathy] Mathewe *1557*

soone after in the stede of those thre score and tenne, he chose

Math. 10

other thre score and tenne dyscyples as I before shewed you, whom he sent about to preche as he had sent his .xii. apostles before.

5   And vnto Iudas yet at this present tyme he gaue a secrete

Luke. 22*

warnyng that he myghte well wytte that hys noughtynesse was knowen, whyche thynge myghte make hym the lesse bolde to synne / and yet he dysclosed hym not openly, bycause he wold not shame hym, 10   and therby make hym happely shamelesse, as many suche wreches waxe / and after that, synne the more boldely.

The .xxv. chapyter.

Chrisosto. hom. 46.
in Iohan.

15

Cyrillus li. 4.
ca. 30 super Io.

THys worde also so spoken to all twelue, was (as saynt Chrisostom sayth and saynt Cyrill [o₂] both) a meruelouse goodly warnyng for them all. These are lo the wordes of saynt Cyrill.

" *Our lord here with sharpe wordes confermyth his apostles and maketh* *them the more dylygent, by puttyng before theyr eyen the perell of theyr ruyne.* 20 *For thys he semeth to saye vnto them. O my dyscyples, mych nede haue you to* *vse mych watche & great study about your saluacyon. The waye of perdicyon* *is very slyper, and not onely wythdraweth a feble mynd from thynkynge of* *theyr fall, by makynge them to forgette them self, but also somtyme deceyueth* *them by vayn delectacyon and pleasure that are of mynde very fyrme and* 25 *stronge. And that thys tale ys trewe that I nowe tell you, you may se well* *prouyd, not by thensample onely of them that are gone abacke, but amonge* *your selfe also that tary and dwell styll wyth me. For I haue you wote well* *chosen* [o₂v] *you twelue as good, well knowynge that in dede you were so.* *For I was not ignoraunt / but beynge god (as I am) very well knew your* 30 *hartes. How be it the deuyll hath deceyued one of you with auaryce, and so*

Man is a fre creture*

pullyd hym awaye. For a man is a free crea- *ture, and may chose his waye as he wyll, eyther* *on the ryght hand or ellys on the lefte yf he wyll.*

" *Our lord therfore maketh them all the more vygylant, bycause that who*

---

30 you] *1557,* yon *1533*

shuld betraye hym he doth not expres by name. But tellynge theym all in a generalty / y^t one of them shold worke suche wyckednesse, he made them all stonde in feare. And by that horrour and drede, lyfted them vp to more vygylaunt dylygence.”

Here haue you herd good reders the wordes of saynt Cyrill. Now shall ye somwhat here what sayeth saynt Crysostome. [o₃]

“ Whan saynt Peter sayd, we byleue: our sauyour not causeles, out of the nomber of them excepted Iudas and sayd:

Chriso. hom. 46
in Ioh.

haue not I chosen you twelue & one of you ys a deuyll. This thyng he sayd to remoue the traytour farre from hys malyce. And where he saw that nothynge dyd auayle hym / yet he went about styll to do wel for him. And se the wysedome of Chryste / for neyther wolde he bewraye hym, nor let hym lurke vntowched. The one, leste he sholde haue waxed shameles and swere naye / the tother leste wenynge that none were ware, he shuld be the bolder in myschyefe.

And afterwarde thys in effecte he sayth. *“ It is not the custome of god by force to make men good whether they*

God maketh no man
good by force*

wyll or no / nor in his eleccion he chosyth not folkes by vyolence, but by good aduyce and mocyon. And that ye may well perceiue that his calling is no constraynt of necessyte, meny [o₃v] *whom he calleth do wyllyngly for all his callyng perysh. And therfore it is euydent, that in our owne wyll is the power sette to chose whyther we wyll be saued or*

It lieth in man to be
lost or saued*

loste. By these admonyssyons therfore, lette vs labour to be sober and vigylant. For yf Iudas which was one of the number of that holy company of thapostles, he that had opteyned so great a gifte, he that had done myracles (for Iudas hym selfe was sent amonge other to cure the lepres, and rayse vp dede men to lyfe) after that he was ones fallen in to the greuous dysease of auaryce: neyther the benefites, nor the gyftes, nor the company of Chryste, nor the seruyce, nor the wasshyng of the fete, nor the felosshyppe of hys own bord, nor the trust in kepynge of the purse, any thyng auayled hym / but all these thynges were wyth hym a passage & a waye to his ponyshement.”

Lo good reders, here haue ye herd [o₄] bothe by saynt Cyrill & saynt Chrysostome, that our sauyour gaue that secrete warnyng of Iudas falshed, and sayed that one of the twelue was a deuyll, to the entent that all folke of what holynesse so euer they were, shulde

12 him.] *1557*, him *1533*   37 shulde] *1533 corr. err.*, such *1533*, should *1557*

Very good counsell* stand euer in drede and fere / and not do
as these heretykes teche, vpon boldnes of
any felynge fayth or fynall eleccyon, presume them selfe so sure of
saluacyon / but that whyle Iudas fell after to naught y^t was onys a
5 holy apostle, there shall no felynge fayth nor prowde hope vppon
fynall eleccyon, sette any man in hys owne harte so sure, but that

Couple fere with hope* with hys good hope he shall all waye
couple some feare, as a brydyll & a bytte
to refrayne and pull hym backe, leste he fall to myschyefe, and
10 folow Iudas in falshed, & waxe a deuyll as Cryst called hym.
Whyche name our sauy[o$_4$v]our gaue him not without good cause.
For y^t deuyllys seruaunt (sayth saynt Cyril) is a deuyll to. For
lykewyse as he y^t is by godly vertues ioyned vnto god, is one spyryt
wyth god / so he that is with deuylysshe vyces ioyned wyth the
15 deuyll, is one spyryte wyth hym.
And therfore good readers, he y^t in suche plyght receyueth the
blessed sacrament wythout purpose of amendement, or wythout
the fayth and bylyefe, that the very flesshe & bloude of Chryste is
in it: he receyueth as saynt Austayne sayth notwythstandyng his
20 noughtynesse y^e very fleshe and bloude of Cryst, the very pryce of
our redempcion. But he receyueth them to hys harme as Iudas
dyd, & eateth and drynketh hys owne iugement & dampnacyon

1. Cori. 11 (as sayth saynt Poule) bycause he dis-
cerneth not our [o$_5$] lordes body. But
25 who so doth on the tother syde (whych I besech god we may all
do) caste out the deuyll & hys wurkes by the sacrament of penaunce and than in the memoryall & remembraunce of Chrystes
passyon, receyue that blessed sacrament / wyth trewe fayth and
deuocyon wyth all honour and wurshyppe, as to the reuerence of
30 Crystes blessed person present in it apperteyneth: they that so
receyue the blessed sacrament, verily receyue and eate the blessed
body of Cryst / & that not onely sacramentally, but also effectually /

Note* not onely the fygure, but the thynge
also / not onely his blessed fleshe in to
35 theyr bodyes, but also his holy spyryte into theyr soules, by
partycypacyon wherof he is incorporate in them & they in hym &
be made lyuely membres of his mysticall body the [o$_5$v] congrega-

---

11 cause.] cause *1533 1557*

cion of all sayntes / of which theyr soules shall (yf they perseuer) attayne y^e fruit and fruicyon clene & pure onys purged after thys transytory lyfe / and theyr flesh also shall Cryst resuscytate vnto the same glory, as hym selfe hath promysed. Of whych hys gracyous promyse, hys hyghe grace and goodnesse vouchesaue to make 5 vs all perteners thorow the merytes of hys bytter passyon. Amen.

And thus ende I good readers my fyrst boke, conteynyng thexposycyon of those wordes in the syxte chapyter of saynte Iohan, wherby you may bothe perceyue by the myndes of holy sayntes, whose wordes I bryng forth, the trewth of our fayth concernynge 10 the blessed body & bloud of Chryst veryly eaten in the blessed sacrament, and may also perceyue and controlle the wyly false folyshe [o$_6$] exposycyon of mayster Masker to the contrary, suche as haue hys boke, and they be not a fewe. And yet that all men may se that I neyther blame hym for nought, nor bylye hym, I 15 shall in my secunde boke shewe you as I promysed, some part of hys fawtes both in falshed and in foly, & his own wordes therwyth.

Here endethe the fyrste boke. [o$_6$v]

---

5 vouchesaue] *1533 corr. err.,* vouchesafe *1557,* so vouchesaue *1533*   8 those] these *1557*   9 by the] *1533 corr. err., 1557,* by these *1533*   16 you] *1533 corr. err., 1557,* yous *1533*

The secunde boke

The .i. chapyter.

I haue good reders in my fyrst boke here before perused you thexposicyon of all that part of ye syxte chapyter of saynte Iohan, which mayster Masker hath expowned you before. And in the begynnyng of thys exposicyon, I haue not brought you forth the wordes of any of the olde expositours, bycause y^t (as I suppose) myne aduersaryes wyll not mych contende wyth me for so farre. But afterwarde concernyng those wordes in which our sauyour expressely speketh of the geuyng of his very flesh & bloud to be veryly eaten & dronken, there haue I brought you forth such authorytees of olde holy doctours & sayntes, y^t ye may well se bothe that [o_7] I fayne you not the mater but expowne it you ryght / & also ye se therby clerely, that mayster Masker expowneth

As heretikes dooe*

it wrong. For though a man may dyuersely expoune one texte and bothe well: yet whan one expowneth it in one trewe maner, of a false purpose to exclude another trouth that is in that wrytynge by the spyryte of god fyrst and immedyately ment, his exposycyon is false all though euery worde were trewe, as mayster Maskers is not.

And therfore syth you se myne exposycion proued you by excellent holy men, and by theyr playne wordes, ye perceyue that the wordes of our sauyour hym self do proue agaynst all these heretykes, the catholyke fayth of Crystes catholyke chyrche very faythfull and trewe, concernyng the very flesshe of Cryste veryly eaten [o_7v] in the blessed sacrament / of whyche eatynge mayster Masker wold with his exposycyon make men so madde, as to wene y^t Cryst spake nothynge at all: now I say by thys exposycyon of myne ye se his exposycyon auoyded clerely for nought, and all the mater clere vpon our parte, though no man wrote one worde more.

And yet wyll I for all that, for ye ferther declaracyon of mayster Maskers handelynge, shewe you some peices of hys exposycyon in

---

13 expowne] expounde *1557*   33 hys exposycyon] *1533 corr. err.*, his exposycion *1557,* thexposycyon *1533*

specyall, by whych ye maye clerely se what credence may be geuen
to the man, eyther for honesty, or lernynge, vertue, wyt or trouth.

The .ii. chapyter.

IN the begynnynge of the second lefe of hys boke, these are
mayster Maskers wordes. [o₈] 5
    "Consyder what thys meate is whyche he bad them here prepare and
seke fore, sayenge: worke take paynes and seke for that meate &c. and
thou shalte se it no nother meate than the bylyefe in chryst. Wherfore he
concludeth that thys meate so often mencyoned is fayth. Of the whyche
meat sayth the prophete, the iuste lyueth. Fayth in hym is therfore the 10
meate whiche chryst prepareth and dresseth, so purely powderynge and
spycyng it wyth spyrytual allegoryes in all thys chapyter folowynge, to
geue vs euerlastynge lyfe thorow it."
    I wyll not laye these wordes to hys charge as heresye / but I
wylbe bolde by hys lycence to note in them a lytle lacke of wytte, 15
and some good store of foly. For though a man may well and wyth

*Faith is a meate
of mans soule**

good reason, call fayth a meate of
mannys soule: yet is it great foly to saye,
that the meate that Chryst speketh of
here ys (as mayster Masker sayth it is) none other meate but fayth. 20
    For mayster Masker maye playnely se, and is not I suppose so
pooreblynde, but that he seeth well in dede [o₈v] that the meate
whych Cryst speketh of here, is our sauyour Cryste hym selfe.
Whyche thynge he so playnely speketh, that no man can mysse to
perceyue it / whan he saith, "*I am my self the brede of lyfe.*" And 25
whan he sayth, "*I am the lyuely brede that am descended from heuyn, he
that eateth of this brede shall lyue for euer.*" And whan he sayth also.
"*That yᵉ meat shold be hys owne fleshe*" (whyche promyse he performed after at his maundye) whych thynge he tolde them playne
in these wordes, "*And the brede which I shall geue you is my flesshe. And* 30
he that eateth my flesshe and drynketh my bloude, hath euerlastyng lyfe, and I
shall resuscytate hym in the last day." And whan he sayed, "*My flessh is*
veryly meate."
    Thus you se good readers how ofte & how playnly that he
declareth [p₁] that the meate whiche he speketh of here, is hym 35
selfe. And now sayth mayster Masker very solempnely, & with

---

6 bad] had *1557*; them] thē *1533*, then *1557*

authoryte byddeth euery man marke it well and consyder it, that
yᵉ meate that Cryste speketh of here is nothynge ellys but bylyefe.

And vpon what colour saith mayster Masker so? bycause (sayth
he) that our lorde bode them labour and wurke for the meate that
wolde not peryshe but abyde into euerlastynge lyfe / and afterward
tolde them that the wurk of god by which they shold wurke &
labour for that meate, was nothynge ellys but fayth and bylyef in
hym.

Fyrste in thys construccyon mayster Masker lyeth very large.
To belieue is the   For though Cryst sayd, that to byleue in
worke of god*   hym was the wurke of god / he sayde not
(as mayster Masker maketh it) [p₁v] that
nothynge ellys was the wurke of god but onely bylyefe.

But now suppose that Cryst had sayd as mayster Masker wold
make it seme, that is to wyt that the wurke of god were nothynge
ellys but the bylyefe: yet ye se well good readers that Cryst in
sayeng that the bylyefe in hym is the wurke by whyche they shall
wurke to gete the meate, sayth that the bylyefe is the meane to gete
the meate, and not that the bylyefe is the meate.

But mayster Masker bycause yᵉ bylyefe is the waye to this meate,
therfore he calleth the bylyefe the meate / as wysely as though he
wold call the kynges strete Westmynster chyrche, bycause it is the
way thytherward yf he come from charing crosse. And bycause
men must spyrytually eate thys meate with fayth: therfor [p₂] he
calleth the fayth the meate as wysely as yf he wold, bycause he
eateth his meate wyth his mowth, therfore call his mowth his
meate. What wyt hath thys man?

But now wyll mayster Masker wax angry with my wordes, and
call me M. mokke as he dothe onys or twyse in hys boke.

But now good readers I wyll not adiure you by goddes holy
names to iudge iustely / but euyn onely desyre you that in waye of
good company, that you wyll say but euyn indyfferently. Were it
not wene you great pytye that a man sholde mokke mayster
Masker, whan euery fole maye perceyue hym in so great a mater
wryte so wysely?

And yet you maye se that I dele wyth hym very gentylly. For in

---

2 bylyefe] byfyefe *1533*, belyefe *1557* 12 (as])as *1557* 23 crosse.] *1557*, crosse *1533*
36 gentylly] *1533 corr. err.*, *1557*, gentyll *1533*

thys poynt wherin by contraryeng of Cri[p₂v]stes own wordes he wryteth playne heresye / I minyshe his borden of that odiouse cryme / & bycause the mater in thys place so serueth me, do couer the boch of his cancred heresye, with this pretty plaster of his pleasaunt frenesie.

And yet I wene the man hath so lytle honesty, that he wyll neuer can me thanke for my curtesye / specyally bycause that (as farre as I can se) the man had leuer confesse hym selfe an heretyke, than be proued a fole. And that appereth well in this. For this lytell scabbe of hys foly he laboreth somwhat to hyde and couer, so that a man muste pull of the clowte ere he can spye the boche. But as for yᵉ boch of hys cancred heresyes without any clowt or plaster he laieth out abrode to shewe, to begge withall amonge the blessed bretherne as beggers laye theyr sore legges out in [p₃] syght that lye a beggynge a frydays aboute saynt sauyour and at yᵉ Sauygate.

But as for raylynge agaynst images, purgatory, and prayenge to sayntes, and agaynst the holy canon of the masse: all this he taketh for tryfles / and wolde we sholde reken all these heresyes of his for poyntes well and suffycyently proued by that that he goth so boldely forth on biyond them & denyeth the blessed body of Cryste it selfe in the blessed sacrament to. And where as he not onely mokketh and iesteth agaynst the olde holy doctours and sayntes of Chrystes catholyke chyrche, but agaynste oure sauyour hym selfe in hys holy sacrament to: yet the sage sad erenest holy man all made of grauite, sadnes, and seueryte, must hym selfe be reuerently reasoned with / & may haue no [p₃v] mokke of his, matched wyth no mery worde of myne in no maner wyse.

But yet lyke as yf a ryght greate man wolde wantonly walke a mummynge, and dysguyse hym selfe, and with nyce appareyle dyssemble hys personage, and with a fonde visour hydde and couer his visage, he muste be content to be taunted of euery good felow that he meteth, as merely as hym selfe lyste to ieste wyth them: so tyll mayster Masker here put of his maskers visour, and shewe forth his owne venerable visage, that I may se hym such an honorable personage, as it may become hym to saye to me what he lyste, and me to requyte hys mockes with no mery worde in this world, but stande styll demurely and make hym lowe curtesy agayne, I wyll

---

5 frenesie.] frenesie *1533*, frenesye *1557*

not let in ye meane tyme, whyle I wote nere what he is, and whyle
[p₄] his wytteles wrytynge maketh men wene he were a wylde
gose, to be so bolde and homely wyth his maystershyp (as sory as I
am for hym whan he playeth the blasphemouse beste) to laugh yet
5   & make mery wyth hym where I se hym playe the fole.

   Yet wyll I now lette passe his repugnaunce, another foly of hys.
For yf euer he defende his foly y^t I haue shewed you / than shall he
be fayne to declare his repugnaunce hym selfe. And therfore I leue
that poynte for hym selfe, that in defendyng his foly he maye shew
10   his repugnaunce / and so for defence of a syngle foly, proue hym
selfe thryes a fole, fyrst in wrytynge foly, secundly in wrytynge
repugnaunce, thyrdly to be so folysshe as in defence of that one
foly, to bryng in the tother to.

   Makynge therfore for thys tyme [p₄v] no lenger tale of his folyes,
15   whiche wold make myne answere ouer long to brynge them in all /
let vs se some pyece of his fruytefull exposycyon.

The .iii. chapyter.

I N the seconde lefe these are his wordes,
   " I am the brede of lyfe, and who so come to me that is to saye, who so is
20   gryffed and ioyned to me by fayth, shall neuer honger, that is who so
byleue in me is satisfyed. It is fayth therfore that stauncheth his honger
and thyrste of the soule. Fayth it is therfore in Cryst that fylleth our
hungry hartes, so that we can desyre no nother yf we ones thus eate and
drynk hym by fayth / that is to say yf we byleue his fleshe and body to
25   haue ben broken, and hys bloude shedde for our synnes, for than are our
sowles satysfyed and we be iustyfyed."

   The worde of Chryst good reader with which he begynneth, is
well and fully fulfylled, yf it be vnderstanden as I haue before
declared, that is to wytte, that who so come onys by well workynge
30   fayth, and perse[p₅]ueraunce therin, vnto the meate that is
Chryste, and attayne the possessyon and fruicion of hym in blysse,
he shall neuer hunger nor thyrste after. And bysydes this, dyuers
good holy doctours expoune these wordes of ye eatynge of our
sauyour in the blessed sacrament also.

35   But surely I byleue that it wyll be very harde for mayster
Masker to veryfye the wordes of his holy exposycyon / ye scant of

---

20 gryffed] graffed *1557*   31 blysse] the blisse *1557*   33 expoune] expounde *1557*

some such piece therof as semeth at the fyrste syghte well sayed as where he sayth yᵗ fayth so fylleth our hungry hartes, and so stauncheth the hunger and thurst of our soule, that we be satysfyed.

For I suppose that men are not satisfied here, neyther with faith 5 alone, nor with fayth and hope and cheryte to / but yet they hunger and thurste styll. For as oure sauyour sayth, [p₅v] He that drynketh me shall yet thyrst styll, & longe sore as he drynketh hym in grace, so to drynke hym in glory. 10

Eccle. 24

But than tempereth mayster Masker hys wordes of neuer thurstyng, with that that he sayth, that yf we eat and drynke god by fayth, we shall neuer hunger nor thyrste / but we be satisfyed / for the fayth so fylleth oure hungry hartys, that we can desyre none other thynge, yf we ones thus eate him & drynke hym by fayth. 15 And than what it is to eate hym & drynke hym by fayth, he forthwith declareth as for the whole somme and exposycyon of fayth and sayth.

"That is to say yf we byleue his fleshe and hys body to haue ben broken, and hys bloude shedde for our synnes, for than are our sowles satysfyed 20 and we be iustyfyed."

Lo here you se good readers that he sayth that who so byleueth thys, here is all that nedeth. For he that [p₆] thus byleueth is iustyfied, and eateth and drynketh Cryst, and so his soule satysfyed / bycause he that so eateth hym ones, can neuer after hunger nor 25 thyrst. And why? For he can desyre none other thynge.

Fyrste I wene that all menne are not agreed, that he yᵗ longeth for none other thing, is not a thurst / if he long styll for more of the same. For if a man drynke a pynt of ale / though he founde hym selfe so well content therwith, that he do not desyre neyther bere, 30 wyne nor water / yet if his appetyte be not so fully satisfied, but that he wold fayne of the same ale, drynk a quarte more, some man wolde saye he were a drye soule & were a thyrste agayne.

But now yf this man ment any good in this mater, and wolde saye yᵗ who so so eateth god as he hath hym [p₆v] well incorpo- 35 rated in hym, shall so haue his hunger and his thurste slaked, that he shall not hunger and thurste after the pleasure of hys body, nor

---

26 thyrst] thryst *1557*; thynge.] thynge *1533*, thing. *1557*   35 who so so] whoso *1557*

after the goodes & ryches, nor after the pompe and pryde of this
wreched worlde: I wolde haue suffred hym go forth with his
exposicyon, and not haue interrupted it. And yet it coulde not (ye
wote well) haue well & fully serued for the texte, syth the texte is,
5 he shall neuer hunger nor thurste, which signyfyeth a takynge
awaye of desyre and longynge. And by this exposicyon though
there be taken awaye the desyre & longyng for other thinges / yet
remaineth there a desyre and longynge for more and more of the
same.
10   But yet I wolde as I say haue lette it passe by and wynke therat,
yf he ment none harme therin. But [p₇] now cometh he after and
declareth by ensample, what he meneth by this his sayenge, that
he that eateth and drynketh god by byleuynge that he dyed for our
synnes, shall thurst and hunger for none other. For he sayth, "he
15 shall desyre none other, he shal not seke by nyght to loue another byfore
whome he wolde laye hys gryefe, he shall not runne wanderyng here and
there to seke dede stockes and stones."
       Lo good readers here is thende of all thys holy mannys purpose /
for which he draweth yᵉ wordes of Cryst from the very thyng that
20 Cryst princypally spake of, vnto another spyrytuall vnderstandynge, in turnyng the meate that Cryst spake of, that is to
wytte the meate of his owne blessed person, his godhed, and his
manhed bothe, in to the meate of fayth, to the entent that vnder
the pretexte of praysyng yᵉ trew fayth, he myght bryng in slily his
25 very false wreched heresies, [p₇v] by whiche he wolde haue no
prayour made vnto sayntes, nor theyr pilgrymages sought, nor
honour done them at theyr images.
       It is euident and playne that our sauyour ment in this place to
speke vnto the Iewes, neyther agaynste images nor sayntes / but
30 rather agaynste the sensuall appetyte yᵗ they had to the fillynge of
theyr belyes with bodily meate / the inordinate desyre wherof
made them the lesse apte and mete for spiritual fode. And therfore
he bode them that they sholde lesse care for that peryshable meate,
and labour and wurk to wynne faith by prayour, and by faith to
35 come to hym. And bycause they so myche hated and fered hunger
and thurste, he wolde geue them hym selfe for theyr meate his very
fleshe and bloude, verily here to eate, not deade but quicke [p₈]

---

11 cometh] comech *1533*, commeth *1557*

with soule and godhed therwith in this worlde / whiche yf they wolde well eate here, with a well wurkyng faith, he wolde geue them the same, so in another worlde, that than shold they neuer haue thurste nor hunger after.

And he ment not that they sholde neuer whan they had ones receyued hym, thurste nor hunger after in this present worlde / in whiche byside that they must bothe hunger and thurste, or elles be euer eatyng and drynking to preuent theyr hunger and thurste, bysyde this I saye they shall hunger and thurste styll after god, yf they be good.

Now yf men wyll saye that the payne of that hunger and thurste is taken away with hope, which greatly gladeth the harte: surely they that neyther hunger nor thurst for heuyn, [p8v] nor care how

This is a very faynt hope*

longe they be thense so that they maye make mery here the whyle, and yet haue an hope that they shal haue heuen to whan they go hens, they fele in theyr faynt hope neyther great pleasure nor payn. But he that hopeth well of heuen, and not onely hopeth after it, but also sore thyrsteth for it, as dyd saynt Poule

Philip. 1

whan he sayd I longe to be dyssolued, that is to haue my soule losed and departed fro my body and to be wyth Cryste / such a man lo, as he findeth pleasure in his hope, so fyndeth he payne in the delaye of

Prouer. 13

his hope. For as Salamon sayth. The hope that is dyffered and delayed, payneth and afflycteth the soule. But whan men shall with wel eatynge of thys meate of Chrystes blessed person, make them mete to eate it, and shall eate it by very fruicyon in heuyn / than all though they shall [q1] neuer be fastidyouse or wery therof, but as they shall euer haue it, so shall euer desyre it (so that of y^t state maye be sayd also, he that drynketh me shal yet thyrste) yet bycause they shall not onely alwaye desyre it, but also alwaye haue it, and so by the contynuall euerlastynge hauynge therof theyr euerlastyng desyre euerlastingly fulfylled, theyr desyre shall euer be wythout any gryefe and payne, & euer full of euerlastynge pleasure /

Psal. 16

so that of y^t state onely the prophete Dauyd sayth: I shalbe saciate or satys-fied, whan thy glory shall appere.

And this ment here our sauioure Chryste / and not that a man

shall by his fayth be fully satysfyed in this wreched worlde, and
neuer hunger nor thyrste after here, as mayster Masker maketh
here by his exposycyon, in turnyng ye saturyte of heuyn [q₁v] into
a saturyte in this lyfe / and turnynge the very meate of Chrystes
5 blessed person, into the onely bylyefe of Chrystes bytter passyon /
& than bryngeth all in conclusyon to thauansynge of his heresye
agaynst the blessed sayntes / as though Chryste in those wordes
hadde ment to speke agaynst the honourynge of his sayntes, wherwith he was so well content, y^t he
Math. 29
10 promysed saynt Mary Mawdeleyn a perpetuall honour in erth, for her deuocyon towarde hym in
bestowynge her costely glasse of oyntement vppon hym / and
promysed his twelue apostles the honour
Math. 19
of .xii. seates, to sytte with hym in iudge-
15 ment vppon the worlde, for the dyshonour and penury that they
sholde sustayne for hym before in the worlde. [q₂]

The .iiii. chapyter.

ᴀɴd se nowe good reader also, howe myche pestylent poyson
mayster Masker hath in thys pyece of his exposycyon put here, by
20 this one syllable onys.

For it is not inough to hym to say, that who so eate Chryste by
fayth shall neuer hunger (whiche wordes he myghte expoune by
perseueraunce and abydynge styll wyth hym after his onys
comynge to hym, as Cryst meneth by his) but he sayth who so
25 come to hym by fayth onys, he shall neuer hunger nor thyrst. And
yet this worde onys, is not there in the texte of Crystes wordes, but
added by mayster Masker in his glose.

And yet if mayster Masker were a good catholyke man, I
wolde not myche marke hys worde, onys. [q₂v] But syth he
30 sheweth hym selfe wel, that he is of mayster Tindals secte, or is
peraduenture mayster Tyndale hym
One of Tyndals
*false heresyes**
selfe, one of whose false heresyes is, that
who so haue ones ye fayth can neuer after
fall therfrom, nor neuer fall after into dedly synne: therfore I can
35 not let mayster Maskers onys, thys onys passe vnmarkyd by me, by

---

22 expoune] expound *1557*

whyche he sayth / that who so come onys to Cryst by faith, that is
to say sayth he, who so byleue onys that Crist suffered hys passion
for our synnes, he shall neuer hunger nor thyrste / but that is he
sayth to be vnderstanden that he shall neuer after desyre none
other.

But now wolde I wyt of mayster Masker onys agayne, what he
meaneth by this worde none other. If he meane that no man that
onys byleueth that Cryste suffred passyon [q3] for vs, shall after at
any tyme desyre any other sauiour, bysyde y^t he sayth one false
heresye in that word onys, (For that fayth maye be onys hadde and
afterwarde loste agayne, as testyfye not
onely all holy doctours & the catholyke
fayth, but the playne scrypture to) he
hath in those wordes I saye bysyde that
false heresye, a very false wyly foly. For
the catholyke chyrche of chrystendome
whych he towcheth in prayenge to
sayntes & goynge in pylgrymages, do
seke no saynt as theyr sauyour / but onely as them whom theyr
sauyour loueth, & whose intercessyon and prayour for them he
wylbe content to here, and whom for his sake he wold they sholde
honour, & whom whyle for his sake they
do honour, the honour that is done them
for his sake, specyally redowndeth to
hym selfe / as hym selfe [q3v] saith, he
that hereth them hereth him, and he that
dyspiseth them dyspyseth hym, and in
lyke wyse he that wurshyppeth them for his sake wurshyppeth
hym.

Hebre. 6
Roma. 11
1. Cori. 10

*How the churche
seeketh sayntes**

*Honour done to
saints doth redoune
to Christ**

Luce. 10

Now yf mayster Masker wyll say that by these wordes, who so
onys byleueth that Chryste dyed for vs, shall neuer after desyre
none other: he meneth that he shall so mynde and desyre euer
after onely Chryst, that he shall not hunger nor thyrst nor desyre
after that any other thynge but god. Than syth mayster Masker in
this boke of his, asketh me so many questyons, and saith so often, I
aske mayster More this: mayster Masker muste of reason geue M.
More leue to aske Mayster masker some questyons agayne.

---

10 onys,] onys. *1533*, ones. *1557*   26 *gloss* Luce. 10] Luke. 10 *1557*

Nowe myghte I aske hym ye se well, whyther he that hath had onys [q₄] that bylyefe, sholde neuer after in suche wyse be an hungred, that he sholde desyre his dyner. But than wold mayster masker cal me maister Mokke, & say that it were but a scoffynge
5 questyon. And yet out of all questyon that same scoffing questyon wold quyte ouerthrow his ernest exposycyon. But now bycause I wyll not angre hym, I wyll lette that scoffyng question go, & I wyll aske hym now another maner thynge, a thynge of yᵗ wayght & grauite, that it wayeth some sowlys downe vnto yᵉ depe pyt of hell.
10 For yf mayster masker be mayster Tyndale, than wyll I aske hym whyther he beyng a preste, desyred none other thynge but onely god, whan synnys yᵗ he sayd he had onys that bylyefe, he hath beynge a preste broken his promyse made onys to god & gone ofter than onys a woynge. [q₄v]
15 And yf mayster Masker be mayster George Ioy / than wold I aske hym whyther that after that bylyefe onys hadde, he desyred nothynge but god, whan beynge a preste he brake his promyse to god / and wedded a wydowe, and by such weddynge neuer made her wyfe, but made her a prestys harlotte.
20 If mayster Maysker be neyther of these twayn, yet syth what so euer he be, he is a dyscyple of Luther and frere Huyskyn both (as contraryouse as they be both eche of them to other) I shall aske hym than, whyther bothe his maysters beynge both professed frerys, and hauynge bothe vowed perpetuall chastyte to god, dyd
25 after that fayth onys had, neuer after desyre any other thynge but onely god, not than whan they brake bothe theyr solempne vowys made [q₅] vnto god, and ran out of relygyone and wedded, the tone a single woman, the tother a nonne, and made theym frerys harlottes bothe? dyd not than frere Luther and frere Huyskyn
30 bothe contrary to mayster Maskers wordes, desyre another, and eche of them go seke by nyght to loue another, byfore whom he wolde lay his gryefe? what answere shal mayster Masker make M. More to thys? he muste eyther confesse agaynste hys owne exposi-cyon, that after that bylyefe had onys, his owne maysters the
35 archeretykes them selfe, thyrsted in the desyre of some other thyng besyde god, or els muste he fall to blasphemy and call a frerys

---

3 that] the *1557*   8 thynge, a] *comma inverted 1533*, thing, a *1557*   17 beynge] he being *1557*

harlot god, or saye that for goddys sake they wedded, and than for
hys sake they wedded agaynste hys wyll, or ellys afferme finally
that the maysters of [q₅v] hys fayth had neuer the faith yet, not the
selfe same fayth that they teche. And why sholde any man than be
so madde to gyue eare to suche heretykes, & byleue theyr fayth-   5
lesse talys?

The .v. chapyter.

Now handelynge hys exposycyon and his doctryne of faith not
onely thus falsely but also thus folyshely to, as ye do now perceyue:
yet as though he hadde wonderfull wysely declared some hygh   10
heuenly mysteryes that neuer man had herde of byfore, in yᵉ fourth
lefe he bosteth his great cunnynge in comparyson of myne and
sayth.

Had mayster more haue vnderstanden thys shorte sentence, who so
byleue in me hath lyfe euerlastyng, and knowen what Paule with the   15
other Apostles preched, especyally Paule beynge a yere & an halfe
amonge the Corinthyes, determynynge not neyther presumynge, not to
haue knowen any other thynge to be preched them (as hym selfe sayth)
then Iesus Cryste, and that he was crucyfyed: had M. More vnderstoden
this poynt, he sholde neuer thus haue blasphemed Cryste and his suffy-   20
cyent scryptures, [q₆] neyther haue so belyed his euangelystes and holy
apostles, as to saye they wrote not all thynges necessarye for our saluacyon, but lefte out thynges of necessyte to be byleued / makynge goddes
holy testament insuffycyent and imperfyte, fyrste reueled vnto our fathers,
wryten efte sonys by Moyses and then by hys prophetes, and at the laste   25
wryten bothe by his holy euangelystes and apostles to. But turne we to
Iohan agayne and let More mocke styll & lye to.

Had maister Masker vnderstanden the selfe same shorte sentence
of Cryst yᵗ he speketh of, & had mayster masker well vnderstanden
also the tother short sentence of saynt Poule yᵗ he now towcheth /   30
& after those two textes well vnderstanden, had loked vpon his
own boke agayne: he wold rather haue eaten his owne boke but yf
he be shamelesse, than euer haue let any man se his false foly for
shame.

For fyrst as for the fyrst text towchyng the brede & the bylief, his   35
false & folysh handelyng ye perceyue more than playn, in yᵗ he
sayth it is nothyng but fayth, where Chryste sayth it is hym selfe.
[q₆v]

Now the place that he towcheth of saynt Poule in hys fyrste

*1. Corin. 2**   pystle to the Corynthyes, I meruayle
                     me mych to se the madnesse of this
Masker, that bryngeth it forth for his purpose here. For as you se,
5   he meneth to make men wene, that by that place it were proued
agaynst my confutacyon, that thapostles left no necessary thynge
vnwryten.

Now of any other apostle ye se well he bryngeth not one worde
for y‸t‸ purpose of his, nor of saynt Poule neyther, but this one place /
10 whyche place syth he bryngeth forth for the profe of theyr heresye,
that there is nothynge necessaryly to be byleued but yf it may be
proued by playne and euydent scripture: it appereth playn that
mayster Masker there mysse taketh saynt Poule, and weneth that
he preched nothyng to them of Crist [q₇] but onely hys passyon.
15 For ellys he myghte notwithstandynge the wordes of that place,
preche to them dyuerse thynges of Cryst by mouth, & leue it with
them by tradycyon without wrytyng to, whych neyther hym selfe
nor none of his felowes neuer wrote any tyme after. And of trouth
so he dyd, as I haue proued at length in my worke of Tyndals
20 confutacyon. Of whiche thynges one is amonge dyuerse other,
the puttyng of the water with the wyne in y‸e‸ chalyce whyche
                     thynge Chryste dyd at his maundy whan
Of puttynge wyne   he dyd instytute the blessed sacrament /
*in the chalyce**   and after he taught the order therof to
25 saynt Poule hym selfe by his owne holy mouth / and saint Poule so
taught it agayne to y‸e‸ Corynthyes by mouth, and lefte it them
fyrste by tradycion without any wrytynge at all. And whan he
wrote [q₇v] vnto them afterward therof, he wrote it rather (as it
well appereth) vppon a certayne occasyon to put them in remem-
30 braunce of theyr dewty in doyng dew reuerence to it, bycause it is
the very blessed body of god, than in that place to teche them the
mater and the forme of consecratyng the sacrament. For he had
taught them that myche more fully before by mouth, than he doth
there by that wrytyng. For as ye wote well though he tell them
35 there what it is whan they drynke it, that is to wyt the bloude of
our lorde: yet he telleth them not there wherof they shall consecrate it. For he neyther nameth wyne nor water. And yet sayth in

---

31 than] the *1557*   32 mater] maner *1557*

the ende that at hys commynge to them agayne, he wyll set an
order in all other thynges. And where wyll mayster Masker shew
me all those thinges wryten, & proue it to be al those? [q₈]

But here you se how madly mayster Masker vnderstandeth y^t
place of saynt Poule, whan he taketh it in that wyse, that he wold   5
therby proue vs that we were bounden to byleue no more but that
Chryst dyed for vs.

And of trouth you se that speking of fayth byfore, thys is his very
conclusyon. In whych whan I redde it and confuted it here now
before: yet marked I not therin so myche as I do now. For though   10
he sayed there,

yf we onys eate hym and drynke hym by faith, that is to saye yf we byleue
hys flesshe and body to haue bene broken, and hys bloud shedde for our
synnys, than are our sowlys satysfyed and we be iustyfyed:

I marked not as I say that he ment so madly as all men maye now   15
se he meneth, that is to wytte that men be bounden to byleue
nothyng ellys, but that Chryst was crucyfyed and dyed for our

*A very shorte crede**   sinnes. Maister masker maketh vs a prety
short crede now. [q₈v]

But that he thus meneth in dede, he now declareth playnely,   20
whan he wolde proue agaynste me that no necessary thynge was

1. Corin. 2   lefte vnwryten, by those wordes of saynt
Poule by which he wryteth to the Cor-
inthyes, that he preched nothynge amonge them but Iesus Chryste
and that he was crucyfyed.   25

And as mayster Masker mysse vnderstandeth those wordes of
saint Poule: so I perceyue that longe before mayster Masker was
borne, there were some suche other folys that mysse toke those
wordes after ye same fonde fasshyon than / and therfore affermed y^t
aduowtry was no dedely synne / as these folyshe folke afferme now   30
y^t it is no dedely synne for a frere to wedde a nonne. And there
argument was that yf auowtry had ben dedely synne, saynt Poule
[r₁] wolde haue preched that poynt vnto the Corynthyes. But he
preched as hym self sayth in his pystle nothyng vnto them but
Chryst and hym crucyfyed / and theruppon they concluded y^t   35
auowtry was no dedely synne.

But saynt Austayne answereth those folys and thys fole to, that
he preched not onely Chrystes crucyfyxion. For than had he lefte
his resurreccyon vnpreched, and his ascencion to, which both we

be bounden as well to byleue as his crucyfyxion, & many other
thynges mo besyde. And therfore as saynt Austayne sayth to preche

Chryste, is to preche bothe euery thynge

What it is to
preche Christ*

that we must be bounde to byleue, and

5   also euery thynge that we muste be
bounden to do to come to Chryste. And not as those folys & this
fole techeth, that we be iustifyed yf we byleue no more but onely
that [r₁v] Chryste was crucifyed and dyed for our synnys.

And whan mayster Masker saith yᵗ by affermyng any necessary
10   pointe to be lefte vnwryten in the scrypture I make goddes holy
testament insuffycyent and vnperfyte, for all that it was fyrst
reueled vnto our fathers, and efte wryten by Moyses, & than by his
prophetes, and at laste wryten bothe by his holy euangelystes and

apostles to: to this I saye that goddes

Gods testament*

15   testament is not insufficyent nor imperfyte, though some necessary thynges be lefte out of the wrytyng.
For I say that his testament is not the wrytyng onely, but all the
whole thynge reueled by god vnto his chyrche, and restynge and
remaynynge therin, parte in wrytynge and parte without wrytynge
20   styll, as it was all together fyrst without writing geuen. [r₂] And se
now good readers the wytte of mayster Masker in this worde of his.
For yf I make the testament of god vnperfyt and insuffycyent,
bycause I saye yᵗ some necessary poyntes therof be not yet wryten:
dothe not he good readers say and afferme therby, that it was all
25   together vnperfyte & vnsufficyent, all the whyle that god taughte it
hym selfe by his owne reuelacyon of spyryte, and that our sauyour
taught it hym selfe by his own blessed mouth, tyll Moyses and the
prophetes & thapostles wrote it wyth the penne?

And whan so euer that mayster Masker is able to proue that al
30   these thynges whiche we be bounden to byleue more than that
Chryst dyed for our synnys, are so fully wryten by Chrystes apostles, that they lefte none of them all vnwryten: whan he [r₂v] shall
haue proued thys, let hym than come hardely and byd maister
More mocke on and lye on to. But nowe whyle he sayeth so, so
35   farre out of season: whyle my worke of Tyndalys confutacyon hath
proued my parte so playnely, that neyther hym selfe nor all the

---

35 confutacyon] confutycyon *1533*, confutacion *1557*

heretikes of them all shall well auoide it whyle they lyue: now may
mayster More be bolde to byd maister masker go mokke on and
lye on to.

And thys maye I nowe saye to mayster masker the more boldely,
syth you se that he vnderstandeth not, or ellys wyllyngly myscon-   5
streweth the place of thapostle that he bryngeth forth hym selfe, &
saynt Iohans gospell to, and wolde make vs wene that it were
inough to saluacyon, to byleue no more but that Chryst was
crucyfyed for our synnys. And than [r₃] sholde we not nede in
dede to byleue that we sholde do penaunce for our synnys our selfe,   10
nor to byleue the presence of Chryst in the blessed sacrament
neyther. Whych poynt they wolde haue now taken for indyfferent,
and many necessary pointes mo. Wherof mayster masker wolde
take awaye the necessyte, bycause saynte Poule sayth he preched
nothynge to the Corynthies but Chryst and hym to be crucyfyed.   15
Which argument of mayster masker were not euyn very stronge, all
though saynt Poule had at that tyme preched them nothynge ellys,
bycause he myght than haue bygonne wyth that, and preche them
many mo thynges after, or sende it vnto them by wrytynge.

But nowe wolde I fayne that mayster masker hadde gone a lytell   20
ferther in the same pystle. For euyn [r₃v] within thre lynes after it
foloweth, " *My prechynge was not among you in persuasyble wordes of
mannes wysdome.*"

These wordes I laye not agaynst mayster Masker / for he kepeth
hym selfe sure inough for that poynt, and is ware well inough that   25
he speke no persuasyble wordes of mannes wysedome. But than
sayth saynt Poule ferther. "*But my prechynge was amonge you in
shewyng of spyryt and of power, to thentent that your fayth shold not be in the
wysedome of men, but in the power of god.*"

Here maye mayster Masker se that saynt Poule bycause he   30
taught straunge doctryne, proued his doctryne not by subtyll phy-
losophycall reasonyng, nor by rethorike & goodly freshe eloquence,
but by myracles & the myghty hand of god. [r₄]

Nowe yf mayster Masker therfore wylbe byleued / reason is that
he do as saynte Poule dyd, syth he teacheth as harde thynges & as   35
straunge to chrysten men, and as farre agaynst the christen fayth as

25 for] fro *1557*

saynte Poule & the other apostles taughte eyther Iewes or Paynyms, thynges hard and straunge & farre from ye fashyon of theyr
false persuasion.

For settynge asyde all the whole hepe of his other heresyes: this
5 one that he setteth forth in this pestylent booke of his, agaynste our
sauyour hym selfe in the blessed sacrament, is as straunge and as
execrable in all good chrysten earys, and euer hath ben synnys
Chrystes dayes, as euer was the prechyng of Chrystes godhed
amonge ye gentylys or ye Iewes eyther. And therfore yf he wyll loke
10 to be byleued as saynt Poule was: [r₄v] reason is that he do myracles as saint Poule dyd.

If he saye that he nedeth not, for he proueth his doctrine by
scrypture: therto fyrst we saye and saye trew, y^t in his so sayeng he
lyeth. And bysyde that we saye that though he proued his doctryne
15 by scrypture in dede: yet syth it semeth to the whole chrysten
nacyons, that the scrypture proueth not his parte but the contrary,
and so haue thought so longe / therfore as our sauyour hym selfe
and his apostles after hym, whych by the scrypture proued theyr
parte very truely to the Iewes, dyd yet for all that proue the trewth
20 of theyr such exposycyon by myracles: so muste mayster masker
proue his exposicions by myracles to be trewe. For ellys syth oure
sauyour though he wolde not wurke myracles at euery man[r₅]nes
bydding, sayd yet of the Iewes, that yf
Iohan. 15
hym self had not done among them
25 suche wurkes as no man ellys had done, theyr infydelyte sholde not
haue ben imputed vnto theym: we maye well be bolde to say to
mayster masker, that excepte he wurke myracles to, he canne of
reason blame no man, that in thexposycyon of holy scrypture beleueth better all the olde holy doctours and sayntes, and all the
30 hole catholyke chyrche than hym.

And therfore whyle mayster masker wolde seme to play saynt
Poule & be an apostle here, to teche englyshe men a new faith as
saynt Poule dyd the Corynthyes / and than techynge thynges as
straunge & as vncredyble to christen men, as his were to the
35 Paynims, & can not do myracles for his doctrine as saynt Poule
dyd for his / but hath against him for our part [r₅v] suche a

---

9 gentylys] Gentyles *1557*   12 for he] *1557*, for be *1533*   16 scrypture] scrypturs *1533*,
scriptures *1557*   23–24 *gloss* Iohan. 15] *om. 1557*

multitude of myracles, that for the profe of any one thynge there
were neuer shewed so many / & whan maister Masker in stede of
myracles proueth his exposycions of scripture so folyshe hym self
and so false, that to suche as marke hym well he maye surely seme
to mene nothynge ellys but to mokke: we may go forth in the   5
mater, and let mayster Masker yet agayne mokke on styll and lye
on to.

The .vi. chapyter.

In the thyrde lefe thus he sayth,
And the cause of thys your blyndenesse is (I wyll not say ouer hardly to   10
yow) that the father hath not drawen you into the knowledge of me or
ellys ye had receyued me. For all that the father geueth me must come to
me.

Mayster maskers exposycyon of these wordes (I wyll not saye
ouer hardely to hym) is I promyse you good readers very bare, and   15
lefte of [r₆] so shortely, and handeled so slenderly, that his owne
frendes coulde here scant thynke any other, than that leuer than he
wold lay hardely to yᵉ Iewes charge the fawte of theyr owne infidelyte, he had leuer lay it in the necke of the father of heuen, &
there leue it.   20

Those wordes and all the wordes of Cryst, in whiche is any
hardnesse, his exposycyon so smothely walketh ouer them, that he
gyueth no lyghte vnto the vnderstandynge of them no more than yf
he neuer touched them.

The bretherne can not bere that my writynge is so longe. But   25
surely it is no maystry for a man to be short, that can fynde in his
harte to do as mayster masker dothe, leue all the harde places
vndeclared.

For he no where stycketh but vppon the places, in whyche he
falsely laboreth by the colour of his exposy[r₆v]cyon of a spyrytuall   30
eatyng by fayth to hyde and withdrawe the very lyterall trewth
and the very fayth in dede, by whiche our sauyour techeth vs to
byleue / that the thynge whych in the blessed sacrament we spyrytually muste eate and bodyly bothe, is his owne very flesshe in
dede.   35

The .vii. chapyter.

In the ende of the fourth lefe he expouneth these wordes of Crist, And this brede that I shall geue you is myne owne flesshe, whyche I shall geue for the lyfe of the worlde.

5 And for as myche as at those wordes specyally bygynneth bytwen hym and me the waye to parte in twayne, and he to go the tone and I the tother / he drawynge it all to that poynt as though Chryst there began to shew them none other thynge of [r₇] his flesshe, but the geuynge it vppon the crosse, and that he nothynge

10 in all those wordes ment to tell them of the geuynge of his fleshe to
Iohn. 6*   eate, that he gyueth in the blessed sacrament / and I there expownynge it that he
there telleth them of bothe, but specyally of the geuynge of his
flesshe to be eaten, whyche he gyueth in the blessed sacrament:

15 therfore at those wordes good readers begynne to take specyall good hede to mayster Maskers fyngers. For there he specyally begynneth to playe a mummers cast with his false dice. And ther-fore conferre his exposycyon vpon the same wordes wyth myne, and than shal ye byd hym caste agayne, for that caste goth for

20 nought. [r₇v]

The .viii. chapyter.

In the fyfthe lefe thus he sayth,
No meruayle was it though these flesshely Iewes abhorred the bodyly eatynge of Chrystes fleshe, albe it our flesshely papystes beyng of the

25 Iewes carnall opynyon, yet abhorre it not.

What thynge more false, more folisshe, or more blasphemouse could any brute beste say than this? For the Iewes had an opinion that he wold haue them eate his fleshe in
August. in enarra.   the very forme of flesshe / and (as saynte
in psalm, 98

30   Austayne sayth) they thought they shod
eate it dede cutte out in gobbettes as shepys flesshe is in the sham-ellys. And now is not mayster masker ashamed to rayle vppon all good chrysten people vnder the name of papystes, and saye that they be all of the Iewes carnall opinion. Doth any man that recey-

---

1 .vii.] *1533*, .vi. *1533 corr. err.*, *1557*   2 expouneth] expoundeth *1557*   12 expownynge]
expounding *1557*   14 he] *1533 corr. err.*, *1557*, ge *1533*   21 .viii.] .vii. *1533 1557*
30 shod] should *1557*

ueth the blessed sacrament, thynke (as y^e Iewes thought) that the
flesshe of Chryste that he re[r$_8$]ceyueth, is in forme of fleshe, cut
out in gobbettes as shepys fleshe is sold in the shamells, and not in
forme of brede? If mayster masker were now bare faced hym selfe,
he were wonderfull shamelesse yf he coulde endure to loke any   5
man in the face for shame.

Now as this was good readers wryten (as you se) moste falsely
that he sayth we be of the Iewes opinion: so where he sayth y^t we
abhorre not to eate Chrystes flesshe in the sacrament / that is yet
wryten ye se well as folysshly.   10

For the wyse goodnes of god hath as the olde holy doctours
declare, geuyn vs his flesshe not in forme of flessh, but in forme of
brede, bycause we sholde not abhorre it. And therefore what
horryble syghte seeth thys fole in y^e blessed sacrament, for whiche
[r$_8$v] he sholde abhorre to receyue it?   15

But where was there euer a more blasphemouse bestely worde
spoken, than this frantyke fole speketh here: y^t mocketh and
rayleth vpon all good chrysten people in this .xv. C. yere. bycause
they do not abhorre to receyue the blessed body of Cryste in such
wyse geuen vs by Chryste, that no creature can abhorre it, but   20
eyther deuyls or deuyls felowes heretikes.

The .ix. chapyter.

THan sayeth mayster Masker ferther in the same place,
Neyther ceace they dayely to crucyfye and offre vp Chryst agayne,
whyche was onys for euer and all, offred vp as Poule testyfyeth Hebre. 9.   25

Lo what lewd boldenes it geueth, whan a man maye walke
about in a vysor vnknowen? Mayster masker careth not what he
sayth whyle hys vysor of dyssymulacyon is on, that [s$_1$] men knowe
hym not. For who sayth that Chryst is dayly new crucyfyed?

Christ is dayly offred *   Trouth it is that the chyrche sayth that   30
                        Chryst is at y^e awter euery daye offered,
                        his owne blessed body in the sacrament.
This of trouth the chyrch sayth, and that Chryste is our dayly
sacryfyce. But no man sayth that he is dayly crucyfied of new, and
dayly put to new payne. But as he was onys crucyfyed and kylled   35

---

21 heretikes.] *1557*, heretikes *1533*   22 .ix.] *1533*, .viii. *1533 corr. err.*, *1557*   31 awter]
aulter *1557*

& offered on the crosse, so is that one deth oblacyon and sacrifice
dayly represented, by the selfe same body, ye onely quicke
sacryfyce and oblacyon that god hath lefte vnto his new chrysten
chyrche, in stede of all the manyfold sacryfyces and oblacyons of
5   his olde synagoge the Iewes. And that ye maye knowe y^t I fayne
you not fantasyes: saynt Crysostom declareth it very playnely,
whose wordes are these. [s₁v]

    "What is that than that we do? Do not we offre dayly? yes forsoth.
    But we do it in remembraunce of hys deth.
        Chriso. hom. 17
10   *And thys hooste is one hooste & not many.*
        in epist. ad Heb.
    How is it one hooste and not many? For
bycause that hooste was onys offered, and was offered into ye holyest taber-
nacle, and this sacryfyce is a copie or example of that. We offer alwaye the
selfe same. Nor we offre not now one lambe, & to morow another, but
15 *stil the same. This sacryfyce therfore is one. For ellys bycause it is offred in*
many places at ones / are there many Christes? nay veryly. For it is but
one Crist euery where, being bothe here hole, & there hole one body. For in
lyke maner as he that is offered euery where, is but one body and not many
bodyes: so it is also but one sacryfyce. And he is our bysshop that offered
20 *the hooste that clenseth vs. We offre nowe also the same hooste whych was*
than offered, and can not [s₂] *be consumed. And thys that we do, is done*
        *Luke. 22**
    in remembraunce of that that was done. For
    (he sayth) do ye this in remembraunce of me.
It is none other sacryfyce / as it is none other bysshop but alwaye we do the
25 *same, or rather we make a remembraunce of that same sacryfyce."*

What wordes can there be clerer, to proue mayster Masker a
very fonde blasphemouse mocker thanne these? by whyche this
holy doctour saynt Crysostome, agaynst mayster Masker mockynge
here the masse, declareth his false foly clerely. And not onely
30 sheweth that it is a sacrifice and an oblacyon: but also sheweth
that it is the dayly representacyon of ye same offryng & sacrifisyng,
by which he was sacrifysed & offred vp on the crosse. And yet to
stoppe maister maskers mouth in ye hole mater: he sheweth y^t this
oblacion, this blessed sacrifice [s₂v] the sacrament of the awter, is
35 all one oblacyon, all one hoste, though it be offred at onys in neuer
so many places. And he sheweth also, that it is y^e very self same
body that was offred on the crosse. And that in thys sacryfyce of

---

2 body,] body *1533 1557*   17 body.] body *1533*, bodye. *1557*   34 awter] aulter *1557*

The Elevation of the Host, from John Lydgate's *The vertue of y* masse,* London,
1520

offerynge vp the selfe same body in the masse, we folow thensample, as a copy is writen after a boke / and do represent the selfe
same sacryfyce, by which Chryst the very selfe same body was
sacryfyed on the crosse.

Howe can mayster Masker be more playnely confuted and con-   5
founded, than saynt Chrysostom here confoundeth hym, vpon
thoccasyon of this folyshe blasphemouse iestynge of his? wyth
whyche he realeth agaynste the chyrche, and sayth that it ceaceth
not dayely to crucyfye Cryst as though the chyrch at this day dyd
[s₃] put Cryst to new payne, bycause his deth is represented in the   10
masse, and of his goodnes his very blessed body offered vp dayly a
swete sacryfyce for our synnys.

Gracian also recyteth in yᵉ decrees for our purpose in euery
point, as effectuall wordes of saynt Ambrose de consecrat. distinc-
tione 2. cap. In Chrysto semel.   15

Saynt Austayne also in the .xvi. booke de ciuitate dei, sayth of
the holy masse in this wyse.

Augu. lib. 16. de   " *That sacryfyce is succeded into the place of*
ciuitate dei   *all those sacryfyces of the old lawe, whyche*
                       sacryfyces were offered for a shadow of the   20
thynge to come. And for yᵗ cause also we knowe that voyce in the .xxxix.
psalme, the prophecye of our medyatour Chryste, where he sayth, Sacryfyce &
oblacyon thou woldest not haue, but the body thou hast perfyted me. For in the
stede of [s₃v] *all those sacryfyces and oblacyons, his body is offered and*
mynistred vnto them that wylbe part takers of it."   25

What speke I of saynt Crysostome and saynt Austayne, all the
old holy doctours and sayntes of chrystes chyrche, without any
excepcion, were euer more clere in thys poynt that mayster Masker
here now denyeth and thus iesteth on, that the blessed sacrament
in the masse is a sacryfyce & an oblacyon.   30

And this can not mayster Masker hym selfe denye. For his owne
                       fyrste mayster Martyn Luther, the late
Luther the welspring   well sprynge of all this flode of heresyes,
*of heresies**   in hys pestylent booke of babilonica,
puttynge forth this heresye that mayster Masker towcheth here, yᵗ   35

---

4 sacryfyed] sacrified *1557*   8 realeth] raileth *1557*   14 point] *1557*, ponnt *1533*
18–20 *gloss* Augu. . . . dei] *Placed a line too low in 1557*   25 part takers] partakers *1557*
26 all] & all *1557*

the blessed sacrament in ye masse is no sacrifice, nor none oblacion, obiecteth agaynst hym selfe & saith thus. [s₄]

Martinus Luther
in capt. babi.

5   *" Now muste we take awaye another occasyon of ruyne, that is that the masse is euery where byleued to be a sacryfyce, that is offered vnto god. And for that opynion, semen to sowne the canon of the masse, where it is sayd, these gyftes, these holy sacryfyces, this oblacyon and offrynge. And therfore is Chryste called the hoste or sacryfyce of the awter. Than cometh there also on this parte the sayenges or sentences of the holy fathers and than*
10   *so many exemples.*

" Agaynst all these thynges bycause they be very fastely receiued, we must very constantely obiecte the wordes & ensample of Chryste at his maundy."

And afterward he sayth agayne,

" What shall we say than to the canon of the masse and to the sayenges of the
15   *olde holy doctours and sayntes: I say that yf we haue nothynge ellys to say: let vs yet rather denye them all, than graunte that the masse shold [s₄v] be any good wurke or any sacryfyce, leste we sholde denye the worde of Cryste, and cast downe fayth & masse and all."*

Thus you se good readers that Luther hym selfe confesseth, that
20   in thys heresye agaynste the sacryfyce and oblacyon of the masse, whyche mayster Masker with two other heresyes to, bryngeth here forth now, the olde holy doctours and sayntes are agaynst hym / and than were we wyse, yf we wolde wene that Martyne Luther & mayster masker euyll chrysten heretykes vnderstand Christes
25   wordes better, than euer dyd all the holy doctours of chrystes chyrch before.

And thus you se good readers what a compendyouse wryter mayster masker is, that hath in lesse than thre lynes, compacted vp together [s₅] such thre abomynable blasphemouse heresyes, as the
30   deuyll hym selfe neuer deuysed wurse.

In the syxte the .vii. the .viii. the ix. the .x. lefe, he hath certayne argumentes agaynst all men in generall, that expoune those wordes of Cryst in the syxte chapyter of Iohan, to be spoken and ment of the very eatynge of his blessed body in the sacrament, and
35   not onely of a spyrytuall eatyng by bylyefe of hys deth. And some solucyons hath he there suche as they be, agaynste myne argument

---

3–5 *gloss* capt.] capit. *1557*   8 awter] aulter *1557*   30 wurse] *1557*, vurse *1533*
32 expoune] expounde *1557*

in specyall made vnto Fryth: All whyche thynges I wyll sorte into
theyr places a parte from his exposycyon, so that ye maye se some
of the fawtes of his exposycyon by them selfe, and his argumentes
answered by them selfe, and his solucyons auoyded by them selfe,
and the notable notes that [s₅v] he maketh of my notable repug- 5
naunces laste of all layed open to you by them selfe, bycause I wyll
laye all thynge in ordre playne before your eyen / so that whan ye
se the thynges in such wyse before you without interlacynge, ruffle,
& confusyon: ye shall the more easyly iudge whyther mayster
Masker in his mummery be an honest man, or ellys a false haserder 10
and play with false dyce.

The .x. chapyter.

In the .xi. lefe, after that in the tother tenne byfore he had
spoken many tymes of fayth alone, and that the onely byliefe of
farre fewer thynges than we be bounden in dede to byleue, whan it 15
were onys hadde, sholde bothe satysfye the soule & also make vs
saufe for euer: it appereth [s₆] in that lefe y^t eyther hys own
mynde beganne to mysse geue hym, or ellys some other wyly
brother gaue hym warnynge, that this maner wrytyng of fayth
alone wolde make all the worlde to wonder on hym. For Luther 20
hym selfe wrytynge fyrste on the same fasshyon, that faythe alone

*Faythe alone pleased
ydle vnthriftes**

was suffycyent for saluacyon, though it
pleased idle vnthryftes very well, that
were glad to be by bare fayth dyscharged
of al good wurkes: it was yet so sore abhorred among all honest 25
men, y^t both hym selfe & all his secte were fayne to seke some
plasters of false gloses, to hele ye foule marmole of theyr skabbed
shynnys, that they hadde gotten by that texte of theyr false fayth
alone.

And than they sayed y^t they ment that maner fayth, that hadde 30
alwaye bothe hope and cheryte wyth it. But than coulde not that
glose serue [s₆v] them. For that maner fayth taughte euer the
comen catholyke chyrch whiche they reproued. And also y^t glose
marred theyr texte, and was clene contrary to all theyr tale. For all
the text of theyr prechynge had ben of fayth alone, and theyr glose 35

---

12 .x.] *1533*, .ix. *1533 corr. err., 1557*   21 fasshyon,] *1557*, fasshyon. *1533*

was of fayth not alone, but encompanied with two good felowes
perdye, ye tone called hope and the tother cheryte.

Now therfore eyther vppon this fere of his owne mynde, or vpon
this aduertysement of some other man: mayster Masker to mende
5 his exposycyon with, and to make all the mater saufe, hath at the
laste in the ende of the .xi. lefe, plastered his marmoll of his onely
fayth on thys fasshyon.

By loue we abyde in god & he in vs. Loue foloweth fayth in the order of
our vnderstandynge, and not in order of successyon of tyme, yf thow
10 lokest vpon the selfe gyftes and not of theyr frutes. So that pryncypally by
fayth wherby we cleue to goddes goodnes and mercy, we abyde in god
and god in vs, as declare [s₇] hys wordes folowynge, sayenge, As the
lyuynge father sent me, so lyue I by my father. And euen so he that
eateth me, shal lyue bycause of me or for my sake. My father sent me,
15 whose wyl in all thynges I obey, for I am hys sone. And euen so veryly
must they that eate me, that is byleue in me, forme and fashyon them
after my ensample, mortefyeng theyr flesshe and chaungynge theyr
lyuynge, or ellys they eate me in vayne and dyssemble theyr bylyefe. For
I am not comen to redeme the worlde onely, but also to chaunge theyr
20 lyfe. They therfore that byleue in me, shall transforme theyr lyfe after
myne ensample and doctryne, and not after any mannys tradycyons.

Thys plaster good readers hath some good ingredyence. But it is
bothe to narow by a great dele to couer his scalde shyn, & hath
also some dede poticary druggys put in hit that can do no good,
25 and some thynge also repugnaunt to his remedy.

But lette vs now consyder hys wordes. Fyrst where he sayth, that
Iohn. 15* by loue we abyde in god and god in vs: he
sayeth trouth, for so sayth the scrypture /
but that is to be vnderstande as longe as [s₇v] we loue hym, and
30 dwell so styll in hym. But whan we breke hys commaundementes,
and therby declare that we loue hym not as ye scrypture also sayth /
agaynst whiche scrypture mayster Tyndale sayth that he that hath
onys a felyng fayth, can neuer fall therfrom, and agaynste the same
scrypture mayster Masker saith that fayth onys had suffiseth for
35 saluacion.

And mayster Masker maketh yet his mater mych wurse than
wyllyam Tyndale. For Tyndale dyd yet at the leste wyse make

---

24 hit] it *1557*   29–30 and dwell] *1533 corr. err., 1557*, and not dwell *1533*   34 had] had,
1557

some bumblyng about a colour for the mater, with a longe processe
of hystorycall fayth & felyng fayth. Whose false wyly foly therin, I
haue so confuted in my confutacyon, y^t though he wryte agayne
therin, as longe as euer he lyueth he shall neuer shake of the
shame.

But mayster Masker handeleth [s$_8$] the mater bothe more
wylyly than Tyndale doth, & yet mych more folysshely to. For
seyng that his sayeng can not be defended: he ruffleth vp all the
mater shortely in a few wordes, bothe for sparynge of labour, &
also bycause he wolde not haue hys wordes well vnderstanden, but
that his wordes myght stande for a short texte, which he wold leue
for euery other good brother to make some good glose therto to
maynteyne it wyth.

For in his nexte wordes folowyng where he sayth, Loue foloweth
fayth in the order of our vnderstandyng, & not in the order of successyon
of tyme, yf thow lokest vpon the selfe gyftes & not vpon theyr frutes: in
these few darke wordes he wolde bothe shewe hys clerklynes before
vnlerned men, and leue them also vndeclared, bycause he wolde
haue them wene y^t his hygh lernyng passeth theyr low capacitees.
[s$_8$v]

But yet in these wordes he iugleth with vs, and may with his
wylynes begile them that wyl take none hede. But who so loke well
to his handes shall perceyue where his galles goo well inough.

For trewe it is that whan so euer god infoundeth eyther thabyt of

*In a quycke faith
there is both hope
and charitye**

fayth, or ye full perfite quycke lyuely
faith that is called fides formata: he
infoundeth in lyke wyse hope and
cheryte bothe. But this is not the fayth
alone. For fayth is neuer such fayth, but whyle he hath his two
felowes with hym. But fayth maye begyn & tary to, before his two
felowes come to hym. As a man maye byleue well longe ere he wull
do well. And fayth may tary also whan both his felowes be gone
from hym, as he that hath had all thre, may by dedely synne fall
from the tother twayne, and haue [t$_1$] fayth alone remayne. And
faith may come and continue styll, and neyther of bothe of his
felowes neuer come at hym at al. As where a man byleueth truely

---

1 bumblyng] bumlyng *1557*   7 wylyly] wyly *1557*   19 capacitees.] capacitees *1533*,
capacities. *1557*   31 wull] wil *1557*

euery article of the fayth / and yet hath neuer ye wyll to wurke well
nor neuer wylbe baptysed, but after dyeth in dyspayre. And in all
these casys is it fayth alone. And bycause it neither wurketh well,
nor hath will to wurke well, neyther in acte nor in habyt: therfore
5   *A dead faith**   is it called fides informis, and a dede
fayth. Not dede in the nature of fayth or
bylyefe / but dede as to the attaynynge of euerlastynge lyfe.

Now wolde mayster Masker iugle & make vs byleue, that he
meneth the fyrste maner of fayth that is quycke and lyuely, by the
10 reason that it hath good hope & cheryte therwith.

But I can not suffre you good [t₁v] chrysten readers to be so
begyled, by suche a fonde false iugler. For yf ye take hede vnto
hym / ye shall soone perceyue that he is euen but a very bungler.

For whan that he fyrste telleth vs what bylyefe is suffycient, &
15 sayth that yf we ones eate & drynke Cryste by fayth, and than
expouneth ye hole somme of all that faythe sayenge, that is to saye,
yf we byleue hys flesshe and his body to haue ben broken, and hys bloud
shedde for our synnys, than are our soules satisfyed & we be iustyfied and
now addeth therunto, that loue foloweth faith in the order of our
20 vnderstandynge and not in the order of successyon of tyme, by
whych he meneth y^t euery man hath cheryte euer more as soone as
he hath faythe: ye may clerely se that he sayth y^t a man hath
cheryte euer as soone as he hath that fayth. So that by hym who so
euer byleueth that Chryste dyed for [t₂] vs: he hath both fayth
25 hope & cheryte, though he byleue nothynge ellys.

But now is thys a very false deuelysshe doctryne. For this is no
full fayth. For a man maye beleue this, & yet leue many a thynge
vnbyleued, whyche we be bounden to byleue bysyde. And therfore
you may well se, that though the theologycall vertue of ful and
30 perfayt fayth, haue alway cheryte togyther infounded with it: yet
mayster Maskers fayth that is neyther perfyt nor full, maye be not
in the begynnyng onely, but also euer after without any cheryte at
all.

Also where he sayth, that ye fayth y^t he describeth onys had, is
35 suffycient / & speketh of no perseueraunce: a man may well se y^t
his sayeng is insuffycyent. For both y^t fayth standynge, a man may

---

5–6 *gloss* A dead faith] *Placed opposite line 3 in 1557*   16 expouneth] expoundeth *1557*
36 y^t] the *1557*

well fall fro cheryte. And than though he had onis cherite as sone
as [t₂v] that fayth (yf that bare faith without more were possyble
to haue cheryte with it) yet myght it lacke cheryte after. And also
that fayth myght it self fall quyte awaye to. For he that onys
byleueth euery artycle of the fayth, and than can fall from any, as   5
mayster Masker is fallen from many: may lytell and lytell fall from
them euerychone. For I dare well say that mayster Masker
byleueth no poynt that he byleueth moste surely, any thyng more
surely now, than he hath byleued ere this, dyuerse of those poyntes
which he now byleueth leste yf he byleue as he wryteth.   10

And thus good readers you se, yᵗ where as his marmole is more
than an handefull brode: thys plaster of his passeth not the bredeth
of a peny. For I dare saye the deuyll byleueth at thys day as mych
as mayster mas[t₃]ker sayth that is suffycyent, that is to wyt that
Chryst dyed for our synne, and yet hath he no cheryte. Nor no   15
more hath no man that wyll byleue no more but that / or though
he do byleue more than that, wyll yet thynke that he byleueth all
the remanaunt but of his courtesye, & not one whyt more of
dewty.

N ow where he sayth ferther,

The .xi. chapyter.   20

So that pryncypally by fayth wherby we cleue to goddes goodnes and
mercy, we abyde in god and god in vs, as declare hys wordes followynge,
sayenge, As the lyuynge father sent me, so lyue I by my father. And euen
so he that eateth me, shal lyue bycause of me or for my sake.   25

This is a very false noughty declaracyon of Chrystes wordes. For
where as the holy doctours do declare those wordes as I byfore
haue shewed you, that lyke as our [t₃v] sauiour had his eternall
lyfe of hys father before any beginnyng of tyme in that his father
eternally before all tyme begate hym, and his flesshe, not of his   30
owne nature but by the coniunccyon that it had with the godhed,
had now the same lyfe and so lyued for the father, so shold he that
eateth that flesshe accordynge to Chrystes instytucyon with dew
cyrcumstaunces of fayth and good hope, and cheryte well wyllyng

---

12 bredeth] bredth *1557*   20 .xi.] *1533*, .x. *1533 corr. err., 1557*   30 hym,] hym *1533*
1557   33 instytucyon] institucion *1557*, iustytucyon *1533*

to worke, attayne euerlastynge lyfe also, by reason of hys coniunccyon and incorporacyon with hys euerlastyng flesshe, so I say
all way if the eater eate it wyth al dewe cyrcumstaunces requisyte /
so y^t lyke as they receyue not his holy flesshe dede as the Iewes had
5 went, but quycke wyth holy spyryte ioyned therto, so theyr soules
may ioyne with his spyryt as theyr flessh ioyneth wyth his: [t$_4$]
where as the holy doctours I say do expoune these wordes thus,
now commeth maister Masker and saith, that in these wordes
Chryst techeth vs that we abyde in hym and he in vs, not pryncy-
10 pally by cheryte but pryncypally by fayth.

Now good reder what one word of those wordes of Cryst, any
thyng sowneth to the mayntenaunce of mayster Maskers exposicyon, that god is in vs and we in hym, pryncypally by fayth?

Iohn. 4* The scrypture sayth, God is cheryte,
15   and he that dwelleth in cheryte dwelleth
in god, & god in hym.

Now yf mayster Masker wolde haue sayd, y^t by fayth a man
myghte eate the flesshe of Chryste, and by fayth myghte dwell in
god: yf mayster Masker were a good catholyke manne, I wolde for
20 so farre fynde no fawte in hys exposycyon. [t$_4$v] For it myghte
haue a menynge good inough, bysyde the lyterall sence of Chrystes
wordes. But now whan he contendeth that this is the lytteral sense,
and therwith wolde shake of the very eatynge that our sauyour
ment in y^e blessed sacrament, and bere vs in hande that our
25 sauyour mente not so, but ment an onely eatynge of his flesshe by a
bare bylyefe of hys deth, and not the very bodyly eatyng at all / &
that in those wordes he ment that though we dwell in god by loue,
yet not pryncypally by loue, but pryncypally by fayth, as to whych
vertu the vertu of cheryte were but a folower and a perpetuall
30 hand mayde, where there is in those wordes of Chryste not one
syllable sownynge towarde it: what good chrysten man can abyde
it? namely whyle the scrypture by playne wordes condempneth

1. Cori. 13   [t$_5$] it, & sayth, fides, spes, charitas, tria
                hec maior horum charitas. Faith, hope,
35 and cheryte, these thre, but the pryncypall of these is cheryte.

---

7 expoune] expound *1557*   12 sowneth] soundeth *1557*   31 sownynge] sounding *1557*
33–34 *gloss* 1. Cori. 13] *om. 1557*

The .xii. chapyter.

Now where he goth good reader forther forth yet vppon these wordes, and sayth,

My father sent me, whose wyll in all thynges I obey, for I am hys sone. And euen so veryly must they that eate me, that is byleue in me, forme and fashyon them after my ensample, mortefyeng theyr flesshe and chaungynge theyr lyuynge, or ellys they eate me in vayne and dyssemble theyr bylyefe.

Though these wordes here seme very good: yet whyle they be all wryten vnto thys one entent, that this gay floryshe sholde so glytter in our eyen, that we myght therby be blynded and not be ware of the perylouse pytte into whyche he goth aboute to caste vs, that is to make vs wene [t₅v] that our sauyour in sayenge that we sholde eate his flesshe, ment no very eatynge therof in yᵉ blessed sacrament but onely a spyrituall eatynge by byleuyng that he dyed for our synnys, as here he declareth agayn, they that eate me that is byleue in me &c: while all draweth I saye to that ende, hys tale is nought all togyther.

And yet it is a worlde also to se, the blyndnesse that the deuyll hath dreuyn into hym, by whyche he can not be suffered to se, that by these selfe same wordes with whyche he wolde auaunce his purpose, he very playnely destroyeth it.

For his purpose is ye wote well, to make vs wene that faith were not onely the pryncypall / but also that fayth hath euer loue waytyng vpon her, and folowynge her as her vnseparable seruaunt / as hete euer fo[t₆]loweth the fyre. And now you se that he sayth here, that who so do not forme and fasshion them after Chrystes ensample, do eate hym in vayne. And than to eate hym he sayth is but to byleue in hym. And so he sayeth wythout good lyuyng, that is to wyt wythout cheryte, the bylyefe is but in vayne. Now to byleue in vayne, is ye wote well to byleue, and yet haue hys bylyefe frutelesse for lacke of that loue, that is the theologicall vertue called cheryte.

And thus ye se good readers how well and cyrcumspectely mayster Masker loketh to hys mater, that whan he hath tolde vs that fayth neuer lacketh cheryte forgetynge hym selfe forthwyth, telleth vs hym self within tenne lynes after, that fayth maye lacke cheryte, and therfore be but in vayne. [t₆v]

5   Now where he sayth, or els they dyssemble theyr bylyefe: I wyll not dyssemble with hym, but tell hym very playne, that as great a dyssembler as he is, he woteth not as it semeth what this worde

What it is to dyssemblyng meneth, or ellys wote I nere
dyssemble* what he meneth therby. For a man dyssembleth the thynge yᵗ he hath and wyll

10   not be a knowen therof / as a man dyssembleth hys hatered, whan he hateth one & fayneth hym selfe his frende to couer his hatered with. And so we say that a man dyssembleth a thynge whan he seeth it and wyll not se it, but maketh as though he saw it not. But no man dissembleth the thynge that he seeth not in dede, nor the

15   thynge that he hath not in dede, but maketh as though he sawe it or had it. For he fayneth or lyeth, and not dyssembleth. As in the latyne tonge (wherof thys englysshe [t₇] worde cometh) ille simulat non dissimulat. And therfore yf mayster masker mene here by these wordes, or ellys they dyssemble theyr bylyefe, any other thing

20   than they fayne a byleyfe, makynge as though they byleued and do not: lette hym not dyssemble with me, but tell me what other thyng he meneth. And yf he mene by those wordes none other thynge than that: than wyll I not dyssemble with hym, but tell hym the playne trewth that he maye peraduenture mene wysely

25   inough, but he speketh but like a fole. For by that worde he sayth the clere contrary that is to wytte that they make as though they byleued not, but yet they do.

The .xiii. chapyter.

But now at laste he concludeth all togyther thus.

30   For I am not comen to redeme the world onely, but also to chaunge theyr lyfe. They therfore that by[t₇v]leue in me, shall transforme theyr lyfe after myne ensample and doctryne, and not after any mannys tradycyons.

I wyll not here holde a longe dyspycyon with maister Masker vpon mannes tradycyons, by whyche word he wold haue all the

35   lawes made by menne vtterly sette at nought / and wolde haue

---

1 hym selfe forthwyth,] himselfe, forthwith *1557*   28 .xiii.] *1533*, .xii. *1533 corr. err.*, *1557*
30 comen] come *1557*

man bounde but eyther by the playne worde of scrypture, or ellys
by his own expresse agrement and consent. For Luther sayth that

Most falsely* neyther man nor angell can make the
bonde of any one syllable vppon any
chrysten man, without his owne expresse consent / so that no lawe 5
can be made by that wise reason, by the prince and the people, to
hange vp eyther thefe or murderer, or to burne vp an heretyke, but
yf the theuys, murderers, and heretykes wyll consent and agree
therto them selfe. Nor no law made thys daye, can bynde hym [t₈]
that shall be borne to morow, tyll he come to good age & agre 10
therto fyrste hym selfe, as our souerayne lorde the kynges grace
most prudentely layed agaynste Luther.

But I lette thys foly of mayster Masker passe / and thys also that
the tradycyons, whiche these heretykes be wurste content withall,
be the tradycyons of the apostles, whych they delyuered to the 15
chyrche, as Chryste not by wrytynge but by tradycyon, delyuered

1. Cori. 11 the thynges to theym. For which saynt
Poule sayth, Ego enim accepi a domino
quod et tradidi vobis, For I haue receyued the thynge of oure lorde
by tradycyon, without wrytyng the which I haue also delyuered 20
vnto you. As though he wold say, as I haue receyued it by tradycyon or delyuery of our lord, so without wrytyng I haue deliuered
it by tradicion to you. [t₈v]

I wyll lette passe all these auauntages (whych I myght as ye se
take agaynst mayster Masker here) and I wyll well allow these 25
wordes of his for thys onys, so that hym selfe wyll stycke and stande
by them styffely, and confesse that they that transforme not theyr
lyfe after Chrystes ensample and doctryne, haue eyther theyr
bylyefe in vayne, or els make as though they byleued, and haue no
bylyefe at all. 30

This onys agreed bytwene hym and me: I yf he wyll rayle vppon
the prestes and prelates of the catholyke chyrche for doynge of the
contrary, let hym name who they be and wherin they do it, and by
my trouth in suche euyll doynge / they shall neuer be defended for me.

But than of reason must mayster Masker gyue me leue agayn, to 35
put [v₁] hym in remembraunce of the prestes and prelates of theyr
heretykes sectes / and I wyll speke of none but by name. Frere

---

19 et tradidi] *1533 corr. err., 1557*, tradidi *1533*   23 you.] *1557*, you *1533*

The prelates
of heretykes*
Luther I wyll name hym the chyefe and
pryncypall authour of theyr heresies. I
wyll name hym frere Lambert / dane
Othe the cartusyan, zuinglius the preste, and the preste Pomeran,
5 & frere Huyskyns the frere brigittane. These be lo the very prelates
and bysshoppes metropolytanys and postles of theyr sectes.

Now wyll I than aske mayster Masker what ensample of Chryste
or what doctryne of Chryste he can shewe, by whyche those holy
prelates of these new sectes, euyll chrysten caytyffes that haue
10 sowed all this sedycyon, haue broken theyr holy vowes and
promyses made vnto god, and runne out of theyr orders / and to
the [v₁v] shame of matrymony & holy orders bothe, speke of the
spyryte, and fall to the flesshe? which whyle they haue all done,
agaynste the doctryne and ensample as well of Chryste as of all
15 holy doctours and sayntes, & of al good chrysten people syth the
deth of Christ vnto this theyr own wreched tyme, and now teche it
forth for a doctryne, reason it is that mayster Masker confesse, that
all the prelates of his sundry sectes, eyther haue but a vayne fayth,
or ellys make as they had faythe and haue no fayth at all. And
20 than are there no mannes tradycyons so euyll as are theyr owne,
beynge theym selfe so euyll men as they be. And why shold we
than here maister Masker preche, eyther theyr fayth or tradycyons
eyther, whyle theyr fayth is eyther vayne fayth or ellys false and
none at all, and theyr [v₂] doctryne as deuylysshe doctryne as
25 them selfe are deuylysshe men / and more deuelysshe I wene is
scant the deuyl hym selfe.

Thus haue I good readers noted you certayne pyeces of mayster
Maskers exposicyon, by whyche as by a taste of a draught or
twayne, ye may se what poysened drynke is in the whole vessell.
30 And now shall I come to hys argumentes, whiche he maketh in
generall agaynst all them that expowne thys place of Chrystes
wordes in the syxte chapiter of saynt Iohan, to be spoken or ment
of that eatynge, by whyche we eate Chrystes blessed body in the
blessed sacrament.

35   Here endeth the seconde booke. [v₂v]

---

5 Huyskyns] Huskyn *1557*   9 sectes,] sectes *1533 1557*   25 selfe] shelfe *1533*, self *1557*
31 expowne] expounde *1557*

The thyrd boke.

The fyrste chapyter.

IN the fyfthe lefe vppon his exposycyon of these wordes, and the brede which I shal geue for the lyfe of the worlde thus he argueth. And euyn her syth Chryste came to teche, to take awaye all dowt and to breke stryfe, he myghte (hys wordes otherwyse declared than he hath declared & wyll hereafter expoune them) haue soluted theyr questyon: sayenge (yf he had so ment as More expouneth) that he wolde haue ben conuayed and conuerted (as our iuglers sleyghtly can conuaye hym with a fewe wordes) into a syngynge lofe, or ellys (as the Thomystycall papystes saye) ben inuisyble wyth all hys dymencyoned body vnder the forme of brede transsubstancyated into it. And after a lyke Thomistycall mystery, the wyne transsubstancyated to into hys bloude, so that they sholde eate his flesh and drynke his bloude after theyr owne carnall vn[v₃]derstandynge (but yet in another forme) to put away all grudge of stomake. Or syth saynt Iohan (yf he had thus vnderstode hys maysters mynde, and toke vpon hym to wryte hys maysters wordes) wold leue this sermon vnto the worlde to be redde, he myghte now haue delyuered vs and them from this dowte. But Chryst wolde not so satysfye theyr questyon, but answered, veryly veryly I say vnto you, excepte ye eate the flesshe of the sone of man and drynke his bloude, ye shall not haue that lyfe in your selues. He that eateth my flessh and drynketh my bloude, hath lyfe euerlastynge, and I shall stere hym vp in the laste daye. For my flesshe is very meate & my bloude the very drynke. He sayth not here that brede shalbe transsubstancyated or conuerted into his body, nor yet the wyne into his bloude.

Lo good chrysten readers thys man here in a folysshe iestynge and mych blasphemouse raylyng maner, agaynst the conuersyon of the brede and wyne into the blessed body and bloude of Chryste in the blessed sacrament, in conclusyon as for a clere confutacyon of me & of saynt Thomas bothe, vppon whyche holy doctour and saynt he folyshely iesteth by name, he argueth as you se, that yf [v₃v] Chryst had entended to haue geuen them his flesshe and his bloude in the sacrament, than myght he haue declared it more

---

7 expoune] expounde *1557*   8 expouneth] expoundeth *1557*   10 wordes] *1557*, worde *1533*   30 blessed] *1557*, hlessed *1533*

openly with mo wordes and more playnly. And than mayster
Masker deuiseth Chryst the wordes that he wold haue had hym say
yf he had so ment. And therin the blasphemouse beste deuyseth,
that he wolde haue had our sauyour say, y^t he wold play as iuglers
5 do, and slyly conuay hym selfe into a singyng lofe / & that our
sauyour so doth, he sayth is myne opinion. Wherin the man is
shameles & shamefully bylyeth me. For I saye as the catholyke
fayth is, that he not conuayeth but conuerteth the brede into his
owne body, and chaungeth it therin to /
Christ conuerteth   and neyther conuayeth (as he speketh)
10   *bread into hys*   his body into the brede (for than were
owne bodye*   the brede and his blessed body bothe
together styll, which [v$_4$] false opinion is Luthers heresy and that
knoweth this man well inough, and therefore sheweth hym selfe
15 shamelesse in layenge that opinion to me) nor also conuerteth not
his blessed body into brede, for that were yet mych worse. For than
remaineth there nothynge ellys but brede styll / & that is ye wote
well mayster Maskers owne heresy for whiche he wryteth agaynste
me / and therfore is he dowble shamelesse (as you se) to say any
20 suche thynge of me.
     But in conclusion theffecte of all his fonde argument is, that euyn
there in that place to breke stryfe & to soyle all theyr dowte, our
lorde myghte & wolde haue done at the selfe communicacion, or
els at y^e lest wyse theuangelist at y^e tyme of his wrytyng, myght
25 and wold haue told them playnly that they shold ete it, not in form
of flesh but in [v$_4$v] forme of bred. But neyther our sauyour than
tolde them so, nor theuangelyste hath tolde vs so in the reportynge
of his wordes spoken to them: ergo it must nedes be that Chryste
ment not so.
30   This is mayster Maskers argument whiche he lyketh so specyally,
that afterwarde in another place, he harpeth vppon the same
strynge agayne. But surely yf the man be in scrypture any thynge
exercysed, than hath he a very poore remembraunce. And whyther
he be scryptured or not he hath a very bare barayne wytte, whan
35 he can wene that this argument were aught.
     For fyrste (as for the scrypture) can he fynde no mo places than
one, in whych our sauyour wolde not tell out playnely all at onys?

---

28 nedes] *1557*, nestes *1533*   34 he be] *1533 corr. err.*, *1557*, be be *1533*

Coulde Chryst of the sacrament [v₅] of Baptysme haue tolde

Iohan. 3

Math. 12

no more to Nichodemus yf he had
wolde? Coulde he to the Iewes that
asked hym a token, haue told them no
more of his deth, sepulture, and resurreccyon, but the fygure of 5

Luke. 11

the prophete Ionas thre dayes swalowed
in to yᵉ whalys bely?

Whan his dyscyples asked hym of the restytucyon of the kyng-

Actu. 1

dome of Israell, and mysse toke his
kyngdome for a worldely kyngdome: 10
dyd he forthwith declare theym all that euer he coulde haue tolde
theym? or all yᵗ euer he tolde them therof at any other tyme after?
nay nor theuangelyste in the rehersynge neyther.

Hath this man eyther neuer redde or ellys forgotten, that all be
it our sauyour came to be knowen for Cryst & somtyme declared 15

*Math. 17**

hym so him self: yet at some other tymes
he forbode [v₅v] his dyscyples to be a
knowen therof? So that as for yᵉ scripturys (excepte he haue eyther
lytell redde, or lytell remembered of them) wold haue made
mayster Masker to forbere thys folysshe argument for shame. 20

But now what wyt hath this man that can argue thus, whan he
sholde (yf he had wytte) well perceyue his argument answered, by
the lyke made agaynste hym selfe vppon the very selfe same place.

For mayster masker sayth here that our lorde ment nothynge
ellys, but to tell them of the geuyng of his flesh to yᵉ deth for yᵉ life 25
of the world, and to make them byleue that. Now aske I therfore
mayster Masker, whyther Chryste coulde not haue tolde them by
more playne wordes than he dyd there (yf it had so ben his [v₆]
pleasure) that he sholde dye for the synne of the world, and in
what wyse also. If mayster Masker answere me no: I am sure euery 30
wyse man wyll tell hym yes. For he spake there not halfe so playnely of the geuynge of his body to be slayne, as he dyd of geuynge it
to be eaten. For as for his deth, not so myche as onys named it, but
onely sayeth, " *And the brede that I shall geue you is myne owne flesshe,*
whyche I shall geue for the lyfe of the worlde." In whyche wordes he not 35
onys nameth deth. But of the eatyng, he speketh so expressely by
and by, and so spake before, all of eatynge, & mych more after-

---

35 worlde] *1533 corr. err.*, *1557*, worde *1533*

warde to, that he gaue them lytle occasyon to thynke that he ment
of his deth any worde there at all, but of the eatynge onely. [v₆v]

   And some great holy doctours also, construe those whole
wordes, And the brede that I shall gyue is my flesshe which I shall gyue
5 for the lyfe of the worlde, to be spoken onely of the gyuynge of hys
blessed body in the sacrament, and neyther the fyrste parte nor the
seconde to be spoken of his deth. But that in the fyrste parte
Chryste sheweth what he wolde gyue them to eate, that is to wytte
his owne flesshe, and in the seconde parte he shewed them why he
10 wolde geue the worlde hys flesshe to eate, and what commodyte
they shold haue by the eatynge of it / sayenge, yᵗ he wolde geue it
men to eate for the lyfe that men sholde haue by the eatynge of it.
And therfore he pursueth forth bothe vpon the eatynge therof, and
vppon the lyfe that they shall lacke that wyll not eate it, and of the
15 lyfe that they shall haue that wyll [v₇] eate it. So that as I saye
Chryste spake and ment after the mynde of some holy cunnynge
men, but of the eatynge onely / but by all good men of the eatyng
specyally, and without any maner questyon of the eatynge moste
playnely, as of whiche he speketh by name expressely. And of hys
20 deth (yf he there spake of it as diuers holy doctours thynke he dyd)
yet he spake it so couertly, yᵗ he rather ment it than sayd it / as the
thynge wherof he nothynge named, but onely the geuynge to eate.
So that where as mayster Masker argueth, yᵗ Chryste nothynge
ment of geuynge of hys flesshe to be eaten in the sacrament, but
25 onely of his flessh to be crucified bycause that yf he hadde ment of
his flesshe to be eatyn in the sacrament, he coulde and wolde haue
tolde them playnely so: ye se now good readers [v₇v] very playne
proued by the self same place, that syth mayster Masker can not
saye nay, but that of his body to be geuyn by deth, Chryst could
30 haue spoken myche more playnely than he dyd in that place, as
well as he could haue spoken more playnely of the geuynge of hys
body to be eaten in the blessed sacrament, mayster Maskers owne
argument (yf it were aught as it is nought) vtterly destroyeth all
his owne exposycyon whole. And therfore ye maye se that the man
35 is a wyse man and well ouer seen in arguynge.

---

16 spake] speake *1557*

The .ii. chapyter.

In the .xi. lefe he hath an other argument, towarde whiche he maketh a blynde induccyon byfore. And bycause ye shall se that I wyll not go about to begyle you: I [v₈] wyll reherse you his induccyon fyrst, and than his argument after. These arre his wordes

Whan the Iewes wolde not vnderstande thys spyrytuall sayenge of the eatynge of Chrystes flessh and drynkynge of his bloude so ofte and so playnely declared: he gaue them a stronge tryppe, and made them more blynde for they so deserued it (suche are the secrete iudgementes of god) addyng vnto all hys sayenges thus. Who so eate my flessh and drynke my bloude, abydeth in me and I in hym. These wordes were spoken vnto the vnbyleuers into theyr farther obstynacyon, but vnto the faythfull for theyr better instruccyon. Now gather of thys the contrary, and saye, who so eateth not my flessh and drynketh not my bloude, abydeth not in me nor I in hym / & ioyne thys to that foresayd sentence, excepte ye eate the flesshe of the sone of man and drynke hys bloude, ye haue no lyfe in you. Lette it neuer fall fro thy mynd chrysten reader, that fayth is the lyfe of the ryghtwyse, and that Chryst is thys lyuynge brede whom thou eatest that is to saye in whom thou byleuest.

Here is mayster Masker fall to iuglynge lo / and as a iugler layeth forth hys trynclettes vpon the table and byddeth men loke on this & loke on that and blowe in hys hande / and [v₈v] than with certayne straunge wordes to make men muse / whurleth his iuglynge stycke about his fyngers to make men loke vpon that / whyle he playeth a false caste and conuayeth with yᵉ tother hand some thynge slyly into his purse or his sleue or somewhere out of syght / so fareth maister Masker here / that maketh Christes holy wordes serue hym for his iugling boxes and layeth them forth vppon the borde afore vs / and byddeth vs lo loke on this texte / and than loke lo vpon this / and whan he hath shewed forth thus two or thre textes and byd vs loke vpon them he telleth vs not wherfore / nor what we shall fynde in them. But bycause they be so playne agaynste hym he letteth them slynke awaye / and than to blere our eyen / and call our mynde fro the mater / vp he taketh his iuglynge stycke the com[x₁]mendacyon of fayth / and whyrleth that about hys fyngers / and sayeth,

27 his sleue] sleue *1557*

Let it neuer fall fro thy mynde chrysten reader that fayth is the lyfe of the
ryghtuouse, and that Chryst is thys lyuynge brede whom thou eatest, that
is to saye in whom thou byleuest.

What are these wordes good chrysten reader to the purpose. All
thys wyll I pray you remember to. But I wyll pray you remember
there with all, where about this iugeler goth, y^t wolde with
byddynge vs loke vppe here vppon fayth / iugle awaye one great
poynt of fayth from vs / and make vs take no hede of Chrystes
wordes playnely spoken here of the very eatyng of his holy flesshe.
And therfore let vs remember fayth as he byddeth. But let vs
remember well therwith specially this piece therof y^t this iugler
with byddynge vs remembre, wold fayne haue vs forgette.

But now after thys induccyon / [x$_1$v] forth he cometh with his
wyse argument in this wyse,

For yf our popystes take eatyng and drynkyng here bodyly as to eate the
naturall body of Chryste vnder the forme of brede / and to drynke his
bloud vnder the forme of wyne / than must all yonge chyldren that neuer
came at goddes borde departed, and al lay men that neuer dranke his
bloude be dampned.

If our sauyour Chryste whyche is the waye to trouth / and the
trouth it selfe, and the very trewe lyfe also / coulde and wold say
false, and breke his promyse by whyche
Math. 18   he promysed his chyrche to be therwith
Iohan. 16   hym selfe vnto the worldes ende, and to
sende it also the spyrite of trouth, that
shold teche it and lede it into al trouth: than wolde there of trouth /
bothe of these wordes of Chryste and these other wordes of his
Iohan. 3   also, But yf a man be borne agayne of
the water and the holy goost he can not
se the kyngdom of god / and of many other wordes of his mo many
greate dowtes aryse / [x$_2$] ryght harde and inexplycable. But now
am I very sure / sith trouth can not be
Psal. 67   but trew / Chrystes promyse shall euer
Iohan. 10   stande and be kepte, & therfore shall his
chyrche euer more by y^e meane of his
holy spyryte which maketh men of one maner and mynde in the
howse of his chyrche / so fall in a concorde and agrement togyther

---

15 popystes] papistes *1557*   23 *gloss* Math. 18] Math. 28 *placed opposite line 20 1557*

The churche cannot
fal into any
*dampnable errour**

vppon the trew sense / and so be led into euery necessary trewth / that by misse takynge of any parte of scrypture, it shall neuer be suffred to fall into any dampnable errour. Whiche thynge what pratynge so euer mayster masker make / I haue so often & so surely proued for the comen knowen catholyke chyrch of good and badde bothe / agaynst Willyam Tindale / y^t neyther he nor all these heretikes among them all, shall neuer be able to voyde it.

Now as for his argument concernynge laye men of age, it were [x$_2$v] a lytell more stronge / yf the blessed body of our lorde were in the blessed sacrament vnder forme of brede with out his bloude /

*Note**

whiche whyle it ys not / nor theyr receyuynge is not the sacryfyce nor oblacyon, which to the integrite therof requyreth bothe the formys / that the thynge sholde agre with the fygure / the fygure I saye of the brede

Gen. 14

and wyne that was offered by Melchysedech / mayster Maskers argument is of a feble force. Of whyche thynge bycause I purpose onys to touche god wyllyng in answerynge to doctour Barons treatyse specyally made of that mater / I wyll holde here mayster Masker for this tyme with no longe tale therof. But to thentent ye may shortely se how lytell wytte is in his wise argument with whych vppon Chrystes general wordes, "but yf you eate [x$_3$] the flesshe of y^e sone of man & drynke his bloude ye shall not haue lyfe in you /" he argueth vniuersally of all men and women & chyldren that dye, and neuer eate his flesshe or neuer drynke his bloude shalbe dampned / by the selfe same forme of arguyng vppon these generall wordes, But yf a man be borne of water and the spyryte, he shall neuer se the kyngedome of god, Mayster Masker may argue generally, that who so dye byfore he be baptysed by water and the spyrite, shalbe dampned. And theruppon conclude that many martyres be dampned for lacke of baptysynge in water, for all theyr baptysynge in theyr owne bloude. And thus you se good readers how substancyall his argument is. [x$_3$v]

5

10

15

20

25

30

35

13–14 receyuynge] receiuing, *1557*   19 Of whyche] Whych *1557*   20 Barons] Barns *1557*
26 of all] that al *1557*   30 god,] *1557*, god. *1533*

The .iii. chapyter.

I̶ₙ the .xii. lefe to proue, yᵗ Cryst ment nothynge to geue his body
to be eaten, mayster masker vppon these wordes that the dyscyples
whiche were offended with his wordes sayde, This is an harde
worde who maye here hym, bryngeth in an other wise argument
5 vnder colour of expownynge yᵉ texte in this wyse. These wordes dyd
not onely offende them that hated Chryst, but also some of his dyscyples.
They were offended sayth the texte and not meruayled as More tryfleth
out of trouth. These wordes good reader of offendynge and
meruaylynge I shall answere anone in a more conuenyent place.
10 whyche dyscyples sayd, Thys is an harde sayenge who may here hym?
These dyscyples stoke no lesse in Chrystes visyble flesshe, and in the barke
of his wordes, than doth now More byleuynge hym to haue spoken of his
naturall body to be eaten wyth theyr teth. [x₄]

15 Here mayster masker maketh as though the catholyke faith in
the blessed sacrament, were but my fayth. But lyke wyse as I do
confesse that his heresye is not onely his, but that he hath felowes
in the same falsed / not onely Fryth and Tyndale, but Wicliffe also
and zuinglius, & frere Huyskyn to, bysyde a lewde sorte of wreched
20 heretykes moo: so must he confesse yf he wyll say trew, that my
fayth is not onely my fayth, but that I haue felowes in the same
fayth / not onely the comen hole multytude of all good chrysten
cuntrees this fyftenne hundred yere, but specyally by name those
holy saintes whose wordes I haue rehersed you before vppon this
25 same mater / as Theophylactus, & saynt Bede, saynte Hyrineus,
and saynt Hilary, and saynte Austayne, saynte Cyryll, and saynt
Chrisostome / the playne wordes [x₄v] of euery one of all whome, I
haue here all redy brought you forth agaynste mayster Masker,
prouynge them selfe felowes of myne in my fayth all redy, now in
30 this answere of this fyrste parte of his. And yet kepe I for mayster
Masker mater inough bysyde, of holy sayntes authorytees, as well
the same sayntes as other, to fyll vp the messys at the seconde
course. And where he bringeth forth for hym in his seconde parte,
Austayne, Tertullyan, and saynte Chrysostom (For in all this his
35 fyrst course he bryngeth forth neuer one) those thre dysshes I

---

6 expownynge yᵉ] expoundynge that *1557*   14 teth.] teth *1533*, teeth. *1557*   29 all
redy, now] al redye nowe *1557*

warraunt you shall whan I come to them, but barely furnysshe hys
borde.

But where mayster masker saith that More stycketh in the
vysyble fleshe of Chryst, to be eaten as those dyscyples and those
Iewes dyd: he [x₅] is bolde to saye what hym lyste bycause he
goth inuysyble. For ellys how coulde he for shame say that we yᵗ
are of the catholyke chyrch, thynke that Chryste geueth vs his
visyble flesshe to eate, as those dyscyples & those Iewys thought /
whan euery man well woteth, that those dyscyples and those Iewes,
thought that they sholde receyue hys flesshe visyble cutte out as
saynt Austayne declareth in visyble dede piecys / and euery man as
well knoweth & mayster Masker to, that we thynke that we do

*For he that doth not
so doth erre**

(and so in dede we do) receyue and eate
his flesshe inuisyble, not in dede pyeces,
but his quycke blessed body whole, vnder

the visible forme of brede. And therfore you se good readers what
trouth is in this man.

But now goth he forth and commeth to hys wyse wurshypfull
ar[x₅v]gument and sayth.

Whyche offence Chryste seynge sayed, doth thys offende you, what than
wyll you saye yf you se the sone of man ascende thyther where he was
before? If it offende you to eate my flessh whyle I am herre: it shall
myche more offende you to eate it whan it shalbe gone out of your syght
ascended into heuyn, there syttynge on the ryght hande of my father,
vntyll I come agayne as I went, that is to iugement.

The exposycyon of these wordes of Chryste, I haue good readers
shewed you before, accordyng to the myndes of holy doctours and
sayntes that by those wordes of his ascencyon he gaue them warnynge before, that he wolde by his ascendyng vp to heuyn, make
them a playne profe that thei were deceiued whan they thought it
could not be that he was descended downe from heuyn, and by his
ascendyng vp with his body hole & vnminyshed, make them a
playne profe yᵗ they were deceiued, whan they thought he wold in
pyeces cut out, and so geue his fleshe to them as he sholde [x₆]
gyue it from hym selfe, & therby lese it hym selfe. For hys whole
body ascendynge, shold well proue yᵗ though his apostles had euery
one eatyn it: yet had he it styll whole hym selfe / yᵗ they sholde

5 hym] hymselfe *1557*

therby not dowt afterward, but that as eche of them had it and
dyd eate it, and yet hym selfe had it styll, and all at onys in .xiii.
dyuerse places in erth, and hym selfe ascended after whole therwith
into heuin: so sholde euer after all good chrysten folke receyue it
5 whole here in erthe, and hym selfe neuer the lesse haue it whole
styll wyth hym in heuyn.

Thys beynge good chrysten readers y^e mynde of our sauiour in
those wordes, as by the holy doctours and sayntes well doth appere
of old: now cometh this new dronken doctour maister masker, and
10 with a wyse exposycyon of hys owne brayne, wolde make vs wene
that those wordes [x_6v] with whiche (as the olde doctours testyfye)
Chryste confermed the sacrament, in declarynge his power by
whyche he wurketh that wonderfull miracle in the sacrament, our
sauiour had hym selfe spoken agaynste his myracles in the sacra-
15 ment. For thus lo doth maister Masker make Cryst expowne his
owne wordes and say,
If it offende you to eate my fleshe whyle I am here: it shall mych more
offende you to eate it whan my body shalbe gone out of your syght
ascended into heuyn, there syttynge on the ryght hande of my father
20 vntyll I come agayne as I went.

There were good readers two causes, for whiche those Iewes and
those dyscyples were offended at the herynge of Cryste, whan he
sayde they shold eate his fleshe. One was, the straungenesse and
the impossybylyte that they thought was therin / y^e tother was the
25 lothsomnes that they had therto. Now yf mayster Masker mene
here for the impossybylyte [x_7] by reason of the dyfference of his
presence and his absence: I can not se why they sholde be more
offended after his ascencyon than before. For yf it be possyble for
hym to make his body to be in many dyuerse places at onys in
30 erth: than it is as possyble for hym to make it at onys in those two
dyuerse places erth and heuyn. For the meruayle standeth not in
the farre dystaunce of the two places a sunder, but in the dyuersyte
of ye two places hauyng in them both one body be they neuer so
nere togyther. And as for the dyfference of his presence here in
35 erth, and his absence hense, by his ascensyon into heuyn: mayster
Masker is more than madde, to put that for a dyfference, as a

cause after thascensyon to make theym more offended to here of
the eatynge of hys body. For yf he make (as he can and [x₇v] doth)
his body to be as well here in erthe as in heuyn: than is hys body
no more absent from hense than from thense, as for the veryte of
hys presence in the place, though it be more absent in consyd-   5
eracyon to vs that se not his body here, but in yᵉ forme of brede.
But the blessed angellys, se that one blessed body of his in heuyn
and here in the blessed sacrament both at onys. And thus you se
that mayster Maskers argument hathe no pyth or strength, yf he
mene for impossybylyte.   10

Nowe yf mayster Masker here mene, that after Chrystes ascensyon into hyuyn, it sholde be a thynge that sholde of reason more
offende the Iewes to eate hys flesshe, than at yᵉ tyme whyle he was
here, as a thyng that wolde be than a mych more lothsome mete:
what deuyll reason hath [x₈] mayster Masker to bere that madde   15
mynde with all, & to thynke that hys gloryfyed flessh shold be
more lothsome to receiue, than yf it were vngloryfyed.

And yet either he meneth thus / or els he lacketh the waye to
fynde the wordes, with which he wold expresse his mynde. For
these are the wordes, that he maketh Chryste to saye, If it offende   20
you to eate my flessh whyle I am here: it shall mych more offende you to
eate it whan my body shalbe gone out of your syghte. You se now that
he sayth it shal more offende you to eate it whan it is gone out of
your syght into heuyn. Now yf he hadde ment in the tother maner
for thimpossibylyte, he wolde haue sayd (except he can not speke)   25
that it sholde more offende theym to here it tolde them that they
sholde than eate his flessh, whan his flessh were so far absent from
them, than to here it told [x₈v] them that they sholde eate it whyle
it were present wyth them / and not say it sholde than more
offende theym to eate it. For they shall not be offended with the   30
eatynge yf they eate it not. And therfore (yf he can tell how to
speke and expresse his owne mynde) he meneth here whyle he
sayth it shal more offend you to eate it, he meneth I saye that they
sholde of reason thynke his flesshe than more lothely to eate after
his gloriouse ascencyon, than it was ere he dyed. Thus it appereth   35
that mayster Masker ment. And verily yf he so mene, he hath a
madde menynge. And yf he mene not so: than hath he a madde

maner of spekynge. And yet bysyde that hys menynge is as madde
that waye as the tother.

For as I haue shewed you, the thyng is no more impossible to
Crist, [y₁] to geue them his body to eate after his ascensyon than
5 byfore / and therfore is maister Masker a fole to say, that it scholde
more offende them to here that they scholde eate it after his
ascencyon than before. For by theyr eatynge he scholde not lese it /
but both men may haue his body here in erth with them, and yᵉ
angelys may haue it in heuyn with them, and hym selfe may haue
10 it both in erth and in heuyn with hym, and all thys at onys.

Wherin leste mayster Masker myghte make some wene, that I
do as he sayth I do, and as in dede mayster Masker doth hym selfe,
that is to wyt mocke in this mater and lye: ye shal good readers
here what holy saynt Chrysostome sayth,

15
　　　Chriso. hom. 2.
　　　ad populum

*" Helyas lefte vnto Heliseus his mantell, as a
very greate enherytaunce. And in very dede a
great enheritaunce* [y₁v] *it was, and more
precyouse than any golde. And Heliseus was a dowble Hely / & there was
than helyas aboue and helyas beneth. I knowe wel that you thynke he was a*
20 *iuste and a blessed man / and you wold fayne eche of you be in his case.
What wyll you say than, yf I shew you a certayne other thynge, that all we
that are seasoned with the holy sacramentes, haue receyued that farre excelleth
helyas mantell. For helias in dede lefte hys dyscyple his mantell. But the sone
of god ascendyng vp, hath lefte vnto vs hys flesshe. And as for helias leuyng*
25 *hys mantell to his dyscyple, lefte it of from hym selfe. But our sauyour Chryst*

　　　*A notable saying
　　　and a true**

*hath bothe lefte it styll with vs, and yet in hys
ascensyon hath taken it wyth hym selfe to. Lette
neuer therfore our hartes fall for fere, nor let vs
not lament and bywayle, nor drede the dyffycultees of the troubelouse tymes.*
30 *For he that neither hath* [y₂] *refused to shede his bloud for vs all, and hath
also bysyde that, geuen vnto vs all his fleshe to eate, & the same bloude
agayne to drynke: he wyll refuse nothynge that maye serue for our saluacyon."*

How say you now good chrysten readers? doth not saynt
35 Chrysostom with these wordes, afferme you playnely the substaunce of that that I say & as playnely destroye all that mayster
masker sayth in his heretycall exposycion of these wordes of Chryst /
whych he constreweth so as he wold therby make a repugnaunce
bytwen the beynge of Chrystes blessed body in yᵉ blessed sacra-

ment, and the beyng of his body by his ascension in heuyn? For
though mayster masker saye they canne not stande together, but is
vtterly repugnaunt that his body sholde be here in erthe before
[y₂v] domys daye, bycause that vntyll domys daye it shalbe styll in
heuyn: yet sayth saynt Chrysostome playnely, that mayster Masker   5
in his exposycyon lyeth. For he sayth that Chrystes blessed body is
bothe in heuyn & also in erth in the blessed sacrament in dede.

And therfore let mayster Masker leue his iestynge with me, & go
ieste and rayle agaynste saynte Chrysostome. For he confuteth you
mayster Masker you se well, a lytell more clerer than I. And than   10
whyther of them twayne ye shal byleue and take for the more
credyble man, mayster Masker or holy saynt Chrysostom, euery
mannys owne wytte that any wyt hath, wyll well serue hym to se.

The .iiii. chapyter.

But mayster Masker to shewe you a ferther declaracyon of his   15
wytte, forthwith vpon his wyse and [y₃] wurshypfull exposycyon of
those wordes of Chryst, he repeteth that fonde argument agayne,
that Chryst ment not of eatynge his flesshe in the sacrament /
bycause that yf he hadde ment it, he coulde and wolde haue
declared his menynge more playnely. And in that mater thus   20
maister Masker sayth.

Here myght Chryste haue enstructe his dyscyples the trouth of the
eatynge of hys fleshe in forme of brede, had thys ben hys menynge. For he
lefte them neuer in any perplexite or dowt, but sought all the wayes by
symylytudes and famylyare examples, to teche them playnely, he neuer   25
spake them so harde a parable, but where he perceyued theyr feble
ignoraunce, anone he helpt them and declared it them. Ye and somtymes
he preuented theyr askynge wyth his owne declaracyon. And thynke ye
not that he dyd not so here? yes veryly. For he came to teache vs and not
to leue vs in any dowt and ignoraunce, especyally the chyefe poynt of our   30
saluacyon, whych standeth in the bylyefe in hys deth for our synnys.
Wherfore to put them out of all dowt as concernyng this eatyng of his
flessh and drynkyng of his bloud, that sholde geue euerlastynge lyfe,
where they toke it for his very body to be eaten with theyr tethe: he
sayed, It is the spyryte that geueth this lyfe. My [y₃v] flesshe profyteth   35
nothynge at all to be eaten as ye meane so carnally: It is spyrytuall meate

---

25 playnely,] plainly. *1557*   36 ye] you *1557*

that I here speke of. It is my spyryt that draweth the hartes of men to me
by fayth, and so refresheth them gostely. Ye be therfore carnal to thynke
that I speke of my flesshe to be eaten bodyly. For so it profyteth yow
nothynge at all. How longe wyll you be wythout vnderstandyng? It is my
5   spyryte I tell you that geueth lyfe. My flesshe profyteth you nothynge to
eate it, but to byleue that it shalbe crucyfyed & suffre for the redempcyon
of the worlde it profyteth. And when ye thus byleue, than eate ye my
flesshe and drynke my bloude / that is ye byleue in me to suffre for your
synnes. The veryte hath spoken these wordes: My flesshe profyteth
10   nothyng at all: it canne not therfore be false. For bothe the Iewes and hys
dyscyples murmured and dysputed of his flessh, how it sholde be eaten /
and not of the offerynge therof for our synnes as Chryst ment. Thys
therfore is the sure anker to holde vs by, agaynst all the obieccions of the
papystes, for the eatynge of Chrystes body as they say in forme of brede.
15   Chryst sayd, My flesh profyteth nothyng, menyng to eate it bodely. Thys
is the key that solueth all theyr argumentes & openeth the waye to shew
vs all theyr false and abomynable blasphemouse lyes vppon Chrystes
wordes, and vttereth theyr sleyght iugelynge ouer the brede to mayntayne
Antichrystes kyngdome therwyth. And thus when Chryste had declared
20   it, and taught them that it was not the bodyly eatynge of hys materyall
body, but the eatynge wyth the spyryte of faythe: he added sayenge, The
wordes whyche I here speke vnto you are spyryte and lyfe / that is to [y₄]
saye, thys mater that I here haue spoken of with so many wordes, must be
spyrytually vnderstanden, to geue ye this lyfe euerlastynge. Wherfore the
25   cause why ye vnderstand me not, is that ye byleue not. Here is lo the
conclusyon of all hys sermon.

    Many a fonde processe haue I redde good chrysten readers, but
neuer redde I neyther a more folysshe nor a more false than this is.
For the effecte and the purpose of al this processe is, that Chryst in
30   all his wordes spoken in thys syxte chapiter of saint Iohan, ment
nothynge of the eatyng of his blessed body in the blessed sacrament, but onely of an allegorycal eatynge of his body / by whyche
he ment onely that they sholde byleue that he sholde be crucyfyed
& shedde his bloude and dye for redempcyon of the worlde.

35   Now that our sauiour bysyde al such allegories & other spirituall
vnderstandinges, playnely ment of yᵉ very [y₄v] eatyng of his
blessed body in the blessed sacrament, you haue good reders all
redy sene, by so many holy doctours and sayntes / whose playn
wordes I haue rehersed you, that no man can dowte but that in the

---

7 ye my] you my *1557*   35 sauiour] *1557*, saniour *1533*

whole conclusyon of his argument and his exposycyon, mayster
Masker hath a shamefull fall / except any man dowt whyther
mayster Masker be better to be byleued alone, or those holy doctours amonge them all.

But now thys false conclusyon of hys, how febly and how
folyshely he defendeth, y^t is euyn a very great pleasure to se.

In this processe hath he .ii. poyntes. The fyrste is that Chryste
coulde & wolde haue made it open and playne in thys place by
clere and euydent wordes, yf he had ment of the eatynge of his
flesshe in the sacrament. [y$_5$] The second is, that by these wordes
"*It is the spyryte that geueth lyfe, my fleshe profyteth nothynge at all, The
wordes that I haue spoken to you be spyryte and lyfe:*" Chryste doth playn
and clerely declare, both that he ment not the eatynge of his flesshe
in the sacrament, and also that he ment onely the bylyefe that he
sholde dye for the synne of the worlde.

Now touchynge his fyrste folysh poynt, I haue confuted it all
redy, & shewed you some samples, where Chryste coulde at some
tyme haue declared the mater mych more openly than he dyd, and
that in great maters of our fayth.

For I thynke the sacrament of baptysme, is a pryncypall poynt
of our fayth. And yet Chryste taught not Nichodemus all that he
coulde haue tolde hym therin as I sayd before. [y$_5$v]

And longeth it nothyng to y^e fayth to byleue the remyssyon of
mortall sinnes? I suppose yes. And yet could Chryste yf he had
Matth. 12   wolde, haue declared more clerely those
                        wordes of his, who so blaspheme the sone
of man it shalbe forgeuen hym. But he that blasphemeth the holy
gooste, it shall neyther be forgeuen him in this world nor in the
world to come.

No good chrysten man thynketh other, but that it is a pryncypall artycle of the chrysten fayth, to byleue y^t Chryst is one equale
god with his father. And yet Chryste (albe it that by all places sette
togyther, he hath declared it clere inough in conclusion, to them
that wyll not be wylfull & contencyouse) yet dyd he not in euery
place where he spake therof, declare the mater so clerely as he
could haue done yf he than hadde wolde. Whiche [y$_6$] appereth
by that that in some other places, he declared it more clerely after.
And yet in all the places of the scrypture set togyther, he hath not,
nor wolde not, declare it in so playne wordes / as he coulde haue

done. For than sholde there neuer haue neded any of those com-
mentes, that all the holy doctours haue made vppon it synnys. And
surely so sayth Luther and these other heretykes, that there neded
none. For all the scrypture (they saye) is open & playne inough.

5   And therfore they put euery manne and
      The which thing   woman vnlerned in boldenesse and
      hath made many   corage, to be in the scrypture sufficyently
         heretikes*   theyr owne maysters them selfe. But
whyle they thus teache them, they forgete that by theyr own
10   techyng they shold holde theyr peace them selfe. And in dede so
were it good they dyd, but yf they taught better. [y₆v]

   And thus for his fyrst poynt, you se good readers that mayster
Masker maketh men perceyue hym for a dowble fole whan it was
not inough for hym to come forth with this foly onys, but he muste
15   a goddes name brynge in this his one foly twyse.

The .v. chapyter.

N ow as towchyng his second poynt, in that it is a worlde to se
how strongly the man handeleth it. For where as Chryst hath by so
many open playne wordes before, taught and declared, that he
20   wolde geue his owne flesshe to be eaten, and his own bloude to be
drunken, and so often repeted it, and in suche effectuall wyse
inculked it, and as who sholde saye bette it into theyr heddes, that
(sauyng for the forme & maner of the eatynge [y₇] whyche he
declared by his word and hys dede at his holy maundye) ellys as
25   for to make men sure that veryly eate it and drynke it they sholde,
there could neuer more clere wordes haue ben of any man desyred,
nor by mayster Masker hym self deuysed: now cometh mayster
Masker forth wyth certayne wordes of Chryst, by whiche he sayth
that Chryste clerely declareth, that he ment clere the contrary that
30   is to wytte that his fleshe shold not be eaten / and also that by thys
worde eatyng of hys flesshe, he ment nothynge ellys, but the
bylyefe of hys deth for mennys synnes.

   Now the wordes of our sauyour that (as mayster masker saith)
proue these two thynges, are these. " *It is the spyryte that geueth lyfe,*
35   *my flesh profyteth nothynge at all. The wordes that I haue spoken to you be*
spyryte and lyfe." [y₇v]

6–7 *gloss* made] mode *1557*   14 this] his *1557*   28 whiche] whithe *1533*, which *1557*

These wordes haue good reders in them selfe neyther any thynge
in dysprofe of the very eatynge of hys flesshe, nor for the profe that
he ment the bylyefe of his deth. For these wordes as saynte Austayne declareth, speke not precysely agaynst ye eatyng of his fleshe,

*Note** as he ment to geue it them wyth the
spyryte and the lyfe therin / but agaynste
the eatynge of his flesshe alone, dede and cutte out in gobbettes, as
they conceiued a false opinion that he ment to make theym eate it.
And as I haue shewed you before, saynt Cyrill expouneth these
wordes after the same maner, and other holy doctours to. And now
yf ye rede agayn mayster maskers wordes here: ye shall fynde that
all that semeth to proue his purpose, is onely the wordes of hym
selfe, & nothynge the wordes of Chryst / but hym selfe [y_8]
expounyng Chrystes wordes in such wyse, that (as I haue shewed
you) saynt Austayne and saynt Cyrill and other holy doctours,
expoune it clere agaynste hym.

If his own argument were aught worth that he layeth against the
interpretacyon of all that expowne those wordes of Chryste, to be
spoken of the very eatynge, by whiche we eate his blessed body in
the sacrament, it wolde make agaynste no man so sore as agaynst
hym self euyn here in this place.

For if it be trew that he sayth, that yf Chryst had ment of the
eatyng of his flesh in the sacrament, he myght & wold haue in this
place told it them playnely / & bycause he told them not that
poynt out playnely, therfore it is clere that he ment it not: than say
I that syth in these wordes / whyche [y_8v] mayster Masker sayth, is
the very anker holde, Cryst doth not so playnely declare, that he
meaneth by the eatynge of his flessh the bylyefe that he sholde dye
for our synnys, as he coulde yf he had wolde, and wolde as mayster
Masker sayth yf he had so ment. Thys is therfore a playne profe by
mayster Maskers argument agaynst mayster Maskers mynde, y^t
our sauyour ment not so / and than is all mayster Maskers mater
go.

Now that our sauyour doth not here declare that poynt clerely /
that he ment nothynge but that they shold byleue that he sholde
dye for theym: I wyll haue mayster Maskers own wordes to bere
me recorde. Whyche wyll I wene make mayster Masker somwhat
wroth wyth hym selfe, for wrytyng them in hym self, so folyshely
agaynste hym selfe. [z_1]

For where he sayth that bothe the Iewes and the dyscyples, murmured and dysputed of his flesshe how it sholde be eaten, and not of the offerynge therof for our synnes: thys declareth and wytnesseth well for our parte agaynste his own / that our sauyour
5 declared more playnely his mynde for the eatynge of his flessh, than for the offerynge therof to the deth for our synnys. And of very trouth so he dyd in dede, though mayster Masker saye naye an hundred tymes. For of the eatyng of his flesh as I haue before said, he spake very precysely, and playnely, and often / and of his
10 offerynge vp vppon the crosse, he neuer spake playnely so mych as one worde.

For as for these wordes whyche maister masker calleth y^e anker hold: *It is the spyrite that geueth this lyfe* [z_1v] *my fleshe profyteth nothynge at all*, hath not one playne word for his purpose at all. For
15 all the vttermost that he coulde take of these wordes, were no more but that Chryste sholde tell them that the spyryte is the thynge

The flesh of Christ without spirite and lyfe is nothing*

that geueth his flesshe the lyfe, with out whiche of it selfe it coulde not profyte them at all / and therfor the wordes that
20 he spake were spyryte & lyfe, and to be vnderstanden spyrytually, that they sholde eate his flesh wyth hys spyryte, and not carnally that they sholde eate hys flessh alone without his spyryte, cut out in dede peces of flesshe, as they had conceyued a fonde opinion therof, out of whyche he sayed all this
25 to brynge them, but yet not so mych as he could haue sayd and he had wold, nor wold not bycause of theyr vnworthynesse to here it / and yet that they shold eate [z_2] his flessh, he tolde them clere inough.

But as I say, what one worde is there in all these wordes of his
30 anchor holde, wherby mayster Masker may take one handefull holde, y^t Chryste here shewed them so clerely, that he ment the offerynge of hym selfe for our synnys? he speketh in al these wordes not one word of offeryng; nor of crucifyeng, nor of deth. And by mayster Maskers owne argument yf he had ment y^t way, as he well
35 could, so he wold also haue told them playnly thus: Sirs I mene not that you shal eate my flessh, but y^t you shall byleue y^t I shall dye for your synnys. And syth he sayd not thus, mayster Maskers

---

5 eatynge] eatyuge *1533*, eating *1557*   13 my] *1533 1557*, My *catchword 1533*

own argument hath cutte of his cable rope, & lost his anchore, &
runne his shyppe hym self agaynst a rocke. For he sayth that yf he
had ment it, he wold haue tolde them playne the tale to put them
out of all dowte. [z₂v]

And here you se now good reders by mo meanys than one, as   5
wel by yᵉ exposycyons of olde holy doctours & sayntes, as by the
wyse argument of mayster masker hym self, to what wyse wurshypfull ende, thys ryall brage of his is come to passe, in whiche he
triumpheth ouer the catholike chyrch & the blessed sacrament,
where he bosteth thus. Thys therfore is the sure anker to holde vs by,   10
agaynst all the obieccions of the papystes, for the eatynge of Chrystes
body as they say in forme of brede. Chryst sayd, My flesh profyteth
nothyng, menyng to eate it bodely. Thys is the key that solueth all theyr
argumentes & openeth the waye to shew vs all theyr false and abomynable blasphemouse lyes vppon Chrystes wordes, and vttereth theyr sleyght   15
iugelynge ouer the brede to mayntayne Antichrystes kyngdome therwyth.
And thus when Chryste had declared it, and taught them that it was not
the bodyly eatynge of hys materyall body, but the eatynge wyth the
spyryte of faythe: he added sayenge, The wordes whyche I here speke
vnto you are spyryte and lyfe / that is to saye, thys mater that I here haue   20
spoken of with so many wordes, must be spyrytually vnderstanden, to
geue ye this lyfe euerlastynge. Wherfore the cause why ye vnderstand me
not, is that ye byleue me not. Here is lo the conclusyon of all hys sermon.
[z₃]

Syth your selfe haue sene good readers, that in this mater and in   25
this whole exposycyon, there are agaynst mayster masker not onely
the catholyke chyrche of our tyme, but also all the olde holy doctours and sayntes, which with one voyce expoune these wordes of
Chryste to be spoken and ment of that eatynge of Chrystes flesshe,
by whyche it is eaten in the blessed sacrament / agaynste whiche   30
poynt mayster masker here rageth in this his furyouse boste,
raylynge vppon them all that so teche or byleue, vnder his spyghtfull name of papystes: I wold wytte of mayster masker, whyther
saynt Bede, saynt Austayn, and saynt Ambrose, saynt Hireneus,
and saint Hilary, Theophilactus, saynt Cyrill, and saynt Chryso-   35
stome, were all papystes or not? If he answere ye, and saye they
were: [z₃v] than shall he make no man (that wise is) asshamed of

---

36–37 they were] *1533 corr. err.*, *1557*, the were *1533*

the name of papystes (as odyouse as he wolde make it) yf he
graunte vs that suche good godly men, & such holy doctours &
sayntes were papystes.

Now yf he answere me nay, and say that they were no papystes:
5 than he maketh it playne and open vnto you good reders, that he
playeth but the part of a folyssh rayler & a iester, and doth but
deceyue and mocke all his owne fraternyte / whan by raylynge
agaynste papystes, whom he wold haue taken for folke of a false
fayth, he dyssembleth the trouth, that his heresye is not onely
10 dampned by them that he calleth papystes, but by them also
whom he confesseth for no papistes, and whom he can not but
confesse for old holy doctours & saintes / nor can not so blynd you,
but that you [z₄] playnely perceyue by theyr own wordes / which
I haue rehersed you, and yet shal hereafter more playnely per-
15 ceyue, by mo holy doctours & sayntes of the same sort, & by mo
playne wordes also of ye same, y^t they do all with one voyce
expoune these wordes of Chryst mencyoned in the syxte chapiter of
saynt Iohan, to be spoken & ment of y^t eatyng of his flesh, by
which we eate it in the blessed sacrament.

20 And thus haue I good reders answered you all mayster Maskers
argumentes, by whych he reproueth in generall vnder the name of
papystes, all those, that is to wytte all the olde holy doctours and
sayntes, that contrary to hys heresye expowne the sayde wordes of
Chryste to be ment of the very eatynge of hys flesshe, and not onely
25 of the byleuynge of his deth for our synne. [z₄v] And now wyll I
come to his subtyll dysputacyons, that he maketh against me by
name in specyall, to soyle such thynges as I in my letter wrote
agaynst Iohan Fryth.

Here endeth the thyrde booke.

The fourth boke

IN the syxte lefe thus he sayth.

Here maketh M. More this argument agaynst the yonge man. Bycause
the Iewes merueyled at this sayenge: my fleshe is very meate & my
bloude drynke and not at this: I am the dore and the very vyne, therfore 5
this text (sayth he) my flesshe &c. must be vnderstanden after the lytterall
sence, that is to wyt euen as the carnall Iewes [z₅] vnderstode it murmurynge at it, beynge offended, goynge theyr wayes from Cryst for theyr so
carnal vnderstandynge therof / and the tother textes, I am the dore &c.
must be vnderstanden in an allegorye & a spyrytual sence, bycause his 10
hearers merueyled no thynge at the maner of speche.

I haue good readers byfore this argument that he speketh of,
another argument in that pystle of myne agaynst Fryth / whyche
all though it went before and was redde before this, yet bycause it
wolde not well be soyled, maister Masker was content to dyssemble 15
it. But I shall afterward anone lay it afore hym agayne, and sette
hym to it with a festue, that he shall not saye but he sawe it.

But now as for this argument of myne, that he maketh the fyrste,
I mysse fortuned to make so feble, that he taketh euyn a pleasure
to playe with it / and therfore he soyleth it and soyleth it agayne / 20
& that full wysely ye may be faste and sure / and so shall [z₅v] you
saye your selfe whan you se all. But yet though he wynne hym selfe
worshyp in the soylynge, yt was no great wysedome to lese his
worshyp in the rehersynge, wyth false beryng in hande, that I saye
that those wordes of Cryste muste be vnderstanden after that 25
lyterall sense that the carnall Iewys toke therin, that murmured
and went theyr way therfore. For they toke yt of hys fleshe, to be
eaten in the self same fleshely forme and as holy saynte Austayne
sayeth that they shold haue eaten his fleshe deade withoute lyfe or
spyryte, as befe or motten is cutte out in bochers shoppys. And I 30
am very sure, that mayster Maskar hathe no such word in my
letter, wherof he maye take hold to say that I say that Chrystes
wordes shold be taken so. But this is no newe fashyon of these

*The vsual fashion
of heretiques**

folkes, to [z₆] reherse other mennes argumentes in suche maner as theym selfe 35
lyste to make them, and then they make

---

3 Here] *1557*, here *1533*   11 no thynge] nothing *1557*   13 pystle] epistle *1557*

149

them such, as them selfe may most easely soyle theym. Whych
whyle mayster Masker hathe done wyth myne, yet hath he lytle
auauntage therby. But to thentent that all thynge shall be the
more open byfore your yien: I shall reherse you fyrste the thynge
that he wolde be content you sawe not, y^t is to wit myne own
wordes as I wrote theym, whyche he reherseth as hym selfe maketh
theym new.

These were good reader my wordes.

And ouer this the very cyrcumstaunces of the places in the gospell, in whych
our sauiour speketh of that sacrament may wel make open the dyfference of his
spech in this mater & of all those other / & that as he spake all those but in
an allegory, so spake he this plainly menyng y^t he spake of his very body &
his very bloud beside al allegories. [z₆v] *For neyther whan our lorde sayde he*
was a very vyne, nor whan he sayde he was the dore / there was none that
herde hym that any thynge meruayled therof. And why? for bycause they
perceyued well that he ment not that he was a materyall vyne in dede, nor a
materyall dore neyther. But whan he sayd that his flesh was very mete, and
his blood was very drynke, and that they shold not haue lyfe in them but yf
they dyd eate his flesshe and drynke his blood / than were they allmoste all in
suche a wonder therof, that they could not abyde. And wherfore? but bycause
they perceyued wel by his wordes and his maner of cyrcumstaunces vsed in the
spekynge of them, that Chryste spake of his very flesshe and his very blood in
dede. For ellys the straungeness of the wordes wold haue made them to haue
taken it as well for an allegorye, as eyther his wordes of the vyne or of the
dore. [z₇] *And than wolde they haue no more meruayled at the tone than they*
dyd at the tother. But now where as at the vyne and the dore they meruayled
nothynge / yet at the eatynge of his flesshe and drynkynge of his blood, they so
sore meruayled, and were so sore moued, and thought the mater so harde, &
the wonder so great, that they asked how coulde that be, and went almoste all
theyr waye. Wherby we maye well se, that he spake these wordes in suche
wyse, as the herers perceyued that he ment it not in a parable nor an allegorye /
but spake of hys very flesshe and hys very bloude in dede.

Lo good readers here I speke of Chrystes very flesshe and his
very bloud (as the trouth is in dede). But here I saye not as
mayster masker sayth I saye, that Christ ment of his flesshe and his

12 an allegory] allegorye *1557*   21 perceyued] preceyued *1533*, perceiued *1557*
22–23 in dede] *1533 corr. err., 1557*, in ded *1533*   30 waye.] way, *1557*   34 dede).] dede)
1533, dede.) *1557*

bloude, in suche wyse [z₇v] as the Iewes thought that forsoke hym
therfore whych thought as you haue herde, that they sholde eate
hys fleshe in the selfe fleshely forme, and also pyecemele in lothly
dede gobettes, without eyther lyfe or spiryt.

And nowe that you haue sene hys trouth in rehersynge: you shal   5
se a shew of his sharpe sotle wit in the soylynge. Wherin fyrst after
his iuglyng fashyon, to carye yᵉ reder wyth wonderynge fro
markynge well the mater, thus he begynneth wyth a great grauyte,
geuynge all the worlde warnynge to be ware of me.

Lo chrysten reader, here haste thou not a taste but a great tunne full of   10
Moris myschyefe, and pernycyouse peruertynge of goddes holy worde.
And as thou seest hym here falsely and pestylently destroye the pure sense
of goddes worde: so doth he in all other places of hys bokes.

Lo good readers, now haue you a great hygh tragycall warnynge, with not a litle taste but a great tunne [z₈] full at onys, of   15
my myscheuouse pernycyouse false pestylent peruertynge and
destroyeng of yᵉ pure sense of goddes holy wordes in this one place,
whych he wyll shall stande for a playne profe that I do the same in
all other places.

Now good readers albe it that yt myght mysse happe me by   20
ouersyght to mysse handle this one place, and yet in some other to
write wel ynough: yet am I content to take the condycyon at
mayster Maskers hand, that if myne handelynge of this one place,
be such an heyghnouse handlyng, as maketh it suche a pernycyouse pestilent, not onely peruersyon, but also destruccyon of   25
the pure sense of goddes holy worde: neuer make examynacyon of
any other worde of myne farther. For I than forthwyth confesse
euen here, that I haue in al other places wryten wronge euery
whyt. [z₈v] But now on the tother syde, though you shold happe to
fynde that in this place, I haue somwhat ouer sene my selfe, in   30
mysse takynge of some one worde for an other, without theffecte of
the mater chaunged: than wyll I requyre you to take my fawte for
no greater than it is in dede / nor mysse truste all my wrytynge for
that one worde in this one place mysse taken, without thempayr-
ynge of the mater. For suche a maner mysse takynge of a worde, is   35

3 fleshe] flleshe 1533, flesh 1557   9 worlde] 1533 corr. err., 1557, worde 1533; be ware]
beware 1557   18 playne] 1533 corr. err., 1557, playnte 1533   23 handelynge] 1533 corr.
err., 1557, hadelyng 1533   26 make] made 1557   31 theffecte] thecfecte 1533, the effecte
1557

not the dystroyeng of the pure sense of goddes holy worde. And
therfore if you fynde my fawte good readers no ferther than suche:
ye wyll I dowte not of your equyte, byd mayster Masker leue his
iniquite, and chaunge his hygh tragicall termes, and turne his great
5   tunne full of pernyciouse pestilent false peruertynge poysen, into a
lytell taste of [A₁] holesome inough, though somewhat smale and
rough rochell wyne. And therfore lette vs nowe se wherin he layeth
this greate hygh hepe of myscheuouse peruertynge. Lo thus good
readers he sayth
10   Fyrste where More sayth, they merueyled at Chrystes sayenge, my flesshe
is very meate &c. that is not so. Neyther is there any suche worde in the
texte, excepte More wyll expoune murmurabant id est mirabantur. They
murmured, that is to saye they meruayled / as he expowneth oportet, id
est expedit et conuenit, he must dye, or it behoueth hym to dye / that is to
15   saye it was expedient and of good congruence that he sholde dye &c. This
poete maye make a man to sygnifye an asse, and blacke whyte, to blere
the symple eyes.
      Now good readers, I wote well that you consider that the cause
wherfore I spake of the meruaylyng that they had, whych herde
20   Chryst speke of the eatynge of his flesshe, was bycause that none of
those that herde hym at other tymes call hym selfe a vyne or a dore
meruayled any thyng therat / so that by the great difference [A₁v]
of the behauour of yᵉ herers, it might well appere that there was
greate dyfference in the spekynge / and that the tother two were
25   well perceyued to be spoken onely by waye of allegorye, and the
thyrde to be spoken of his very flesshe in dede / where as Fryth
helde opinion yᵗ thys was none otherwyse spoken, but onely by way
of an allegorye as the tother twayne were.
      Now good readers, yf you reade my wordes agayne, & in euery
30   place of them where I write they merueyled, it wolde lyke you to
put out that worde they merueyled, and set in this worde, they
murmured, in the stede therof: ye shall fynde no chaunge made in
the mater, by that chaunge made in the wordes. But you shal se
myne argument shal stand as strong with that worde, They mur-
35   *Iohan. 6*   mured / [A₂] as with this worde, they
                          merueyled. For whan at the herynge of
Chrystes wordes spekynge of the eatynge of his flesshe, the
          Iohan. 15   euangelyste sheweth that many of the
                          herers murmured / and neyther at the

callynge of hym selfe a vyne, nor at the callynge of hym selfe a

Iohan. 10

dore, none of his herers murmured for y^t
maner of spekynge: it appereth as well
the dyfference in Chrystes spekynge, by the dyfference of dyuerse
his herers at ye tone word murmurynge, and at the tother two not   5
murmurynge, as at the tone meruaylynge, and at the tother two
not meruaylynge.

Lo thus you se good readers, that in this mater in whyche
mayster masker maketh his great out cry vppon me, for
chaungynge of this worde murmuryng, into this word meruaylyng,   10
syth there is no chaunge in the [A$_2$v] mater by the chaunge of the
worde, but myne argument as stronge with the tone worde as with
the tother: I neyther haue done it of any fraude for auauntage of
myne owne parte in the mater / nor yet syth the chaunge is but in
the worde without chaunge of the mater, I haue not therby per-   15
nycyousely and pestylently by the whole tunne full of falshed at
onys, peruerted and destroyed the pure sense of goddes holy worde.
But it appereth well on the tother syde, that mayster Masker hath
geuyn vs here, I wyll not be so sore to saye a tunne full, but at the
leste wyse a lytell prety taste of hys lytell prety falshed, wyth   20
whyche a lytell he pretyly belyeth me. [A$_3$]

The .ii. chapyter.

But yet shall you now se his wyt and hys truth bothe a lytell
better tryed, euyn vpon thys same place, in whiche with hys huge
exclamacyons he maketh hys parte so playne.   25

As for oportet of whyche he speketh here, we shall talke of after
in another place. But now towchynge this worde they meruayled /
mayster Masker sayth thus. That is not so, nor there is no suche worde
in the texte. So you se good readers that he sayth two thynges. One
that it is not so, and another that there is no such worde there in y^e 30
texte. As for the word good reader I wyll not greatly stryue with
hym. But where he sayth it is not so, and therin affermeth that
they meruayled not: I thynke the wordes of the text wyll wel
mayntayn my sayeng. [A$_3$v] For good reader, whan they sayde,
How can he geue vs his flesh to eate? And whan they sayd, *Thys word is*   35

---

2 murmured] murmouren *1557*

harde and who can here it: Do not these wordes proue that they meruayled and thought it straunge, whan they called it so hard y^t no man might abide to heare it, & asked how he could do it, bycause they thought it impossible?

5   Now you se good readers, y^t the gospell sayth the selfe same thynge that I say, though it say not the self same worde / and therfore lyeth mayster Masker in sayenge it is not so.

But by thys wyse waye of mayster Masker, yf I had wryten that

2. Reg. 13

10   Absolon was angry with Ammon his brother for violatynge his syster Thamar: mayster Masker wolde say, lo good reader here thou hast not a taste but a tunne full of Morys pernicyouse peruertyng of goddys holy [A₄] word / & as thou seest hym here falsely and pestilently destroye the pure sense of goddes worde, so doth he in all other
15 places of his workes. For where he sayth y^t Absolon was angry with Ammon, it is not so, neyther is there any such worde in the texte / except More wyl expoune oderat eum, id est irascebatur ei / he hated him, y^t is to saye, he was angry with hym / as he expouneth murmurabant id est mirabantur / they murmured, that is to say
20 they meruayled. And thus maye thys poete make a man to sygnyfye an asse. For the bybble sayeth not as More sayth, that Absolon was angry with Ammon. For the texte sayeth no more, but that Absolon hated Ammon, and caused hym to be kylled.

How lyke you now good reders this wyse solucyon of mayster
25 Masker? This proueth not hym a poete [A₄v] that can make a man signyfye an asse but proueth hym rather in stede of a poete, and in stede of a man, a very starke asse in dede.

The .iii. chapyter.

B̶ut of very trouth good reader, not without a good cause and a
30 great, I dyd rather touche the thyng y^t was the cause of the Iewes murmur and theyr dyssensyon whan they dysputed vppon the mater, than I dyd theyr murmure and theyre dyssensyon. For of

5 the gospell] *1533 corr. err.,* *1557,* gospell *1533*   6 though] *1557,* thought *1533*
9 Ammon] *1533 corr. err., (though there* Anmon *is corrected to* Ammon), *1557,* Amnon *1533*
13 & as] as *1557*   16 Ammon] *1533 corr. err., 1557,* Amnon *1533*   20 they] *1557,* the *1533*
22 Absolon] *1533 corr. err., 1557,* Asolon *1533;* Ammon] *1533 corr. err., 1557,* Amnon *1533*
23 Absolon] *1533 corr. err., 1557,* Asolon *1533;* Ammon] *1533 corr. err., 1557,* Amnon *1533*

Iohan. 10

trouth where he sayd of hym self that he was a· dore: there grew dyssensyon amonge his herers vppon that worde of hys, and vpon other wordes that he spake therwith at yᵉ same tyme / so yᵗ the gospel sayth,

Iohan. 6

" *And there was dyssensyon among the Iewes* 5 *vpon these wordes / some sayenge that the deuyll was in hym and some sayeng nay, and that the deuyll* [A₅] *was not wont to make blynd men se* " / as there was here dissensyon and dysputynge vppon these wordes of eatynge of his fleshe. But in the .x. chapyter they nothynge meruayled of his callynge hym selfe a dore for he 10 expowned yᵉ parable at length so that they perceyued well that he called hym selfe a dore, but onely by waye of an allegory. And therfore of callynge hym self a dore they meruayled not of that worde when he declared yt, for they perceyued it for a parable. But they dysputed vppon that worde and vppon his other wordes also, 15

Iohan. 10

wherein he sayde that no man could kyll hym agaynst his wil, and that he wolde dye for his shepe, and that he had power to put awaye his soule and take it agayn. Of these thynges they dysputed, and thought theym straunge and meruaylouse to. [A₅v] But not for the wordes 20 or the maner of spekynge, but for the very mater. For all they vnderstode the wordes metely wel / but many of them byleued them not. But not one of theym dyd so take that worde, I am a dore, as that they meruayled howe that could be. And therfore none of them for any suche meruayle sayd there, how can he be a dore? as 25 these Iewes said here, howe can he geue vs his fleshe to eate? And therfore as I saye, therin apperreth well that our sauyour in the tone place called hym selfe a dore by waye of a parable / and in the tother spake of the eatynge of his owne very fleshe yt selfe, besydes all parables. Whyche well appered I saye by hys audyence. 30 For the tone worde they perceyued for a parable, and therfore none of theym meruayled of the maner of the spe[A₆]kynge of that worde, though they meruayled and murmured and dysputed at the thynge that the parable ment. But in the tother place, many meruayled at the thynge by the selfe same name that he gaue 35 therto, sayenge, howe can he geue vs hys fleshe to eate? whereby yt well apperreth that they perceyued that he spake of very eating of

---

6 these] those *1557*   11 expowned] expowneth *1557*

his fleshe in dede / & in ye tother place appereth not y^t they
thought he ment that he was a very dore in dede, but the contrarye playn appereth. For Chryste by his playn and open
exposycyon of that parable, delyuered theym clene from all
5   occasyon of thynkynge that he ment hym selfe to be a very dore in
dede. But in these wordes of eatynge of hys fleshe, bycause he
wolde geue hys very fleshe to be eaten in very dede, therfore he
more [A$_6$v] and more tolde them styll the same / & also tolde
theym hym selfe was god, and therfore able to do yt / and ouer
10 that gaue theym warnynge that they sholde not eate it in dede
gobbettes, but sholde eate it quycke with spyryt and lyfe. For his
wordes were spyrit and lyfe. For his fleshe sholde ellys auayle
*Note** nothyng. And that though his bodye
sholde be eaten by many sundry men in
15 many sundry places, yet sholde yt neuer the lesse be also styll
Ioh. 6 whole and sounde, where so euer he
wolde besyde. Whych he declared by his
ascensyon wyth his body perfyte into heuen, not withstandynge
that it sholde be byfore that, eaten of many men in erthe.

20 And thus haue I good reders as for this solucyon of maister
Masker, made open and playne vnto you / his falsed and his foly
both / and made yt [A$_7$] clere for all his hygh pernycyouse pestylent wordes, both that I haue handled this place of the scripture
right, & also taken rather the sentence than the word. And I haue
25 also by occasyon of his wise solucyon, caused you to perceyue that
in myne argument was and is more pyth and more strength, then
peraduentur euery man perceyued before. And therfore thus much
worshyp hath he wonne by thys his fyrste solemne solucyon.

The .iiii. chapiter.

30 But in his seconde solucyon, he specyally sheweth hys depe
insyghte and cunnynge, and myne ouersyght to shamefully. For
therein lo thus he sayth.
But yet for hys lordely pleasure, let vs graunt hym that they murmured, is
as myche to saye as they meruayled, bycause perchaunce the one may
35 folowe at the tother. And than do I aske hym whyther [A$_7$v] Chrystes

---

33 But] *1557*, Bnt *1533*   34 bycause] bycanse *1533*, because *1557*   35 tother] other *1557*

dyscyples and hys apostles, herde hym not and vnderstode hym not, when
he sayde I am the dore and the vyne, and whan he sayde my fleshe &c. If
he saye no or naye, the scrypture is playn agaynst hym Ioh. 6.10.15. If he
saye ye or yes: then yet do I aske hym whyther his dyscyples & apostles,
thus herynge and vnderstandynge his wordes in all these thre chapyters,   5
wondered and meruayled as mayster More saythe, or murmured as hath
the texte at theyre maysters speche. What thynke ye More must answere
here? here may you se whither this old holy vpholder of the popes chyrch
is brought, euyn to be taken in his owne trappe. For the discyples & hys
apostles neyther murmured nor meruayled, nor yet were not offended   10
with theyr mayster Chrystes wordes and maner of speche.

Lo good readers, here mayster Masker bycause he thynketh yt
not ynough for his worship, to shew him selfe ones a fole by his
fyrst solucion, cometh nowe farther forth to shewe him self twise a
fole, ye thryse a fole, by the secunde.   15

And fyrst for a way to come thereto, he sayth he wyll graunte
me for my lordely pleasure, that they murmured is as mych to say
as they mer[A₈]uayled. In whych grauntynge he doth me no great
lordly pleasure. For I haue as you haue herde well, proued hym al
redy that I nede not hys grauntynge therin. But veryly in the cause   20
that he addeth therto, when he sayth bycause perchaunce the tone
maye folowe at the tother, therin he doth me a very great lordely
pleasure. For yt is euyn a pleasure for a lord and for a kyng to, to
se hym play so farre the fole, as without necessytie to wryte in that
worde hym selfe, which helpeth myn argument agaynst hym self,   25
and maketh all his wonderynge yᵗ he hath in his fyrst solucyon
vppon me, fal in his own necke. For yf theyr murmuryng folowed
vppon theyre meruaylynge, as hym selfe here sayth that peraduenture yt dyd: than playeth he fyrste peraduenture the fole, to make
suche an oute[A₈v]crye vppon me for sayenge that they meruailed,   30
where the texte saith they murmured / as though I wyth that word
vtterly destroyed yᵉ pure sense of goddes holy word. For that word
dothe not so pestylently peruerte the sense, yf yt maye stande with
the sentence, as yt maye in dede, yf mayster Masker saye trewe
that peraduenture the tone maye folow vppon the tother / that is   35
to wit the murmuryng vppon the meruaylynge, for so he meaneth
therby. For as madde as he is, he is not I thynke so madde yet, as

7 speche. What] *1557*, speche what *1533*   15 secunde] secnnde *1533*, second *1557*
28–29 peraduenture] *1557*, peaduenture *1533*

to meane that the meruaylynge folowed vppon the murmurynge.
For they meruayled fyrst and murmured after. And nowe syth this
one worde of his therfore, ouer throweth all his wondering, that he
hath made on me, and proueth hym selfe willyngly and wyttyngly
5   in all his hygh tragycall [B₁] exclamacyon agaynst his own conscy-
ence, and his own very knowledge to bylye me: he hathe therin as
I saye done me a very special pleasure, to se him so farre play the
fole, as to bring forth that worde hym self / specyally where there
was no nede at all, but euen for a garnyshe of his induccion, wyth
10 a shewe of his cunnynge, to make men know that he hadde not so
lytle lernynge, but that he wyst well ynough hym selfe that he had
shamefully bylyed me in all that euer he hadde cryed oute agaynst
me, concernynge any mysse constrewyng of that place of holy
scrypture.

15   The .v. chapyter.

N owe after thys hys double folye well and wysely putte forth at
ones, he bryngeth me to myn opposycyon. And therin he handeleth me so hardly, yᵗ I can not scape, which [B₁v] waye so euer I
take, whether I say that Chrystes dyscyples and apostles herde and
20 vnderstode theyr maysters wordes in all the thre places, or that I
saye that in any one of those thre places they vnderstode him not.
For here to be sure to holde me in on both sydes that I scape not,
he sheweth what daungeour I fal in, whyche waye so euer I take.
For he sayeth that on the tone syde I denye the gosspell yf I
25 answere no or naye, and on the tother syde I am taken in myn
owne trappe, yf I saye ye or yes.

And surely here he playeth the wysest poynte and the moste for
hys owne suertye, that I sawe hym play yet. For ye shall vnderstand that in the fyrste parte of my Confutacyon in the thyrd boke
30 the .clxxx. syde, for as myche as Tyndale hathe ben so longe out of
England, that he could [B₂] not tell howe to vse these englyshe
aduerbys, naye and no, ye and yes: I gaue hym a rule and a
certayne samples of yᵉ rule, wherby he mighte lerne where he shold
answere naye, and where no, and where ye & where yes.

35 Nowe mayster Masker whan he wrote hys boke, neyther
hauynge my boke by hym, nor the rule by hart thoughte he wolde

---

19 take, whether] take. whether *1533*, take. Whether *1557*

be sure that I sholde fynde no suche faute in hym / and therfore on the tone syde for the answere, assygneth ye and yes both / and on the tother syde bothe naye and no / leuynge the choyce to my selfe, whyche he durst not well take vpon him, lest he myght shew therin suche congruytie in the Englyshe tonge, as he sheweth in some other thynges wherin he speketh englyshe as congrewe, as a man myghte that [B₂v] hadde lerned his englishe in a nother lande.

But now muste I answere hym to his subtyll questyons. His fyrste questyon is thys.

He asketh me, whether Chrystes dyscyples and his apostles, hard him not and vnderstode hym not, whan he sayde, I am the dore, and whan he sayde, I am the vyne, and whan he sayde, my fleshe is veryly meate &c.

Mayster Maskar is so wyly that I must nedes take better hede what I answere him, than I shold nede, yf I were to answere a good plain man of the countrey. For maister Maskar in y^e .29. lefe bosteth hym selfe of his connynge ryally and sayth. It ys veryly the thyng that I desyre euen to be wryten agaynste in thys mater. For I haue the solucyons of al theyr obieccyons redy.

Now syth therfore this man is so cunnynge, and hath his answerys so [B₃] redy for all obieccyons that men may lay to hym: he can not be by lykelyhed but wonderfull sure & redy, with subtyll replycacions, agaynst all answeres that men maye make to those opposycions that he deuiseth agaynst other men him self. I wyll therfore be as ware of him as I can. And fyrst I say that his questyon is captiouse. For he asketh one answere to thre thynges at onys / and in eche of the thre he asketh me two questyons at ones. For he asketh of ye dore, and the vyne, and of his fleshe, all thre at ones. And yet of eche of these not a double question as I told you / but a quatreble questyon at ones. For he asketh both of his apostles and the disciples / and not onely whether all these herde Chryste at all thre tymes, but also whyther all these vnderstode hym. And all twelue questyons [B₃v] mayster Masker wylyly to bygyle suche a symple soule as I am, asketh in one questyone at ones. And therfore leste he betrappe me, I shall some what at the leste wyse dyuyde theym.

1–2 on the] *1557*, onthe *1533*   5 Englyshe] Englishe *1557*, Englyhhe *1533*
22 lykelyhed] lyklelyded *1533*, likelihod *1557*

And than I saye to the fyrste questyon whyther Chrystes dyscyples and apostles harde hym not and vnderstode hym not, when
he sayde I am the dore: because the questyon ys yet double and
captyouse, I purpose to make sure worke & answere, that I can not
5 tel, I thinke that some dyd and some dyd not, for some of them I
wene were not there.

Nowe yf he saye that he meaneth onely them that were there: so
wold I to haue taken hym, yf he were a good playne soule, and not
suche a sotle sophystre that longeth to be arguynge, and hath all
10 thynge so redy [B₄] vppon his fyngers endes.

But go to nowe, though I could yet haue other answeres for hym
yf I wolde: yet for hys lordely pleasure I shalbe content to graunt
hym, that they bothe herde hym and vnderstode hym / wherin I
graunte hym more yet I promyse you, than he can precysely bynde
15 me to by the texte. All thys grauntynge for this place geueth hym
no grounde yet. For here I am well contente, not onely to say al
that he sayth, that is yᵗ his apostles and his discyples vnderstode
that Chryste calleth hym selfe the dore but by a parable / and
therfore meruailed not at yᵗ maner of speking. But I saye more to,
20 that so dyd also the Iewes that reproued hym and repugned
agaynste hym. And saye also that they repugned so myche the
more agaynste hym, and so myche [B₄v] the more murmured and
disputed agaynst the mater, in how myche they more vnderstode
the maner of yᵉ spekynge and that it was but a parable. For they
25 wyste well that worde of the dore, was spoken by a parable, for
Christ playnly expowned it. But they murmured myche at that yᵗ
no man might well come in but by hym.

Let vs now to yᵉ secund than. And where he asketh me whyther
Chrystes dyscyples and his apostles, herde hym not and vnderstode
30   Ioh. 15   him not, when he sayde, I am the very
                                     vyne: here I wolde for myne owne
suertye aske hym, whyther he meane by Christes discyples and
apostles, some of both sortes, or ellys those disciples onely that were
both dyscyples & apostles. How be it yf I shold aske him thus he
35 wolde say I dyd but tryfle / & that [B₅] euery man maye well
wytte by the puttynge of hys questyon, that he meneth of eyther

---

17 his discyples] dis discyples *1533*, his Disciples *1557*   24 that it was but a parable] *1533*
corr. err., *1557*, that parable *1533*   34 apostles.] apostles, *1533*, Apostles. *1557*

sorte some. For els he wolde haue sayd no more but apostles which
had ben inough if he had ment but them. And also it were
agaynste his purpose, yf Chrystes other dysciples vnderstode hym
not, though his apostles dyd. Well I am content than to take it so.
And than vnto the questyon, whyther his discyples and apostles   5
harde not Chryste and vnderstode hym not, whan he sayd I am
the very vyne: to this questyon copulatyue I answere no.

But than mayster Masker replyeth, that the scrypture is playne
agaynste me. But vnto that replycacyon I say naye. For I saye that
the scrypture there wyth saynt Marke & saynt Luke set vnto it,   10
proueth myne answere trewe. For it appereth well [B₅v] amonge
them thre, that bysyde thapostles, none of his other dyscyples
vnderstode hym, for none of his other dyscyples herde hym, for
none of his other dyscyples were there, nor yet all his .xii. apostles
neyther / for Iudas was gone before. So that in this parte of his   15
fyrste questyon, mayster Masker hath geuen hym selfe a fall in the
subtyll proponynge of his questyon. As to the vnderstandynge, I
agre that they that were there vnderstode hym, whiche maketh
nothynge agaynst me.

Now to the thyrde place whan he asketh me whyther Chrystes   20
dyscyples & his apostles herd hym not and vnderstode hym not,
whan he sayed, my flesh is very mete &c. Fyrste as for his dyscyples I saye no not all. Than sayth mayster Masker that yf I say
nay or no, the scrypture is [B₆] playne agaynst me. Iohan. 6. But
to that say I agayne, that whan I saye no, yᵉ scripture is euyn there   25
with me. For as the gospell there playnely telleth, many of his
dyscyples though they herd hym well, dyd vnderstand hym amysse.
For though they vnderstode hym ryght, in that they perceyued
that he spake of the very eatyng of his very fleshe: yet they vnderstode hym wronge, in that they toke hym that they shold eate it in   30
the self flesshely forme & in dede pyeces with out lyfe or spyryte /
and therfor they went theyr waye from hym and lefte hym, and
walked no more after with hym. Here hath mayster masker
another fall in thys place to, towchyng his fyrst questyon as for yᵉ
dyscyples.

But what saye we than for thapostles? dyd not they vnderstand   35
hym? what yf I here wolde say naye? than [B₆v] except mayster
Masker could proue yes, ellys is not onely his fyrst questyon gone,
whyche he maketh for a waye to the secunde / but his secunde

questyon is clerely gone to, wherwith he wolde make me be taken
in myne owne trappe. And therfore fyrste for argument sake, I
denye that thapostles them selfe vnderstode Chrystes worde. How
wyll now mayster Masker proue me y^t they dyd, Mary sayth he;
5   for they were well acquaynted wyth suche phrasys. And answered theyr
mayster Chryst whan he asked theym, wyll you go hense fro me to? Lorde
sayd they to whom shall we go, thou hast the wordes of euerlastynge lyfe /
& we byleue that thou arte Chryste the sone of the lyuynge god.

Now good reader I thynke there be some textes in scrypture that
10 mayster Masker vnderstandeth not no more than other pore men.
But yet yf he wyll not agre that, but say that he vnderstandeth
them all: yet yf we wolde [B$_7$] put y^e case that there were some
such one texte, he wold I thynke admytte the case for possible. Let
vs than put him hardely none other, but euyn the same wordes of
15 Chryste that we be now in hande wythall. For no man vnderstandeth any word wurse than he vnderstandeth those, euyn yet whyle
he wryteth on them. If hym selfe had ben than of that flocke, and
had sene all other thynges in Chryst that his apostles saw, and had
byleued in hym, and had not mysse trusted Chryste, but ben redy
20 to do what he wolde byd hym do, and byleue what he wolde byd
hym byleue / but had yet as for those wordes of eatynge Chrystes
flesshe thought them hard to perceyue what Chryste ment by
theym / but though he fully vnderstode them not as he thought,
yet he dowted not but that good they were [B$_7$v] that god spake,
25 and that Chryst if he taryed hys tyme, wold tell hym ferther of the
mater at more leysour: yf now whan other went theyr waye,
Chryst wolde haue sayde vnto hym, wylte thou mayster Masker go
thy waye fro me to? whyther wold than mayster Masker haue
letted to saye euyn the selfe same wordes that the apostles sayd
30 with other lyke, whyther sholde I go fro the good lorde? Thou
haste the wordes of euerlastynge lyfe, & I byleue and knowe that
thou arte Chryst the sone of the lyuyng god, and art able to do
what thou wylte, and thy wordes be holy and godly whyther I
vnderstande them or no / and thou mayst make me perceyue them
35 better at thy ferther pleasure. Wold mayster masker haue ben
contented to saye thus: or ellys wolde he haue sayd? Nay by my

---

11 agre] agre to *1557*   11–12 vnderstandeth them all] *1533 corr. err.*, *1557*, vnderstandeth
1533   30 the good] thee good *1557*

fay [B₈] good lorde, thou shalte tell me this tale a litel more playnly y^t I may better perceyue it by & by, or els wyll I go to the deuyll with yender good felowes, and lette theym dwell wyth the that wyll.

Now yf mayster Masker wolde (as I wene he wolde but yf he were starke madde) haue sayde the same hym selfe that saynt Peter sayde / or be content at the lest that saynt Peter sholde saye it for hym, though hym selfe hadde not well and clerely perceyued what Chryste ment by those wordes: How can he nowe proue by the same wordes of theyrs, that thapostles vnderstode hys wordes than.

Thus you se good readers, that of his two questyons, the fyrst haue I so answered that it is come to nothynge / (yf I wolde stycke wyth [B₈v] hym styll at hys answere) tyll he haue better proued me than he hath yet, that thapostles in the syxte chapyter of saynt Iohan dyd vnderstand Cristes wordes. And now therfore tyll he haue better handeled hys fyrst questyon, he can agaynste me neuer vse his secunde, wherby he bosteth that I coulde make none answere, but suche as sholde take my self in myne own trappe. From whych syth I am clene ascaped all redy, by the answerynge of his fyrste questyon, you may good readers se, that mayster Masker goth as wylyly to worke to take me, as a man myghte sende a chylde about wyth salt in hys hand, and byd hym go cache a byrde, by layenge a lytell salt on her tayle / & whan ye bird is flowen, comforte hym than to go cache another, and tell hym he hadde caught y^t and it had taryed a lytell. [C₁]

The .vi. chapyter.

But yet to se now how craftely he could betrappe me if I wold let hym alone: Let vs graunte hym for hys lordly pleasure, that the dyscyples and apostles vnderstode Christes wordes well in all thre

	places, not onely whan he sayd he was
Iohan. 10	the dore / and whan he sayde he was the
Iohan. 15	vyne / but also whan he sayde, my flesshe
	is veryly meate. What now? Mary than

sayth mayster Masker,

If More answere ye or yes: than do I aske hym ferther, whyther Chrystes dyscyples and apostles thus herynge and vnderstandynge hys wordes in al the thre chapyters, wondered & merueyled (as More sayth) or murmured (as hath the texte) at theyr maysters speche. What thynke you More

muste answere here? here maye you se whyther this olde holy vpholder of
the popys chyrche is brought, euyn to be taken in hys own trappe. For the
dyscyples and hys apostles neyther murmured nor meruayled, nor yet
were not offended wyth this theyr mayster Chrystes wordes and maner of
5 spekynge.

In what trappe of myne owne or his eyther, hath mayster
Masker [C₁v] caught me here? Mine

Iohan. 10   argument was ye wote well, yᵗ at the

Iohan. 15   herynge Cryst saye, I am the dore, & I
10   am the very vyne: no man meruayled at
the maner of spekynge, bycause that euery man perceyued his

Ioh. 6   wordes for allegoryes & parables. But in
the thyrd place where he sayde, *" My
flesshe ys veryly meate, And the brede that I shall geue you is my flesshe. And
15 excepte you eate the flesshe of the sone of man, and drynke his bloude, you
shall not haue lyfe in you:"* so many meruayled bycause they perceyued well it was not a parable but that he spake of very eatynge
of his flesshe in dede, that of all his herers very few could abyde it,
but murmured & sayd how can he gyue vs his flesshe to eate. And
20 his own dyscyples sayd, Thys worde is harde, who maye here hym /
and went almost all theyr way. Now whan theffecte of myne [C₂]
argument is, that in this poynt many meruayled at the thynge, as a
thynge playnely spoken, and not a parable, but a playne tale that
men sholde veryly eate his flesshe / and that no man meruayled at
25 the tother two maner of spekynges, bycause they perceyued them
for parables: what maketh it agaynste me, that in the thyrde place
there were some that meruayled not nor murmured not syth that
though some dyd not, yet many dyd, & bothe meruailed & murmured & went theyr way, & that farre the moste part, and saue
30 the apostles almost euerichone. And veryly the tother dyscyples as
saynt Chrysostome sayth, those that than were present (agaynst
mayster maskers sayeng) went theyr wayes all the maynye.

Where is now good readers thys trappe of myne owne makynge,
that [C₂v] I am fallen in? hath mayster Masker caste me downe so
35 depe, with prouynge me that some meruayled not, where I sayd
many dyd? Be these two proposicions so sore repugnaunt and so
playne contradyctory: Many meruayled, and some meruailed not,
that bycause I sayd the fyrste, and he proueth the secund, therfor
I am quyte caste and caught in myne owne trappe? This man is a
40 wyly shrewe in argument I promyse you.

The .vii. chapyter.

Bvt now that I haue good readers so fayre escaped my trappe I
truste with the helpe of some holy saynt, to cach mayster Masker
in his owne trappe, that his maystershyppe hath made for me.

Ye wote well good readers, that the trappe whiche he made for
me, [C₃] were these two wyly capcyouse questyons of his, with
whych he thought to cache me / that is to wytte, fyrste whyther the
dyscyples and apostles hard and vnderstode our sauyour in all thre
places / and than vpon myne answere ye or yes, his other questyon
ferther, whyther they meruayled or murmured. Vnto whyche
whyle I haue answered no: now by the trappys of his questyons he
rekeneth me dreuyn to be caught in myne owne, bycause I sayd
that many merueyled / as though many other might not bycause
the apostles dyd.

Now before I shewe you howe hym selfe is taken in his own
trappe ye shall here his owne gloryouse wordes with which he
bosteth yᵗ he hath taken me, & wolde make men wene it were so.
Lo these are his wordes.

Here may you se, whether thys olde holy vpholder of the popys chyrche is
brought, euyn to be taken in [C₃v] hys owne trappe. For the dyscyples
and his apostles neyther murmured nor meruayled, nor yet were not
offended wyth this theyr mayster Chrystes wordes and maner of speche.
For they were well acquainted wyth such phrases, & answered theyr
mayster Cryst when he asked theym, wyll ye go hence fro me to? Lorde
sayd they to whome shall we go? thou haste the wordes of euerlastyng
lyfe, & we byleue yᵗ thou art Chryste the sone of the lyuynge god. Lo
mayster more, they neyther merueyled nor murmured. And why? For
bycause as ye saye, they vnderstode it in an allegorye sence, and perceyued well that he ment not of hys materyall body to be eaten wyth
theyr teth / but he ment it of hym selfe to be byleued to be very god and
very man, hauynge flesshe and bloude as they had, and yet was he the
sone of the lyuynge god. Thys bylyefe gathered they of all hys spyrytuall
sayenges, as hym selfe expouneth hys owne wordes sayenge, My flesshe
profyteth nothynge, meanynge to be eaten: but it is the spyryte that
geueth this lyfe. And the wordes that I speke vnto you are spyryte and
lyfe. So that who so byleue my flesshe to be crucyfyed and broken, and
my bloude to be shede for hys synnes, he eateth my flesshe and drynketh
my bloud, and hath lyfe euerlastyng. And thys is the lyfe wherwyth the
ryghtuouse lyueth euen by fayth. Abacuk .2.

---

12 dreuyn] drieuen 1557

Lo good reader here haue I rehersed you his wordes whole to thende. And yet bycause you shall se that I wyll not hyde from you any pyece of [C₄] hys, that may make for any strength of his mater: I shal reherse you ferther his other wordes wryten in his 13.

5 lefe, whyche I wolde haue touched before, sauynge that I thought to reserue it for hym, to strength withall thys place of his, where it myght do hym best seruyce / where he wold proue agaynst me to trappe me with, that the cause why the dyscyples and apostles merueyled not, nor murmured not, nor were not offended, was

10 bycause they vnderstode Chrystes wordes to be spoken not of very eatynge of hys flesshe, but onely of the bylyefe of his passyon by waye of a parable or an allegorye / as he spake those other wordes whan he sayed, I am yᵉ dore, & whan he

Iohan. 10   sayd, I am the vyne. The wordes lo of M.

15   *Iohan. 15*   Masker with which he setteth forth the
profe of this point in his .13. lefe be these, in [C₄v] the ende of all his exposycyon vpon the syxt chapyter of saynt Iohan.

Here is lo the conclusyon of all thys sermon. Chryst very god and man

20 had set hys flesshe byfore them to be receyued with fayth, that it sholde be broken and suffre for theyr synne. But they coulde not eate it spiry-tually, bycause they byleued not in hym. Wherfore many of hys dyscyples fyll from hym and walked no more wyth hym. And than he sayd to the .xii. wyll ye go away to? And Symon Peter answered: Lorde to whome

25 shall we go? Thou haste the wordes of euerlastynge lyfe, and we byleue and are sure that thou arte Chryste the sone of the lyuynge god. Here it is manyfest what Peter and his felowes vnderstode by this eatynge and drynkynge of Chryste. For they were perfytely taught that it stode all in the bylyefe in Chryst, as theyr answere here testyfyeth. If this mater had

30 stode vppon so depe a myracle as our papystes fayne, wythout any word of god not comprehended vnder any of theyr comen senses, that they shold eate hys body vnder forme of brede, as longe, depe, thycke, and as brode as it hangeth vppon the crosse, they beynge yet but feble of fayth not confermed with the holy goost, muste here nedes haue wondered,

35 stonied, and staggered, and haue ben more inquisytyue in and of so straunge a mater, than they were. But they neyther dowted, nor mer-ueyled nor murmured, nor nothynge offended wyth this maner of speche, as were the other that slypte away / but they answered fermely: Thou

---

21 But] *1533 corr. err., 1557,* Cut *1533*   23 fyll] fell *1557*   35 stonied] stonned *1557*

hast the wordes of euerlastynge lyfe, and we byleue &c. Now to the exposycyon of the wordes of our lordes sowper. [C₅]

Lo good readers, ye wyll I trow nowe bere me recorde, that I dele playnly with mayster Maskar here, and hyde nothynge of his a syde that maye do hym any substancyall seruyce / towarde the 5
profe of hys purpose. And I warraunt you yt shalbe long ere you fynde hym or any of all that secte, deale in suche playne maner wyth me.

But nowe good Christen reader, reade al these whole wordes of hys in both yᵉ places as often as you lyst, and consyder theym well / 10
and than shal you perceyue in conclusyon, yᵗ he proueth hys purpose by none other thynge in all this worlde, than onely by his owne wordes expownynge al way the wordes of Chryste as mayster Maskar lyste hym self. And vppon that that hym selfe sayeth, that the cause wherfore the disciples [C₅v] and apostles meruayled not, 15
nor murmured not at these wordes of Christ, *The brede yᵗ I shall geue you is my flesh &c.* was bycause they perceyued that Chryste spake yt in a parable (as I say of his other wordes, I am the dore, and I am the very vyne) vppon these wordes of mayster Maskers owne, mayster Maskar concludeth for his purpose, the selfe same thynge 20
that he fyrste presupposeth, the thyng that he shold not presuppose but preue, that is to wyt that Chryst spake yt but by way of a parable.

But agaynste mayster Maskar and his presumptuouse presup-
posynge, the mater appereth playne. For 25
Iohan. 10   as I haue byfore sayde, our sauyour
Iohan. 15   whan he sayd, I am the dore, and when
he sayde, I am the very vyne, dyd so
prosecute and declare in [C₆] bothe the places his owne wordes,
that there coulde no man haue cause to meruayle at the maner of 30
spekynge for his owne declaracyon in prosecutynge his owne
wordes was suche, that it muste nedes make any man (but yf he
were an idiote or an asse) perceyue that Chryste spake in those two
places yᵗ he was the vyne & the dore but by waye of a parable.
And this may euery man sone se yᵗ lyst to loke on yᵉ places. And 35
therfore no man sayd howe can he be a vyne, nor how can he be a

---

12 worlde] worde *1533*, word *1557*   21 presupposeth,] *1557*, presupposeth *1533*
22 preue] prooue *1557*   24 presumptuouse] presumpteous *1557*   27 *gloss* Iohan, 15]
Iohan. 51 *1533*, Iohn. 15 *1557*

dore, as many sayd in the thyrde place, *"How can he geue vs his fleshe to eate."* Whyche wordes, yf they were so clerely spoken but by waye of parable, as the tother twayne were, yt were farre vnlykely that so many wyse men wolde haue taken it so farre
5   otherwyse euer synnes, that take the tother twayne / [C₆v] for none other. And namely such holy doctours and sayntes, as are well acquaynted wyth Chrystes phrases and parables / and in the studye therof, haue spent the great parte of all theyr lyues. And therfore mayster Maskar agaynst so many wyse men and so good, goynge
10 about nowe to proue this poynte but a parable, by none other substancyall meane, than onely by thauthoryte of hys owne worshyp-full worde, proueth vs hys purpose very faynte and slender, for all his lo Mayster More, as though hys purpose appered very clear.

The .viii. chapyter.

15 Howe be yt for to furnyshe hys mater with, and to set it the better forth, bycause he wolde not haue yt seme to stande all vppon his owne onely exposycyon, that ys to [C₇] wyt vppon his owne onely worde: he setteth vnto his owne bare word, hys owne bare balde reason, and sayth.
20 If thys mater had stode vppon so depe a myracle as oure papystes fayne, without any worde of god not comprehended vnder any of theyr commen sensys, that they shold eate his body beynge vnder the forme of brede, as longe, depe, thykke, and as brode as yt hanged vppon the crosse: they beyng yet but feble of fayth, not confyrmed wyth the holy goste, muste
25 here nedes haue wondered, stonned, and staggred / and haue ben more inquysytyue in and of so straunge a mater than they were. But they neyther meruayled nor murmured / nor nothynge offended wyth thys maner of speche / as were the other that slypte awaye, but they answered fermely. Thou haste the wordes of euerlastynge lyfe, and we byleue &c.
30 Now to the exposycyon of the wordes of our lordes souper.

Here hath mayster Maskar geuen vs a maior of an argument, and a minor to. His maior is his fyrste parte vnto these wordes, But they &c. and his minor is al the remnaunt. But we maye nowe aske hym ergo what? For conclusyon he setteth none vnto theym. If he
35 thynke the conclu[C₇v]syon folowe so clere that he neded not, but

---

21 worde of god] *1533 corr. err.*, *1557*, worde *1533*   33 remnaunt] remaunt *1533*, remenant *1557*

euery man muste nedes se what foloweth vppon his two premysses:
in good fayth for my parte yf I sholde set ergo to yt, that ys the
comen note of the consequente, I se not what wold folow any more
then the commen verse of the compute manuell, Ergo ciphos
adrifex, he hathe made his maior so folyshely.   5

    In whych that fyrst yt pleaseth his maystershyppe to tryfle &
mocke in this great mater, & make vs pore people wene / that
euery thynge that any doctour sayth in dyspycyons, or holdeth by
way of probleme, were delyuered vs to byleue as a necessary
poynte of our fayth: he doth but play the false fole for his pleasure.   10

We be not bounde
to belieue all
*these thinges**

For as for the maner how the blessed
bodye of Chryste is in the blessed
sacrament, whyther with his dymen-
sy[C₈]ons, as long, thycke, and brode, as
he hanged on the crosse, or with his dymensyons proporcionable to   15
the forme of brede, as his blessed bodye was as veryly his bodye in
the fyrst moment of his holy concepcyon, as yt euer was at his
passion / and yet was yt than neyther so thycke, so longe, nor so
brode / or whyther his body be there in his naturall substaunce,
without any dymensyons at all / or whyther he be there in all his   20
distynctyons of the members of his holy bodye, or there haue al his
members without any distinctyon of place at all: these thinges and
suche other in whiche lerned men maye moderately and reuerently
dyspute and exercyse theyr witte and lernynge, the catholyque
chyrche in suche wyse leueth at large, that yt byndeth not the   25
people to any suche strayghtes in the mater, but onely to the
poyntes that we be bounden [C₈v] by certayne and sure reuelacyon, to byleue / that is to wytte, that vnder what maner so euer yt
be there, veryly there yt is, his very fleshe and hys very blood.
And in the forme of brede veryly eate hys very bodye there we do,   30
when we receyue the very blessed sacrament. Thus farre haue we
by certayne and sure reuelacyon, bothe by holy scrypture, and by
the tradycyon also, by whych Chryst taught yt to hys apostles
and they to the chyrche, as saynte Poule dyd to the

1. Cori. 11

Corinthyes, and the chyrch to the people   35
by succession from age to age euer syn
thapostles dayes vnto our owne tyme.

---

21 bodye] *1557*, hodye *1533*; al his] his *1557*   35–36 *gloss* 1. Cori. 11] *om. 1557*

And therfore wyth those mockes and iestes, mayster Maskar mocketh no man but hym selfe / saue that vnder the name of papystes, he mocketh all the catholyque chyrche [D₁] of this .xv. hundred yere both clergy and temporaltye, men and women, and
5 all / and amonge the remanaunt, all the olde holy doctours and sayntes that haue wythout doute or questyon both byleued and taught, that Crist ment not to speke those wordes: *My fleshe is very meate*, by waye of a parable, as mayster Masker sayth he onely ment / but that he veryly spake and ment of the very eatynge of
10 hys fleshe in dede.

But now shall you se that as I sayd, his maior is so folishely made, that al the world may wonder where his wytte was when he made yt. For he sayth that yf the mater stode in dede, vppon such a great myracle as the catholyque chyrche (whyche he calleth the
15 papystes) byleue, that is to wyt that his very bodye sholde be eaten in forme of brede / and that [D₁v] also (whyche he putteth for a necessary parte of our fayth) as longe, as depe, as thycke, and as brode as yt was whanne yt hanged on the crosse: than the dyscyples and apostles (bycause they were yet but feble in the fayth)
20 muste nedes haue wondered, stonned, and stagerd, and haue bene more inquysytyue therein then they were. Nowe woteth well euery chylde good reader, that Chryst dyd not in that place, playnely tell theym in what maner that they shold eat yt / that is to wyt that they shold eate yt in forme of brede. For though he gaue them an
25   *Iohan. 6*   insynuacyon & sygnyfycacyon therof, in
                                 that he sayde, *And the brede that I shall gyue you is my flesshe* / whyche wordis coupled with his dede when he dyd
            Mat. 26   instytute it in dede at hys maundy, myghte then make theym clerely per-
30 ceyue that they [D₂] sholde eate hys flesshe in forme of brede: yet at the tyme when the worde was fyrste spoken, yt was not so playne for that mater, but yt myght seme to theym that he vsed that worde brede but by maner of allegorye to sygnyfye there his fleshe, bycause they sholde veryly eate yt as men eate brede.
35 Now se than good reader the madnesse of mayster Maskar, that

---

25 insynuacyon] insinuacion *1557*, insynnacyon *1533*   27 wordis] woorde is *1557*
28 instytute it] *1533 corr. err.*, *1557*, instytute *1533*   28–29 *gloss* Mat. 26] Math. 16 *1557*
30 eate hys flesshe] *1533 corr. err.*, *1557*, eate fleshe *1533*

sayeth here, that that thyng must nedes haue made thapostles
wonder, stonned, and stagger, at the time when Christ spake those
wordes in the sext chapyter of saynt Iohan / at whych tyme euery
chyld knoweth, y^t they though they well perceyued that they
sholde veryly eate his fleshe, yet they knew not that they shold eate   5
it in forme of bred. And how could it than haue made them
wonder (that thyng I say that [D$_2$v] he spekethe of, and so sore
exaggerateth to encrease the wonder) that ys to wytte that his
fleshe sholde be eaten in forme of bred, and that as long as thycke,
as depe, and as brode, as yt was whan yt hanged on the crosse.   10
Howe coulde thys thyng I saye haue made theym wonder at that
tyme, at whyche tyme they thoughte not of the eatynge therof in
the forme of brede? Herd euer any man suche a madde argument,
as mayster Maskar hathe made vs here.

Nowe yf Chryste had there told theym in dede, all that mayster   15
Maskar hath here putte in so folyshely, to make the mater the
more wonderful: than wolde I denye hys maior. And so wyll I do if
hym self putte al that oute agayne, and leue no more in hys maior
than Chryste sayde in dede, [D$_3$] that is that they sholde veryly
eate his fleshe & haue life therby, & y^t they shold not onely eate it   20
bodyly but also spyrytually / nor in dede gobettes wythoute lyfe or

How Chrystes
*fleshe gueth lyfe**

spyryte, but quycke and ioyned wyth the
lyuely spyryte, by whyche yt sholde geue
lyfe, and wythoute whyche his fleshe of
hys owne proper nature to the geuynge of lyfe, coulde not auayle.   25
Nowe saye I that yf mayster Masker hadde made his maior of this:
all this had ben no cause for hys apostles to wonder, nor to be
stonned and stagger, nor to murmure and grudge as they dyd that
slypte awaye. For as feble as mayster Maskar maketh thapostles in
the fayth of Crist: yet at that tyme wythoute any suche maner of   30
meruayle, as myght make theym stonne and stagger and slyppe
away from hym, they byleued suche [D$_3$v] other thynges as were
as harde to byleue as this, and that wythout any farther inquysycyon at all.

For elles why sholde they not at the same time haue meruayled   35
of his ascensyon vppe to heuen, and bene more inquysytyue therof.

For that was no lytle meruayle neyther, and was one of the thynges /
that made ye Iewes and those disciples to stonne and stagger, that
there slypte awaye from hym.

Also they byleued y^t he was god / and hadde no such wonder
5 therof, as made theym stonne and stagger or be more inqisytyue
therof, whyche was as straunge a mater as was al the tother / and
which poynt ones byleued, yt was ethe to byleue the tother without
any suche maner of meruaylyng, as shold make them eyther stonne
or stagger therat. [D_4]

10 Nowe as for beynge inquisytyue therof: holy saint Chrisostome
saith, that as straunge as the thing was of eatynge his fleshe, (For y^t
men hadde ben rysen from deth they had herd of in y^e scripture
before / but y^t one shold eate a nothers flesh saith saint Chrisostome, that had they neuer herd of) yet they byleued Christes word
15 and folowed forth styll, & confessed y^t he had the wordes of euerlastyng lyfe, and wold not be by & by curiouse and inquisytiue as
mayster Maskar saith they wold, yf they had byleued hym that he
ment of eatyng of his flesh in dede. For saynt Chrysostome sayth,

That is y^e parte of a discyple, what so
The part of a
20 *disciple**   euer his mayster affermeth, not to be
curyouse and inquysytyue therof, nor to
make serche therin, but to heare and byleue, and yf they wolde
any thynge forther be enformed / abyde a conuenyent tyme. For

they that dyd [D_4v] otherwyse & were
Crisosto. hom. 45.
25 *in. 6. cap. Iohan.*   inquisytyue, went awaye backe, and that
thorow theyr foly. For sayth saynt
Chrysostome,

" *Whan so euer it comth in the mynde, to aske the questyon how the thynge*
may be done: than cometh there in to the mynde incredulyte therwith. So was
30   *Nichodemus troubled & asked, How maye a*
Note*   *man be borne agayne whan he is olde? Maye a*
Iohan. 3   *man entre agayne into his mothers bely and be*
borne agayn? And so the Iewes sayd here to:
how can he gyue vs his flesh to eate? But thou Iewe yf thou aske that, why
35 *dydest thou not aske that in lyke wise in the myracle of the fyue louys: why*
dydest thou not than aske how can he fede so many of vs with so lytell mete.

---

11 fleshe, (For] fleshe. For *1533*, fleshe. (For *1557*   18 eatyng of] eating *1557*
23 forther] further *1557*   28 comth] commeth *1557*

nunquid docibiles erant dei? Quid hoc in loco eximium eft? Quod tunc per homines res di
uinas docebantur,nunc per unigenitum & fpiritum fanctum:deinde inquit, Non quia pa c
trem uidit quifquam,nifi is qui à deo eft.)Non fecundum caufæ rationem hic loquitur, fed
fecundum modum fubftantiæ.Nam fi diceret,Omnes à deo fumus:ubi præftantia & diffe
rentia filij? Sed quare non apertius dixit? Propter illorum imbecillitatem.Etenim fi dicen
do,de cœlo defcendi,tantum fcandalizati funt:quidnam feciſſent fi id addidiſſet? Pane au
tem uitæ feipfum appellat,quoniam uitam noftra & hanc & futuram corroborat.Et inquit:
    Si quis manducauerit ex hoc pane,uiuet in æternu.)Panem uero fiue doctrinam hoc in lo
co & falute & fidem in fe,fiue corpus fuum dicit.Vtrunq; enim animam fortiore reddit.At
qui alibi dixit:Si quis fermonem meu audierit,mortem non guftabit,& perturbati funt: hic
non itidem,quia iam ob panis miraculum eum reuerebantur. Animaduerte aute quam fa
ciat huius panis & mannæ differentia,ab utriufq; fcilicet fine. Quod enim manna nihil ma
gnum præberet,addidit: Patres ueftri manducauerunt manna in deferto,& mortui funt.)
inde fubdit maxima perfuafionem,quod longe pluris,maioribus illis patribus Mofe & cla
ris illoru temporu uiris ipfi habiti fint. Cum enim dixiſſet mortuos qui mana comediſſent,
profecutus eft: Hic eft panis de cœlo defcendes,ut fi quis ex ipfo manducauerit,non mo
riatur.Ego fum panis uiuus, qui de cœlo defcendi,qui manducat ex hoc pane, uiuet in æter
num.)Illa præterea particula,In deferto,manna nó diu duraſſe,neq; in terram promiſſionis
ueniſſe fignificat.Hic aute panis non eft eiufmodi. Et panis quem ego dabo,caro mea eft
pro mundi uita.)Merito hoc in loco dubitare quifpiam poſſet,cur hæc nunc Chriftus loque
retur,cum nihil proficeret,nihil ædificaret,imo eſſet ædificatis nocumeto? Ex hoc enim,in
quit,multi ex difcipulis fuis retro abierunt:&,Durus eft hic fermo,quis poteft eum audire?)
Erant igitur hæc folis difcipulis comunicanda, ut Matthæus priuatim cum ipfis loqui tefta
tur.Quid ad hoc dicemus? Quænam horum uerborum utilitas? Magna quidem & neceſſa
ria.Cum enim in petendo cibo inftaret,& patribus fuis datum memorarent,& manna tan
quam magnum quiddam laudarent,omnia illa figuram & umbram fuiſſe, rerum autem ue D
ritatem præfente oftendit.Ideo fpiritalis cibi meminit.Sed erat,inquit dicendum:Patres ue
ftri manducauerunt manna in deferto,ego autem uobis pane præbui.Sed magna fane diffe
rentia:minus enim hoc quàm illud uifum eſſet. Mannæ miraculum extuliſſet,fuum de pa
nibus depreſſiſſet.Cum ergo de cœlo cibum quæreret, ideo frequenter de cœlo fe defcediſſe
teftatur.Quod fi quis percotaretur,cur myfterioru fermonem adduxerit . Refpondebimus
quod horum nunc maxime tepus erat. Obfcurius enim dictu femper auditorem erigit & at
tentiore reddit.Nó ergo perturbari debebat,fed interrogare & quærere,Sed abierut.Quod
fi prophetam eum arbitrabatur,credere eius uerbis oportebat.Itaq; ftultitia fua, non fermo
nis Chrifti obfcuritate perturbabantur:tu aute confydera,quomodo eos ad fe paulatim tra
hit.Nam fe,non patre dediſſe dicit:&,panis que ego dabo,caro mea eft pro mudi uita. Sed
aliena quæda doctrina erat,inquies,& diuerfa.Atqui Ioanes fuperius hoc fignificauit,agnu
ipfum appellans,fed nó intellexerunt.Non me latet,non tamen difcipuli diffidebant.Nam
fi de refurrectione nondum quicq; norant,& propterea ignorabant quid fibi uellet.Soluite
templu hoc,& in tribus diebus fufcitabo illud:multo magis quæ hic dicutur,quæ obfcuriora
funt.Quod enim prophetæ fufcitaſſent,norat,quauis non tam manifefte locutæ fint fcriptu
ræ:quod aut carne quis comederit,núquam quifquam illoru dixerat. Veruntamen perfuafi
funt,& fequebatur, & habere eum uerba uitæ cofitebantur. Hoc difcipuli eft, quæ magifter
aſſerit,nó curiofius inueftigare,fed audire & credere,& idoneu folutionis tempus expectare.
Quid igitur aiunt contrariu accidiſſe? Abierunt retro,hoc propter coru ftultitiam.Quando
enim fubit quæftio quomodo aliquid fiat,fimul fubit & incredulitas.Ita & Nicodemus per
turbatus eft inquiens: Quomodo poteft homo in uentrem matris fuæ iterato introire? Iti
dem & hi nunc:Quomodo poteft hic nobis carne fuam dare ad manducandu?Nam fi hoc
inquiris,cur nó idem in quinq; panu miraculo dixifti,quomodo eos in tantum auxit?Quia
tunc tantum faturari curabant,non cófyderare miraculum.Sed res ipfa tunc docuit,inquies.
                                                                        Ergo

John Chrysostom, *Opera quae hactenus uersa sunt omnia*, Basel, 1530–31, vol. 3,
sig. F*F$_5$v (reduced)

Ergo ex eo & hæc credere oportuit ei facilia factu esse . Propterea id prius fecit miraculum,
A ut per illud non essent amplius increduli his quæ postmodum diceret.Illi quidem tunc tem
poris nihil ex his dictis,nos ipsius beneficij utilitatem cepimus.Quare necessario dicendum
quàm admirãda mysteria,& cur data sint,& quænam eorum utilitas.Vnum corpus sumus,
& membra ex carne,& ossibus eius. Quare initiati eius præceptis parêre debent.Vt autem
non solum per dilectionem,sed re ipsa in illam carnem conuertamur,per cibum id efficitur,
quem nobis largitus est . Cum enim suum in nos amorem indicare uellet, per corpus suũ se
nobis cõmiscuit,& in unum nobiscũ redegit,ut corpus cum capite uniretur. Hoc enim aman
tium maxime est.Hoc Iob significabat de seruis,à quibus maxime amabatur,qui suũ amo/
rem præ se ferentes dicebant:Quis daret nobis ut eius carnibus impleremur ? Quod Chri/ Iob ʒɪ
stus fecit ut maiori nos charitate adstringeret,& ut suum in nos ostenderet desiderium,non
se tantum uideri permittens desiderãtibus,sed & tangi,& manducari,& dentes carni suæ in/
figi,& desiderio sui omnes impleri . Ab illa igitur mensa tanquam leones ignem spirantes,
surgamus diabolo formidolosi,& caput nostrũ intelligamus,& quã in nos præ se tulit chari
tatem.Parentes sæpenumero liberos suos alijs alendos dederunt,ego autem mea carne alo,
me his exhibeo,omnibus faueo,omnibus optimam de futuris spem præbeo. Qui in hac ui/
ta ita se nobis exhibet,multo magis in futura . Vester ego frater esse uolui, & cõmunicaui
carnem propter uos & sanguinem:& per quæ uobis cõiunctus sum,ea rursus uobis exhibui.
Hic sanguis facit,ut imago in nobis regia floreat: hic sanguis pulchritudinem atqʒ nobilita
tem animæ, quam semper irrigat & nutrit, languescere non sinit. Sanguis enim à cibo non
fit repente, sed prius aliud quiddam: hic quamprimum irrigat animam, eamcʒ ui quadam
magna imbuit. Hic mysticus sanguis dæmones procul pellit, angelos & angelorum domi/
num ad nos allicit . Dæmones enim cum dominicum sanguinem in nobis uident,in fugam
uertuntur,angeli autem procurrunt.Hic sanguis effusus,uniuersum abluit orbem terrarum,
de quo multa Paulus ad Hebræos prosecutus est. Hic sanguis abdita & sancta sanctorum
B purgabat. Quod si eius figura tantã habuit uim in templo Hebræorum,in medio Ægypto
liminibus aspersus,longe magis ueritas.Hic sanguis aureũ altare significauit.Sine hoc prin/
ceps sacerdotum in penetralia ingredi non audebat.Hic sanguis sacerdotes faciebat,hic san/
guis in figura peccata purgabat, in qua si tantam habuit uim, si umbram ita mors horruit,
quantopere quæso ipsam formidabit ueritatem? Hic nostrarũ animarum salus est,hoc la
uatur anima, hoc ornatur,hoc incenditur, hic igne clariorem nostram mentĕ reddit,& auro
splendidiorem.Huius sanguinis effusio cœlum peruium fecit.Admiranda sanè ecclesiæ my/
steria,admirabile sacrarium. Ex paradiso fons scaturijt,à quo sensibiles fluuij emanarent. A
mensa hac prodijt fons,qui fluuios spiritales diffundit:iuxta hũc fontĕ nõ steriles salices ger
minant,sed quercus cœlum ipsum attingĕtes,quæ fructus tĕpestiuos & solidos semper pro/
ducunt:si quis æstuat,ad hunc fontem se conferat,& recreabitur. Mũdat squalorĕ & sordes,
æstus mitigat,non solares,sed quos ignitæ sagittæ imprimunt.Etenim ortum suum supernĕ
habet,inde radicem unde irrigatur . Multi huius fontis riui,quos paracletus diffundit, & fi
lius arbiter est, neqʒ bidente,aut ligone uiam facit, sed animos nostros aperit. Hic fons lucis
diffundens radios ueritatis,huic supernæ adstiterũt uirtutes fluctuum eius pulchritudinem
inspicientes. Nam manifestius quam nos illæ propositorum uirtutem & fulgorem inaccessi
bilem intuentur.Quemadmodum enim si quis liquefacto auro manum ,uel linguã inijciat,
quamprimum deauratur:ita hæc nobis proposita animam auream reddunt.Resurgit enim
uehementius igne fluuius,neqʒ incendit,sed abluit tantum quicquid cõprehenderit.Hic san
guis præfiguratus est semper in altaribus,in iustorum cædibus:hic orbis terrarum decus est,
hic est quo Christus emit,quo uniuersam ornauit ecclesiã.Vt enim homo seruos auro emit,
& ornat, ita nos sanguine suo Christus. Qui huius sanguinis sunt participes, cũ angelis &
archangelis,& supernis uirtutibus cõmorantur,ipsam regiã Christi stola induti,spiritalibus
armis muniti.Sed nihil dixi,imò ipsum induti sunt regem.Sed sicut magnũ est,& admirabi
le:ita si pure accesseris, ad salutem accessisti: sin praua conscientia,ad pœnam & supplicium.
Qui

John Chrysostom, *Opera quae hactenus uersa sunt omnia*, Basel, 1530–31, vol. 3,
sig. F*F₆ (reduced)

Why dydest thou not aske, by what meane he wolde & dyd encreace it so myche. The cause was bycause they cared but for the meate, and not for the myracle. But thou wylte peraduenture saye, the thynge [D₅] *at that tyme declared and shewed itselfe. But than I say agayne, that of that manifest open myracle that they saw hym there wurke, they shold haue byleued that he coulde* 5 *do these thynges to, that is to wyt these thynges that they now murmured at whan they sayd, how can he gyue vs hys flesshe to eate. For therfore* (saythe saynt Chrysostome) *dyd our sauiour wurke the tother myracle of his fyue louys byfore, bycause he wolde therwith induce them that they shold not dystruste those thynges that he wold tell them after,"* that is to wytte good 10 readers of hys godhed, and of the geuynge of hys fleshe to eate.

The .ix. chapyter.

N̄ow good Christen readers here you se by saynt Chrysostome, that though thapostles vnderstode well that Chryste spake of the [D₅v] very eatynge of his flessh: yet there was no cause why they 15 shold eyther dowtfully wonder, stonne, or stagger or be by and by curyouse and inquysitiue therof / & so destroyeth he playne mayster Maskers reason / but yf it be to suche as are dysposed for theyr pleasure, better to byleue mayster masker than saynt Chryso-stome. 20

For euery man may here well se, that saynt Chrysostom meneth here, that Chryste in those wordes bysyde all parables and alle-goryes, spake and ment of the very eatynge of his very flesshe in dede. Whyche thynge lest mayster Masker myghte as he is shame-lesse, brynge yet in question and controuersye: I shall reherse you 25 a fewe lynes ferther of saynte Chrysostome in this self same place. Lo thus there sayth he ferther. [D₆]

" Those Iewes at that tyme toke no commodyte / but we haue taken the profyte of that benefyte. And therfore is it necessare to declare how meruelouse are these mysteryes" (that is to wytte of the blessed sacrament) *" and why* 30 *they be geuen vs, and what is yᵉ profyte therof. We be one body & membrys of Chrystes flesshe and his bonys. And therfore they that are chrysten, are bounden to obaye his preceptes. But yet that we sholde be not onely by loue, but also in very dede turned in to yᵗ flesh of his, that thyng is done by the*

---

11 of the geuynge] geuyng *1557*   13 Christen] *1557*, Chrsten *1533*   27 there sayth he]
he sayth here *1557*   29 necessare] necessarye *1557*   31 membrys] menbrys *1533*,
members *1557*   34 yᵗ] the *1557*

meate that his lyberalyte hath gyuen vs. For whyle he longed to declare and
expresse hys loue that he bore towarde vs, he hath by his owne body mengled
hym selfe wyth vs, and hath made hym selfe one wyth vs, that the body sholde
be vned with the hedde. For that is the greateste thynge that louers longe for
5 *(that is to wytte to* [D₆v] *be (if it were possyble) made both one) And that*
thynge sygnyfyed Iob of his seruauntes, of whom he was most hartely beloued.
Which to expresse the vehement loue that they bare towarde hym, sayde who
coulde gyue vs the gyfte, that we myghte haue oure bodyes euyn fulfylled with
hys flesshe: whyche thynge Chryst hath done for vs in dede / bothe to thentent
10 *to bynd vs in the more feruent loue towarde hym, and also to declare the*
feruent loue and desyre that hym selfe bare towarde vs. And therfore hath he
not onely suffered hym selfe to be sene or loked vppon by them that desyre and

Note*
                 longe for hym, but also to be touched and eaten,
                 and the very teth to be infyxed into his flesshe,

15 *and all folke to be fulfylled in the desyre of hym. From goddes borde therfore*
let vs ryse like lions that blew out fyre at the mouth suche as the deuyll maye
be aferde to beholde vs / & let vs consyder Chryst [D₇] *our hed, & what a*
loue he hath shewed vs. The fathers and the mothers oftentymes put out theyr
chyldren to other folke to nurse. But I (may our sauyour say) nuryshe & fede
20 *my chyldren with myne owne flesshe. I geue them here myne own selfe / so*
fauour I them all. And suche greate hope I geue theym all, agayne the tyme
that shall come. For he that in suche wyse gyueth vs hym selfe in this lyfe
here: mych more wyll he gyue vs hym selfe in the lyfe that is to come. I
longed (sayd our lorde) to be your brother. And for your sakes I haue
25 *communycated and made comen vnto you my flesh and my bloud. The thynges*
by whyche I was ioyned with you, those thynges haue I exhybyted agayne and
geuen to you" (yᵗ is to saye the very fleshe and bloude, by which I
was made natural man with you, that same haue I in the sacrament exhybyted & geuen agayne vnto you) [D₇v] *" Thys bloud*
30 *causeth* yᵉ *kinges image to floure in vs. This bloude wyl not suffre the bewty*
and the noblynes of the soule (whych it euer watereth & nuryssheth) to
wyther or fade & fall. The bloud that is made in vs of our other comen
meate, is not by and by bloude / but before it be bloude it ys somwhat ellys.
But this bloude of Chryst out of hande watereth yᵉ *soule & with a certayne*
35 *meruelouse myght and strength seasoneth it by and by. This mystycall or*
sacramentall bloud" (that is to saye thys bloud of Christ in the

---

6 sygnfyed] fygnyfved *1533*, signified *1557*; his] *1557*, hio *1533*   7 hym, sayde] hym sayde,
1557   16 deuyll] denyll *1533*, deuil *1557*   25 comen] commen *1557*   31 of]
1557, of of *1533*   32 comen] commen *1557*

sacrament) " *dryueth the deuyls farre of and bryngeth to vs not angellys onely, but the lorde of all angellys to. The deuyls whan they byholde and se the bloud of Chryst within vs, they fle farre from vs, and the angellys runne as faste towarde vs.*"

And yet saynt Chrysostome ceaceth not wyth all thys, but goth 5 forth with a lenger processe, declaryng the [D₈] great benefyte of this bloud, both by the shedyng on the crosse, and by the receyu-yng in the sacrament / whyche whole processe I shall peraduenture hereafter in some other place reherse.

But for this mater good chrysten readers thus mych dothe more 10 then suffyse. For by lesse than this ye may more than playnely perceyue, that thys olde holy doctour saynt Chrysostom, many-festely declareth & sheweth, that our sauyour in those wordes that he spake to the Iewes, mencyoned in the syxte chapyter of saynte Iohan, veryly spake and ment of the very eatynge of his 15 flesshe. Whyche thynge he promysed there, and which promyse

Math. 26   he performed after at hys maundy, whan he there instituted the blessed

sacrament. [D₈v]

The .x. chapyter.

    20

Nd nowe good readers to fynyshe at laste this mater of mayster Maskers agaynste my secunde argument (whyche he calleth my fyrste, bycause my fyrste is suche as he is lothe to loke vppon) I retorne ones agayne to mayster maskers two sore captyouse ques-tyons / and lykewise as he hath asked theym of me, and I haue as 25 you se so well auoyded his gynnys and his grinnes and all his trymtrams, that he hathe not yet trayned me into no trappe of myne owne, as you se him solempnely boste: so wyll I now be bolde to aske of hym fyrst, whyther saynt Chrisostome, here, ye and saynt Austayne to, and saynte Cyrille, saynte Bede, saynte 30 Hyreneus, and saynt Hilary, were of the mynde, that thapostles vnderstode theyr mayster Chry[E₁]stes wordes whan he sayd,

Ioh. 6   " *And the brede that I shall gyue you is my fleshe &c. And my flesh is very meate &c. And I tell you very trouth, except you eate the flesh of ye sone of man &c.*"   35

---

6 lenger] longer *1557*   9 reherse.] *1557*, reherse *1533*   29 here, ye] here ye, *1557*
30 Bede,] *1557*, Bede *1533*   33–34 *gloss* Ioh. 6] *om. 1557*

If mayster masker answer me to thys questyon naye or no, than
shall he make me bolde to answere ye same to hym. For than shall
he not fere me wyth his owne sayenge, that the gospell sayth
contrary in the syxte chapyter of saynte Iohan, yf he graunte and
5   confesse hym selfe / that all those holy doctours saye therin
agaynste his owne sayenge / whyche amonge them all, vnderstode
that gospell as well as hym selfe alone, ye & though he take Fryth
and frere Huyskyn. to hym to. And therfore yf he answere naye or
no: than is he quyte ouerthrowen as you se / and his secunde
10   questyon quyte gone to, for than can [E_1v] he neuer come to it.

Now on the tother syde, yf he answere me ye or yes: than se
good readers wherto mayster Masker bryngeth hym self euyn to be
taken in his owne trappe. For than he marreth all hys mater. For
syth you se clerely good readers, that all these holy doctours and
15   sayntes, openly do declare by theyr playne wordes which your selfe
haue here all redy herde, that Chryste in those wordes veryly spake
and ment of the very eatynge of his very flesshe in dede: it muste
nedes folow agaynste mayster Maskers mynde (in the earys & the
hartes of al such as byleue better al those holy doctours than hym)
20   that this is the ryght vnderstandynge of Chrystes wordes / and that
thapostles yf they vnderstode his wordes, vnderstode them after the
same fashyon / that is [E_2] to wyt, that he spake & ment of y^e very
eatyng of his very flesh in ded. And so serueth hym his secunde
questyon of nought. For the cause why they meruayled not in any
25   murmurynge maner, was bycause they byleued it well at theyr
maysters word, whych mayster masker doth not / and y^e cause why
they were not by & by curyouse & inquisitiue, was as you haue
herd saint Chrysostome declare, bycause they were meke and
obedyent, and not so presumptuouse and malapert, as maister
30   Masker wolde haue ben.

Lo mayster masker here may you se lo, what wurship you haue
wonne with your questions / with which you haue not onely missed
of trayning me into myn own trappe, as you triumphe & boste, but
are also dreuyn into your own trap your self, out of which you can
35   neuer clymbe vp your self nor al [E_2v] the bretherhed be able to
drawe you vp, as longe as the deuyll the very father of your lyenge
bretherhed, lyeth in the depe denne of hell.

---

23 ded] dede *1557*   27 they] *1533 corr. err., 1557*, the *1533*   34 dreuyn] dryuen *1557*
36 lyenge] *1533 corr. err., 1557*, lyuynge *1533*

Thus haue I good readers my fyrste argument (as he calleth it) that he bosteth to haue twyse so substancially soyled, that he maketh me therin such a feble babe, that I were not able to stande in his strong hand: that argument haue I so strongely now defended, and geuyn hym in his owne turne so many gret & fowle 5 fallys, in euery part of his processe, that if this great clerke had so many so great fallys geuen hym at Clerkenwell at a wrestelynge, he wolde haue had I wene neyther rybbe, nor arme, nor legge lefte hym hole longe ago, nor at thys laste lyfte, his necke vnbroken neither. And now therfore let vs loke how he soyleth my thyrde 10 argument, [E₃] whych hym selfe calleth my second, bycause he wold haue yᵉ fyrst forgoten.

The .xi. chapyter.

Lo thus good readers goeth mayster Masker forth.
The secunde argument of More.   15

After thys texte thus wysely proued to be vnderstanden in the lyterall sense wyth the carnall Iewes, & not in the allegoryke or spyrytuall sense with Cryst and hys apostles: The whole somme of Morys confutacyon of the yonge man, standeth vppon this argument, a posse ad esse / that is to wytte, God maye do it, ergo it is done. God may make his body in many 20 or in all places at onys, ergo it is in many or in all places at onys. Whyche maner of argumentacyon how false and naught it is, euery Sophyster & euery man that hath wytte, perceyueth. A lyke argument. God may shew More the treuth and call hym to repentaunce as he dyd Paule for persecutyng hys chyrche, ergo More is conuerted to god. Or god may lette 25 hym runne of an indurate harte with Pharo, and at last take an open and sodayne vengeaunce vppon hym for persecutynge hys worde, & burnyng hys pore membres: ergo it is done all redy.

In all thys tale good reders you se, that mayster Masker is yet at the leste wyse constant & nothynge chaun[E₃v]geth his maners. 30 For as falsely as he rehersed myne other argumente before (wherin what falshed he vsed you haue your selfe sene) as falsely now reherseth he this other. For rede good readers all my letter thorowe your selfe, and whan you fynde that fashyoned argument there, than byleue mayster masker in this mater / & in the meane whyle 35 byleue but as the trouth is, that with his lyes he mocketh you. And

---

12 forgoten.] forgoten *1533*, forgotten. *1557*   20 his body] *1533 corr. err.*, *1557*, thys body *1533*   26 Pharo] Pharao *1557*

sith he maketh vs first a lowde lye for his fundacion, & buyldeth
after his argumentes vppon the same, wherwith he skoffeth so plea-
sauntly at me, y^t it as properly becometh the man to taunt, as it
becometh a camell or a bere to daunce: I wyl not with hym argue,
5 a posse ad esse / & say he can lye ergo he doth lye / but I wil turne
the fashyon, & argue ab esse ad posse / & saye that he doth lye,
ergo he [E$_4$] can lye, & so commende his wyt. Lo this forme of
arguyng can he not denye. And thantecedent shall you fynd as
trewe whan you rede ouer my letter as hym self can not say nay,
10 but that the consecucyon is formall.
     But than goth mayster Masker forth on and sayth.
Mayster More muste fyrste proue it vs by expresse wordes of holy scrypture, and not by his owne vnwryten dremys, that Chrystes body is in
many places or in all places at ones. And than though our reasyn can not
15 reche it, yet our fayth measured and dyrected wyth the worde of fayth
wyll both reche it, receyue it, and holde it faste to / not bycause it is
possyble to god, & impossyble to reason, but bycause the wryten worde of
our fayth sayth it. But whan we rede goddes wordes in mo than twenty
places contrary, that hys body sholde be here: More must geue vs leue to
20 byleue hys vnwryten vanitees, verytees I wolde say, at laysour.
     Here ye se good reders how many thynges mayster masker hath
tolde vs here, and how fresshely he floryssheth them forth.
     The fyrst is that I muste proue it hym, that the body of Chryste
is [E$_4$v] in many places at onys, or in all places at onys.
25   The secunde is, y^t I muste proue it by expresse wordes of scrypture.
     The thyrde is, that I maye not proue it by myne owne vnwryten
dremys.
     The fourth is, that yf I proue it so by expresse wordes of scryp-
30 ture, than he wyll bothe reche it, and receyue it, and holde it fast
to.
     The fyfth is that he fyndeth .xx. places of scrypture and mo, to
the contrary, prouynge that hys body is not here.
     The syxth is, y^t therfore I must geue hym leue to byleue myne
35 vnwryten vanytees, verytees, he wold saye, at laysore.
     Now for the fyrste good readers where mayster Masker sayth y^t
maister More muste fyrst proue it hym, [E$_5$] that Chrystes bodye

1 fundacion] foundation *1557*

is in many places at once or in all places at ones: I saye that as for
all places at ones, mayster More muste not proue at al. For (sith y^e
sacrament is not in al places at ones) whyther his blessed bodye
may be in al places at ones, is no poynte of our mater.

Now as touchynge the beynge of hys blessed body in many   5
places at ones, where mayster Maskar sayth that ere he be bounde
to byleue yt, I muste proue yt: he is very farre out of reason and
oute of the ryght way. For is mayster Maskar nor father Frith
byfore hym, bounden to byleue no more, than mayster More were
able to proue them? I saye agayn to father Fryth and mayster   10
Maskar bothe, that yf eyther of theym bothe, or any suche other
fonde felowe as they be, begynne to denye nowe [E5v] any such
playn artycle of ye fayth, as all good chrysten nacyons, are & long
haue be full agreed vppon, so longe and so full as they haue bene
vppon this, and so longe rekened the contrarye byleuers for here-   15
tyques: eyther mayster More or any man els, might well with
reason reproue them therof, and rebuke theym therfore, and onely
answere the folysh argumentes that they make agaynste the trouth,
and shold not ones nede to go aboute the profe of the ful receiued
& vndouted trouth, as though it were become douteful vpon euery   20
proud heretikes blasphemouse folyshe argument.

For if master maskar wold nowe bryng vppe the Arrianes
heresye agayne, agaynst the godhed of Christ, which he might as
wel as this frantike heresye of frere Huskyn & wycleffe agaynst the
blessed sacrament / or yf [E6] he wold now begyn the tother folysh   25
heresy, wherof the prophete speketh in the psalter. Dixit insipiens

Psal. 13

in corde suo non est deus. The fole sayd
in his harte there is no god, which he
might as well begynne as any of the tother twayne: yf he wold now
for the furnyshynge of this heresye, come forth with suche vnrea-   30
sonale reasons, as some folysh folosophers broughte in therfore of
olde, were yt not ynough for me to confute those folyshe argumentes wherwyth he wold blynd symple soulis? Must I nedes
besyde y^t go make myche a do, & proue y^t there were a god, or els
graunt thys gose y^t there were no god at all, bycause hym self wold   35
say so styll, when his fond reasons were soyled?

---

3 in] *1533 corr. err.*, *1557*, ta *1533*   8 nor] or *1557*   15 byleuers] *1533 corr. err.*, *1557*,
byleues *1533*   20 vndouted] *1557*, vndonted *1533*   36 fond] found *1533*, fonde *1557*

Now to his seconde poynt, where it is not inough for him to say
that I muste proue it (wherin as ye se I haue proued hym [E₆v] a
very fole) but he assygneth me also what maner of profe I must
make / and none maye serue hym, but suche as hym selfe lyst
5 assygne / & that therfore I must proue it hym by expresse wordes
of holy scrypture: I aske hym than whyther he wylbe content yf I
proue yt hym by expresse wordes of Chryste wryten in all the foure
euangelystes, saynt Mathew, saynt Marke, saynt Luke, and saint
Iohan? yf he saye ye as I suppose he wyll, than aske I hym farther
10 wherfore he wyll byleue the wrytyng of them foure. Wherto what
will he answere, but bycause yᵗ those gospells of theyrs are holy
scrypture. But than shall I farther desyre hym to shewe me, howe
he knoweth that those foure bokes or any one of all four, is the
boke of hym, whose name yt bereth, or ys the holy scrypture of god
15 at all. To [E₇] this questyon lo (but yf he can go farther than holy
saint Austayne could, or the mayster captayne of his owne heresyes
Martyne Luther eyther) he muste saye that he knoweth those
bokes for holy scrypture, bycause the commen knowen catholique
chyrch hath so told hym. Now whan he shal haue ones answered
20 me thus: euery chyld may sone se what I shall aske hym agayne.
For than shall I saye, tell me than mayster Maskar I beseche you,
syth you byleue this commen knowen catholyque chyrche in that
one great verytie, wherupon by your owne saynge all the other
wryters depende: why sholde you not as well byleue yt in thys
25 other artycle, whyche yt as playnely telleth you, and yet you do
denye yt? why sholde you not I saye mayster Maskar byleue the
chyrche as wel, whan yt tel[E₇v]leth you god hath taught his
chyrche that this is his very body, as you byleue the same chyrch
when yt telleth you, god hath taught his chyrch that this is his very
30 scripture, namely syth there are wryten in yᵉ same scrypture other
thynges, to mannes reason as harde to conceyue and as incredyble
to byleue as that.

Here you se good readers, to what poynte I haue brought master
Maskar. I haue set hym here so fast in the myre, that therin shall
35 he stycke and neuer clene wade oute whyle he lyueth.

Moreouer mayster maskar can not denye me this, but that the

---

11 gospells] gospell *1533*, ghospels *1557*   30 scripture] *1557*, scriture *1533*

ryght bylyef in y^e sacrament / & dyuers other thynges mo, were
ones taughte and byleued, and christen men bounden to byleue
them to, without expresse wordes of holy scripture layed forth for
[E$_8$] the profe, before any word of y^e new testament was wryten
and after peraduenture to / where tharticles were preached, and 5
wryten gospelles not there. Now yf suche thynges were at one tyme
not onely byleued, but men also bounden to the belief therof
without expresse wordes of scripture for the profe: mayster Maskar
must than, though there be come wrytynge synnes, yet either profe
vs by expresse wordes of scrypture, that of all that god wyl we shall 10
byleue, there is nothynge left out / but euery such thyng there
writen in with expresse wordes, or els may he neuer make him self
so sure, & face it out a this fashion with expresse wordes, that
sauyng the very playne expresse wordes of scripture, we be no man
of vs bounden to byleue nothynge ellys. 15

Now this am I sure inough, that suche expresse wordes shall he
neuer [E$_8$v] fynde in scrypture, that tell hym expressely that all is
wryten in. And than syth he can not proue vs this poynte by
scrypture, but that at the leste wyse we maye be bounden to byleue
some suche thynges as in holy scrypture is not expressely writen / 20
which thynges those may be and which not, of whome wyll god we
shall lerne, but of his knowen cathylyque chyrch by whiche he
teacheth vs whiche be the very scripture?

Nowe as for the thyrde poynte, that mayster maskar toucheth, in
whiche he wyl allowe for no suffycient profe myne owne vnwryten 25
dremys, he geueth my dremys I thanke hym of his courtesye,
myche more authoryte than euer I loked for. For whyle he reiecteth none of theym, but suche as are vnwryten, he sheweth hym
selfe redy to byleue them, yf I wold [F$_1$] vouchesaufe to wryte
them. 30

In the fourth point he promiseth, y^t yf I do by expresse wordes of
scrypture proue that it is so: than (though yt be aboue the reche of
his reason) yet wyl he by belyefe, bothe reche yt, and receyue yt, &
hold it fast to. Wold god mayster Maskar wolde abyd by this
worde. For now I aske hym agayn, whyther he wyl be content, yf I 35

---

13 face it] *1533 corr err., 1557*, face in *1533*   19 scrypture] *1533 corr. err., 1557*, scrypturer
1533   24 that mayster] *1533 corr. err., 1557*, mayster *1533*   31 fourth] *1557*, fonrth *1533*

proue it him by expresse wordes of some one of the foure
euangelystes. And if he be content with expresse wordes of any one,
than will I do more for hym, proue yt by all foure.

For saynte Iohan reherseth, that our sauyour sayd hym selfe
5   *Iohn. 6**   he wold geue theym his fleshe to eate.
And that he ment of the sacramente,
you se all redy proued here byfore.

And the tother thre reherse, that Chryste sayde hym selfe whan
he [F₁v] gaue theym the sacrament, thys is my body that shal be
10 broken for you. What wordes can there be more playn and
expresse than these?

But here sayth mayster Maskar that these be not expresse
wordes. For he sayth that these wordes be spoken but by way of
allegory. And he proueth it as Frith doth, by yᵗ our sauiour sayd of
15 hym self, I am the dore, and I am the vyne.

Nowe remember good readers, that master Maskar bylyed me
right nowe, and sayd that all my second argument was, a posse ad
esse, it may be so, ergo yt is so. But now consyder good christen
reders your selfe, whyther this argument of his be not a posse ad
20 esse in dede. For by those places, I am the dore, and I am the
vyne, and suche other: he concludeth that these other places of
eatynge hys [F₂] fleshe and geuynge of hys bodye, was spoken by
an allegorye to. And howe concludeth he that yt ys so? but
bycause yt maye be so. And thus ye se good readers, that the selfe
25 same kynde of arguynge which mayster Maskar fayneth hym selfe
to fynd with me, & falsely belyeth me therin (for I neded there
none other thynge to do, but answere the thynges that Fryth layed
forthe agaynst the catholyque fayth) the selfe same kynde of
arguynge I saye mayster Maskar vseth hym selfe / and so dothe
30 yonge father Fryth hys felow in folye to.

But than agayne whan they argue thus, These places maye be so
vnderstanden by an allegorye onely, as those other places be, ergo
they be to be so vnderstanden in dede: I haue proued al redy that
his entent is false, and that they maye not be vnder[F₂v]standen in
35 an allegory onely as the tother be / but the playne and open
difference betwene the places appere vppon the cyrcumstaunces of
the texte. This haue I proued agaynst Frith al redye / and that in
suche wyse, as your selfe hath sene here, that mayster Maskar can
not auoyde yt / but in goynge about to defende Frythes foly, hathe

wyth his two solucyons of myne one argument, ofter than twyse
ouerthrowen him self, & made myne argument more than twyse so
stronge.

But yet good readers, bycause I say that those wordes of Crist,

Iohan. 6

The brede y^t I shal geue you is my flesh, 5
which I shal geue for the lyfe of the
world / and my flesh is verily meat, and my blood veryly drynke /
and, But if you eate the fleshe of the son of man, and drynke hys
bloode, you [F$_3$] shal not haue life in you / and so forth al such
wordis as our sauyour spake hym selfe, mencyoned in the syxte 10
chapyter of saynte Iohn / and those wordes of our sauyour at hys
maundye wryten wyth all the tother thre euangelystes. Thys is my
bodye that shall be broken for you, be playn and expresse wordes
for the catholyque fayth / and mayster maskar sayth that they be
not wordes playne and expresse, but expowneth them all another 15
waye: therfore to breke the stryfe therin betwene him and me, I
haue brought you forth for my parte in myne exposycyon, the
playne expresse wordes of dyuerse olde holy sayntes, by whych you
may playne & expressely se, that they al sayd as I saye.

And mayster maskar also can not hym selfe say naye / but that 20
agaynst [F$_3$v] other heretyques before his dayes and myne, dyuerse
whole generall counsayles of chrystendome, haue playnely and
expressely determyned the same to be trew that I saye.

And all the countreys chrystened can also testyfye, that god
hathe hym self by manyfold open miracles, playn & expressely 25
declared for the blessid sacrament, that this is the trewe fayth
which mayster Maskar here oppugneth / and that god hath by
those myracles expowned his own wordes hym self, to be playne &
expressely spoken for our part.

And therfore nowe good christen reders, yf mayster maskar wil 30
make any more stickyng with vs, & not graunt Christes wordes for
playn & expresse / & accordynge to hys promyse, reche & receyue
y^e trew faith & hold it faste to: ye may playne & expressely tel
him, there shal neuer trew man, trust his false promyse after. [F$_4$]

Now touchyng the fyfth poynte, where he saith that he findeth 35
.xx. places in scripture & mo to, prouyng that Christes body is not
here in erth: remember this wel good reder agaynst he bryng them

forth. For in his second part when we come to the tale, ye shal fynd
his mo than twenty, farre fewer than fyftene, & of al yᵗ shal wel
serue hym, ye shall fynd fewer than one.

Then where he concludeth in the laste poynt vpon these fyue
5   poyntes afore (whyche fyue howe well they proue good chrysten
readers you se) that I muste geue hym leue to byleue myne vnwryten vanyties (veryties he wold saye) at leysour: yf the thynges that
he calleth vnwryten verities were in dede vnwriten and inuented
also by me, than he might be yᵉ bolder to cal them myne vnwriten
10   vanities, & (as he calleth them before) myn vnwriten dremis to.
But on yᵉ tother syde syth you se [F₄v] your selfe, that I haue
shewed you theym writen in holy saintes bokes, and that a thousand yere before that I was borne / & your self seeth it writen in
the playne scrypture to, proued playn & expresse for our part
15   against hym, by tholde exposycyon of all the holy doctours and
sayntes, and by yᵉ determinacyons of dyuerse generall counsayles
of Christes whole catholyque chyrche / and proued playn for our
parte also, by so many playn open myracles: mayster maskar must
nedes be more then madde to cal nowe suche wryten veryties myne
20   vnwryten vanytes, or myne vnwryten dremys either / except he
proue both all those thynges to be but an inuencyon of myne / and
ouer that all those writynges to be yet vnwriten / and that holy
doctrine both of holy saintes and of holy scripture vanities, & also
that [F₅] all the whyle that al those holy folke were awurke ther-
25   with, they neyther wrote nor studyed nor dyd nothynge but dreme.

Now whyle mayster More must therfore vppon suche consydera-
cions, geue maister Masker leue to byleue thys vnwryten vanyte,
whiche is in all the .iiii. euangelystes an expresse wryten verite:
whyle I must I say therfore vppon suche folysh false consydera-
30   cyons, geue hym leue to byleue the trewe fayth at leysour / yf he
had put it in my choyce, I wold haue ben loth to geue hym any
lenger leysour therin, for he hath ben to longe out of ryght bylyefe
all redy. But syth he sayeth I muste, I maye not choyse. Wherof I
am as helpe me god very sory. For excepte he take hym selfe that
35   leysour bytyme, leuynge the busynesse that he dayly taketh in
wry[F₅v]tyng of pestylent bokes to the contrary: he shal els not

9 cal them] calt hem *1533*, call theym *1557*   12 writen] *1557*, writem *1533*   19 veryties]
vetyties *1533*, verities *1557*   33 choyse] choose *1557*

faile to byleue ye trew fayth at a longe leysour ouer late, y^t is to
wytte whan he lyeth wrechedly in hell / where he shall not wryte
for lacke of lyght and burnynge vp of his paper, but shall haue
euerlastyng laysour from all other worke to byleue there that he
wolde not byleue here, and lye styll & euer burne there, in euer-   5
lastynge fyre, for his formar vngracyouse obstinate infydelyte / out
of whyche infydelyte I beseche god geue hym the grace to crepe
and gete out bytyme.

And thus you se good readers what a goodly piece mayster
masker hath made you / which pleased him I warraunt you very   10
well, whan he wrote it. But it wyl not I wene please him now very
well, whan he shall after this myne answere rede it. [F₆]

The .xii. chapyter.

B̲ut now goth he ferther against me with a specyall goodly piece
wherin thus he sayth.   15
Here mayst thou se chrysten reader wherfore More wolde so fayne make
the byleue that thapostles left aught vnwryten of necessyte to be byleued,
euyn to stablysshe the popes kyngdome, whych standeth of Morys vnwryten vanytees / as of the presence of Chrystes body, and makynge therof in
the brede, of purgatory, of inuocacyon of sayntes, wurshyppyng of stonys   20
and stockys, pylgrymages, halowynge of bowes and belles, and crepynge
to the crosse &c. If ye wyll byleue what so euer More can fayne wythout
the scrypture: than can thys poete fayne ye another chyrch then Chrystes,
and that ye muste byleue it what so euer it teach you / for he hath fayned
to that it can not erre, though ye se it erre and fyght agaynst it selfe a   25
thowsand tymes / ye yf it tell you blacke is whyte, and good is badde, and
the deuyll is god, yet muste ye byleue it or ellys be burned as heretykes.

Styll ye se the wisdome good reders, & the trouth of maister
masker, in euery piece of his mater. For here you se that all these
thynges / that he [F₆v] speketh of, as that the chyrch can not erre,   30
and the crepynge to the crosse, wyth all other ceremonyes of
the chyrche, inuocacyon of sayntes, goynge on pylgrymage,
wurshyppyng of images, byleuynge of purgatory, byleuynge the
body of our sauyour present in the blessed sacrament: all these
thynges he calleth myne vnwryten vanitees, and maketh as though   35
these thynges were all of my faynynge. Is not this wene you wysely

21 bowes] *1533 corr. err., 1557,* vowes *1533*   33 byleuynge the] belieuing of the *1557*

fayned of hym, that the thynges comenly vsed this .xiiii. C. yere byfore I was borne, sholde now be fayned and imagyned by me. But yet shall it be as long after my dayes and his to, ere mayster Masker and all the mayny of them shall amonge theym all, be able
5   to confute the thynges y^t my selfe haue in these maters wryten. And yet hange not the maters vpon [F$_7$] my wrytynge, but vppon the treuth it selfe, reueled vnto Christes knowen catholyke chyrche, bothe by Chryste hym self and his apostles after him, by tradycyon and by wrytynge both, and by many myracles confyrmed, & wyth
10 the secrete instyncte and inspyracyon of his holy spyryte, wrought & brought into a full & whole catholike agrement and consent, as necessary poyntes of the trewe chrysten fayth.

This is also by mayster masker wonderfull wysely fayned, y^t More hath fayned all these thynges, euyn to the entent to
15 stablysshe the popes kyngdome. But now what greate cause sholde moue me, to bere that greate affeccyon to the pope, as to fayne all these thynges for stablyshement of his kyngdome: that thynge mayster masker telleth you not, as y^e thynge that is so playne and euydent [F$_7$v] that he nedeth not. For he thynketh y^t euery man
20 knoweth all redy, that the pope is my godfather, & goeth aboute to make me a cardynall.

But now good chrysten readers, they that wolde at the counsayle of this euyll chrysten caytyfe, cast of all suche maner thynges as all good chrysten peple haue euer taken for good, and now neyther
25   *No more thei do but*   crepe to the crosse, nor set by any
        *against their wille**   halowed thynge, dispyse pylgrymages,
                                   and set holy sayntes at nought, no more
reuerence theyr images than an horse of wax, nor reken theyr relykes any better than shepys bonys, scrape clene the letany out of
30 euery boke, with our lady matens & the dyryge to, and away with our ladys psalter, & cast the bedys in y^e fyre & beware also y^t we wurshyp not the sacrament, nor take it for no better thyng than vnblessed brede, & byleue [F$_8$] that the chyrch erreth in euery thyng y^t it teacheth, and all that holy sayntes haue taught therin
35 this .xiiii. C. yere (for all they haue taughte all these thynges y^t this

---

5 these maters] *1533 corr. err.*, the maters *1533 1557*   6 wrytynge] writinges *1557*
26 dispyse] *1533 corr. err.*, *1557*, dyspute *1533*; pylgrymages] pysgrymages *1533*, pilgrimages
1557

man nowe dispyseth) than wolde there wax a mery world, ye very
kyngdom of ye deuyl him self.

And veryly it semeth y^t they wold set the people vppon myrth.
For penaunce they shake of as a thynge not necessary. Satisfaccion they call gret synne / & confessyon they call ye deuils dryft. 5
And of purgatory by two meanes they put men out of drede. Some
by slepyng tyll domys daye, & some by sendyng all strayt to
heuyn, euery soule that dyeth & is not dampned for euer. And yet
some good comforte geue they to the dampned to. For tyll they se
somtyme to deny hell all vtterly, they goo aboute in the meane 10
season to putte oute the fyre. [F$_8$v] And some yet boldely forthwith
to say there is none there, that they dred a lytell / and therfore for
the season they brynge the mater in questyon, & dyspute it abrode
& say they wyll not vtterly afferme and say the contrary / but the
thynge is they say but as problema neutrum, wherin they wold not 15
force whyther parte they shold take / & yet yf they sholde chose,
they wold rather holde nay than ye / or though there be fyre in
eyther place, that yet it neyther burneth sowle in helle, nor
payneth sowle in purgatory. But Chryst I

Math. 13. 18. &. 25   wote well in many places sayth there is 20
fyre there / & his holy sayntes after hym afferme and saye the same /
and with that fyre he frayed his owne dyscyples, byddyng them
fere that fyre, that they fell not therin.

Now though that clerkes maye [G$_1$] in scolys hold problems
vppon euery thynge: yet can I not perceyue what profyte there can 25
come, to call it but a probleme amonge vnlerned folke, and
dyspute it out abrode, and brynge the people in dowte, & make
them rather thynke that there is none than any / and that this
worde fyre is spoken but by parable, as these men make the
eatynge of Chrystes blessed body. Thus shal they make men take 30
bothe paradyse, and heuyn, and god, and all togyther, but for
parables at laste.

Though fere of hell alone be but a seruyle drede: yet are there
all redy to meny that fere hell to lytell, euyn of theym that byleue
the truthe, and thynke that in hell there is very fyre in dede. How 35
many wyll there than be that wyll fere it lesse, yf such wordes onys
maye make theym wene, [G$_1$v] that there were in hell no very fyre

---

16 & yet] and *1557*   22 that] the *1557*

at all, but that the payne that they shall fele in hell, were but after
the maner of some heuy mynde, or of a troublous dreme.

If a man byleue Chrystes word, that in hell is fyre in dede, and
make the feare of that fyre, one meane to kepe hym thense: than
5   though there were no fyre there, yet hath he nothynge loste / syth
good he can gete none there, though the fyre were thense. But yf
he byleue suche wordes on the tother syde, and catche therby

*As many doe**   suche boldenesse that he sette hell at
                        lyght, and by the meanes therof fall
10   boldely to synne, and theruppon fynally fall downe vnto the
deuyll: yf he than fynde fyre there as I am sure he shall, than shall
he lye there and curse them that tolde hym those false talys, as
longe as [G₂] god with hys good folke sytteth in the ioye of heuyn.

And therfore good chrysten readers, wysedome wyll we byleue
15   Chrystes owne wordes, and let such vnwyse wordes and deuelyshe
deuyces passe.

The .xiii. chapyter.

Bvt nowe after thys pleasaunt dyscourse of his into the rehersall
of this hepe of heresies that you haue herde, for whyche as for lytell
20   tryfyls hys harte freteth sore, that any heretyke sholde be burned:
he goth on agaynst me and sayth.

But let vs returne to our propose. To dyspute of goddes almighty absolute
powre, what god may do wyth hys body, it is great foly and no lesse
presumpcyon to More, syth the pope whiche is no hole god but halfe a
25   god, by theyr owne decrees hath decreed no man to dyspute of his power.
But chrysten reder be thou content to knowe that godes wyll, his word,
and his power, be all one, and repugne not. And neyther wylleth he, nor
maye not do any thynge inclu[G₂v]dynge repugnaunce, imperfeccyon, or
that shuld derogate mynysshe or hurte hys glory and his name. The glory
30   of hys godhed is, to be present and to fyll all places at onys essencyally,
presently wyth his almyghty power, whych glory is denyed to any other

*Esay. 42**   creature / hym selfe sayenge by his prophete:
                         I wyll not geue my glory to any other crea-
ture. Now therfore syth hys manhed is a creature, it can not haue this
35   glory whiche onely is appropryed to the godhed. To attrybute to his
manhed that propertye / whyche onely is appropryed to hys godhed / is to
confounde bothe the natures in Chryste. What thynge so euer is euery
where after the sayd maner / that muste nedes be infynyte / without

---

13 in the ioye of] in *1557*

begynnynge and ende / it muste be one alone / and almyghty: whiche
propertyes onely are appropryed vnto the gloryouse maiesty of the
godhed. Wherfore Chrystes body may not be in all or in many places at
onys. Chryste hymselfe sayenge as concernynge his manhed: He is lesse

Iohn. 10*   than the father / but as towchynge his   5
godhed the father and I be bothe one thynge.

And Paule recytynge the Psal. affyrmeth: Cryste as concernynge his
manhed to be lesse then god / or lesse than angellys as some texte hath it.
Here is it playne that all thynges that More imagyneth and fayneth / are
not possyble to god / for it is not possyble for god to make a creature egall   10
vnto hym selfe / for it includeth repugnaunce and derogateth his glory.

Now haue you lo good chrysten readers herde a very specyall
piece, wherin mayster masker (as you se) [G₃] solempnely fyrste
rebuketh the foly and yᵉ presumpcyon of me, for that I was so
bolde in my letter agaynste his felow father Fryth, to dyspute of   15
goddes almighty absolute power. But now good readers whan you
shall se by the mater, yᵗ it was Fryth whyche argued agaynst
goddes almyghty power, denyenge that Cryst coulde make his
owne body in many places at onys / & that I dyd in effect
nothynge ellys but answere hym, & sayd and affermed that god   20
was able to do it, and that Fryth was but a fole so to strayte & to
limite the power of almyghty god, but yf he could proue repugnaunce (which agaynste goddes owne word playne spoken in his
holy gospel father Frith coulde neuer do) whan you se this good
readers, I dowte not but yė wyll saye, that it is neyther foly nor   25
presumpcyon for the [G₃v] symplest man or woman in a towne, to
mayntayne that god maye do this thyng or that (namely the thyng
that god hath sayed hym selfe he doth) agaynste hym that is so
folyshe as to presume, agaynst the playne worde of god, to determine by his own blind reason the contrary / & specyally syth the   30
thynge is suche in dede, as though god had not spoken therof, yet
had he none holde to say that god coulde not do it, for as myche as
it implyeth no suche repugnaunce as shold make the thynge
impossyble vnto god.

But now se ferther good reders the wysedome and the mekenesse   35
of mayster Masker here. Which as sone as he hath scant fynysshed
his hygh solempne rebukyng of me; for suche disputyng of goddes
almighty power, that I sayd he was in dede so mighty that he
coulde do the thynge that we [G₄] dysputed vpon agaynst hym

---

39 dysputed] dispute *1557*, dyspute *catchword 1533*

that sayd nay, falleth hym selfe forthwith in ye same fawte that he
fyndeth / and yet not in the same fawte (for the fawte that he
founde was none) but in the fawte that he wolde seme to fynde.
For he dysputeth and taketh the part agaynst goddes almyghty
5 power in dede / and argueth as you se that god in dede can not do
it.

And this poynt he argueth in such maner fashyon, that in my
lyfe I neuer sawe so folyshe an argument, so solempnely set vp an
hygh. Fyrste he maketh his reason thus. It is y^e glory of the godhed
10 and appropryed onely therunto, to be present and to fyll all places
at onys, essencially, presently, with his almyghty power / and is
denyed to any creature. But Chrystes manhed is a creature. Ergo it
can not haue this glory that is appropryed to the godhed. [G$_4$v]

Here is a wise argument. God hath many gloryes. And his chyefe
15 glory standeth not in beyng presente at onys essencyally in euery
place. And though he wyl not geue his glory from hym, yet of his
glory he maketh many creaturs in many greate partes of it, to be
partiners with him. It is one parte of his glory to lyue & endure in
eternall blysse / & though no creature be without begynnynge, yet
20 maketh he many a thowsande possessours of ioy without endynge.

How proueth mayster masker y^t to be present at onys in all
places, is such a kynde of glory so appropred vnto god, y^t god can
not geue y^t gyfte to any creature. The scrypture semeth to
appropre vnto god alone, the knowlege
*Psalm 7**   of mannes secrete thought. And yet can I
25 not se but y^t god might geue y^t knowlege to some creature to [G$_5$]
and yet abyde god styll hym selfe.

T The .xiiii. chapyter.

HAN maketh mayster Maskar an other argument, wherwyth he
30 wolde as it semeth somwhat strength the fyrst, as yt hath of trouth
no lytle nede, beynge as yt is so feble of yt selfe.

His other argument therfore is (as you haue herd) this. What
thyng so euer is euery where after the sayd maner, that muste
nedes be infynyte withoute begynnynge and ende. It muste be one,
35 and alone, and almyghtye. Whyche propertees are appropryed

---

1 y^e] that *1557*   2 not in] not *1557*   8 vp an] vp on *1557*   18 him.] *1557*, him *1533*
22 appropred] appropried *1557*

vnto the gloryouse maieste of the godhed. But Chrystes manhed ys not suche (as hym selfe wytnesseth in holy scrypture) ergo his manhed can not be in all or in many places at ones.

Fyrste (that we labour not about [G₅v] noughte) we muste consyder what mayster Maskar meaneth by these wordes, after the sayde maner. He sayde you wote well in the tother argument before, that the glory of god, is to be present, and to fyll all places at ones, essentyally, presently, with hys almyghtye power. And therfore whan he saythe nowe, what so euer thynge is euery where at ones after the sayde maner, he meaneth (you se well) present, and fyllynge all places at ones, essencyally, presently, wyth his almyghtye power.

I let passe here his word presently, whose presence nedeth not in that place for ought that I can se. For whan he sayd byfore, present and fyllynge all places at ones essentyally: his other worde presently may take his leue and be absent wel ynough. For howe can he be present & essen[G₆]tyally fyll the place, and not presently? But nowe whan he sayeth by hys almyghtye power: what ys thys to the mater? For yt is ynough agaynste hym, yf any creature maye be present in euery place at ones, and essencyally fyl the place / not by hys owne almyghtye power, but by the almyghty power of god / and yet not so fyll the place neyther, but that yt maye haue a nother wyth yt in the same place. For I trowe he wyl not denye, but that there be many creatures in those places, whyche god wyth his owne presence essencyally fylleth full.

Therfore as for these wordes after the sayde maner whyche he putteth in to make vs amased: mayster Maskar must put out again. Now yᵗ being put out, reherse & consyder well master maskars argument. What thynge so [G₆v] euer is in euery place at ones, that thynge muste nedes be infynyte without begynnynge and ende / it must be one, and alone, and almyghty / which propretyes are appropryed to the gloryouse maiestie of the godhed. But the manhed of Chryste is a creature and not god: ergo Chrystes manhed can not be in all places or in many places at ones. And yet consyder here that though he leue oute that odyouse worde: yet muste his conclusyon be in dede, that god can not make yt so, as you se plain by his begynnyng, where he sheweth that yt implyeth repugnaunce, & that therfore god can not do yt.

Now good readers consyder wel his fyrste proposycyon, whyche

we call the maior, that is to wyt that god can not make any thynge
created to be euery where at ones. Let vs [G₇] pray hym to proue
yt, and geue hym one yeres leysour to yt. But here he taketh vppon
hym to proue yt, and layeth for the reason, that god can not make
5 any creature to be in all places at ones, bycause yt shold than be
infynyte, and therby god almyghties mate and hygh felow. Lette
hym as I saye proue vs this in two yere, that yt sholde than be
infynyte, wythoute begynnynge, and wythout ende, and almyghty.
In good fayth eyther am I very dull, or elles doth mayster Maskar
10 tel vs herein a very madde tale.

I thynke he wyll not denye, but that god whyche coulde make
all this worlde, heuen, and erthe, and all the creatures yᵗ he
created therin, coulde yf yt so had pleased hym, haue created onely
one man, and let all the remanaunt alone vncreated, and haue
15 [G₇v] kept hym styll, and neuer haue made heuen nor erth nor
none other thyng, but onely that one man alone. The soule nowe
that than hadde ben created in that man, hadde yt not than ben in
all places at ones? I suppose yes. For there hadde bene no mo
places than that mannys bodye / and therein hadde there ben
20 many places in many diuerse partes of the man / in all whyche that
soule sholde haue bene present at ones, and the whole soule in
euery parte of all those places at ones. For so is euery soule in euery
mannes bodye nowe. And yet hadde that soule not ben infynyte,
no more than euery soule is now.

25 If god wolde nowe (as yf he wolde he coulde) create a newe
spyryte that sholde fulfyll all the whole worlde heuyn and erthe
and all, as myche as euer ys created, that in [G₈] suche wyse
sholde be whole present at ones in euery parte of the worlde, as the
soule is in euery parte of a man, and yet sholde not be the soule of
30 the worlde: I wyll here aske mayster Maskar, were that newe
created spyryte infynyte? If he answere me naye: than hathe he
soyled hys owne wyse reason hym selfe. For thanne no more were
the manhed of Chryste, though yt were present in all those places
of the whole world at ones. If he answere me ye: than syth that
35 spyryte were no more infynyte than the worlde ys, wythin the
lymytes and boundes wherof yt were conteyned, yt wolde folowe
therof, that the worlde were infynyte all redye, whyche is false.

10 herein] *1557*, here in *1533*

And also yf yt were trewe, thanne wold yt folow by mayster
Maskers reason, that god almyghtye hadde [G₈v] a mache all
redy, that is to wyt a nother thyng infynyte besyde hym self,
whyche is the inconuenience that maketh mayster Maskar afferme
yt for impossyble, that god coulde make Chrystes manhed to be in   5
all places at ones.

Thus you se good readers vpon what wyse grounde mayster
Maskar hath here concluded, that god can not make Chrystes
bodye to be in all places at ones.

But yet is yt a worlde to consyder how madly the man con-   10
cludeth. His conclusion is this ye wote wel, Wherfore Chrystes body
can not be in all places, or in many places at ones. All his reason ye
wote well goth vppon beynge in all places at ones, bycause that
theruppon wolde yt by his wyse reason folowe, that yt shold be
infynyte. And nowe is that poynte of trouthe no [H₁] parte of our   15
mater. For we saye not that Chrystes bodye is in all places at ones,
but in heuyn, and in suche places in erth as the blessed sacramente
ys. And therfore where as his reason goeth nothynge agaynste
beynge in many places at ones, but onely agaynste beynge at ones
in all places: he concludeth sodaynely agaynste beynge in many   20
places, towarde whyche conclusyon no pyece of his premisses
hadde any maner of mocyon. And so in all this his hygh solemne
argument, and his farre fet reason, neyther is his maior trew, nor
his argument toucheth not the mater, nor his premysses any thynge
proue his conclusyon. And yet after thys goodly reasonyng of his,   25
he reioyceth in his harte hyghly to se how iolyly he hathe handeled
yt, and sayeth,
Here yt is playne that all thynges that More yma[H₁v]gyneth and
fayneth are not possyble to god. For yt ys not possyble to god to make a
creature egall to hym selfe, for yt includeth repugnaunce and derogateth   30
hys glorye.

Mayster maskar speketh myche of myne vnwryten dremys and
vanytees. But here haue we hadde a wryten dreme of hys, and
therein this folyshe boste also so ful of vayn gloryouse vanytie / that
yf I hadde dremed yt in a fyt of a feuer, I wold I wene haue ben   35
a shamed to haue tolde my dreme to my wyfe when I woke. And
nowe shall you good readers haue here a nother pyece as proper.

---

17 places in erth as] *1533 corr. err.*, *1557*, places as *1533*

God promysed and swore that all nacyons shuld be blessed in the deth of
that promysed sede whych was Chryste: god had determyned and

Gala. 3* decreed yt before the world was made: ergo
Cryste must nedys haue dyed / and not to
5 expowne this worde oportet as More mynseth it. For it was so necessary
that the contrary was impossyble: excepte More wolde make god a lyer,
whyche is impossyble. Paule concludeth that Cryst must nedes haue dyed /

Hebre. 9* vsynge this latin terme Necesse. Sayeng
where so euer is a testyment, there muste the
10 deth of the testyment maker go betwene: [H₂] or ellys the testament is
not ratyfyed and sure / but ryghtuousnes and remyssyon of synnes in
Chrystes blood is his new testament, wherof he is medyatour: ergo the
testyment maker muste nedes haue dyed. Wreste not therfore (mayster
More) this word oportet (though ye fynde potest for oportet in some
15 corrupte copy) vnto your vnsauery sence. But let oportet sygnyfye, he
muste or yt behoueth hym to dye. For he toke our very mortall nature for
the same decreed counsayle: hym selfe sayenge Iohan. 2. & .12. Oportet
exaltari filium hominis &c. It behoueth, or the sonne of man muste dye /
that euery one that beleue in hym peryshe not &c. Here may ye se also
20 that yt is impossyble for god to breke hys promyse. It is impossyble to god
whych ys that verytie to be found contrarye in hys dedes and wordes: as
to saue them whome he hath damned / or to dampne them whome he
hathe saued. Wherfore all thynges ymagyned of Mores brayne are not
possyble to god. And when More sayeth, that Chryste had power to lette
25 hys lyfe and to take yt agayne, and therfor not to haue dyed of

Iohn 10* necessyte: I wonder me, that his scolematter
here fayled hym, so connynge as he maketh
hym selfe therin: whyche graunteth and affermeth (as trewe yt is) that
wyth the necessarye decreed workes of goddes forsyghte and prouydence
30 standeth ryght well hys free lybertye. [H₂v]

The .xv. chapyter.

IF this pyece were good readers any thynge to the purpose of our
pryncypall mater, concernynge the blessed sacrament: mayster
Maskar had here geuyn me holde ynough to geue hym four or fyue
35 suche foule falles on the backe, that his bones sholde al to burste
therwyth. But for as myche as you shall perceyue by the readynge
of my letter, that all this gere is but a bye mater, rysen vppon a

---

4 and not to] *1533 corr. err., 1557,* and to *1533*   11 ryghtuousnes] righteousenes *1557*
16 For] *1557,* for *1533*

certayne place of saynte Austayne whyche Fryth alledged imperfytely: I purpose not to spende the tyme in vayne dyspycyons wyth
mayster Maskar, in a thynge out of our mater. And namely syth
the man hath after his long bablyng agaynst me, yet in the ende
answered him self wel and suffycyently for me. [H₃]   5

For whan he hathe sayde a great whyle, that yt was in suche
wyse necessarye that Chryste muste dye, that the contrary therof
was impossyble: at laste as though he wold mocke me therwyth
and shew myne ignoraunce, he bryngeth in his own, and sheweth
that for any thynge that god hath eyther forsene or decreed and   10
determyned therin, he had left Chryst at hys lybertye to dye or
lyue yf he wolde. And than yf he was at hys lybertye not to dye but
yf he had wolde: than was it not impossible for hym to haue lyued
yf he hadde wolde. But the kepynge of hys lyfe was the contrarye of
hys dyenge: ergo hys dyenge howe necessarye so euer yt was for   15
mannes redempcyon, that ys to wytte so behofull thereto, that
wythoute yt we sholde not haue ben saued: yet mayster Maskar
here to [H₃v] shewe hym selfe a great scoles man in respecte of me,
confesseth hym selfe agaynste hym selfe, that Christ to dye was not
in suche wyse necessaryly constrayned, that the contrarye therof,   20
that is to wytte Cryst to lyue, was impossyble to hym yf he hadde
wolde / whyle mayster maskar can not saye naye, but muste nedes
geue place to the scryptures that I layed hym, and therfore must
confesse and so he dothe, that Chryst coulde by no constraynte be
compelled to dye, but was offred bycause hym selfe so wolde.   25

But the dyspytyons of thys poynte ys as I saye good reader all
besyde our pryncypall mater / and therfore I wyll let hys other
folyes that I fynde in this pyece passe by.

Than goeth mayster Maskar forthe and sayth. [H₄]
But mayster More sayth at laste, yf god wolde tell me that he wolde make   30
eche of bothe theyr bodyes to (meanynge the yonge mannys bodye and
Chrystes) to be in fyftene places at ones / I wolde byleue hym I, that he
were able to make hys worde trewe in the bodyes of bothe twayne / and
neuer wolde I so myche as aske hym whether he wolde gloryfye theym
bothe fyrste or not: but I am sure, gloryfyed or vngloryfyed, yf he sayde   35
yt, he is able to do yt. Lo here maye ye se what a feruent fayth thys olde
man hath, and what an ernest mynde to byleue Crystes wordes yf he
hadde tolde hym: but I praye ye mayster More, what and yf Chryste

---

26 dyspytyons] dispicion *1557*   37 an] a *1557*

neuer tolde yt you, nor sayde yt nor neuer wolde / wolde ye not be as
hastye to not beleue yt? yf he told it you / I pray ye tell vs where ye speke
wyth hym, and who was by to beare ye recorde: and yet yf you bryng as
false a shrewe as your selfe to testyfye thys thynge: yet by your owne
5 doctryne, muste ye make vs a myracle to conferme your tale / ere we be
bounde to byleue you, or yet to admytte this your argument, God may
make hys bodye in many places at ones, ergo yt ys so.

The .xvi. chapyter.

Rᴇade good readers in my letter the .xxi. lefe, and thanne
10 consyder mayster Maskars goodly mocke that he maketh here, and
you [H₄v] shall fynde yt very folyshe. But nowe mayster Maskar
asketh me, where I spake with Cryst whan he told me yᵗ he wold
make his owne bodye in two places at ones, as though Christe
coulde not speke to me but if I spake to hym, nor coulde not tell
15   *Luke, 24**   me the tale but yf he appered to me face
                           to face, as he dyd after his resurreccyon
to his dyscyples. This questyon of mayster Maskar cometh of an
hygh wyt I warraunt you. I answere master maskar therfore, Crist
tolde yt at hys maundy to other good credyble folke, and they
20 tolde yt forth to the whole catholique chyrch, and the whole
chyrche hathe tolde yt vnto me / and one of theym that was at yt,
that is to wytte saynte Mathew, hathe putte yt in wrytynge as the
                           same chyrche telleth me. [H₅] For ellys
       The church dothe   were I not sure whyther that gospel were
       teache vs which is
25   *scripture**   his or not, nor whyther it were any parte
                           of holy scrypture or not. And therfore I
can lacke no good and honest wytnesse to bere me recorde in that
point that wyll depose for me, that I fayne not the mater of myne
owne hed. And I haue a testymoniall also of many olde holy
30 doctours and sayntes, made afore a good notary the good man god
hym selfe, whiche hath with hys seale of many an hundred myracles, both testyfyed for the trouth of those men, & also for the
trouth of the pryncypall mater it selfe / that is to wytte that
Chrystes very body is in the blessed sacrament, though the sacra-
35 ment be eyther in two or in .x. thowsande places at onys. And thus
mayster Maskers questyons concernyng Chrystes blessed body, that

8 chapyter] capyter *1533*, chapiter *1557*

Chryst hath tolde [H₅v] me that he wolde make it be in two places
at onys, is I truste suffycyently answered. But now as for Frythys
body (whyche wryteth that Christes body can be no more in two
places at onys than his) though I wolde haue byleued yᵗ Chryst
coulde haue made it in two placys at onys yf Chryste had so tolde   5
me: yet syth Chryste hath now tolde me, by hys whole catholyke
chyrche, and by wrytynge of the olde holy sayntes of the same, &
by his own holy scrypture to, which scrypture by the same chyrche
& the same holy sayntes I know, and also se declared and
expowned, and ouer that hath by many wonderfull myracles   10
manyfestly proued & testyfyed, that thopinions in which Fryth
obstynately & therwith very folishly dyed, were very pestylent
heresyes, wherby he is perpetually seuered from [H₆] the lyuely
body of Chryst, and made a ded member of the deuyll: I byleue
therfore and very surely knowe as a thynge taught me by god, that   15
the wreched body of that felow shall neuer be in two places at onys /
but whan it shall ryse agayne and be restored to that wreched
obstynate soule, shall therwith lye styll euer more in one place,
that is to wyt in theuerlastyng fyre of hell. From whych I beseche
our lorde turne Tyndale & George Iay, wyth all the whole breth-   20
erhed, and mayster Masker amonge other (who so euer he be) by
tyme.

Now vpon his aforesayd suche a proper handeled mocke as you
haue herde, mayster masker goeth on, and geueth me ryght holsom
admonicyon, that I medle no more with such hygh maters, as is   25
the great absolute almyghty power of god / & therin thus he sayth
vnto me [H₆v]
Syr you be to bysy wyth goddes almyghty power, and haue taken to great
a burden vppon your weke shuldren.

H The .xvii. chapyter.   30

Ere he sholde haue rehersed what one worde I had sayd of
goddes almyghty power, in whyche worde I was to bysy. Rede my
letter ouer, and you shall clerely se that I saye nothynge ellys, but
that god is almyghty, & that he therfore may do all thynge. And
yet (as you shall here mayster Masker hym selfe confesse) I sayed   35

5 at] *1557*, as *1533*

not that god coulde do thynges that imply repugnaunce. But I
sayd that some thynges may seme repugnaunt vnto vs, which
thynges god seeth how to sette togyther well inough. Be these
wordes good reader ouer hyghly spoken of goddes almighty power?
5 May not a pore vnlerned man be bolde to saye that god is able to
do so myche? [H₇] And yet for sayeng thus mych, sayth mayster
Masker that I am to besy, and haue taken to great a burden vppon
my weke sholdren, and haue ouer laded my selfe with myne owne
harneyse and wepons, & many gaye wordes mo to vttre his elo-
10 quence with all. But mayster Masker on the tother syde is not hym
selfe to bysy at all with goddes almyghty power, in affermynge that
god hath not the power to make hys owne blessed body in many
places at onys. Hys myghty stronge sholdren take not to mych
weyght vppon them, whan in stede of omnypotent, he proueth god
15 impotent / and that by suche impotent argumentes, as you se your
selfe so shamefully halte, that neuer lame cryple yᵗ lay impotent by
yᵉ wallys in crepyng out vnto a dole, halted halfe so sore. But than
goth he ferther for [H₇v] the prayse of yonge Dauyd & sayth.
You haue ouerladen your selfe wyth your owne harneyse and weapons /
20 and yonge Dauyd is lyke to preuayle agaynst you wyth hys slynge & his
stone.
    As for mayster Maskers yonge mayster Dauyd, who so loke
vppon his fyrst treatice & my letter together shall sone se yᵗ his
sling and his stone be beten both about hys earys. And whan so
25 euer his new sling & his new stone (which is as I nowe here saye
very lately come ouer in prent) come onys into my handes, I shall
turne his slynge into a cokstewe, & his stone into a fether, for any
harme that it shalbe able to do, but yf it be to suche as wyllyngely
wyll putte out theyr owne eyen, to whych they neuer nede neyther
30 stone nor slynge, but wyth a fether they maye do it and they be so
madde.
    But an heuy thynge it is to here of his yonge folyshe Dauyd, that
[H₈] hath thus wyth his stone of stobburnesse, stryken out his
owne brayne / & with the slynge of hys heresyes, slongen hym selfe
35 to the deuyll.
    Yet mayster Masker can not leue me thus, but on he goth ferther
in his raylynge rethoryke & thus he sayth.

---

10 on] *1557*, vn *1533*   16 lame] *1533 corr. err.*, *1557*, lambe *1533*   18 goth he] he goeth
1557   34 slongen] slonken *1557*

God hath infatuated your hygh subtyll wysdome / your crafty conuayaunce is espyed. God hath sent your chyrche a mete couer for suche a
cuppe, euyn such a defender as you take your selfe to be, that shall lette
all theyr whole cause fall flatte in the myre, vnto bothe your shames and
vtter confusyon. God therfore be praysed euer amen.   5

The .xviii. chapyter.

As for wysdome I wyll not compare wyth mayster Masker
therin / nor wolde waxe myche the prowder in good faythe though
menne wolde saye that I had more wytte than he. I praye god
sende vs bothe a lytell more of his grace, and make vs bothe good.   10
[H₈ᵛ]

But where as he iesteth concernynge my defence of the chyrch:
who so loke my bokes thorow, shall fynde that the chyrch, in the
treuth of whose catholyke fayth concernynge the blessed sacrament
I wryte agaynst Fryth and Tyndale, and mayster Masker and such   15
false heretykes mo, is none other chyrch but the trewe catholyke
chyrche of Cryst, the whole congregacyon of al trew chrysten
nacyons / of whyche chyrche I take not my selfe to be any specyall

*It is euerye true
mannes part to
defend the church* *

defender, how be it to defende it / is in
dede euery good mannys parte. And as   20
for hytherto, the thynges that I haue
wryten are (I thanke god) stronge
inough to stand, as it is playnely proued agaynst all these heretykes
yᵗ haue wrestled therwith, wherof they coulde neuer yet ouer-
throwe one lyne / and no man more shamefully sowsed in yᵉ myre /   25
[I₁] than mayster Masker here hym self that bosteth his victory
while he lieth in the dyrte. But the catholyke chyrche hath another
maner defender than is any erthely man. For it hath god hym selfe
therin, and his holy spyryt, permanent and abydyng by Crystes
own promise to defende it from falshed vnto thende of the worlde.   30

Math. 28

And therfore it can not fall flatte in the
myre / but god maketh heretykes fall
flatte in the fyre.

Yet to thentent good readers / that you sholde well se that I lefte
not vntowched the point of repugnaunce, with whych mayster   35
Masker hath al this whyle set out his hygh solempn reason agaynst

20 good] gook *1557*

goddes almyghtynes: hym selfe sheweth here at laste, that of
repugnaunce I dyd speke my self. How be it in dede, somwhat
more moderately than he / as ye shall not [I₁v] onely perceyue by
the wordes of my letter, but also by the wordes of mayster Masker
5 hym selfe whyche be these.
Then sayth maister More / though it semeth repugnaunt bothe to hym
and to me / one body to be in two places at onys: yet god seeth how to
make theym stonde togyther well inough. This man wyth hys olde eyen
10 and spectacles seeth farre in goddes sight / and is of his preuey counsell:
that knoweth belyke by some secrete reuelacyon how god seeth one body
to be in many places at onys / includeth no repugnaunce. For worde hath
he none for hym in all scrypture no more then one body to be in all places
at onys. It implyeth fyrst repugnaunce to my syght & reason / that all
15 thys worlde shulde be made of nothynge: & that a vyrgyn sholde brynge
forth a chyld. But yet when I se it wryten wyth the wordys of my fayth /
whyche god spake / and brought it so to passe: then implyeth it no
repugnaunce to me at all. For my fayth recheth it and receyueth it
stedfastly. For I knowe the voyce of my herdeman / whyche yf he sayd in
20 any place of scrypture that hys body shulde haue bene contayned vnder
the forme of brede and so in many places at onys here in erth / and also
abydynge yet styll in heuyn to / Veryly I wolde haue byleued hym I / as
sone and as fermely as mayster More. And therfore euen yet / yf he can
shew vs but one sentence truely taken for hys parte, as we can do many
25 for the contrary / we muste gyue place. For as for his vnwryten verytees
and thautoryte of his [I₂] antichrysten synagoge, vnto whyche (the scrypture forsaken) he is now at laste wyth shame inough compelled to flee:
they be proued starke lyes and very deuelrye.

The .xix. chapyter.

30 Is not thys a wyse inuented scoffe that mayster Masker mocketh
me wythall / and sayth that with myne olde eyen & my spectacles
I se farre in goddys syghte, and am of goddys pryuy counsayle, and
that I knowe bylyke by some secrete reuelacyon, how god seeth
that one body to be in many places at onys includeth no repug-
35 naunce. It is no counsayle ye wote well that is cryed at the crosse.
But Chryst hath cryed and proclamed this hym selfe, and sent hys
heraldys, hys blessed apostles, to cry it out abrode, & hath caused
his euangelistes also to wryte yᵉ proclamacion, by which all yᵉ
world was [I₂v] warned that hys blessed body, hys holy fleshe and
40 his bloude, is veryly eaten and dronken in the blessed sacrament.
And therfore eyther all those places be one in whyche the blessed

sacrament is receyued at onys, or els god may do the thynge that is
repugnaunt, or els he seeth that his body to be in dyuerse places at
onys, is not repugnaunt. For well I wote / he sayth he doth it, in all
the .iiii. euangelystes. And well I wote also, that he can not say but
soth. And therfore neyther nede I to see very farre for this poynt,   5
nor nede no secrete reuelacyon neyther, syth it is the poynt, that to
the whole worlde, god hath bothe by worde, wrytynge, and myracles, reueled and shewed so openly. Where is mayster Masker now?

For where he sayeth I haue no worde of scrypture for Chrystes
[I₃] body to be in many places at onys, no more than to be in all   10
placys at onys: yf I hadde not, yet yf god had otherwyse than by
wrytynge reueled the tone to hys chyrche and not the tother, I
wolde and were bounde to byleue the tone, and wolde not nor
were bounden to byleue the tother / as I byleue and am bounde to
byleue now that the gospell of saynt Iohan is holy scrypture, and   15
not the gospell of Nichodemus. And yf god hadde reueled bothe
twayne vnto the chyrche: I wolde and were bounde to byleue
bothe twayne / as I byleue now that the gospell of saynte Iohan is
holy scrypture, and the gospell of saynt Mathew to.

But now of trouth mayster masker abomynably bylyeth the   20
worde of god, whan he sayeth that we haue not the worde of god,
no more for the [I₃v] beynge of Chrystes body in many places at
onys, than in all places at onys. For as for the beynge therof in all
places at onys, we fynde no word playnely wryten in the scrypture.
But for the beynge therof in many places at onys, Chrystes wordes   25
in his last souper, and byfore that in the syxte chapyter of saynt
Iohan, be as open, as clere, and as playne as any man well coulde
wyth any reason requyre / excepte any man were so wise as to
wene yᵗ dyuerse mennys mowthes were all one place. And therfore
whan mayster Masker in his wordes folowynge, maketh as though   30
he wolde byleue it, as well as he byleueth the creacyon of the
world, and Chrystes byrth of a virgine (whiche seme also to hys
reason repugnaunt) yf Chryste in any playne place of scrypture
sayd it, the trouth appereth [I₄] otherwyse. For vnto hym that is
not wyth his own frowardnesse blynded by the deuyll, the thynge   35
that he denyeth is as playnely spoken, as are the tother twayne that
he sayth he byleueth. And some other wreches such as hym selfe is,
in foly and stoburnnesse denye bothe the tother twayne, for the

---

37 is,] is *1557*   38 stoburnnesse] stubbernes, *1557*; twayne,] twain *1557*

repugnaunce, as well as he doth this / whiche thynge you haue
herde hym al redy, with very folysh reasons declare for so repug-
naunte, that he sayeth that god can not do it, bycause it were as he
sayth a geuyng awaye of his glory. And therfore his harte onys sette
5 and fyxed on the wronge syde the deuyll causeth hym so to delyte
in suche fonde folysshe argumentes of hys owne inuencyon, that he
can not endure to turne hys mynde to the trowthe / but euery texte
be it neuer so playne, ys darke [I₄v] vnto hym / thorow the darke-
nesse of his owne brayne.

The .xx. chapyter.

10   Bvt now for bycause he sayeth, that he wylbe content and
satysfyed in thys mater with any one texte truely taken: whyle I
shall say that the textes that I shall bryng hym, be by me truely
taken, and he shall saye naye, and shall saye that I take them
15 amysse & vntreuly: whyle he and I can not agre vppon the
takynge, but vary vppon thexposycyon and the ryght vnderstandynge of them: by whom wyll he be iudged, whyther he or I
take those textes truely? If by the congregacyon of chrysten
people: the whole chrysten nacyons haue thys fyftene hundred yere
20 iudged it agaynste hym. [I₅] For all this while haue they beleued,
yᵗ Chryst at his maundy, whan he sayd this is my bodye, ment that
yt was his very body in dede / and euer haue byleued and yet do,
that yt was so in dede. If he wyll haue yt iudged by a generall
counsayle, yt hath ben iudged for me agaynste hym, by mo then
25 one all redye, before his dayes and myne bothe. If he wyl be
iudged by the wrytynges of the olde holy doctours and sayntes: I
haue al redye shewed you suffycyentely, that they haue al redye
iudged this poynte agaynste hym. If he and I wolde varye vppon
the vnderstandyng of the olde sayntes wordes, bysydes that you se
30 them your self so playne, that he shal in that poynte but shewe
hym selfe shameful and shamlesse: yet the general counsayles
(whych hym selfe denyeth not) hauyng redde and [I₅v] sene those
holy doctours them selfe, and many of those holy sayntes beynge
present at those counsayles them selfe, haue therby iudged that
35 poynt agaynste hym to. For no wyse man wyll doute, but that

16 the ryght] ryghte 1557

amonge theym they vnderstode the doctours than as well as
mayster Maskar doth nowe. If he saye that he wyll wyth his other
mo then twenty textes of scrypture of whyche he spake before,
dysproue vs the textes one or two that I brynge for the blessed
sacrament: than cometh he (you se well) to the self same poynt 5
agayne, wherin he is ouerthrowen al redye. For all the corps of
chrystendome of thys .xv. hundred yere before vs, and all the olde
holy doctours & sayntes, and al the general counsayles, and all the
meruaylouse myracles that god hath shewed for the blessid sacrament [I₆] yerely almost, and I wene dayly to, what in one place 10
and other / al whyche thynges proue the textes that I lay, to be
ment and vnderstanden as I say. Al they do therby declare agaynst
hym also, that none of his mo than twenty textes, can in any wyse
be wel and ryght vnderstanden as he sayth. For ellys shold yt
folow, that dyuerse textes of holy scrypture, not onely semed 15
*In scripture is
no repugnaunce**
(whyche may well be) but also were in
dede (whyche is a thynge impossyble and
can not be) contraryouse & repugnant
vnto other.

Now good chrysten readers here you se, that in his shyft that he 20
vseth, where he sayeth that he wyl byleue any one text trewly
taken: we bryng hym for the trew takyng vppon our parte, all
these thynges that I haue here shortely rehersed you / of whych
thynges hym selfe denyeth very [I₆v] fewe / that is to wyt, the olde
holy doctours to holde on our parte / and the people of theyr tyme. 25
But therin haue I shewed you diuerse of yᵉ beste sorte agaynst
hym. And the fayth of the people of the dyuerse tymes appereth by
theyr bokes and by the counsayles. And than that the generall
counsayles and the myracles are on our parte, of these two thynges
he denyeth neyther nother. But syth he can denye none of them, he 30
dyspyseth bothe. And the holy counsayles of Chrystes chyrche he
calleth the Antichrysten synagoge. And goddes myracles both
Fryth and he be fayne to cal the workes of the deuyl. And therfore
good chrysten readers, whyle you se all thys: ye se well ynough
that the textes of the gospell whyche we laye for the blessed bodye 35
of Chryste in the blessed sacrament, [I₇] be clere and playne for
the purpose / and mayster Maskar wyll not agre yt so, but sayth

that we take theym not trewly, onely bycause he will not perceyue
and confesse the trouth.

[The .xxi. chapyter.]

Nowe where as mayster Maskar sayth of me ferther thus.

5   As for his vnwryten verytees, and thautoryte of hys Antichrysten synagoge, vnto whyche the scrypture forsaken he is now at laste wyth shame
ynough compelled to fle: they be proued starke lyes and very deuylrye.

Consyder good chrysten readers that in these wordes mayster
maskar telleth you two thynges. Fyrste that I am wyth shame
10   ynough compelled to fle fro the scrypture to myn vnwryten
veryties, and to thauthoryte of thantichrysten synagoge, by whyche
he meaneth the tradycyons and the determynacyons of the
catholyque chyrche. The tother that the tradycyons and [I₇v]
determinacyons of the chyrch, be all redy proued starke lyes and
15   very deuylrye. For the fyrste poynte you se that in this mater of the
blessed sacrament, whyche ys one of the thynges that he meaneth,
he hath not yet compelled me to fle fro the scrypture. For I haue
wel all redye proued you this poynt, & very playne and clerely, by
the selfe same place of scrypture, whyche mayster Maskar hathe
20   expowned & falsely wolde wreste it a nother way, that is to wyt the
wordes of Chryst wryten in the syxt chapyter of saynt Iohan. Nowe
yf I do for the profe of thys poynte, lay the tradycyon of yᵉ whole
catholyque chyrche besyde, whyche thynge ys also suffycyent to
proue the mater alone: ys that a fleynge fro the scrypture? If that
25   be a fleynge fro the scryp[I₈]ture, than myghte the olde heretyques very wel haue sayde the same vnto al the olde holy doctours, that this new heretyque sayeth nowe to me. For this woteth
wel euery man (that any lernynge hathe) that those old holy doctours and sayntes, layed agaynste those old heretykes not the scryp-
30   ture onely, but also the tradycyons vnwryten, byleued and taughte
by the chyrche. And yf mayster Maskar whan he shal defende hys
boke, dare denye me that they so dyd: I shall brynge you so many
playn proues therof, that be he neuer so shamelesse he shal be
ashamed thereof. And yf he can not say naye but that they so dyd,

---

7 fle] flye *1557*   21 syxt] sixth *1557*   34 And yf he] *1533 corr. err.*, *1557*, And he *1533*

as I wote wel he can not: than you se wel good reders y^t by master
maskers wise reason, those old heretikes might haue sayd agaynst
eche of those old holy doctours & saintes as [I$_8$v] mayster Maskar
sayth agaynste me now, that they hadde made him with shame
ynough, fle fro the scrypture, bycause he besyde the scrypture   5
proued the trew faith and reproued their false heresyes, by thauthoryte of the catholyque chyrche. Suche strength haue alwaye lo,
mayster maskers argumentes.

Nowe touchyng the secund point, where he calleth the catholyke
chyrch the antichrysten synagoge, and the vnwryten veryties starke   10
lyes and deuylrye: he hathe al redy shewed and declared partely
which thynges they be that hym self meaneth by y^t name. For he
hath before specyfyed purgatorye, pylgrimages, and prayenge to
sayntes, honourynge of ymages, and crepynge to the crosse, and
halowyng of belles agaynst euyl spirites in tempestes, and boughes   15
on palme sone[K$_1$]daye, and byleuynge in the blessed sacrament.
And Tyndale that ys eyther hym selfe or his felow, mocketh vnder
the same name the sacrament of anelyng / and calleth the sacrament of confyrmacyon the butterynge of the boyes forhed, & had
as lyefe haue at his chrystenynge sande put in hys mouth as salt /   20
and mocketh mych at fastyng. And as for lent, father Frith vnder
name of Brightwell in the reuelacyon of Antichrist calleth it y^e
folishe fast / which ieste was vndoutedly reueled father Fryth by
the spyryt of the deuyll hym selfe, the spirituall father of Anti-
chryste.   25

So that you maye se good readers that to saye the latenye, or our
ladye matens, and crepe to the crosse at Ester, or praye for all
christen soules: these thynges & such other as I haue rehersed you,
mayster Maskar [K$_1$v] saith are all redy proued starcke lyes and
very deuylrye. But he sheweth vs no such profe yet, neyther of lyes   30
nor of deuylrye. But euery man may sone se, that he whych sayeth
so myche and nothyng proueth, maketh many a starke lye / & that
thus to raile agaynste god and al good men / and holy sayntes, and
helpynge of good chrysten soules / and raylyng agaynst the blessed
bodye of Chryste in the blessed sacrament, callynge ye bylyef therof   35
deuylrye: yf suche raylyng in mayster maskar be not (as I wene it

---

8 maskers] maykers *1533*, Maskers *1557*   26 latenye] letany *1557*   31 deuylrye] del-
uylrye *1533*, deuilrye *1557*

is) very playne and open deuylrye, yt can be no lesse yet at the leste wyse than very playne and open knauery.

The .xxii. chapyter.

5 Master Maskar cometh at last to the mockynge of those wordes of my pystle, wherin I shewe [K₂] that yf men wolde denye the conuersyon of the brede and wyne into the blessed bodye and blood of Chryste, bycause that vnto his owne reason the thynge semeth to implye repugnaunce, he shal fynde many other thynges bothe in scrypture, and in nature, and in hande craftes to, of the
10 trouthe wherof he nothynge douteth, whyche yet for any solucion that hys owne reason coulde fynde, other than the omnipotent power of god, wolde seme repugnant to / of whych maner thynges, other good holy doctours haue in the mater of the blessed sacrament vsed some ensamples byfore.

15 Nowe for as myche as in these wordes I speke of the apperynge of the face in the glasse, and one face in euery pyece of the glasse broken in to twenty: mayster Maskar hath [K₂v] caughte that glasse in hand and mocketh and moweth in that glasse, and maketh as many straunge faces and as many pretye pottes therin,
20 as yt were an olde ryueled ape. For these are his wordes lo.

Then sayth he, that ye wote wel that many good folke haue vsed in thys mater many good frutefull exsamples of goddes other workes: not onely myracles, wryten in scrypture / vnde versus? (where one I praye ye?) but also done by the comen course of nature here in erth. (If they be
25 done by the comen course of nature: so be they no myracles) And some thynges made also by mans hande. As one face beholden in dyuerse glasses: and in euery pyece of one glasse broke into twenty &c. Lorde howe thys pontyfycall poete playeth hys parte. Because (as he sayeth) we se many faces in many glasses: therfor maye one bodye be in many
30 places / as though euery shadowe and symylytude representynge the bodye / were a bodyly substaunce. But I aske More / when he seeth his owne face in so many glasses / whyther all those faces that appere in the glasses be hys own very face hauynge bodely substaunce, skynne, fleshe, and bone, as hathe that face / whyche hathe hys very mouth, nose, yien,
35 &c. wherwyth he faceth vs oute the trouthe thus falsely wyth lyes? and yf

---

they be al hys very faces / than in very dede there ys one body in many places / & he hym selfe beareth as many faces in one hoode. But accordynge to hys purpose / [K₃] euen as they be no very faces / nor those so many voyces, sownes, and symylytudes multyplyed in the ayer betwene the glasse or other obiecte and the body (as the phylosopher proueth by naturall reason) be no very bodyes: no more is yt Chrystes very bodye, as they wolde make the byleue in the brede in so many places at ones:

Now good reders to thende that you may se the custumable maner of mayster Maskar in rehersynge my mater to his owne aduauntage / syth my wordes in my letter that touche this poynt be not very longe / I shall reherse them here vnto you my self / lo good reders thus shal you fynd yt there in the .xxvi. lefe.

I wote well that many good folke haue vsed in this mater many good frutefull examples of goddes other workes, not onely myracles wryten in scrypture, but also done by the comen course of nature here in erth and some thynges made also by mannys hand as one face byholden in dyuers glasses & in euery pyece of one glasse [K₃v] broken into .xx. and the merueyle of the makynge of the glasse it selfe such mater as it is made of. And of one worde comyng whole to an hundred earys at onys and the syghte of one lytell eye present and beholdynge an whole great cuntrey at onys wyth a thousande such other merueyles mo, such as those that se them dayly done and therfore merueyle not at theym, shall yet neuer be able no not thys yonge man hym selfe, to geue suche reason by what meane they maye be done / but that he maye haue such repugnaunce layed agaynste it that he shall be fayne in conclusyon for the chyefe and the moste euydent reason to say that the cause of all those thynges is bycause god that hath caused theym so to be done, is almyghty of hym selfe and canne do what hym lyste.

Lo good Chrysten readers here you se your selfe, that I made none [K₄] suche argument as mayster Maskar bereth me in hand. Nor no man vseth vppon a symilytude, to conclude a necessarye consequence, in the mater of the blessed sacrament / vnto whyche we can brynge nothynge so lyke, but that in dede it muste be farre vnlyke, sauynge that it is as semeth me some what lyke in this, that god is as able by his almyghty power, to make one body be in twenty places at ones, as he is by comen course of nature which hym self hath made, able to make one face kepynge styll hys owne fygure in hys owne place, caste yet and multyply the same fygure of yt self, into xx. pyeces of one broken glasse / of whyche pyeces eche hathe a seuerall place. And as he is able by the nature that

hym selfe made, to make one self worde that the speker hath
brethed oute in the spekynge to be forth with [K₄v] in the eares of
an whole hundred persones, eche of theym occupyeng a seuerall
place, and that a good dystaunce a sundre. Of whyche two thynges
5 (as natural and as comen as they both be) yet can I neuer cease to
wonder, for all the reasons that euer I redde of the phylosopher.
And lyke wyse as I veryly truste, that the tyme shall come, whan
we shall in the clere syght of Christes godhed, se this great myracle
soyled, and wel perceyue howe yt ys, and howe yt maye be, that
10 his blessed bodye ys bothe in heuyn and in erth, and in so many
places at ones: so thynke I veryly that in the syght of hys godhed
than, we shall also perceyue a better cause of those two other
thynges than euer any phylosopher hath hytherto shewed vs yet /
or ellys I wene for my parte I shall neuer [K₅] perceyue theym
15 well.

But nowe where as mayster Maskar mocketh myne argument,
not whych I made, but whyche hym selfe maketh in my name /
and maketh yt feble for the nonce, that he maye when he hathe
made yt at hys owne pleasure soyle yt, as chyldren make castelles
20 of tyle shardes, and than make theym theyr passe tyme in the
throwynge downe agayne: yet is yt not euyn so, so feble as his own,
where he argueth in the negatyue, as I laye the sample for thaffyr-
matyue. For as for the tone that he maketh for me: though thargu-
ment be nought for lacke of forme, yet holdeth it somwhat so so, by
25 the mater in that the consequent that is to wytte, that god may
make one body to be at ones in many places, is what so euer
mayster masker bable, a trouth with[K₅v]out questyon necessary.

But where he argueth for hym selfe in the negatyue, by that that
the bodyly substaunce of the face is not in the glasse, that therfore
30 the bodyly substaunce of our sauyoure Chryste is not in the blessed
sacrament: that argument hath no maner holde at all. For thantecedent is very trewe / and (excepte goddys worde be vntrewe) ellys
as I haue all redy by the old holy expositours of the same, well and
planely proued you, the consequent is very false.

35 Now yf he wyll saye that he maketh not that argument, but
vseth onely the face in the glasse for a sample & a symylytude:

6 phylosopher] phylopher *1533*, Philosopher *1557*   24 so so,] so so *1557*   25 mater]
matter, *1557*; consequent] consequent, *1557*

than he sheweth hym selfe to playe the false shrewe, whan of my
bryngynge in the selfe same sample, he maketh that argument for
me. And therfore now whan [K$_6$] vppon those facys in the glasse,
he maketh and faceth hym selfe that lye vppon me, and than
scoffeth that I face out the trouth with lyes, and than proueth 5
neuer one: he doth but shew what prety wordes he coulde speke,
and how properly he coulde scoffe, yf the mater wolde serue hym.

And yet I pray you good readers consyder well the wordes of
that argument that he maketh in myne name. We se many faces in
many glasses: therfore may one body be in many places. Now spake not 10
I you wote well of many faces sene in many glassys (as he bothe
falsely & folysshely reherseth me) but of one face sene at onys in
Note this* many glassys. For that is lyke to the
mater. For like as all those glasses, whyle
onely one man loketh in them / he seeth but hys owne one face in 15
all those places / so be (as saynt Chrysostom declareth) [K$_6$v] all
the hostes of the blessed sacrament beynge in so farre dystaunt
seuerall places a sondre, all one very body of our blessed sauyour
hym selfe, and all one hoste, one sacryfyce, and one oblacyon.

And as properly as mayster masker scoffeth at that sample and 20
symylytude of the glasse: I wolde not haue mysse lyked myne owne
wytte therin, yf thinuencyon therof had ben myne owne. For I
fynde not many samples so mete for the mater, to the capacite of
good and vnlerned folke, as it is. For as for the poynt of which
mayster Masker maketh all the dyfficultye, that one substaunce 25
beynge but a creature myghte be in many places at onys: euery
man that is lerned seeth a sample that satisfyeth hym shortely. For
he seeth and perceyueth by good reason, that the soule [K$_7$] is
vndiuisyble and is in euery parte of the body, and in euery parte it
is whole. And yet is euery member a seuerall place. And so is the 30
blessed substaunce of the spyrytuall body of Chrystes flesshe & his
bonys, whole in euery parte of the sacrament.

But thys sample of the soule can not euery man vnlerned conceyue and imagyne ryghte / but of the glasse hath for his capacite a
more metely symilitude, & that y^t in one poynt also doth more 35
resemble the mater. For the soule forsaketh euery member y^t is

---

9 myne] my *1557*   33 can not] cannt *1557*

clene deuided from the body. But the blessed body of our sauyour

Note*   abydeth styll whole in euery parte of the
blessed sacrament, though it be broken
into neuer so many partes / as the image and forme of the face
5   abydeth whole styll to hym that byholdeth it, in euery parte of the
broken [K₇v] glasse. And thus good readers as for thys sample and
symylytude of the face in the glasse, mayster Masker maye for his
folyshe facynge yt out, be myche ashamed yf he haue any shame,
whan so euer he loketh on his owne face in the glasse.

10   And for conclusyon, thys beynge of the body of Chryste in
dyuers places at ones, syth the olde holy doctours and sayntes sawe
and perceyued, that the soule of euery man whyche is a very
substaunce, and peraduenture yet of lesse spirituall power, than the
flesshe and bones of our sauyour Chryste be now, and yet very
15   flesshe for all that and very bonys also styll: they rekened not that
the beynge therof in dyuers places at ones, wolde after theyr dayes
begyn to be taken for so straunge and harde a thynge as these
heretykes make yt [K₈] nowe. And therfore they made nothyng so
great a mater of that poynt / but the thynge that they thought men
20   wolde moste meruayle of, was the conuersyon and turnyng of the
brede and the wyne into Chrystes very flesshe and bloud. And
therfore to make that poynte well open, and to make it synke into
mennys brestes: those olde holy doctours and sayntes (as I sayde in
these wordes whyche maister maskar mocketh) vsed many mo
25   good samples of thynges done by nature.

     But than were they no myracles sayth mayster Masker. And
what than good master Masker? Myghte they not serue to proue yᵗ
god myght do as mych by myracle, as nature by her comen
course? Those wordes lo were by maister masker (you se wel) very
30   well and wysely put in. [K₈v]

The .xxiii. chapyter.

Over this towarde the perceyuyng and bylyefe of that point of
conuersyon of the brede and the wyne into the very flesshe and
bloud of Chryste: I sayd that those holy doctours and sayntes, vsed

---

4 partes] *1533 corr. err.*, *1557*, places *1533*

ensamples of other myracles done by god, and wryten in holy
scrypture.

Now at thys word mayster masker asketh me Vnde versus? where
one I pray you? you haue herd all redy good readers in the .xv.
chapyter of the fyrste boke, the wordes of that holy doctour saynt 5
Cyryll, in whyche for the credence of that poynt, that is to wytte
the chaungynge of the brede and the wyne into Chrystes flesshe
and hys bloud, he bryngeth the myracles that god wrought in the
olde lawe, as the chaungyng of the water into bloude, [L₁] and the
chaungyng of Moses rodde into a serpent, and dyuers other 10
chaunges and myghty myracles mo.

Yow haue herde also before, how saynt Chrysostome agaynste
them yᵗ wolde dowte, how Chryste coulde geue them hys flesshe
to eate, layeth forth the myracle of the
Math. 14* multiplyeng of fyue louys so sodaynly, to 15
.xii. basketes full more than the suffycyent fedynge of fyue thousand folke.

Here be lo some verses yet mayster Masker, & mo than one
miracle perdye, that those holy doctours and sayntes haue vsed in
this mater of the blessed sacrament. And yet suche other mo shall I 20
brynge you at another leysour, ere I haue done wyth your second
course, that it shall greue you to se them. And surely where properly you scoffe at me wyth my many facys in one hode: I haue here
[L₁v] in thys fyrste parte all redy brought you for the trew fayth of
the catholyke chyrche, agaynste your false heresye, wherwith you 25
wolde face our sauyour out of yᵉ blessed sacrament: I haue
brought agaynst you to your face, saint Bede and Theophilactus,
saynt Austayne, and saynt Hylary, saynt Hyreneus, saynt Cyryll,
and saynt Chrysostome, so many suche good facys into this one
hode, that al the shameful lyes yᵗ your shamelesse face can make, 30
shall neuer agaynste these facys be able to face out the trouth. And
thus ende I good readers my fourth boke.

Here endeth the fourth booke. [L₂]

---

16 suffycyent] fuffycyent *1533*, sufficient *1557*

The fyfth booke
and the laste of the
fyrste parte.

The fyrste chapyter.

5 Now come I good chrysten readers to the last poynte that I
spake of, the two contradyccyons of myn owne, that mayster
Masker hath hyghly layed vnto my charge / whose wordes I shall
good reders fyrst reherse you whole. Lo these they be god saue
them.

10 At laste note chrysten reader, that mayster More in the thyrde boke of
hys confutacyon of Tyndale, the 249. syde, to proue saynt Iohans gospell
vnperfyte & insuffycyent, for leuyng out of so necessary a poynt of our
fayth, as he calleth the last souper of Chryste hys maundye: sayth that
Iohan spake nothynge at all of thys sacrament. And now se agayne in
15 these [L₂v] hys letters agaynste Fryth / how hym selfe bryngeth in Iohan
6. cap. to impugne Frythes wrytyng / and to make all for the sacrament,
euen thus / My flesshe is veryly meate, and my bloude drynke. By lyke
the man had there ouershette hym selfe fowle / the yonge man here caus-
ynge hym to put on his spectacles and poore better and more wysshely
20 wyth his olde eyen vppon saynt Iohans gospell to fynde that thynge there
now wryten, whyche before he wolde haue made one of hys vnwryten
verytees. As yet yf he loke narowly he shall espye that hym selfe hath
proued vs by scrypture, in the 37. lefe of his dyaloge of quod he and quod
I our ladyes perpetuall virgynyte expownynge non cognosco, id est, non
25 cognoscam / whych now wryten vnwryten veryte he nombereth a lytell
before amonge hys vnwryten vanytees. Thus maye ye se how thys olde
holy vpholder of the popes chyrche / hys wordes fyghte agaynste them
selfe into his owne confusyon, in fyndynge vs forth hys vnwryten wryten
vanitees veritees I shulde saye. But returne we vnto the exposycyon of
30 saynt Iohan.

Now haue you good christen readers herd his whole tale, concernyng my two contradyccyons. Of whyche twayne I wyll fyrst
answere yᵉ last, that concerneth yᵉ perpetual virginite of our lady.

---

8 whole.] *1557*, whole *1533*   18 ouershette] ouershotte *1557*   25 nombereth] uombereth
1533, noumbreth *1557*   26 vanytees.] vanytees *1533*, vanities. *1557*

Which point I haue towched towarde the ende of the .xxv. [L₃]
chapyter of the fyrst boke of my dyalogue, wherin master masker
mocketh me for quod I and quod he / and wolde I se well in no
wyse, that in the rehersyng of a communycacyon had bytwene my
selfe & another man, I shold not for shame say quod I and quod   5
he / but rather reherse our two talkinges, with quoth we and quoth
she.

   I haue also spoken of that poynt in mo places than one of my
wurke that I wrote of Tyndals confutacyon / whiche places who so
lyste to rede shall fynde thys poynt of contradyccyon answered all 10
redy, yᵗ maister masker now layth to my charge dyssymulynge such
thynges as I haue answered it wyth.

   And of this contradyccyon I am so sore ashamed, yᵗ for all
mayster maskers wordes euyn here before in my fyrst boke of this
wurke, I haue not [L₃v] letted the beste that my wytte wyll serue   15
me this vnwryten veryte, to proue yet agayne by the selfe same
place of saynte Lukes holy writyng.

   For why, to saye the trouth I do not so myche force to haue that
artycle taken for an vnwryten veryte, with good catholyke folke for
the mayntenaunce of my word, as to haue it for the honour of our   20
lady, taken & byleued for an vndowted trowth, with catholykes
and those heretykes to, that wyll take it for no such trouth but yf it
be wryten in scrypture.

   Now doth the clere certaynte of thys artycle in dede depende
vppon the tradycyon of thapostles, continued in the catholyke   25
chyrche. For all be it that my selfe thynke, that I fynd some wordes
wryten in scrypture that wolde well proue it / and vppon those
wordes lette not to wryte myn [L₄] owne mynde, and dyuers olde
holy doctours to: yet whyle I se that holy saynt Hierome hym selfe,
a man far otherwyse sene in scrypture than I, arguynge for the   30
defence of that artycle agaynst that heretyke Heluidius dyd onely
soyle the scryptures that Heluidius layed agaynste it, and layeth no
scripture hym selfe for yᵉ profe of his part, but resteth therin to
thauthoryte of Chrystes catholyke chyrche, whyche mayster
Masker here calleth yᵉ antichrysten synagoge: I neyther dare nor   35
wyl take so mych vpon my selfe, as to afferme surely that it is

---

proued to be a wryten veryte. And thys lacke of takynge lo so
myche vpon my selfe, is the thynge y^t mayster Masker calleth so
shameful repugnaunce to my great confusion.

And therfore in that place of my dyaloge, though I vpon that
5   worde [L₄v] of our lady, " *In what wise shall thys thyng be done for I
know not a man* " do reason and shew my mynde, that it proueth for
this parte, as in dede me thynketh it doth: yet I am not so bold
vpon myne owne exposicion therin, as to afferme that the scripture
saith there openly & playnely, that she was a perpetuall virgyne.
10   For yf it hadde ben a very precyse playne euydent open profe of
that mater, myne own mynde geueth me, y^t saynt Hierom wolde
not haue fayled to haue found it before me.

I shall also for this poynte haue maister masker hym self to say
some what for me, though he do therin (as he is often wont to do)
15   speke somewhat agaynst hym selfe. For he sayth here him self, y^t if
a man loke narowly than he shal espye y^t I haue my selfe proued
our ladyes perpetual virginite. [L₅] Nowe syth that mayster
Maskar sayth that a man can not spye yt but yf he loke narowly:
he sayth you se well hym selfe, that yt is no playne open profe. And
20   than is yt no profe to theym you wote wel. For they receyue no
scrypture for profe of any purpose, but onely playne open and
euydent.

And therfore by mayster Maskars owne tale, though I proued yt
suffycyently a wryten verytie vnto good catholyques: yet rested yt
25   vnproued styll a wryten verite, vnto suche heretyques, and agaynst
them ye wote wel wrote I.

How be it here wyll I demaund of mayster masker touchyng the
perpetuall virgynyte of our lady to be playnely wryten in holy
scrypture, whyther I proue that poynt well or not? If not / than
30   maye I well inough [L₅v] notwithstandynge any such profe of
myne, saye styll that it is an vnwryten veryte. If he wyll confesse
that I proue it well: I wylbe content with that prayse of hym selfe
to abyde his rebuke of that contradyccyon. For I sette more as I
sayde by the profyt of his soule in fallynge from the contrary
35   heresye to the ryght bylyefe of our ladyes perpetual vyrgynyte,
than I sette by myne owne prayse & commendacyon of abydynge
well by my wordes.

But yet if he wyl allow my profe made of that poynt: I meruayle
me mych but yf that he allow nowe my profe made for the blessed

body of Chryste present in the blessed sacrament. For I am very
sure I haue proued mych more clerely, by myche more open and
playne wordes of the scrypture, and the sense of those wor[L₆]des
by dyuers olde holy doctours other maner of men than my self,
than I haue proued or any man elles, yᵉ perpetuall vyrginyte of   5
our blessed ladye.

Howe be yt of trouthe though I proued wel that poynte of the
perpetual vyrginyte of our ladye, to be a verytie wryten in scrypture, and that many other also proued yt mych better than I, as I
thynke there do / and that my selfe hadde affermed yt neuer so   10
strongely for neuer so clere a wryten verytie: yet syth Wyllyam
Tyndale agaynste whome I specyally wrote, taketh yt, as in his
wrytynge well and playne apperethe, for no wryten veryte, and yet
agreeth that yt is to be byleued, but not of necessyte / and yet after
vppon hys owne wordes I proue hym that of necessyte to: I maye   15
wythoute any contradyccyon or repugnaunce at [L₆v] all, laye yt
agaynste hym for an vnwryten verytie, for as myche as hym selfe so
taketh yt.

Moreouer all the profe that I make of our ladyes perpetual
vyrginyte, is no more, but that she was a perpetual vyrgyne except   20
she brake her vowe. And surely as I saye, yt semeth to my selfe
that I proue this very clerely. And this beynge proued, is indede
ynough to good chrysten folke, for a ful profe that she was a
perpetual vyrgyne. But yet vnto these

*Heretikes set
not by vowes
of virginitie**

heretyques agaynste whome I wrote, syth   25
they set nought by vowes of vyrgynyte,
but saye that they that make theym do
bothe vnlawfully make theym, and maye whan they wil lawfully
breke them / and yᵗ therfore freres may runne oute of relygyon and
wedde nunnes: this profe of myne ys to theym no maner [L₇] profe   30
at al. And therfore I maye to theym wythoute contradycyon or
repugnaunce, laye yt for an vnwryten verytie styl.

And thus I truste you se good readers, that as for this repugnaunce turneth to mayster Maskars confusyon and not myne.

---

4 doctours] doctours, *1557*   24 perpetual] perpepetual *1533*, perpetuall *1557*

The secunde chapyter.

Nowe come I than good readers to the tother contradyccyon
that he layeth agaynst me, his wordes wherin, byfore myne
answere I praye you rede ones agayne. And lest ye sholde be loth
5   to turne backe and seke theym / here shall you haue them agayne,
lo these they be.

At laste note chrysten reader, that mayster More in the thyrde boke of
hys confutacyon of Tyndale, the 249. syde, to proue saynt Iohans gospell
vnperfyte & insuffycyent, for leuyng out of so necessary a poynt of our
10   fayth, as he calleth the last souper of Chryste hys maundye: sayth that
Iohan spake nothynge at all of thys sacrament. And now se agayne in
these [L₇v] hys letters agaynste Fryth / how hym selfe bryngeth in Iohan
6. cap. to impugne Frythes wrytyng / and to make all for the sacrament,
euen thus / My flesshe is veryly meate, and my bloude drynke. By lyke
15   the man had there ouershette hym selfe fowle / the yonge man here caus-
ynge hym to put on his spectacles and poore better and more wysshely
wyth his olde eyen vppon saynt Iohans gospell to fynde that thynge there
now wryten, whyche before he wolde haue made one of hys vnwryten
verytees.

20   Whan my selfe good reader redde fyrste these wordes of his, all
be it that I was sure ynough, that in the thinges that I purposed
there was no repugnaunce in dede: yet seynge that he so dylygent-
ly layed forth the lefe in whyche my faute shold be founde, I very
playnly thought that I had not so circumspectely sene vnto my
25   wordes as wysedome wold I shold. And taking therfore myne
ouersyght for a very trouth, I neuer vouchesaufede to tourne my
booke and loke.

But afterwarde yt happed on a day [L₈] I sayde in a certayne
company, that I was somwhat sorye, that yt hadde mysse happed
30   me to take in this one poynte no better hede to myne hand, but to
wryte therin two thynges repugnaunt and contrary. Where vnto
some of theym made answere, yᵗ such a chaunce happeth
sometyme ere a man be ware in a longe worke. But yet quoth one
of theym a gentylwoman, haue you consydered well the place in
35   your boke, and sene that he sayth trouth. Nay by my trouthe quod

---

9 out of] out *1557*   11 thys] his *1557*   15 ouershette] ouershotte *1557*
26 vouchesaufede] vouchefaufede *1533*, vouchesaued *1557*   33 quoth] quod *1557*
34 theym] them, *1557*; gentylwoman] gentle woman *1557*

I that haue I not. For yt yrketh me to loke vppon the place agayne
nowe whan yt ys to late to mende yt. For I am sure the man wolde
nat be so madde, to name the very lefe, but yf he were well sure y^t
he sayd trew. By our lady quod she, but syth you haue not loked yt
your [L$_8$v] selfe, I wyl for al the lefe layed out by hym, se the
thynge my selfe ere I byleue his wrytynge, I knowe these felowes
for so false. And therwythal she sent for the boke, and turned to
the very .249. syde, and wyth that nomber marked also. And in
good fayth good readers, there founde we no suche maner mater,
neyther on the tone syde of the lefe nor on the thother.

Howe be yt of trouth I can not denye, but that in a syde after
mysse marked with the nombre of .249, whyche sholde haue ben
marked wyth the number of .259, there we founde the mater in
that place. But therin found we the moste shamefull, eyther foly or
falsed of mayster Maskar, that euer I saw lyghtly in any man in
my lyfe. Whych bycause ye shal not seke farre to fynde: I shal
reherse you [M$_1$] here the very wordes of that place. Lo good
readers these they be.

But now bycause of Tyndale, let vs take some one thing. And what thing
rather then the last souper of Chryst, hys maundye with his apostles, in
whiche he instytuted the blessed sacrament of the aulter hys owne blessed body
and bloode. Is this no necessary poynt of fayth? Tyndale can not denye it for
a necessary poynt of faith & though it were but of his own false fayth,
agreynge with Luther, Huyskyn, or Suynglyus. And he can not saye that saynt
Iohan speketh any thynge therof, specyally not of the instytucyon. Nor he can
not saye that saynt Iohan speketh any thyng of the sacrament at all, syth that
hys secte expressely denyeth, that saynt Iohan ment the sacrament in hys
wordes where he speketh expressely therof in the .vi. chapyter of his gospell.

Where haue you euer good chry[M$_1$v]sten readers sene any
fonde felowe byfore thys, handle a thynge so falsely or so folyshely,
as maister maskar here handeleth this? He telleth you that I sayde
here, that saynt Iohn spake nothynge of the sacrament at all. Nowe
you se that mayster Maskar in that poynte bylyeth me. For I sayd
not here that saynt Iohn spake nothynge therof / but fyrste I sayde
there that Tyndale agaynste whom I there wrote, could not say
that saynte Iohan wrote any thynge of the blessed sacrament,

---

28 gospell.] gospelli *1533*, ghospell *1557*   34 nothynge] notkynge *1533* nothing *1557*

specyally not of the instytucyon therof. And this is very trouthe.
For as touchynge thinstytucyon therof at Chrystes laste souper and
maundye, neyther Tyndale nor no man ellys can saye that saynte
Iohan any thynge wrote therof in his gospell.

5   Than sayde I farther there (as [M₂] you se) not that saynte
Iohan speketh nothyng of the sacrament, but yᵗ Tyndale can not
saye that saynte Iohan speketh of the sacrament any thynge at all.
And that I ment not in those wordes, to saye myne owne selfe that
saynte Iohan spake nothynge therof: I declare playnely there
10   forthwyth, by that I shew the cause why Tyndale can not say that
saynt Iohan spake any thynge of the sacrament at all, that is to
wyt bycause that al his sect expressely denyeth, that any thynge
was ment of the sacrament in the wordes of Chryste wryten in the
.vi. chapyter of saynt Iohan.

15   By this ye may se playnely good readers, that mayster Maskar
playnly belyeth me. For I sayde not my selfe that saynt Iohan
spake nothyng of the sacrament / but that Tyndale bycause of
thopynyon of all his secte [M₂v] in that poynt, coulde not saye yᵗ
saynt Iohan spake any thyng therof. Which was ynough for my
20   purpose, whyle Tyndale was the man agaynste whome I wrote,
though my selfe wolde for myne owne parte saye the contrary. For
yt is yᵗ kynde of argument that is in the scoles called argumentum
ad hominem. And thus you se good reders, mayster Maskar in this
thyng eyther shamefully false, or very shamefully folish / shame-
25   fully false, if he perceyued & vnderstode my wordes, and than for
al that thus bylyeth me / shamefully folyshe yf the thyng beynge
spoken by me so playne, his wyt wold not serue hym to perceyue it.

       But now as clere as ye se the mater all redy by this, to thentent
yet that mayster Maskar shal haue no mater left hym in all this
30   worlde to make any argument of for hys excuse therin: [M₃] rede
my wordes agayn good reders, and byd maister Maskar marke wel
my wordes therin, where I saye expressely that saynte Iohan spake
expressely therof in the .vi. chapyter of his gospel. For these wordes
are as you se there the very last wordes of al.

35   *Nor Tyndale can not say, that saynt Iohan speketh any thyng of the sacra-*
ment at all, syth that his sect expressely denyeth that saynt Iohan ment the

---

18 yᵗ] yᵉ *1533*, that *1557*   22 kynde] kyude *1533*, kynd *1557*; argument] *1557*, argumten
1533   30 worlde] *1533 corr. err.*, *1557*, word *1533*   34 al.] al *1533*, all. *1557*

sacrament in his wordes (where he speketh expressely therof) in the .vi.
chapyter of his gospell.

Whose wordes are these? where he speketh expressely therof?
Are not these wordes myne? And do I not in these wordes
expressely say, y^t saynte Iohan expressely speketh of the blessed   5
sacrament in the syxt chapiter of his gospel, in whych place
Tindals secte saith expressely that he nothyng spake therof. And
now saith M. mas[M₃v]kar that I sayde there, that saynte Iohan
spake nothynge therof at all. And layeth it for a foule repugnaunce
in me, that in my letter agaynst Fryth I saye therof the contrary.   10

But how nowe mayster maskar? What haue you nowe to saye?
wyth what shameful shyft wyl your shamlesse face, face vs oute this
folyshe lye of yours, that you make vppon me here? If you lyed so
loude wyttyngly: howe can you loke that any man shold trust your
worde? If for lacke of vnderstandynge: howe can you loke than for   15
shame that any man sholde truste your wyt? Why sholde we
thynke that your wyt wyll perse into the perceyuynge of harde
wordes in the holy scripture of god, whan yt wyll not serue you to
perceyue suche pore playne wordes of myne.

Ye wryte that the yonge man hath [M₄] here made me done on   20
my spectacles and loke more wyshly on the mater, to fynde now
writen therin the thyng that I sayde byfore was not wryten therin.
But nowe muste you loke more wyshely vppon my wordes, on
whych you make here so loude a lye, and pore better on theym
wyth your spectacles vppon your Maskars nose.   25

I wyste ones a good felow, whyche whyle he daunsed in a maske,
vppon boldenesse that no man coulde haue knowen hym, whan he
perceyued that he was well espyed by hys euyll fauored daunsynge: he waxed so ashamed sodaynly, y^t he softly said vnto his
felowe, I pray you tell me doth not my visour blosh rede? Now   30
surely good reders, M. maskar here, yf he were not vtterly paste
shame, [M₄v] hathe cause ynough to be in thys poynt so sore
ashamed, that he myght wene ye glowyng of his vysage shold euyn
perse thorow his visor, & make it rede for shame.

Thus haue I now good christen readers, answered at the full in   35
these fyue bokes of my fyrst parte, the fyrst part of mayster maskars

---

8 saith] *1557*, sath *1533*   21 wyshly] wisely *1557*   23 wyshely] wyselye *1557*   29 y]
1557, y^e *1533*

worke / and taken vp the fyrst course of mayster maskars souper,
whych he falsely calleth the last souper of the lorde / whyle he
hathe with his own poysened cokery, made yt the souper of the
deuyl. And yet wold the deuyl I wene dysdayne to haue his souper
5   dressed of such a rude ruffyn, suche a scald Colyn coke, as vnder
the name of a clerke, so rybaldyousely rayleth agaynst the blessed
bodye of Chryste in the blessed sacrament of thauter. [M₅]

The .iii. chapyter.

But one thynge wyll I yet reherse you, that I haue hytherto
10   dyfferred, that is to wytte my fyrste argument agaynst Fryth,
whiche (as I shewed you before) mayster Masker lette go by, as he
hath done many thynges mo, and made as though he saw them
not. That argument good readers was thys,

   In this heresye besyde the comon fayth of all catholyke chrysten regyons, the
15   *exposycyons of al the old holy doctours & sayntes be clere agaynste Fryth, as*
whole as agaynste any heretike that euer was hitherto herd of. For as for the
wordes of Chryste of whyche we speke touchynge the blessed sacrament /
though he maye fynd some olde holy men that bysyde the lytteral sence doth
expowne them in an allegorye, yet he shal neuer fynde any [M₅v] *of them*
20   *that dyd as he doth now after wicliffe, Ecolampadius, Tyndale, & Suin-*
glius, denye the lyterall sence / and say that Chryste ment not that it was his
very body & hys very bloud in dede / but the olde holy doctours & exposy-
tours bysyde all suche allegoryes, do playnely declare & expoune, that in those
wordes our sauyour as he expressely spake, so dyd also well and playnely
25   *mene, that the thynge whych he there gaue to his discyples in the sacrament,*
was in very dede hys very flesh and bloud. And so dyd neuer any of the olde
exposytours of scrypture expowne any of those other places in whyche Chryste
is called a vyne or a dore. And therfore it appereth well, that the maner of
spekynge was not lyke. For yf it had / than wold not the olde exposytours
30   *haue vsed suche so farre vnlyke fashyon in the expownynge of them.*

   Thys was lo good readers the [M₆] fyrste argument of myne
that maister Masker mette with, and whiche he sholde fyrste therfore haue soyled. But it is suche as he lysted lytle to loke vppon.
For where as he maketh mych a do to haue it seme that bothe

---

7 thauter] the aultare *1557*   25 to] vnto *1557*

these wordes of our sauyour at hys laste souper, *thys is my body*, and
his wordes of eatynge of his fleshe, and drynkynge of his bloude,
wryten in the syxte chapyter of saynte Iohan, sholde be spoken in a
lyke phrase and maner of spekyng, as were his other wordes, I am
the dore and I am the very vyne: I shewed there vnto Fryth   5
(whome mayster masker maketh as though he wolde defende) y^t by
thexposycyons of all the olde holy doctours & sayntes y^t haue
expowned all those .iiii. places before, y^e difference well appereth,
syth none of them declare hym to be a very material dore, [M$_6$v]
nor a naturall very vine. This saith no man not so myche as a very   10
naturall fole. But that in the sacrament is his very naturall body,

Wherein no
faithful christian
*dooth stagger**

his very flesshe and his bloude, this
declare clerely all the olde holy exposytours of the scrypture, whiche were good
men and gracyouse, wyse and well lerned   15

bothe. And therfore as I sayd the difference may sone be perceyued, but yf mayster masker lyste better to byleue hym self than
all them. Which yf he do (as in dede he doth) than is he myche
more fole than a naturall fole in dede.

For as for his .iii. places of saynt Austayne, Tertulyane, and   20
saynte Chrysostome, whom he bryngeth in his secunde parte: I
shall in my secunde parte in takynge vp of his secund course, whan
we come to frute, pare hym I warraunt you those thre [M$_7$] perys
so nere, that he getteth not a good morcell amonge them. And yet
peraduenture ere I come at it to.   25

For so is it now good reders, that I very certaynly knowe, that y^t
boke whiche Fryth made laste agaynst the blessed sacrament, ys
come ouer into thys realme in prente, and secretely sent abrode
into the bretherns handes and some good systers to. And for as
mych as I am surely enformed for trouth, that Fryth hath in to   30
that boke of his, taken many textes of old holy doctours wylyly
handeled by false frere Huyskyn byfore, to make it falsely seme
that tholde holy doctours and sayntes were fauerours of theyr false
heresye: therfore wyll I for the whyle sette mayster maskers secund
part asyde tyll I haue answered that pestylent peuyshe booke of   35
Iohan Frith / about which I purpose [M$_7$v] to go as soone as I can

---

3 syxte] sixth *1557*   33 fauerours] *1533 corr. err., 1557* fauerouse *1533*

gete one of them / whych so many beyng abrode, shall I truste not
be longe to. And than shal I by the grace and helpe of almyghty
god, make you the foly & the falshed of Fryth and frere Huyskyn
bothe as open and as clere, as I haue in thys wurke made open and
5 clere vnto you, the falshed and the foly of mayster Masker here.

And where as I a yere now passed and more, wrote and put in
prynte a letter agaynste the pestylent treatyse of Iohan Fryth,
whyche he than had made and secretely sent abrode amonge the
bretherne agaynste the blessed sacrament of thaulter, which letter
10 of myne as I haue declared in myn apology, I nathelesse caused to
be kepte styll and wolde not suffre it to be put out abrode into
euery mannes handes, bycause Frythes treatyse [M8] was not yet
at that time in prente: yet now syth I se that there are comen ouer
in prente, not onely Frythes boke, but ouer that this maskers boke
15 also / and that eyther of theyr bothe bokes maketh mencyon of my
sayde letter, and wolde seme to soyle it, and laboreth sore there
about: I do therfore nowe suffre the prenter to putte wyth thys
boke my sayd letter also to sale.

And for as myche also as those authorytees of saynt Austayn,
20 saynt Chrysostome, and Turtuliane, whych master maysker layeth
in hys secunde parte, I shall of lykelyhed fynde also in Frythes
boke, and therfore answere theym there, and all mayster Maskers
whole mater to, before I retourne to his secund part, whyche yet I
wyll after all thys [M8v] (god wyllyng) not leue nor let go so: in
25 the meane while may mayster maskar (syth it is as he saith so great
pleasure to hym to be wryten agaynst, hauynge as he bosteth all
solucyons so redely) loke and assay whither he can soyle these
thynges wyth whyche I haue in this fyrst parte ouerthrowen his
whole heresye, and proued hym very playne, a very false fole all
30 redye. Of whose false wyly foly to be ware our lorde geue vs grace /
and of all suche other lyke, whych with folyshe argumentes of
theyre owne blynde reason, wresting the scripture into a wronge
sense, agaynste the very playn wordes of the text, agaynst thexposycyons of all the olde holy sayntes, agaynste the determynacyons
35 of dyuers whole generall counsayles, agaynste the full consent of all
trewe chrysten nacyons this .xv. [N1] hundred yere before theyr
days, and agaynste the playne declaracyon of almyghty god hym

---

3 falshed] _1557_ fashed _1533_   11 put out] put _1557_   30 be ware] beware _1557_

self, made in euery chrysten countrey by so many playn open
myracles, labour now to make vs so folyshely blynde and madde,
as to forsake the very trew catholike fayth, forsake ye socyetie of the
trew catholyque chyrche, and wyth sundry sectes of heretikes fallen
out therof, to set both holy dayes & fastyng days at nought, & for
the deuyllis pleasure to forbere & abstayne from all prayer to be
made either for soules or to sayntes, iest on our blessed lady y^e
immaculate mother of Chryste, make mockes at all pylgrymages,
and crepynge of Chrystes crosse, the holy ceremonyes of the
chyrche and the sacramentes to, turne theym into tryflynge, wyth
lykenynge theym to wyne garlandes and ale polys / and fynally by
[N$_1$v] these wayes in the ende and conclusyon, forsake our sauyour
hym selfe in the blessed sacramente / and in stede of his own
blessed bodye & his blood, wene there were nothynge but bare
brede and wyne, and call it ydolatrye there to do hym honour. But
woo may suche wreches be. For this we may be sure, that who so
dyshonour god in one place wyth occasyon of a false fayth: standynge that false bylyefe and infydelyte, all thonour that he dothe
hym any where besyde, ys odyouse and dyspyghtfull and reiected
of god, and neuer shall saue that faythlesse soule from the fyre of
hel. From whiche our lorde geue theym grace trewely to tourne in
tyme, so that we and they to gether in one catholyque chyrche,
knytte vnto god to gether in one catholyque fayth, fayth I saye, not
fayth alone as [N$_2$] they do, but acompanyed wyth good hope,
and wyth her chyefe syster well workynge charytie, maye so
receyue Chrystes blessed sacramentes here, and specyally that we
may so receyue hym selfe, his very blessed bodye, very fleshe and
blood, in the blessed sacrament our holy blessed howsyll, that we
maye here be wyth hym incorporate so by grace, that after the
shorte course of this transytorye lyfe, wyth hys tender pytye
powred vppon vs in purgatorye, at the prayour of good people,
and intercessyon of holy sayntes, we maye be wyth them in theyr
holy felyshyppe, incorporate in Chryste in hys eternall glorye
Amen.

5

10

15

20

25

30

Finis. [N$_2$v]

35

---

7 sayntes,] *1557*, sayntes *1533*   9 of Chrystes] to Christes *1557*   12 these] the *catchword*
1533   21 whiche] whcche *1533*, which *1557*   28 sacrament] sacramente, *1557*

COMMENTARY

COMMENTARY

The following bibliography includes works and abbreviations cited frequently in the Introduction and the Commentary. The titles of works referred to only once or occurring only in a brief cluster of references are given in full as they occur. Unless otherwise noted, references to the Bible and Latin quotations from it are from the Clementine Vulgate. In citing and quoting the glosses of de Lyra in the Froben Bible of 1498, we have given modern verse numbers (which are not present in the Froben Bible) instead of volume, page, and column, because the numbered verses can be easily located in the Froben Bible and provide the briefest, most accurate way of referring to the glosses. Unless otherwise noted, quotations from classical authors are taken from the texts of the Loeb editions, which are cited here with the permission of the Harvard University Press. For quotations from *The Souper of the Lorde*, the reader is referred to Appendix A, where this pamphlet is reprinted.

BIBLIOGRAPHY AND SHORT TITLES

Alberigo, Giuseppe, et al., eds., *Conciliorum oecumenicorum decreta*, 2nd ed., Basel, 1962. Cited as "Alberigo."

Alford, Henry, ed. *The Greek New Testament*, 4 vols., Boston, 1873.

Allen. *See* Erasmus.

Althaus, Paul. *The Theology of Martin Luther*, trans. R. C. Schultz, Philadelphia, 1966.

Answer. See Tyndale.

Aquinas, Thomas. *Catena aurea in quatuor evangelia, Opera omnia*, vols. 11–12, Parma, 1861–62; reprint, New York, 1949. Cited as "*Catena aurea*."

———. *Commentum in Matthaeum et Joannem evangelistas, Opera omnia*, vol. 10, Parma, 1865. Cited as "*Commentum*."

———. *Summa theologica, Opera omnia*, vols. 1–4, Parma, 1852–54. Cited as "*Summa theologica*."

ASD. See Erasmus.

Barge, Hermann. *Andreas Bodenstein von Karlstadt*, 2 vols., Leipzig, 1905.

Barlow, William, *A dyaloge descrybyng the orygynall ground of these Lutheran faccyons* ..., London, William Rastell, 1531; *STC* 1461.

Biblia latina. [*Biblia*] *cum glosa ordinaria et expositione lyre literali et morali: necnon additionibus ac replicis* ..., 6 vols., John Peter and John Froben, Basel, 1498. Bible text interlined with the Gloss of Anselmus Laudunensis, the Glosses of Walafrid Strabo and others, the Postillae and Moralitates of Nicholas de Lyra, the Additiones of Paulus de Santa Maria (Bishop of Burgos; 1354–1435), with Matthias Döring's replies.

Butterworth, Charles C., and Allan G. Chester. *George Joye, 1495?–1553: A Chapter in the History of the English Bible and the English Reformation*, Philadelphia, 1962. Cited as "Butterworth and Chester."

Catena aurea. See Aquinas.

CCSL. Corpus Christianorum: Series Latina, 70 vols. to date, Turnholt, 1954–.

Chrysostom, John. *D. Ioannis Chrysostomi . . . opera, quae hactenus uersa sunt omnia*, 5 vols., Basel, 1530–31. Cited as "*Opera*, 1530."

CIC. See Richter and Friedberg.

Clarke, Francis, S.J. *Eucharistic Sacrifice and the Reformation*, London, 1960. Cited as "Clarke."

Clebsch, William A. *England's Earliest Protestants, 1520–1535*, New Haven, 1964. Cited as "Clebsch."

Clichtove, Josse. *De sacramento eucharistiae, contra Oecolampadium, opusculum* ..., Paris, 1526.

Commentum. See Aquinas.

CRM. See Melanchthon.

Cross, F. L. *The Oxford Dictionary of the Christian Church*, 2nd ed., London, 1974. Cited as " Cross."

CRZ. See Zwingli.

CSEL. Corpus Scriptorum Ecclesiasticorum Latinorum, 88 vols. to date, Vienna, 1866–.

CW. See More.

Cyril. *Divi Cyrilli archiepiscopi alex. opera*, trans. George of Trebizond, 3 vols., Basel, 1528. Cited as " tr. Trapezontius, 1528."

de Lyra, Nicholas. *Expositio literalis et moralis*, in *Biblia latina*. Cited as " de Lyra."

DTC. Dictionnaire de théologie catholique, 15 vols., Paris, 1908–50.

Emden, A. B. *A Biographical Register of the University of Oxford*, A.D. *1501–1540*, Oxford, 1974. Cited as " Emden."

Erasmus, Desiderius. *Ausgewählte Werke*, ed. Annemarie Holborn and Hajo Holborn, Munich, 1933.

————. *The Enchiridion of Erasmus*, trans. Raymond Himelick, Bloomington, Ind., 1963.

————. *Opera omnia*, ed. J. Clericus (Leclerc), 10 vols., Leiden, 1703–06; reprint, Hildesheim, 1961. Cited as " *Opera omnia*."

————. *Opera omnia Desiderii Erasmi Roterodami*, ed. J. H. Waszink et al., 11 vols. to date, Amsterdam, 1969–. Cited as *ASD*.

————. *Opus epistolarum Des. Erasmi Roterodami*, ed. P. S. Allen, H. M. Allen, et al., 12 vols., Oxford, 1906–58. Cited as " Allen."

Essential Articles. See Sylvester and Marc'hadour.

EW. See More.

Fisher, John. *De veritate corporis et sanguinis Christi in eucharistia*, Cologne, Peter Quentel, 1527. Cited as " Fisher, *De veritate*."

Freys, Ernst, and Hermann Barge. " Verzeichnis der gedruckten Schriften des Andreas Bodenstein von Karlstadt," *Zentralblatt für Bibliothekswesen, 21* (1904), 153–79, 209–43, 305–31. Cited as " Freys and Barge."

Frith, John. *A boke made by Iohn Frith prisoner in the tower of London / answeringe vnto M mores lettur which he wrote agenst the first litle treatyse that Iohan Frith made concerninge the sacramente*, Münster [Antwerp?] Christoffel van Ruremund, 1533; *STC* 11381.

————. *A christen sentence and true iudgement of the moste honorable Sacrament of Christes body & bloude declared both by the auctorite of the holy Scriptures and the auncient Doctores*, London, Richard Wyer, 1548?; *STC* 5190. Cited as " *A Christian Sentence*."

Fulop, Robert E. " John Frith and His Relation to the Origin of the Reformation in England," Ph.D. Dissertation, University of Edinburgh, 1956.

Gibson, R. W., and J. Max Patrick. *St. Thomas More: A Preliminary Bibliography of His Works and of Moreana to the Year 1750*, New Haven and London, 1961. Cited as "Gibson."

Glossa ordinaria. See Strabo.

Gordon, Walter M. "A Scholastic Problem in Thomas More's Controversy with John Frith," *Harvard Theological Review*, *69* (1976), 131–49.

Gratian. *See* Richter.

Himelick. *See* Erasmus.

Holborn. *See* Erasmus.

Hume, Anthea. "English Protestant Books Printed Abroad, 1525–1535: An Annotated Bibliography," in *CW 8*, Appendix B, pp. 1065–91. Cited as "Hume."

Joye, George. *The Subuersion of Moris false foundacion*, Antwerp?, 1534; *STC²* 14829.

Köhler, Walther. *Zwingli und Luther: Ihr Streit über das Abendmahl nach seinen politischen und religiösen Beziehungen*, 2 vols., Quellen und Forschungen zur Reformationsgeschichte 6, Leipzig, 1924–53. Cited as "Köhler."

Kronenberg, M. E. "Forged Addresses in Low Country Books in the Period of the Reformation," *The Library*, 5th Series, *2* (1947), 81–95.

A Letter against Frith. See More.

Luther, Martin. *D. Martin Luthers Werke*, 94 vols. to date, Weimar, 1883–. Cited as *WA*.

———. *Works*, ed. Helmut T. Lehmann and Jaroslav Pelikan, 54 vols. to date, Philadelphia, 1955–.

Marc'hadour, Germain. *The Bible in the Works of Thomas More*, 5 vols., Nieuwkoop, 1969–72. Cited as "Marc'hadour, *The Bible*."

———. "Le Masque et le visage," *Moreana*, *18* (1968), 111–18.

———. *Thomas More et la Bible*, Paris, 1969.

Martz, Louis L. "Thomas More: The Sacramental Life," *Thought*, *52* (1977), 300–318.

Melanchthon, Philippus. *Opera quae supersunt omnia*, ed. Karl G. Bretschneider and Heinrich E. Bindseil, 28 vols., Corpus Reformatorum 1–28, Halle/Saale and Braunschweig, 1834–60. Cited as *CRM*.

Miller, Edward W., and Jared W. Scudder. *Wessel Gansfort: Life and Writings and Principal Works*, 2 vols., New York and London, 1917. Cited as "Miller and Scudder, *Gansfort*."

Missale ad usum insignis et praeclarae ecclesiae Sarum, ed. F. H. Dickinson, Burntisland, 1861–83. Cited as "*Sarum Missal*."

More, Thomas. *The Correspondence of Sir Thomas More*, ed. Elizabeth F. Rogers, Princeton, 1947. Cited as "Rogers."

———. *A letter ... impugnynge the erronyouse wrytyng of Iohan Frith ...*, London, William Rastell 1533 [1532]; *STC²* 18090; Rogers, no. 190. Cited as "*A Letter against Frith*."

————. *The workes of Sir Thomas More Knyght, ... wrytten by him in the Englysh tonge*, London, 1557; *STC*² 18076. Cited as *EW*.

————. *The Yale Edition of the Complete Works of St. Thomas More*: Vol. 2, *The History of King Richard III*, ed. R. S. Sylvester; Vol. 3, Part 1, *Translations of Lucian*, ed. C. R. Thompson; Vol. 3, Part 2, *Latin Poems*, ed. C. H. Miller, L. Bradner, C. A. Lynch, R. P. Oliver; Vol. 4, *Utopia*, ed. Edward Surtz, S.J., and J. H. Hexter; Vol. 5, *Responsio ad Lutherum*, ed. J. M. Headley, trans. Sister Scholastica Mandeville; Vol. 6, *A Dialogue Concerning Heresies*, ed. T. M. C. Lawler, Germain Marc'hadour, and R. C. Marius; Vol. 8, *The Confutation of Tyndale's Answer*, ed. L. A. Schuster, R. C. Marius, J. P. Lusardi, and R. J. Schoeck; Vol. 9, *The Apology*, ed. J. B. Trapp; Vol. 12, *A Dialogue of Comfort against Tribulation*, ed. L. L. Martz and Frank Manley; Vol. 13, *Treatise on the Passion, Treatise on the Blessed Body, Instructions and Prayers*, ed. G. E. Haupt; Vol. 14, *De Tristitia Christi*, ed. C. H. Miller; New Haven and London, 1963–. Cited as *CW* followed by volume number.

Obedience. See Tyndale.

Oecolampadius, Johannes. *De genuina verborum domini, Hoc est corpus meum, iuxta vetustissimos authores, expositione liber*, Basel [Strassburg], 1525; Staehelin, "Oekolampad-Bibliographie," no. 113. Cited as "*De genuina ... expositione.*"

————. *Quid de eucharistia veteres tum Graeci tum Latini senserint dialogus ...*, Basel, 1530; Staehelin, "Oekolampad-Bibliographie," no. 164. Cited from the Heidelberg edition of 1572, Staehelin, "Oekolampad-Bibliographie," no. 218. Cited as "*Quid veteres senserint.*"

OED. The Oxford English Dictionary, ed. J. A. H. Murray et al., 13 vols., Oxford, 1933.

Payne, John B. *Erasmus: His Theology of the Sacraments*, [Richmond, Va.], 1970. Cited as "Payne."

Pelikan, Jaroslav. *The Christian Tradition: A History of the Development of Doctrine*, 4 vols. to date, Chicago and London, 1971–. Cited as "Pelikan, *The Christian Tradition.*"

PG. Patrologiae Cursus Completus: Series Graeca, ed. J.-P. Migne, 161 vols., Paris, 1857–66.

Pineas, Rainer, "George Joye's Controversy with Thomas More," *Moreana, 38* (1973), 27–36.

PL. Patrologiae Cursus Completus: Series Latina, ed. J.-P. Migne, 221 vols., Paris, 1844–1903.

Richter, Emil L., and Emil A. Friedberg, eds. *Corpus Iuris Canonici*, 2 vols., Leipzig, 1879, reprint, Graz, 1959. Cited as *CIC*.

Rogers. See More.

Rupp, Gordon. *Patterns of Reformation*, Philadelphia, 1969. Cited as "Rupp."

Sarum Missal. See Missale ... Sarum.

Souper. The Souper of the Lorde by George Joye. *See* Appendix A.

Staehelin, Ernst, ed. *Briefe und Akten zum Leben Oekolampads*, 2 vols., Quellen und Forschungen zur Reformationsgeschichte 10 and 19, Leipzig, 1927 and 1934. Cited as " Staehelin, *Briefe und Akten*."

———. "Oekolampad-Bibliographie: Verzeichnis der im 16. Jahrhundert erschienenen Oekolampaddrucke," *Basler Zeitschrift für Geschichte und Altertumskunde, 17* (1918), 1–119; reprint, Nieuwkoop, 1963. Cited as " Staehelin, ' Oekolampad-Bibliographie.' "

STC. A Short-Title Catalogue of Books Printed in England, Scotland, & Ireland and of English Books Printed Abroad, 1475–1640, comp. A. W. Pollard and G. R. Redgrave, London, 1926.

STC². Revised ed. of *STC*, ed. W. A. Jackson, F. S. Ferguson, and Katharine F. Pantzer, vol. 2, London, 1976; vol. 1, in press.

Stow, John. *A Survey of London*, ed. C. L. Kingsford, 2 vols., Oxford, 1908. Cited as " Stow."

Strabo, Walafrid. *Glossa ordinaria*; in *PL* 113–114.

Summa theologica. See Aquinas.

Sylvester, Richard S., and Germain P. Marc'hadour, eds. *Essential Articles for the Study of Thomas More*, Hamden, Conn., 1977. Cited as " *Essential Articles*."

Tilley, M. P. *A Dictionary of the Proverbs in England in the Sixteenth and Seventeenth Centuries*, Ann Arbor, 1950. Cited as " Tilley."

Trapezontius, 1528. *See* Cyril.

Tyndale, William. *An answere vnto Sir Thomas Mores dialoge*, [Antwerp], 1531; *STC²* 24437; Hume, no. 25. Cited as " *Answer*."

———. *The obedience of a Christen man and how Christen rulers ought to governe* ..., Marburg [Antwerp], 1528; *STC²* 24446; Hume, no. 7. Cited as " *Obedience*."

———. *The Whole workes of W. Tyndale, Iohn Frith, and Doct. Barnes*, ed. John Foxe, London, 1573; *STC²* 24436. Cited as *WW*.

———. *Works*, ed. Henry Walter, 3 vols., Parker Society 42–44, Cambridge, 1848–50.

WA. See Luther.

Whiting, Bartlett J. *Proverbs, Sentences, and Proverbial Phrases from English Writings Mainly before 1500*, Cambridge, Mass., 1968. Cited as " Whiting."

Williams, George H. *The Radical Reformation*, London, 1962. Cited as " Williams, *The Radical Reformation*."

Wordsworth, John, Henry White, et al., eds. *Nouum Testamentum ... secundum editionem Sancti Hieronymi*, 3 parts, Oxford, 1889–1949. Cited as " Wordsworth-White."

WW. See Tyndale.

Zwingli, Ulrich. *Huldreich Zwinglis sämtliche Werke*, ed. Emil Egli et al., 14 vols., Corpus Reformatorum 88–101, Leipzig, 1905–59. Cited as *CRZ*.

3/27–29 **thapostles . . . you.** Eph. 5 : 3: "Fornicatio autem, et omnis immunditia, aut avaritia, nec nominetur in vobis, sicut decet sanctos."

3/31–4/3 **after tyme y^t . . . dekaye.** An identical syntactic structure occurs in *CW 8*, 254/14–21. Cf. Joseph Delcourt, *Essai sur la langue de Sir Thomas More d'après ses oeuvres anglaises* (Paris, 1914), p. 404, and "*after,* prep.," in the Glossary, below.

4/3–5 **thapostle . . . maners.** 1 Cor. 15 : 33: "Nolite seduci: corrumpunt mores bonos colloquia mala." Paul is quoting Menander (*Thais* 218K), as More pointed out in *The Debellation of Salem and Bizance (EW,* sig. P$_4$v): "Which wordes though the greke Poete Menander meant by the communicacion of other fleshly lewdnesse: yet the blessed apostle vsed them and aplyed them specially, to the lewde communicacyon of heresies, which with such bold naughty talking crepeth furth and corrupteth (as saint Paule also saith) like a corrupt canker."

4/29–32 **And agaynst . . . resurreccion.** 1 Cor. 15 : 12.

4/34–37 **And such . . . cankar.** 2 Tim. 2 : 17: "et sermo eorum ut cancer serpit."

5/12–17 **Saynt Poule . . . hym.** Titus 3 : 10–11: "Haereticum hominem post unam et secundam correptionem devita: sciens quia subversus est, qui eiusmodi est, et delinquit, cum sit proprio iudicio condemnatus."

5/20–23 **no sayth . . . them.** 2 John 10–11: "Si quis venit ad vos, et hanc doctrinam non affert, nolite recipere eum in domum, nec Ave ei dixeritis. Qui enim dicit illi Ave, communicat operibus eius malignis."

5/31–32 **yet . . . yet.** The first "yet" means "moreover" (OED "yet" 1); the second, "hereafter" (OED "yet" 5).

6/1–2 **And this . . . there be.** Hume lists 30 books printed abroad before December 1533; still others may be presumed to have been lost. A search at Oxford for heretical books in 1528 uncovered about 100 titles in circulation there. See *CW 8*, 1173.

6/8–9 The marginal gloss, which appears only in the Huntington copy of *1533*, is incorrect; it was perhaps carried over from the previous page.

6/7–8 **vayne curyouse.** On the fear of vain curiosity in the late Middle Ages, see Heiko Oberman, *Contra vanam curiositatem*, Theologische Studien 113 (Zurich, 1974). See *CW 6*, Commentary at 74/34–75/2.

6/12 **bokes . . . forboden.** For a discussion of censorship procedures, see A. W. Reed, "The Regulation of the Book Trade before the Proclamation of 1538," chapter 7 of his *Early Tudor Drama* (London, 1926), pp. 160–86; and D. M. Loades, "The Press under the Early Tudors," *Transactions of the Cambridge Bibliographical Society*, 4 (1964–68), 29–50. Until 1530, the power to prosecute the writers, printers, and readers of heretical books and translations rested exclusively with the bishops and diocesan courts. This power stemmed from the statute " ex officio " of an Act of Parliament of 1510, which sanctioned the procedures drawn up in the provincial constitutions of the synod at Oxford under Archbishop Thomas Arundel in 1407. It was under these provisions that Tunstall and More (under Tunstall's license) pursued their campaign against heretical works in the 1520s. Regulation of heretical books began to shift to the king and secular authorities with the royal proclamation of March 6, 1530, 20 Henry VIII, which enforced existing statutes against heresy and prohibited unlicensed preaching and heretical literature. See Paul L. Hughes and James F. Larkin, *Tudor Royal Proclamations*, 2 vols. (New Haven, 1964), *1*, 181–86, no. 122; see also pp. 193–97, no. 129. The document is misdated 1529 by Hughes and Larkin; see G. R. Elton, *Studies in Tudor and Stuart Politics and Government*, 2 vols. (London, 1974), *1*, 162, note 1.

6/20 **bretherne.** On More's repeated use of this term, in ironical mockery of the reformers, see *CW 9*, Commentary at 7/28, 9/12, and 14/23.

6/23–29 **sauynge . . . deuyl.** See Frederick C. Avis, " Book Smuggling into England during the Sixteenth Century," *Gutenberg-Jahrbuch*, 1972, pp. 180–87; " England's Use of Antwerp Printers, 1500–1540," *Gutenberg-Jahrbuch*, 1973, pp. 234–40. Tyndale alludes to the possible subsidy of George Joye's work in a letter to Frith: " George Ioye would haue put foorth a treatise of the matter [i.e., the real presence], but I haue stopt hym as yet, what he will doe if he get money, I wotte not " (*WW*, sig. CC₄).

6/31 **Fryth.** For Frith's controversy with More over the eucharist, see the Introduction, pp. xxxi–xxxvi. John Frith, one of the most learned and winning of the early English Protestants, was born c. 1503 in Westerham, Kent, the son of an innkeeper, and was raised at nearby Sevenoaks. After attending Eton, he spent several years at Cambridge (c. 1520–25), where he was associated with the Protestant circle of the White Horse Inn, a group that included Thomas Bilney, Robert Barnes, Thomas Arthur, Hugh Latimer, Matthew Parker, and George Joye. He was admitted B.A. in 1525. Frith was then invited to join the faculty of Cardinal's College, Oxford, recently founded by Wolsey; he served there until 1528, when, after being released from house arrest at Cambridge, he left England for Antwerp and possibly Marburg in order to escape prosecution for heresy and to join Tyndale, whom he had met earlier, in promulgating the Protestant cause from abroad. In 1529 he published a translation of Luther's *The Reuelation of Antichrist* together with a prefatory epistle and a series of comparisons between the Pope and Antichrist, based on the *Passional Christi und Antichristi* (Wittenberg, 1521), written by Melanchthon and illustrated with woodcuts by Lucas Cranach the elder (*STC* 11394; Hume, no. 11; see also *CW 9*, Commentary at 89/20), and in 1531 a translation of Patrick Hamilton's *Loci communes* (or *Dyuers frutful gath-eringes* . . . , *STC* 12732) and a tract against John Rastell, More, and Fisher, *A disputacion of purgatorye* (*STC* 11388; Hume, no. 24).

Before his arrest in 1532, Frith completed two works in addition to his sacramentarian tracts: *The Testament of master Wylliam Tracie esquier* (*STC*² 24167; Hume, no. 40), which addresses divisive theological issues such as the state of the soul between death and resurrection and the doctrine of double justification; and *An other boke against Rastel* (*STC* 11385; see Hume, p. 1091), another work on purgatory, which apparently played a part in the conversion of Rastell to the Protestant cause. From the Tower, Frith composed (in addition to the book against More) three works: *A Letter vnto the faythfull followers of Christes gospel* (*STC* 11386), concerning the consolations of suffering for the sake of true religion; *A mirrour or glasse to know thyselfe* (*STC* 11390), which, like *A Letter*, defines the nature of a good Christian and discusses Frith's view of justification by faith; and *A myrroure or lokynge glasse wherin you may beholde the Sacramente of baptisme described* (*STC* 11391), which refutes both the Catholic and the Anabaptist positions; for the publication of these works, see Hume, p. 1091. Frith may have had a hand in Tyndale's *An answere vnto Sir Thomas Mores dialoge* (Antwerp, 1531; *STC*² 24437).

For the biography of Frith, see Clebsch, pp. 99–136; Robert E. Fulop, "John Frith and His Relation to the Origin of the Reformation in England" (Ph.D. Dissertation, University of Edinburgh, 1956); and Emden, pp. 218–20.

6/36–7/1 **a nother . . . sacrament.** *The Souper of the Lorde . . . wheryn incidently M. Moris letter agenst Iohan Frythe is confuted* (*STC*² 24468; reprint-ed below in Appendix A) bears the colophon "Imprinted at Nornburg by Niclas twonson. 5 April. An. 1533." *STC*² suggests, however, that this is not the original edition, but a reprint made around 1546 by the London printer Nicholas Hill. M. E. Kronenberg suggests that the original edition was printed by Simon Cock in Antwerp; see "Forged Addresses in Low Country Books in the Period of the Reformation," *The Library*, 5th Series, *2* (1947), 81–95. More's quotations from the text do not vary substan-tively from *STC*² 24468. Three later editions of the work were issued in London around 1547 (*STC*² 24469–71). The disputed authorship of the book is examined by Michael Anderegg (Appendix B, below), who con-cludes that the most likely author is George Joye. On Joye, see note to 7/22–8/4.

7/19–21 **But some . . . forthe.** See *WW*, sig. CC₄v: "Finally if there were in me any gift that could helpe at hand, & ayde you if nede required: I promise you I would not be farre of, and commit the end to God: my soule is not faynt, though my body be wery." This is one of two letters of advice and encouragement that Tyndale wrote to Frith when Frith was imprisoned in the Tower. Both were intercepted by More; see *The Apology*, *CW 9*, 91/9.

At the time of More's writing, Tyndale had completed his most influential works. His translation of the New Testament (*STC* 2824; Hume, no. 2), completed in 1525, was published in 1526; his version of the Pentateuch followed in 1530 (*STC* 2350; Hume, no. 13). *The obedience of a Christen man and how Christen rulers ought to governe* (*STC²* 24446; Hume, no. 7), perhaps Tyndale's most influential work after the New Testament, appeared in 1528. In 1531, Tyndale challenged More in *An answere vnto Sir Thomas Mores dialoge*, which refutes the arguments More advanced in *A Dialogue Concerning Heresies* (*CW 6*; 1529, 1531). More, in turn, responded with his *Confutation of Tyndale's Answer* (*CW 8*; 1532, 1533), the lengthiest of his polemical works.

In his letter to Frith, Tyndale cautions him not to write on the eucharist, a divisive issue that Tyndale wished to downplay in order to preserve a show of Protestant unity: "Of the presence of Christes body in the Sacrament, medle as litle as you can, that there appeare no diuision among vs. Barnes will be whote [i.e., hot] agaynste you. The Saxons be sore on the affirmatiue, whether constant or obstinate, I [c]omit it to God. Philippe Melancton is sayd to be with the French king. There be in Antwerpe that say, they saw him come into Paris with an c. and l. horses, and that they spake with hym. If the Frenchmen receiue the worde of God, hee will plant the affirmatiue in them. . . . I would haue the right vse preached, and the presence to be an indifferent thyng, till the matter might be reasoned in peace at laysure, of both parties. If you be required, shew the phrases of the Scripture, and let them talke what they will. For as to beleue y' God is euery where, hurteth no man that worshyp him no where but within, in the hart, in spirite and verity: euen so to beleue that the body of Christ is euery where (though it can not be proued) hurteth no man that worshippeth hym no where saue in the fayth of hys Gospell. You perceiue my minde: how beit if God shew you otherwise, it is free for you to do as he moueth you" (*WW*, sig. CC₄).

For the biography of Tyndale, see Clebsch, pp. 137–204; Emden, pp. 567–69; J. F. Mozley, *William Tyndale* (New York, 1937); C. H. Williams, *William Tyndale* (London, 1969). On the doctrine of "indifferent things," see Bernard J. Verkamp, *The Indifferent Men: Adiaphorism in the English Reformation to 1554*, Studies in the Reformation 1 (Detroit, 1977).

Tyndale's advice may be responsible for Frith's not having answered the letters that George Joye addressed to him in the Tower; see Joye's *Apology* (London, 1535; *STC²* 14820; Hume, p. 1090), sig. E₁.

7/22–8/4 **Howe be yt . . . purpose.** For Tyndale's letter, see *WW*, sig. CC₄: "George Ioye would haue put foorth a treatise of the matter, but I haue stopt hym as yet, what he will doe if he get money, I wotte not. I beleue he wold make many reasons litle seruyng to the purpose. My mynde is, that nothyng be put forth till we heare how you shal haue spede."

George Joye (Gee, Geach, Jay) was born c. 1495 at Renhold, near

Bedford. He proceeded B.A. at Cambridge in 1513, and M.A. in 1517. He was ordained in 1515 and was made a fellow of Peterhouse, Cambridge, in 1517. He was summoned, with Bilney and Arthur, for examination on charges of heresy in November 1527, having been betrayed by a friend, John Ashwell, but his case never came to trial, and he sailed to voluntary exile on the Continent, where, in his words, he lived in a "strange lande amonge rude and boisterous people, with whose maners I can not wel agre." See Joye's surprisingly lighthearted account of his summons in *The letters whyche Iohan Ashwell . . . sente secretely to the Byshope of Lyncolne* (Antwerp, 1531; *STC* 845; Hume, no. 23).

From Antwerp Joye produced a string of biblical and liturgical translations: the Psalter in 1530 (*STC* 2370; Hume, no. 12), after the Latin version of Bucer (1529); Isaiah in 1531 (*STC* 2777; Hume, no. 21), from Zwingli's Latin; and in late 1529 or early 1530, the first English primer, now lost. The primer was reissued in 1530 with the title *Ortulus anime. The garden of the soule* (*STC²* 13828.4; Hume, no. 14). More refers to the primer in *The Confutation* and *The Apology* (*CW 8*, 11/6–23; *CW 9*, 9/20–21).

Joye's theological works begin with *The letters whyche Iohan Ashwell . . . sente*, a defense of Joye's early Lutheran beliefs. After *The Souper of the Lorde*, Joye published *The Subuersion of Moris false foundacion* (Antwerp, 1534; *STC²* 14829; Hume, no. 31), a reply to More's *Confutation*. He may have been the author of *The praier and complaynte of the ploweman vnto Christe* (Antwerp, 1531; *STC²* 20036; Hume, no. 20). Joye returned to translation with versions of Proverbs (based on Melanchthon's) and of Ecclesiastes; the original edition was lost, but a second one was issued in London in 1535 (*STC* 2752). In 1534, Joye produced a translation of Jeremiah (*STC* 2778; Hume, no. 33), based on Zwingli's Latin, and a second translation of the psalter (*STC* 2372; Hume, no. 34), also based on Zwingli's. In 1534 he also brought out a revised edition of Tyndale's New Testament (*STC* 2825), a work that enraged Tyndale, who shortly thereafter produced his own revision (*STC* 2826; Hume, no. 36), in which he defends himself against Joye's alterations. Joye replied in a second edition of Tyndale's New Testament (*STC* 2827), and in *An apologye made . . . to satisfye . . . w. Tindale* (London, 1535; *STC²* 14820; see Hume, p. 1090). Also in 1535 Joye published a translation (*STC²* 14821) of the *Summa totius sacrae scripturae* of Johannes Graphaeus (1533).

Joye returned to England in 1535 and remained there until 1540, when the requirement that married clergy put away their wives drove him back to Antwerp, where he remained until the accession of Edward VI in 1547. He spent his final year in England, where he died in 1553. During the later part of his career, Joye produced still more controversial works, including two books written against Stephen Gardiner, and two defending clerical marriage.

On the biography of Joye, see Butterworth and Chester; Clebsch, pp. 205–28; Rainer Pineas, "George Joye's Controversy with Thomas More," *Moreana, 38* (1973), 27–36, his "George Joye's Polemical Use of

History in his Controversy with Stephen Gardiner," *Nederlands Archief voor Kerkgeschiedenis*, New Series, 1972, pp. 125–26, and his "George Joye's *Exposicion of Daniel*," *Renaissance Quarterly, 28* (1975), 332–42.

8/9–11 Mayster mocke . . . inough. *Souper*, Appendix A, 339/33–35.

9/13 Barons. More himself knew that Robert Barnes (c. 1495–1539) was an unlikely candidate for the authorship of *The Souper*. Not only had he read in Tyndale's letter to Frith that Barnes would be "whote agaynste you" (see note to 7/19–21), but in 1532 he himself had received a letter from Barnes in which the reformer strenuously denied holding the sacramentarian position; see note to 135/20. Although Joye was indeed held in little respect by Tyndale (see note to 7/22–8/4), there is no evidence that Barnes was accounted a fool by his brethren, even though he retained a conservative Lutheran view of the eucharist. More often speaks of Barnes disparagingly, however. For example, in *The Apology, CW 9*, 5/35–38: "For as for frere Barons I perceyue by sundry wayes, that the bretherhed speke myche lesse of hym, eyther for that they find hym in theyr owne myndes well and fully answered, or ellys y^t they take him in respect of Tindale but for a man of a secunde sorte." See also *CW 8*, 831/8–15. Barnes spent several months in England under Henry's safe conduct in 1531, a visit that More strongly opposed (*CW 8*, 1394–95). Although Barnes was in Germany in early 1533, he may have made a secret visit to England in October 1533 (*CW 8*, 1396). For a full account of Barnes, see James P. Lusardi, "The Career of Robert Barnes," *CW 8*, 1367–1415. See also Clebsch, pp. 42–77.

9/27–28 the booke . . . to prent. That is, Frith's answer to More, *A Boke . . . answeringe vnto M mores lettur*; see Introduction, pp. xxxii, lix, and note to 6/31.

10/9 withoute . . . salte. That is, "without a grain of wit."

10/16 the fyrste parte. *Souper*, Appendix A, 305/1–318/21.

10/20 secunde parte. *Souper*, Appendix A, 318/22–340/4.

11/14 two placys. *Souper*, Appendix A, 315/15–34.

12/17–19 But he . . . awaye. In January 1525 Erasmus advised the town council of Basel to forbid books not identified by author, printer, and place of publication and to punish those who imported, printed, or sold such books (Allen, *6*, 8).

13/1–10 mayster Mummer . . . Masker. The traditional European Christmas and Easter mummings, which combined dumb-show, music, sword-dance, parade, and disguise, probably have their origin in ancient vernal folk rituals but survive in England to this day. Formalized versions of such mummings, most often called disguisings, were brought to court in the late fourteenth and early fifteenth centuries; at court, they often included allegory, elaborate scenery, and expensive costumes. Dicing was occasionally introduced, and E. K. Chambers concludes that in the early sixteenth century the terms *mumming* and *mummery* were specialized; they referred specifically to presentations that included "mumchance," that is, dicing (*The Elizabethan Stage*, 4 vols. [Oxford, 1923], *1*, 151). The original distinction between a disguising or mumming and the masque seems to have been that the masque was an Italianate form in which the audience participated (as they had in primitive folk mummings). Edward Hall claims that the mask was brought to England by Henry VIII himself on Twelfth Night 1512: "the kyng with a .xi. other were disguised, after the maner of Italie, called a maske, a thyng not seen afore in Englande, thei were appareled in garments long and brode, wrought all with gold, with visers and cappes of gold, & after the banket doen, these Maskers came in, with sixe gentlemen disguised in silke bearyng staffe torches, and desired the ladies to daunce, some were content, and some that knew the fashion of it refused, because it was not a thyng commonly seen. And after thei daunced and commoned together, as the fashion of the Maske is, thei tooke their leaue and departed, and so did the Quene, and all the ladies"; *The Vnion of the two noble and illustrate famelies of Lancastre & Yorke* . . . (London, 1548; *STC* 12721), sig. CCc₄. As this passage makes clear, maskers spoke; hence More chooses this name for his opponent rather than the silent "mummer." On mummings, see E. K. Chambers, *The Medieval Stage*, 2 vols. (Oxford, 1903), *1*, 205–27; Alan Brody, *The English Mummers and Their Plays* (Philadelphia, 1970). On the early court masque see Chambers, *The Elizabethan Stage*, *1*, 149–57; Enid Welsford, *The Court Masque* (London, 1927). See also Germain Marc'hadour, "Le Masque et le visage," *Moreana, 18* (1968), 111–18.

16/2–7 **all those wordes . . . Capharnaum.** The miracle of the feeding of the five thousand at Galilee is related in John 6 : 1–15. John 6 : 24–71 tells of Jesus' discussion of the miracle the next day at Capernaum. The synoptic accounts of the miracle occur in Matt. 14 : 13–21; Mark 6 : 30–44; Luke 9 : 10–17.

16/7–11 **fyrst rebuke . . . perysshe.** John 6 : 25–27: "Et cum invenissent eum trans mare, dixerunt ei: Rabbi, quando huc venisti? Respondit eis Iesus, et dixit: Amen, amen dico vobis: quaeritis me non quia vidistis signa, sed quia manducastis ex panibus et saturati estis. Operamini non cibum, qui perit, sed qui permanet in vitam aeternam, quem Filius hominis dabit vobis."

16/12–15 **what they sholde do . . . sent.** John 6 : 28–29: "Dixerunt ergo ad eum: Quid faciemus ut operemur opera Dei? Respondit Iesus, et dixit eis: Hoc est opus Dei, ut credatis in eum quem misit ille."

16/17–23 **what token . . . heuen.** John 6 : 30–32: "Dixerunt ergo ei: Quod ergo tu facis signum ut videamus et credamus tibi? quid operaris? Patres nostri manducaverunt manna in deserto, sicut scriptum est:

Panum de caelo dedit eis manducare. Dixit ergo eis Iesus: Amen, amen dico vobis: Non Moyses dedit vobis panem de caelo, sed Pater meus dat vobis panem de caelo verum." On manna in the wilderness, see Exod. 16.

16/23-27 **all the remanaunt . . . synnes.** See especially John 6 : 35, 48, 50-58.

17/23 **flesshely . . . mysse toke it.** John 6 : 52.

17/25 **institucion.** Matt. 26 : 26-29; Mark 14 : 22-25; Luke 22 : 19-23.

17/27-18/6 **It is . . . chyrche.** More alludes to the four senses of scripture, first distinguished by St. John Cassian (*Collationes* 14.8; *PL 49*, 962-65). There is one literal or historical sense, and three spiritual senses: the allegorical, which applies the passage to Christ and the church on earth (the church militant); the tropological, or moral, which interprets the passage in terms of the soul and its virtues; and the anagogical, which relates a passage to heavenly realities. Cassian's example became classic. Historically, Jerusalem is a city of the Jews; allegorically it is the church of Christ; tropologically it is the soul of man, "which under this name the Lord often threatens or praises," and anagogically it is the heavenly City of God. See Marc'hadour, *Thomas More et la Bible*, pp. 459-63, and *CW 14*, Commentary 2, note on 21/5-7.

18/13-23 **Of this maner . . . bysyde.** See *A Letter against Frith* (1532), sigs. c₃v-c₄v; Rogers, no. 190, p. 446, lines 200-20.

18/35-19/5 **Genesis . . . remanaunt.** Allegories of Gen. 2 : 10-14 began as early as Philo Judaeus (*Questions and Answers on Genesis* 1.12). Ambrose, in his elaborate allegory (*De Paradiso* 3.12-18; *PL 14*, cols. 279-82), apparently relied on lost writings of Origen. The *Glossa ordinaria* (*PL 113*, 87) quotes allegories by Gregory, Bede, and Isidore. One constant feature of such allegories is the interpretation of the four rivers as the four cardinal virtues. More's insistence on both literal and allegorical interpretation resembles Augustine's view of how Genesis should be interpreted (*De Genesi ad literam*, 8.1.1; *PL 34*, 371). Giovanni Pico della Mirandola allegorized the six days of creation in his *Heptaplus*, but he links the days to the whole history of man's fall and redemption and does not mention paradise or its rivers.

19/15-31 **Sampson . . . story.** This allegory of Judges 15 : 4-5 is perhaps closest to Augustine's *Sermones* 364 (*PL 39*, 1641-42): "Quid est aliud vulpes capere, nisi haereticos divinae legis auctoritate revincere, et sanctarum Scripturarum testimoniis velut quibusdam vinculis alligare atque constringere? Vulpes capit, ligatis ignem caudis apponit. Quid sibi volunt caudae vulpium colligatae? Caudae vulpium quid sunt, nisi posteriora haereticorum, qui prima habent blanda et deceptoria: ligata, id est, damnata, et ignem in fine trahentia; ut eorum fructus et opera consumant, qui suis seductionibus acquiescunt? . . . Videte ergo judicium haereticis retro, quomodo non vident post se. Habent blandimenta, ut mulceant, primas partes suas liberas ostendunt: in judicio Dei in ligatis caudis, id est, in posterioribus suis ignem trahunt, quia improbitas praecedit poenas suas." Cf. Augustine's *Enarrationes in Psalmos* 80.13 (*CSEL 39,* 1128–29): "Vulpes insidiosos, maximeque haereticos significant. . . . Sed omnes hi [sc. vulpes aut haeretici] in posterioribus consentiunt, id est, simili vanitate detinentur." Cf. also Ambrose (*PL 15,* cols. 1707–08) and Paschasius (*PL 120,* col. 357). Samson in some circumstances was taken as representative of sinners (Gregory, *PL 75,* col. 787); more often he is a figure of Christ (for example, Gregory, *PL 76,* cols. 491, 1173). He was never, so far as we know, taken as a figure of the devil as More seems to do here.

20/26–27 **My flesshe . . . drynke.** John 6 : 56: "Caro enim mea vere est cibus: et sanguis meus, vere est potus."

21/9–12 **somwhat before . . . shippes.** John 6 : 16–24: "Ut autem sero factum est, descenderunt discipuli eius ad mare. Et cum ascendissent navim, venerunt trans mare in Capharnaum: et tenebrae iam factae erant et non venerat ad eos Iesus. Mare autem, vento magno flante, exsurgebat. Cum remigassent ergo quasi stadia viginti quinque aut triginta, vident Iesum ambulantem supra mare, et proximum navi fieri, et timuerunt. Ille autem dicit eis: Ego sum, nolite timere. Voluerunt ergo accipere eum in navim et statim navis fuit ad terram, in quam ibant. Altera die, turba, quae stabat trans mare, vidit quia navicula alia non erat ibi nisi una, et quia non introisset cum discipulis suis Iesus in navim, sed soli discipuli eius abiisent: aliae vero supervenerunt naves a Tiberiade iuxta locum ubi manducaverant panem, gratias agente Domino. Cum ergo vidisset turba quia Iesus non esset ibi, neque discipuli eius, ascenderunt in naviculas, et venerunt Capharnaum quaerentes Iesum."

21/13–17 **hard allegory . . . heretykes.** See Alcuin (*PL 100,* 827, drawing upon Bede, *PL 92,* 711) in *Catena aurea* on John 6 : 22–24 (p. 332): "Una autem navis est una Ecclesia: sed et aliae naves quae superveniunt, sunt conventicula haereticorum qui 'quae sua sunt quaerunt, non quae Jesu Christi': Philipp. 2."

21/17–19 **And yet . . . to gyther.** Disciples of Christ (including the apostles) came over in the single ship symbolizing the church. After his speech about giving them his flesh to eat, his disciples abandoned him, and among the remaining apostles was the traitor Judas (87/18–26).

21/34–35 **For . . . heuyn.** John 6 : 33: "Panis enim verus est" was the received reading in More's time (as in the Froben *Biblia latina* of 1498). Later, more correct editions of the Vulgate have "Panis enim dei est." See Wordsworth–White, *1,* 546. In his *Nouum Testamentum* Erasmus finally chose "Dei" over "verus" (*Opera omnia, 6,* 366).

22/11 **& shall reyse hym.** Cf. John 6 : 40: "et ego resuscitabo eum."

More translates the same phrase as "and I shall reyse him" at 22/17 and 22/30.

22/13 **the sone of Ioseph.** John 6 : 42. "Iesus filius Ioseph" is now the accepted reading, but *Biblia latina* and other manuscript traditions in More's time omitted "Iesus" (Wordsworth–White, *1*, 548). Erasmus' *Nouum Testamentum* has "Iesus" (*Opera omnia, 6*, 366).

23/6 **ye byleuers.** John 6 : 64. More follows the presently accepted reading "credentes," but many Greek and Latin manuscripts support "non credentes," the reading chosen by Erasmus in his *Novum Testamentum* (*Opera omnia, 6*, 368). See Wordsworth–White, *1*, 551.

23/28–29 **iii. times . . . shepe.** John 21 : 15–17.

23/31–34 **Thou . . . agaynste yt.** Matt. 16 : 16–19. Cf. John 1 : 41.

24/5–9 **warnyng . . . general resurreccyon.** See Matt. 16 : 21, 27; 17 : 21–22; 20 : 18–19; 25 : 31–33; Mark 8 : 31, 38; 9 : 30; 10 : 32–34; Luke 9 : 22, 26, 44; 18 : 31–33.

24/13–14 **not very wel byleued . . . dyscyples.** See Mark 9 : 31; Luke 9 : 45; 12 : 40; 18 : 34.

24/24–26 **Nichodemus . . . Iewes.** See John 3 and 62/3–34, below.

26/21–24 **syrs . . . belyes.** John 6 : 26. Note the lively colloquialism of More's paraphrase: "syrs I tell you very trewth" ("Amen, amen dico vobis"); "well eaten and well fylled your belyes" ("manducastis . . . et saturati estis").

26/25–29 **In these wordes . . . harte.** In the *Catena aurea* on John 6 : 6 (p. 328), Chrysostom cites "Scrutatur corda hominum" (Rom. 8 : 27) to confirm Christ's omniscience (*In Ioannem homiliae* 42; in *PG 59*, 240). The *Catena aurea* on John 6 : 65 (p. 340) gives the following comment of Theophylactus: "Volens per hoc nobis Evangelista ostendere quod ante constitutionem mundi omnia cognoscebat; quod divinitatis erat indicium."

26/28–29 **our lorde . . . harte.** See 1 Kings 16 : 7; 3 Kings 8.39; 1 Par. 28 : 9; Ps. 7 : 10; Jer. 17 : 10. The gloss is incorrect.

27/3–4 **prophecye . . . prophetes.** For Moses' prophecy, see Deut. 18 : 15–22. For other messianic prophecies see, for example, Isa. 7 : 14; 9 : 6; 11; Jer. 23 : 5–8.

27/21–26 **By these wordes . . . after.** See Augustine, *In Iohannis evangelium* 25.9 (*CCSL 36*, 252): "Seipsum enim insinuat istum cibum, quod in consequentibus illucescit." Cf. de Lyra on John 6 : 26: "Respondit eis iesus. Posito signo de cibo corporali. hic convenienter ponitur doctrina de cibo spirituali. Cibus autem spiritualis est ipsum verbum incarnatum principaliter ratione deitatis: et ex consequenti ratione assumpte carnis: qui nobis datur in cibum in sacramento eucharistie."

27/22 **insinuate.** As *1557* and the passage from Augustine in the preceding note show, "insumate" is a printer's error caused by a series of minims in his manuscript copy. See 50/2 and *CW 6*, 146/22 and Commentary.

28/5–7 **The meate . . . tother.** 1 Cor. 6 : 13–14: "Esca ventri, et venter escis: Deus autem et hunc et has destruet, corpus autem non fornicationi, sed Domino: et Dominus corpori. Deus vero et Dominum suscitavit: et nos suscitabit per virtutem suam." This passage is cited by Aquinas on John 6 : 27 (*Commentum*, p. 408).

28/18 **mete . . . meate.** Here and at 28/31–32 More plays on "mete" ("fitting") and "meate" ("food").

28/19–23 **that is . . . heuyn.** Cf. Aquinas on John 6 : 27 (*Commentum*, p. 408): ". . . qui quidem cibus est ipse Deus, inquantum est veritas contemplanda, et bonitas amanda, quibus reficitur spiritus. . . . Et hoc inquantum est conjuncta Verbo Dei, quod est cibus quo Angeli vivunt." Cf. also *Glossa ordinaria* on John 6 : 33 (*PL 114*, 382): "Angeli purum verbum solidum cibum comedunt: nos vero verbum, sed in lac versum, quia si non possumus comedere, possumus sugere. Nisi enim incarnaretur, a nobis non cognosceretur, a nobis non gustaretur."

28/33–29/12 **But . . . lyfe."** Cf. de Lyra on John 6 : 27: "Si enim cibus corporalis maneat in propria forma non nutrit: sed magis nocet corpori. Sed si nutriat oportet quod a propria natura pereat et conuertatur in membra. econuerso autem cibus spiritualis manet et conuertit in seipsum sementem [*for* sumentem], quia deus nos sibi incorporat et non econuerso. vnde Augustinus loquens in persona huius cibi dicit: Cibus sum grandium: non me mutabis in te: sed tu mutaberis in me" (*Confessions* 7.10.16). Cf. also Aquinas on John 6 : 27 (*Commentum*, p. 408): "Virtus illius cibi consideratur in hoc quod non perit. Unde sciendum est circa hoc, quod corporalia sunt quaedam similitudines spiritualium, utpote ab eis causata et derivata; et ideo imitantur ipsa spiritualia aliquo modo: unde sicut corpus sustentatur cibo, ita illud quo sustentatur spiritus, dicitur ejus cibus, quicquid sit illud. Illud autem quo sustentatur corpus, cum transeat in corporis naturam, corruptibile est: sed cibus quo sustentatur spiritus, est incorruptibilis, quia non mutatur in ipsum spiritum, sed potius e converso spiritus in cibum. Unde dictum est Augustino 'Cibus sum grandium; cresce, et manducabis me; nec tu me mutabis in te, ut cibum carnis tuae, sed mutaberis in me,' ut dicitur lib. Confess." Cf. *De civitate Dei* 21.15 (*CCSL 48*, 781).

29/13–16 **But yet . . . therfore.** See note to 32/32–33/3.

29/23–32 **And therfore . . . you.** Cf. Alcuin on John 6 : 27 in the *Catena aurea* (p. 332): "Quando autem per manum sacerdotis corpus Christi accipis, non sacerdotem quem vides, sed illum quem non vides attende. Sacerdos est dispensator hujus cibi, non actor. Filius hominis seipsum dat nobis, ut nos in ipso et ipse in nobis maneat." We have not been able to find this passage in the extant works of Alcuin.

30/10–12 **For hym ... creaturs.** Cf. Alcuin (*PL 100*, 828) on John 6 : 27 in the *Catena aurea* (p. 332): "Istum Filium hominis nolite sic accipere quasi alios filios hominum: sequestratus est enim quadam gratia, et exceptus a numero omnium."

30/14–33 **For ... hym selfe.** See Hilary (*PL 10*, 269) on John 6 : 27 in the *Catena aurea* (p. 332). "Signaculorum autem natura est ut omnem impressae in se speciei explicent formam, et nihil minus ex eo in se habeant unde signantur; et dum totum accipiunt quod imprimatur, totum ex se praeferunt quidquid impressum est. Verbum igitur hoc ad divinae nativitatis non proficit exemplum: quia in signaculis et materies sit, et diversitas, et impressio, per quam mollioribus naturis, validiorum generum species imprimuntur. Unigenitus vero Deus et per sacramentum salutis nostrae hominis Filius, volens proprietatis nobis paternae in se signare speciem, signatum se a Deo ait, ut per hoc postestas in eo dandae ad aeternitatem escae intelligi possit, quia omnem in se paternae formae plenitudinem signantis se Dei contineret." For Cyril see *PG 73*, col. 483.

30/21–22 **Crist ... father.** Col. 1 : 15: "qui est imago Dei invisibilis, primogenitus omnis creaturae."

31/5 **anonynted.** The gloss refers to Ps. 44 : 8.

31/26–30 **As the woman of Samary ... for euer.** Cf. Augustine (*CCSL 36*, 255) in the *Catena aurea* on John 6 : 34 (p. 333): "Sicut enim Samaritana cui dictum est, supra 4: *Qui biberit de hac aqua, non sitiet unquam*, secundum corpus accipiens, et carere indigentia volens, *Da mihi*, inquit, *Domine, de hac aqua*: sic et isti dicunt: Da nobis panem qui reficiat et non deficiat." De Lyra and the *Glossa ordinaria* (*PL 114*, 382), commenting on John 6 : 34, also make the parallel with the Samaritan woman in John 4 : 5–26.

32/6–7 **Esca ... destruet.** 1 Cor. 6 : 13: "Esca ventri, et venter escis: Deus autem et hunc et has destruet." The *1557* gloss is incorrect.

32/13–19 **they ... scratchyng.** Cf. *Utopia, CW 4*, 176/7–11.

32/32–33/3 **And our lorde ... owne.** More refers to Chrysostom (*PG 59*, 249), quoted in the *Catena aurea* on John 6 : 27 (p. 332): "Sed quia quidam, eo quod volunt pigre nutriri, abutuntur hoc verbo; necessarium est inducere id quod est Pauli Ephes. 4: 'Qui furabatur, jam non furetur; magis autem laboret operando manibus suis, ut habeat unde tribuat necessitatem patienti.' Sed et ipse Corinthum veniens morabatur apud Aquilam et Priscillam et operabatur. Dicendo autem, *Ne operemini cibum qui perit*, non insinuat quod oporteat pigritari, sed quod oporteat operari et dare; hic enim est cibus qui non perit: operari autem cibum qui perit, est affici saecularibus rebus. Hoc igitur dixit, illi nullam fidei curam habuerunt, sed solum volebant ventrem implere, nihil laborantes; et hoc decenter cibum qui perit vocavit."

33/3–5 **Lord . . . welle.** More paraphrases John 4 : 15: "Domine, da mihi hanc aquam, ut non sitiam, neque veniam huc haurire."

33/10–15 **whan . . . lyuynge.** Gen. 2 : 15; 3 : 19.

33/25–26 **vale . . . terys.** Cf. Ps. 83 : 7; Eccles. 3 : 4.

34/14 **bely ioy.** For discussion of a similar phrase, see *CW 6*, Commentary at 73/13.

35/12–13 **Our . . . eate.** See Exod. 15 : 16; Ps. 77 : 24.

35/26–31 **But agaynst . . . eyer.** Cf. de Lyra on John 6 : 32: "non dedit vobis moyses panem de celo, scilicet proprie dicto: quia non de celo sedereo et empyreo sed de celo aereo: quia descendebat vt ros vel pruina." Cf. also Aquinas on John 6 : 31 (*Commentum*, p. 410): "Item contra hoc quod dicit, *Non dedit vobis panem de caelo*, est quod dicitur in Psalm. 77, 24: 'Panem caeli dedit eis.' Respondeo: Caelum accipitur tripliciter. Quandoque pro aere. Matth. 13, 4: 'Volucres caeli comederunt illud.' Et in Psal. 17, 14: 'Intonuit de caelo Dominus.' Quandoque pro caelo sidereo, secundum illud Psal. 113, 16: 'Caelum caeli Domino.' Et Matth. 24, 19: 'Stellae cadent de caelo.' Quandoque vero pro ipsis spiritualibus bonis. Matth. 5, 12: 'Gaudete, et exultate, quia merces vestra est in caelo.' Manna ergo de caelo fuit non sidereo seu spirituali, sed aereo. Vel dicitur de caelo inquantum erat figura veri panis caelestis Domini nostri Jesu Christi."

36/26 **the very . . . angelles fede.** See note to 28/19–23.

36/36–37/33 **Good . . . byd theym.** For the relation of faith to the two other theological virtues, see notes to 121/6–123/19 and 119/13–120/2, below.

37/1–4 **olde heresye . . . reproue.** Jas. 2 : 14–26, which contains James's famous dictum "fides sine operibus mortua est," and Gal. 5 : 6. See *CW 6*, Commentary at 149/6–7.

37/25–26 **he . . . byleue.** Heb. 11 : 6: "Credere enim oportet accendentem ad Deum quia est, et inquirentibus se remunerator sit."

38/3–12 **Saynt Iohan . . . wagys.** Luke 3 : 10–14.

38/30 **vertuouse.** The sense requires a plural noun (virtues) rather than an adjective, but the spelling is unusual for the noun. The spelling "vertuose" for the plural noun also occurs in *CW 12*, 127/16 and in *The Supplication of Souls* (London, 1529; *STC²* 18093), sig. I₃v.

38/32–37 **There are . . . cheryte.** See Aquinas on John 6 : 47 (*Commentum*, p. 416): "Si ergo ille qui credit in Christum habet vitam, manifestum est quod manducando hunc panem vivificatur: ergo iste panis est panis vitae: et hoc est quod dicit: *Amen amen dico vobis, qui credit in me,* fide scilicet formata, quae non solum perficit intellectum, sed etiam affectum (non enim tenditur in rem creditam nisi ametur) *habet vitam aeternam.* Christus autem est in nobis dupliciter: scilicet in intellectu per fidem, inquantum fides est; et in affectu per caritatem, quae informat fidem." See also de Lyra on John 6 : 35: "Qui venit ad me, per fidem formatam charitate." On *fides formata,* see below, note to 121/6–123/19.

38/36 dede fayth. Jas. 2 : 20. The gloss is incorrect.

39/1–16 And therfore sayth holy saynt Austayne . . . wurketh. More translates a passage from Augustine (*CCSL 36,* 254) included in the *Catena aurea* on John 6 : 29 (pp. 332–33): "Non autem dicit, Ut credatis ei, sed *ut credatis in eum*: non enim continuo qui credit ei, credit in eum; nam et daemones credebant ei, et non credebant in eum; et nos credimus Paulo, sed non in Paulum. Credere ergo in eum, est credendo amare, credendo diligere, credendo in eum ire, et ejus membris incorporari. Ipsa est fides quam de nobis exigit Deus, quae per dilectionem operatur. Discernitur tamen ab operibus fides, sicut dicit Apostolus Rom. 3: 'Justificari hominem per fidem sine operibus legis.' Et sunt opera quae videntur bona sine fide Christi, et non sunt bona, quia non referentur ad eum finem ex quo sunt bona: 'finis enim legis Christus ad justitiam omni credenti;' Rom. 10 et ideo noluit discernere ab opere fidem; sed ipsam fidem dixit esse opus Dei: ipsa est enim fides quae per dilectionem operatur."

39/9–10 a man . . . lawe. Rom. 3 : 28.

39/12–13 For . . . byleue. Rom. 10 : 4.

39/15–16 fayth . . . wurketh. Gal. 5 : 6.

39/31–34 Lo thus . . . byleue. Cf. Chrysostom (*PG 59,* 253), quoted in the *Catena aurea* on John 6 : 36 (p. 333): "Vel per hoc quod dicit, *Dixi vobis,* insinuat testimonium Scripturarum. . . . Hoc autem quod dicit, *Quia vidistis me,* signa occulte insinuat."

40/23–32 For but . . . at me. More's reading of this passage draws upon Augustine's discussion of John 6 : 45, parts of which More paraphrases below (see 48/2–22). Cf. esp. "Non enim quisquam dicere potest, Credidi, ut sic vocarer: praevenit quippe eum misericordia Dei, quia sic est vocatus ut crederet." On "preventing" or prevenient grace, see Aquinas, *Summa theologica,* Iª–IIᵃᵉ, q. 111, a. 3.

41/12 Arryane. Arianism, named for its founder, Arius (c. 250–336), an Alexandrian priest, denied the divine nature and co-eternity of Jesus Christ. The heresy was condemned by the first Council of Nicaea in 325, which reaffirmed belief in the trinity by defining Jesus as "homoousios," of one substance with the Father. The struggle between Arianism and orthodoxy divided the church and the empire through much of the fourth century. A moderate Arian creed was accepted by a council of eastern and western bishops at Sirmium in 357, the orthodox position was reaffirmed under Theodosius I, and the heresy was suppressed.

41/13–14 **as . . . often.** See, for example, Matt. 11 : 25; Mark 14 : 36; Luke 2 : 49; John 4 : 34.

42/14–43/3 **But nowe . . . god also.** Cf. de Lyra on John 6 : 38: "Quia descendi de celo etc. non est per hoc intelligendum quod voluntas Christi in aliquid discordet a voluntate patris: quia secundum naturam diuinam eadem omnino est voluntas patris et filii. similiter secundum naturam humanam voluntas eius non poterat a voluntate diuina discordare. cum anima Christi esset coniuncta verbo: non solum per fruitionem sed per realem vnionem: et sic voluntas Christi nullo modo poterat a voluntate patris discrepare. et ideo facere voluntatem patris et suam est idem secundum rem et econuerso. quando ergo dicit: Descendi de celo non vt facerem voluntatem meam etc. est communis modus loquendi apud homines. illius qui onmino sequitur voluntatem alterius. et est sensus: Descendi de celo etc. ac si diceretur: non veni ad declinandum in aliquo a voluntate patris, et per consequens, veni ad proficiendum salutem electorum quia hec est voluntas patris ipsos praedestinantis. ideo sequitur: Hec est enim voluntas eius qui misit me patris. . . ." Cf. also Aquinas on John 6 : 38 (*Commentum*, p. 412): "Sciendum est autem, quod in Christo fuit duplex voluntas. Una secundum humanam naturam, quae est sibi propria, et natura, et voluntate Patris; alia secundum naturam divinam, quae est eadem cum voluntate Patris. Voluntatem ergo suam, scilicet humanam, ordinavit sub voluntate divina, quia obedientiam suam sub effectu paternae voluntatis ostendit ipse, volens voluntatem Patris explere." More returns to this theme in *De Tristitia*; see *CW 14*, text and Commentary at 175/7–185/14 and 219/1–9.

43/6–8 **No man . . . heuyn.** John 3 : 13.

44/6–9 **incorporatynge . . . incorporated.** The *OED* gives only later uses of "incorporate" as applied to the eucharist (*OED*, "incorporate" *v.* 2).

45/3–6 **whan god . . . names.** Phil. 2 : 8–9: "Humiliavit semetipsum factus obediens usque ad mortem, mortem autem crucis. Propter quod et Deus exaltavit illum, et donavit illi nomen, quod est super omne nomen."

46/9–16 **All . . . eyre.** Cf. Chrysostom (*PG 59*, 257), quoted in the *Catena aurea* on John 6 : 41 (pp. 334–35): "Judaei existimantes se comestione carnali potiri, non turbabantur, usquequo postea diffisi sunt: unde dicitur: *Murmurabant ergo Judaei de illo, quia dixisset: Ego sum panis vivus, qui de caelo descendi.* Videbantur quidem turbari in hoc quod dixerat eum de caelo descendisse; sed non hoc erat quod turbationem faciebat, sed hoc quod non expectabant potiri mensa corporali."

46/23–30 **fore fathers . . . sauour.** Exod. 16 : 2–8; Num. 21 : 5.

47/32–34 **prophete . . . teth.** Ps. 31 : 9 and note to 94/8–9.

48/2–22 **And if . . . within you.** More paraphrases loosely parts of two passages from Augustine given in the *Catena aurea* on John 6 : 45 (pp. 335–36). The first is from *In Iohannis evangelium tractatus 124 (CCSL 36,* 263): "Omnes regni illius homines docibiles erunt Dei, non ab hominibus audient: Et si hic ab hominibus audiunt, tamen quod intellegunt, intus datur. Strepitum verborum ingero auribus vestris, nisi reuelet ille qui intus est." The second is from *De praedestinatione sanctorum (PL 44,* 970–71): "Omnes autem docibiles Dei veniunt ad Filium, quoniam audierunt et didicerunt a Patre per Filium: unde subditur: *Omnis qui audivit a Patre, et didicit, venit ad me.* Si autem omnis qui audivit a Patre et didicit, venit, profecto omnis qui non venit, non audit a Patre nec didicit. Valde remota est a sensibus carnis haec schola, in qua Pater auditur et docet, ut venia-tur ad Filium; nec agit hoc cum carnis aure, sed cordis, ubi est et ipse Filius; quia ipse est Verbum ejus per quod Pater sic docet. . . . Non enim quisquam dicere potest, Credidi, ut sic vocarer: praevenit quippe eum misericordia Dei, quia sic est vocatus ut crederet."

48/10–11 **all . . . god.** See Isa. 54 : 13; cf. John 6 : 45.

48/17–18 **wysdome . . . harte.** Sap. 1 : 4. The gloss is incorrect.

49/7–11 **For euery man . . . ellys.** John 6 : 46: "Non quia Patrem vidit quisquam, nisi is, qui est a Deo, hic vidit Patrem."

50/6–7 **Alcuinus . . . Cyrill.** For Alcuin and Aquinas see notes to 29/23–32 and 28/19–23. More has not yet quoted Theophylactus and Cyril on this point, but he will do so shortly (52/9–33, 63/32–65/21, 66/22–67/13, 71/12–31, 72/14–18).

51/5–8 **same very flesshe . . . deth.** The marginal gloss refers to 1 Cor. 11 : 24.

51/20 **Luther.** In 1527 Luther had briefly applied John 6 to the eucharist (*WA 23,* 205), but in his sermons on John 6–8 (delivered between 1530 and 1532 but not printed till 1565) he made no mention of the sacrament and asserted that "to eat" in John 6 means "to believe," in order to insist on faith alone without works (*WA 33,* 209–10).

51/21–24 **Fryth . . . poynt.** *A Boke . . . answeringe vnto M mores lettur,* sigs. C₆v, D₂v–D₃.

52/9–33 **Consyder . . . wyth.** The passage translated may be found in Theophylactus' *In quatuor Euangelia enarrationes . . . Ioanne Oecolampadio interprete* (Basel, A. Cratander, 1527), sig. E₄ (*PG 123,* 1308). The brack-eted sentences are omitted from the version cited in the *Catena aurea* on John 6 : 52 (p. 337). "Attende autem quod panis, qui a nobis in mysterijs manducatur, non est tantum figuratio quaedam carnis domini, sed ipsa caro domini. Non enim dixit, panis quem ego dabo, figura est carnis: sed, caro mea est. Transformatur enim arcanis verbis panis ille per mysticam benedictionem, & accessionem sancti spiritus, in carnem domini. [Et ne quem conturbet, quod credendus sit panis caro. Etenim & in carne ambulante domino & ex pane alimoniam admittente, panis ille qui manducabatur, in corpus eius mutabatur, & similis fiebat sanctae eius carni, & in augmentum & sustentationem conferebat, iuxta humanum morem. Igitur & nunc panis in carnem domini mutatur.] Et quomodo, inquit, non apparet nobis caro, sed panis? Vt non abhorreamus ab eius esu. Nam si quidem caro apparuisset, insuauiter affecti essemus erga communionem. Nunc autem condescendente domino nostrae infirmitati, talis apparet nobis mysticus cibus, qualibus alioquin assueti sumus."

53/4 **me.** In *1533* the comma has been displaced upward in the Bodleian, Oscott, and Huntington copies; the Lincoln copy has it in the regular position.

53/6–7 **as saint Poule doth.** 1 Cor. 11 : 26: "Quotiescumque enim manducabitis panem hunc, et calicem bibetis, mortem Domini annuntiabitis donec veniat."

53/29–33 **serpent . . . magycianis.** Exod. 7 : 9–13.

55/4–21 **Et panis . . . world.** The phrase is repeated in many Greek texts of John 6 : 51 and by many of the fathers; see *The Greek New Testament*, ed. Henry Alford, 4 vols. (Boston, 1873), *1*, 766. Erasmus' *Novum Testamentum* has the repeated phrase in Greek and Latin (*Opera omnia*, 6, 366).

56/30–33 **Now yf . . . sacrament.** *Souper*, Appendix A, 309/36–310/8.

57/20–26 **saint Bede . . . crosse.** Bede, quoted in the *Catena aurea* on John 6 : 51 (p. 337): "Hunc panem tunc Dominus dedit, quando mysterium corporis et sanguinis sui discipulis tradidit, et quando semetipsum Deo Patri obtulit in ara crucis." We have not been able to find this passage in the extant works of Bede.

58/9–14 **Saynt Bede . . . shoppys.** Bede, *In S. Ioannis evangelium expositio* 6 (*PL 92*, 720): ". . . prout voluerunt, ita intellexerunt, et more hominum quibus caput non erat Jesus, quasi hoc disponeret Jesus, carnem, qua indutum erat Verbum, velut in frusta concisam distribuere credentibus in se. Durus est, inquiunt, hic sermo, quis potest eum audire?" Here Bede follows the language of Augustine, who does not, however, have the phrase "in frusta" (*In Iohannis evangelium tractatus*, 27.2, *CCSL 36*, 270). The following comment on John 6 : 53 is also attributed to Bede in *Catena aurea* (p. 337): "Putabant ergo Judaei quod Dominus particulatim carnem suam divideret et eis ad manducandum daret: et ideo litigabant, quia non intelligebant." See note to 80/26–27. The same idea appears in a medley of passages from Augustine given in Gratian's *Decretum* (De consecratione 2.44; *CIC 1*, 1330).

58/19–30 **our lady ... gospell.** For Mary asking "how" see Luke 1 : 26–38; for Nicodemus, see John 3 : 1–20.

58/31–59/4 **For thangell ... afterwarde.** More borrowed the argument from St. Augustine's *De sancta virginitate* 4 (*CSEL 41*, 237–38). In *Explanatio symboli* (Basel, March 1533), written at the request of Sir Thomas Boleyn, to whom it was dedicated, Erasmus propounded the same argument as an example of a doctrine that must be believed because of the *consensus fidelium*, even though it cannot be clearly proved from scripture (*ASD 5/1*, 245/189–246/213). Erasmus also expressed the same idea in *Modus orandi deum* (Basel, October 1524; *ASD 5/1*, 146/887–147/891).

58/31–32 **shalt conceyue.** Luke 1 : 31: "ecce concipies in utero, et paries filium, et vocabis nomen eius Iesum."

59/1 **as I ... dialoge.** See *CW 6*, 150–51.

59/23–24 **goddes ... ordynaunce.** Gen. 1 : 28: "Crescite et multiplicamini."

60/16–17 **deuyl ... angel of light.** Cf. 2 Cor. 11 : 14: "Et non mirum: ipse enim Satanas transfigurat se in angelum lucis."

61/30–37 **zachary ... chyld.** Luke 1 : 18–20: "Et dixit Zacharias ad angelum: Unde hoc sciam? ego enim sum senex, et uxor mea processit in diebus suis."

62/3–14 **Nichodemus ... goost.** John 3 : 3–8.

62/32–34 **Nichodemus ... with hym.** John 7 : 50–51.

62/35–63/12 **Now Cryste ... vnsoyled.** John 3 : 8–21.

63/2–3 **for y^t ... diuersely.** In his note on "Spiritus ubi vult spirat" (John 3 : 8) Erasmus cites Valla, Chrysostom, Cyril, Theophylactus, and Augustine to show that the invisible but efficacious movement of the air is here applied metaphorically to the Holy Spirit (*Opera omnia, 6*, 351EF).

63/32–65/21 **The Iewes ... your wordes.** Cyril, *In Iohannis evangelium*, 4.2 (*PG 73*, cols. 573–76); tr. Trapezontius, 1528, sig. n$_1$v: ". . . contra omnino faciunt: Et quomodo potest hic carnem suam nobis dare? De deo non sine magna impietate conclamant, nec in mentem uenit nihil esse impossibile apud deum. Nam quum animales essent (ut ait Paulus) spiritalia intelligere non poterant. Sed fatuitas quaedam tam magnum sibi uidetur mysterium: sed nos magnum quaeso a peccatis aliorum profectum faciamus, & firmam fidem mysterijs adhibentes, nunquam in tam sublimibus rebus, illud quomodo, aut cogitemus, aut proferamus. Iudaicum enim hoc uerbum est, et extremi supplicij causa. Ideo Nicodemus etiam quum diceret: Quomodo haec fieri possunt? merito audiuit: Tu es magister in Israel, & haec ignoras? Aliorum igitur, ut diximus, culpa perdocti, quum deus operetur, non quaeramus quomodo, sed operis sui uiam atque scientiam illi soli concedamus. Nam quemadmodum, quamuis nullus nouit quidnam secundum naturam deus sit, iustificatur tamen per fidem, quum credat praemia illum redditurum quaerentibus eum: sic etsi operum eius rationem ignorat, quum tamen fide omnia illum posse non dubitet, non contemnenda probatatis huius praemia consequetur. Ita profecto nos affici per prophetam Esaiam dominus ipse hortatur? Non enim sunt consilia mea, inquit, ut consilia uestra, nec sicut uiae uestrae uiae meae sunt, dicit dominus: sed sicut exaltatur coelum a terra, sic exaltatae sunt uiae meae a uijs uestris, & cogitationes meae a cogitationibus uestris. Qui autem sapientia a uirtute & deo excellit, quomodo non operabitur ita miraculose, ut operum suorum ratio mentem nostram effugiat? Nonne uides quid saepenumero mechanici faciunt? Incredibilia uidentur nobis nonnunquam enarrare: sed tamen quia similia ipsos fecisse uidimus, posse peragi ab ipsis facile credimus. Quomodo igitur summis cruciatibus digni non erunt, qui rerum omnium opificem deum ita contemnunt, ut quomodo, in operibus suis dicere audeant? quem totius sapientiae largitorem esse non ignorant: quem omnia posse scriptura nos docuit. Si uero tu o Iudaee, quomodo, etiam nunc clamas: hanc tuam imperitiam ego quoque sequutus, libenter quomodo ex Aegypto exiuisti rogabo: quomodo in serpentem Mosaica fuit uirga conuersa? quomodo lepra manus affecta, uno momento temporis in pristinum statum restituta iterum fuit? quomodo in naturam sanguinis aquae transierunt? quomodo patres tui per media maria, ut per aridam effugerunt? quomodo per lignum amaritudo aquarum in dulcedinem recidit? quomodo e lapide fontes aquarum fluebant? quomodo stetit Iordanis? quomodo solo clamore inexpugnabilis Hierico cecidit? innumerabilia sunt, in quibus si quomodo quaeris, uniuersam euertere tibi scripturam necesse erit, prophetarum doctrinam & ipsius Mosis scripta contemnenti. Quare credidisse Christo potius uos oportuit, & si quid arduum uidebatur, ab eo humiliter petere, quam ueluti temulentos exclamare: Quomodo potest hic nobis suam carnem dare? Nonne uidetis, quia quum haec dicatis, statim quum [i.e. cum] ista uoce arrogantia magna significatur?" This passage is also quoted by Oecolampadius, *Quid veteres senserint*, sigs. C_5v–C_7.

63/35 **vnderstande spyrytuall thynges.** 1 Cor. 2 : 14: "Animalis autem homo non percipit ea quae sunt Spiritus Dei: stultitia enim est illi et non potest intelligere."

64/5–7 **Nicodemus . . . thynges.** John 3 : 9–10.

64/12–14 **yet . . . hym.** Germain Marc'hadour suggests an echo of Hab. 2 : 4 (*The Bible, 5,* 187).

64/19–21 **My . . . your deuyces.** Isa. 55 : 8–9.

64/31 **workes.** Both the context and the Greek (ὧν ἂν ἐργάζηται) show that "wordes" in *1533* and *1557* is a misprint. Phillip E. Pusey's edition of Cyril's *In S. Joannis Evangelium* (3 vols., Oxford, 1872) has no variants of the Greek phrase (*1*, 527). The Latin of Trapezontius' translation has "operibus" (see note to 63/32–65/21).

65/1–14 **how ... trumpettes.** See Exod. 4 : 6–7 ("Moyses rodde"); Exod. 4 : 6–7 ("hand ... restored"); Exod. 7 : 20 ("waters ... bloude"); Exod. 14 : 21–22 ("thorow the mydde sees"); Exod. 15 : 25 ("bytter water"); Exod. 17 : 5–6 ("water ... out of the stone"); Joshua 3 : 16–17 ("Iordane stode styll"); Joshua 6 : 20 ("walles of Ieryco").

65/30 **hand crafted men.** This formulation does not appear in the *OED*, and the editor of *1557* found it unusual enough to substitute "handy craft men" for it.

66/22–67/13 **Cryst ... faythe of Chryste.** Cyril, *In Iohannis evangelium*, 4.2 (*PG 73*, cols. 576–77); tr. Trapezontius, 1528, sigs. n₁v–n₂: "Misericors certe ac mitis Christus est, ut a rebus ipsis uidere licet. Non enim aspere ad crudelitatem eorum respondit, nec ullo modo contendit: sed uiuificantem huius mysterij cognitionem iterum atque iterum in mentibus eorum imprimere studet: & quomodo quidem carnem suam dabit ad manducandum, non docet: quia intelligere illi non potuerunt: quam magna uero bona, si cum fide manducabunt, adipiscentur: id iterum atque iterum aperit, ut aeternae desiderio uitae ad fidem compellantur, per quam etiam doceri facilius poterint. Sic enim Esaias dixit: si enim, inquit, non credideritis, nec intelligetis. Oportebat igitur fidei primum radices in animo iacere, deinde illa quaerere quae homini quaerenda sunt. Illi uero, anteque crederent, importune quaerebant. Hac igitur de causa dominus, quomodo id fieri possit non enodauit, sed fide id quaerendum hortatur: sic credentibus discipulis fragmenta panis dedit, dicens: Accipite & manducate, hoc est corpus meum. Calicem etiam similiter circuntulit, dicens: Bibite ex hoc omnes, hic est calix sanguinis mei, qui pro multis effundetur in remissionem peccatorum. Perspicis, quia sine fide quaerentibus, mysterij modum nequaque explanauit, credentibus autem etiam non quaerentibus exposuit. Audiant haec, qui ex arrogantia nondum Christi fidem suscipere uolunt. . . ." This passage is also quoted by Oecolampadius, *Quid veteres senserint*, sigs. C₇–C₇v.

66/32–33 **But ... vnderstande.** Isa. 7 : 9. Cyril's version is that of the Septuagint; cf. Vulgate "si non credideritis, non permanebitis." See Marc'hadour, *The Bible, 1*, 201–02.

67/5–9 **he gaue ... synnes.** Matt. 26 : 26–28.

68/7–18 **As the turnynge ... there.** Exod. 7 : 20 ("water into bloude"); Exod. 4 : 3 ("Aarons rod"); Num. 21 : 8–9 ("brasyn serpent"). On the transformation of Aaron's rod as a figure of transubstantiation, see *CW 5*, text and Commentary at 456/17–19. In the *Catena* *aurea* (pp. 295–96) Chrysostom, Theophylactus, and Augustine explicate John 3 : 14 on the brazen serpent as a type of Christ.

69/10 **dede peces.** See notes to 58/9–14 and 80/26–27.

69/13 **Cyrill.** See 67/2–4.

69/16 **Theophilactus.** See 52/9–33.

69/18 **Cyrill.** See 67/5–12.

70/2–3 **and haue . . . wrytynge.** "Suche poysen" refers to the denial of some parts of scripture (as Luther doubted the genuineness of the Epistle of James) and some doctrines of Christian faith. No reformer had written a total denial of scripture and the Christian faith.

70/11–15 **He answered . . . saued.** Cf. Chrysostom, *In Ioannem homiliae* 46; (*PG 59*, 263), cited in the *Catena aurea* on John 6 : 55 (p. 338): "Hoc autem dicit, aut ut credant his quae dicta sunt, ut non aestiment aenigma et parabolam esse, sed sciant quoniam omnino oportet manducare corpus Christi; aut vult dicere, quod verus cibus est hic qui animam salvat."

70/15–23 **As though . . . bloude to.** Cf. Augustine (*CCSL 36*, 267), cited in the *Catena aurea* on John 6 : 53 (p. 337): "Quasi dicat: Quomodo quidem edatur et quisnam sit modus manducandi illum panem ignoratis; verumtamen *nisi manducaveritis carnem Filii hominis et biberitis ejus sanguinem, non habebitis vitam in vobis.*"

70/35–71/4 **For as . . . wyth hym.** Augustine (*CCSL 36*, 266), cited in the *Catena aurea* on John 6 : 51 (p. 337): "Quando autem caperet caro quod dixit panem carnem? Norunt autem fideles corpus Christi, si corpus Christi esse non negligant: fiant corpus Christi, si volunt vivere de spiritu Christi: de spiritu enim Christi non vivit nisi corpus Christi. Numquid enim corpus meum vivit de spiritu tuo? Hunc panem exponit Apostolus dicens. 1 Corinth. 11: 'Unum corpus multi sumus.' O sacramentum pietatis, o signum unitatis, o vinculum caritatis! Qui vult vivere, accedat, credat, incorporetur ut vivificetur."

71/12–31 **Chryste . . . god hym selfe.** Cyril, *In Iohannis euangelium*, 4.2 (*PG 73*, cols. 581–84); tr. Trapezontius, 1528, sig. n_2v: "Distinguit rursus inter mysticam benedictionem & manna, & aquarum fluenta ex lapide & calicis sancti communicationem. Ita iterum eadem repetit, ne magis mannae miraculum admirentur: sed ipsum potius suscipiant, qui coelestis panis est, & aeternae uitae largitor. Patres enim, inquit, uestri manducauerunt manna in deserto, & mortui sunt. Hic est panis qui de coelo descendit, ut aliquis ex ipso comedat & non moriatur. Mannae nanque alimentum non aeternam uitam, sed breue famis remedium afferebat. Non ergo erat cibus uerus, id est panis de coelo. Sanctum vero Christi corpus, ad immortalitatem & uitam aeternam nutriens cibus est: ita inquit: Sed aquam illi ex petra biberunt. Quid igitur inde lucrati sunt, qui mortui fuerunt? non igitur potus ille uerus, sed uerus potus est sanguis Christi, quo radicitus mors euertitur atque destruit? Non enim hominis simpliciter sanguis est, sed eius qui naturali uitae coniunctus, uita effectus est. Propterea corpus & membra Christi sumus: quia per hanc benedictionem mysterij, ipsum filium dei suscipimus." This passage is also quoted by Fisher, *De veritate*, sig. S$_6$.

71/26 **the very ... Chryste.** The Greek shows that "drynke of Chryste" is a misprint for "bloude of Chryste": ἀληθὴς δὲ κατ' ἀλήθειαν εὑρίσκεται πόσις τὸ τίμιον αἷμα χριστοῦ. Phillip E. Pusey's edition of Cyril's *In S. Joannis Evangelium* (3 vols., Oxford, 1872) gives no variants for this Greek phrase (*1*, 534). The Latin translation of Trapezontius, 1528 has "sanguis Christi."

72/14–18 **Lyke as ... Chryst.** Cyril, *In Iohannis evangelium*, 4.2 (*PG 73*, col. 584); tr. Trapezontius, 1528, sigs. n$_2$v–n$_3$: "Sicuti enim, si quis liquefactae cerae aliam ceram infuderit, alteram cum altera per totum commisceat: necesse est, si quis carnem & sanguinem domini recipit, cum ipso ita coniungatur, ut Christus in ipso, & ipse in Christo inueniatur." The passage is quoted by Fisher, *De veritate*, sig. R$_3$v, and by Oecolampadius, *Quid veteres senserint*, sig. C$_5$.

72/26–36 **But this ... sayntes.** Augustine (*CCSL 48*, 344), cited in the *Catena aurea* on John 6 : 57 (p. 338): "Hoc est, illi qui non sacramento tenus tantum, sed revera corpus Christi manducant, et sanguinem bibunt." Cf. also Augustine (*CCSL 36*, 267), cited in the *Catena aurea* on John 6 : 54 (p. 338): "Hunc itaque cibum et potum societatem vult intellegi corporis et membrorum suorum, quod est Ecclesia in praedestinatis et vocatis et justificatis et glorificatis sanctis et fidelibus ejus."

72/27–28 **sacramentally ... effectually.** Cf. *CW 13*, 194/17–19.

72/31 **trew fayth.** Cf. *CW 13*, 196–97.

72/32 **trew repentaunce ... lyuyng.** Cf. *CW 13*, 193/7–15.

72/37 **Theophilactus before.** See 52/9–33.

73/2–3 **Frithis answere ... prented.** See note to 9/27–28.

73/12–16 **but they ... lorde.** 1 Cor. 11 : 29.

73/17–22 **And therfore ... presumpcyon.** Prosper, *Liber sententiarum ex operibus S. Augustini delibatarum* 343 (*PL 51*, 481); Augustine, *CCSL 36*, 268: "Escam vitae accipit, et aeternitatis poculum bibit, qui in Christo manet, et cujus Christus habitator est. Nam qui discordat a Christo, nec carnem ejus manducat, nec sanguinem bibit: etiam si tantae rei sacramentum ad judicium suae praesumptionis quotidie indifferenter accipiat." It is clear that Frith used Prosper's version and not Augustine himself, whose text differs markedly.

73/23–24 **This text . . . communycacyon.** See *A boke . . . answeringe vnto M mores lettur*, sig. D$_2$. Frith could have taken the Augustine text from Prosper's *Sententiae* in Gratian's *Decretum* (De consecratione 2.64, *CIC 1*, 1338). Even though he had not yet seen Frith's *A boke . . . answeringe vnto M mores lettur* in printed form (see 73/2–3), More could have seen a manuscript of it or heard that Frith had made use of this text.

73/31–32 **sacramentally . . . effectually.** Cf. *CW 13*, 191/8, 194/17–19.

74/4–7 **whyther Iudas . . . he dyd.** Augustine seems to have asserted uniformly that Judas did receive the eucharist with the other apostles at the Last Supper (*Epistolae* 44.5 [*PL 33*, 178]; *Enarrationes in Psalmos* 3.1 and 10.6 [*CSEL 38*, 7–8, 79]; *Sermones* 71.11 [*PL* 38, 453]). In *In Iohannis evangelium tractatus* 62.3 (*CCSL 36*, 482), Augustine says Judas received the eucharist together with the others before Christ gave him the dipped morsel which identified him as a traitor (John 13 : 26).

74/11–19 **"Lyke as Iudas . . . hym selfe."** Augustine, *De baptismo contra Donatistas* 5.8 (*PL 43*, 181): "Sicut enim Judas, cui buccellam tradidit Dominus, non malum accipiendo, sed male accipiendo locum in se diabolo praebuit (*Joan.* XIII, 27); sic indigne quisque sumens dominicum Sacramentum non efficit ut quia ipse malus est, malum sit, aut quia non ad salutem accipit, nihil acceperit. Corpus enim Domini et sanguis Domini nihilominus erat etiam illis quibus dicebat Apostolus, *Qui manducat indigne, judicium tibi manducat et bibit* (I *Cor.* XI, 29)." The passage is given by Gratian (De consecratione 2.68, *CIC 1*, 1338–39).

74/29–35 **he writeth . . . body.** Augustine, *Epistolae*, 43.8 (*PL 33*, 171) and 44.5 (*PL 33*, 178).

74/36–75/4 **Frith . . . frere Huyskyns boke.** Oecolampadius' *Quid veteres senserint*, praised by Frith in his *Boke . . . answeringe vnto M mores lettur*, sigs. D$_2$v–D$_3$. But More might also be referring to Oecolampadius' *De genuina . . . expositione liber* (Basel, 1525) which also cites many passages from Augustine. But the text from Prosper's collection of Augustine's *Sententiae* (73/18–22) is not quoted in either of these books by Oecolampadius.

75/17–35 **saynte Austayne . . . wordes.** *Sermones* 71 (*PL 38*, 453): "Illud etiam quod ait, *Qui manducat carnem meam, et bibit sanguinem meum, in me manet, et ego in illo*, quomodo intellecturi sumus? Numquid etiam illos hic poterimus accipere, de quibus dicit Apostolus quod judicium sibi manducent et bibant; cum ipsam carnem manducent, et ipsum sanguinem bibant? Numquid et Judas magistri venditor et traditor impius, quamvis primum ipsum manibus ejus confectum Sacramentum carnis et sanguinis ejus cum caeteris discipulis, sicut apertius Lucas evangelista declarat, manducaret et biberet, mansit in Christo, aut Christo in eo? Tam multi denique, qui vel corde ficto carnem illam manducant et sanguinem bibunt, vel cum manducaverint et biberint, apostatae fiunt, numquid manent in Christo; aut Christus in eis? Sed profecto est quidam modus manducandi illam carnem, et bibendi illum sanguinem, quo modo qui manducaverit et biberit, in Christo manet, et Christus in eo. Non ergo quocumque modo quisquam manducaverit carnem Christi, et biberit sanguinem Christi, manet in Christo, et in illo Christus; sed certo quodam modo, quem modum utique ipse videbat, quando ista dicebat."

75/23–27 **Dyd Iudas ... handes.** That Judas also received the bread and wine from the hands of Christ at the Last Supper is implied by the "omnes" of Matt. 26 : 27 and Mark 14 : 23 but it is even clearer in the account of Luke (22 : 21). See *CW 14*, Commentary 2 at 277/4–279/4, 277/7–279/1.

76/6–8 **he playnely ... bysyde.** See Augustine, *In Iohannis evangelium tractatus* 27.5 (*CCSL 36*, 268); *Sermones* 92 (*PL 5*, 1229); *Enarrationes in Psalmos* 142.16 (*CCSL 40*, 2071).

76/28–31 **is one lofe ... declareth.** Cf. Augustine, *Iñ Iohannis evangelium tractatus* 26.17 (*CCSL 36*, 268): "Propterea ... Dominus noster ... corpus et sanguinem suum in eis rebus commendauit, quae ad unum aliquid rediguntur ex multis. Namque aliud in unum ex multis granis confit, aliud in unum ex multis acinis confluit." Cf. *CW 13*, text and Commentary at 143/29–144/10.

77/30–78/2 **For syth ... Chryste.** Cyril, *In Iohannis evangelium* 4.3 (*PG 73*, col. 586); tr. Trapezontius, 1528, sig. n₃: "sic qui manducatione carnis meae me recipiet, uiuet profecto totus ad me reformatus, qui uiuificare possum, quoniam ex uiuo patre sum, a patre autem se carnem factum esse affirmat, cum scriptum sit: spiritus sanctus superueniet in te, & uirtus altissimi obumbrabit tibi." See also the quotation from Cyril at 71/12–31.

78/5–7 **Not meanynge ... opynyon.** Cf. Theophylactus on John 6 : 63 in *Catena aurea* (p. 339): "Non ergo propter hoc putes quod de caelo corpus Christi descenderit: hoc enim Marciani [i.e., Marcionis] haeretici et Apollinaris est dictum; sed quia unus et idem erat Filius Dei et hominis." Marcion (d. about 160) preached a docetic theology, holding that the humanity of Christ was merely an appearance. Apollinaris (c. 310–c. 390) apparently held that Christ was fully divine, but not fully human because his human spirit was supplanted by the Logos. More may also be thinking of the Valentinians of the second century, who were thought to have held that the body of Christ was celestial (see, for example, Aquinas, *Summa theologica*, III, q. 5, a. 2).

78/18–19 **Thou ... heuyn.** Ps. 77 : 24–25.

78/33–79/7 **For manna ... for a whyle.** Cf. Chrysostom, *In Ioannem homiliae* 45 (*PG 59*, 259), quoted in the *Catena aurea* on John 6 : 47 (p. 336): "Quia vero turbae instabant, cibum corporalem petentes, et ejus cibi qui patribus eorum datus erat reminiscentes: ut ostendat quod omnia illa figura erant hujus veritatis praesentis, mentionem de cibo spirituali facit, dicens: *Ego sum panis vitae.* Panem quidem vitae se ipsum vocat, quoniam vitam nostram continet, et hanc, et futuram." Cf. also Augustine (*CCSL* 36, 266), quoted in the *Catena aurea* on John 6 : 47 (p. 337): " De caelo descendit et manna; sed manna umbra est, iste veritas est."

80/26–27 **Austayn . . . treatices.** Augustine, *In Iohannis evangelium tractatus* 27.2–4 and especially 27.5 (*CCSL 36*, 272): ". . . carnem quippe sic intellexerunt [Iudaei], quomodo in cadauere dilaniatur, aut in macello uenditur, non quomodo spiritu uegetatur." See note to 58/9–14. The number 168 in the marginal gloss is an error for 98. In *Enarrationes in Psalmos* 98.9 (*CCSL 39*, 1385–86) Augustine says the Jews " acceperunt illud stulte, carnaliter illud cogitauerunt, et putauerunt quod praecisurus esset Dominus particulas quasdam de corpore suo, et daturus illis, et dixerunt, Durus est hic sermo." Augustine's " serm. 2 de verbis apostoli " (on John 6 : 54–66), mentioned in the gloss, is sermon 131 in the modern classification of the sermons (*PL 38*, 729). The pertinent passage is: " Quid sibi vult, *Hoc vos scandalizat?* Putatis quia de hoc corpore meo quod videtis, partes facturus sum, et membra mea concisurus, et vobis daturus? Quid, *si ergo videritis Filium hominis ascendentem ubi erat prius?* Certe qui integer ascendere potuit, consumi non potuit " (*PL 38*, 729).

81/6–7 **For though . . . do it.** See *Souper*, Appendix A, 309/17–31, 317/2–20.

82/35–83/6 **" The spyryt . . . spyryte."** Augustine, *In Iohannis evangelium tractatus* 27.5 (*CCSL 36*, 272): " Proinde sic dictum est: *Caro non prodest quidquam,* quomodo dictum est: *Scientia inflat.* Iam ergo debemus odisse scientiam? Absit. Et quid est: *Scientia inflat?* Sola, sine caritate. Ideo adiunxit: *Caritas uero aedificat.* Adde ergo scientiae caritatem, et utilis erit scientia; non per se, sed per caritatem. Sic etiam nunc, *caro non prodest quidquam,* sed sola caro; accedat spiritus ad carnem, quomodo accedit caritas ad scientiam, et prodest plurimum."

83/1–3 **as cunnyng . . . pride.** 1 Cor. 8 : 1; 2 Cor. 13 : 1–13.

83/11–14 **which . . . theyr way.** Chrysostom, *In Ioannem homiliae* 47(46).2 (*PG 59*, 264).

83/16–35 **" Wene . . . receyue it."** Cyril, *In Iohannis evangelium* 4.3 (*PG 73*, 604); tr. Trapezontius, 1528, sig. n₅v: " Putatis, inquit, me dixisse, uiuificum natura sui terrestre hoc esse corpus. Ego uero de spiritu, & de uita aeterna loquutus sum: non enim natura carnis uiuificum reddit spiritum, sed spiritus uirtus uiuificam carnem efficit. Verba ergo quae uobis loquutus sum, spiritus, id est, spiritalia, & de spiritu & uita, id est, de uiuifica & naturali uita sunt. Sed quod modo diximus, id iterum repetere non erit inutile. Natura carnis ipsa per se uiuificare non potest: quid enim maius natura deitatis haberet? Nec sola in Christo esse intelligitur, sed habet filium dei sibi coniunctum, qui consubstantialiter uita est: quando igitur uiuificam Christus ipsam appellat, non ita illi, ut sibi, siue proprio spiritui uim uiuificandi attribuit. Nam propter seipsum spiritus uiuificat, ad cuius uirtutem per coniunctionem caro conscendit: quomodo autem id fiat, nec mente intelligere, nec lingua dicere possumus: sed silentio, atque firma fide id suscepimus."

84/16–17 **but . . . vnderstand.** Isa. 7 : 9. See note to 66/32–33.

84/33–85/9 **But lykewyse . . . syt.** In *De consolatione philosophiae* (5, pr. 3.10–13) Boethius used the example of seeing a man sitting to prove that God's foreknowledge destroys free will: "Etenim si quispiam sedeat, opinionem, quae eum sedere coniectat veram esse necesse est; atque e converso rursus, si de quopiam vera sit opinio quoniam sedet, eum sedere necesse est. In utroque igitur necessitas inest, in hoc quidem sedendi, at vero in altero veritatis. Sed non idcirco quisque sedet, quoniam vera est opinio, sed haec potius vera est, quoniam quempiam sedere praecessit. Ita cum causa veritatis ex altera parte procedat, inest tamen communis in utraque necessitas." Later (5, pr. 6.27–30), Philosophy solves this difficulty by distinguishing between simple (or natural) and conditional (or contingent) necessity: "Duae sunt etenim necessitates, simplex una, veluti quod necesse est omnes homines esse mortales, altera condicionis, ut, si aliquem ambulare scias, eum ambulare necesse est. Quod enim quisque novit, id esse aliter ac notum est nequit, sed haec condicio minime secum illam simplicem trahit. Hanc enim necessitatem non propria facit natura sed condicionis adiectio; nulla enim necessitas cogit incedere voluntate gradientem, quamvis eum tum cum graditur incedere necessarium sit. Eodem igitur modo, si quid providentia praesens videt, id esse necesse est, tametsi nullam naturae habeat necessitatem." More refers to the same argument in *De consolatione philosophiae* tangentially in *CW 8*, text and Commentary at 938/30–939/16, 1331–32.

85/16–22 **"Thynke not . . . receyue it."** Chrysostom, *In Ioannem homiliae* 47(46) (*PG 59*, 266); *Opera*, 1530, *3*, sig. G*G$_1$v: "Spontaneam dispensationem hoc in loco Euangelista, & eius patentiam significat. Et illa particula, Ab initio, non simpliciter hic ponitur, sed ut eius praescientiam intelligas, & quod ante haec uerba, non post eorum murmurationem & scandalum, proditorem norat, quod diuinitatis erat. Inde inquit, Nisi fuerit ei datum a patre meo: suadens eis ut suum patrem deum, non Ioseph arbitrarentur: & in se ostendens nihil sua interesse, si non crederent: quasi dicat, non mouent me, neque perturbant, qui mihi non credunt, noui ea omnia antequam fierent, noui quibus dedit pater. Cum autem audieris dedisse patrem, noli simpliciter priuilegium arbitrari, sed illi crede, quod qui se accipiendi dignum exhibet, ipse accipit."

85/22–27 **Cyryll . . . fayth.** Cyril, *In Iohannis evangelium* 4.3 (*PG 73*, 608); tr. Trapezontius, 1528, sig. n$_6$: ". . . qui bonis moribus apud eos uiuebant, quique ueritatis amatores erant, gratia dei opitulante salutem per

fidem adepti sunt. Arrogantes autem pharisaei, & durae ceruicis pontifi-
ces, senioresque populi, quamuis Mosis & prophetarum scripturis docti
fuissent, credere tamen noluerunt: sed malignis eorum consilijs indigni
aeterna vita comperti, dei patris illuminationem non receperunt."

85/28–33 **This gyfte . . . erre.** The passage More refers to is attributed
to Augustine in the *Catena aurea* (p. 340): "Ergo et credere datur nobis:
non enim nihil est credere. Si autem magnum quid est, gaude quia cred-
idisti, sed noli extolli: 'quid enim habes quod non accepisti?' 2 Corinth.
4. Hoc autem donum quibusdam dari et quibusdam non dari omnino non
dubitat qui non vult manifestissimis sacris litteris repugnare. Cur autem
non onmibus detur, fidelem movere non debet, qui credit ex uno omnes
esse in condemnationem justissimam; ita ut nulla Dei esset justa reprehen-
sio, etsi nullus inde liberaretur; unde constat magnam esse gratiam quod
plurimi liberantur. Cur autem istum potius quam illum liberet, inscruta-
bilia sunt judicia ejus, et investigabiles viae ejus." Only the first two
sentences ("Ergo . . . accepisti?") appear in the modern editions of
Augustine's *In Iohannis evangelium tractatus* (*CCSL 36*, 273; *PL 35*, 1619).
But they do contain a passage similar to the rest in another part of
Augustine's *In Iohannis evangelium tractatus* (*CCSL 36*, 455).

85/34–35 **soule helthe.** The form "soule" here is a survival of an Old
English genetive singular (*OED* "soul" 18).

85/37–86/1 **Lo I . . . with me.** Rev. 3 : 20.

86/2–7 **Seke . . . forgeuenesse.** Isa. 55 : 6–7.

86/8–9 **Aske . . . lette in.** Matt. 7 : 7.

86/10–13 **that no man . . . draw hym.** John 6 : 44, 66.

86/18–19 **Lette hym . . . fall.** 1 Cor. 10 : 12.

86/26–30 **saint Austayn . . . drawe yᵉ.** See *In Iohannis evangelium tractatus*
26.4 (*CCSL 36*, 261–62). For More's views on free will see further *CW* 8,
1319–22.

87/22–24 **dyscyples . . . ten.** In a passage quoted in the note to 80/26–
27 Augustine interpolates "septuaginta ferme" into his paraphrase of
John 6 : 61: "Scandalizati sunt discipuli eius quidam, septuaginta ferme,
et dixerunt: *Durus est hic sermo; quis potest eum intellegere?*" (*Enarrationes in
Psalmos* 98.6; *CCSL 39*, 1385). Cf. 91/34–35.

87/25–26 **.iii. score . . . before.** Luke 10 : 1. The manuscript traditions
of the Vulgate and the Greek are about evenly divided between seventy
and seventy-two in this text. See Wordsworth–White, *1*, 371, and Bruce
M. Metzger, "Seventy or Seventy-two Disciples?" *New Testament Studies*,
5 (1958–59), 299–306.

87/28–34 **He neyther . . . wyth hym.** Cf. Chrysostom, *In Ioannem homi-*

liae 47(46).3 (*PG 59*, 266), quoted in the *Catena aurea* on John 6 : 67 (p. 340): "Per hunc autem modum oportebat eos trahi: nam si eos laudasset, passi essent aliquid humanum, existimantes se gratiam Christo facere, eum non relinquendo: ostendens vero se non indigere eorum sequela, magis eos detinuit. Non autem eis dixit, Abite: hoc enim esset eos expellere; sed interrogavit eos an vellent abire, auferens eis vim et necessitatem, et nolens eos verecundia coactari: ex necessitate enim detineri par esset ac si abirent."

89/15–90/6 **And dyuerse . . . gesse.** Aquinas notes (*Commentum*, p. 424) that Augustine and Ambrose both believed that Christ chose Judas as his disciple even though Judas was evil from the beginning; Aquinas refers to Augustine's *In Iohannis evangelium tractatus* 26.18 (*CCSL 36*, 268) and to Ambrose's *Expositio evangelii secundum Lucam* 5.45 (*PL 15*, 1648). Both Augustine and Ambrose appear to be more concerned with God's foreknowledge of Judas's evil than with the predestination of Judas as evil. For a recent treatment of the problem, see Roman B. Halas, *Judas Iscariot: A Scriptural and Theological Study of His Person, His Deeds, and His Eternal Lot*, Catholic University of America Studies in Sacred Theology 96 (Washington, D.C., 1946), pp. 53–56. De Lyra (on John 6 : 70) notes, like More, that the answer to the question of whether or not Judas was evil from the beginning of his discipleship is hidden from men, and that in such occult questions one must choose the answer that best accords with holy scripture and with reason. De Lyra quotes Augustine and Bede in support of the position that Judas was evil from the beginning; on the other side he refers to John 17 : 12, quoted by More at 89/35–90/2. For the fathers that More brings to the argument, see Theophylactus, *Enarratio in evangelium Marci* 14/16–21 (*PG 123*, 649); Chrysostom, *In Ioannem homiliae* 47 (*PG 59*, 267–68); and Cyril, *In Iohannis evangelium* 4.4 (*PG 73*, 632).

91/7 **well.** Despite the unusual spelling, this word stands for "weal" (wellbeing).

91/27–29 **hys owne . . . Mathy.** Acts 1 : 23–26.

91/31 **Chrisostom sayth.** See *In Ioannem homiliae* 47.3 (*PG 59*, 266).

91/34–35 **were . . . tenne.** See notes to 87/22–24 and 87/25–26 which (together with Augustine's "septuaginta ferme") suggests that "aboue" here may be a misprint for "about."

91/36–92/4 **And he . . . before.** Commenting on John 6 : 66, de Lyra refers to the seventy-two of Luke 10 : 1. See the notes to 87/22–26.

92/5–6 **Iudas . . . warnyng.** John 6 : 71–72; Luke 22 : 21.

92/18–93/4 **Our lord . . . dylygence.** Cyril, *In Iohannis evangelium* 4.4 (*PG 73*, 629–32); tr. Trapezontius, 1528, sig. o₂v: "Acrioribus eos confirmat uerbis, diligentioresque facit, periculo ante oculos posito: sic enim dicere uidetur: Magna uobis o discipuli uigilantia, magnoque studio ad salutem opus est. Lubrica enim admodum perditionis est uia: non imbecillam solummodo distrahens mentem, uerumetiam firmos nonnunquam animos uoluptate decipiens: quod autem ita sit, non eorum qui retro abierunt, sed uestri exemplo confirmatur. Ego enim uos ut bonos elegi, non ignorabam, sed cognoscebam ut deus corda vestra: sed rapuit unum uestrum auaritia deceptum diabolus. Liberum enim homo animal est, & potest, siue dextrum, siue sinistrum uelit iter (uirtutem dico, aut uitium) eligere. Vigilantiores ergo facit omnes, quia quis traditurus sit, clare non dicit: sed uni generaliter tantae impietatis onus imminere affirmans, solicitos omnes reddit, & horrore ad maiorem uigilantiam erigit."

93/7–33 **Whan saynt Peter . . . ponyshement.** Chrysostom, *In Ioannem homiliae* 47(46) (*PG 59*, 267–68); *Opera*, 1530, *3*, sigs. G*G₁v–G*G₂: "Nonne ego, inquit, uos duodecim elegi, & unus ex uobis diabolus est?) Cum enim dixisset Petrus, & nos credidimus, eximit e numero Iudam. Alibi enim nihil de discipulis dixit, sed cum Christus diceret: Vos autem quem me dicitis? respondit, Tu es Christus filius dei uiui: hic autem dicente eo, Et nos credidimus: merito ex ipsorum numero Iudam exemit: hoc autem dixit, ut longe proditoris malitiam propulsaret, & cum nihil ei proficere uideret, ei tamen consulebat. Et intuere Christi sapientiam. Neque eum manifestauit, neque latere uoluit. Illud, ne impudentius contenderet: hoc, ne latere arbitratus, licentius auderet. . . . Non enim ui & necessitate quadam deus bonos facere consueuit, neque electio eius uiolenta est, sed suasoria. Vt enim intelligas, inquit, non cogi uocationem, multos uocatos perire continget. Quam ob rem constat, in nostro esse arbitrio, an saluemur, an perdamur. His igitur admonitionibus & sobrij esse, & uigilare contendamus. Nam si is qui in sanctum illum chorum connumeratus erat, qui tantum donum consecutus, qui signa fecerat (etenim ipse Iudas cum alijs ad suscitandos mortuos, & mundandam lepram mittebatur, ex quo grauissimo auaritiae morbo captus est) nihil ei neque beneficia, neque dona, neque Christi consuetudo, non obsequium, non lotio pedum, non mensae participatio, non loculorum custodia profuit, sed omnia haec aditus ei ad supplicium fuerunt."

93/8–10 *gloss* **Chriso . . . . Ioh.** Most of the type in the *1533* marginal gloss must have been almost entirely lost during printing. See Introduction, p. xci, note 3.

94/8–9 **brydyll . . . backe.** Marc'hadour, *The Bible 5*, 188, has noticed an echo here of Ps. 31 : 9. See also 47/32–34; *CW 6*, 492; *CW 14*, 207/6–8.

94/12–15 **For yᵗ . . . hym.** Cyril, *In Iohannis evangelium* 4.4 (*PG 73*, 632); tr. Trapezontius, 1528, sig. o₃: "Diabolum uero diaboli ministrum appellauit. Nam sicut qui domino coniungitur, unus cum eo spiritus est; sic contra quoque fieri non est negandum." This is the conclusion of a chapter of Cyril from which More translated above, 92/18–93/4. The sense and the Latin suggest that "y^t" (line 12) in 1533 (which is pretty clearly not "y^e" and was printed "that" in *1557*) may well be a misprint for "y^e."

94/19–21 **he receyueth . . . redempcion.** See 73/38–74/35.

94/22 **eateth . . . dampnacyon.** 1 Cor. 11 : 29.

97/6–13 **Consyder . . . thorow it.** *Souper*, Appendix A, 305/21–29.

97/9–10 **Of the whyche . . . lyueth.** Hab. 2 : 4: "Iustus autem in fide sua vivet."

97/21–22 **For . . . pooreblynde.** Here More mocks the Masker's accusation that More's vision is failing (*Souper*, Appendix A, 315/19–26).

98/22–23 **kynges strete . . . charing crosse.** Stow (*2*, 102) mentions this street in his description of Westminster. Charles Kingsford, the editor of Stow's *Survey of London*, states in a note: "Till long after Stow's time it was the only way to Westminster from the north. The last part of it has now been covered by the new Government offices in Parliament Street" (*2*, 374). Charing Cross, north of Westminster, was one of a series of monumental crosses set up by Edward I to commemorate the funeral procession of his queen (Stow, *1*, 265–66).

98/29 **M. mokke.** *Souper*, Appendix A, 339/33.

99/7 **can me thanke.** That is, "thank me." For the construction see F. T. Visser, *A Syntax of the English Language of St. Thomas More*, 3 vols., Materials for the Study of the Old English Drama nos. 19, 24, 26 (Louvain, 1946–56), *1*, 155.

99/14–15 **beggers . . . Sauygate.** The beggars More mentions were probably attached to a leperhouse called "the Loke" in Southwark, on Kent Street near St. Savior's Church (Stow, *2*, 66–68), or to the Hospital of the Savoy in the Liberty of Lancaster (Stow, *2*, 95). More mentions the beggars sitting at Saint Sauours in *The Supplication of souls* (1529; *STC*² 18093), sig. C₃. See also *CW 9*, Commentary at 73/20.

100/19–26 **I am . . . iustyfyed.** *Souper*, Appendix A, 306/6–13.

100/28–34 **as I have . . . also.** See 36/36–39/26, 119/13–120/2, 121/6–123/19, and notes.

101/8–10 **He that . . . glory.** Ecclus. 24 : 29: "Qui edunt me adhuc esurient, et qui bibunt me adhuc sitient." The words are spoken by Sapientia about herself, but Christ, the wisdom of the Father, was often identified with her. In his commentary on the first verses of Ecclesiasticus, de Lyra explains that Sapientia often speaks in the person of the Word, and he refers to this introductory explanation in his glosses on Ecclus. 24.

102/14–17 **"he . . . stockes and stones."** *Souper*, Appendix A, 306/20–22.

103/20 **I longe to be dyssolued.** Phil. 1 : 23.

103/24–26 **The hope . . . soule.** Prov. 13 : 12.

103/31 **he that . . . thyrste.** See 101/8–10 and note.

103/37–38 **I shalbe . . . appere.** Ps. 16 : 15.

104/10–13 **Mary Mawdeleyn . . . vppon hym.** Matt. 26 : 12–13; Mark 14 : 8–9. The marginal gloss "Matt. 29" is incorrect. In 1519 John Fisher, Jacques Lefèvre d'Etaples, and Josse Clichtove disputed at length about whether Mary of Magdala (Luke 8 : 2), Mary the sister of Lazarus (John 12 : 1–9), and the penitent woman who annointed Jesus' feet (Luke 7 : 36–50) were one person or three. Here More simply accepts the view commonly held in the western church that the three passages refer to the same woman—a view elaborately defended by Fisher. See Edward Surtz, S.J., *The Works and Days of John Fisher* (Cambridge, Mass., 1967), pp. 5–7, 274–89.

104/13–16 **twelue apostles . . . worlde.** Matt. 19 : 28.

104/20 **this one syllable onys.** *Souper*, Appendix A, 306/10–11: ". . . we can desyre no nother yf we once thus eat and drynke hym by faythe. . . ." More cited the entire passage on p. 100.

105/12–13 **all holy doctours . . . scrypture.** See, for example, Aquinas's discussion of faith and the heretic, *Summa theologica*, II^a–II^{ae}, q. 5, a. 3: ". . . dicendum, quod in haeretico discredente unum articulum fidei non manet fides neque formata, neque informis." See also the *Summa theologica* on infidelity, II^a–II^{ae}, qq. 10–16. On faith, see 121/6–123/19 and note. The marginal gloss suggests references to Heb. 6 : 4–6; Rom. 11 : 20–21; 1 Cor. 10 : 12.

105/25–29 **he that . . . hym.** Luke 10 : 16: "Qui vos audit, me audit: et qui vos spernit, me spernit. Qui autem me spernit, spernit eum qui misit me." Cf. *CW 6*, text and Commentary at 48/35–49/4. For the Masker's attack on the invocation of saints, see *Souper*, Appendix A, 312/4–5.

106/10–107/6 **For yf . . . talys?** Either not knowing or not caring to make known the name of the author of the *Souper*, More directs against all the likely suspects a diatribe on the marriage of priests, one of his favorite polemical topics; see, for example, *CW 6*, 165/16–19, 304/9–10, 346/13; *CW 8*, 585/30–586/21; *CW 9*, 29/22, 45/21. In the West, celibacy was gradually imposed as a canonical obligation on those in major orders. Attempting to discourage concubinage, which was widespread in the tenth and eleventh centuries, the Second Lateran Council (1139) declared the marriage of a cleric in major orders to be invalid; hence More's repeated insistence that the wives of the reformers were not wives at all but "harlots". See Alberigo, p. 174, canon 7. Tyndale, in contrast to most of the reformers, remained unmarried, but he nonetheless upheld the

right of a priest to marry; see, for example, *Obedience*, sigs. I₇v; *Answer*, sig.
M₈v. According to Joye's modern biographers, Butterworth and Chester
(p. 205), More is the sole source of information on Joye's marriage. The
name of his wife is not known; his only son was born in 1543. Given
More's reference to Joye's marriage in *The Confutation* (1531), it may be
supposed that Joye married more than once; see *CW 8*, Commentary at
7/33. Although Luther at first supported clerical celibacy (see, for
example, his letter of January 17, 1522 in Luther's *Briefwechsel*, ed. G.
Bebermeyer and O. Clemen, 12 vols. [Weimar, 1930–67], *2*, 430–34), he
had reversed his position later in 1522, when he published his *De votis
monasticis*. Luther himself married Katherina von Bora, a former Cis-
tercian nun, on June 13, 1525. Oecolampadius was married in March
1528 to Wilbrandis Rosenblatt, the widow of Ludwig Keller; after Oecolampadius' death she became in turn the wife of his friends Wolfgang
Capito and Martin Bucer (see Staehelin, *Briefe und Akten*, *2*, 143–44). By
late November 1524, at the start of the eucharistic controversy, Oecolampadius is known to have broken with Luther over the real presence; see
Staehelin, *Briefe und Akten*, *1*, 331–32, no. 230.

107/14–27 **Had mayster . . . lye to.** *Souper*, Appendix A, 308/4–18.

107/14–15 **who so . . . euerlastyng.** John 6 : 47.

107/16 **a yere & an halfe.** Acts 18 : 11.

107/17–19 **not to . . . crucyfyed.** 1 Cor. 2 : 2: "Non enim iudicavi me
scire aliquid inter vos, nisi Iesum Christum, et hunc crucifixum."

107/19 **vnderstoden.** *Souper* has "vnderstod" (Appendix A, 308/9).
Though the northern or Scottish form "vnderstooden" was used in the
sixteenth century (OED "stand" A 5), it is probably a misprint here
either for "vnderstonden" or "vnderstod."

108/6 **agaynst my confutacyon.** In the third book of *The Confutation*
(*CW 8*, 223–383) More discusses "whyther the chyrche were before the
gospell, or the gospell before the chyrch / & whyther the apostles lefte
ought vnwryten, that is of necessyte to be byleued" (p. 223).

108/20–21 **Of whiche . . . chalyce.** See *Confutation*, *CW 8*, 318–20 and
the Commentary at 319/30–32, where More's principal authority for
Christ's mixing water with the wine at the Last Supper is a letter of
Cyprian: "Nobis vero non poterit ignosci, qui nunc a Domino admoniti
et instructi sumus ut calicem Dominicum vino mistum, secundum quod
Dominus obtulit, offeramus; et de hoc . . . ubique lex evangelica et traditio Dominica servetur, et ab eo quod Christus et docuit et fecit non
recedatur" (*Epistolae* 63; *PL 4*, col. 399). Although none of the gospels
mentions the mixing of the wine with water, the practice was supported
by reference to the blood and water that flowed from Christ's side on the
cross (John 19 : 34).

108/24–109/2 **taught . . . thynges.** See 1 Cor. 11 : 23–34, especially verses 23 ("Ego enim accepi a Domino quod et tradidi vobis") and 34 ("Caetera autem, cum venero, disponam").

109/12–14 **yf we . . . iustyfyed.** See 100/23–6.

109/28–110/8 **folys . . . synnys.** In *De fide et operibus* Augustine refutes those who claim that faith is the only prerequisite for baptism, without any moral requirements. His opponents did not deny that adultery was a serious sin, but they did assert that someone who refuses to give it up after baptism would nevertheless be saved (*PL 40*, 197, 202–03). To their argument that Paul preached nothing but Christ crucified (1 Cor. 2 : 2) Augustine replies (*PL 40*, 206–07): "Si ergo ille qui per Evangelium genuit . . . nihil eos amplius docuit quam Christum crucifixum; quid si dicat aliquis, nec resurrexisse Christum eos audisse, quando per Evangelium geniti sunt? Unde est igitur quod eis dicit, *Tradidi enim vobis in primis, quia Christus mortuus est secundum Scripturas, et quia sepultus est, et quia resurrexit tertia die secundum Scripturas* (1 Cor. 15 : 3–4), si nihil nisi crucifixum docuerat? Si autem non ita intelligunt, sed hoc quoque ad Christum crucifixum pertinere contendunt; sciant in Christo crucifixo multa homines discere, et maxime quod *vetus homo noster simul crucifixus est, ut evacuetur corpus peccati, et ultra non serviamus peccato* (Rom. 6 : 6). . . . Proinde attendant, et videant quemadmodum doceatur atque discatur Christus crucifixus, et ad ejus crucem noverint pertinere quod etiam nos in ejus corpore crucifigimur mundo; ubi intelligitur omnis coercitio malarum concupiscentiarum: ac per hoc fieri non potest ut eis qui cruce Christi formantur, professa adulteria permittantur."

111/22–29 **My prechynge . . . of god.** 1 Cor. 2 : 4–5.

112/23–26 **yf hym . . . theym.** John 15 : 24: "Si opera non fecissem in eis quae nemo alius fecit, peccatum non haberent: nunc autem et viderunt, et oderunt et me, et Patrem meum." The second numeral of "15" in the marginal gloss is blurred in all copies we have seen and might be misread as "3."

113/10–13 **And the cause . . . to me.** *Souper*, Appendix A, 306/27–30.

113/12–13 **all . . . me.** John 6 : 37: "Omne quod dat mihi Pater, ad me veniet."

114/3–4 **And this . . . worlde.** See *Souper*, Appendix A, 308/32–34.

114/5–12 **And for . . . blessed sacrament.** As More says, the Masker reads John 6 : 52 only in regard to the passion (*Souper*, Appendix A, 308/35–42.

114/17 **mummers . . . dice.** See note to 13/1–10.

114/23–25 **No meruayle . . . not.** *Souper*, Appendix A, 309/12–14.

114/29–30 **saynte Austayne sayth.** See notes to 58/9–14 and 80/26–27.

115/24–25 **Neyther . . . Hebre. 9.** More adds the reference to Hebrews 9 : 28 to the Masker's "as Paule testifyeth"; *Souper*, Appendix A, 309/14–16. On the Reformation controversy about the sacrifice of the mass, see Clarke.

116/8–25 **What is . . . same sacryfyce.** Chrysostom, *Homiliae in Epistolam ad Hebraeos* 17 (*PG 63*, 131), *Opera*, 1530, *4*, sig. m*₅v: "Quid ergo nos? Nonne per singulos dies offerimus? Offerimus quidem, sed ad recordationem facientes mortis eius. Et una est haec hostia, non multa. Quo modo una est & non multae? Et quia semel oblata est illa, oblata est in sancta sanctorum: hoc autem sacrificium exemplar est illius, idipsum semper offerimus. Nec nunc quidem alium agnum, crastina alium, sed semper idipsum. Proinde unum est hoc sacrificium, alioquin hac ratione, quoniam in multis locis offertur, multi Christi sunt? Nequaquam, sed unus ubique est Christus, & hic plenus existens, & illic plenus, unum corpus. Sicut enim qui ubique offertur, unum corpus est, & non multa corpora: ita etiam & unum sacrificium. Pontifex autem noster ille est qui hostiam mundantem nos obtulit: ipsam offerimus & nunc, quae tunc oblata quidem, consumi non potest. Hoc autem quod nos facimus, in commemorationem quidem fit eius quod factum est. Hoc enim facite, inquit, in meam commemorationem. Non aliud sacrificium, sicut pontifex, sed idipsum semper facimus: magis autem recordationem sacrificij operamur."

In the English passage "hooste" means "victim," as the Greek θυσία shows; but Christ, the victim of the sacrifice, is also present under the appearance of the eucharistic bread, which was also called " host."

This passage is also quoted by Fisher, *De veritate*, sig. H₃v; by Oecolampadius, *De genuina . . . expositione*, sig. C₄v: and by Clichtove, *De sacramento eucharistiae*, sig. n₈.

116/23 **do ye . . . of me.** Luke 22 : 19.

117/13–15 **Gracian . . . semel.** The passage More cites from Gratian's *Decretum* (De consecratione 2.53 [In Christo semel], *CIC 1*, 1333) is in fact another rendering of the passage from Chrysostom that More has just translated (116/8–25). Both Gratian and Peter Lombard (*Sentences*, 4.12.5) identify the source as Ambrose, *In Epistolam ad Hebraeos*. Of the passage in the form quoted by Gratian and (with slight variations) by Lombard, Clarke states: ". . . no text was more constantly quoted by the Catholic theologians, both before and during the Reformation, to explain the doctrine of the Mass" (p. 75).

117/16–30 **Saynte Austayne . . . oblacyon.** The reference to book 16 in the text and margin is incorrect. See *De civitate Dei* 17.20 (*CCSL 48*, 588): " Id enim sacrificium successit omnibus illis sacrificiis ueteris testamenti, quae immolabantur in umbra futuri; propter quod etiam uocem illam in psalmo tricensimo et nono eiusdem Mediatoris per prophetiam loquentis agnoscimus: *Sacrificium et oblationem noluisti, corpus autem perfecisti mihi*; quia

pro illis omnibus sacrificiis et oblationibus corpus eius offertur et partici-
pantibus ministratur." The Vulgate version of Ps. 39 : 7 is: "Sacrificium
et oblationem noluisti; aures autem perfecisti mihi."

117/32–118/18 **Martyn Luther . . . masse and all.** *De captivitate Babylonica, WA 6,* 523–24: "Iam et alterum scandalum amovendum est, quod
multo grandius est et speciosissimum, id est, quod Missa creditur passim
esse sacrificium, quod offertur deo. In quam opinionem et verba Canonis
sonare videntur, ubi dicitur 'haec dona, haec munera, haec sancta sacrifi-
cia,' et infra 'hanc oblationem.' Item, clarissime postulatur, ut acceptum
sit sacrificium, sicut sacrificium Abel &c. Inde Christus hostia altaris
dicitur. Accedunt his dicta sanctorum patrum, tot exempla tantusque
usus per orbem constanter observatus. His omnibus, quia pertinacissime
insederunt, oportet constantissime opponere verba et exemplum Christi.
. . . Quid ergo dicemus ad Canonem et autoritates patrum? Primum
respondeo: Si nihil habetur quod dicatur, tutius est omnia negare quam
Missam concedere opus aut sacrificium esse, ne verbum Christi negemus,
fidem simul cum Missa pessundantes." Luther's public opposition to the
sacrifice of the mass dates from this work (1520), and from a sermon given
the same year (*WA 6,* 522–24). See Clarke, p. 100, and N. M. Halmer,
"Der literarische Kampf Luthers und Melanchthons gegen das Opfer der
heiligen Messe," in *Divus Thomas* (Fribourg, 1943), pp. 63–78.

118/21 **two other heresyes.** One of these is the denial of the real presence in the eucharist. In the immediate context, the other is the assertion
that papists believe Christ is repeatedly crucified at mass.

118/31–119/9 **In the syxte . . . confusyon.** *Souper,* Appendix A, 310/9–
315/34. More treats the Masker's objections to *A letter against Frith* in Book
4, pp. 149–211.

119/13 **.xi. lefe.** See *Souper,* Appendix A, 315/35–316/32.

119/13–120/2 **In the .xi. lefe . . . cheryte.** On the eleventh leaf of the
Souper (Appendix A, 316/12–27), quoted by More below (120/8–21), the
Masker attempts to reconcile the doctrine of justification by faith alone
with a particularly stubborn text, 1 John 4 : 16: "Deus charitas est: et qui
manet in charitate, in Deo manet, et Deus in eo." The Masker's gloss,
which alludes to scholastic tradition, provokes More's outrage, and he
devotes chapters 10, 11, and 12 to refuting the Masker's position. More
claims that the Masker, like Luther and Tyndale, has attempted to
bolster the doctrine of *sola fides* by perverting traditional teaching about
the three theological virtues: faith, hope, and charity.

Contrary to More's suggestion (119/20–120/2), Luther never retreated
from his original stand on justification by faith alone. He denied repeatedly the scholastic doctrine of *fides formata charitate* (see *WA 39/1,* 318; *WA
39/2,* 2). And from the beginning he argued that love and hope were the
necessary fruits of faith, and he frequently spoke of how they accompany

faith. In *De captivitate Babylonica* (1520), for example, he states: "But God has need of this: that we consider him faithful in his promises, and patiently persist in this belief, and thus worship him with faith, hope, and love" (Luther, *Works*, ed. Jaroslav Pelikan, 54 vols. [St. Louis, 1955], *36*, 42; *WA* 6, 516). More's assertion that Luther and his followers changed their definition of faith probably reflects the shifting emphasis of the Lutheran program in the 1520s and 1530s, especially in the aftermath of the Peasants' Rebellion of 1525. Seeing that the doctrine of *sola fides* was misconstrued by Müntzer, Karlstadt, and other radical Protestants (More's "idle vnthryftes"), Luther stressed that justification by faith alone does not diminish the ethical value of good works, which he had always viewed as the necessary fruits of faith and righteousness. Like the love of God and hope in God, good works follow necessarily from faith: "First of all there is God's Word. After it follows faith; after faith, love; then love does every good work. . . ." (*Works*, Pelikan, *36*, 39; *WA 6*, 514; see also, for example, *WA 12*, 282; *10/3*, 225).

In *An exposicion vppon the .v. vi. vii. chapters of Mathew* . . . (Antwerp, 1533?; *STC²* 24440), Tyndale attempted to explain how faith, as he understood it, always includes hope and love (sigs. a₄v–a₆).

119/19–20 **fayth alone.** See, for example, *Souper*, Appendix A, 306/22–23, 308/20–21, 309/40–310/8.

119/27–28 **marmole ... shynnys.** Cf. Chaucer's "General Prologue" to *The Canterbury Tales*, I (A), 385–86:

> But greet harm was it, as it thoughte me,
> That on his shyne a mormal hadde he.

An allusion to Chaucer's dishonest cook is especially appropriate to the Masker, who prepares a false banquet and who is called "Colyn coke" at 220/5.

120/8–21 **By loue ... tradycyons.** *Souper*, Appendix A, 316/12–27. 1 John 4:16: "Deus charitas est: et qui manet in charitate, in Deo manet, et Deus in eo."

120/26–121/5 **But lette ... shame.** Even Tyndale, More argues, had said that in order to be saved a man needed not merely "historycall faith," that is, a faith based on the honesty of the teller or common consent, but a "feeling faith," a faith felt for certain in the heart of the believer; see Tyndale's *Answer* (*STC²* 24437), sigs. D₅–D₆v. Tyndale extends a distinction made by Melanchthon. More answers the argument in the second half of Book 7 of *The Confutation*; see *CW 8*, 741–829, and Commentary at 396/10–11; see also *CW 9*, Commentary at 37/35–38/1.

120/30–35 **But ... saluacion.** As it stands this sentence is incomplete. Perhaps "But" should be taken to mean "except"; or "and" may be a misprint for "we"; or the main clause may have been dropped by the

compositor. The scriptural passage to which More refers is probably John
14 : 15: "Si diligitis me, mandata mea servate."

121/6–123/19 **But mayster ... dewty.** The Masker's own gloss on
1 John 4 : 16 makes several brief allusions to the complex relation drawn
in scholastic theology between faith, hope, and charity; see *Summa theologica*, Iᵃ–IIᵃᵉ, qq. 62, 65; q. 66, a. 6; IIᵃ–IIᵃᵉ, qq. 1–7 (faith); qq. 17–22
(hope); qq. 23–33 (charity). According to the order of generation (in the
Masker's words "the order of our vnderstandyng"), faith, resident in the
intellect, precedes hope and charity, resident in the will: "No human
appetite is for anything, either by hoping or loving, unless it be appre-
hended by sense and mind. Now it is by faith that the mind apprehends
what it hopes for and loves. And so in the sequence of coming to be [*ordine
generationis*], faith has to precede hope and charity" (Iᵃ–IIᵃᵉ, q. 62, a. 4).
Yet these habitual dispositions are all infused together by the grace of
God and begin simultaneously in time; by commonly received doctrine
they are said to be infused at baptism—a doctrine approved by the
Council of Vienne in 1312 (see Alberigo, p. 337). Thus the Masker,
as More recognizes, distinguishes between the "order of our
vnderstandyng" and the "order of successyon of time" in order to argue
that love and charity always accompany faith, and that "pryncypally by
fayth wherby we cleue to goddes goodnes and mercy, we abyde in god
and god in vs." The Masker's other distinction, between "the selfe
gyftes" and "theyr frutes," relies on a further refinement of scholastic
doctrine. While, in the order of generation, faith, as a habitual disposition
given by God, precedes hope and charity, charity precedes hope and faith
in the order of perfection or excellence, for both faith and hope are
completed and made perfect as virtues (not merely as habits) only
through charity.

More's distinction between *fides informis* and *fides formata* and his treatment of the relation between the three theological virtues reflects
Aquinas's analysis of the theological virtues, especially his discussion of
faith as an intellectual habit and virtue (*Summa theologica*, IIᵃ–IIᵃᵉ, qq.
4–7). While in the beatific vision man will see God face to face, faith
allows man to believe in God unseen and thus to move towards eternal
life. Except for the beatific vision, faith is the only means through which
man may attain supernatural knowledge of God. God infuses into man
the grace of faith, calling forth belief; ". . . since in assenting to the things
of faith a person is raised above his own nature, he has this assent from a
supernatural force influencing him; this source is God. The assent of faith,
which is the principal act, therefore, has as its cause God, moving us
inwardly through grace" (q. 6, a. 1). Man can respond fully to God's
grace only in belief (*credere*), the act of faith, which issues from two
faculties of the human soul: the intellect, which assents, and the will,
which moves the intellect to assent. The act of faith thus requires the
virtue of charity (infused, like faith, through grace) which penetrates and

suffuses man's will with the love of God, drawing him toward union with God. Charity is thus said to be the "form" or shaping principle of faith; "the act of faith is completed and shaped [*perficitur et formatur*] by charity" (q. 4, a. 3). Without the full adhesion of the will to God through charity, faith is unformed (*informis*) and incomplete; it remains a mere disposition to believe but does not constitute a full commitment to God; hence it is a dead faith that does not lead toward eternal life; only when the gift of faith is formed by charity does it become a theological virtue. Charity, moreover, is preceded in the order of generation by hope. Hoping to be rewarded by God, one becomes inspired to love him (II^a–II^ae, q. 17, a. 8; q. 62, a. 4). More thus asserts that faith is formed only "but whyle he hath his two felowes with hym."

121/14–16 **Loue ... frutes.** The Masker expands Zwingli's sentence: "Sed amor fidem sequitur intellectus ordine" (*CRZ 3*, 781/17).

121/23 **galles.** More probably refers to oak-galls or oak-apples, which were used by jugglers in their tricks. See *CW 9*, Commentary at 22/20–21.

122/4 **acte nor in habyt.** See *CW 14*, 319/3–323/6.

122/36–123/4 **For both ... awaye to.** The words "y^t fayth standynge" are a nominative absolute meaning "while that faith stands." The change to the second half of the both/and construction is at "And also" (123/3). The clause "And than ... cheryte after" is merely a parenthetical refinement of the preceding clause.

123/4–7 **For he ... euerychone.** See note to 105/12–13.

123/13 **the deuyll byleueth.** See James 2 : 19 ("Daemones credunt, et contremescunt") and *Summa theologica*, II^a–II^ae, q. 5, a. 2: "... dicendum, quod fides quae est donum gratiae inclinat hominem ad credendum secundum aliquem affectum boni, etiamsi sit informis; unde fides quae est in daemonibus, non est donum gratiae, sed magis coguntur ad credendum ex perspicacitate naturalis intellectus."

123/28–32 **lyke as ... father.** The absence of a comma after "hym" in *1533* and *1557* makes it seem that "flesshe" is the object of either "had" (line 28) or "begate" (line 30), whereas it is actually the subject of "had" (line 32).

124/14–16 **God ... hym.** 1 John 4 : 16.

124/33–34 **fides ... horum charitas.** 1 Cor. 13 : 13.

125/4–8 **My father ... bylyefe.** *Souper*, Appendix A, 316/19–23.

126/4–27 **I wyll not dyssemble ... they do.** The Latin *dissimulo* was not used in the sense "to feign," and that meaning does not appear to be common for either "dissemble" or the earlier "dissimule." But the *OED* notes the meaning "feign" in Caxton (1483) and Starkey (1538); see

OED, s.v. "dissemble," 5; "dissimule," 5. Zwingli, from whose Latin the Masker is here translating, has *simulare*: "Frustra edetis, hoc est: frustra vos credere simulabitis, nisi et vitam immutetis" (*CRZ, 3*, 781/24–25).

127/2–5 **For Luther sayth . . . consent.** *De captivitate Babylonica*, WA 6, 536: "Dico itaque: neque Papa neque Episcopus neque ullus hominum habet ius unius syllabae constituendae super Christianum hominem, nisi id fiat eiusdem consensu." More quotes and answers the passage in the *Responsio*, *CW 5*, 270/12–282/9.

127/18–21 **Ego . . . you.** 1 Cor. 11 : 23.

128/3 **frere Lambert.** François Lambert (1486–1530) was born into a distinguished family in Avignon, where he entered the Franciscan Observants in 1501. After meeting Zwingli in 1522, he left his order and moved to Wittenberg. Luther obtained a position for him in 1523. He married on July 23, 1523. From 1524 to 1526 he lived in Metz and Strassburg, but in 1526 Landgraf Philip made him rector of Hesse, where he rose to prominence as a reformer, aligning himself more and more with the Zwinglian position on the eucharist. Among his several exegetical and polemical works is an attack on Erasmus, *De arbitrio hominis vere captivo*, published in 1525. See *CW 9*, Commentary at 29/10.

128/3–4 **dane Othe the cartusyan.** Otho Brunfels (c. 1488–1534) left the Carthusian order in 1521, entering the service of Ulrich von Hutten, whom he defended against Erasmus in his *Pro Ulricho Hutteno defuncto* (Strassburg, 1523). He and Erasmus were reconciled in 1525. Although he remained aligned with the Lutheran party throughout his life (despite a brief flirtation with Karlstadt), his major interests were scholarly, and he is often regarded as the "father of botany." See Allen, *5*, 367–68. The honorific title "dane" (= "don," "master"), customarily applied to members of religious orders, is ironical here.

128/4 **zuinglius.** Zwingli married on April 2, 1524. See *CW 9*, Commentary at 125/12.

128/4 **preste Pomeran.** Johann Bugenhagen, Luther's confessor and one of his closest advisers, was born in Wollin, Pomerania, in 1485 (hence his Latin name, Pomeranus). After pursuing humanist studies at the University of Greifswald, becoming a Premonstratensian canon, and serving as rector of the school at Treptow, he was ordained a priest in 1509 and made a lector in the Bible and the church fathers at Belbuck in 1517. He was converted by Luther's *De captivitate Babylonica* and moved to Wittenberg in 1521, where he married in 1522 and quickly became a leading member of the Lutheran movement. He was pastor of Wittenberg from 1523 to 1527 and professor of theology at the university from 1535. He published several polemical works and biblical translations in the 1520s and 1530s. Between 1527 and 1544 he became the founding father of the Lutheran church in northern Germany and in Denmark, where he consecrated the "overseers" of the Danish church, reconstituted the University of Copenhagen, and, in 1537, crowned King Christian III. Throughout the eucharistic controversy, Bugenhagen supported Luther and Melanchthon; he published a refutation of Zwingli in 1525. That same year he also addressed an exhortatory *Epistola . . . ad Anglos,* answered by More in his *Letter to Bugenhagen* (1526; Rogers, no. 143; see *CW 8,* 1152–55).

128/5 **Huyskyns.** See note to Introduction, pp. xlviii–liv, and note to 106/10–107/6.

129/5–26 **And euyn . . . his bloude.** *Souper,* Appendix A, 309/17–38.

129/9 **sleyghtly.** *Souper* reads "sleyghly" and *1533* has "slyly" when More paraphrases this passage at 130/5. At 142/18 and 147/15 *1533* again has "sleyght" where *Souper* has "sleighe" (317/34). But the obsolete adjective "sleight" was formed from the noun "sleight," which corresponds to the adjective "sly," so that the adjectives "sleight" and "sly" were practically synonymous.

129/10 **wordes.** The reading "worde" of *1533* is merely a misprint, as the sense and "wordis" in *Souper* (309/22) show.

129/10 **syngynge lofe.** The communion wafer; see *OED,* s.v. "singing," *vbl. sb.,* "singing bread," "singing cake." See also s.v. "sing," 3, 11: "to chant or entone," "to say mass."

129/23 **stere . . . vp.** That is, "stir up, arouse" Cf. John 6 : 44: "resuscitabo."

130/8–20 **not conuayeth . . . of me.** More seizes upon the illogicality of the Masker's sloppy language in "convayeth and conuerteth." As More suggests, the two terms are contradictory. "Convey" implies that both the body and the bread remain present; Luther held that in the eucharist the body and blood coexist with the bread and wine, just as fire and iron are united but unchanged when iron is heated red-hot in a fire (see *WA 6,* 510; *11,* 408). Wyclif held a similar view (see note to 136/18, below). The doctrine of transubstantiation was accepted as *de fide* by the Fourth Lateran Council in 1215. As Aquinas defined the doctrine later in the thirteenth century, the substance of the bread and wine is replaced by mere quantity, which maintains the accidents (that is, the appearance) of the bread and wine, while the substances of the bread and wine become Christ's body and blood. Scotus held that the substances of the bread and wine are annihilated and become Christ; the accidents are maintained by God's power. The Masker's distinction between what More "expouneth" and what the "Thomystycall papystes saye" is inaccurate, since More agrees with Aquinas.

130/31 **another place.** *Souper,* Appendix A, 317/2–12.

130/31–32 **harpeth . . . strynge.** Whiting, S839; Tilley, S936.

131/1–3 **Coulde . . . wolde?** John 3 : 1–20.

131/3–7 **Coulde . . . bely?** Matt. 12 : 38–41; Luke 11 : 29–32.

131/8–13 **Whan . . . neyther.** Acts 1 : 6.

131/14–18 **Hath . . . therof?** Matt. 12 : 16; 16 : 20. The gloss in *1557* is incorrect.

132/3–22 **some greate holy doctours . . . eate.** Aquinas (*Commentum*, p. 417) and de Lyra, for example, appear to apply John 6 : 51 only to the sacrament. Aquinas states: " Sic ergo quod dixit supra, *Ego sum panis vivus*, pertinet ad virtutem Verbi; hic vero quod subdit pertinet ad communionem sui corporis, scilicet ad eucharistiae sacramentum." For "diuers holy doctours" who state, as More himself does, that the passage refers primarily to the eucharist and indirectly to the crucifixion, see notes to 57/20–26, 63/32–65/21, 66/22–67/13.

133/7–20 **Whan the Iewes . . . byleuest.** *Souper*, Appendix A, 315/35– 316/8.

133/9 **tryppe.** Perhaps a misprint for "strype" (or lash) the reading of *Souper*. The phrase the Masker was translating from Zwingli is "potentius eos ferit" (*CRZ 3*, 780/36). The word "tryppe" could refer to the move by which a wrestler overthrows his opponent. Cf. 177/6–12.

134/15–19 **For yf . . . be dampned.** *Souper*, Appendix A, 316/8–12.

134/20–21 **waye . . . lyfe.** John 14 : 6.

134/22–24 **his promyse . . . ende.** Matt. 28 : 20.

134/25–26 **sende it . . . trouth.** John 16 : 13.

134/28–30 **But yf . . . god.** John 3 : 5.

134/28–31 **But yf . . . inexplycable.** In *A Treatise on the Passion* (*CW 13*, 33–44), More discusses at length the difficult question of what happens to unbaptized infants and virtuous pagans after they die.

134/36–37 **holy spyryte . . . chyrche.** Cf. Ps. 67 : 7. See Marc'hadour, *The Bible*, *1*, 155–56.

135/6–8 **I haue . . . Tindale.** See *Confutation*, *CW 8*, 62, 108–109, 132–34, 223, 341, 387–91, 561, 564, 616–18, 675, 677, 680, 689–90, 872, 910–11, 915–19, 1031.

135/16–18 **brede . . . Melchysedech.** Gen. 14 : 18–20.

135/20 **doctour Barons treatyse.** In *The Confutation* (*CW 8*, 302) More accused Barnes of holding the sacramentarian position. In *A Letter against Frith* More happily announced that Barnes had protested against the accusation in a letter: " For at hys laste beynge here, he wrote a letter to me of hys own hand, wherin he wryteth that I lay that heresye wrongfully to his charge . . . and sheweth hym self so sore greued therwyth, that any man shold so repute hym by my wrytyng, that he sayth he wyll in my reproche make a boke agaynst me, wherin he wyll professe and proteste hys fayth concernyng thys blessed sacrament" (Rogers, no. 190, p. 461, lines 782–90). No such work of Barnes survives, but More either knew or supposed that the book advanced the utraquist position that Barnes held in his *Supplication* of 1531 (*STC* 1470; Hume, no. 27, sigs. Q₃–R₄v) and in his *Sentenciae ex doctoribus collectae* (see Clebsch, p. 50).

135/30–35 **Mayster . . . argument is.** More concludes his dismissal of the Masker's rigid interpretation of John 6 with a resounding irony, underscored by the full stop after "dampned" in line 32. If we follow the Masker's reasoning, More argues, then a passage like John 3 : 5 would, absurdly, damn martyrs and children, when we all know (More implies) that traditional doctrine provides for both baptism by desire and baptism by blood as forms of the sacrament of baptism. See *Summa theologica*, III^a, qq. 66–71.

136/6–14 **These wordes . . . teth.** *Souper*, Appendix A, 316/33–39. More quotes here less accurately than usual, but the only change which modifies the sense is the substitution of "of trouth" for "the trouth" in line 9.

136/18 **Wicliffe.** John Wyclif, the Oxford reformer (c. 1330–84), departed from received opinion on the eucharist late in his career; the condemnation of his eucharistic views led to his withdrawal from Oxford in 1381; he returned to the subject frequently in his last years, most extensively in *Wyclif's Latin Works*, vol. 12, *Tractatus de apostasia*, ed. M. H. Dziewicki (London, 1888), and vol. 16, *De eucharistia tractatus maior*, ed. I. Loserth (London, 1892). Although Wyclif never denied the real presence per se, he did not accept the metaphysical explanations of these doctrines given by Aquinas or Scotus. Wyclif affirmed that the bread and wine continued to exist as substances and accidents after the consecration. After consecration, Wyclif held, the bread remains; it coexists with the body of Christ. The bread remains naturally; it becomes the body of Christ sacramentally, through the faith of the recipient; the words of the consecration are not the agent of the eucharistic change, but the efficacious sign of Christ's presence. See Gordon Leff, *Heresy in the Later Middle Ages; The Relation of Heterodoxy to Dissent c. 1250–1450*, 2 vols. (Manchester, England, and New York, 1967), 2, 549–58.

136/25 **Theophylactus.** See 52/9–33.

136/25 **Bede.** See 57/20–26.

136/25–26 **Hyrineus . . . Hilary.** More has neither mentioned nor quoted Irenaeus against the Masker, but he quoted and translated passages from Irenaeus in *A Treatise on the Passion* (*CW 13*, 161/28–162/5).

More has alluded to Hilary's interpretation of Christ as the seal of the Father, without quoting or translating him (30/14–33 and note). In *A Treatise on the Passion* he quoted and translated another passage from Hilary to prove the real presence (*CW 13*, 163/17–165/7; see also xxviii–xxx).

136/26 **Austayne.** See 39/1–16, 74/11–19, 74/29–35, 75/17–35, 82/33–83/6, 85/30–33, 87/23–26, 117/16–25.

136/26 **Cyryll.** See 63/32–65/21, 66/21–67/13, 71/11–31, 72/13–18, 83/15–35, 85/22–27, 92/17–93/4.

136/27 **Chrisostome.** See 85/16–22, 93/6–33, 116/6–25.

136/30–33 **And yet . . . course.** Many of these passages from the fathers on the institution of the eucharist at the Last Supper finally appeared in More's *Treatise on the Passion* (*CW 13*, 160/21–170/34, 178–88), though perhaps not in exactly the form he intended (*CW 13*, xxviii–xxx).

136/33–137/2 **And where . . . borde.** In *Souper* (Appendix A, 332/23–28), the Masker, wrongly believing that More was the true author of William Barlow's *A dyaloge descrybyng the orygynall ground of these Lutheran faccyons . . .* (London, 1531; *STC* 1461), points out that this book impugns Oecolampadius' use of the fathers, accusing him of "allegynge Tertulliane, Chrisostome & saynt Austen for hys authorite, whom he vnderstandyth a mysse and recyteth falsly / somtyme addynge more to theyr wordes, somtyme takynge awaye from theyr sentencyes" (*A dyaloge*, sigs. f₄v–g₁). In order to vindicate Oecolampadius, the Masker quotes and translates passages from these three authors (*Souper*, Appendix A, 332/38–334/10): Tertullian, *Adversus Marcionem* 4.40.3 (*CCSL 1*, 656); Augustine, *Contra Adamantum* 12 (*PL 42*, 146); and Chrysostom, *Commentarius in S. Matthaeum* 82 (83) (*PG 58*, 743). The passage from Tertullian appears in Oecolampadius' *De genuina . . . expositione* (sigs. C₅v–C₆), though the Masker omits a genuine seven-word clause given by Oecolampadius. The passage from Augustine was also quoted by Oecolampadius in *Quid veteres senserint* (sig. Q₆); but Oecolampadius makes his point by bringing together sentences separated by more than seven hundred words in their original context. The Masker quotes the passage in a slightly fuller form, but he makes the same leap (and one or two other besides). The last passage given by the Masker is not from Chrysostom but from Oecolampadius' *Quid veteres senserint* (sigs. H₂–H₂v); the first four words are from a passage of Chrysostom quoted by Oecolampadius; the rest is Oecolampadius' own explanation, which the Masker puts forth as Chrysostom's own words.

The marginal reference to Chrysostom's *Opus imperfectum* in *Souper* is erroneous, though Oecolampadius does quote another passage from this work in *Quid veteres senserint* (sig. N₇), a passage which Erasmus singled out as heretical in its eucharistic teaching in his 1530 edition of Chrysostom's

Opera (I have consulted volume 2 of *Opera Divi Ioannis Chrysostomi* . . . , Basel, Ioannes Hervagius and Ioannes Erasmius Frobenius, 1539, *2*, sig. R*₃v). The *Opus imperfectum in Matthaeum* was an Arian work falsely ascribed to Chrysostom, as Erasmus, More, and presumably Oecolampadius knew (see *CW 8*, Commentary at 685/8–11, text and Commentary at 933/1–18).

The Masker goes on to defend Oecolampadius against the charge of distorting the fathers by asserting that if he had done so his opponent Luther would have pointed it out. The Masker was apparently unaware that Luther's ally Melanchthon had accused Oecolampadius of distorting patristic texts in a letter written to Oecolampadius on April 8, 1529, separately published at Grossenhain in the same year (*CRM 1*, 1050) and published at Basel in 1530 as part of Oecolampadius' *Quid veteres senserint*. Fisher had taken Oecolampadius to task in great detail and at great length for the same vice in *De veritate*.

For a discussion of Barlow's authorship of the *Dyaloge*, see *The Works of William Barlowe*, ed. A. M. McLean (Appleford, 1981).

137/3–16 **But where . . . brede.** In the work of Zwingli from which the Masker borrowed most of *Souper*, *De vera et falsa religione commentarius* (*CRZ 3*, 776–81; see introduction to Appendix A, pp. 299–300), Zwingli argues at length against a position he wrongly attributes to his Catholic opponents on the basis of the condemnation of Berengarius at Rome (*Decretum*, De consecratione 2.42, *CIC 1*, 1328–29); the belief that Christ is perceptible to the senses in the eucharist. See Walter M. Gordon, "A Scholastic Problem in Thomas More's Controversy with John Frith," *Harvard Theological Review*, *69* (1976), 140–41.

137/20–25 **Whyche . . . iugement.** *Souper*, Appendix A, 316/39–317/2.

137/26–27 **The exposycyon . . . before.** See 81/12–38.

139/7–8 **blessed angellys . . . at onys.** See *Summa theologica*, IIIᵃ, q. 76, a. 7.

139/15 **what deuyll.** Equivalent to the modern "what the devil." Cf. *CW 6*, 271/1.

139/20–22 **If it . . . syghte.** *Souper*, Appendix A, 316/41–317/1.

140/15–33 **Helyas . . . saluacyon.** Chrysostom, *Homiliae XXI de Statuis ad populum Antiochenum habitae* (*PG 49*, 46); *Opera 1530*, *4*, sigs. F₃v–F₄: "Tanquam maximam haereditatem Helisaeus meloten suscepit: etenim uere maxima fuit haereditas, omni auro preciosior. Et erat duplex Helias ille, & erat sursum Helias & deorsum Helias. Noui qui iustum illum beatum putatis, & uelletis quisque esse, ut ille. Quid igitur, si uobis demonstrauero quid aliud, quod illo multo maius omnes sacris mysterijs imbuti recepimus? Helias nempe meloten quidem discipulo reliquit. Filius autem dei ascendens, suam nobis carnem dimisit: sed Helias quidem exutus, Christus autem & nobis reliquit, & ipsam habens ascendit. Ne igitur decidamus, neque lamentemur, neque temporum difficultatem timeamus. Qui enim sanguinem suum pro omnibus effundere non recusauit, & carnem suam, & rursus ipsum sanguinem nobis communicauit: nihil pro salute nostra recusabit."

140/24–25 **And as for . . . hym selfe.** The absence of a pronoun subject such as *he* in sentences beginning *as for* was quite common and idiomatic in More's time; see F. T. Visser, *A Syntax of the English Language of St. Thomas More*, 3 vols., Materials for the Study of the Old English Drama, New Series 19, 24, 26 (Louvain, 1946–1956), *1*, 33–34.

141/22–142/26 **Here myght . . . sermon.** *Souper*, Appendix A, 317/2–42.

143/26–29 **who so . . . come.** Matt. 12 : 32.

144/4 **For all . . . inough.** See *CW 8*, Commentary at 157/14–15.

145/3–7 **saynte Austayne . . . gobbettes.** See notes to 58/9–14 and 80/26–27.

145/9 **saynt Cyrill.** See 63/32–65/21 and 66/21–67/13.

146/12–14 **For as for . . . at all.** See note to 140/24–25.

147/10–23 **Thys therfore . . . sermon.** *Souper*, Appendix A, 317/29–42.

149/3–11 **Here . . . speche.** *Souper*, Appendix A, 310/9–17. The biblical references ("I am . . . vyne") are to John 10 : 9 and 15 : 1.

149/13 **another argument.** More correctly accuses the Masker of ignoring the first argument advanced in More's *Letter against Frith* (1532), sigs. e₂v–e₃v (Rogers, no. 190, p. 447, lines 236–56). See the Introduction, pp. lxxiv, lxxvii, and 220/9–33, below.

149/28 **holy saynte Austayne.** See notes to 58/9–14 and 80/26–27.

150/9–32 **And ouer . . . dede.** See *A Letter against Frith* (1532), sigs. d₂–d₃v (Rogers, pp. 447–48, lines 257–85).

150/18–19 **haue . . . allmoste.** For " haue lyfe in them" the 1533 [1532] edition of More's *Letter against Frith* has "be saued"; for "allmoste all" it has merely "all." The first change has no bearing on More's argument but the second does, since in replying to the Masker More is willing to admit that though many marveled, some did not (164/26–40).

151/10–13 **Lo . . . bokes.** *Souper*, Appendix A, 310/17–21.

152/10–17 **Fyrste . . . eyes.** *Souper*, Appendix A, 310/21–29.

152/16 **make . . . whyte.** "To make black white" was proverbial.

(Tilley, B440; Whiting, B330). Cf. *CW 6*, 169/15–16; *CW 8*, 137/34; *CW 12*, 33/25.

153/28–29 **That is ... texte.** *Souper*, Appendix A, 310/22–23.

154/9–10 **Absolon ... Thamar.** 2 Kings 13 : 22; "Porro non est locutus Absalom ad Amnon nec malum nec bonum: oderat enim Absalom Amnon, eo quod violasset Thamar sororem suam." At 154/9, 16, 22 and 23 the corrector of *1533* has changed "Amnon" (or "Anmon") to "Ammon." Absalom's brother is regularly called Amnon in the Vulgate (including the *Biblia latina* of 1498) and Ἀμνών in the Septuagint, though one ancient and authoritative codex, the Codex Alexandrinus, has Ἀμμών. More does not mention the name elsewhere. It seems unlikely that the name was changed to conform to a subsidiary manuscript tradition of the Septuagint. It was perhaps changed by a press corrector who was misled by a series of minims (see note to 27/22) and the name Ammon, progenitor of the Ammonites, who is mentioned frequently in the Old Testament. It may be, however, that More possessed his own copy of the Septuagint, one which was later owned by his protégé, the physician John Clement: this copy was described by Plantin as "très ancienne et beaucoup différente de celles qui sont imprimées" (*Correspondance de Christophe Plantin*, ed. Max Rooses, 9 vols. [Antwerp, 1883–1918], *1*, 227); see also Germain Marc'hadour, "1968 Remembers," *Moreana*, *18* (1968), 77–78.

154/23 **caused ... kylled.** 2 Kings 13 : 23–29.

155/5–8 **And there ... men se.** John 10 : 19–21: "Dissensio iterum facta est inter Iudaeos propter sermones hos. Dicebant autem multi ex ipsis: Daemonium habet, et insanit: quid eum auditis? Alii dicebant: Haec verba non sunt daemonium habentis: numquid daemonium potest caecorum oculos aperire?"

155/17–19 **that he ... agayn.** John 10 : 15, 18.

156/33–157/11 **But ... speche.** *Souper*, Appendix A, 310/29–311/1.

157/3 **Ioh. 6.10.15.** John 6 : 53; 10 : 9; 15 : 1.

158/35–159/7 **Nowe ... lande.** See *CW 8*, text and Commentary at 231/18–232/12; there More asserts that according to good usage "nay" and "yea" are the proper answers to questions posed in the affirmative; "no" and "yes," to those posed in the negative. In some places the Masker's English does sound unidiomatic, particularly in matters of agreement ("congruytie"): for example, Appendix A, 316/37–38, 321/26–27, 326/38.

159/10–13 **He asketh ... meate &c.** *Souper*, Appendix A, 310/32–34.

159/17–19 **It ys ... redy.** *Souper*, Appendix A, 336/10–12.

161/10 **scrypture . . . Luke.** Mark 14 : 17, 43; Luke 22 : 14, 47; see also Matt. 26 : 20, 47.

162/11 **agre that.** The change to "agre to" in *1557* is unnecessary. Here and at 203/37 More uses agree in an absolute transitive sense "to accept favorably" (*OED* "agree" *v.* 2).

162/28 **whyther.** Used to introduce a simple direct question (*OED* "whether," II, 2).

163/21–25 **as a man . . . lytell.** Whiting, S40; Tilley, B401.

163/35–164/5 **If More . . . spekynge.** *Souper*, Appendix A, 310/35–311/1.

164/31–32 **saynt Chrysostome . . . maynye.** Chrysostom does not explicitly state that all the disciples departed, but he does imply that only the twelve apostles remained with Christ (*PG 59*, 266). Augustine says that "almost seventy" of the disciples went away (see note to 87/22–24).

165/13–14 **many . . . dyd.** The sense seems to require "dyd not," and in the convolutions of the argument the printer might easily have dropped "not" by a false analogy with such a contrast as 164/35–36.

165/19–39 **Here may . . . Abacuk. 2.** *Souper*, Appendix A, 310/39–311/17.

165/38–39 **the ryghtuouse . . . fayth.** Hab. 2 : 4.

166/19–167/2 **Here is lo . . . sowper.** *Souper*, Appendix A, 317/41–318/21.

167/12 **worlde.** The errata of *1533* corrected "worde" to "worlde" at 131/35 and 218/30 but neglected to do so here.

168/20–30 **If thys . . . souper.** *Souper*, Appendix A, 318/10–21.

168/31–169/5 **Here hath . . . folyshely.** For an explanation of More's use of the terms *major* and *minor*, see *CW 8*, Commentary at 346/6–7. More accuses the Masker of giving only the first two terms of a syllogism (for example, "Every B is A"; "Some C is B") without drawing from them any conclusion ("*Ergo* some C is A"). The conclusion More mockingly suggests is part of a verse from a mnemonic, "De festis fixis," in the *Compotus manualis ad vsum Oxoniensium* (Oxford, C. Kyrfoth, 1519; *STC* 5613), sig. A₃v. The verse itself is nonsense, but the initial letters of each of the syllables correspond to letters on a table that is shaped like a hand and that, when used with other mnemonic verses, enables the user to compute the dates of the fixed feats of the Christian year:

> Postea de festis fixis sit regula talis
> A.B.C. sunt extra. G. supra. D.E.F. manet infra
> Radices dant .D. mediie / sed et F. tibi terne
> Mensis cuiusque ceptum versus dabit iste
> A / dam / de / ge / bat / er / go / ci / fos / a / dri / fex.

169/11–22 **For as for . . . at all.** In his article "A Scholastic Problem in Thomas More's Controversy with John Frith," *Harvard Theological Review*, *69* (1976), 131–49, Walter Gordon assigns three of the hypotheses mentioned by More to their scholastic sources: "Elements of three different theories can be discerned in this passage. There is the Ockhamist view which posits a bodily presence 'without any dimensions at all.' This theory, although attributed to Ockham, does not seem to have originated with him, because Scotus, who antedates Ockham by almost half a century, argues against it in his *Quaestiones in librum quartum sententiarum* (dist. 10, qu. 2, *Opera omnia*, 8.504). There Scotus contends for the extension and shape necessary for a truly vitalized body or, as More puts it, for Christ's body 'with his dimensions.' Finally, the last theory mentioned, that of a corporeal presence 'without any distinction of place,' suggests, among others, the Thomistic view" (p. 145). See also Clarke, pp. 318–21. In Karlstadt's *Dialogus oder ein gesprechbüchlin von dem grewlichen vnnd abgöttischen missbrauch des hochwirdigsten sacraments Iesu Christi* (1524; see p. xxii, note 3, above), a reactionary insists that Christ's body in the host is as large as it was when it hung on the cross and one of Karlstadt's spokesmen denies it, adding that he would find it easier to believe that Christ's body in the host is as small as when he was born or conceived (p. 12).

169/22–26 **these thinges . . . mater.** Erasmus frequently ridiculed the fine-spun questions of scholastic theologians, including some about Christ's presence in the eucharist (for example, *Moriae encomium*, *ASD 4/3*, 148/404–06). But in a letter of March 25, 1532 (and elsewhere) he agreed essentially with what More says here: "De veritate Corporis Dominici nihil ambigendum est. De modo praesentiae licet aliquo pacto dubitare, quoniam de hoc Ecclesia disputat verius quam pronunciat, aut certe in genere credere quod credit Ecclesia, praesertim homini laico" (Allen, *9*, 472).

169/26–29 **but onely . . . blood.** The real presence, long a part of traditional doctrine, was affirmed for the first time under the terminology of transubstantiation by the Fourth Lateran Council in 1215: "Una vero est fidelium universalis ecclesia, extra quam nullus omnino salvatur, in qua idem ipse sacerdos et sacrificium Iesus Christus, cuius corpus et sanguis in sacramento altaris sub speciebus panis et vini veraciter continentur, transsubstantiatis pane in corpus et vino in sanguinem potestate divina, ut ad perficiendum mysterium unitatis accipiamus ipsi de suo, quod accipit ipse de nostro" (Alberigo, p. 206).

169/34–35 **saynte Poule . . . Corinthyes.** 1 Cor. 11 : 23–34.

170/27–28 **his dede . . . maundy.** Matt. 26 : 26–29; Mark 14 : 22–25; Luke 22 : 18–20.

172/28–175/9 **Whan so euer . . . reherse.** Chrysostom, *In Ioannem homiliae* 45 (*PG 59*, 260–61); *Opera*, 1530, *3*, sigs. F*F₅v–F*F₆: "Quando enim

subit quaestio quomodo aliquid fiat, simul subit & incredulitas. Ita &
Nicodemus perturbatus est inquiens: Quomodo potest homo in uentrem
matris suae iterato introire? Itidem & hi nunc: Quomodo potest hic nobis
carnem suam dare ad manducandum? Nam si hoc inquiris, cur non idem
in quinque panum miraculo dixisti, quomodo eos in tantum auxit? Quia
tunc tantum saturari curabant, non consyderare miraculum. sed res ipsa
tunc docuit, inquies. Ergo ex eo & haec credere oportuit ei facilia factu
esse. Propterea id prius fecit miraculum, ut per illud non essent amplius
increduli his quae postmodum diceret. Illi quidem tunc temporis nihil ex
his dictis, nos ipsius beneficij utilitatem cepimus. Quare necessario dicendum quam admiranda mysteria, & cur data sint, & quaenam eorum
utilitas. Vnum corpus sumus, & membra ex carne, & ossibus eius. Quare
initiati eius praeceptis parere debent. Vt autem non solum per dilectionem, sed re ipsa in illam carnem conuertamur: per cibum id efficitur,
quem nobis largitus est. Cum enim suum in nos amorem indicare uellet,
per corpus suum se nobis commiscuit, & in unum nobiscum redegit, ut
corpus cum capite uniretur. Hoc enim amantium maxime est. Hoc Iob
significabat de seruis, a quibus maxime amabatur, qui suum amorem prae
se ferentes dicebant: Quis daret nobis ut eius carnibus impleremur? Quod
Christus fecit, ut maiori nos charitate adstringeret, & ut suum in nos
ostenderet desiderium, non se tantum uideri permittens desiderantibus,
sed & tangi, & manducari, & dentes carni suae infigi, & desiderio sui
omnes impleri. Ab illa igitur mensa tanquam leones ignem spirantes,
surgamus diabolo formidolosi, & caput nostrum intelligamus, & quam in
nos prae se tulit charitatem. Parentes saepenumero liberos suos alijs
alendos dederunt, ego autem mea carne alo, me his exhibeo, omnibus
faueo, omnibus optimam de futuris spem praebeo. Qui in hac uita ita se
nobis exhibet, multo magis in futura. Vester ego frater esse uolui, &
communicaui carnem propter uos & sanguinem: & per quae uobis coniunctus sum, ea rursus uobis exhibui. Hic sanguis facit, ut imago in nobis
regia floreat: hic sanguis pulchritudinem atque nobilitatem animae,
quam semper irrigat & nutrit, languescere non sinit. Sanguis enim a cibo
non fit repente, sed prius aliud quiddam: hic quamprimum irrigat
animam, eamque ui quadam magna imbuit. Hic mysticus sanguis daemones procul pellit, angelos & angelorum dominum ad nos allicit. Daemones enim cum dominicum. sanguinem in nobis uident, in fugam
uertuntur, angeli autem procurrunt." This passage is also quoted by
Fisher *De veritate*, sigs. F₃v, X₃–X₃v.

172/30–33 **Nichodemus . . . agayn?** John 3 : 4.

174/6–9 **Iob . . . flesshe.** Job 31 : 31: Si non dixerunt viri tabernaculi
mei: Quis det de carnibus eius, ut saturemur? "

174/16 **blew.** Perhaps a misprint for "blow." The Latin is "ignem spirantes, surgamus."

174/20 **I geue . . . selfe.** Perhaps More's Latin text had "hic" for "his" in the clause "me his exhibeo."

175/8–9 **whyche . . . reherse.** More did not quote or translate this passage from Chrysostom (*PG 59*, 261–62) among the patristic passages in *A Treatise on the Passion* (*CW 13*, 160–70, 178–88) nor in any of the other works he wrote before his death. But he may have planned to include it in his projected replies to Barnes (135/20), the second half of *Souper* (10/30–31, 136/30–33), or Frith's *Boke . . . answeringe vnto M mores lettur* (198/24–31, 221/21–222/5).

175/17–19 **hys maundy . . . sacrament.** Matt. 26 : 26–29; Mark 14 : 22–25; Luke 22 : 19–20.

175/31 **Hyreneus.** More probably refers to *Contra haereses*, 4.18 (*PG 7*, 1027–28), quoted and translated in *CW 13*, 161/28–162/5. The same passage is discussed by Fisher in book 4, chapter 21 of *De veritate*, sigs. T₄–T₄v, and part of it is given by Melanchthon in *Sententiae veterum aliquot scriptorum de coena Domini* (Wittenberg, 1530; *CRM 23*, 742–43). On Irenaeus and Hilary, see note to 136/25–26.

177/7 **Clerkenwell.** Skinnerswell, near Clerkenwell, was a traditional location for St. Bartholomew's Day wrestling matches. The two wells, near London on the north side, were only a short distance apart and their names became almost interchangeable. Clerkenwell or Clerks' well was so called either because the well was frequented by scholars and youths of the city "in sommer euenings, when they walke forth to take the aire," or because it was the site of an annual pageant play presented by the parish clerks of London. See Stow, *1*, 15–16, 95, 104. Cf. the elaborate comparison of disputation to a wrestling match in More's *Letter to Brixius* (*CW 3/2*, 606/25–608/13).

177/16–28 **After thys . . . redy.** *Souper*, Appendix A, 311/18–32.

177/19 **a posse ad esse.** On this kind of fallacy, see Petrus Hispanus (Pope John XXI), *Tractatus (Summule logicales)*, ed. L. M. de Rijk (Assen, 1972), Tractatus VII, 68–69, pp. 122–23.

177/24–25 **Paule . . . chyrche.** Acts 9 : 4–7.

177/25–28 **Or god . . . membres.** See Exod. 9 : 12; 10 : 1, 27; 11 : 10. For the Lord's "open and sodayne vengeaunce vppon" Pharaoh, see Exod. 14 : 28.

178/4 **camell . . . daunce.** Erasmus, *Adagia* 1666 (*Opera omnia, 2*, 630A); Whiting, C15; Tilley, C30.

178/8–10 **And thantecedent . . . formall.** That is, "And you shall find the antecedent so true, when you read over my *Letter against Frith*, that the Masker himself will not be able to deny that my conclusion has been carried out according to correct logical form." See *OED*, s.v. "consecution," 1; "formal," 1 d.

178/12–20 **Mayster . . . laysour.** *Souper*, Appendix A, 311/32–41.

178/37–179/4 **Chrystes . . . mater.** In *De genuina . . . expositione*, Oecolampadius reports an argument communicated to him by a minister friend of his to the effect that a man cannot be in many places at once because only the creator, not any creature, can be everywhere at once. Oecolampadius points out that advocates of the real presence require that Christ's body be in many places, not all places, at once, though he goes on to say: "Apparet tamen, si demus, posse esse simul in diversis locis, quod sequatur etiam posse esse in omnibus locis . . ." (sig. K₈). He makes similar remarks in *Quid veteres senserint*, sig. P₆.

179/15–16 **longe rekened . . . heretyques.** Berengarius of Tours was condemned by councils at Rome (1050, 1059, 1079), Vercelli (1050), and Paris (1051); his recantation of 1059 entered canon law (*Decretum*, De consecratione 2.42, [Ego Berengarius]; *CIC 1*, 1328–29). For the condemnation of Wyclif and Hus, see note to 183/21–23.

179/22–23 **Arrianes heresye.** See note to 41/12.

179/24 **wycleffe.** See note to 136/18.

179/26–27 **Dixit . . . deus.** Ps. 13 : 1; 52 : 1.

179/31 **folosophers.** The fusion of "fool" and "philosopher" was suggested by μωρόσοφος used by Lucian (*Alexander* 40), Erasmus (*Moriae encomium*, *ASD* 4/3, 74/76 and commentary), and More (*Utopia*, *CW 4*, 64/2). Cf. "folosophy" in *A Letter against Frith* (Rogers, p. 462, line 811).

180/6–32 **I aske . . . that.** This is one of More's favorite arguments for the authority of the church (cf. *Responsio*, *CW 5*, 674–83; *Confutation*, *CW 8*, 675–81). Here, as in these works, More refers to a famous passage in Augustine: "Evangelium mihi fortasse lecturus es, et inde Manichaei personam tentabis asserere. Si ergo invenires aliquem, qui Evangelio nondum credit, quid faceres dicenti tibi, Non credo? Ego vero Evangelio non crederem, nisi me catholicae Ecclesiae commoveret auctoritas. Quibus ergo obtemperavi dicentibus, Crede Evangelio; cur eis non obtemperem dicentibus mihi, Noli credere Manichaeis? Elige quid velis" (*Contra epistolam Manichaei* 1.5; *PL 42*, 176). See *CW 5*, 742–43. For Luther's use of the same passage from Augustine, see *WA 10/2*, 216–18. For a discussion of More's use of the passage, see Marc'hadour, *The Bible*, 4, 201–06.

180/34 **in the myre.** Whiting, M573; Tilley, M989.

182/8–10 **And the tother thre . . . you.** Luke 22 : 19: "Hoc est corpus meum, quod pro vobis datur: hoc facite in meam commemorationem." Cf. Matt. 26 : 26 and Mark 14 : 22: "hoc est corpus meum."

183/21–23 **dyuerse . . . saye.** The Council of Constance (1414–18) condemned the eucharistic doctrines of Wyclif and Hus; see Alberigo, pp. 387–407. For the Fourth Lateran Council see note 169/26–29.

185/16–27 **Here mayst . . . heretykes.** *Souper*, Appendix A, 311/41–312/12.

185/21 **halowynge . . . belles.** In More's time there was an elaborate rite for the blessing of flowers and the branches of palms and other trees on Palm Sunday. In the ensuing procession, saints' relics and a consecrated host in a pyx were carried. See *Sarum Missal*, cols. 255–58. The blessing of bells was an elaborate ceremony performed by a bishop. Water was blessed and the bell was washed, anointed, and incensed. The prayers included a petition against evil spirits, lightning, thunder, and storms (see *The Pontifical of Magdalen College*, ed. H. A. Wilson, Henry Bradshaw Society, 29 [London, 1910], p. 145).

185/21–22 **crepynge . . . crosse.** The rite for Good Friday included the veneration of the cross, often called creeping to the cross (see *OED*, s.v. "creep," verb, B 1 c); the clergy and the congregation proceeded on their knees to the sanctuary steps, where they kissed a crucifix. See Cross, p. 1431; *Sarum Missal*, cols. 330–31; 223/9, below; and *CW 8*, text and Commentary at 33/28.

185/26 **blacke is whyte.** See note to 152/16.

186/29 **shepys bonys.** Cf. Chaucer's Prologue to the Pardoner's Tale, VI (C) 347–51:

> Thanne shewe I forth my longe cristal stones,
> Ycrammed ful of cloutes and of bones—
> Relikes been they, as wenen they echoon.
> Thanne have I in latoun a sholder-boon
> Which that was of an hooly Jewes sheep.

The passage is quoted by More in *A Dialogue Concerning Heresies, CW 6*, 98/14–15.

186/29–32 **scrape clene . . . sacrament.** "Our lady matens" refers to the first hour in the office of the Blessed Virgin. The "dyryge" refers to the office for the dead, so called from the opening antiphon of matins taken from Ps. 5 : 9: "Dirige Domine Deus meus in conspectu tuo viam meam." Both these offices and the litany of the saints were generally included in the books of hours, as they were in the one used by More; see V. Leroquais, *Les Livres d'heures manuscrits de la Bibliothèque Nationale*, 4 vols. (Paris, 1927–43) *1*, iii–ix; *Thomas More's Prayer Book*, ed. Louis L. Martz and Richard S. Sylvester (New Haven, 1969), pp. xxvi–xxvii. These devotions were often written on parchment, from which ink could be scraped off. "Our ladys psalter" is the rosary, which contains as many

recitations (150) of the "Ave Maria" as there are psalms; see *OED*, s.v.
"psalter," B I 3. The adoration of the blessed sacrament in the tabernacle
began in the twelfth century, when the church, in response to the denial
of the real presence by Berengarius, wished to stress the divinity of the
consecrated host. The practice was common in monasteries by the end of
the fourteenth century, and it quickly spread among the laity: see *New
Catholic Encyclopedia*, 16 vols. (New York, 1967), *2*, 610. The feast of
Corpus Christi, which commemorates the institution of the Lord's
Supper, was instituted by Urban IV in 1264; Thomas Aquinas composed
hymns for the feast and arranged the order of the liturgy. See Cross, p.
349, and *New Catholic Encyclopedia*, *4*, 345–47.

187/4–5 **penaunce . . . dryft.** Contrition, satisfaction and confession are
the three essential elements of the sacrament of penance; see *Summa theologica*, supp., qq. 12–13.

187/6–8 **Some . . euer.** Luther held that souls sleep between death and
the last judgment (Paul Althaus, *The Theology of Martin Luther*, tr. R. C.
Schultz [Philadelphia, 1966], pp. 413–15). Joye held that souls went
straight to heaven or hell at death; for his quarrel with Tyndale on this
point see Butterworth and Chester, pp. 176–79, and Clebsch, pp. 219–23.
See *CW 9*, Commentary at 88/9–10 and 89/37–90/1; *CW 8*, Commentary
at 288/9–10 and 625/36–626/4.

187/8–19 **And yet . . . purgatory.** Luther held that the fiery punishment
of hell consisted essentially in the pain of a bad conscience (Althaus, *The
Theology of Martin Luther*, pp. 177–78). In *A disputacion of purgatorye* (*STC*
11387) Frith claimed that fire in a text cited by More in support of
purgatory (1 Cor. 3 : 15) should not be interpreted as material fire but as
an allegory of temptation and persecution (sigs. $H_8v–I_1v$). In *The Confutation* (*CW 8*, 290/8–11) More replied to Tyndale's accusation that
papists quench the fire of purgatory by paying money: "And yf the fere of
purgatory were so clere gone, bycause it myghte be quenched wyth the
coste of thre halfepence: then were the fere of hell gone to by Tyndales
techynge / syth bare fayth and sleyght repentyng putteth out that fyre
clene, wythout the cost of a peny." But before the time of Calvin (who
held that the fires of hell are metaphorical, not real) Protestants in
England and on the continent did not discuss at length the reality of
hellfire. See *CW 8*, Commentary at 625/30–31.

187/19–21 **But Chryst . . . there.** The gloss presents as examples Matt.
13 : 42, 50; 18 : 8–9; 25 : 41. Marc'hadour, *The Bible*, *5*, 189, suggests
Matt. 3 : 10.

187/30–32 **Thus . . . laste.** Melanchthon makes a similar argument in
Sententiae veterum aliquot scriptorum de coena Domini (*CRM 23*, 749).

188/22–189/11 **But let . . . glory.** *Souper*, Appendix A, 312/12–40.

188/22–23 **absolute powre.** Scotus, Ockham, and their followers observed a theoretical distinction between *potentia dei absoluta* (the power of God to do anything that is not logically contradictory) and *potentia dei ordinata* (the power of God within the order of the natural law that God has ordained); see Heiko Oberman, *The Harvest of Medieval Theology: Gabriel Biel and Late Medieval Nominalism* (Cambridge, Mass., 1963), pp. 30–56. Scotus ascribes the miracle of multilocation in the eucharist to God's absolute power, observing that the miracle does not present a contradiction (*Quaestiones in librum quartum sententiarum*, dist. 10, q. 2; *Johannis Duns Scoti . . . Opera omnia iuxta editionem Waddingi*, 26 vols. [Paris, 1891–95], *17*, 197–98).

188/24–25 **pope . . . power.** Since the time of Boniface VIII (1294–1303) and especially since the Council of Constance (1414–18) there had been considerable struggle and disputation about the power of the papacy, as opposed to that of temporal rulers, other bishops, and a general council (*DTC 13*, 308–17; *CW 8*, 1297–99). Leo X's bull *Exsurge* (June 15, 1520) condemned those who denied that Christ himself established the successors of Peter in the Roman see over all churches in the whole world (*DTC 13*, 318–19).

188/30–31 **to be present . . . power.** See *Summa theologica*, I, q. 8, a. 3.

188/33–34 **I wyll . . . creature.** Isa. 42 : 8.

189/4–6 **Chryste . . . thynge.** John 10 : 30; 14 : 28.

189/7–8 **And Paule . . . hath it.** Heb. 2 : 7; Ps. 8 : 6.

189/15 **letter . . . Fryth.** See *A Letter against Frith* (1532), esp. sigs. d₄v–h₃v (Rogers, pp. 448–56, lines 310–614).

190/23–25 **The scrypture . . . thought.** Ps. 7 : 10.

192/16–23 **The soule . . . nowe.** The argument is based on Augustine: "Creatura quoque spiritalis sicut est anima est quidem in corporis comparatione simplicior; sine comparatione autem corporis multiplex est, etiam ipsa non simplex. Nam ideo simplicior est corpore quia non mole diffunditur per spatium loci sed in unoquoque corpore, et in toto tota est et in qualibet parte eius tota est. . . ." (*De trinitate* 6.6; *CCSL 50*, 237). The formula describing the rational soul as "tota in toto et tota in qualibet parte corporis" (which Augustine again uses in *De immortalitate animae* 16; *PL 32*, 1034), became well known in the Middle Ages. For example, *Summa theologica*, I, q. 8, a. 2: "sicut anima est tota in qualibet parte corporis, ita Deus totus est in omnibus et singulis."

194/1–3 **God . . . made.** Gal. 3 : 8, 16, 29; Gen. 18 : 18, 22 : 18; Acts 3 : 25.

194/1–195/5 **God . . . me.** The Masker's twisting argument is, as More suggests (194/37), merely a "bye mater" of More's extended controversy with Frith. In his manuscript sketch of his views on the eucharist (printed about 1548 as *A christen sentence and true iudgement of the moste honorable Sacrament of Christes body & bloude* . . . ; *STC* 5190), Frith quoted a sentence from Augustine to show that Christ's body could be in only one place, heaven, after the ascension: "Corpus in quo resurrexit in vno loco esse oporteth" (sig. A₄v). This sentence from Augustine was an important text for Zwingli in his arguments against the real presence (*CRZ 5*, 655). In his *Letter against Frith*, More wished Frith had identified the quotation from Augustine: "For why to seke out one lyne in all hys bokes, were to go loke a nedle in a medew" (sig. e₃v; Rogers, p. 450, lines 367–68). In *A Boke . . . answeringe vnto M mores lettur* (sigs. F₁v–F₂), Frith admitted he had quoted Augustine from Gratian's *Decretum* (De consecratione 2.44; *CIC, 1*, 1330). The passage in Gratian is a conflation from three different works of Augustine, and the sentence quoted by Frith (from Augustine's *In Ioannis evangelium* 30.1) has, in its original context, little or no bearing on the eucharist, as Melanchthon had already pointed out (*Sententiae veterum aliquot scriptorum de coena Domini*, Wittenberg, 1530; *CRM, 23*, 747).

In *A Letter against Frith* (1532), More suggests that Augustine's "oportet" means not "it must be" but "it behooves to be," and he asserts that merely because Christ's body must be in one place at one time does not mean that it may not be in many (sigs. e₄v–f₂; Rogers, p. 451, lines 389–418). To support this reading, More cites Luke 24 : 26: "Nonne haec oportuit pati Christum, et ita intrare in gloriam suam," arguing that to read "fulle and precyse necessyte" in "oportuit" would deprive Christ of the choice whether or not to die.

The Masker argues (194/1–24) that it was necessary for Christ to die, since the contrary of this, that Christ live, is impossible: God had promised redemption through the death of Christ, and for Christ to live would thus have made a liar of God, who is truth. The Masker concludes (194/24–30) with a passing allusion to scholastic doctrine, affirming that the necessity of what God had decreed (that is, that Christ's death redeem man) is perfectly compatible with Christ's freedom of will. More finds a contradiction between this last statement and the Masker's initial argument (195/6–25). If Christ had liberty of choice, then it was possible for him to have lived. The Masker's original claim in his argument from the contrary was that this was impossible. More recognizes the scholastic origin of the Masker's reasoning, but he declines to argue the point like a schoolman. The necessity of the atonement, a doctrine formulated by Anselm in his *Cur deus homo*, was later modified by many scholastic theologians. Aquinas distinguishes between several kinds of necessity, and between absolute and hypothetical possibility. Christ's death was not intrinsically necessary (that is, by reason of his very nature), nor was it extrinsically necessary by reason of compulsion (that is, by God's decree). It was, however, extrinsically necessary in view of its end: the deliverance of man, the exaltation of Christ, and the fulfillment of God's word. The distinction between absolute and hypothetical possibility creates a similar refinement. It is possible, in an absolute sense, that God could have saved man without the passion of Christ, since all things are possible with God. But given the hypothesis that God had decreed Christ's passion, it was impossible for Christ not to suffer: see *Summa theologica*, III^a, q. 46, aa. 1–2; see also q. 47, aa. 2, 4.

More considers the Masker's argument irrelevant to the eucharist, the central issue, but before dismissing it he briefly points out that "in the ende" (195/4) the Masker has destroyed his own argument by admitting that Christ was at liberty not to die. See Appendix A, 312/40–313/25.

194/7–13 **Paule . . . dyed.** Heb. 9 : 15–17.

194/14–15 **oportet . . . copy.** Melanchthon had noted that "vulgate codices" had "potest" for "oportet" in the text from Augustine, but he rejected it as "lectionem mendosam" (*Sententiae veterum aliquot scriptorum de coena Domini, CRM 23*, 747). The best modern edition of *In Iohannis evangelium tractatus* accepts "potest" (*CCSL, 36*, 289).

194/17–19 **Johan. 2. &. 12 . . . peryshe not &c.** John 3 : 14: "Et sicut Moyses exaltavit serpentem in deserto, ita exaltari oportet Filium hominis." John 12 : 34: "Oportet exaltari Filium hominis." The Masker's reference to John 2 is incorrect.

194/24–25 **Chryste . . . agayne.** John 10 : 18.

195/30–196/7 **But mayster . . . ys so.** *Souper*, Appendix A, 313/25–41.

196/9 **.xxi. lefe.** See *A Letter against Frith*, (1532), sigs. f₄v–g₁v; (Rogers, p. 453, lines 473–88): "But I say yet agayn of theyr bodyes both twayne, yf he sayed that he wold do it / I wold not dowt but he could do it. And yf he coulde not do it but yf he glorified them fyrst / than were I sure that he wold gloryfye them both. And therfore yf it were trewe, that he coulde not make hys owne body to be in two places at ones at maundy, but yf it were than gloryfyed / than syth I am sure that he there dyde it, I am therby sure also that he than for the tyme glorifyed it. For that thynge was in hys owne power to do as ofte as he wolde, as well before hys deth as at hys resurreccyon / & yet to kepe hys gloryfycacion from perceyuyynge, as he dyd from his two dyscyples, whyche for all his gloryfyed body toke hym but for a pylgryme. And therefore as I saye, yf Chryste sayd vnto me that he wolde make bothe hys body and this yong mannes to, ech of them to be in a thousande places at ones / I wolde putte no dowte therin, but that by some maner meanes he were able inough to do it."

196/16–17 **as he dyd . . . dyscyples.** Matt. 28 : 16–20; Mark 16 : 12–17; Luke 24 : 36–53. John 20 : 19–30; 21 : 1–25.

196/21–23 **one of theym . . . me.** Matt. 26 : 26–29.

196/23–26 **For ellys . . . not.** See note to 180/6–32.

196/30 **good man.** That is "goodman," a title prefixed to designations of occupation (*OED*, s.v. "goodman," 3 a).

197/28–29 **Syr . . . shuldren.** *Souper*, Appendix A, 313/41–42.

197/32–198/3 **Rede . . . inough.** See *A Letter against Frith* (1532), sig. f₄; (Rogers, p. 452, lines 458–63): "Whan our sauyour sayde, that it was as possible for a camel or a great cable rope to entre thorowe a nedles eye, as for a ryche man to entre into the kyngdome of heuen, and after tolde hys apostles that though those two thinges were both impossyble to men, yet all thyng was possyble to god: I thynke that he ment that neyther the sample nor the mater was to god impossyble."

198/19–21 **You . . . stone.** *Souper*, Appendix A, 313/42–314/2. See 1 Kings 17 : 40–54. "Yonge Dauyd" is John Frith; the first treatise is the manuscript outline of Frith's views on the eucharist; his new sling and new stone are the *Boke . . . answeringe vnto M mores lettur* (1533).

198/27 **cokstewe.** Perhaps a misprint for "cockstele," a stick to throw at a cock at Shrovetide (*OED*, "cock" *sb.*¹, 23). See More's Pageant Verses, "Chyldhod," line 12 in *The History of Richard III and Selections from the English and Latin Poems*, ed. Richard S. Sylvester (New Haven and London, 1976), p. 114.

199/1–5 **God . . . amen.** *Souper*, Appendix A, 314/2–7.

199/2–3 **a mete . . . cuppe.** Whiting, C487; Tilley, C742, C906. Erasmus, *Adagia* 972 (*Opera omnia*, 2, 387C). A. Otto, ed., *Die Sprichwörter und sprichwörtlichen Redensarten der Römer* (Leipzig, 1890), no. 1355.

199/29–30 **Crystes . . . worlde.** Matt. 28 : 20.

200/6–28 **Then sayth . . . deuelrye.** *Souper*, Appendix A, 314/8–29.

200/19 **For I knowe . . . herdeman.** Cf. John 10 : 14–16.

200/35 **cryed . . . crosse.** Proclaimed at a market cross, especially St. Paul's Cross in London.

201/16 **gospell of Nichodemus.** An apocryphal gospel dating from the fourth or fifth century. See *CW 6*, Commentary at 229/23–24.

202/21 **this is my bodye.** See note to 182/8–10.

202/23–25 **generall . . . bothe.** See notes to 183/21–23 and 130/8–20.

202/33–34 **sayntes . . . counsayles.** For example, Cyril was present at the Council of Ephesus (431), which adopted a letter by him to Nestorius asserting the doctrine of the real presence (Alberigo, p. 43; Gratian, *Decretum*, *CIC 1*, 1346).

203/8 **general counsayles.** See, for example, the decrees of the Councils of Ephesus (431), Lateran IV (1215), Constance (1415), and Florence (1439) in Alberigo, pp. 43, 49, 206, 387, 398, 402, 523. In *De veritate*, sigs. L_2v–L_3, Fisher mentions these and other councils.

203/9–11 **myracles . . . other.** In *De veritate*, sigs. L_3–L_4, Fisher gives accounts of eucharistic miracles from Eusebius (*Historia ecclesiastica* 6.44; *PG 20*, cols. 629–34); Cyprian (*De lapsis*, 24–26; *CCSL 3*, 254–56); Ambrose (*De excessu fratris sui Satyri*, 26–31; *PL 16*, 1298–1300); Augustine (*De civitate Dei*, 22.8, *CCSL 48*, 820); Gregory (*Dialogi* 3.3; *PL 77*, 223); and others. Stories about miracles proving the real presence in a consecrated host were common both before More's time and afterwards. See E. Cobham Brewer, *A Dictionary of Miracles* (Philadelphia, 1884), pp. 489–95; and *Medieval Sermon-Stories*, ed. Dana C. Munro, Translations and Reprints from the Original Sources of European History, vol. 2, no. 4 (Philadelphia, 1901), pp. 18–20. The thirteenth-century miracle of Bolsena, in which blood from the chalice stained a corporal to form an image of Christ's face, is not well authenticated, but it was sufficiently renowned in More's time to have been the subject of one of Raphael's frescoes in the Vatican Stanze. More mentions a spurious miracle about a host in *CW 6*, text and Commentary at 87/17–19. Two of the miracles narrated by Cyprian are quoted and translated in *CW 13*, 180. See also *CW 8*, text and Commentary at 276/27–28.

204/5–7 **As for . . . deuylrye.** *Souper*, Appendix A, 314/26–29.

205/12–16 **For he . . . sacrament.** See 185/19–22.

205/15 **halowyng . . . tempestes.** See note to 185/21. In a series of poems written by Erasmus for six new churchbells, the bell dedicated to Saint Peter says of itself:

Petro sacra fugo cacodaemonas, arceo fulmen,
  Funeraque et festos cantibus orno dies.

See *The Poems of Desiderius Erasmus*, ed. Cornelis Reedijk (Leiden, 1956), no. 54, p. 259.

205/17–21 **Tyndale . . . fastyng.** See *CW 8*, 79; and Tyndale's *Obedience* (STC^2 24446), sigs. O_3–O_4v.

205/21–23 **Frith . . . fast.** In a translation (1529) of Luther's *Revelatio Antichristi* (1524), preceded by a prefatory letter by Frith under the pseudonym Richard Brightwell (*STC* 11394; Hume, no. 11), Lent is called a foolish fast (sig. I_3). See note to 6/31 and *CW 8*, Commentary at 631/12–13.

206/21–207/8 **Then sayth . . . ones.** *Souper*, Appendix A, 314/30–315/9.

207/2 **beareth . . . hoode.** "Two faces in one hood" was proverbial for duplicity (Whiting, F13; Tilley, F20). Cf. *CW 6*, 399/19–20.

207/5–6 **the phylosopher proueth.** Cf. Aristotle, *On Sense and Sensible Objects*, Loeb edition, trans. W. S. Hett (Cambridge, Mass., 1935), 446b22–27: "The original cause of the original movement such as the bell, or the incense, or the fire, which all perceive is the same and numerically one, but each perceives a quality which is different numerically though the same in form, for many see, smell, and hear it at the same time. These are not bodies, but are an affection or movement of some kind (for otherwise it would not occur), though not apart from a body."

207/14–28 **I wote . . . lyste.** Cf. *A Letter against Frith* (1532), sigs. g₃-g₄ (Rogers, p. 454, lines 524–40). The simile of the broken mirror, which appears in Innocent III, *De sacro altaris mysterio* 4.8 (*PL 217*, 861), is discussed by Bonaventure, *In Sent*, 4, dist. 10, p. 1, a. 1, q. 5 (*Opera omnia*, 11 vols., Quaracchi, 1882–1902, *4*, 224); by Albertus Magnus, *In Sent*. 4, dist. 13, a. 11 (*Opera omnia*, 38 vols., ed. Auguste Borgnet, Paris, 1890–99, *29*, 351); and by Aquinas, *Summa theologica*, III, q. 76, a. 3. The analogy to the voice comes from *De sacro altaris mysterio* 4.27 (*PL 217*, 875).

208/23–34 **For as for . . . false.** The contrast between the affirmative syllogism attributed to him by the Masker and the Masker's own negative syllogism will be clearer if both are reduced to schematic form:

More

A particular face can be in many places (glasses) at once.
That particular face is a particular body.
Therefore a particular body can be in many places at once.

The Masker

A particular face cannot be in many places (glasses) at once.
A particular face is a particular body.
Therefore Christ's body cannot be in many places at once.

Both syllogisms are "nought for lacke of forme" (on the allowable forms of the syllogism in figure and mood, see *CW 8*, Commentary at 346/6–7) because the third figure, to which both belong, does not allow the mood III (More's) or OIO (Masker's). But the conclusion ("consequent") of the syllogism falsely attributed to More does necessarily follow; that of the Masker's does not because the indefinite predicate of the minor (some one body or other) has been changed to a single, definite body in the conclusion.

209/16–19 **as saynt . . . oblacyon.** See Chrysostom, *In I Cor. homiliae* 24 (*PG 61*, 200), *Opera*, 1530, *1*, sigs. z₂-z₂v: "Quoniam unus panis & unum corpus multi sumus.) Quid enim appello, inquit, communicationem? Idem ipsum corpus sumus. Quidnam significat panis? corpus Christi. Quid autem fiunt qui accipiunt corpus Christi? Non multa, sed unum corpus. Nam quemadmodum panis ex multis granis unitur, ut minime grana appareant, sed tamen grana sunt, uerum incerta discretione coniuncta inuicem Christo coniungimur. Non enim ex altero corpore tu, ex altero ille educatur, sed ex eodem omnes."

209/28–30 **soule . . . whole.** See *Summa theologica*, I, q. 76, a. 8. Since the soul is united to the body as its substantial form, it is essentially present in the whole body and it is essentially in each part of the body. See note to 192/16–23.

211/10–11 **chaungyng . . . mo.** See note to 65/1–14.

211/14–17 **layeth . . . folke.** See note to 172/28–175/9.

211/23 **scoffe . . . hode.** See note to 207/2.

211/27–29 **Bede . . . Chrysostome.** See notes to 136/25–27.

212/10–30 **At laste . . . Iohan.** *Souper*, Appendix A, 315/15–34; *Confutation*, *CW 8*, 312/25–314/16; *A Dialogue Concerning Heresies*, *CW 6*, 150/1–151/28. The passage about Mary's perpetual virginity occurs on leaf 37 of *A Dialogue* only in the 1529 edition (in the 1531 edition it begins on leaf 48). At 213/1–2 More locates the passage by the book and chapter numbers to avoid the confusion caused by the different foliation in the two editions.

212/15 **these hys letters.** The plural is used in a singular sense (OED "letter" *sb.*[1] 4 b). More wrote only one letter against Frith.

213/8–12 **I haue . . . wyth.** See, for example, *CW 8*, 287/3–288/20; 312/36–314/28; 472/19–474/34; 1005/27–1006/12.

213/14–17 **euyn here . . . writyng.** See 58/19–61/29.

213/28–29 **dyuers . . . to.** See note to 58/31–59/4. Two scriptural texts frequently cited to prove Mary's virginity were Isa. 7 : 14 and Ezek. 44 : 2. See Aquinas, *Summa theologica*, III, q. 28, aa. 1–4.

213/29–34 **yet whyle . . . chyrche.** Jerome answered the fourth-century heretic Helvidius in *De perpetua virginitate . . . adversus Helvidium* (*PL 23*, cols. 183–206).

214/4–6 **And therfore . . . mynde.** *CW 6*, 150/6–34.

215/9 **many other.** See notes to 58/31–59/4 and 213/28–29.

215/33–34 **as for . . . turneth.** See note to 140/24–25.

216/7–19 **At laste . . . verytees.** *Souper*, Appendix A, 315/15–26.

217/7–10 **And therwythal . . . thother.** *CW 8*, 313–14; *The confutacyon of Tyndales answere . . .* (London, William Rastell, 1532; *STC*[2] 18079), sig. L₄. As More says, the page is misnumbered 249: it should be 259.

217/19–28 **But now . . . gospell.** *CW 8*, 313/3–14.

218/19–23 **Which . . . hominem.** An "argumentum ad hominem" is one which depends on the opinions or personality of a particular opponent rather than on the subject matter itself ("ad rem"). The earliest example in the *OED* (supp. s.v., "ad hominem") is 1599, and we have not been able to find the phrase in the *Summulae logicales* of Peter of Spain or the *Compendium totius logicae* of Jean Buridan. In the fifteenth century Rudolph Agricola wrote of two kinds of refutations: "ad rem" and "ad hominem." Of "solutiones ad hominem" he says: "Ad eas refugimus, quando ex re parum speramus auxilij. Quia firmior est argumentatio, quam ut aliqua parte infringi labefactarive possit. Vel quia datur occasio de aduersario dicendi, quem quia possumus acrius retundere, malumus in ipsum rationem quam in rem ingerere" (*De inventione dialectica* 2.15, Strassburg, Johann Knoblouch, 1521, sig. R₂). Johannes Capreolus (d. 1444), a defender of Aquinas at the University of Paris, says that he prefers Aquinas' discussion of a particular problem in one work rather than in others because he sticks to the problem itself in that work whereas in the others he proceeds "respondendo magis ad hominem quam ad rem" (*Defensiones theologiae divi Thomae Aquinatis*, 7 vols., Tours, 1900–08, reprint Frankfurt, 1967; 7, 29).

220/5 **ruffyn.** Though perhaps related to "ruffian," this word is older. In the Chester mystery plays it was the name of a fiend, but it came to mean "the devil" (*OED*, "ruffin").

220/5 **Colyn coke.** More is probably playing on the name "Collin," the noun "cullion" ("base rascal"), and the adjective "colly" ("grimy, coal-black").

220/14–30 **In this . . . of them.** *A Letter against Frith* (1532), sig. d₁–d₂; (Rogers, p. 447, lines 236–56). Here More alters slightly the opening line: "Agaynste which, beside the comon fayth of all catholyque christen regyons, the expositions of the old holy doctours and saintes be clere agaynste thys yonge mannes mynd in thys mater. . ." (sig. d₁).

221/20–21 **.iii. places . . . Chrysostome.** See *Souper*, Appendix A, 332/38–334/10; for the passages that the Masker quotes and translates, see note to 136/33–137/2.

221/26–222/5 **For so . . . here.** For Frith's *A boke . . . answeringe vnto M mores lettur* (Hume, no. 30), see Introduction, pp. xxxi–xxxv. More here accuses Frith of borrowing his patristic evidence from Oecolampadius' books on the eucharist: the two which included copious passages from the fathers were *De genuina . . . expositione* (Staehelin, "Oekolampad–Bibliographie," no. 113) and *Quid veteres senserint* (Staehelin, "Oekolampad–Bibliographie," no. 164; I have consulted the Heidelberg edition of 1572, Staehelin, no. 218). In *A Boke* Frith praises the second of these under the title "quid ueteres senserint de sacramento eucharistiae" and seems to acknowledge his debt to it (sigs. D_2v–D_3). That he did make use of it is certain: he draws from it two brief quotations from Haymo and Druthmarus (*A boke*, sigs. E_5v–E_6; *Quid veteres senserint*, sigs. Q_6–Q_6v) and includes in a passage of Augustine an interpolation by Oecolampadius (*A boke*, sig. D_7; *Quid veteres senserint*, sig. Q_6). At least three-quarters of Frith's quotations can be found in Oecolampadius' two books, and if we add to them Gratian's collections of patristic passages in *Corpus iuris canonici* (*Decretum*, De consecratione 2.33–97; *CIC 1*, 1324–52) almost all of Frith's passages could probably be accounted for. But Frith quotes a passage from Chrysostom in a different Latin translation from that given by Oecolampadius (*A boke*, sig. E_4v; *Quid veteres senserint*, sig. N_1), and he frequently supports his argument with passages from Ambrose's *De sacramentis*, which Oecolampadius rejected as spurious (*De genuina . . . expositione*, sig. E_7v). Frith also avoids some of the more problematic authors discussed by Oecolampadius, such as Cyril, Irenaeus, and Hilary.

222/7 **treatyse . . . Fryth.** Frith's book on the eucharist, which More saw only in manuscript, was later printed under the title *A christen sentence and true iudgement of the moste honorable Sacrament of Christes body & bloude . . .* (London, 1548?; *STC* 5190).

222/9–11 **letter . . . styll.** See Introduction, p. xxxii, *CW 9*, 123/25–29 and Commentary at 90/3–5.

222/14 **Frythes boke.** Frith's *A boke . . . answeringe vnto M mores lettur . . .* (Antwerp, 1533; *STC* 11381).

222/17–18 **I do . . . sale.** More provides the correct date for the publication of his *Answer to a Poisoned Book* in his letter to Cromwell of February 1, 1534, where he defends himself against the charge that he had written a book against the *Articles devised by the Whole Consent of the King's Council* (Rogers, p. 468, lines 11–23): "For of trouth the last boke that he printed of mine was that boke that I made against an vnknowen heretike which hath sent ouer a worke that walketh in ouer many mens handes named the Souper of the Lord, against the blessed sacrament of the alter. My aunswere whereunto albeit that the printer (vnware to me) dated it Anno 1534, by which it semeth to be printed since the Feast of the Circumcision, yet was it of very trouth both made and printed and many of them gone before Christmas. And my selfe neuer espied the printers ouersight in the date, in more then three wekes after. And this was in good faith the last boke that my cosin [i.e., William Rastell] had of myne. Which being true as of trouth it shalbe founde, suffiseth for his declaracion in this behalfe."

222/19–20 **Austayn . . . Turtuliane.** See note to 136/33–137/2.

223/9 **crepynge . . . crosse.** See note to 185/21–22. The usual expression is "creeping to the cross" or "creeping the cross," but "creeping of the cross" is recorded in 1511 (*OED*, "creeping" 1 b).

223/11 **wyne . . . polys.** Clebsch (p. 120) points out that Tyndale (1528), Barnes (1531), and Frith (1533) had compared the distinction between *sacramentum* and *res* to that between an alepole with its green bush and the ale or wine to be obtained within the tavern, noting that none of Frith's cohorts used it "with such pungency" as he did. But any or all of them could have found the simile in Oecolampadius' *Ad Bilibaldum Pykraimerum* [sic], *de Eucharistia, Ioannis Husschin, cui ab aequalibus a prima adolescentia Oecolampadio nomen obuenit, Responsio posterior* (Basel, Cratander, March 1527; Staehelin, "Oekolampad-Bibliographie," no. 140): "Hedera res est, et in aperto rem absentem, uinum scilicet uenale, ex hominum institutione annunciat" (sig. a_6).

223/17-18 **standynge . . . infydelyte.** A nominative absolute construction meaning "as long as that false belief and lack of faith persist."

223/22-34 **so that . . . Amen.** More's concluding prayer is shaped like the postcommunion of a mass. See, for example, the postcommunions for Holy Thursday and Corpus Christi (*Sarum Missal*, cols. 308, 747*).

APPENDIX A

The Souper of
the Lorde (1533)

WITH A HEADNOTE
BY CLARENCE H. MILLER

APPENDIX A

The Souper of the Lorde (*1533*)

It has long been recognized that the Masker's treatise relies on the eucharistic theology of Ulrich Zwingli.[1] In fact, the opening pages (305/1–310/8) are directly translated (with some additions and omissions[2]) from the section entitled "De eucharistia" of Zwingli's *De vera et falsa religione commentarius* (Zürich, 1525).[3] Three editions of a German translation of the eucharistic section, entitled *Von dem Nachtmal Christi . . .* , appeared in 1525.[4] But a comparison of the Latin, German and English texts shows that the Masker translated from the Latin, not the German.[5] After his digression defending Frith (310/9–315/34), the Masker returned to Zwingli's text (315/35–317/42), translating more freely and substituting longer sections of his own.

All the arguments of the Masker in the rest of his treatise, with a few exceptions, can be found in "De eucharistia" and Zwingli's other treatises on the eucharist published between 1525 and 1527.[6] Even in the

---

[1] William A. Clebsch claimed that *The Souper* was "simply a digest and translation of Zwingli's 1526 treatise *On the Lord's Supper*" (Clebsch, p. 216). Clebsch repeated essentially the same information in "More Evidence That George Joye Wrote the Souper of the Lorde," *Harvard Theological Review*, 55 (1962), 64. The only work of Zwingli that appeared in 1526 and has a title similar to the one Clebsch gives is *Eine klare Unterrichtung vom Nachtmahl Christi* (*CRZ, 4*, no. 75). This treatise has been translated into English in *Zwingli and Bullinger*, tr. G. W. Bromiley, The Library of Christian Classics 24 (Philadelphia, 1953), pp. 185–238. Though it contains an exposition of John 6, it is not the treatise from which the Masker translated the first part of *The Souper*.

[2] The Masker's major additions are 308/4–17, 309/17–31, 309/38–310/8. The major omissions are *CRZ 3*, 779/39–780/7, 780/17–27.

[3] *CRZ 3*, 776–81.

[4] *CRZ 3*, 625–27.

[5] I have examined a microfilm of *Von dem Nachtmal Christi / & vidergedechtnus / oder dancksagung Huldrychen Zuinglis meinung . . .* (Zürich, Christopher Froschouer, March 23, 1525). The German follows the Latin very closely, but the Masker has a few words found in the Latin text but not in the German: "to al the worlde" (306/6), "And as for me" (306/31), "ancore" (307/35). Also it is hard to see how the Masker could have derived "in the ordyr of our vnderstandinge" (316/13–14) (*intellectus ordine*) from "*so vil als menschliche vernunfft verston mag*" (sig. C₂).

[6] *CRZ 3*, no. 41; *4*, nos. 63, 67, 77; *5*, no. 104. The parallel between circumcision/baptism and passover/eucharist (322/5–325/2) may also owe something to Zwingli's *Von der Taufe* (1525; *CRZ 4*, 227–28).

digression on Frith, the argument that Christ's human nature is a creature limited to one place (heaven, after the ascension) is frequently propounded by Zwingli. The passages from Tertullian, Augustine, and
Chrysostom quoted and translated by the Masker (332/23–334/12) are
drawn from Oecolampadius and Frith, as the Masker himself notes. One
biblical example of "eating" in the sense "believing" (321/34–42) and
one of "is" in the sense "signifies" (325/27–36) do not appear in Zwingli
and may be original.[1] His argument from John 6 : 53 that the Catholic
position would damn children who die before receiving the eucharist
(316/1–12) is touched briefly by Oecolampadius.[2] But his insistence that,
if Christ had meant what the Catholics say, he and the evangelists would
have said so more fully and specifically (317/2–25) does not seem to
derive from Zwingli and may be original (if anything could still be original in 1533 after the deluge of eucharistic controversy from 1525 on).
The Masker's argument that the apostles had already received and consumed the bread and wine before Christ spoke the words of consecration
(318/22–319/5, 320/16–26) is not proposed by Zwingli and probably
derives from Karlstadt.[3] The liturgy described by the Masker (337/16–
339/29), who does not present an actual liturgy in detail as Zwingli[4] and
others had done, is also presumably original with him.

I have reprinted *The Souper of the Lorde* (dated April 5, 1533 in its
colophon; STC^2 24468)[5] from a photocopy of the copy in the Bodleian
Library at Oxford, omitting the epistle by Robert Crowley[6] from a later
edition (London, 1547?; STC^2 24469) which is bound after *The Souper* in
the Bodleian copy. Abbreviations have been silently expanded (except
"&" and *y* abbreviations like "y^e") and obvious misprints silently corrected. In a few places the punctuation has been corrected to make the
sense clearer, and lowercase letters at the beginnings of sentences have
been capitalized (especially *w*, for which the printer seems to have lacked

---

[1] They also do not appear in Oecolampadius' *De genuina verborum domini, Hoc est corpus
meum . . . expositione* (Basel, 1525).

[2] *De genuina . . . expositione*, sigs. F₅–F₅v.

[3] Hermann Barge, *Andreas Bodenstein von Karlstadt*, 2 vols. (Leipzig, 1905), 2, 166–67. The
argument might also have been suggested by Erasmus' note on Mark 14 : 24) (*Opera omnia*,
6, 206). So too the argument of 319/5–11 may derive from Erasmus' note on 1 Cor. 11 : 24
(*Opera omnia*, 6, 716).

[4] *CRZ 4*, no. 51.

[5] For a full description see Hume, no. 29 (*CW 8*, 1083).

[6] On Crowley's career see John N. King, "Robert Crowley: A Tudor Gospelling Poet,"
Yearbook of English Studies, 8 (1978), 220–37, and the same author's *English Reformation
Literature: The Tudor Origins of the Protestand Tradition* (Princeton, N.J., 1982), pp. 319–57;
for some additional biographical details, see Mark Eccles, "Brief Lives: Tudor and Stuart
Authors," *Studies in Philology, 79* (1982), 27–28.

the uppercase form). Sidenotes have been italicized and inset into the text; all final periods in these notes have been removed. In some sidenotes a few letters have been trimmed away; they are conjecturally restored here. The pilcrows used to mark paragraphs have been replaced by indentation.

Katharine Pantzer (STC^2 24468) points out, on the basis of the initial *W* on sig. A_1v, that this edition may be a reprint (by Nicholas Hill, London) of the 1533 edition (presumably lost) and not the 1533 edition itself. More's quotations of *The Souper* present only slight variations from the edition reprinted here, no greater than when he is quoting from a known edition,[1] so that these variations give us no reason to believe that he is quoting from a lost edition.

---

[1] See *CW 8*, 1052–54.

The Souper
of the Lorde.

wher vnto, that thou mayst be the better prepared and
suerlyer enstructed : haue here firste the declaracion
of the later parte of the .6. ca. of S. Iohan,
beginninge at the letter C. the fowerth lyne
before the crosse, at these wordis : Verely
here .&c. wheryn incidently M. Moris
letter agenst Iohan Frythe
is confuted. [A₁v]

WHan Cryste sawe those glotons sekynge theyr belyes flockinge so faste vnto hym Aftyr hys wonte maner (the occasion taken to teche and preche vnto them of the thynge now moued) he sayde. Verely verely I saye vnto you: ye seke me not because ye haue sene my myracles, but because ye haue eten of the loues and were well fylled. But as for me, I am not comen into thys worlde onely to fill mennis belyes: but to feed and satysfye their souls. Ye take grete paynes to folowe me for the meate of your belyes: but o slougherdis, worke, take paynes and labour rather to get that meate that shall neuer perysshe. For thys meat that ye haue sought of me hytherto, perysheth wyth your belyes: but the meat that I shall geue you is spiritual and may not perysshe but abydeth for euer geuinge lyfe euerlastynge. For my father hath conseygned and confyrmed me with hys assuered testimony to be that assuered sauuyng helthe and ernest peny of euerlasting lyfe. Whan the Iwes vnderstode not what Cryste ment bydding them to worke & labour for that meat that shuld neuer peryssh, they asked hym what shal we do that we myght worke the workis of God? supposynge that he had spoken of some vtwarde worke requyred of them. Wherfore Iesus answerde sayng. Euen thys is the worke of God, to beleue and truste in hym whom the father hath sent. Lo, here maye ye see that worke of God whyche he requyreth of vs euen to beleue in Cryste. Also consyder agen [A₂] what this meate is, whiche badde them here prepare & seke for sayng: worke, take paynes & seke for that meat &c. and thou shalt se it no nother meate then the beleif in Criste wherfore he concludeth that this meat so oft mencioned, is faithe: of the whiche

Abacuk, 12   meate saith the Prophet the iuste lyueth. Faith in him is therefore the meat whiche Cryste prepareth & dresseth so purely: powldering & spycyng it with spiritual allegoryes in al this chapiter folowinge to geue vs euerlasting lyfe thorow it.

Then sayd the iues vnto him. What token doist thou wherby we might knowe that we shulde beleue in the? Do some what that we might beleue the? what thinge workest thou that we might knowe the to be god? Thou knowest wel ynoughe that our fathers did ete brede or Manna in the deserte as it is wryten, he gaue them brede frome aboue. Iesus answered

Psal. 7   Verely verely I saye vnto you: Moses gaue ye not that brede frome heuen: for thoughe it fil down frome the ayer: yet was it not heuenly fode, for it did but fede the belly. But this brede of god that is descenden frome heuen whom my father geueth, refressheth the soule so abundantly that it geueth lyfe vnto the worlde. Whan the iwes vnderstode not this saynge, whiche was not els then the declaring of the gospel (for by the etinge of this brede he ment the beleif of this his gospel): they sayd. Sir geue vs this brede euermore. Iesus sayd vnto them. I am the brede of lyue, and who so come to me,

shal not honger: and who so beleue in me shal neuer thriste. Whan the
iwes herde Cryste saye the brede that descended from heuen shulde ge-
[A₂v]ue lyfe to the worlde: they desyerd to haue this brede gyuen them
for euer. And Iesus perceyuing that they vnderstod not the sense of this
5   gospel, he expowned them who was this so lyuely brede that geueth lyfe
to al the worlde sayng: I am the brede of lyfe, & who so come to me, that
is to saye, who so is gryffed & ioyned to me by fayth shal neuer honger,
that is, who so beleue in me is satisfyed. It is faith therfore that stancheth
this honger and thirste of the soule. Fayth it is therfore in Crist that filleth
10   our hongerye hartis, so that we can desyre no nother yf we once thus eat
and drynke hym by faythe, that is to saye, yf we beleue hys flesshe & bodi
to haue ben broken and his blood shed for our synnes. For then ar our
soulis satisfyed and we be iustified.

Ouer this it folowith. But I haue tolde ye this because ye loke vpon me
15   & beleue me not that is, ye be offended that I sayed, he that cometh to
me shal nether honger nor thirste, seyng that your selues being present, be
yet bothe hongry & thirste. But this cometh because ye haue sene me with
your bodelye eyes, & ye see me & beleue not in me. But I speke not of
suche syght nor comyng: but of the lyght of faithe, whiche who so hath,
20   he shal no nother desyer he shal not seke by night to loue a nother before
whom he wolde laye his greif: he shal not run wandering here & there to
seke dede stockis & stones. For he is certifyed by hys fayth to whom he
shal cleaue: he is coupled by faithe vnto me his very spouse & lyuely food
the onely tresure of his soule neuer more to thirste for any other. This
25   lyght of faith ye haue not, for [A₃] ye beleue not nor truste in me:
wherfore ye vnderstande not how I am the veri bred & meate of youre
soulis, that is to saye, your fayth and hope. And the cause of thys your
blyndenes is (I wyl not saie ouer hardly to you) that the father hath not
drawne you into the knowlege of me, or els ye had receyued me. For all
30   that the father geueth me, muste come vnto me.

And as for me, I caste out noman that cometh to me. For I am not
comen downe from heuen to do my wyl, whiche ye attribute vnto me as
vnto eche any other man, for I am verely a very man: and accordyng to
that nature I haue a special proper wyl: but miche more obedient to my
35   father than one of you. For youre wyll ofte resisteth & repugneth gods
wyl, but so do myne neuer. I am therfore comen downe to do his wil that
hath sent me. And to do ye to wete what his wyll is. This (I saye) is my
fathers wyll that hathe sent me. That of all that he hath geuen me, I leese
non: but muste rease him vp agayn in the laste daye: & to be playne.
40   This is his wyll that sent me That who so se that is knowe the sone and
beleue in hym, he must haue lyfe euerlasting: & I shall stere hym vp in
the laste day. Here may ye se what meat he speketh of. God sent his sonne

ergo Iudæi: Quid signi facis, quo sciamus, uidelicet tibi fidendum esse, & credamus? Quid operaris; quo te Deum esse agnoscamus, cui uni hærere Lex præcipit? Non enim te latet, ut patres nostri cœlitus deplutum pa nem in Eremo ederint, nam in Psalmis ea res cãtata est. Panem de cœlo dedit eis. Respondit Iesus: Vere uere di co uobis, Moyses non dedit uobis panem de cœlo: nam & si superne decideret, non tamen cœlestis erat, sed pa ter meus dat uobis panem de cœlo uerum: panis enim Dei est qui de cœlo descendit, & dat uitam mundo. Pa nis Moseos uitam sustinebat corporalem, sed panis quẽ pater dat, animum reficit: tamq; abundans & efficax est, ut mundo uniuerso uitam det. Qum ergo Iudæi nõ caperent Christi sermonem, qui nihil aliud erat quàm **Edere pro** Euangelij explicatio: per panem enĩ edere, uerbo Euan **credere** gelij credere intelligit. Dicunt ad eum: Domine, sem= **Euange** per da nobis panem hunc. Dixit ergo eis Iesus: Ego sum **lio.** panis uitæ, qui ad me uenit, nullatenus esuriet: & qui me fidit, non sitiet unquam. Cum audissent ergo Iudæi Christum dicere quod panis, qui de cœlo descenderet, uitam daret mundo, optabãt sibi semper hunc panem dari. Iesus autem intellegens quod sensum Euangelij nõ caperent, exponit quis nam sit iste panis tam uiuificus, ut mundũ totũ possit uitalẽ facere, & dicit: Ego sum pa nis uitæ, qui ergo ad me uenit, hoc est qui mihi iseritur, qui me recipit, nullatenus esuriet. Qd' aũt hic uenit pro
recipit

Ulrich Zwingli, *De vera et falsa religione commentarius*, Zurich, 1525, sig. P₁v
(reduced)

recipit accipiatur, ſequẽtia uerba indicãt. Qui me fidit
nõ ſitiet. Fides ergo eſt, quæ famem ac ſitim omnẽ ſedat:
ſed quam famẽ, aut quã ſitim? animæ nimirũ. Fides ergo
in Chriſtum ſola eſt quæ mentẽ ſatiat ac potat, ut nihil
amplius deſit. Proſequitur Chriſtus : Sed dixi uobis, qđ
me uidiſtis, & nõ fiditis. Quid hoc porrò aliud eſt, ꝗ,
Vos miramini quidẽ, qđ dixi eũ qui ad me ueniat, neꝗ
eſuriturũ neꝗ ſititurũ, cũ tamẽ uos iã nunc præſto apud
me adſitis fami ac ſiti obnoxij. Hoc inde prouenit, qđ
me quidẽ carnis oculis uidiſtis, dudũ et etiamnũ uidetis:
ſed ego de hoc uiſu uel acceſſu nõ loquor, ſed de fidei lu
ce: eam ſi quis habeat, nihil deſiderabit: nõ quæret per
noctẽ quẽ diligat, cui æſtus ſuos queratur: nõ uagus oĩꝗ
pererrabit: certus eſt eni eum quem tenet, uerũ animæ
ſꝓſum eſſe, unicũꝗ theſaurũ, nec alium ſitiet. Hãc uos
fidei luce nõ habetis, nõ .n. fiditis me: hinc nõ intelligitis
quo pacto ego ſim aniæ cibus, hoc eſt ſpes. Cauſa uero   Cibus aĩæ
huius ueſtræ cæcitatis eſt, ut nihil durius dicã, qđ pater   ſpes certa
nõ traxit uos in mei cognitionẽ, alióqui reciperetis me.   & iſta fi=
Nam omne qđ mihi pater dat, ad me ueniet. Quod uero   des eſt.
ad me adtinet, Ego nullum qui ad me uenit, foras eijcio.
Nõ eni deſcẽdi de cœlo, ut meã uoluntatẽ, quã uos mihi
haud aliter tribuitis quàm alijs hominibus: ſum equidẽ
uerus homo, atꝗ ſecundum eam naturam peculiarem
etiam uoluntatẽ habeo, ſed longe obtẽperantiorẽ ꝗ uos
habeatis: ueſtra enim uoluntas Dei uoluntati frequẽtꝛ

P ij

Ulrich Zwingli, *De vera et falsa religione commentarius*, Zurich, 1525, sig. P₂
(reduced)

into thys worlde that we myght lyue thorow him. Who lyueth by hym? they that eat his flesshe & drynke his blood. Who eat his flesshe & drynke hys blood? thei that beleue his body crucifyed and his blood shed for theyr synnes, these cleaue vnto his gracious fauour. But how coud thei cleaue thus vnto him except thei knew hym? And therfore he hadded 5 sayng: Euery man that [A₃v] seith the sonne: that is to saye, vnderstandeth wherfore the sonne was sent into this worlde & beleueth in him, shal haue euerlastynge lyfe.

Here it pered to the carnall iwes that Criste had taken to myche vpon

The cause of the iwes murmur

himselfe, to saye: I am the brede of lyfe, 10 whiche am comen downe frome heuen to geue lyfe to the worlde. Wherfore the flesshe, that is to saye the iwes now murmured, & not merueled (as M. More seweth hys owne dreme to a nother texte folowynge whiche I shal touche anon) they murmured at this sayng of Cryste. I am the brede which am comen 15 from heuen, sayng. Is not this Iesus Iosephs sonne whose father & mother we knowe well ynoughe? How then sayth he, I am comen from heuen? Iesus answered saing Murmur not among your selues. Herd ye not what I told ye euen nowe? All that my father geueth me, come to me? your vnbeleif, wherof foloweth this false vnderstanding of my wordis spiritually 20 spoken compelleth me to tell ye one thyng more then once or twyse. This therfore it is: Noman maye come to me thonely ernest penye and pledge of your saluacion onlesse my Father that sent me drawe him: and whom he draweth vnto me, that is ioyneth vnto me by faith, him shal I stere vp in the laste daye. I wonder ye take my wordis so strangelye beleuing them 25 to be some harde rydels or derke parables, when I say nothinge els then is

Isay. 54
Iere. 31

wryten in your owne prophetis, bothe in Isaye & Ieremye, sayng that all shalbe taught off the lorde. Sith euen your prophetis testifye thys knowlege to be geuen ye of my father: what can be spoken 30 more playnly then to saye: what [A₄] my father geueth me, that cometh to me? or this, noman may come to me, excepte my father drawe him: & yet haue it more manifestly. Who so haue herde my father and is lerned

Heb. 6

of him, he cometh to me as vnto the very onely ancore of his saluacion. Not that any 35 man hath sene the father, leste peraduenture ye mistake these wordis to here & to lerne, as thoughe they perteyned to the vtwarde sensis, and not rather to the mynde and inwarde illumininge of the soule. For noman euer sawe the father althoughe he worketh secretely vpon his hearte, so that what so euer he willeth, we muste hear & lerne, Noman (I saye) 40 seith him, but he that is sent of God, as I sayde before of my selfe, he it is that seith the father. Now therfore say I vnto you so verely verely as

playnely playnly. That who so beleue & truste in me, he hath lyfe euerlastinge. Now haue ye the some of this my doctrine, euen my very gospel
the wholl tale of al my legacye and message wherfore I am sent in to the
worlde. Had M. More haue vnderstande this shorte sentence, who so
5   beleue in me hathe lyfe euerlastynge, and knowne what Paule with the
other apostles preched: especially Paule being a yere and an halfe
amonge the Corinths, determininge not nether presuminge not to haue
knowne anye other thinge to be preched them (as him selfe saythe) then
Iesus Cryste, and that he was crucyfyed. Had M. More vnderstod this
10   *1. Cor. 2*   pointe, he shulde neuer haue thus blasphemed
Cryste and his sufficient scryptures, nother
haue so belyed hys euangelistis and holy apostles, as to saye, they wrote
not al thinges necessa[A₄v]ry for our saluacion, but lefte out thinges of
necessite to be beleued, makynge gods holy testament insufficient and
15   vnperfite: firste reueled vnto our fathers writen eft sence by Moses, and
then by his prophets, and at laste wryten bothe by his holy euangelestis
and apostles to.
      But turne we to Iohan ageyn and let More mocke stil and lye to. I am
the brede of lyfe saith Cryste. And noman denyeth that our fathers and
20   elders dyd ete Manna in the deserte, & yet ar thei dede. But he that eteth
of this brede: that is to saye beleuethe in me, he hathe lyfe euerlastynge.
For it is I that am this lyuely brede whiche am comen from heuen, of
whom who so ete by faithe, shal neuer dye. Here therfore it is to be noted
diligently that Cryste meaneth, as euery man may se, by the etinge of this
25   brede non other thinge then the beleif in him selfe offred vp for our
sinnes: whiche faithe onely iustifyethe vs: which sentence to declare more
playnely, and that he wolde haue it noted more diligently, he repeteth it
yet agene sayng, It is I that am the lyuely brede, which am comen downe
from heuen: who so eteth of this brede, shal lyue euerlastinge. And to put
30   ye clere out of doute, I shal shewe you in few wordis, what this mater is,
and by what wayes I muste be the sauiour and redemer of the worlde to
geue it this lyfe so ofte reherced. And therfore now take good heed. This
brede which I speke of so myche, and shall geue it you: It is myn own
flesshe whiche I muste laye forthe and paye for the lyfe of the worlde.
35   Here is it now manifest, that he shuld suffer [A₅] dethe in his owne flesshe
for our redempcion to geue vs this lyfe euerlastinge. Thus now may ye se
how Cristis flessh, whiche he called brede, is the spirituall food & meate of
our soulis. When our soulis by faith see god the father not to haue spared
his onlye so dere beloued sonne but to haue deliuered hym to suffer that
40   ignominious and so paynfull dethe to restore vs to lyfe, then haue we eten
his flesshe and dronke his blood, assuered fermely of the fauour of God,
satisfyed and certefyed of our saluacion.

Aftyr this communicacion, that he sayd, The brede whiche I shal geue
you, is my flesshe, whiche I shall paye for the lyfe of the worlde: yet were
the carnall iwes neuer the wyser. For their vnbeleif and stourdy hatered
wold not suffer the very spiritual sence & mynde of Crystis wordis to enter
into their hertis. Thei coulde not see that Crystis flesshe broken and 5
crucifyed, & not bodely eaten, shuld be our saluacion, and this spiritual
meat: as our soules to be fed and certifyed of the mercy of God &
forgeuenes of our synnes thorow his passion, and not for any eatinge of his
flesshe withe our tethe. The more ignoraunt therfore and flesshly they
were the more fyerce were they ful of indignacion stryuinge one agenst a 10
nother sayng. How may this felow geue vs his flessh to ete it? Thei stoke
fast yet in his fleshe before their eyes: these flesshely iwes. Wherfore no
meruel thoughe they aborred the bodely etinge therof: although our flesshely papistis being of the iwes carnall opinion, yet aborre it not, nether
ceasse thei dayly to crucifye and offer him [A₅v] vp agen whyche was once 15
for euer & al offered as Paule testifyeth.

Hebr. 10

And euen here, sythe Cryste came to teche,
to take a way all doute, and to breke stryfe, he myght, hys wordis
otherwyse declared then he hath declared and wyl heraftyr expowne
them, haue soluted theyr question: sayng, yf he had so ment as More 20
meanethe, that he wolde haue bene conuayed & conuerted, as oure iuggel-
ers sleyghly can conuaye hym wyth a fewe wordis, into a syngynge lofe
orels, as the thomisticall papistis saye, bene inuisyble wythe al hys dymen-
cioned body vnder the forme of brede transsubstauncyated into it, And
aftyr a lyke thomysticall mystery, the wyne transsubstancyated to, into 25
hys blood: so that they shulde eate hys flesshe & drynke his blood aftyr
their owne carnal vnderstandyng, but yet in a nother forme, to put awaye
al gruge of stomach. Or sith saynt Iohan, yf he had thus vnderstod hys
masters mynde, and toke vpon hym to wrytte hys wordis, wolde leue thys
sermon vnto the world to be redde: he myght now haue delyuered vs and 30
them from thys doute. But Cryste wolde not so satisfye theyr questyon:
but answerde. Verely verely I saye vnto you: except ye ete the flesshe of
the sonne of man and drynk hys blood, ye shal not haue that lyfe in youre
selues. He that eteth my flesshe & drynketh my blood, hath lyfe euerlastynge: and I shall stere hym vp in the laste daye: for my flesshe is very 35
meat & my blood the very drynke. He saythe not here that brede shalbe
transsubstancyated or conuerted into hys body, nor yet the wyne into hys
blood: but now conferre thys saynge to hys purpos at the begynnyng,
[A₆] where he bad them worke for that meate that shuld neuer perysshe:
tellinge them, that to beleue in him whom God hath sente, was the worke 40
of God, and whoso beleueth in him shuld neuer thirste nor honger, but
haue lyfe euerlastinge. Conferre also this that foloweth and thou shalt se it

playne that his wordis be vnderstanden spiritually of the beleyfe in hys
flesshe crucyfyed and his blood shede, for whych beleif we be promysed
euerlasting lyfe: himself sayng who so beleueth in me hath lyfe euerlastynge. Here therfore their question, how maye this man geue vs hys
5   flesshe to ete it, is soluted: euen when he gaue his bodye to be broken and
his blood to be shed. And we ete & drynke it in dede, when we beleue
stedfastly that he dyed for the remission of our synnes: Austen and Tertulliane to witnesse.

But here maketh More hys argument agenste the yonge man. Because
10 the iwes merueled at this sayng: My flesshe is very meate, and my blood
drynke. And not at thys: I am the dore and the very vyne, therfore this
texte (sayth he) My flesshe &c. muste be vnderstanden aftyr the litterall
sence, that is to wytte euen as the carnall iwes vnderstode it, murmuryng
at it being offended goyng ther ways from Cryste, for theyr so carnall
15 vnderstanding therof. And the tother textis, I am the dore .&c. muste be
vnderstanden in an allegorye and spirituall sence, because his hearers
merueled nothinge at the maner of the speche. Lo crysten reder, her hast
thou not a taste: but a gret tunne full of Moris myscheif & perniciouse
peruertinge of Goddes holy worde: and as thou seist [A₆v] him here
20 falsely & pestelently destroye the pure sence in Goddes worde, so dothe he
in al other placis of hys bokis. Firste where he saythe they marueled at
this Cristis sayng. My flesshe is very meat &c. that is not so, nether is
there any siche worde in the texte, excepte More wyll expowne Murmurabant, id est, mirabantur, they murmured, that is to saye, they merueled,
25 as he expowneth. Oportet, id est, expedit et conuenit. He muste dye, or it
behoueth him to dye, that is to say, it was expedient & of good congruence that he shulde dye, &c. Thus this poet may make a man to

Moris fyrst signifye an asse and blak whyght to blere the
reson confuted symple eyes? But yet for his lordely plesure,
30 let vs graunte hym that they murmured is
as myche to saye as they merueled: because perchaunce the one may
folowe at the tother. And then do I aske hym: whether Cristes disciples &
his apostels herd him not, and vnderstode him not when he sayde. I am
the dore and the vyne: and when he said My flesshe &c. yf he say no or
35 nay then scripture is playn agenst him. Io. 6. 10. 15 yf he saye ye or yisse.
Then yet do I aske hym whether his disciples and apostles thus hearynge
and vnderstandinge his wordes in al these .3, sayd chapiters wonderd and
marueled (as More sayth) or murmured (as hath the texte) at their
masters speche: what thynke ye More muste answer here? here may ye se
40 whother this olde holy vpholder of the popis chirche is brought: euen to
be taken in his owne trappe. For the disciples & his apostles nether
murmured nor merueled, nor yet were not offended wyth this their master

Crystes wordis and maner [A₇] of speche: for thei were well aqueaynted
wyth siche phrases: and answerd theyr master Cryst when he asked them,
wyll ye go hence fro me to? Lorde sayd they to whom shal we go? thou
haste the wordis of euerlastynge lyfe: and we beleue that thou art Cryste
the sonne of the lyuyng God. Lo M. More, they nether merueled nor   5
murmured. & why? For because as ye saye they vnderstode yt in an
allegory sence, & perceyued well that he ment not of hys materiall body
to be eaten wythe their tethe, but he ment it of hym selfe to be beleued, to
be very God & very man hauyng flesshe and blode as they had and yet
was he the sonne of the lyuynge God. Thys beleyf gatherd they of all hys   10
spirituall sayngis as hym selfe expowned hys own wordis sayng. My flesshe
profiteth nothing, meanyng to be eaten, but it is the spirit that geueth
thys lyfe. And the wordis that I speke vnto you ar spirit and life: so that
whoso beleue my flesshe to be crucyfyed and broken, and my blood to be
shede for hys synnes, he eateth my flesshe and drynketh my blood, and   15
hathe lyfe euerlastynge. And thys is the lyfe wher wyth the rightwyse
lyuethe euen be faithe. Abac.2.

The secounde argument of More.

Aftyr this texte thus wyselye proued to be vnderstanden in the lyterall
sence wyth the carnall iwes, and not in the Allegoryke or spirituall sence   20
wyth Cryste and hys Apostles: The hole some of Moris confutacyon of the
yonge man standeth vpon thys argument. A Posse ad Esse. That is to
wytte, God maye [A₇v] do it, ergo it is done. God maye make his body in
many, or in all places at once, ergo it is in many or in all placis at once.
Which maner of argumentacion, how false and naught it is euery soph-   25
ister, & euery man that hath wit perceyueth. A lyke iugement: God may
shew More the trouthe and call hym to repen-
The confutacion
of hys .2. argument   taunce as he did Paule for persecutinge his
chirche: ergo More is conuerted to God?
Or, God may let him runne of an indurate hert with Pharao and at laste   30
take an open and soden vengance vpon him for persecutinge his worde &
burninge his pore members: ergo it is done all redy? M. More must first
proue it vs by expresse wordis of holy scripture, and not by his owne
vnwryten dremes, that Crystis bodye is in many placis or in all placis at
once: & then, thoughe our reason cannot reche it, yet our faith mesured   35
and directed with the worde of faith will bothe reche it, receyue it, &
holde it faste to: not because it is possible to God, and impossible to
reson: but because the wryten worde of our faith sayth it. But when we
rede gods worde in mo then xx. places contrary, that his body shulde be
here, More muste geue vs leue to beleue his vnwryten vanites, verities I   40
shulde saye, at laysour. Here maist thou se Crysten reder wherfore More

wolde so fayne make the beleue that thapostles left aught vnwryten of
necessite to be beleued euen to stablesshe the popis kingdom whiche
standeth of Moris vnwryten vanites, as of the presence of Crystis body and
making therof in the brede, of purgatory, of inuocacion of sayntes, wor-
5   shiping of stones and stockis, pylgrimagis, halowing [A₈] of bowes and
bellys and crepyng to the crosse &c. If ye wyll beleue what so euer More
can fayne wythoute the scripture, then can thys poet fayne ye a nother
chyrche then Crystis & that, ye muste beleue it what so euer it teche you,
for he hath fayned to that it can not erre, thoughe ye se it erre & fyght
10 agenst it selfe a thousande tymes. Ye yf it tell ye blak is whighte, good is
badde, and the deuel is god: yet muste ye beleue it, orels be burned as
heretyks. But let vs retourne to our propose.

    To dispute of Gods almighty absolute powr, what God maye do wyth
hys body, it is grete foly and no lesse presumpcion to More, syth the pope
15 whyche is no hole god but halfe a god by theyr own decrees haue decreed
noman to dispute of hys power. But Crysten reder, be thou content to
knowe that gods will, his worde, and his power be all one and repugne
not. And nether wylleth he, nor may not do any thynge includyng repugnance, imperfeccion, or that shulde derogate mynessh or hurte hys glory
20 and hys name. The glory of hys godhed is to be present & to fyll all placis
at once essencyally presently wyth hys almyghty power, whyche glory is
denyed to any other creature, hym selfe sayng by hys Prophete: I wyll not

Isa. 42   geue my glorye to any other creature: nowe
therfore sithe hys manhed is a creature, it
25 cannot haue thys glory whyche onely is appropryed to the godhed. To
attrybute to hys manhed that property whych onely is appropried to his
godhed is to confounde bothe the natures of Cryste. What thynge so euer,
is euery where aftyr the sayd maner, that muste nedis be infinite, wyth-
[A₈v]oute begynnynge and ende, it muste be one alone, and almyghty:
30 whych propertys onely ar appropryed vnto the gloriouse maiestye of the
godhed. Wherfore Crystis body maye not be in al or in many places at

              once. Cryste hymselfe saynge as concernyng
Ioan. 14   his manhed: He is lesse then the father, but
Ioan. 10
Hebr. 2   as touchyng hys godhed, the father and I be
35   bothe one thyng. And Paule recytyng the
Psal affirmeth: Cryste as concernyng his manhed to be lesse then god: or
lesse then angellis as some texte hathe it: Here it is playne that all thyngis
that More ymagineth and fayneth are not possible to God, for it is not
possible for God to make a creature egall vnto hymselfe, for it includeth
40 repugnaunce & derogateth his glorye. God promysed and swore that all
nacions shulde be blessed in the dethe of that promysed sede whyche was
Cryste. God had determyneth and decreed it befor the worlde was made:

ergo Cryste muste nedis haue dyed, and not to expowne thys worde
oportet as More mynseth it. For it was so necessary that the contrary was
impossible: except More wolde make God a lyer, whyche is impossible.
Paule concludeth that Cryste muste nedys haue dyed, vsynge thys latyn
terme Necesse. Sayng: wherso euer is a teste-
ment, there muste the dethe of the testement
maker go betwene: or els the testement is not ratyfyed and suer but
ryghtuosnes & remyssion of sinnes in Crystis blood is hys new testement,
where of he is mediatour: Ergo the testement maker muste nedis haue
dyed. Wreste not therfore (M. More) thys worde Oportet (thoughe ye
fynde potest for oportet in some corrupt copye) vnto that [B₁] your
vnsauery sence. But let oportet signifye, he must or it behoueth hym to
dye. For he toke our very mortall nature for the same decreed counsel:
hymself sayng. Io. 2 & 12 Oportet exaltari filium hominis &c. It
behoueth, or the sonne of man must dye, that euery one that beleue in
hym perysshe not &c. Here may ye se also that it is impossible for God to
breke hys promyse. It is impossible to God whyche is that verite to be
fownde contrary in hys dedis and wordis: as to saue them whom he hathe
dampned, or to dampne them whom he hathe saued, wherfore all thinges
imagyned of Moris brayne ar not possible to God. And when More sayth,
that Christe had powr to let hys lyfe and to take it agayn, and therfore
not to haue dyed of necessite: I wonder me, that hys scollematter here
fayled hym, so conynge as he maketh hym selfe theryn: which graunteth
and affirmeth (as trewe it is) that wythe yᵉ necessary decreed workis of
gods forsyght and prouidence standeth ryght wel hys fre lybertie. But M.
More sayth at laste, If God wolde tell me that he wolde make eche of
bothe their bodyes too (meanynge the yonge mannys body and Christis)
to be in fyften placis at once, I wolde beleue hym I, that he were able to
make hys worde trewe in the bodyes of both twayn, and neuer wolde I so
mych as aske hym whyther he wolde gloryfye them bothe first or not: but
I am suer gloryfyed or vnglorifyed, if he sayd it, he is able to do it. Lo
here may ye se what a feruent faythe thys olde man hathe, and what an
ernest mynde to beleue Christis wordis if he had tolde him: but [B₁v] I
praye ye M. More, what and yf Cryste neuer tolde it you, nor sayd it nor
neuer wolde: wolde ye not be as hasty to not beleue it? yf he tolde it you:
I pray ye tel vs wher ye speke wyth hym, and who was by to bere ye
recorde: & yet yf ye brynge as false a shrewe as your self to testifye this
thing: yet by your owne doctryne, must ye make vs a myracle to
confyrme your tale, ere we be bownde to beleue you: or yet to admit this
your argument, God may make his body in many placis at once, ergo it is
so. Syr ye be to besy with gods almighty powr, & haue taken to grete a
burden vpon your weke shuldern, ye haue ouerladen your self with youre

Heb. 9

own harnes and weapens: & yonge Dauid is lykely to preuayle agenste ye
wyth hys slynge & stone. God hath infatuaded your highe subtyl wysedome. Your crafty conuayance is spyed. God hath sent your chyrche a
met kouer for siche a cuppe, euen siche a defender as ye take vpon your
5 selfe to be, that shal let all their wholl cause fall flatte in the myer vnto
bothe your shames and vtter confusion. God therfore be praysed euer
Amen.

Then sayth M. More, thoughe it semeth repugnant both to him and to
me, one body to be in two placis at once: yet God seith howe to make
10 them stonde to gither well ynough. Thys man with his olde eyen and
spectacles seithe farre in goddis syght, and is of his preuey counsell: that
knoweth belyke by some secrete reuelacion how god seyth one body to be
in many placis at once, includeth no repugnance. For worde hathe he non
for hym in all scripture nomore then one body to be in all placis [B₂] at
15 once. It impllyeth first repugnance to my syght and reason, that al this
worlde shulde be made of nothing: and that a virgen shulde bringforth a
chylde. But yet, when I se it wryten with the wordis of my faithe, which
God spake: and brought it so to pas: then implieth it no repugnance to
me at all. For my faithe recheth it and receyueth it stedfastly. For I
20 knowe the voyce of my herdeman: which if he sayd in any place of
scripture that his bodye shuld haue bene contayned vnder the forme of
brede and so in many placis at once here in erthe, and also abydinge yet
still in heauen to, Verely I wolde haue beleued him I, as soone and as
fermely as .M. More. And therfore euen yet, if he can shewe vs but one
25 sentence truly taken for his parte, as we can do many for the contrary, we
muste geue place. For, as for his vnwryten verites, & thautorite of his
anticristen synagoge, vnto whiche (the scripture forsaken) he is now at
laste with shame ynoughe compelled to flee: thei be prouede starke lyes
and very deuelrye.

30 Then saith he, that ye wote well that many good folke haue vsed in this
mater many good frutefull exsamples of gods other workis: not onely
myracles, wryten in scripture. vnde versus? (where one I praye ye?) but
also done by the comen course of nature heare in erthe. (if they be done
by the comen course of nature: so be thei no miracles) And some thingis
35 made also by mannis hande. As one face beholden in dyuerse glasses: and
in euery pese of one glasse broke into twenty &c. Lorde how this pontifi-
call poete playeth his parte. Be[B₂v]cause (as he sayth) we se many facis
in manye glasses: therfore maye one body be in many placis, as thoughe
euery shadew and similitude representinge the bodye, wer a bodely sub-
40 stance. But I aske More, when he seith his owne face in so mani glasses,
whither al those faces that apere in the glasses be his owne very facis
hauinge bodely substance skynne flesshe & bonne, as hathe that face,

whiche hath his very mouthe nose yen &c. wherwith he faceth vs out the
trouthe thus falsely with lyes? and if thei be all his very faces: then in very
dede there is one body in many placis, and he himselfe barethe as many
faces in one hoode. But acordinge to his purpose, euen as they be no very
faces, nor those so mani voyces, sownes, and similitudes multiplied in the 5
ayer betwene the glasse or other obiecte and the body (as the philosopher
proueth by naturall reson) be no very bodyes: no more is it Crystis very
bodye: as thei wolde make the beleue in the brede in so many places at
once. But the brede broken and eaten in the souper monessheth & putteth
vs in remembrance of his dethe, and so exciteth vs to thankis geuing to 10
laude and prease: for the benefit of our redempcion, and thus we there
haue Cryste present in the inwarde eye and sight of our faithe. We ete hys
body & drinke his blode, that is, we beleue suerly that his bodi was
crucified for our sinnes and his blood shed for our saluacion.

At laste, note, Cristen reder, That M. More in the 3 boke of his 15
confutacion of tyndall the 249 syde, to proue S. Iohans gospel vnperfit
and insufficient for leuinge out of so necessa[B₃]ry a poynt of our faithe,
as he callethe the laste souper of Criste hys maundye: saythe that Iohn
spake nothynge at al of this sacrament: And now see agayn in these his
letters agenst Frythe, how him selfe bryngethe in Iohn the 6 cap. to 20
impugne frythes wrytinge, and to make all for the sacrament, euen thus,
My flesshe is verely mete, and my bloode drynke. Belyke the man had
there ouershette himselfe fowle, the yonge man here causyng him to put
on his spectacles and poore better and more wysshely with his olde eyen
vpon saynt Iohans gospell to fynde that thinge there nowe wryten, 25
whyche before he wolde haue made one of his vnwryten verites. As yet yf
he loke narowly he shall espye that hymselfe hathe proued vs by scripture,
in the 37 lefe of his dialoge of quod he and quod I, our ladys perpetual
virginite expowninge non cognosco, id est, non cognoscam, whiche now
writen vnwrytten verite he nowmbereth a lytel before emonge his vnwry- 30
ten vanites. Thus may ye se how this olde holy vpholder of the popis
chirch, his wordis fight agenst themselfe into his owne confusion, in fynd-
inge vs forthe his vnwryten wryten vanites verites I shulde saie. But
returne we vnto thexposicion of S. Iohan.

Whan the iwes wolde not vnderstande this spirituall sayng of the etinge 35
of Cristis flesshe and drynkinge of his blood, so oft and so playnely
declared: he gaue them a stronge strype and made them more blynde, for
thei so deserued it (siche are the secret iudgements of god) addinge vnto
all his sayngis thus. Who [B₃v] so ete my flesshe and drynke my blode:
abydeth in me and I in him. These wordis were spoken vnto these vnbe- 40
leuers into theyr farther obstinacion, but vnto the fayth full for theyr better

instruccion. Now gather of this the contrary, and saye, whoso eteth not
my flesshe and drinketh not my bloode: abydeth not in me, nor I in him,

Abac. 2   and ioyn this to that forsayd sentence
Except ye eat the flesshe of the sonne of
5 man, and drynke his bloode, ye haue no lyfe in you. Let it neuer fal fro
thy mynde Christen reder, that faythe is the lyfe of the ryghtwyse, & that
Christe is this lyuynge bred whome thou etest that is to saye, in whom
thou beleuest. For yf our papistis take eting & drinking here bodely, as to
eate the naturall body of Criste vnder the form of brede and to drinke his
10 bloode vnder the forme of wyne: then muste al yonge chyldren that neuer
came at Godes borde departed, and all laye men that neuer dranke hys

Ioh. 4   blode be dampned. By loue we abyde in God
and he in vs. Loue foloweth fayth in the
ordyr of our vnderstandinge and not in order of succession of tyme, yf
15 thou lokest vpon the selfe giftis and not of their fruites. So that princypally by faythe wherby we cleue to gods goodnes and mercy, we abyde
in God, and God in vs, as declare his wordis folowing, sayng, as the
lyuing father sent me, so lyue I by my father. And euen so he that eatethe
shall lyue because of me, or for my sake. My father sent me whose wyl in
20 all thynges I obaye, for I am his sonne. And euen so verely muste they
that ete me, that is beleue in me, forme and fasshion them aftir my
ensample mortifyng their [B₄] flesshe and changyng theyr lyuynge: orels
thei eat my in vayne and dessemble theyr beleif. For I am not comen to
redeme the worlde onely, but also to change theyr lyfe. They therfore that
25   beleue in me shall transforme theyr lyfe aftyr
Cristen relygion   my example and doctryne, and not aftyr any
is fayth, and a   mannys tradicions. This is the brede comen
lyfe correspondent   frome heuen, as theffecte selfe declareth,
whom whoso eteth shall lyue euer. But he that etith bodely brede lyueth
30 not euer, as ye may se of your fathers that eit Manna, and yet ar they
dede. It is not therfore no materiall brede nor bodely food that may geue
you lyfe eternall.

These wordis did not onely offende them that hated Cryst, but also
some of hys discyples (they where offended sayd the texte and not mer-
35 ueled as More tryfleth oute the trouth) whyche sayd Thys is an harde
sayng. Who maye here thys? These discyples yet stoke no lesse in Crystis
visyble flesshe, and in the barke of hys wordis, then did the other iwes: &
as do now More, belyuyng hym to haue had spoken of hys naturall body
to be eaten wyth their tethe. Whyche offence Chryst seyng, sayd: Do thys
40 offende ye? what then wyll ye saye, if ye se the sone of man ascende
thyther wher he was before? If it offende ye to ete my flesshe whyle I am
here, it shall myche more offend ye to ete it whan me body shalbe gone

oute of your syght ascended into heuen there syttyng on the ryght honde
of my father vntyll I come ageyn as I went, that is to iugement. Here
myght Cryst haue enstructed hys disciples the trouthe af the etinge of hys
flesshe in forme of brede, [B₄v] had thys ben his meaninge. For he left
them neuer in any perplexite or doute: but sought all the wayes by   5
similitudes and familiare examples to teche them playnely. He neuer
spake them so harde a parable, but where he perceyued their feble ignorance, anon he helpt them and declared it them. Ye & some tymes, he
preuented theire askinge with his owne declaracion, and thinke ye not
that he did not so here? yisse verelye. For he cam to teche vs, and not to 10
leue vs in any doute and ignorance, especially in the chefe poynt of our
saluacion, whiche standethe in the beleif in his dethe for our synnes. Wher
for, to put them out of all dout as concerning this etinge of hys flesshe,
and drinkinge of his blood, that shulde geue euerlastinge lyfe: where thei
toke it for his very body to be eten with their tethe: he sayd, It is the 15
spirit that geueth this lyfe, My flesshe profiteth nothing at all, to be eten
as ye mean so carnally. It is spirituall meat that I here speke of. It is my
spirit that draweth the hertis of men to me by faith and so refressheth
them gostely, ye be therfore carnall to thinke that I speke of my flesshe to
be eten bodely, for so it profitethe you nothing at al. How longe wyl ye be 20
without vnderstandinge? It is my spirit I tell you that geueth lyfe, My
flesshe profiteth you nothinge to eate it: but to beleue that it shalbe
crucifyed and suffer for the redempcion of the worlde it profyteth, And
when ye thus beleue, then ete ye my flesshe & drinke my blood, that is ye
beleue in me to suffer for your synnes. The verite hathe spoken these 25
wordis My flesshe profiteth nothing at all: it cannot therfo[B₅]re be false.
For bothe the iwes and his disciples murmured and disputed of his flesshe
how it shulde be eaten, and not of the offering therof for our synnes as
cryste ment. This therfore is the suer ancor to holde vs by agenst all the
obieccions of the papists for the eting of Cristes bodye as they say in forme 30
of breade. Cryste sayd My flesshe profyteth nothing: meaning to ete it
bodely. This is the keye that solueth all their argumentis & openeth the
waye to shew vs al their false and abominable blasphemous lyes vpon
Cristis wordis, & vttereth their sleighe iuggelynge ouer the brede to
mayntayn anticrystes kyngdom ther with. And thus when Criste had 35
declared it and taught them that it was not the bodely eatinge of his
material body: but the eating with the spirit of faithe: he added sayng.
The wordis which I here speke vnto you ar spirit, and lyfe. That is to
saye, this mater that I here haue spoken of with so many words must be
spiritually vnderstanden to gyue ye this lyfe euerlasting. Wherfore the 40
cause why ye vnderstande me not is that ye beleue not. Here is lo the
conclusion of all this sermon. Cryste very God and man, had set his

flesshe before them to be receyued with faithe that it shuld be broken and
suffer for their synnes, but thei coulde not ete it spiritually because they
beleue not in him. Wherefore many of his disciples fill from him and
walked nomore with him. And then he sayd to the twelue. Wyll ye go a
5   waye to? And Symon Peter answerde: Lorde, to whom shall we go? Thou
haste the wordis of euerlastinge lyfe, and we beleue, and ar suer, that
[B₅v] thou art Cryst the sonne of the lyuynge god. Here is it manifest
what peter & hys felowes vnderstode by this etinge & drynkinge of
Cryste. For they were perfitly taught that it stode all in the beleif in
10 Cryste as their answer here testifieth. If this mater had stode vpon so depe
a myracle, as our papistis fayne with oute any worde of god, not comprehended vnder any of their comon sensis, that they shuld eat his bodye
beynge vnder the fourme of bred as longe, depe thycke and as brode as it
hanged vpon the crosse, thei beyng yet but feble of fayth not confirmed
15 with the holy goste, muste here nedis haue wondred, stonned and stag-
gerd, and haue ben more inquisytyue, and of so strange a mater then they
were. But thei nether douted nor marueled, nor murmured, nor nothyng
offended withe this maner of speche, as were the other that slipte awaye,
but they answerde fermely. Thou haste the wordis of euerlastynge lyfe:
20 and we beleue &c. Now to the exposicion of the wordis of oure lordis
souper.

Amonge the holy euangelistis, wrytinge the story of Cristis souper:

Mat. 26
Math. 14
25 *Luck. 22*

Iohan, because the other thre had wryten it
at large, dyd but make a mencion therof in
hys 13. cap. Mattheu Marke and Luke declaryng it clerely, orderly and with iuste
nowmber of wordis. With whom Paule agreeth, thus wryting vnto the

1 Co. 11

Corynthis. Our lorde Iesus, the same nyght
he was betrayed: he toke the brede, and
30 after he had geuen thankis: he brake it, saynge: Take ye it, eat it. This is
my boodye, whiche is for you broken. Here is nowe to be noted the
or[B₆]dyr of this accion or acte. Firste Criste toke the brede in his handis,

The order of
the accion

secondarylye he gaue thankis, thirdelye he
brake it: fowertly he raught it them sayng,
35 take it, fiftely he bad them eate it. At laste
after all this he sayd. This is my bodye whiche is for you broken, this
thinge do ye into the rememberance of me. Her ye se, that this breade
was firste broken deliuered them, and they were commaunded to eate it
to: ere Criste sayde This is my boodye. And for because it is to suppose
40 verely, that they toke it at his hande as he bad them, and dyd eat it to,
when they had it in their handis, their master (whose wordis they did euer
obaye) commandinge them, It muste nedis folow (yf these be the wordes

of the consecration) that they were houseled with vnconsecrated brede, or
els now eaten, or at leste wyse parte of it, ere Cryste consecrated it, ye it
foloweth that it was oute of Cristis handis and in theyr mouthes when
Criste consecrated it, and so to haue consecrated it when it was now in
hys disciples handis or in their mouthes or rather in theyr belyes. Here it 5
is manifest that Cryste consecrated no breade, but delyuered it to his
disciples, & bad them ete it. In somyche that S. Thomas theyr owne
doctour, that made their transsubstanciacion confesseth that some there
were, that sayd that Criste did firste consecrate with other wordis, ere he
nowe reching the breade to his disciples sayd, This is my bodye .&c. and 10
yet calleth he it no heresye so to saye. Nowe sithe in all this acte and
souper, ther be no wordis of consecracion, but of the delyuering [B₆v] of
the brede broken after thankis geuying with a commandement to eat it:
brynge vs your wordis of consecracion? and shew vs by what wordes God
promised you & gaue ye powr to make hys bodye? There is nether 15
commandement, nor yet any wordis lefte in all the scripture to make or to
consecrate Christes body, to bringe it into the brede. But therbe the
wordis of God lefte in the fyrst cap. of Genesys, wherby he made al the
worlde: with which wordis, all be it we yet haue them: yet is it denyed vs
to make that thing that he made with them. Now, sith we hauyng his 20
wordis of the creacion, cannot yet make any newe creature of nothyng:
how then shall we with out any wordis of consecracion and makinge,
make yᵉ maker of all thyngis?

Vnto thys accion or souper or delyuerance of the brede, he added a
reason and significacion of thys signe or sacrament, and what also is the 25

The vse of vse therof: as thoughe any shulde aske them
yᵉ souper theraftir: what sacrament, religion, or ryte is
this? They shulde answer euen in a lyke
maner of spech as it was commanded their fathers to make answere to
theyr chyldren at the eatyng of the olde passouer wherof this new pass- 30
ouer was the veryte, and that the figure sayng. When your chyldern aske
ye what religion is thys? ye shal answer them. It is the sacrifyce of the
passyngby of the lorde &c. Lo here the lambe that signifyed, and did put
them in rememberance of that passyngby in Egypte the Israelitis spared,
and the egypcians smy[B₇]ten, was called in lyke phrase the selfe thynge 35
that it represented, signifyed and did put them in remembrance of: No
notherwyse then if Chrystes disciples, or any man els, seyng in that
souper, the brede taken, thankys geuen, the brede broken distributed &
eaten: shulde haue asked hym. What sacrament or religion is thys? He
had to answer them yᵗ Christe sayd. This is my bodye whych is for you 40
broken. This thing do ye into the rememberance of me, that is to saye, so
ofte as ye celebrate thys souper, geue thankis to me for your redempcion.

In whych answere he callethe the vtwarde sensible signe or sacrement,
that is the brede wyth all ye other accion, euen the same thinge that it
sygnifyeth, representeth, and putteth syche eaters of the lordis souper in
remembrance of. For when he sayd, whyche is broken for you, euery one
5 of them sawe that then it was not his body that was ther broken: but the
brede: for as yet he had not suffered, but the brede broken was diuided
into pesis euery one of the twelue takyng & eatinge a peace before he
sayde. This is my bodye &c.

Nowe sith M. More wil steke so faste in hys literall sense vpon these
10 wordis. This is my bodye &c. Then do I aske him, what thynge he
Mores letterall   shewethe vs by this first worde and pro-
sence is lost   nowme demonstratyue Hoc, in englysshe
                               (this)? If he shewe vs the brede: so is the
brede Christis bodye, and Christis body the brede, whiche sayng in the
15 literall sense is an hyghe heresye aftir them. And for thys sayng thei
burned Lorde Cobham. Also I aske whither [B$_7$v] Cryste speking these
wordis This is my bodye &c. had then the brede in his handis wherwith
he houseled his disciples or no? That he had it not, but had now delyuered it them: and had commaunded them to ete it to, the ordyr and
20 wordis of the texte playnly proue it, as is declared before. And S. Marke
Mar. 14   telleth the story also in this ordyr. The
                               Cuppe taken in his handis, aftyr he had
geuen thankis, he gaue it them, and thei all dranke therof. And he sayd to
them. This is my bloode of the new testament: whiche is shed for many.
25 Here is it manifest that thei had all dronken therof first ere he said the
wordis of consecracion (if they be the wordis of any consecracion.) Besydis
this yet: if ye be so sworne to the litterall sense in this mater, that ye wyl
not in these wordes of Cryste. This is my body &c. admitte in so playne a
speche no troope (for Allegorye ther is none, if ye knew the proper differ-
30 ence of them both, whiche euery grammarion can teche you) then do I
laye before your olde eyen and spectacles to, Crystes wordis spoken of the
Cuppe bothe, in Luke cap .22. and Paule .1. Co 11. sayng. This Cuppe is
the newe testament thorow my bloode which is shed for you. Here Cryste
calleth the wyne in the cuppe the selfe cuppe which euery man knoweth is
35 not the wyne. Also he calleth the cuppe the newe testament, and yet was
not the cuppe, nor yet the wyne contayned theryn the newe testament,
and yet he calleth it the newe testament conteigned and confirmed with
his blood, here ye se he called not the cuppe his blode but the testament.
40 Where is now your litterall sense [B$_8$] that ye wolde so fayne frame for
your papistis plesure? If ye wyll so sore steke to the letter: why do youre
faccion leue here the playne letter: sayng that the letter slayeth: goinge

aboute the busshe wyth thys exposicion and circumlocucion, expownyng
Thys is my bodye. that is to saye, This is conuerted and turned into my
bodye, and thys brede is transsubstancyated into my bodye? How farre
lo, M. More is thys your strange thomisticall sence frome the flatte letter?
If ye be so addicte to the letter: why fraye ye the comon peple frome the 5
letterall sence wyth thys bugge, tellyng them the letter slayeth? but ther is
nether letter nor spirit that maye brydle and holde your styfe necked
headis.

Also ye shall vnderstande that Christe rebuked the iwes .Io. 6, for theyr
litteral sense and carnal vnderstandyng of hys spiritual wordis Sayng My 10
flesshe profiteth you nothynge at all to eate it .&c. And their litterall
takyng of hys spirituall wordis was the cause of theyr murmure .&c. For
euen there, as also lyke in other placis, To ete Crystis flesshe .&c. aftyr the
comon phrayse of the scripture, is not els, then to beleue that Cryste

To ete cristis flesshe is to beleue in·hym

suffred dethe, and shede hys blode for vs. 15
Rede ye .1. Coryn .10. that our fathers all
dyd ete the same spyritual meate and
dranke the same spirytuall drynke that we
nowe ete and drynke? Here I thinke M. More muste leue hys litteral
sence and materiall meat, or els denye Paule, and denye to that our 20
fathers did ete Cryst and dranke hys blode, whyche all here Paule saythe,
for to eate and to drynke thys spyrituall meat and drin[B₈ᵛ]ke, was as
himselfe declarethe to eate and drinke Christe. Thei dranke of the stone
(saith Paule) that went with them. Whiche stone was Christe. And we ete
and drinke the very same stone. Whiche is not els, then to beleue in 25
Christe. Thei beleued in Christ to come and we beleue in hym comen and
haue suffred. Where is now thinke ye M. Moris litterall sence for the eting
of Christis materiall bodye? Our fathers were one, and the same chyrche
with vs, vnder the same testament and promyse, & euen of the same
faithe in Christe, And euen as they eate hym and dranke his bloode euen 30
the same spirituall meat and drynke that we do ete and drinke: so do we
now in the same faithe. For what els was signifyed by thys maner of
speche our fathers did eate and drinke Chryste, then that they beleued in
Christe to be incarnated & to suffer dethe? what els ment the pore
woman of Chanane by eatynge, then to beleue? when she answerde 35

Mat. 15

Christe, saynge, Ye saye sothe my lorde. But
yet do the lytell whelpis ete of the crummes
that fall frome theyr maisters table? This did she answer in an allegory
accordyng to Christis first answer vnto her, she meaning by the etinge of
the crummes, the beliefe of his wordis and gospel to be scatred among the 40
gentyls as Christe answering, comfirmed hir meaning saing: O woman
grete is thy faithe. He sayd not, thou arte a grete eater and deuowerer of

brede. Here is it playne that to ete in escripture is taken to beleue: as
Chryste himself expowneth it Io. 6. so ofte, and so plentuously: and I am
here compelled to inculke and iterat it with so many wordis, to satisfye if
it were [C₁] possible this carnall flessh vowerer and flesshely iwe.

5   Nowe to examyn and to discusse this mater more depely and playnly, I
shall compare the olde passouer with the newe and souper of the Lorde.
And to shewe ye how the figuris corresponde theyr verites: I wyll begyn
my comparison at Baptysme comparyng it with the lordis souper whyche
be the two sacramentis lefte vs now vnder the grace of the gospell. And
10   aftirwarde, to set forthe both these sacramentis playnely, I wyll compare
Cyrcumcision with baptysme: and the passe lambe with Crystis souper.

By baptysme, as we testyfyed vnto the congregacion our enterynge into

1. Co, 10, 11, & .12
Ro. 6
15   *Ephe. 4*

the bodye of Criste (take here Crystis bodye,
as dothe Paule for his congregacion) to dye,
be buryed, and to ryse wyth hym, to mortifye
our flesshe, and to be reuyued in spirit, to
caste of the olde man, and to do vpon vs the newe: euen so, by the

Eucharystia thanksgeuynge

thankys geuynge (for so did the olde greke
doctours call thys souper) at Goddis borde,
20   or at the lordis souper (for so doth Paule call it) we testifye the vnite

1. co, 10, 11

and communion of oure hertis, glued vnto
the hole bodye of Cryst in loue: ye and
that in siche loue as Cryste at thys, hys laste souper expressed: what tyme
he sayde, hys bodye shulde be broken and hys blod shede for the remis-
25   sion of our synnes, And to be short: As baptisme is the badge of oure
faythe so is the lordis souper the token of our loue to god and oure

1. Tim. 1

neghbours: wher vpon standeth the lawe and
prophetis. For the ende of the precepte, is
loue out of a pure herte, and good [C₁v] conscience and faith vnfained.
30   So that by Baptisme we be iniciated & conseigned vnto the worship of
one god in one faith: And by the same faithe and loue at the lordis
souper, we shewe our selues to continew in our possession, to be incorporated and to be the very members of Crystis bodye.

Bothe these sacramentis were fygured in Moses lawe. Baptysme was
35   fygured by circuncisyon: and the lordis souper, by the etynge of the
passelombe, where lyke as by cyrcuncysion, the people of Israel were
rekened to be goddis people, seuerall frome the gentyls: so be we now by
baptisme rekened to be: conseigned vnto Crystis chyrche seueral frome
iwes paynyms &c. And as their passouer, that is to saye their solempne
40   feste yerely in etynge their passelombe, was an vtwarde token of their
perseuerance in their relygion, and in remembrance of theyr passage out

of egypte into the londe of Chanaan: so is
now the etinge of the lordis souper (whyche
Cryst and Paule called our passouer) a
token of our perseuerance in our crysten profession at baptisme: and also
thankis geuynge wyth that ioyfull remembrance of our redempcion from 5
synne, dethe, & helle by Crystis dethe. Of the fygure of thys souper, our
new passouer: thus is it wrytten. Aftir ye be
entred into that lande whyche the lorde God
shal geue you accordyng to thys promyse: ye shal kepe thys ceremony.
And when your chyldren aske ye: what relygion is thys? ye shall answer 10
them. It is the sacryfice of the passyngouere of the lorde, when the lorde
passed forebye the houses of the chyldern of Israel in egipte, smy[C_2]ting
the gipcians and delyuering our houses. This etinge therfore of the passe
lambe was the figure of the lordis souper, which fygure whan the howr
was comen that he wolde it to ceasse & geue place vnto the verite, as the 15
shadewe to vanisshe awaye at the presence
of the bodye: He sayde thus. With a feruent
desyer do I longe to eate this passouer with you ere I suffer.

Agene, let vs compare the fygure wyth the trwthe, the olde passouer
with the newe, and diligently consyder the properte of spekinge, in and of 20
ether of them. Let vs expende the succession, imitacion, & tyme, howe the
newe succeding the olde, the mediatour Criste betwene bothe sitting at
the souper celebratinge bothe with his presens, dyd put out the olde and
bryngyng the newe. For ther is in ether of them syche lyke composicion of
wordis, siche affinite and proporcion in speche, syche symilitude and 25
propertie in them bothe, the newe so corresponding in all thingis the olde,
that the olde declarethe the newe, what it is, wherfore it was instituted, &
what is the very vse therof. And to beginne
at circuncision the fygure of baptisme. Ye
shall vnderstande That in syche rytes and 30
sacraments ther ar two thingis to be consyd-
ered, that is to wit. The thinge, and the sygne of the thinge. The thynge is
it wherfore the sygne is instituted to sygnifye it: as in circuncision, the
thinge is the couenant to be of the peple of God and the sygne is, the
cuttyng of the foreskinne of the preuey member. In the passouer, the 35
thinge was, the rememberance wyth thankis geuinge for the delyue-
[C_2v]rance out of the harde seruitute of egipt: but the sygne was, the
lambe rosted with siche ceremones as were ther prescrybed them. So in
baptisme: The thynge is, the promyse to be of the chirche of Cryste: the
sygne is, the dippinge into the water withe the holy wordis. In oure 40
Lordis souper, the very thinge is, Cryste promysed and crucifyed, and of

Luc. 22
1. Cor. 5

Exo. 12

Luc. 22

2. thinges to
be consydered
in the sacramentis

fayth thankis geuinge vnto the father for his sonne geuen to suffer for vs.
But the sygne is, the dealyng and distributing or rechinge forth of the
bred and wyne, with the holy wordis of our lorde spoken at his souper,
after he had thus dealte the brede and wyne, vnto his disciples.

5   And here is it diligently to be noted: That sithe in all these rites,
                                 ceremones, or sacramentes of God thus insti-
        The sygne is
        called the thinge.   tued: these two thynges that is to weite the
                                 thinge sygnyfyed, and the sygne that signi-
fiethe be concurrent and inseperable: it is the comen vse and propertye of
10   the speche in the scripture, to call the sygne, the thynge, as is circumcision
                                 called the couenant. Euery manchylde muste
        Gen. 17
                                 be cyrcumcysed that my couenant myght
be in your flesshe for a perpetual bonde. And yet was it onely but the
vtwarde sygne and seal of the couenant, that the sead of Abraham shuld
15   be his especial chosen people, and that he
        Exo. 12
                                 wolde be their God. The lambe, that was but
the sygne, was called the passouer: and yet was not the lambe the passyng
ouer, but the sygne onely excitinge & monesshinge them to remember
that delyuerance by the angell passynge by the Israelitis in egipt, smyting
20   thegipcians. And sithe this trope or maner of speche the scripture dyd vse
w[C₃]yth so grete grace in the olde rytes and ceremones that figured our
sacramentis: why may it not wyth lyke grace, for that analogye & proper
congruence of the fygures wythe theyr verites, vse the same phrase and
maner of speche in their verites? Yf the scripture called the sygne the
25   thynge in circumcision and passouer, why shuld we be offended wythe the
same speche in our baptisme and in the lordis souper? sithe siche maner
of speche haue no lesse grace and fulnes here then there to brynge the
thynge sygnifyed into our hertis by siche vtwarde sensible signes. For
when that sygne of circumcision was geuen the chyld: then were they
30   certified (as an vtward token maye certifye) that the chylde was of the
peple of Israel. And therfor dyd the sygnes then, as they do nowe bere
the names of the thynges which they signified as the lambe eten in theyr
passouer was called the sacrafyce and the selfe passouer, no nother wyse
than in our new passouer, that is the lordis souper, the breade broken &c.
35   is called the bodye of Cryste, and the wyne powerd forthe and distributed
to eche man, the blood of Cryste, because the brede so broken and dealte
signifieth vnto the receyuers and putteth them in rememberance of the
sacrifyce of his bodye one the aulter of the crosse and of his blood
powerde forthe for our redempcion. So that this maner of speche in
40   thadministracion & vse of the souper of our lorde: to saye This is my
bodye, and this is my bloode: is as miche to saye as, This signifyeth my
body, thys sygnifyethe my bloode. Whiche souper is here celebrated to

put vs in rememberance of Cristes dethe, and [C₃v] to excyte vs to
thankis geuinge.

Nether let it not offende the, o crysten reder, That Est is taken for
Est is taken significat: that is to saye, This is that, is as
for significat miche to saye, as this signifyethe that. For
this is a comen maner of speche in many
placis of scripture, and also in our mother tonge: as when we se many
pictures or images, whiche ye knowe well are but sygnes to represent the
bodyes whom they be made lyke: yet we saye of the image of our ladye.
This is our ladye. & of .s. Kataryne, this is saynt Kataryne. and yet do
they but represent and sygnyfie vs our ladye or saynt Kataryne. And as it
is wryten Genesis .40. ca. The thre branches ar thre dayes. The .3. baskettes ar .3. dayes. which was not els but they sygnyfyed thre dayes. Also
in the .28. ca. Iacob sayde This stone whiche I haue set vp an ende,
shalbe goddis house, which stonne yet was neuer gods house, nor neuer
shalbe: but only did signifye goddis house to be buylded in that same
place. Agayn, Pharao dremed to haue sene .7. fayer fatt oxen, & efte sone
.7. pore lene oxen. Whiche Ioseph expowning sayd: The .7. fatte oxen ar
.7. plentuouse yeris: and the .7. lene are 7. deare yeris, in whiche phrase
or maner of speche euery man seithe that the oxen were no yeres: but
they signifyed siche yeris. Meruel not therfore thoughe Est lyke wyse in
thys sentence: Hoc est corpus meum. be taken for significat, as miche to
saye, as this signifyeth my bodye. And yet for because the scriptures
conferred togither expowne them selfe as saith S. Austen. And Peter .2.
pe. 1. That we haue before a ferme and suer propheticall speche vnto
whiche [C₄] yf ye attende as vnto a lyght set vp in a derke place, ye do
wel: I shal shew ye a lyk phrase in Ezechiel where the destruccion of
Eze. 5 Ierusalem was thus fygured: God command-
inge Ezechiel to take a swerde as sharpe as
raser, & shaue of his head and berde, and then take a certayne waight of
the hearis deuyded into .3. partes: of the one, he shulde burne in the
myddes of the cyte a nother he shuld cutte rowndabout, and the thirde
caste it vp into the wynde .&c. whiche done he sayd: Thus sayth the lord
god This is Ierusalem. Which acte and dede so done, was not Ierusalem:
but it signifyed & preched vnto the beholders of it, Ierusalem to be
destroyed: no nother wyse then the brekinge & distributing of the brede
and wyne called Crystis body and blode signifyeth and precheth vs the
dethe of Cryste, the fygure and sygne beringe the name of the thinge
signifyed as in the prophetis speche, sayng: This is Ierusalem: whiche did
Ioan. 2 but signifye Ierusalem. When Cryste did
brethe into his disciples sayng. Take ye the
holy goste: the same brethe was not the holy goste, but signifyed and

represented them the holy gost, with a thousand lyke maner of speche in the scripture.

In the olde passouer thankis were geuen for the slaughter of the firste begoten, wheryn the kyngis posterite of egipte fill a waye, the Hebrews
5   spared, passed ouer, and delyuered. But in the newe passeouer, thankis ar gyuen, that the only begoten sonne of the most hyghest was crucified, wherby al faithful ar spared passed ouer, and not smyten with the swerde of dampnacion: but delyuered and saued in the [C₄v] lambis blood that haue taken awaye the synne of the worlde. In the olde passouer, The
10 lambe or festes is called the lordis passouer, and yet was nether the lambe nor the feste his passyng ouer: but the sygne and commemoracion of his passyngby. And euen so is it nowe in yᵉ newe souper of our lorde. It is ther called the body of our lorde, not that ther is any thinge wheryn his very natural body is contayned so longe and brode as it hanged on the
15 crosse, for so is it ascended into heuen and sitteth one yᵉ right hande of the father: but that thinge that is there done in that souper, as the breking & dealing & eting of the brede, and the wholl lyke accion of the wyne, signifyeth representeth and puttethe into our hertis by the spirit of faithe this commemoracion, ioyful rememberance, and so to geue thankis
20 for that inestimable benefit of our redempcion, wheryn we se with the eye of our faithe presently his bodye broken, and his bloode shed for our synnes. This is no small sacrament, nor yet irreuerently to be entreted: but it is the moste gloriouse and hyghest sacrament, with all reuerence & worsehip, withe thankis geuinge to be ministred, vsed receyued, preched
25 & solempnely in the face of the congregacion to be celebrated: of whose holy administracion and vse I shal peraduenture speke in the ende of thys souper.

But in the mene ceason (Crysten reder) let these sensible signes signifye and represent the his dethe, and prynte it
The vse of
30 *the souper*   in thy herte, geuinge thankis incessantly vnto God yᵉ father for so incomparable a benefit, that hathe geuen yᵉ his owne onely so dere beloued sone our saui[C₅]our Iesus Cryste to dye for thy synnes, ye & that when we were not his chyldern but his enmyes. Crystis disciples
Luk. 22
35 sayd to the man, where is this geste chamber where I might ete the passing by with my disciples? and thei prepared the passouer. And yet cryste eit not the passouer, but the lambe with his disciples, where it is playne, the signe to do on the name of the thing.

40 At laste, consyder vnto what ende all thingis tended in that last souper, how the fygure teched the verite, the shadew the bodye, and how the verite abolesshed the fygure, and the shadewe gaue place to the bodye. Loke also with what congruence, proporcion, and similitude bothe in the

accion and the speche, all thinges were consonant and finesshed, and all
to lede vs by siche sensible sygnes frome the fygure vnto the verite, from
the flesshe vnto the spirit, And take thou here this infallible and assuered

Lu. 22
sayng of Cryste neuer to fall fro thy mynde
in this last souper. Do ye this into the remem-   5
berance of me. And also of Paule, sayng 1. co. 11. So oft as ye shal ete this
brede, lo this heretike calleth it brede euen aftyr the wordis of the popis
consecracion, and drincke of this cuppe, prayse, declare, and geue thankes
for the dethe of the lorde, vntyl he shal come agene to iugement. Remember thou also: what Cryste sayd to the carnall iwes takinge the etinge of   10

Iohan. 6
Abac. 2
his flesshe and drinkinge of his blood so carnally, answeringe them. My flessh profiteth
not, mening to ete it bodely but the spirit
maketh lyfe. And to this set the prophet Abacuke sentence. The iuste
lyueth of his faithe. [C₅v]   15

And now (Crysten reder) to put the clene oute of doute, that Crystis
bodye is not here present vnder the forme of brede (as the papistis haue
mocked us many a daye) but in heuen, euen as he rose and ascended,
Thou shalt knowe that he tolde his disciples almoste twenty tymes
betwene the .13. and .18. cap. of Iohan, that he shulde, and wolde go   20
hence, and leue this worlde. Where to conforte them agene for that thei
were so heuy for his bodely absence, he promised to sende them his holy
goste to be their conforter, defender, and techer: in whom, and by whom,
he wolde be present with them and all faithful vnto the worldis ende. He
sayd vnto his disciples. I go hence, I go to the father, I leue the worlde,   25
and now shal I nomore be in the worlde. But ye shall abyde stil in the
worlde. Father I come to the. Pore men haue ye euer with you, but me

Act. 2
shall ye not alwais haue with you. And when
he ascendid vnto heuen, thei did beholde him
and sawe the clowde take his bodye out of their syght: and thei fastening   30
their eyes aftir him, the two men clothed in whight, sayd vnto them. ye
men of galyle, wherfore stande ye thus lokinge vp into heuen? This is
Iesus that is taken vp frome you into heuen, whiche shal so come agene,
euen as ye haue sene him goynge hence. Here I wolde not More to flitte
from his litteral playn sense. All these so playne wordis be sufficient, I   35
trowe, to a crysten man to certifye his conscience that Cryste went his
waye bodely ascending into heuen. For when he had tolde his disciples so
ofte of his bodely departing from them: they were meruelouse he[C₆]uy

Io. 14. & 16
and sadde. Vnto whom Cryste sayd. Because
I tolde ye that I go hence, your herts ar ful   40
of heuenes. If they had not beleued hym to haue spoken of hys very
bodely absence: they wolde neuer haue so morned for hys goyng away
And for because they so vnderstode hym, and he so ment as hys wordis

sowned: He added (as he shulde haue sayde) be ye neuer so heuye or how
heuely so euer ye take my goyng hence, yet do I tell ye trouthe. For it is
expedyent for you that I go hence. For if I shuld not go hence, that
counforter shall not come vnto you. But and if I go hence, I shal sende
5   hym vnto you. And agayn in the same Cap. I am comen frome the father,
and am comen into the worlde, and shall leue the worlde agene and go to
my father. What mystery, thynke ye, shulde be in these so manyfeste
wordis? Dyd he speke them in any darke parables? Dyd he mean other
wyse then he spake? Dyd he vnderstande by goyng hence so ofte repeted,
10   to tary here styll? or dyd he mene by forsakyng and leuyng the worlde to
be but inuisible beyng styll in the worlde wyth hys bodye? No suerly. For
he ment as faithfully and as playnely as hys wordis sowned, and euen so
dyd hys disciples wyth out any more meruelynge vnderstode him. For
they answerd him sayng: Lo now spekest thou apertely: nether spekest
15   thou any prouerbe. But what a derke prouerbe and subtyle rydle had it
bene: if he had ment by hys goynge hence to haue taryed here styll? and
by forsakynge the worlde, to abyde styll in the worlde? and by hys goyng
hence to hys father by hys very bodely ascencion, to be but inuisible?
Who wolde in[C₆v]terprete thys playne sentence thus? I go hence, that is
20   to saye: I tarye here styll. I forsake the world and go to the father, that is
to saye I wyll be but inuisible and yet here abyde styll in the worlde
bodely? For as concernyng hys godhed, whiche was euer wyth the father,
and in all placys at once, he neuer spake syche wordis of it. Whan Cryste
sayde, hys dethe now at hande, vnto hys disciples: now agene I forsake
25   the worlde and go to my father, but ye shall tary styl in the world. If they
wyl expowne by hys forsakyng the worlde, to tarye here styl bodely, and
to be but inuysyble: why do they not by lyke exposicion interprete the
tarynge here styl of the disciples at that tyme, to be gone hence bodely
and to be here visible? For Crist did set these contraryes one agenst
30   another to declare eche other, as if to tarye here styll, dyd signyfye to the
disciples that they shulde abyde in the worlde, as it dothe in dede: then
muste nedis his goyng hence & forsakyng the worlde signifie his bodely
absence as both the wordis plainely sowne, Cryste ment, & they vnderstode them. But in so playne a mater what nede all these wordis? Be thou
35   therfore suer, Crysten reder, that Crystis glorified body is not in this
worlde, but in heuen, as he thyther ascended in whiche body he shall
come euen as he went gloriously wythe powr and grete maiestye to iuge
all the worlde in the laste daye. Be thou therfore assuered, that he neuer
thus iugeled nor mocked hys so dere beloued disciples so ful of heuines
40   now for hys bodely departynge. For if he had so ment as our papistis haue
paruerted his sayngis, his disciples wolde haue wondered at so [C₇]
strange maner of speche, and he wolde haue expressed his mynde playnly,

sithe at thys tyme he was so full set to leue them in no doute, but to
counfort them with hys playne and confortable wordis. And yf he wolde
haue bene but inuisible and still bodely present: he woulde neuer haue
couered himselfe wyth the clowde shewynge them and testifyenge also by
those two men his very bodely ascension oute of theyr syghtis. We maye   5
not make of his very bodely ascension, siche an inuysyble iugelynge caste
as oure papistis fayne, Fasshoning and fayning Cryste a bodye nowe
inuisible, now in manye placis at once, and then so greate and yet in so
lytel a place, not discerned of any of our sensis, nowe glorified, now.
vngloryfied, now passible, and then impassible, and I wote ner what they   10
imagyn and make of theyr maker, and all with oute any worde, ye clene
agaynste all the wordis of holy scripture. For suerly, in thys theyr imaginacion and so sayng thei bringe in a fresshe the heresye of that great
heretik Marcyon, whiche sayd that Criste toke but a phantasticall bodye,
and so was nether verely borne, nor suffered, nor rose, nor ascended   15
verelye, nether was he very man. Whiche heresye Tertullian confuteth.
Cryste toke verely oure nature, siche a passible and mortal body as we
bere aboute with vs, saue that it was with oute all maner of synne. In
siche a body he suffred verely, & rose agen frome dethe in siche a glorifyed body now immortall &c. as euery one of vs shall ryse in at the   20
general iudgement. It is appropryed onely to his godhed to be euery
where and not to be circumscribed nor contaned in no place. And as for
our papistis prophane [C7v] voyde voyces, his bodye to be in many places
at once, indiffinitiue incircumscriptiue non per modum quanti neque
localiter &c. whiche includeth in it selfe contradiccion, of whiche Paule   25
warned Timothe .1. Timo. 6: & .2. Tim. 2 callyng them thopposicions of
a false named scyence (for that their scolasticall diuinite muste make
obieccions agaynste euery trouthe, be it neuer so playne wyth pro &
contra: whych scyence many that professe it saith Paule .1. Tim. 2. haue
erred from the faithe) as for this contencion and bataill aboute wordis   30
profitable for nothynge els, but to subuerte the herers, I care not for
them. For I haue the almyghty testymony of theuerlastinge worde of God
redy to soyle all their madde and vnreasonable reasons, to wype them
clene a waye, & to turne them into their owne confusion.

And for because they holde them so faste by Paule .1. Co. 11. I shall   35
loose their holde, expownynge the lordis souper aftir Paule, whyche
addeth immediatly vnto the cuppe, this that Luke there leaued forthe: Do
ye this in to my rememberance. This doth Paule repete so ofte to put vs in
mynde, that these thankis geuyng and souper is the commemoracion and
the memoriall of Crystis dethe. Wherfore aftir all he repeteth it yet   40
agayne the thirde tyme saynge. So oft as ye shall ete this brede (he calleth
it styll brede euen aftir the popis consecracion) & drinke the cuppe (he

saith not drynke this blood) se that ye geue thankes, be ioyouse and preche the dethe of the lorde, for so myche sygnifieth annunciate in this place, vntyll he come, that is to saye, fro the tyme of hys deathe & [C₈] ascencion vntyll he come agayne to iugement. Forthermore, saith Paule,

5 whoso ete thys brede, he calleth it styll brede, or drynke of the cuppe of the lorde vnworthely: he is gilty the bodye and blode of the lorde. The bodye & blood of the lorde Paule calleth here the congregacion assembled toghyther to ete the lordis souper. For they ar hys body and blood whych ar remeded wyth his body and blode, as he sayde in the .10. cap. before.

10 The cuppe of thankis geuynge whyche we receyue wyth thankis: is it not the felowship of the blood of Cryste? The brede whyche we breke, is it not the felowship of the bodye of Cryst? For we beyng many togither ar one brede, euen one bodye. Lo here Paule expownyng hymselfe vseth the same forme of speche that is vsed in these wordis This is my bodye,

15 takyng Is, for signifieth. We are one brede euen one bodye, that is to saye, we ar signified be one lofe of bred to be one bodye, he shewethe the cause, adding because we be all partakers of one lofe or pese of brede. And in the .12. cap. folowing, he sayth playnely. Ye be the bodye of Cryste and hys partyclar members, and in the firste cap. to thephesians. God dyd set

20 Cryste to be the head ouer all vnto hys congregacion whyche hys bodye .&c.

And because the comparyson in the .10. cap. betwene the lordys borde & hys cuppe, and the deuillys borde and hys cuppe, do declare thys mater. I shall recyte Paulys wordis saynge ye maye not drynke the cuppe

25 of the lord, & the cuppe of the deuyll bothe togyther. Ye may not be partakers of the lordis borde & the deuylls borde bothe at once. The deuyls bord and his [C₈v] cuppe was not hys body and blode, but the etynge and drynkynge before theyr images and Idolls as dyd the haithen in the worshyp and thankys of thyr Gods, of whyche thynge thou maist

30 gather what Paule ment by the lordis borde and his cuppe. Now let vs retourne to Paule in the .11. cap. Thei eate thys brede and drynke of this cuppe vnworthely, that come not vnto thys borde with suche faithe and loue as they professed at theyr baptisme. They ete vnworthely that thrusted them selues in among thys congregacion hauyng not the loue

35 that this sacrament and sygne of vnyte techethe & sygnyfyeth, whych maner of people Paule in thys same ca. rebukethe, & bendethe all hys sermon agenste them: for that they were contensyouse, and came togyther not for the better but for the worse. So that thyr comyng togither whyche shuld haue bene a token of faithe and loue, was turned into thoccasyon

40 and mater of dissencion and stryfe: because euery man dyd ete (as Paule sayth) hys owne souper and not the lordys souper: wheryn the brede and drynke is comon as well to the pore as to the ryche. But here the ryche

dysdayned the pore and wolde not tarye for them, so that some (as y^e
ryche) wente theyr waye dronken and ful: and the pore departed hongrye
& drye, whyche was a token of no egal distrybucion of the brede and
drynke: and that the ryche comtemned the pore and so became sclaunderouse and gyltie of y^e body and blode of Cryste: that is to wite, of y^e 5
pore congregacion redemed wyth Crystis body and blode. Thus they that
came togyther aperyng to haue had that loue whyche the sou[D$_1$]per
signifyed, and had it not, vttered them selues by thys contenciouse &
vnlouynge dealyng not to be members of Crystys bodye, but rather gyltye
& hurtfull vnto them. As if a soudyer of our aduersaryes parte shulde 10
come in among vs wythe our lordis badge, hauynge not that herte faythe
and loue to our capitayne that we haue, we wolde (if we espyed it by any
token) take hym for a spye and betrayer rather then one of vs.

Let a man therfore sayth Paule proue him selfe well before, whyther he
hathe thys faythe to Cryste and loue to God and hys neghbour whych all 15
he professed at baptisme, & thys souper signyfyed: and so come in
emonge the congregacion to ete of thys brede & drynke of this cuppe (he
calleth it styll brede & wyne: and nether hys body nor blode). For he that
etith and drinketh vnworthely, etheth & drynketh his own dampnacion:
because he discryueth not the lordis bodye. He calleth styll the lordis 20
bodye the congregacion redemed wyth Crystis body, as he dyd before,
and also in the chap. folowynge fetchyng hys analogy and simyletude at
the naturall bodye. In whyche althoughe ther be diuerse members one
exellynge a nother, one inferior, vyler & more contemptible then a nother
yet may not the bodye want them: but must kouer them reuerently, & 25
holde them in honour. Ageyn, in the bodye, thoughe therbe dyuerse
members of diuerse offices: yet is ther no discorde emonge them: but
euery member, be it neuer so low & vyle: yet dothe it mynister & serue a
nother, and al togither holde vp & helpe the wholl bodye. This consider-
acion with these com[D$_1$v]parysons so eloquently, so playntuously, so 30
lyuely dothe Paule set forthe in that .12. chap. that noman can desyer any
more. And all to bringe vs into the consyderacyon & discrecyon of the
bodye of Cryste whyche is hys congregacyon: wythout whyche consyderacion & discrecion, if we thrust our selues yn wyth this signe & cognisans
faynedly: we be but hypocrites and ete and drynke our owne iugement. 35
For thys cause many are syke amonge you, and many ar a slepe, that is,
ar dede. Here it semeth some plage to haue bene caste vpon the Corinth
for this abuse in the etyng of the lordis souper. For bothe the lawe and
prophetis thretened vs plages as pestilence, famyne: & swerde for our
synnes. For yf we had iuged our soules, that is, If we had dilygently 40
examined our owne lyuinge and repented: we shulde not haue ben iuged,
that is to saye, punisshed of the lorde. But whyle we be punyshed, we be

corrected of the lorde leste we shuld be condempned wythe the worlde.
Wherfore my brethern, when ye come togyther to eate, tary one for a
nother. Here is the cause of all thys dissention wherfor Paule rebuketh
them. But here myght some of them obiecte & tell Paule, Syr we come
5   hyther hongry & may not tarye so longe. Wher vnto Paulle answereth as
he dyd before: saynge, Haue ye not houses to ete & drynke yn? Do ye
contempne the congregacyon of God & shame them that haue non? Here
he calleth the pore, the chyrche of god, whom aftyrward he called the
body of the lorde: and now at laste he sayth. If any man be so hongry, let
10 hym ete somwhat at home, & so delaye hys honger that he may the beter
ta[D2]ry for the pore, leste ye come togither vnto your condempnacyon.
And as for other thyngys I shall dispose and set in ordyr when I come.
These other thynges were concerning this souper, & siche as were out of
frame emong them whyche yf ye rede the wholl pystle, ar efte esye to se:
15 & that they were no necessary trouthes for their saluacion, for al syche
trouthes Paule had preched them before and wrytten them to. Nether
were these other thyngys lente, faste, thassumpcion of our lady, halowyng
of bowes bellis and asshes, halowyng of vestymentis, & crepynge to the
crosse, wyth siche other vnwryten vanites, as M. More listethe to ieste and
20 tryfull out the trouthe.

Now haue ye the very pure sence of these Crystis wordis. Thys is my
bodye, that is to say. Thys signifyethe or representethe my bodye, takynge
Est for significat. As M. More hymselfe vttered it in hys Dyaloge put
forthe in wylliam Barlows name, reciting the opinyons of Ecolampadius &
25 zwinglius: saynge, thys is my body, is as miche to saye as thys sygnyfyeth
my body, wher he sayth that Ecolampadius allegeth for hym Tertulyan,
Chrystostome, and Austen, but falsely somtyme addynge more to their
wordis, sometyme takynge awaye frome their sentencis. Whych sayng is
playne false, and he belyethe the man now departed, for fyrste hys incom-
30 parable lernynge and very spirituall iugement wolde not suffer hym to be
ignorant in the vnderstanding of these olde holy doctours (whom I dare
saye) he vnderstode as well as More. And his conscience & faythfulnes
wold not suffer him falsely to peruerte [D2v] them as More belyethe and
peruertethe Cryste and Paule & all holy scripture. And yf this man had
35 thus delte wyth these doctours sayngis: Luther agaynste whome he dyd
contend in this mater wolde not haue lefte it vntolde him.

But (Christen reder) to put the oute of doute haue here these Doctours
owne wordis bothe in latyne & in englysshe. And firste heare Tertullyan,
where thou muste fyrste vnderstande that there was an heretyk called
40 Marcyon, sayng that Cryste toke not to him the very bodye of man, but
an imagined and phantasticall bodye, to put of, and on, whan he lysted:
& so not to haue ben borne verely of the virgen Marye, nor yet to haue

Tertulyan suffered verely dethe &c. Agenst whom, thus wrytteth Tertullian in hys .4. boke.

Professus itaque se concupiscentia concupisse edere pascha, vt suum acceptum panem & distributum discipulis corpus suum illum fecit, hoc est corpus meum dicendo: id est figura corporis mei. Figura autem non fuisset, nisi veritatis esset corpus. Ceterum, vacua res, quod est phantasma, figuram capere non posset. Whyche wordis are thus in englishe spoken of Cryste. Whiche acknowleginge himselfe wyth how feruent desyer he longed to ete the passouer, as his brede taken & distributed to hys disciples: made it his bodye saynge: This is my bodye: that is to saye, the fygure of my bodye. For fygure had it be none, excepte it were a verye bodye. For a voyde thinge whiche is a phantasye can receue no fygure. Here is it playne, that This is my bodye after olde holye doctours is as miche to saye as this is the fygure or signe that representeth or signifyeth my bodye. [D₃]

Also, thus sayth Austen. Lex dicit non esse manducandum sanguinem,
Austen ca. 12 agaynste adimant quod anima sit sanguis. Quod lex dicit, sanguis est anima: esse positum dicimus, sicut alia multa et pene omnia scripturarum illarum sacramenta signis et figuris plena future predicationis, que iam per dominum nostrum Iesum Christum declarata est &c. Possum etiam interpretari preceptum illud in signo esse positum. Non enim dubitauit dominus dicere: Hoc est corpus meum, quum signum daret corporis sui. Sic est enim sanguis anima, quomodo petra erat Christus. Nec tamen quum hec diceret, ait: petra significabat Christum, sed ait: petra erat Christus. Que rursus ne carnaliter acciperetur, spiritualem illam vocat. id
Gen. 9 Leui. 7 Deut. 12 est spiritualiter intelligi docet. Whiche wordis ar thus in englisshe. The lawe sayth that blood shuld not be eten, because the lyfe is bloode. Whiche precept of the lawe and because that bloode is lyfe: we affirme it to be sette lyke as many of her almost innumerable sacramentis of those scriptures, full of sygnes and fygures of the prechinge to come: whiche nowe is declared by our lorde Iesu Cryste &c. And I maye interprete that precept to be layed in a sygne. For the lorde douted not to saye This is my body: when he gaue the sygne of his bodye. And euen so is the blode lyfe, as the stone was Cryste. And yet when he said these wordes: he sayd not the stone signifyed Cryste: but he sayd, the stone was Criste. Whiche leste they shulde be taken carnally, he callethe it spirituall, that is to saye, he techeth it to be vnderstande spiritually. Where is now Moris litterall sence, and materiall meat? [D₃v]

Now shal ye heare Chrysostome. Nihil sensibile tradidit Christus: licet

Hom. 83 operis
imperfecti

dederit panem et vinum: non quod panis &
vinum non sint sensibilia, sed quod in illis
mentem herere noluit. Nam in suum corpus,
quod est panis vite, subuehit dicens. Hoc est corpus meum: perinde ac
5   dicat Hoc licet panis sit, significat tamen tibi corpus. Thus it is in
englysshe. Cryste geuinge brede and wyne, gaue no sensible thynge: not
that brede and wyne be not sensible: but that he wolde not our mynde to
steke styll in them, For he lyfted vs vp into his bodye, whiche is the brede
of lyfe: sayng. This is my bodye: as though he shuld saye. Thoughe this
10 be but brede, yet it signifyethe vnto the, my bodye. Now iudge thou
(Christen reder) whither M More reportethe ryghte, of thys man that
alleged these olde holy doctours, or no.

Nowe haue ye the pure vnderstandynge of the wordis of the lordes

The confutacion
of the
papistes gloses

souper confirmed wyth the olde holy doctours. That this is my bodye, is as miche to
saye, as this signifyeth my body. And this
is my bloode: is, this sygnyfyethe my bloode:
But yet was there neuer siche maner of speking in the scripture This is
that That is to saye, This is conuerted & transsubstanciated into that. Or
20 this is contayned in that: the thinge conuerted and changed, kepping styll
her forme, qualites, quantite &c. As to saye. This is my body, that is to
saye. This brede is conuerted into my bodye, the brede abyding styll in
his fasshion, taste, colour, waight &c. For Cryste when he conuerted
water into wyne, dyd not leue the forme, colour, and taste styll in the
25 water. For so had it bene no [D4] changing. But let our couetouse conuerters choppe and change brede & wyne tyll we there fele se and taste
nether brede nor wyne, & then wyll we beleue them so thei bringe for
them the worde of god. For as for their false iugelinge we fele it at our
fyngers ende: we se it, had we but halfe an eye: we cast it at our tongues
30 ende, and know it with all our wittis and vnderstanding so manifestly,
that we parceyued them openly longe a goo, to be the very anticrystis, of
whom Cryste and his apostles warned vs to come in this laste tyme.

And if they saye. That this conuersion is made by miracle. Then muste
euery one of them as ofte as he say a misse make vs many a miracle the
35 very markis of Moris chirche. For it is one grete miracle that Crystis body
shulde come so sodenly inuisible and so ofte out of heuen, and that suche
a miracle as the worde of god neuer knew: a nother that to [i.e., so] grete
a body shuld be contayned in so litel a place, and that one bodye shulde
be at once in so many placis and two bodyes in one place, an other that it
40 is eten nether the eter feling it, nor the bodye eten suffering nor feling the
tethe of the eter. which [with?] as many mo meruelouse and lyke miracles
or rather absurdites of the brede & wyne, that there muste be the forme,

coloure, taste, waight, broken &c. and yet nether to be brede nor wyne in
our belife except we wilbe burned of them because we beleue not their
iugelinge castis. O mischeuous miracle makers. O cruel conuerters. O
blodye vouchers [i.e., bouchers].

But herke, Crysten reder, and I shal lerne the to knowe Crystis playn & 5
trwe miracles, [D₄v] from the sleighthy iugglinge of these crafty conuay-
ers. Cryste wolde neuer haue done miracle had men beleued him onely by
his wordis, but when he sayd firste these wordis. This is my bodye, noman
douted at them, no man was in any vnbeleife of them. Wherfore these
wordis muste nedis be playne single & pure without miracle, as these. The 10
.3. branchis ar .3. dayes: withoute any subtyle transsubstanciacion, siche
insensible conuersion, or any false miracle. Cryste wrought al his miracles
for the glorye of god to declare him selfe bothe god and man so that all
Crystis miracles were comprehended vnder mannes sences or comon
wites, which brynge in siche knowlege vnto the vnderstondyng. As when 15
he changed water into wyne, the miracle was firste receyued withe the
syght, open at the eye, tasted withe the mouthe and so conuayed vnto the
vnderstonding. And now, thoughe we nether se nor taste that miracle, yet
we heare it, se it, rede it, and so vnderstonde that it was once a miracle
done of cryste: when he restored the syght to the blynde, heled the lame, 20
clensed the leprose, reared the deade: all was seen, herde and so comprehended vnder our most suerest sensis: that his very enimes were compelled to confesse them for miracles, But our miracle makers, that make
dayly so ofte and so many, ar so farre from this clere poynt: that their
miracles in this mater, be not, nor neuer shalbe contayned nor com- 25
prehended vnder any of our 5 wyttes, but thei rather delude and deceyue
bothe sight, taste, felinge, hering, and smellinge: ye our faith & vnderstanding to. Beware therfore of these mis[D₅]cheuous miracle makers for
their owne glorye and profit: and will kyll the to, if thou beleueste not
their lyes. Beware I saye of those marchants that wil sell the wares, 30
whiche thei wil not suffer the to se, nor to taste, nor to touche: but when
thei shewe the whight, thou muste beleue it is blak: If they geue the
brede, thou muste beleue it withoute any worde of thy faithe, that it is
Crystis body, & that of their owne makinge. If thou taste, se, & fele it
brede yet thou muste saye it is none though the scripture calleth it brede 35
.xx. tymes. Beware beware I saye of Anticryste: whose cominge sayd
Paule .1. thess .2, (he is come al redy saith Iohn .1. Ioan, 2. & now ar
there many anticrystis) shalbe aftir the workinge of Satan with an
almighty powr, withe false sygnes & wonders lyinge miracles, and with al
deceite of vnrightuousnes .&c. 40

To be to curiouse in so playn a sacrament and sygne, to cauill Crystis
clere wordis with sophistical sophismes, & to tryful out the trouthe withe

tauntis & mockis, as More dothe, is no crysten maner. And if our Papistis,
& scolasticall sophisters will obiecte & make answer to this souper of the
lorde, bringing yn for them, their vnwryten wordis, dede dremes (for we
haue compelled More withe shame to flitte frome the scripture) strewed
5   withe their vayn strange termes whiche Paule damneth, & geueth
Timothe warning of. I shall, by goddis grace, so set the almighty worde of
god agenst them that all christen shall se their falshed & deceite in this
sacrament: & so disclose their deuilessh doctryne & sleighe iugelynge,
that all that can [D₅v] rede englysshe, shall se the trouthe of Goddis
10 worde openly bere downe their vnwryten lyes. For it is verely the thinge
that I desyer, euen to be wryten agenste in this mater, for I haue the
solucions of al their obieccions redye. And knowe right wel, that the more
thei stere this sacrament, the broder shal their lyes be sprede, the more
shal their falshed apere and the more gloriously shal the trowthe tri-
15 umphe: as it is to se this daye by the longe contencion in this same, and
other lyke articles: whiche the papistis haue so longe abused, & how
More hys lyes vtter the trwthe euery daye more & more. For had he not
come begging for the clergye from purgatory, withe his supplicacion of
soulis, and Rastel & Rochester had they not so wysely playd their partis:
20 purgatory paraduenture had serued them yet a nother yere: nether had it
so sone haue ben quenched, nor the pore soule & proctour ther be with
his blody bisshop crysten catte so farre coniured into his owne Vtopia
with a sechel about his necke to gather for the proude preistis in Synagoga papistica.
25   Whan Cryste was ascended into heuen: and had sent his Apostles the
spirit of trouthe, to leade them into all trouthe perteyning vnto our saluacion euen in to him that sayd: I am the trouthe of whyche trouthe he
enstructed them aftir his resurrection. Luk. 24. and thei had preched the
same trouthe nowe in Ierusalem Act .2. at which preching ther were that
30 receyued their wordes & where baptized, abouthe 3 .M. his apostles
rememebringe how their master Cryste at his last souper did institute &
leue them this holy sacrament of his body [D₆] & blood to be celebrated
& done in hys rememberance emonge siche as had receyued his gospell,
were baptized, had professed his faythe, and wolde perseuer in his religi-
35 on, dyd nowe in this firste congregacion celebrate the lordis souper brekinge the brede & etinge it as Cryste dyd teche them, whiche souper,
Luke & Paule called afterwarde the brekinge of the brede. As Acto, 2.
saynge. That they which gladly had nowe receyued Peters acte, & were
baptized: were perseuerynge in the doctrine of the apostles, and in the
40 communion, & in the breakinge of the brede, and in prayer, whiche
sacramente was now a token of the perseuerance in theyr cristen religion
nowe professed. Off thys brekinge of brede, Luke wrytynge of Paule

coming vpon Troadem, sayth Act. 20. also, that there vpon a sabbot daye, when the disciples were come togyther vnto the brekinge of the brede: Paule made a sermon during to mydnight &c. And that this was no comen nor prophane vse but an heuenly sacrament and a reuerent ryte and vsage, the circumstancis of the action declare, bothe in Luke and Paule, shewyng it to be the very institucion that Cryste ordened at his soupere, Paule thus recytynge this brekeynge of the brede: sayng. The brede which we breke, is it not the felawship of the bodye of Cryste? that is to saye dothe it not signify vs to be the bodye of Criste that is his congregacion and his peple, as dothe the wordes folowinge declare? Paule addinge the cause saynge For we being many are all togyther signifyed by the one lofe to be one bodye: for that we be partakers of the same brede. Also before, he [D₆v] callethe in the same souper, the cuppe of thankis geuinge the felawshyp of the blode of Cryste, that is to saye, the congregacion redemed with Crystis bloode.

Thys holy sacrament therfore, wolde god it were restored vnto the pure vse, as thapostles vsed it in theyr tyme. Wolde God, the seculare prynces whyche shulde be the very pastours and hed rulers of their congregacions committed vnto their cure, wolde fyrste commaunde or suffer the trwe prechers of goddis worde to preche the gospell purely and plainly wyth discrete lyberte: and constitute ouer eche particulare parysshe syche curatis as can and wolde preche the worde, and that once or twyse in the weke, apoyntynge vnto their flocke certayne dayes aftyr their discrecion and zele to godwarde, to come to gyther to celebrate the lordis souper. At the whyche assemble the curate wolde propowne and declare them fyrste thys texte of Paule. 1. Corynth .11. So ofte as ye shal ete this brede and drinke of this cuppe: se that ye be ioyouse, prayse, and geue thankys prechyng the dethe of the lorde .&c. whyche declared, and euery one exhorted to prayer, he wolde preche them purely Cryste to haue dyed and ben offred vpon the altare of the Crosse for their redempcion: whyche onely oblacion to be a sufficyent sacryfice to peace the fathers wrathe, and to purge all the synnes of the worlde. Then to excyte them wyth all homble dilygence euery man vnto the knowlege of him selfe and hys synnes: and to beleue and truste to the forgeuenes in Crystis blode: and for this so incomparable benefyt of oure redempcion [D₇] (whiche were solde bondmen to synne) to gyue thankis vnto God the father for so mercyfull a delyuerance thorowe the deathe of Iesu Cryste, euery one, some synginge and some saynge deuoutely, some or other psalme or prayer of thankes geuinge in the mother tonge. Then, the brede and wyne set before them in the face of the chirche vpon the table of the lorde purely and honestly layed, let hym declare to the people the significacions of those sensyble signes, what the accion and dede mouethe, techethe and

exhortethe them vnto: and that the brede and wyne be no prophane
comen signes: but holy sacraments reuerently to be consydered and
receyued with a depe faithe and rememberance of Crystis dethe and of
the shedynge of his blood for our synnes, those sensible thinges to rep-
5 resent vs the very bodye and bloode of Cryste, so that whyle euery man
beholde with his corporall eye those sensible sacramentis: the inwarde eye
of his faithe maye se and beleue stedfastlye Cryste offred and dying vpon
the crosse for his synnes, how his bodye was broken & his blood shed for
vs, and hathe geuen himselfe wholl for vs, himselfe to be all oures, & what
10 so euer he dyd, it to serue vs, as to be made for vs of hys father our
rightwysnes, our wysdome, holynes, redempcion satisfaccion &c. 1.
Corinth .1.

Then let thys preacher exhorte them louingly to drawe nere vnto thys
table of the lorde, and that not onelye bodelye, but also (their hertes
15 pourged by faythe, garnyshed with loue and innocencye) euerye man to
forgeue eache other vnfaynedlye, and to expresse [D₇v] or at lestwyse to
endeuour them to folow that loue whiche Cryste dyd set before our eyes
at his laste souper when he offred himselfe willingly to dye for vs his
enymes. Whiche incomparable loue to commende, brynge in Paulis argu-
20 mentis. Roma. 5. so that thus, thys flocke maye come togyther, and be
ioyned into one bodye, one spirite, and one peple. Thys done, let him
come downe: and accompaned honestely wyth other ministers come
forthe reuerently vnto the lordis table, the congregacion nowe set rownd
aboute it, & also in their other conuenient seatis, the pastour exhortinge
25 them all to praye for grace faithe and loue, whyche all this sacrament
signifyethe and puttethe them in mynde of. Then let ther be redde apertely and distinctly the .6. cap. of Iohan in theyr mother tongue: wherby
they maye clerely vnderstand, what it is to eate Crystis flesshe and to
drynke his bloode. This done, and some breyfe prayer and prayse songe
30 or redde, lette one or other minister rede the .11. chap. of the fyrste to the
Corinths, that the peple myghte perceyue clerely of those wordis the
mystery of thys Crystes souper, & wherfore he dyd institute it.

These wyth siche lyke preparacions and exhortacions hadde, I wolde
euery man presente shuld professe the articles of oure faythe openly in our
35 mother tongue, and confesse his synnes secretly vnto God, praynge intier-
ly that he wolde nowe vouchsafe to haue mercy vpon him, receyue his
prayers, glwe his harte vnto hym by faythe and loue encrease his fayth,
geue him grace to forgeue and to loue hys neyghbour as himselfe, to
garnesshe his life with pu[D₈]renes ond innocencye, and to confyrme hym
40 in al goodnes and vertu. Then agen it behoueth the curate to warne &
exhorte euery man depely to consyder and expende wyth hym selfe the

sygnificacyon and substance of thys sacrament so that he sytte not downe
an ypocryte & a dissembler, sith god is sercher of herte and raynes
thoughtis and effectis: and see that he come not to the holy table of the
lorde wythout that fayth whych he professed at hys baptisme, and also
that loue whych the sacrament precheth & testifyeth vnto hys herte, leste   5
he now fownde gyltie the body & blood of the lorde, that is to wytte a
dessembler wyth Crystis dethe & sclaunderouse to the congregacyon, the
body & blode of Cryste: receyue hys owne dampnacion. And here let
euery man fall downe vpon his knees sayng secretely wyth al deuocion
their Pater noster in englysshe, their curate as ensample knelyng downe   10
before them. Whyche done, let hym take the brede & efte the wyne in the
syght of the peple herynge hym with a lowde voyce, wyth godly grauite,
& aftir a crysten relygiouse reuerence rehersynge distinctely the wordis of
the lordis souper in theyr mother tongue. And then distrybute it to the
ministers, whyche takynge the brede wyth grete reuerence, wyl deuyde it   15
to the congregacyon euery man breking & rechyng it forthe to hys nexte
neghbour and member of the mystik body of Cryst, other mynisters folowyng wythe the cuppis powering forthe & dealynge them the wyne, all
togyther thus beynge now partakers of one brede & one cuppe, the
thynge therby sygnifyed & precheth prynted fast in their hertys, But in   20
this meane [D₈v] whyll, must the minister or pastour be readyng the
communicacion that Cryste had wyth his disciples aftyr hys souper. Io.
13. begynnynge at the wasshynge of their fete: so redynge tyll the brede
& wyne be eten & dronken and all the accion done. And then let them all
fal downe on their knees geuinge thankis highely vnto god the father, for   25
thys benyfyt & dethe of hys sone, wherby nowe be faithe euery man is
assuered of remyssion of hys synnes, as this blessed sacrament had put
them in mynde & preched it them in thys vtwarde accion & souper. This
done, let euery man commende and geue them selfe whol to god, &
departe.   30

I wolde haue herto put mi name, good reder, but I know wel that thou
regardest not who wryteth, but what is wryten thou estemest the word of
the veryte, & not of the autor. And as for M. Mocke, whom the veryte
most offendeth, & doth but mocke it oute when he can not soyle it: he
knowth my name well inoughe. For the deuyl hys gardian, as hym selfe   35
sayth, cometh euery daye into purgatory, yf therby [i.e., ther be] there
any day at all, wyth hys emnyouse & enuyouse laughter, gnasshyng his
tethe & gryning, tellyng the proctour wyth hys popis presoners, what so
euer is here done or wryten agenst them, both hys persone & name to.
And he is now, I dare saye, as gret wyth hys gardian, as euer he was.   40

If any man tell ye, lo here is Cryste, or ther is he beleue hym not, For

Mat. 24   ther shal aryse false crystes false anoynted
geuyng grete miracles. Take hede, I haue
tolde ye before, yf thei therfore tel ye: lo, he is in the deserte, go not forth:
lo he is in the preuye pixe, beleue it not.

5   Inprinted at Nornburg by Niclas twonson.
.5. April. An. 1533.

APPENDIX B

The Probable Author of
The Souper of the Lorde:
George Joye

BY MICHAEL ANDEREGG

APPENDIX B

The Probable Author of The Souper of the Lorde: *George Joye*

The authorship of *The Souper of the Lorde* has been in doubt ever since, sometime after the early spring of 1533, Thomas More first read this new addition to a long list of heretical books and began to compose an answer. That an answer was required, More never doubted: the anonymous tract not only presented a strong, unequivocal denial of Catholic eucharistic dogma, but the author also claimed to have confuted (as the full title states) *M. Moris letter agenst Iohan Frythe.* More might nevertheless have been excused for ignoring an anonymous work; as he was beginning to discover (and no doubt lament), to the refuting of heretical writings there was no end. His 1529 *Dialogue concerning Heresies,* aimed primarily at Tyndale, had given impetus to Tyndale's *Answere vnto Sir Thomas Mores dialoge* (1531), which in turn fed the massive counterblast of More's *Confutation* (1532–33). This last work would then be attacked in George Joye's *Subuersion of Moris false foundacion* (1534). The war of words seemed to be self-generating and endless.

The eucharistic controversy threatened to entangle More in a long and drawn-out dispute similar to his battle with Tyndale; nevertheless, he forged bravely on. Before Christmas 1533, *The answere to the fyrst parte of the poysened booke* issued from Rastell's press. Though far longer than *The Souper,* More's *Answer* undertook to counter only the first half of that "blasphemouse, and ... bedelem rype" work (7/2–3). One of More's initial concerns in responding to *The Souper* was the problem of authorship: "whose yt is," he writes, "I can not surely say"; some say Tyndale, some George Joye (7/18–23). But More turns his ignorance to his own advantage. Learned men, he writes, think *The Souper* to be Joye's, because Tyndale had once remarked that if Joye published a work on the eucharist, "there shold be founden in it many reasons & very few to the purpose" (7/35–8/4). However, More continues, this cannot be the work in question, for "in this boke be there very fewe reasons, and of them all neuer one to the purpose" (8/6–7). In any case, More cannot be expected to tell one mad foolish book from another. Maybe the author is neither

Tyndale nor Joye, but "some yonge vnlerned fole" (8/31). On second thought, More hastens to add, both Tyndale and Joye are quite capable of such folly. Of course, there is one good reason to ascribe the work to Joye: he (like Barnes) was held in so little regard by the brethren that he would naturally be afraid of putting his name to such a work.

Even though More continues in this vein, on and off, throughout *The Answer*, he decides early on to refer to his opponent as "Master Masker." That More could not discover the author's name is in itself somewhat surprising, since he knew so much about the doings of the Protestant exiles. Indeed, the author of *The Souper* had remarked that "M. Mocke . . . knowth my name well inoughe" (Appendix A, 339/33–35). But we have no reason to suspect More of indulging in a pose; had he known the name of his adversary, he would certainly have exploited his knowledge. Without making too great a point of the author's failure to identify himself (as he hardly could, having himself published the *Responsio* pseudonymously on two occasions), More does benefit rhetorically from his opponent's anonymity. Occasionally, More hints that he might actually know who the Masker is. More claims that Master Masker "maketh yet his mater mych wurse than wyllyam Tyndale" (120/36–37). At another point, he shows that the Masker "is of mayster Tindals secte, or is peraduenture mayster Tyndale hym selfe" (104/30–32). But in fact he leaves the matter open throughout *The Answer*, using the guessing game more for polemical emphasis than as a genuine contribution toward unmasking his adversary. He prefers to leave us with the impression that all heretics are pretty much alike.

Other Investigators

The Souper of the Lorde has been ascribed to Tyndale, Joye, and (on at least one occasion) Coverdale. By the nineteenth century, Tyndale seemed to have pretty well won the contest. In our own time, however, the controversy has been rekindled and new arguments have been advanced in favor of both Tyndale and Joye. Proponents of each view have put forward their claims with a great deal of assurance, but the paucity of hard factual information belies such certainty. Tyndale's case has been argued most ably in the writings of his first twentieth-century biographer, J. F. Mozley. Joye has been championed by, among others, W. D. J. Cargill Thompson and William A. Clebsch. Mozley has found support in Joye's modern biographers, Charles C. Butterworth and Allan G. Chester.

On the other hand, a recent student of Tyndale, Norman Davis, believes that *The Souper* is " very probably the work of George Joye."[1]

The arguments in favor of Tyndale's authorship (principally Mozley's) may be outlined briefly:

1. John Foxe, in his edition of *The Whole workes of W. Tyndall, Iohn Frith, and Doct. Barnes* (1573), suggests that Tyndale wrote *The Souper* and reprints it along with the rest of Tyndale's works.

2. Tyndale was a close friend of Frith, and hence the logical person to defend Frith against More's attacks.

3. *The Souper* does not tally with Tyndale's description of the eucharistic tract he ascribed to Joye in his letter to Frith (c. January 1533).

4. *The Souper* is Zwinglian; Joye was not a likely Zwinglian.

5. *The Souper* is too able a work for Joye's pen.

6. *The Souper* contains specifically Tyndalian themes: More is a poet; attack on the *Utopia*; reference to More's use of "quod he" and "quod I" in his *Dialogue*.

7. Several allusions in *The Souper* point to Tyndale. Specifically, the reference to "blody bisshop crysten-catte" (Appendix A, 336/22) as a description of Stokesley would more probably be known to Tyndale, who was at Oxford when Stokesley was, than to Joye, who was not. Also, the reference to More's use of "yea" and "nay" points to Tyndale, whom More had accused of misusing those words.

8. The style and wording of *The Souper* are "Tyndalian."

9. Burnet's list of forbidden books, which ascribes *The Souper* to Joye, is not a reliable source.

10. Foxe, who ascribes the work to Tyndale, is as good a source as John Bale, who ascribes it to Joye.

It soon becomes apparent that few of these points are of much objective value. Point 1 is undoubtedly the strongest. But even this is undercut by

---

[1] Mozley presents his arguments in *William Tyndale* (New York, 1937), pp. 223, 252–53; "Tyndale's 'Supper of the Lord,'" *Notes and Queries*, *183* (21 November 1942), 305–06 and *185* (31 July 1943), 87; "George Joye, or Gee," *Notes and Queries*, *185* (23 October 1943), 252–53; *Coverdale and His Bibles* (London, 1953), p. 342; "The Supper of the Lord 1533," *Moreana*, *10* (1966), 11–16. For Thompson, see "Who Wrote 'The Supper of the Lord'?" *Harvard Theological Review*, *53* (1960), 77–91. For Clebsch, see "More Evidence That George Joye Wrote the Souper of the Lorde," *Harvard Theological Review*, *55* (1962), 63–66, and *England's Earliest Protestants: 1520–1535* (New Haven, 1964), pp. 96, 213. Butterworth and Chester ascribe *The Souper* to Tyndale in *George Joye: 1495?–1533* (Philadelphia, 1962), p. 93. For Norman Davis, see *William Tyndale's English of Controversy*, Chambers Memorial Lecture (University College, London, 1971), p. 5.

Foxe's uncertainty: he reprints *The Souper* only as an appendix to Tyndale's works. Point 2 has value if we assume that *The Souper* was written exclusively and specifically to aid Frith, but we have no real evidence that this was so; indeed, Tyndale's letter to Frith suggests that controversy will endanger rather than help him. In any case, we need not argue that only a close friend of Frith's would have defended his views and tried to save his life. Point 3 attempts only to deny that Joye is the author; it assumes, illegitimately, that if Joye wrote a treatise on the eucharist, it would have to fit Tyndale's description. The fourth point raises a complex issue; certainly, as we shall see, *The Souper* is "Zwinglian" in effect, but that Joye was not a likely Zwinglian would be difficult to prove. Points 5 and 8 are purely subjective. The sixth argument is stronger but other Protestant polemicists, including Joye and Frith, have made reference to More's status as a poet and to the "lies" of *Utopia*. By the same token, anyone could make fun of More's "quod he and quod I and quod your friend." Point 7 is weak, for the reasons just alleged. The ninth point may be accepted without any advancement of Tyndale's case, and the final argument adds very little one way or the other: Foxe is tentative, whereas Bale is quite definite.

The evidence favoring Joye's authorship may be similarly catalogued. The following outline has been abstracted primarily from articles and references by Thompson and Clebsch.

1. John Bale's *Scriptorum summarium* (1548) and *Scriptorum . . . catalogus* (1557) ascribe *The Souper* to Joye.
2. Tyndale's letter to Frith, written sometime after Christmas 1532, suggests that Joye was planning to publish a work on the eucharist.
3. Unlike other known works by Tyndale, *The Souper* contains no references to the original tongues of the Bible.
4. Bonner's list of forbidden books (reprinted in Burnet)[1] ascribes *The Souper* to Joye.
5. *The Souper* was not associated with Tyndale until 1573 (by Foxe).
6. More's opinion in *The Answer to a Poisoned Book* weighs in Joye's favor.
7. Robert Crowley, who wrote a preface to the 1548 edition of *The Souper*, does not say that the author was a martyr, as Tyndale (but not Joye) was.
8. In 1533 Tyndale was opposed to any discussion of the sacrament.
9. Joye was in the habit of publishing his works anonymously; Tyndale was not.

---

[1] See p. 351, n. 1, below.

10. No work on the sacraments by Joye is extant; but both Tyndale and More refer to such a work by Joye.

11. The doctrinal ideas in *The Souper*—particularly the appeal to civil authorities and the suggestion of a model eucharistic service—conflict with Tyndale's known views.

12. The style of *The Souper* resembles Joye's rather than Tyndale's.

13. The long, elaborate title points to Joye's practice.

14. *The Souper* is a patchwork job, and hence fits More's hypothesis that Joye has enlarged a former treatise "by a pyece that he hath patched in agaynst me" (7/31–32).

15. The method of citing from the New Testament in *The Souper* is peculiar to Joye.

16. *The Souper* refers to Frith as "the young man"; Tyndale, who greatly admired Frith, would not have done so.

17. Joye, as would be expected if he were the author of *The Souper*, responded to More's *Answer* in his *Subuersion of Moris false foundacion* (a signed work).

The proponents of Joye's cause seem, generally speaking, to offer more evidence than do those who champion Tyndale. But many of their arguments are quite weak, and a few completely lack substance. Points 1 and 4 are the strongest single pieces of external evidence; against them, we must place the evidence of Foxe and Mozley's comments on Bale and on Burnet's list of forbidden books. Point 6 would also be a strong piece of external evidence if the conclusion were justified, but, as I have already argued, the evidence does not bear such an interpretation. It is amusing (and instructive) to note that Henry Walter, in his introduction to the Parker Society edition of *The Souper*, claims that More takes for granted throughout *The Answer* "that the writer to whom he is replying is none other than Tyndale."[1] Mozley, in his biography of Tyndale, makes very much the same comment.[2]

Points 2 and 14 should be taken together, for they both hinge on Tyndale's letter to Frith. These arguments are sound only if we assume Tyndale is describing something he has actually read or heard about in some detail. But, clearly, Tyndale's comments are not so much a description as a prediction based on his low opinion of Joye's capabilities. "George Ioye," Tyndale wrote, "would haue put foorth a treatise of the matter, but I haue stopt hym as yet, what he will doe if he get money, I

---

[1] William Tyndale, *Works*, ed. Henry Walter 3 vols., Parker Society 42–44 (Cambridge, 1848–50), *3*, 218.

[2] *William Tyndale*, p. 253.

wotte not. I beleue he wold make many reasons litle seruyng to the purpose."[1] We cannot conclude from Tyndale's words that he had actually seen Joye's treatise. By the same reasoning, More's comment— based on Tyndale's words—that Joye could have written *The Souper* because "in this boke be there very fewe reasons, and of them all neuer one to the purpose" (8/6–7) hardly proves Joye's authorship. Even if *The Souper* is "a patchwork job" as Clebsch insists, Joye need not have been the author of it. Point 3 was anticipated, and answered reasonably well, by Mozley. Certainly, the briefness of *The Souper* makes it both difficult and dangerous to apply to it the "characteristic" habits of any particular writer. Still, this remains one of the strongest pieces of presumptive evidence against Tyndale's authorship, although it does little to advance Joye's cause.

Points 5, 7, 8, 11, and 16 are advanced to tell against Tyndale rather than for Joye. The fifth point proves little except that we have no record that *The Souper* was ascribed to Tyndale before 1573. The evidence of Crowley's preface carries weight only if we could demonstrate that Crowley himself knew who the author was; but his vague allusions to "the author" are made for ease of reference and are totally impersonal in tone. Point 8 again refers to Tyndale's letter to Frith; his exact words are: "I would haue the right vse [of the sacrament] preached, and the presence to be an indifferent thyng, till the matter might be reasoned in peace at laysure, of both parties."[2] Mozley counters this by suggesting that once Tyndale heard Frith was in extreme danger and unable to answer More's arguments, he stepped into the breach and came to his friend's aid. Mozley quickly adds that the passage is "indecisive," which is true enough. The argument of point 11 is quite important, opening up as it does a broad field of inquiry which will be taken up in its place. Point 16 nicely illustrates what can happen when we ignore the literary and rhetorical structure of a work in our concern for other matters: the author of *The Souper* refers to Frith as "the young man" in direct and sarcastic echo of More, who in *A Letter against Frith* constantly appeals to his own wisdom and that of other sage and learned men as against Frith's relative inexperience and youth.

The remaining arguments (9, 10, 12, 13, 15, and 17) are all meant to support Joye's authorship. The issue of anonymity is a valid one. As Anthea Hume notes, "there is no evidence that Tyndale ever published works anonymously after 1526."[3] But a good half-dozen of Joye's tracts

---

[1] *WW*, sig. CC₄.

[2] *WW*, sig. CC₄.

[3] *CW 8*, 1078.

and translations were issued either anonymously or pseudonymously throughout the 1530s and 1540s. The tenth point proves little, and Thompson, who advances it, himself presents part of the counter-argument:

> It should, however, be pointed out that Bale mentions two other treatises on the eucharist in his list of Joye's works—De Baptismo et Eucharistia . . . , which is listed in both editions of his Catalogue . . .; and De Eucharistia . . . which is only mentioned in the 1557 edition . . . . These works are not recorded in the Short-Title Catalogue and appear to be otherwise unknown.[1]

To this should be added the opinion of Butterworth and Chester that a work entitled *A frutefull treatis of baptyme and the Lordis souper* (1541) is "possibly by Joye." The argument from style (12), presented without supporting evidence, holds no more weight than Mozley's equally strong assurance that *The Souper* is "Tyndalian." The long and elaborate title does suggest Joye's practice, but long titles were very common among sixteenth-century writers: witness Frith's *A disputacion of purgatorye* (*STC* 11388) and Tyndale's *An exposicion vppon the. v. vi. vii. chapters of Mathew* (*STC²* 24440). Clebsch's assertion (15) that the New Testament citations in *The Souper* are peculiar to Joye, who usually paraphrased Tyndale's version of the New Testament, is not precisely accurate: at least one other polemicist, as we shall see, cited scripture the same way—Tyndale himself. The final point (17), even if acceptable in theory, again falls down in fact; Joye's *Subuersion* responds not to More's *Answer* (which he evidently had not yet seen) but to other works by More, particularly his *Confutation* and *Apology*.

The findings of previous investigators, then, still leave the matter of authorship uncertain, although the arguments favoring Joye have, in the last few years, convinced many students of the English Reformation either to champion Joye or at least to reject Tyndale. Anthea Hume, Norman Davis, and Rainer Pineas,[2] among others, have advanced Joye's claim

---

[1] "Who Wrote 'The Supper of the Lord'?" p. 87, n. 35. It is clear, however, that "De Eucharistia" refers specifically to *The Souper*. John Bale's notebook, edited by Reginald Lane Poole under the title *Index Britanniae Scriptorum* (Oxford, 1902), lists *The Souper* as *De Eucharistia*. The *incipit*—"Non mirandum, chari fratres, si Sathan"—translates the beginning of Robert Crowley's preface to a reprint of *The Souper*. "De Eucharistia" is the title of the section partly translated by the Masker from Zwingli's *De vera et falsa religione commentarius*. The *Index* also attributes to More "Laruam, aduersus Georgium Ioye."

[2] For Pineas, see "George Joye's Controversy with Thomas More," *Moreana*, *38* (1973), 27–36.

without, however, presenting any new evidence. The issue has all along been clouded somewhat by the stated or unstated prejudices of the investigator. Mozley's conclusions, for example, depend to some extent on his generally low opinion of George Joye, whom he dismisses at one point as "a conceited and ignorant fellow."[1] Yet poor Joye hardly fares better at the hands of his supporters. According to Clebsch, Joye "possessed a reckless pen and, on the whole, a minor intelligence. . . ."[2] Even Joye's biographers warn us that their subject was "not cast in the heroic mold."[3] In short, Joye has almost always been treated as a minor and disreputable figure, if not an actual embarrassment to the Protestant cause. Those who ascribe *The Souper* to Joye, then, must implicitly admit that the treatise falls short of being a first-rate polemical work, whereas the claim for Tyndale's authorship is made with the conviction that *The Souper* is "too able and powerful a work to have proceeded from [Joye's] pen."[4]

Whatever preconceptions or prejudices have impeded the search for the author of *The Souper*, the fact remains that the evidence, both internal and external, is sparse and contradictory. It must also be noted that the whole question of how one goes about settling problems of disputed authorship has never been satisfactorily settled. How much weight ought we to give to external evidence? What exactly constitutes internal evidence? Does a series of coincidences "add up" to more than their sum? Is it true, as one writer has averred, that only very strong internal evidence can buttress weak or contradictory external evidence? Or should we accept the view of another writer that the value of internal evidence outweighs any other? What kind of use can be made of statistical analysis in the determination of style? To what extent are we hindered by poor texts of the works we wish to analyze and compare?[5] All of these questions (and many others) need to be kept in mind as we sift through what evidence we have. We cannot hope to reach any absolute conclusions about an action that took place over four hundred years ago, but we can, if we take elementary care, build up a presumptive case one way or another. The remainder of this essay reassesses the evidence and introduces some new points worth consideration, particularly through stylistic analysis.

---

[1] *William Tyndale*, p. 273.

[2] *England's Earliest Protestants*, p. 226.

[3] *George Joye*, p. 15.

[4] Mozley, "The Supper of the Lord 1533," p. 15.

[5] Many of these points are raised and discussed in *Evidence for Authorship: Essays on Problems of Attribution*, ed. David V. Erdman and Ephim G. Fogel (Ithaca, N.Y., 1966).

External Evidence

Thomas More, as we have seen, was the first to explore the problem of authorship, and he left the question open, only suggesting that the author of *The Souper* must be either Tyndale or Joye; subsequent investigations have centered primarily on these two names virtually to the exclusion of other candidates. Neither Tyndale (who was burned at the stake in 1536) nor Joye (who lived until 1553) ever laid claim to the work. What must be the earliest definite attribution occurs in an appendix to the list of "books prohibited" reprinted in Bishop Burnet's *History of the Reformation*. The original list was drawn up in 1542; the appendix, taken from "Bonner's register," is not separately dated and hence may be assumed to belong to the same year and may even belong to the same list. The germane entry reads: "The Supper of the Lord, of George Joye's doing."[1] The question that naturally arises is who made the list and on what basis. Mozley finds little value in such evidence:

> ... such lists have small authority when they supply names to anonymous books. What else can they do but follow hearsay and vague rumour? This very list gives us "The Matrimony of Tyndale; the exposition of Tyndale upon IV (a slip for VII) Corinthians." Here we have one and the same book twice described. The second title (The Exposition etc) is correct; the first is a popular description of its contents. But the book is not Tyndale's; the author sharply distinguishes himself from "the good man who translated" the New Testament.[2]

Mozley's point is well taken. Still, we cannot but wonder why *The Souper* would have been ascribed to Joye. Was it just hearsay? Or the evidence of spies or turncoats? We can only guess.

The next attribution to Joye was made by John Bale in his two catalogues of English authors, *Illustrium maioris Britanniae scriptorum summarium* (Ipswich, 1548; *STC* 1295) and *Scriptorum illustrium maioris Brytanniae catalogus* (Basel, 1557). In both works, Bale gives the title and *incipit*: "De coena domini, li I. Cum uidisset epulones Christus." There can be little doubt that the work here cited is *The Souper*. Under More's works in the *Scriptorum summarium* Bale also gives "Laruam aduersus G. Ioye," clearly referring to *The Answer to a Poisoned Book*. Bale, as Mozley himself points

---

[1] Gilbert Burnet, *The History of the Reformation*, ed. Nicholas Pocock, 7 vols. (Oxford, 1865), *4*, 518. I have not been able to discover the whereabouts of the original list.

[2] "The Supper of the Lord 1533," p. 13.

out, was in a good position to have had inside information, having
"certainly" known Joye at Cambridge and "doubtless also in the reign
of Edward VI."[1] But for Mozley, the words of Foxe, an intimate friend of
Bale's just at the time when the latter was compiling his index, cancel out
this piece of evidence. At the very least, Mozley concludes, Foxe did not
accept Bale's opinion. Mozley is not very convincing here, but it must be
added that others have questioned the accuracy of Bale's work. Bale's
biographer acknowledges the customary view that Bale's catalogues "are
marred by an excess of zeal for Protestantism and by many errors," but
he does add that "entirely too much emphasis, perhaps, has been laid on
such points."[2] Whatever we may think of Bale's general accuracy, his
attribution remains the strongest piece of external evidence in favor of
Joye's authorship.

Our next witness, the martyrologist John Foxe, also knew George Joye,
having crossed polemical swords with him over the issue of whether adul-
terers should be punished by death. The memory of this quarrel may or
may not have influenced Foxe when he ignored Bale's attribution of *The
Souper* to Joye. In any case, Foxe, in John Daye's folio of *The Whole workes
of W. Tyndall, Iohn Frith, and Doct. Barnes* (and not, it should be noted, of
Joye), reprints *The Souper of the Lorde* as an appendix to the works of
Tyndale and adds this note:

> Here foloweth a short and pithy treatise touching the Lordes Supper,
> compiled, as some do gather, by M. William Tyndall, because the
> methode and phrase agree with his, and the tyme of writyng are
> concurrent, which for thy further instruction & learnyng (gentle
> Reader) I haue annexed to his workes, lest the Church of God should
> want any of the paineful trauels of godly men, whose onely care &
> endeuour was to aduaunce the glory of God, & to further the salua-
> tion of Christes flocke committed to their charge.[3]

Mozley makes much of this, but Foxe clearly does not know the author's
identity, and simply wants to make sure that no possible work of
Tyndale's go unnoticed. Hence, it seems hardly just to claim that Foxe
attributes *The Souper* to Tyndale. Furthermore, as Thompson points out:

> It is also significant that Foxe does not mention 'The Supper of the
> Lord' in his account of Tyndale's life in the 'Acts and Monuments.'
> He does state there that Tyndale wrote a treatise on the sacraments,

---

[1] "The Supper of the Lord 1533," p. 13.

[2] Jesse W. Harris, *John Bale: A Study in the Minor Literature of the Reformation*, Illinois
Studies in Language and Literature 25, 4 (Urbana, Ill., 1940), p. 114.

[3] *WW*, sig. CC₄v.

but adds that he put it aside and refrained from publishing it, on the ground that the people were not yet prepared for such advanced teaching. The work which he describes must refer to another book of Tyndale's on the sacraments, whose authorship has never been in question, 'A Fruitful and Godly Treatise on the Sacraments': for there is no suggestion in Foxe's memoir that Tyndale composed two works on the sacraments.[1]

By reprinting *The Souper* along with Tyndale's works, however, Foxe virtually ensured that Tyndale's claim would remain strong in the succeeding centuries.

The only other sixteenth-century source worthy of attention is Robert Crowley, who wrote a preface to a reprint of *The Souper*.[2] Crowley (c. 1518–1588), author, printer, and divine, worked (from about 1548) for the printer John Day. His epistle gives a brief summary of *The Souper*'s main points and concludes with an attempt to reconcile the eucharistic views of the early English and continental reformers. Unfortunately, Crowley does not identify the author of *The Souper* and his vagueness suggests that he did not know the author's name. If he knew, he failed to tell his friend John Foxe, who was uncertain of the matter as late as 1573. In short, Crowley does not help to solve our problem.

One significant piece of indirect external evidence may, in the long run, carry more weight than even direct attributions: Tyndale's letter to Frith. However we interpret Tyndale's words, at least two points remain incontestable: George Joye had worked on a eucharistic treatise at some period before Tyndale wrote his letter, and Tyndale himself was reluctant, as late as January 1533, to discuss publicly a doctrinal issue which continued to divide the Protestant ranks. If Tyndale—as Mozley suggests—changed his mind under the pressure of events and wrote *The Souper* to help Frith, he must have done so with great reluctance. We may further question exactly how *The Souper* could have helped Frith. A heretical treatise, written in a harsh tone more offensive to Catholics than Frith ever adopted, a work which insulted and belittled the former lord chancellor of England, seems ill suited to soften the hearts of Frith's prosecutors. It seems more likely that only someone unaware of Frith's predicament would have chosen to enter the lists with such a weapon. *The Souper of the Lorde* does indeed support Frith's eucharistic theories, but this is not the kind of aid Frith now required. The very fact that Frith could enlist other heretics under his banner was one reason his judges would require him to be burned at the stake some three months after *The Souper* came off the

---

[1] "Who Wrote 'The Supper of the Lord'?" p. 81.
[2] *STC*² 24469–71.

press. All in all, Tyndale's letter to Frith argues rather strongly against Tyndale's authorship of *The Souper*.

Finally, the form in which the text of *The Souper* has survived is as problematic and inconclusive as almost everything else about it. The octavo volume (STC^2 24468) which has long been accepted as the first edition bears the following colophon: " Imprinted at Nornburg by Niclas twonson. 5 April. An. 1533." M. E. Kronenberg believed this to be a false imprint and tentatively assigned *The Souper* to Symon Cock at Antwerp.[1] The assumption that STC^2 24468 is indeed the first edition gains credibility from references in More's *Answer* which fit the physical description of the text we have. Recently, however, Katharine Pantzer has suggested, primarily on the basis of the ornamental initial which begins the text, that STC^2 24468 is in fact a later reprint by the London printer Nicholas Hill of the now lost first edition.[2] If Pantzer's theory be accepted, we are bereft of any copy of the genuine first edition, although we have good reason to believe that, if STC^2 24468 is in fact a reprint, it is one that bears a substantial resemblance to the original. We may then conclude that *The Souper* was first printed in April 1533, probably at Antwerp. But since both Tyndale and Joye (as well as Coverdale) were living in Antwerp in early 1533, the provenance of the first edition does not help us to determine its authorship.

The external evidence, then, is ambiguous but suggestive. Little of what has been presented thus far is new: most of these points have been brought forward by previous investigators wishing to show that either Tyndale or Joye wrote *The Souper of the Lorde*. Some of the evidence has in the past been used carelessly; some of the facts do not prove what those who have made use of them wished to prove. No single point, taken alone, is conclusive. The cumulative effect of all these bits of information, however, tends to make George Joye at least a more likely candidate than William Tyndale. A consideration of the internal evidence helps to strengthen this likelihood.

Internal Evidence

Doctrine and Sources

Even a cursory reading of *The Souper of the Lorde* must lead an informed student to conclude that the doctrine there developed is Zwinglian in its position on the eucharist, rejecting at least by implication both the tran-

---

[1] " Forged Addresses in Low Country Books in the Period of the Reformation," *The Library*, 5th Series, *2* (1947), 81–94, 89.

[2] See STC^2 24468.

substantiation of the Catholics and the consubstantiation of the Lutherans. William Clebsch claims that *The Souper* represents little more than a translation of Zwingli's 1526 treatise *Eine klare Unterrichtung vom Nachtmal Christi*, with a few potshots at More tacked on for good measure.[1] His point is essentially correct, though the actual facts are somewhat more complicated (see headnote to Appendix A, pp. 299–300). Certainly *The Souper* reflects Zwingli's ideas. In one respect only does it differ fundamentally from Zwingli: the latter quite clearly intends as much to refute the Lutherans as he does the Catholics. *The Souper*, on the other hand, tactfully avoids any direct reference to the Lutherans; it is aimed solely at the papists.

For Zwingli, the Lord's supper is essentially "eucharist" or thanksgiving;[2] the sacraments are little more than signs and ceremonies. The sign and the thing signified cannot be the same; hence it is meaningless to speak of the presence of the body of Christ in the Lord's supper. Zwingli's key text was not (as it was for Luther) "this is my body" but rather (from John 6) "the flesh has nothing to offer." Zwingli rejected the concept of the multilocality of Christ's body: Christ had ascended to heaven and therefore could not be present in the bread and wine of the sacrament. All of these ideas, it should be noted, are reflected in the eucharistic writings of John Frith, and most of them were taken up by More in his *Letter against Frith* (1532). Frith uses many of the same analogies and examples Zwingli uses, and some of them are repeated in *The Souper*: specifically, the equating of the bread and wine to the paschal lamb; the similarity in wording (and hence in meaning) between "this is my body" and other statements by Christ such as "I am the door" and "I am the vine"; the warning against false messiahs in Matthew 24; and some others.

Clebsch describes the shape and contents of *The Souper* primarily to advance the case for Joye's authorship. In his view, *The Souper* as it stands nicely fits More's comments in *The Answer*:

> Nowe of trouthe George Ioye hath longe hadde in hande and redy lyenge by hym, his boke agaynst the sacrament. And nowe yf this be yt / he hathe somwhat enlengthed yt of late, by a pyece that he hath patched in agaynst me, wherin he wolde seme to soyle myne argumentes, whyche in my letter I made in that mater agaynst the deuelyshe treatyce of Fryth (7/28–33).

Clebsch insists that these remarks prove More knew that Joye's treatise

---

[1] In "More Evidence," p. 64.
[2] See Jacques Courvoisier, *Zwingli: A Reformed Theologian* (Richmond, Va., 1963), p. 67.

existed independently of Tyndale's reference in his letter to Frith. "That More knew Joye had patched pieces onto an earlier treatise," Clebsch continues, "would be astonishing but for the fact that More knew more about English Protestant writers and writings than anybody else in his day. He tacitly ascribed Souper to Joye in the name of 'diuers that are learned and haue redde the booke' who took it to be from Joye's hand."[1] There are several problems with this statement. First of all, we have no reason to believe that More knew anything about Joye's book aside from what Tyndale reports. His elaboration of Tyndale's comments could easily have been deduced from both the title and the shape of *The Souper* itself. More's hypothesis, by suggesting that *The Souper* was hastily thrown together from various sources for a specific occasion, is good polemics. Clebsch's argument goes in circles and illegitimately attempts to stretch one piece of evidence (Tyndale's comment to Frith) to fit a variety of purposes. Nor is it fair to say that More " tacitly ascribed *Souper* to Joye "; More's comment forms part of a rhetorical ploy, a joke, in fact, at the expense of *The Souper*.

A potentially more decisive test of authorship would be to compare the doctrine in *The Souper* with the known eucharistic beliefs of Tyndale and Joye. Here again, however, matters are not as simple as we might wish. Tyndale discusses the Lord's supper at length only in his so-called *Briefe declaration of the sacraments*, a work not published until about 1548. We cannot now ascertain when Tyndale composed this treatise, or for what specific purpose, if any. Whatever its date, the doctrine of *A Briefe declaration* quite definitely echoes the beliefs of Ulrich Zwingli and John Frith. Tyndale denies the real presence in any form and insists on the purely symbolic nature of the sacraments. Moreover, Tyndale enforces the analogy between the Passover and the Lord's supper:

> And hereof ye se that our sacramentes are bokys of storyes only and that ther is none other vertu in them then to thestyfye the couenauntes and promysses made in chrysts bloud. And here of ye perceyue that where nought is vnderstand by the sacrament or ceremonyes / ther they be clene vnprofitable.[2]

Later he deals briefly with John 6, showing that Christ's words "except ye ete the flesshe of the sonne of man and drynk hys blood, ye shal not haue lyfe in youre selues" were meant in a purely spiritual sense: "But though it is that the ryghtuos lyueth by his fayth: ergo to beleue and trust in christes bloude is y^e eatynge that ther was meant as y^e text well

---

[1] " More Evidence," p. 63.
[2] *A Briefe declaration of the sacraments* (1548; *STC*² 24445), sig. B₅.

proueth " (sig. D$_1$). Tyndale expresses similar beliefs in his other works. In *Obedience*, for example, he asserts that sacrament means only "holy sygne" (sig. O$_8$v). And in his *Answer* to More's *Dialogue*, he speaks of the eucharist as "but the memoriall of the very sacrifice of christ once done for all" (sig. O$_6$v).

Tyndale's eucharistic theology, then, seems quite consistent with the views expressed in *The Souper*. As C. W. Dugmore notes, "it is difficult to discover any great divergence from the views here expressed in those writings on the Eucharist which are unquestionably Tyndale's." It is true, Dugmore adds, that Tyndale "employs the Lutheran idea of the testament, and at times uses language which is less obviously sacramentarian than that of *The Supper of the Lorde*." Nevertheless, if Tyndale "did not write *The Supper of the Lorde*, his belief is indistinguishable from that of the author of it."[1]

And yet, as Clebsch and others have insisted, Tyndale's views seemingly diverge from those expressed in *The Souper* on at least one issue. In the oft-mentioned letter to Frith, Tyndale had written: "I would haue the right vse preached, and the presence to be an indifferent thyng, till the matter might be reasoned in peace at laysure, of both parties."[2] Frith claimed that beliefs about the eucharist should be classed among *adiaphora* or things indifferent. Tyndale's tone here suggests that for him such a concept was at least politic if not governing. Elsewhere he remarks that "it is wyckednes to make it a necessary artycle of our fayth. And to sley them that can not think that it ought to be beleued." He goes on to say:

> Notwythstandyng all these reasons and the dampnable Idolatrye whych ye papistes haue commytted wyth the sacrament / yet whether they affyrme the body and bloud to be present w^t the bread and wyne, or the bread & wyne to be turned and transsubstancyate into the body and bloud, I am therwyth content (for vnityes sake) yf they wyll there cease, & let hym be there, onely to testyfye & confyrme the testament or couenaunt made in chrysts bloud and body for which cause onely Chryst instituted the sacrament.[3]

Yet unlike Frith, whose beliefs might lead to greater religious toleration, Tyndale tends to take away with one hand what he grants with the other. How much latitude, for example, does he allow in the following paragraph?

---

[1] *The Mass and the English Reformers* (London, 1958), pp. 104–05.

[2] *WW*, sig. CC$_4$.

[3] *A Briefe declaration*, sig. E$_4$v.

> Wherfor to avoyd thys endeles braelynge whych y^e deuelles, no
> dowbt, hath styrred vp, . . . methynketh that the Parte that hathe
> professed the fayth of chryste, and the loue of hys neybour ought of
> dutye to Beare eche other as longe as the otheres opinyon is not
> playne wicked through false ydolatrye nor contrarye to the saluacion
> that is in Chryste. Nor agaynste the open and manyfest doctrin of
> chryst & his apostls Nor contrarye to the generall artycles of the
> faythe of the generall churche of chryste whych are confyrmyd wyth
> open scrypture. In whyche artycles Neuer a trew churche in any
> lande dyscentyth.[1]

The tone of *The Souper* differs considerably from Tyndale's. The author,
like Zwingli himself, takes a hard line. No allowance for opposing views,
no gestures in the direction of conciliation disturb the author's single-
minded insistence on the purely symbolic nature of the eucharist. Though
the author makes no specific reference to Lutherans, he clearly considers
their views as repugnant as those of his papist opponents. A harsh,
unyielding, sarcastic, militant tone dominates throughout. The following
example is characteristic:

> To be to curiouse in so playn a sacrament and sygne, to cauill Crystis
> clere wordis with sophistical sophismes, & to tryful out the trouthe
> withe tauntis & mockis, as More dothe, is no crysten maner. And if
> our Papistis, & scolasticall sophisters will obiecte & make answer to
> this souper of the lorde, bringing yn for them, their unwryten wordis,
> dede dremes, (for we haue compelled More withe shame to flitte
> frome the scripture) strewed withe their vayn strange termes whiche
> Paule damneth, & geueth Timothe warning of. I shall, by goddis
> grace, so set the almighty worde of god agenst them that all christen
> shall se their falshed & deceite in this sacrament: & so disclose their
> deuilessh doctryne & sleighe iugelynge, that all that can rede
> englysshe, shall se the trouthe of Goddis worde openly bere downe
> their vnwryten lyes. (Appendix A, 335/41–336/10)

Given the tone of this and other passages, it is hard to see how Mozley
could characterize *The Souper* as pleading "for mutual toleration of rival
views."[2] Certainly the very opposite is true.

Of course, as Mozley and others would point out, ideas and beliefs
change with time and circumstance. The early English Protestants often
groped in the dark, forging their views in the heat of debate, anxiously

---

[1] *A Briefe declaration*, sigs. E$_7$–E$_7$v.
[2] "Tyndale's 'Supper of the Lord,'" p. 305.

discarding the old without always knowing what to put in its place. It is not rare, nor should it be surprising, to find contradictions and confusions not only within the same man but even within the same work. And yet, when these objections have been duly weighed, we still cannot easily reconcile Tyndale's statement of about January 1533 that the presence be regarded "an indifferent thyng" with the unyielding and unequivocal tone of a treatise published three or four months later. If Tyndale wrote *The Souper of the Lorde*, he must have undergone a very rapid and extreme change of mind indeed.

George Joye's sacramental views cannot be determined from his known writings; the topic comes up, of course, from time to time, but never in sufficient length or depth for the reader to conclude anything more than that Joye's views were Protestant. A brief work entitled *A frutefull treatis of baptyme and the Lordis souper* (*STC*^{2} 24217), published anonymously in 1541, has been ascribed (quite tentatively) to Joye by Butterworth and Chester. Unfortunately, *A frutefull treatis* does not provide us much help; it is not controversial and reads more like a catechism than a sustained argument. The author seems primarily interested in giving a brief, clear, and fairly simplistic exposition of the purpose and function of sacraments: he notes on the title page that his treatise will present information "necessary to be knowne of all Christen men" (sig. A$_1$). The doctrine presented is no doubt Zwinglian in its emphasis on the symbolic nature of the water, bread, and wine used in the sacraments. If we were "al togi-ther spirituall / immortall gloriouse et cetera," the author insists, we would not need to "be thus fed / with siche sensible / elements / symbols / rytes or Sacraments" (sig. A$_3$). Although the author carefully distin-guishes his views from the teachings of papists, he does not bother to engage Catholic dogma directly and he makes no attempt to differentiate his position from that held by any other Protestant. The temperate tone of *A frutefull treatis* distinguishes it not only from *The Souper* but indeed from nearly all the extant eucharistic tracts written in the 1530s. If Joye is the author, this must be considered one of his least characteristic works. In any case, nothing in this treatise conflicts with the arguments present-ed in *The Souper of the Lorde*; if Joye wrote one, he could have written the other.

Style

Stylistic analysis, seemingly an ideal way of resolving questions of authorship, in fact remains the most dubious, least firm area of evidence. No one quite knows what "style" is or how to define it. Computer-aided statistical analysis, a potentially fruitful means of determining stylistic constants, has thus far yielded mixed results. In any case, an accurate

count of stylistic variables depends on sound, reliable texts, and we do not
have these for either Tyndale or Joye.[1]

Recently, William Tyndale's prose style has attracted some attention,
as we would expect for the writings of a man who had such an enormous
influence on the King James Bible and hence on the development of
modern English prose. Mozley, in his biography of Tyndale, devoted
considerable space to a discussion of Tyndale's translations, a specialized
instance of stylistic analysis. Several years ago, Norman Davis wrote a
brief but suggestive study, *William Tyndale's English of Controversy* (London,
1971). Although much of what he says falls under the category of intelligent and educated "impressionism," he does make one foray into statistical analysis. Davis does not concern himself with questions of
authorship; he merely wishes to suggest something about the development
of Tyndale's polemical style. He therefore selects three of Tyndale's works
representing the early, middle, and late "periods" of Tyndale's career
and counts the number of times Tyndale chooses between "to" and
"unto" in order to determine which form Tyndale seems to prefer. Using
the number 84 as a base, Davis produces the following results:

	to	unto
Prologue to Romans (1526)	58	26
Obedience (1528)	41	43
Practice of Prelates (1530)	23	61

This chart seems to show a decided shift in Tyndale's preference (presumably unconscious) for one form over the other. But several objections
must immediately be raised. As Davis himself warns, "such variations
might be due at least in part to printers concerned with length of lines."[2]
In addition, as a glance at the dates of the works shows us, Tyndale's
career as a polemicist was so brief as to render the whole question of
"development" rather dubious. Nevertheless, it may be of some value to
apply the same test to *The Souper* and to several works by Joye, setting
these next to Tyndale's *Practice of Prelates* as nearest in date to *The Souper*
itself, and using Davis's base number of 84.

	to	unto
Tyndale's *Practice of Prelates* (1530)	23	61
The Souper of the Lorde (1533)	51	33
Joye's *Subuersion* (1534)	60	24
Joye's *Apology* (1535)	41	43

---

[1] See Rebecca Posner, "The Use and Abuse of Stylistic Statistics," *Archivum Linguisticum*,
15 (1963), 111–139.

[2] *William Tyndale's English of Controversy*, p. 9, n. 1.

The figures seem to favor Joye, but the whole pattern may be the result of pure chance. Tyndale's usage varies even more than Davis's figures show: in a sample passage of *A Briefe declaration of the sacraments* (of uncertain date, but first published after Tyndale's death), "to" occurs 72 times, "unto" only 12.

For the rest, Davis's findings do not help us much in isolating stylistic features peculiar only to Tyndale. He notes that Tyndale does not much favor doublets, though they occur in his works. He points to Tyndale's fondness for certain expressions: "clene contrary," "juggle" and "juggler," "bo peepe." But he adds that "clene contrary" was also used by other writers of the period, including Thomas More. The same can be said of "bo peepe," which is used not only by More in *A Letter against Frith* but also at least three times by Joye in his *Apology* (1535).[1] Claims that a particular author uses certain "characteristic" expressions are always difficult to sustain and must be treated with great caution.

One of the major difficulties in the use of comparative stylistics lies in deciding precisely what discriminating details ought to be investigated. *The Souper*, however, appears to provide its own set of discriminators in the English translations of scriptural texts that dot its pages. Indeed, this factor might seem at first to be decisive. Tyndale, after all, had translated the entire New Testament only a few years before *The Souper* appeared. We ought to be able to determine at the very least whether or not the author of *The Souper* is Tyndale or someone using Tyndale's *New Testament*. But again we run into troublesome complications. Tyndale, as is well known to students of his writings, seldom employed his own translations when he quoted scripture in his polemical works; instead, as might be expected of a man in a hurry, he retranslated ad hoc. We cannot hope, then, that the scriptural translations in *The Souper* will provide an absolute test for authorship or even eliminate Tyndale from consideration. But we might reasonably expect Tyndale's ad hoc renderings to bear a fairly close relationship to his own version of the New Testament, especially when we consider that the Bible was a work long and intimately familiar to him, the sentences and words of which he must have rendered into English many times before he even began working on a translation. In brief, we would expect Tyndale's various translations from scripture to be closer to each other than to renderings by someone not familiar with the Tyndalian *New Testament*. We should recall, however, that our other candidate for authorship, George Joye, was undoubtedly quite familiar with Tyndale's translation, although it was over a year after the pub-

---

[1] Sigs. A$_7$, B$_5$, D$_4$.

lication of *The Souper* that Joye issued his now infamous "corrected" edition of Tyndale's *New Testament*.

Keeping these qualifications in mind, we can compare the scriptural citations in *The Souper* with the same passages as translated in various places by Tyndale and (in the few instances I could find) by Joye. In the first group (which is reasonably complete) scriptural citations from *The Souper* are juxtaposed with Tyndale's *New Testament* version and with at least one other version of the same passage from the works of either Tyndale or Joye. In every case, I have compared both editions (1525 and 1534) of Tyndale's translation and noted significant variants.

1 Cor. 2 : 2

Souper

nether presuminge not to haue knowne anye other thinge to be preched them (as him selfe saythe) then Iesus Cryste, and that he was crucyfyed. [308/7–9]

Joye, *Subuersion*

For I professed myselfe than beinge w^t you nothing els to knowe but Iesus Cryste & that he was crucified. [sig. D$_4$v]

Tyndale, *New Testament*

Nether shewed I my selfe that I knewe eny thinge amonge you save Iesus Christ, even the same that was crucified.

1 Cor. 11 : 24

Souper

Our lorde Iesus, the same nyght he was betrayed: he toke the brede, and after he had geuen thankis: he brake it, saynge: Take ye it, eat it. This is my boodye, whiche is for you broken. [318/28–31]

Joye, *A frutefull treatis*

Take it / eat it / this is my bodye which is broken for you. [sig. B$_8$v]

Tyndale, *Briefe declaration*

(1) The lorde Iesus the nyghte he was betrayed / toke breade and gaue thankes and broke it, and sayde: Take and eate, thys is my bodye that shalbe geuen for you. [sig. B$_3$]

(2) How that the lord Iesus that same nyghte he was betrayed. toke bread and gaue thankes and brake and sayd. Take ye and eate, thys is my body that shalbe delyuered for you. [sig. C$_5$]

Tyndale, *Obedience*

This is my body y^t is broken for you. [sig. M$_1$]

Tyndale, *New Testament*

For the lorde Iesus the same nyght in which he was betrayed, toke breed: and thanked and brake, and sayde. Take ye, and eate ye: this is my body which is broken for you.

1 Cor. 11 : 26

Souper

So oft as ye shal ete this brede, . . . and drincke of this cuppe, prayse, declare, and geue thankes for the dethe of the lorde, vntyl he shal come agene to iugement. [327/5–8]

Tyndale, *Briefe declaration*

As oft sayth paul as you shall eate of thys Breade and drynke of thys cuppe ye must declare or preache the lordes death untyll he come. [sigs. C$_5$–C$_5$v]

John 6 : 26

Souper

Verely verely I saye vnto you: ye seke me not because ye haue sene my myracles, but because ye haue eten of the loues and were well fylled. [305/3–5]

Tyndale, *Obedience*

ye seke me not / because ye saw the myracles: But because ye ate of the bred and were fylled. [sig. C$_6$v]

Tyndale, *New Testament*

verely verely I saye vnto you: ye seke me, not because ye sawe the myracles: but be cause ye ate of the loves [ofthebreed, *1525*], and were filled.

John 6 : 39

Souper

This (I saye) is my fathers wyll that hathe sent me. That of all that he hath geuen me, I leese non: but muste rease him vp agayn in the laste daye. [306/37–39]

Tyndale, *Testament of William Tracy*

This is the wyll of my father wich sent me / that I lose nothinge of all that he hath geuen me / but that I rayse hit vp againe in the last daye. [sig. c5]

Tyndale, *New Testament*

And this is the [my, *1525*] fathers will which hath sent me, that of all which he hath geven me, I shuld loose no thinge: but shuld rayse it vp agayne at the last daye.

John 6 : 45

Souper

all shalbe taught off the lorde (307/28–29).

Tyndale, *Exposition of John I*

For they must be al taught of God (D_8).

Tyndale, *Answer to More*

They shalbe all taught of God (D_6).

Tyndale, *New Testament*

that they shall all be taught of God [And they shall all be taught of God, *1525*].

John 6 : 48–51

Souper

I am the brede of lyfe . . . our fathers and elders dyd ete Manna in the deserte, & yet ar thei dede. But he that eteth of this brede . . . he hathe lyfe euerlastynge. For it is I that am this lyuely brede which am comen from heuen, of whom who so ete by faithe, shal neuer dye. . . . This brede which I . . . shall geue . . . you: it is myn own flesshe . . . whiche I . . . paye for the lyfe of the worlde. [308/18–34]

Tyndale, *New Testament*

I am that breed of lyfe. Youre fathers dyd eate Manna in the wild-erness and are deed. This is that breed which commeth from heaven, that he which eateth of it [that he wich of it eateth, *1525*], shuld also not dye. I am that lyvinge breed which came doune from heaven. Yf eny man eate of this breed, he shall live forever. And the breed that I will geve, is my flesshe, which I will geve for the lyfe of the worlde.

John 6 : 53–55

Souper

Verely verely I saye vnto you: except ye ete the flesshe of the sonne of man and drynk hys blood, ye shal not haue that lyfe in youre selues. He that eteth my flesshe & drynketh my blood, hath lyfe euerlastynge: and I shall stere hym vp in the laste daye: for my flesshe is very meat & my blood the very drynke. [309/32–36]

Tyndale, *Briefe declaration*

Except ye eate the flesh of the son of man & drink his bloud ye shal haue no lyfe in you. [sig. D₁]

Tyndale, *New Testament*

Verely, verely I saye vnto you, except ye eate the flesshe of the sonne of man, and drinke his bloude, ye shall not have lyfe in you. Whoso-ever eateth my flesshe, and drinketh my bloude, hath eternall lyfe: and I will rayse him vp at the last daye. For my flesshe is meate in dede: and my bloude is drynke in dede.

John 6 : 63

Souper

It is the spirit that geueth this lyfe, My flesshe profiteth nothing at all, to be eten as ye mean so carnally. It is spirituall meat that I here speke of. [317/15–17]

Joye, *A frutefull treatis*

My wordis ar spirit and lyfe / the flesshe profiteth not / It is the spirit yᵗ geueth this lyfe wherof yᵉ iuste lyueth. [sig. C₁v]

Tyndale, *Obedience*

the wordes which I speake are sprite & lyfe. [sigs. P₃v–P₄]

Tyndale, *Exposition of John I*

The wordes whiche I speake ar sprite & life / & the fleshe profiteth not at al. [sig. A₈v]

Tyndale, *Answer to More*

. . . it is the spirite that quikeneth / the flesh profiteth nothynge at all / the wordes whych I speake sayth he / ar spirite and life. [sig. O₇]

Tyndale, *New Testament*

It is the sprete that quyckeneth, the flesshe proffeteth nothinge. The wordes that I speake vnto you, are sprete and lyfe.

Mark 14 : 24

Souper

And he sayd to them. This is my bloode of the new testament: whiche is shed for many. [320/23–24]

Tyndale, *Briefe declaration*

And he sayde, Thys is my bloud of the newe Testamente. [sig. C₄v]

Tyndale, *New Testament*

And he sayde vnto them: This is my bloude of the new testament which is sheed for many [which shalbe sheed for many, *1525*].

Matthew 26 : 27

Souper

Take ye it, eat it. This is my boodye. [318/30–31]

Tyndale, *Briefe declaration*

. . . take and eat thys is my body. [sig. C₂v]

Tyndale, *New Testament*

Take, eate, this is my body.

2 Peter 1 : 19

Souper

That we haue before a ferme and suer propheticall speche vnto whiche yf ye attende as vnto a lyght set vp in a derke place, ye do well. [325/25–27]

Joye, *Ieremy the prophete*

. . . the light set vp in a derke place. . . . [sig. A₆v]

Tyndale, *Obedience*

. . . we have (saith he) a moare sure worde of prophesie / where vnto if ye take hede / as vnto a lighte shininge in a darke place / ye doo well. [sig. S₂]

Tyndale, *New Testament*

We have also a right [more, *1525*] sure worde of prophesye wher vnto yf ye take hede, as vnto a lyght that shyneth in a darke place, ye do well.

With so little evidence from Joye, no firm conclusions can be based on these examples. Several points may be noted, however. For one thing, Tyndale invariably prefers to omit the direct object (and often the indirect as well) in the words of consecration from 1 Cor. 11 : 24 and Matthew 26 : 27. So Tyndale has "Take, eate," "Take and eate," "Take ye and eate," and "Take ye, and eate ye," whereas *The Souper* has "Take ye it, eat it" (which is close to "Take it / eat it" from *A frutefull treatis*). *The Souper* also seems more circumstantial (or simply more wordy) than Tyndale. The author writes "vntyl he shal come agene to iugement" where Tyndale twice renders the same passage as "untyll he come." We may also compare (in John 6 : 53–55) *Souper*'s "lyfe in your selues" to Tyndale's two renderings "lyfe in you." These are small details, of course. In some instances (as in Mark 14 : 24), Tyndale and *The Souper* differ hardly at all. But in general it seems fair to say that the most striking variations in translation are not among Tyndale's various versions but between Tyndale and *The Souper*. Particularly noteworthy are John 6 : 39 (Tyndale's "it vp" follows the Vulgate; *The Souper*'s "him vp" does not) and John 6 : 63 (*The Souper*'s "My flesshe," indicating specifically the body of Christ, and Tyndale's more abstract and generalized "the flesh").

My second group of examples has less evidentiary value; these are passages that, as far as I could determine, were not translated by Joye at all and by Tyndale only in his *New Testament* and *Pentateuch*. All that can be compared, then, are *The Souper* and Tyndale's translations of scripture. (This list is representative; the number of passages could be doubled.)

Genesis 17 : 12–14

Souper

Euery manchylde muste be cyrcumcysed that my couenant myght be in your flesshe for a perpetual bonde. [324/11–13]

Tyndale, *Pentateuch*

And euery manchilde . . . shall be circumsysed amonge you . . . that my testament may be in youre flesh, for an everlastinge bonde.

Exodus 12 : 25–28

Souper

Aftir ye be entred into that lande whyche the lorde God shal geue you accordyng to thys promyse: ye shal kepe thys ceremony. And when your chyldren aske ye: what relygion is thys? ye shall answer them. It is the sacryfice of the passyngouere of the lorde, when the lorde passed forebye the houses of the chyldern of Israel in egipte, smyting the gipcians and delyuering our houses. [323/7–13]

Tyndale, *Pentateuch*

And when ye be come in to the land which the Lorde will geue you acordinge as he hath promysed, se that ye kepe this seruice. And when youre childern axe you what maner off seruice is this ye doo. Ye shall saye, it is the sacrifice of the Lordes passeouer which passed ouer the housses of the childern of Israel in Egipte, as he smote the Egiptians and saued oure housses.

1 Cor. 10 : 3–4

Souper

. . . our fathers all dyd ete the same spyritual meate and dranke the same spirytuall drynke that we nowe ete and drynke. [321/16–19]

Tyndale, New Testament

. . . and dyd all eate of one spirituall meate, and did all drincke of one maner of spirituall drincke.

Heb. 9 : 16–18

Souper

. . . wherso euer is a testement, there muste the dethe of the testement maker go betwene: or els the testement is not ratyfyed and suer but ryghtuosnes & remyssion of sinnes in Crystis blood is hys new testement, where of he is mediatour. . . . [313/5–9]

Tyndale, New Testament

For whersoever is a testament, there must also be the deeth of him that maketh the testament. For the testament taketh auctoritie when men are deed: For it is of no value as longe as he that made it is a live. For which cause also, nether that fyrst testament was ordeyned with out bloud.

John 6 : 32–34

Souper

Verely verely I saye vnto you: Moses gaue ye not that brede from heuen: for thoughe it fil down frome the ayer: yet was it not heuenly fode, for it did but fede the belly. But this brede of god that is descenden frome heuen whom my father geueth, refressheth the soule so abundantly that it geueth lyfe vnto the worlde. [305/35–40]

Tyndale, New Testament

. . . verely, verely I saye vnto you: Moses gave you [you not, 1525] breed from heaven: but my father geveth you the true breed from heaven. For the breed of God is he [For he is the breed of God, 1525] which commeth doune from heaven and geveth lyfe vnto the worlde.

John 6 : 41–44

Souper

. . . they murmured at this sayng of Cryste. I am the brede which am comen from heuen, sayng. Is not this Iesus Iosephs sonne whose father & mother we knowe well ynoughe? How then sayth he, I am comen from heuen? Iesus answered saing Murmur not among your selues. . . . Noman maye come to me . . . onlesse my Father that sent me drawe him: and whom he draweth vnto me, that is ioyneth vnto me by faith, him shal I stere vp in the laste daye. [307/15–25]

Tyndale, *New Testament*

The Iewes then murmured at him [The iewes murmured attitt, *1525*], because he sayde: I am that breed which is come doune from heaven. And they sayde: Is not this Iesus the sonne of Ioseph, whose father and mother we knowe? How ys yt then that he sayeth, I came doune from heaven? Iesus answered and sayde vnto them. Murmur not betwene youre selves. No man can come to me except the [my, *1525*] father which hath sent me, drawe him. And I will rayse him vp at the last daye.

John 6 : 67–69

Souper

And then he sayd to the twelue. Wyll ye go a waye to? And Symon Peter answerde: Lorde, to whom shall we go? Thou haste the wordis of euerlastinge lyfe, and we beleue, and ar suer, that thou art Cryst the sonne of the lyuynge god. [318/4–7]

Tyndale, *New Testament*

Then sayde Iesus to the twelue: will ye alsoo goo awaye? Then Simon Peter answered [answered hym, *1525*]: Master to whom shall we goo? Thou haste the wordes of eternall lyfe, and we beleve and knowe [And wehave beleved, and knowen, *1525*], that thou arte Christ the sonne of the lyvinge God.

Luke 22 : 11

Souper

. . . where is this geste chamber where I might ete the passing by with my disciples? [326/35–36]

Tyndale, *New Testament*

. . . where is the gest chamber, where I shall eate myne ester lambe with my disciples?

Matthew 15 : 27

Souper

Ye saye sothe my lorde. But yet do the lytell whelpis ete of the crummes that fall frome theyr maisters table? [321/36–38]

Tyndale, *New Testament*

. . . truthe [it is truthe, *1525*] Lorde: nevethelesse the whelpes eate
of the crommes, which fall from their masters table.

One might argue from these examples that, at least in the majority of
cases, the author of *The Souper* sounds very unlike Tyndale as we have him
in his scriptural translations. But at other times Tyndale and *The Souper*
substantially agree. Since Tyndale was quite capable of translating the
same verses differently at different times, the issue becomes one of degree,
of how far we can allow Tyndale to diverge from himself based on his
known practice. Unfortunately, we cannot impose any hard and fast rules
on the translating habits of a sixteenth-century controversialist: time,
circumstances, and contexts play their part in determining the way a
scriptural passage will be rendered in a particular text. The tendency of
many writers—including Tyndale and Joye—to provide loose paraphrases rather than strict translations when it suits their purposes further
complicates our investigation. The citation from 1 Cor. 10 : 3-4 provides
a perfect example of conscious distortion. Tyndale (and Paul) mean that
all who were there ate the same food. The author of *The Souper* (like
Zwingli) means that our fathers ate what we now eat, a paraphrase that
supports his argument but alters the text. In any case, neither Joye's Old
Testament translations nor his "corrections" of Tyndale's *New Testament*
coincide with any of the verses quoted in *The Souper*. Without Joye's
testimony, it would be rash to conclude very much from this group of
parallel passages.

In the end, we are perhaps compelled to fall back on very unscientific
impressions, as other students of authorship questions usually do. Certainly, as Mozley has insisted, there are significant and obvious qualitative
differences between the literary styles of Tyndale and Joye. Few readers
would question the conclusion that, at his best, Tyndale excels Joye as a
writer of English prose. Although the "joyous, lyric quality" that C. S.
Lewis[1] attributes to Tyndale emerges primarily in the non-controversial
works, Tyndale can be a vigorous polemicist. His style takes fire from his
obvious fervor and indignation: clauses pile on clauses, sentences follow
each other with furious inevitability and rhetorical force. His is an
excited, mocking, scornful, nervous style, a style which often sacrifices
logic and reason to the pleasure of sarcasm and taunts. Of course, this is
Tyndale at his controversial best; at his worst (as, in my opinion, he is in
The Parable of the Wicked Mammon and much of *The Practice of Prelates*), he

---

[1] *English Literature in the Sixteenth Century Excluding Drama* (Oxford, 1954), p. 192.

is dull, repetitive, petty, and totally lacking in either spiritual generosity or stylistic elegance.

As a writer, Joye seems more of a piece than Tyndale; his virtues are inextricably tied to his vices. He, too, can be dull, repetitive, and petty (as all sixteenth-century polemicists were, at some time or other), but he does have a nice feeling for colloquial expressions and narrative drive. Joye is at his best when he is most personal, whether on the defense or the attack. For all of the opprobrium heaped on it, Joye's *Apology* in many ways makes for delightful reading, because its circumstantial and breezy style sometimes brings a dead controversy vividly and personally to life. The mixture of self-pity, injured innocence, and self-righteous scorn which emerges from such works as *An Apology* and *The refutation of the byshop of Winchesters derke declaration* (*STC*^{2} 14828.5) attracts and repels the reader in almost equal measure. On the other hand, Joye's treatment of theological issues is often tedious, unedifying, or downright confusing. Butterworth's brief characterization of Joye's traits as a translator—"his fervor, his extravagant mode of expression, and withal the fresh effect of his unstudied and offhand approach"—applies as well to the high points of his controversial style.[1]

The Souper of the Lorde seldom if ever reaches the literary quality which Tyndale and Joye at their best could achieve. The bulk of this treatise seems mechanical and uninspired; even as a piece of scurrilous and bitter polemic, it remains—after repeated readings—uninteresting. *The Souper* does present its major points forcefully and unequivocally; although some details may be muddy, the overall argument—in spite of a somewhat loose and unsystematic organization—emerges with sufficient clarity to have the desired polemical impact. But the author seldom relieves his insistent, dogmatic tone with either spiritual feeling or worldly humor. It seems pointless to argue that such a style is either too good for Joye or not good enough for Tyndale. Both men were quite capable of having written *The Souper*, as both were capable of much better work. Relying on impressionistic response alone, an unprejudiced reader would be hard put to commit himself for or against either candidate.

One other approach to stylistic discrimination may be suggested here. Both Tyndale and Joye, at various times, engaged in direct polemical controversy with Thomas More; perhaps we could differentiate their method of attack and rebuttal. Mozley has already concluded that such an investigation would support Tyndale's authorship:

---

[1] Charles C. Butterworth, *The English Primers (1529–1545)* (Philadelphia, 1953), p. 37.

We meet . . . in the 'Supper' some of Tyndale's favourite points, e.g. the hits at More as a poet who feigns anything he pleases, a jester who mocks out the truth, a forger of "unwritten verities," a proctor of purgatory. We find again the old sarcasms at More's 'Utopia,' and, above all, the scornful phrase "Quod he" used to describe More's 'Dialogue.' . . . To add one more point—the pun "unwritten written vanities—verities I should say " is highly Tyndalian; so is the frequent alliteration. . . .[1]

But, as we have noted, the findings of Pineas and others clearly demonstrate that these primarily ad hominem arguments against More quickly became the common property of Protestant polemicists.[2] In fact the evidence, such as it is, favors Joye over Tyndale. In his *Subuersion of Moris false foundacion* (1534), in particular, Joye echoes several phrases and arguments from *The Souper*. In *The Souper*, the author ironically picks up on More's insistence that scripture must be understood in the light of church tradition, or "vnwritten . . . verities," by several times mentioning More's "vnwryten dremes" (311/34) and his "vnwryten vanites, verites I shulde saye" (311/40–41). In *Subuersion*, Joye writes of More's "vnwryten deed dremes" (sig. A$_3$v), "vnwryten vanites" (sig. B$_7$v), and even his "wauering vnwryten vanites" (sig. H$_7$). Indeed, Joye seems to have liked this kind of phrasing; so we have, for example, "vnwryten verities" (*Ieremy the prophete*, sig. A$_3$; *The vnite and scisme of the olde chirche*, sig. A$_6$v) and "deade dreames" (*The vnite and scisme*, sig. B$_1$; *Refutation of . . . Winchesters . . . declaration*, sig. C$_7$v; *Our sauiour Iesus Christ*, sig. B$_1$), as well as other variations of the same thought in a number of his writings. Joye also echoes *The Souper*'s reference to More as "M. Mocke" in *Subuersion*, noting that "M. Mok playd y^e proctour of purgatory creping forth groning out his Supplicacion of soules" (sig. B$_5$). This last reference to More's tract against Simon Fish also has a parallel in *The Souper*:

For had he not come begging for the clergye from purgatory, withe his supplicacion of soulis, and Rastel & Rochester had they not so wysely playd their partis: purgatory paraduenture had serued them yet a nother yere: nether had it so sone haue ben quenched, nor the pore soule & proctour ther be with his blody bisshop crysten catte so farre coniured into his owne Vtopia with a sechel about his necke to gather for the proude preistis in Synagoga papistica. (336/17–24)

---

[1] *Notes and Queries 183* (21 November 1942), 306 and *185* (31 July 1943), 87.
[2] See Rainer Pineas, "Thomas More's *Utopia* and Protestant Polemics," *Renaissance News*, *17* (1964), 197–201 and *Thomas More and Tudor Polemics* (Bloomington, Ind., 1968).

The *Supplication* furnishes both *The Souper* and *Subuersion* with yet another allusion:

Souper	*Subuersion*
For the deuyl hys gardian, as hym selfe sayth, cometh euery daye into purgatory, yf therby there any day at all, wyth hys emnyouse & enuyouse laughter, gnasshyng his tethe & gryning, tellyng the proctour wyth hys popis presoners, what so euer is here done or wryten agenst them, both hys persone & name to. And he is now, I dare saye, as gret wyth hys gardian, as euer he was. (339/35–40)	But yet into these trouthes did not ye holy goste lede any man / for into ye trouth y^t ye Supplicacion of beggers was wryten & who wrote it / More saith himselfe in his supplicacion of soules / y^t ye deuyl led him. wherfore it is not the spirit of trouth y^t leadeth into euery trouth / for ther be some trouthes / as they be vnworthy the holy gostis ledinge / so be ther some agayne so aperte vnto our eyes & eares y^t thei nede not his ledinge: of y^e which kinde of trouthes (& reken not his lyes) be all Mores vnwryten trouthes which he sayeth be of necessite to be beleued. (sig. B$_5$)

And Joye exhibits a fondness for alliteration—"blody blynd bisshops," "the very tryed tryacle agenst y^e vyrulent venome," "conuenient kouers for sich a cuppe" (*Subuersion*, sigs. A$_8$v, B$_8$v, A$_7$v)—which seems to equal if not surpass Tyndale's.

Although the verbal and other parallels between *The Souper* and *Subuersion* may prove nothing more than that Joye had read the former before writing the latter, we may equally assume that Joye's less than creative imagination—witness his poor jest that "Moros in Greke is stultus in Latyn / a fool in Englysshe" (*Subuersion*, sig. A$_1$)—led him to repetition rather than variation. Furthermore, some of Joye's seemingly characteristic traits, such as the often ludicrous use of alliteration ("this popisshe prowed parkers peuissh examinacion," "deuellisshe doctryne drawne forthe of these dampnable deluers," "the humble pore pure persecuted precher"),[1] appear throughout his writing career. That the evidence hurts Mozley's case for Tyndale cannot be denied.

---

[1] The phrases are cited from *A present consolacion for the sufferers of persecucion* (1544; *STC*^{2} 14828), sig. E$_8$; *Ieremy the prophete* (1534; *STC* 2778), sigs. A$_4$–A$_4$v; and *George Ioye confuteth / Winchesters false articles* (1543; *STC*^{2} 14826), sig. b$_3$v.

My discussion thus far has been almost exclusively concerned with the likelihood that either William Tyndale or George Joye wrote *The Souper of the Lorde*, but of course the possibility remains that neither of them is responsible for this work. No evidence, however, has ever been brought forth in favor of another candidate. Christopher Anderson, it is true, noted in his *Annals of the English Bible* (London, 1845) that *The Souper* had once been mistakenly ascribed to Miles Coverdale,[1] but he does not tell us when or by whom. Mozley's remarks on this question are apropos:

> Is there any other possible candidate for the authorship beside Joye and Tyndale? I can think of none. Coverdale indeed was probably at Antwerp in 1533, but there is nothing to connect him with *The Supper of the Lord*. John Rogers seems to have been still in England. Simon Fish and William Roye were dead. William Barlow and George Constantine were possibly at Antwerp, but they lacked the deep conviction and steadiness of purpose that mark our tract.[2]

Although his last sentence is arguable, Mozley's conclusions seem just. At the very least, we can say that the author of *The Souper* was not a totally obscure figure: his assumption that Thomas More would know him precludes that possibility. Only some striking new piece of evidence, internal or external, would make it worth our while to bring someone other than Tyndale or Joye into the controversy at this late date.

The arguments presented here, though not conclusive, virtually eliminate Tyndale's claim to authorship of *The Souper of the Lorde*. Mozley's case for Tyndale, whether based on questions of doctrine, on stylistics, or on biographical and historical data, does not stand up to careful scrutiny. Similarly, the supporters of Joye, admittedly less partisan than Mozley, frequently show certainty where skepticism would be more in order. In the end, although the case for Joye seems the more attractive of the two, the verdict must remain "not proven." If we were certain that the only possibilities were Tyndale and Joye, then Joye would be the only reasonable choice.

---

[1] *I*, 350.

[2] "The Supper of the Lord 1533," p. 16.

APPENDIX C

Table of Corresponding Pages:
The 1533 Edition, the 1557 Edition,
and The Yale Edition

APPENDIX C

Table of Corresponding Pages

Signatures in 1533 edition	Page numbers in 1557 edition	Page numbers in Yale edition
Aa₁	1035	1
Aa₂	1035	2
Aa₂v	1035	3
Aa₃	1035	3–4
Aa₃v	1035	4
Aa₄	1035–1036	4–5
Aa₄v	1036	5
Aa₅	1036	5
Aa₅v	1036	5–6
Aa₆	1036	6
Aa₆v	1036	6–7
Aa₇	1036–1037	7
Aa₇v	1037	7
Aa₈	1037	7–8
Aa₈v	1037	8
Bb₁	1037	8
Bb₁v	1037	8–9
Bb₂	1037	9
Bb₂v	1038	9
Bb₃	1038	9–10
Bb₃v	1038	10
Bb₄	1038	10–11
Bb₄v	1038	11
Bb₅	1038	11
Bb₅v	1038–1039	11–12
Bb₆	1039	12
Bb₆v	1039	12
Bb₇	1039	12–13

Signatures in 1533 edition	Page numbers in 1557 edition	Page numbers in Yale edition
Bb_7v	1039	13
a_1	1039	15
a_1v	1039–1040	15
a_2	1040	15–16
a_2v	1040	16
a_3	1040	16
a_3v	1040	16–17
a_4	1040	17
a_4v	1040–1041	17–18
a_5	1041	18
a_5v	1041	18
a_6	1041	18–19
a_6v	1041	19
a_7	1041	19
a_7v	1041–1042	19–20
a_8	1042	20
a_8v	1042	20
b_1	1042	20–21
b_1v	1042	21
b_2	1042	21–22
b_2v	1042–1043	22
b_3 (missigned b_2)	1043	22
b_3v	1043	22
b_4	1043	22–23
b_4v	1043	23
b_5	1043–1044	23–24
b_5v	1044	24
b_6	1044	24
b_6v	1044	25
b_7	1044	25
b_7v	1044	25–26
b_8	1044	26
b_8v	1044–1045	26
c_1	1045	26–27
c_1v	1045	27
c_2	1045	27–28
c_2v	1045	28
c_3	1045	28
c_3v	1046	28–29

Signatures in 1533 edition	Page numbers in 1557 edition	Page numbers in Yale edition
c$_4$	1046	29
c$_4$v	1046	29
c$_5$	1046	29–30
c$_5$v	1046	30
c$_6$	1046	30–31
c$_6$v	1046–1047	31
c$_7$	1047	31
c$_7$v	1047	31–32
c$_8$	1047	32
c$_8$v	1047	32–33
d$_1$	1047	33
d$_1$v	1047–1048	33
d$_2$	1048	33–34
d$_2$v	1048	34
d$_3$	1048	34
d$_3$v	1048	34–35
d$_4$	1048	35
d$_4$v	1048–1049	35–36
d$_5$	1049	36
d$_5$v	1049	36
d$_6$	1049	36–37
d$_6$v	1049	37
d$_7$	1049	37
d$_7$v	1050	37–38
d$_8$	1050	38
d$_8$v	1050	38–39
e$_1$	1050	39
e$_1$v	1050	39
e$_2$	1050–1051	39–40
e$_2$v	1051	40
e$_3$	1051	40
e$_3$v	1051	40–41
e$_4$	1051	41
e$_4$v	1051	41
e$_5$	1051–1052	41–42
e$_5$v	1052	42
e$_6$	1052	42–43
e$_6$v	1052	43
e$_7$	1052	43

Signatures in 1533 edition	Page numbers in 1557 edition	Page numbers in Yale edition
e_7v	1052	43–44
e_8	1052–1053	44
e_8v	1053	44
f_1	1053	44–45
f_1v	1053	45
f_2	1053	45
f_2v	1053	45–46
f_3	1053–1054	46
f_3v	1054	46–47
f_4	1054	47
f_4v	1054	47
f_5	1054	47–48
f_5v	1054	48
f_6	1054–1055	48
f_6v	1055	48–49
f_7	1055	49
f_7v	1055	49
f_8	1055	49–50
f_8v	1055	50
g_1	1055–1056	50–51
g_1v	1056	51
g_2	1056	51
g_2v	1056	51–52
g_3	1056	52
g_3v	1056	52
g_4	1056	52–53
g_4v	1056–1057	53
g_5	1057	53
g_5v	1057	54
g_6	1057	54
g_6v	1057	54–55
g_7	1057	55
g_7v	1057–1058	55
g_8	1058	55–56
g_8v	1058	56
h_1	1058	56
h_1v	1058	56–57
h_2	1058	57
h_2v	1058–1059	57

Signatures in 1533 edition	Page numbers in 1557 edition	Page numbers in Yale edition
h₃	1059	57–58
h₃v	1059	58
h₄	1059	58–59
h₄v	1059	59
h₅	1059	59
h₅v	1059–1060	59–60
h₆	1060	60
h₆v	1060	60
h₇	1060	60–61
h₇v	1060	61
h₈	1060	61
h₈v	1060–1061	61–62
i₁	1061	62
i₁v	1061	62
i₂	1061	62–63
i₂v	1061	63
i₃	1061	63–64
i₃v	1061–1062	64
i₄	1062	64
i₄v	1062	64–65
i₅	1062	65
i₅v	1062	65
i₆	1062	65–66
i₆v	1062–1063	66
i₇	1063	66–67
i₇v	1063	67
i₈	1063	67
i₈v	1063	67–68
k₁	1063	68
k₁v	1063–1064	68
k₂	1064	68–69
k₂v	1064	69
k₃	1064	69–70
k₃v	1064	70
k₄	1064	70
k₄v	1064–1065	70–71
k₅	1065	71
k₅v	1065	71
k₆	1065	71–72

Signatures in 1533 edition	Page numbers in 1557 edition	Page numbers in Yale edition
k_6v	1065	72
k_7	1065	72
k_7v	1065–1066	72–73
k_8	1066	73
k_8v	1066	73
l_1	1066	73–74
l_1v	1066	74
l_2	1066–1067	74–75
l_2v	1067	75
l_3	1067	75
l_3v	1067	75–76
l_4	1067	76
l_4v	1067	76
l_5	1067–1068	76–77
l_5v	1068	77
l_6	1068	77
l_6v	1068	77–78
l_7	1068	78
l_7v	1068–1069	78–79
l_8	1069	79
l_8v	1069	79
m_1	1069	79–80
m_1v	1069	80
m_2	1069	80
m_2v	1069–1070	80–81
m_3	1070	81
m_3v	1070	81
m_4	1070	81–82
m_4v	1070	82
m_5	1070	82
m_5v	1070–1071	82–83
m_6	1071	83
m_6v	1071	83–84
m_7	1071	84
m_7v	1071	84
m_8	1071–1072	84–85
m_8v	1072	85
n_1	1072	85
n_1v	1072	85–86

Signatures in 1533 edition	Page numbers in 1557 edition	Page numbers in Yale edition
n₂	1072	86
n₂v	1072	86–87
n₃	1072–1073	87
n₃v	1073	87
n₄	1073	87–88
n₄v	1073	88
n₅	1073	88
n₅v	1073	88–89
n₆	1073–1074	89
n₆v	1074	89–90
n₇	1074	90
n₇v	1074	90
n₈	1074	90–91
n₈v	1074–1075	91
o₁	1075	91
o₁v	1075	91–92
o₂	1075	92
o₂v	1075	92–93
o₃	1075	93
o₃v	1075–1076	93
o₄	1076	93–94
o₄v	1076	94
o₅	1076	94
o₅v	1076	94–95
o₆	1076	95
o₆v	1077 (misnumbered 1078)	96
o₇	1077	96
o₇v	1077	96–97
o₈	1077	97
o₈v	1077	97
p₁	1077–1078 (misnumbered 1076)	97–98
p₁v	1078	98
p₂	1078	98–99
p₂v	1078	99
p₃	1078	99
p₃v	1078–1079	99–100
p₄	1079	100

Signatures in 1533 edition	Page numbers in 1557 edition	Page numbers in Yale edition
p4v	1079	100
p5	1079	100–01
p5v	1079	101
p6	1079	101
p6v	1079–1080	101–02
p7	1080	102
p7v	1080	102
p8	1080	103
p8v	1080	103
q1	1080	103–04
q1v	1080–1081	104
q2	1081	104
q2v	1081	104–05
q3	1081	105
q3v	1081	105–06
q4	1081	106
q4v	1081–1082	106
q5	1082	106–07
q5v	1082	107
q6	1082	107
q6v	1082	108
q7	1082–1083	108
q7v	1083	108–09
q8	1083	109
q8v	1083	109
r1	1083	109–10
r1v	1083	110
r2	1083–1084	110
r2v	1084	110–11
r3	1084	111
r3v	1084	111
r4	1084	111–12
r4v	1084	112
r5	1084–1085	112
r5v	1085	112–13
r6	1085	113
r6v	1085	113–14
r7	1085	114
r7v	1085	114–15

Signatures in 1533 edition	Page numbers in 1557 edition	Page numbers in Yale edition
r_8	1085–1086	115
r_8v	1086	115
s_1	1086	115–16
s_1v	1086	116
s_2	1086	116
s_2v	1086	116–17
s_3	1086–1087	117
s_3v	1087	117–18
s_4	1087	118
s_4v	1087	118
s_5	1087	118–19
s_5v	1087	119
s_6	1087–1088	119
s_6v	1088	119–20
s_7	1088	120
s_7v	1088	120–21
s_8	1088	121
s_8v	1088–1089	121
t_1	1089	121–22
t_1v	1089	122
t_2	1089	122–23
t_2v	1089	123
t_3	1089	123
t_3v	1089–1090	123–24
t_4	1090	124
t_4v	1090	124
t_5	1090	124–25
t_5v	1090	125
t_6	1090	125–26
t_6v	1090–1091	126
t_7	1091	126
t_7v	1091	126–27
t_8	1091	127
t_8v	1091	127
v_1	1091	127–28
v_1v	1091–1092	128
v_2	1092	128
v_2v	1092	129
v_3	1092	129

Signatures in 1533 edition	Page numbers in 1557 edition	Page numbers in Yale edition
v₃v	1092	129–30
v₄	1092–1093	130
v₄v	1093	130–31
v₅	1093	131
v₅v	1093	131
v₆	1093	131–32
v₆v	1093	132
v₇	1093–1094	132
v₇v	1094	132–33
v₈	1094	133
v₈v	1094	133
x₁	1094	133–34
x₁v	1094–1095	134
x₂	1095	134–35
x₂v	1095	135
x₃	1095	135
x₃v	1095	136
x₄	1095	136
x₄v	1095–1096	136–37
x₅	1096	137
x₅v	1096	137
x₆	1096	137–38
x₆v	1096	138
x₇	1096	138–39
x₇v	1096–1097	139
x₈	1097	139
x₈v	1097	139–40
y₁	1097	140
y₁v	1097	140
y₂	1097	140–41
y₂v	1097–1098	141
y₃	1098	141
y₃v	1098	141–42
y₄	1098	142
y₄v	1098–1099	142–43
y₅	1099	143
y₅v	1099	143
y₆	1099	143–44
y₆v	1099	144

Signatures in 1533 edition	Page numbers in 1557 edition	Page numbers in Yale edition
y_7	1099	144
y_7v	1099–1100	145
y_8	1100	145
y_8v	1100	145
z_1	1100	146
z_1v	1100	146
z_2	1100	146–47
z_2v	1100–1101	147
z_3	1101	147
z_3v	1101	147–48
z_4	1101	148
z_4v	1101	148–49
z_5	1101–1102	149
z_5v	1102	149
z_6	1102	149–50
z_6v	1102	150
z_7	1102	150–51
z_7v	1102	151
z_8	1102–1103	151
z_8v	1103	151–52
A_1	1103	152
A_1v	1103	152
A_2	1103	152–53
A_2v	1103–1104	153
A_3	1104	153
A_3v	1104	153–54
A_4	1104	154
A_4v	1104	154–55
A_5	1104	155
A_5v	1104–1105	155
A_6	1105	156–56
A_6v	1105	156
A_7	1105	156
A_7v	1105	156–57
A_8	1105	157
A_8v	1106	157–58
B_1	1106	158
B_1v	1106	158
B_2	1106	158–59

Signatures in 1533 edition	Page numbers in 1557 edition	Page numbers in Yale edition
B_2v	1106	159
B_3	1106–1107	159
B_3v	1107	159–60
B_4	1107	160
B_4v	1107	160
B_5	1107	160–61
B_5v	1107	161
B_6	1107–1108	161
B_6v	1108	161–62
B_7	1108	162
B_7v	1108	162–63
B_8	1108	163
B_8v	1108	163
C_1	1108–1109	163–64
C_1v	1109	164
C_2	1109	164
C_2v	1109	164–65
C_3	1109	165
C_3v	1109–1110	165–66
C_4	1110	166
C_4v	1110	166–67
C_5	1110	167
C_5v	1110	167
C_6	1110–1111	167–68
C_6v	1111	168
C_7	1111	168
C_7v	1111	168–69
C_8	1111	169
C_8v	1111–1112	169–70
D_1	1112	170
D_1v	1112	170
D_2	1112	170–71
D_2v	1112	171
D_3	1112	171
D_3v	1112–1113	171–72
D_4	1113	172
D_4v	1113	172–73
D_5	1113	173
D_5v	1113	173

Signatures in *1533 edition*	*Page numbers in* *1557 edition*	*Page numbers in* *Yale edition*
D_6	1113	173–74
D_6v	1113–1114	174
D_7	1114	174
D_7v	1114	174–75
D_8	1114	175
D_8v	1114	175
E_1	1114–1115	175–76
E_1v	1115	176
E_2	1115	176
E_2v	1115	176–77
E_3	1115	177
E_3v	1115	177–78
E_4	1115–1116	178
E_4v	1116	178
E_5	1116	178–79
E_5v	1116	179
E_6	1116	179–80
E_6v	1116–1117	180
E_7	1117	180
E_7v	1117	180–81
E_8	1117	181
E_8v	1117	181
F_1	1117	181–82
F_1v	1117–1118	182
F_2	1118	182
F_2v	1118	182–83
F_3	1118	183
F_3v	1118	183
F_4	1118	183–84
F_4v	1118–1119	184
F_5	1119	184
F_5v	1119	184–85
F_6	1119	185
F_6v	1119	185–86
F_7	1119–1120	186
F_7v	1120	186
F_8	1120	186–87
F_8v	1120	187
G_1	1120	187

Signatures in 1533 edition	Page numbers in 1557 edition	Page numbers in Yale edition
G_1v	1120	187–88
G_2	1120–1121	188
G_2v	1121	188–89
G_3	1121	189
G_3v	1121	189
G_4	1121–1122	189–90
G_4v	1122	190
G_5	1122	190–91
G_5v	1122	191
G_6	1122	191
G_6v	1122	191–92
G_7	1122–1123	192
G_7v	1123	192
G_8	1123	192–93
G_8v	1123	193
H_1	1123	193
H_1v	1123–1124	193–94
H_2	1124	194
H_2v	1124	194–95
H_3	1124	195
H_3v	1124	195
H_4	1124–1125	195–96
H_4v	1125	196
H_5	1125	196–97
H_5v	1125	197
H_6	1125	197
H_6v	1125–1126	197–98
H_7	1126	198
H_7v	1126	198
H_8	1126	198–99
H_8v	1126	199
I_1	1126	199–200
I_1v	1126–1127	200
I_2	1127	200
I_2v	1127	200–01
I_3	1127	201
I_3v	1127	201
I_4	1128	201–02
I_4v	1128	202

Signatures in 1533 edition	Page numbers in 1557 edition	Page numbers in Yale edition
I$_5$	1128	202
I$_5$v	1128	202–03
I$_6$	1128	203
I$_6$v	1128–1129	203
I$_7$	1129	203–04
I$_7$v	1129	204
I$_8$	1129	204
I$_8$v	1129	204–05
K$_1$	1129	205
K$_1$v	1129–1130	205–06
K$_2$	1130	206
K$_2$v	1130	206
K$_3$	1130	206–07
K$_3$v	1130	207
K$_4$	1130–1131	207–08
K$_4$v	1131	208
K$_5$	1131	208
K$_5$v	1131	208–09
K$_6$	1131	209
K$_6$v	1131	209
K$_7$	1131–1132	209–10
K$_7$v	1132	210
K$_8$	1132	210
K$_8$v	1132	210–11
L$_1$	1132	211
L$_1$v	1132	211
L$_2$	1132–1133	212
L$_2$v	1133	212–13
L$_3$	1133	213
L$_3$v	1133	213
L$_4$	1133	213–14
L$_4$v	1133–1134	214
L$_5$	1134	214
L$_5$v	1134	214–15
L$_6$	1134	215
L$_6$v	1134	215
L$_7$	1134	215–16
L$_7$v	1134–1135	216
L$_8$	1135	216–17

Signatures in 1533 edition	Page numbers in 1557 edition	Page numbers in Yale edition
L₈v	1135	217
M₁	1135	217
M₁v	1135	217–18
M₂	1135	218
M₂v	1135–1136	218
M₃	1136	218–19
M₃v	1136	219
M₄	1136	219
M₄v	1136	219–20
M₅	1136	220
M₅v	1136–1137	220
M₆	1137	220–21
M₆v	1137	221
M₇	1137	221
M₇v	1137	221–22
M₈	1137	222
M₈v	1137–1138	222
N₁	1138	222–23
N₁v	1138	223
N₂	1138	223

GLOSSARY

GLOSSARY

This glossary is intended to contain only words whose meanings or forms (not merely spellings) are obsolete or archaic according to *The Oxford English Dictionary*. It also includes a few words which might be puzzling because of their spelling or some other ambiguity. In general, if a word recurs more than twice, only the first instance, followed by "*etc.*," is given. Unusual spellings of proper names have also been included.

a *prep.* on 99/15; in 181/13

abacke *adv. gone abacke* lapsed 92/26

Abacuk *n.* Habakkuk 165/39

abide *v. See* **abyd(e)**

abominacyon *n.* abhorrence, loathing 59/23

about(e) *adv.* all round 6/28 *etc.*; *bysy about. See* **bysy**

aboute *prep.* concerned or occupied with 34/9

abrode *adv.* abroad, at large 4/25 *etc.*; *laieth out abrode. See* **lay**

abyd(e), abide *v.* tolerate, put up with 3/26 *etc.*; wait for 6/27, 172/23; remain 21/25 *etc.*; stand by 71/4 *etc.*

abydyng(e) *vbl. n.* remaining 87/30

accompted *pp* reckoned 3/20

adiure *v.* change under oath 98/30

a do *n.* stir, trouble 220/34

aduaunce *v.* promote 9/30

aduenture *n.* risk 6/27

aduertysement *n.* admonition, warning 120/4

aduowtry *n. See* **a(d)uowtry**

aduysed *v. pt.* pondered 61/3

aferde *ppl. a.* afraid 174/17

affeccyon, affeccion *n.* attraction 60/21, *pl.* **affeccions** feelings 32/26, 46/32

affeccyonate *adj.* disposed, inclined 46/7

afore *adv.* before 77/19, 189/5

afore *prep.* before 53/13 *etc.*

after *prep.* according to 3/19 *etc.*; *after time y* after 3/31

after *adv.* afterward 6/9 *etc.*

agayne *adv.* in reply 26/20 *etc.*; *prep.* in anticipation of 174/21

agaynst *conj.* against the time at which 183/37

agre *v.* agree 21/5 *etc.*; accept favorably 162/11, 203/37

a hungred, an hungred *adj.* hungry 32/17 *etc.*

a knowen *ppl. a. be a knowen (of)* confess, avow, acknowledge 126/10, 131/17–18

all in great. *See* **great**

albe it, al(l) be it, all be yt, albe yt *conj.* albeit, although 4/9 *etc.*

ale polys *n. pl.* poles set up as the signs of alehouses 223/11

all *adv.* completely 8/35 *etc.*; *all were there* although there were 15/15

alledged *v. pt.* adduced, cited 73/23, 195/1

allegorye sence *phr.* allegorical sense 165/23

allegoryke *adj.* allegorical 177/17

all thynge *n. phr.* everything, all things 43/11–12

almoyse *n.* alms 38/6

al(l) way(e), alway(e) *adv.* always 22/1 *etc.*

amende *v. trans.* change, correct 9/29; *intrans.* repent, improve 84/25 *etc.*

amonge *adv.* occasionally, now and then 13/2

and *conj.* if 163/25, 198/30

anelyng *vbl. n.* anointing, extreme unction 205/18

anone *adv.* immediately 65/20; soon 136/10

antecedent *n.* statement in logic upon which any consequent statement depends 178/8, 208/31–32

anythyng(e) *adv.* in any way, to any extent 3/20 *etc.*

a pace, apace *adv.* swiftly 35/9

a payed *ppl. a.* contented, pleased 46/18

apostatas *n. pl.* apostates 75/29

apostleshyp *n.* office or position of an apostle 91/28

apperteyneth *v. pr. 3 s.* is appropriate 94/30

appropre *v.* assign or attribute as proper to 190/24

appropr(y)ed *ppl. a.* appropriate 188/35 *etc.*

ascaped *ppl. a.* escaped 163/19

assygne *v.* prescribe, appoint authoritatively 180/5; *pt.* **assigned** 35/20; *pr. 3 s.* **assygneth** 159/2, 180/3

astonied *ppl. a.* benumbed 76/35

at *prep.* on 156/35, 157/22; in 40/10; with 40/11; to 48/24

auansynge *vbl. n.* advancing 104/6

auaunce *v.* advance 125/21

aulter *n. See* **autare**

a(d)uowtry *n.* adultery 109/30 *etc.*

auoyde *v.* nullify 96/30 *etc.*

Austayn(e) *n.* Augustine 39/1 *etc.*

autare, aulter, awtre, awter, auter *n.* altar 10/7 *etc.*

awne *adj.* own 10/23 *etc.*

a woynge *vbl. n. See* **wowyng**

awtre, awter *n. See* **autare**

a wurke, awurke *adv.* at work 184/24; *sette a wurke* roused to action 48/7

axe *v.* ask 65/1

bad *v. pt. See* **byd**

bandes *n. pl.* bonds 19/30

bare *adj.* mere, simple 7/12 *etc.*; naked, poor 9/33 *etc.*

barke *n.* external part, bark 136/12

Barons *n. poss.* Barnes's 135/20

bartlemew tyde *n.* St. Bartholomew's Day (August 24) 6/34

be *v. pr. 3 pl.* are 6/2 *etc.*

becom(m)eth, bycometh *v. pr. 3 s.* suits, is proper (for) 90/34 *etc.*; *where yt bycometh*

what becomes of it 7/17; *pt.* **bycame** suited 12/35, 90/35

bedelem *n.* Bedlam, St. Mary of Bethlehem hospital for the insane in London; *bedelem rype* ready for an insane asylum 7/3

bedys *n. pl.* rosary 186/31

begate *v. pt.* begot 77/23 *etc.*

behauour *n.* behavior, conduct 152/23

behofull *adj.* behoveful, necessary, 195/16

beholden, byholden *ppl. a.* beheld 206/26, 207/15

behoueth *v. pr. 3 s.* behooves, befits, requires 152/14 *etc.*

bely *n.* belly 28/3 *etc.*; *theyr (your) bely ioy* the satisfaction of their (your) bellies 34/14, 47/35; *your bely meat* the food for your bellies 47/36; *pl.* **belyes** 16/10 *etc.*

belyed *pp. See* **bylye**

belyeth *v. pr. 3 s. See* **bylye**

belyke *adv. See* **by lyke**

bent *pp.* turned 7/16

bere *n.* beer 101/30; bear 178/4

bere *v.* endure, bear 113/25 *etc.*; *bere . . . in hande* maintain or assert against 84/7 *etc.*; *pt.* **bare** bore 174/7, 174/11; *bereth me recorde. See* **recorde**

beshrew *v.* curse 7/6

besy *adj. See* **bysy**

besyde(s), bysyde(s), by syde *adv.* besides, over and above 10/8 *etc.*

besyd(e), bysyde *prep.* besides, in addition to 17/13 *etc.*

betrappe *v.* entrap 159/35, 163/27

betrayeng *vbl. n.* betrayal 24/5–6

bewraye *v.* expose 93/13

blere *v.* deceive, blind 133/35, 152/16

blosh *v.* blush 219/30

blynd(e) *v.* deceive 20/37 *etc.*

boch(e) *n.* boil, ulcer 99/4 *etc.*

bo(u)chers *n. pl.* butchers 58/14 *etc.*

bode *v. pt. See* **byd**

bodyly, bodely *adv.* corporeally, bodily 134/15 *etc.*

bond *adj. bond slauys* bondslaves 46/30

bonde *n.* binding agreement 59/33, 127/4

bord(e) *n.* table 7/9 *etc.*

borne *ppl. a.* natural 4/15

both(e) *adj.* two 27/25 *etc.*; *theyr(e) bothe of them both* 31/2 *etc.*; *any of the bothe* either 42/20–21

bounde(n) *ppl. a.* bound, obligated 61/13 *etc.*

bowes, boughes *n. pl.* boughs 185/21, 205/15

brage *n.* show, display 147/8

brasyn *adj.* brass 68/14

breke *v.* break 19/30 *etc.*; remove, halt 129/6 *etc.*; *pt.* **brake** 106/26, 215/21

bretherhed *n.* brotherhood 9/15 *etc.*

brethern(e) *n. pl.* brethren, brothers 6/20 *etc.*

brigittane *adj.* Brigittine, belonging to the order of the Brigittines 128/5

broke *ppl. a.* broken 206/27

bryng(e) *v.* *brynge forth* give birth to, bear, yield, produce 12/8 *etc.*; express, put forth, advance 15/9 *etc.*; *bryng(e) in* introduce 11/13 *etc.*

bumblyng *vbl. n.* blundering 121/1

but *adv.* only 6/7 *etc.*

but *conj.* that 68/5, 68/27; *but if, but yf* unless 15/28 *etc.*, *but that* that 4/17

by *prep.* through, by means of 3/30 *etc.*; in the possession of 7/29; concerning 8/5 *etc.*; because of 42/6 *etc.*; *conj. phr.* **by that that,** by the fact that 30/2–3, 99/19; *by the way(e).* See **way(e)**

by & by, by and by *adv.* immediately, at once 35/22 *etc.*

bycame *v. pt.* See **becom(m)eth**

bycometh *v. pr. 3 s.* See **becom(m)eth**

byd *v.* ask, exhort, command 5/1 *etc.*; wish 5/21 *etc.*; *pt.* **bad** 32/33, 33/11; *pt.* **bode** 34/7 *etc.*; *pr. 3 s.* **byddeth** 5/1 *etc.*

byddyng(e) *ppl. a.* asking, exhorting, commanding 23/29 *etc.*

byddynges *vbl. n. pl.* commands 5/24

bye mater *n.* something beside the main business 194/37

bylye *v.* belie, slander 47/20 *etc.*; *pp.* **belyed, bylyed** 107/21, 158/12; *pr. 3 s.* **belyeth, bylyeth** 153/21 *etc.*

by lyke, belyke, bylyke *adv.* perhaps, possibly 200/11 *etc.*

bysinesse, bysynes(se) *n.* busyness, activity 33/18 *etc.*

bysy, besy *adj.* concerned (with or to) 5/8 *etc.*; meddlesome 198/7

bytyme, by tyme *adv.* early, in good time 184/35 *etc.*

bywayle *v.* bewail 140/29

cach(e) catch *v.* seize on 5/6; catch 163/24 *etc.*

can *v.* *can . . . thanke.* See **thanke**

cancred *ppl. a.* cankered, ulcerated 99/4, 99/12

cankar *n.* spreading malignancy, cancer 4/37

canon *n.* portion of the mass containing the words of consecration 99/17 *etc.*

Cap(h)arnaum *n.* Capernaum 16/7 *etc.*

capcyouse *adj.* See **captiouse**

captiouse, captyouse, capcyouse *adj.* fallacious, sophistical 159/26 *etc.*

care *v.* mind, be anxious, be concerned 12/24

cartusyan *adj.* Carthusian 128/4

case *n.* condition, plight 62/19, 140/20; *pl.* **casys** instances 122/3

caste *v.* **caste . . . awaye** *v. phr.* waste 48/28

cast(e) *n.* throw (of dice) 13/2 *etc.*; trick 133/21

cause *n.* reason 6/1 *etc.*

causeles *adv.* without reason 93/7

caytyfe *n.* villain 186/23; *pl.* **caytyffes** 128/9

chapyter, chapiter *n.* chapter 10/18 *etc.*

character *n.* stamp 30/21

charge *n.* *laye . . . charge.* See **lay(e)**

chekys *n. pl.* jawbones 47/34

chese, chose, choyse *v.* choose, select 89/30 *etc. pr. 3 s.* **chosyth** 93/18

christen *adj.* See **chrysten**

christened *v. pp.* Christianized 41/12

chrysten, christen, crysten *adj.* Christian 3/4 *etc.*

chrystenly *adv.* in a Christian way 37/24

chylderne, chyldren *n. pl.* children 90/17 *etc.*

ciuilyte *n.* politeness 5/26

clawing *ppl. a.* scratching 32/19

clene *adj.* pure 75/16, 95/2

clene *adv.* completely, altogether 7/15 *etc.*

clennesse *n.* purity 3/30, 4/2

clere *adv.* clearly 144/29 *etc.*; *comp.* **more clerer** more clearly 141/10

clerke *n.* cleric, scholar 187/24, 220/6

clerklynes *n.* scholarliness 121/17

cleue *v.* cling 120/11, 123/22

closely *adv.* secretly, privately 8/17

clowt(e) *n.* cloth, bandage 99/11, 99/12

coke *n.* **Colyn coke** Colin cook 220/5. *See n.*

cokery *n. See* **coquery**

cokstewe *n.* 198/27. *See n.*

colour *n.* show of reason, specious or plausible reason or ground 98/3 *etc.*

Colyn coke *n. See* **coke**

come *ppl. a. come ouer* arrived 9/36

come(n) *v.* approach, arrive 3/26 *etc.*; *come at* reach (with implied effort) 40/32 *etc.*; *come of* come along 35/8; *come to* arrive at, attain 40/5 *etc.*; *pp.* **come(n)** 6/35 *etc.*; *pr. 3 s.* **com(m)eth** 5/7 *etc.*; *cometh me* comes to me 56/24

comely *adj.* appropriate, seemly 17/9

com(m)en *adj.* common, customary 4/15 *etc.*; ordinary 36/24 *etc.*

com(m)en *adv.* commonly 135/6, 180/18

come(n) *pp. See* **come**

commodyte *n.* advantage, benefit 12/12, 132/10

communycacyon, communicacyon, communicacion *n.* action of communicating or imparting 3/23 *etc.*; interchange of speech, conversation 4/4 *etc.*

compacted *pp. compacted up* packed 118/28

compendiously *adv.* succinctly 5/12-13

compendyouse *adj.* succinct 28/12, 118/27

compte *n.* estimation 3/19

compute manuell *n.* set of tables for calculating astronomical occurrences and the movable feasts of the calendar 169/4

conceyue *v.* understand 43/27, 180/31; conceive (a child) 58/21-22 *etc.*; *pp.* **conceyued, conceiued** imagined, formed 58/10 *etc.*; *pp. pass.* **conceyued** made pregnant 58/35 *etc.*

conclusyon *n. in conclusyon* finally 46/20 *etc.*

condempneth *v. pr. 3 s.* condemns 124/32

condycyon *n.* provision, stipulation 151/22; *pl.* morals 85/23

confermyth *v. pr. 3 s.* strengthens 92/18; *pt.* **confermed** established 138/12; *pp.* **confermed, confyrmed** 59/9, 186/9

conferre *v.* compare 11/22, 114/18

confesseth for *v. pr. 3 s.* acknowledges as 148/11

confounde *v.* confute 117/5-6; confuse 188/37

confusyon, confusion *n.* ruin, overthrow 199/5 *etc.*

confute *v.* refute 6/32 *etc.*

congrewe *a.* grammatically correct 159/6

congruens *n. of good congruence* as is fitting or reasonable 90/10, 152/15

congruytie *n.* grammatical correctness 159/5

coniunccyon, coniunccion *n.* union, joining 28/25 *etc.*

connynge *adj. and n. See* **cunnyng(e)**

consecucyon *n.* sequence of reasoning, train of logic 85/3, 178/10

consequency *n.* conclusion of an argument 85/3

consequent *adj.* following 85/1

consequent(e) *n.* conclusion of a syllogism 169/3 *etc.*

conseruacion *n.* preservation 28/8

conserue *v.* preserve 3/31 *etc.*

consonaunt *adj.* in agreement (with) 91/17

constantely *adv.* steadfastly 118/12

construccyon *n.* interpretation 98/9

consyderacyon, consyderacion *n.* regard 139/5-6

contagyon, contagion *n.* contagious disease, plague 3/22, 4/36

contend(e) *v.* argue 58/4 *etc.*

contingent *adj.* happening by chance 85/2

contradyccyon *n.* opposition, denial 62/31 *etc.*

contraryed *pp.* contradicted 11/16, 15/10-11

contraryeng *vbl. n.* contradicting 99/1

contraryouse *adj.* mutually opposed, antagonistic 106/22, 203/18

controll(e) *v.* restrain 6/18, 9/31; check on 95/12

contynue *v.* persist in being 73/5

conuayaunce *n.* sleight of hand 199/1-2

conuayth *v. pr. 3 s. See* **conuey**

conuenient, conuenyent *adj.* proper, fitting, suitable 18/3-4 *etc.*

conuey, conuay(e) *v.* carry, remove 7/10 *etc.*; transmit 129/9 *etc.*; *pr. 3 s.* **conuayth** 7/7

copulatyue *adj.* including a connecting conjunction such as " and " 161/7

coquery, cokery *n.* cookery 10/27, 220/3

corage, cowrage *n.* boldness 4/23 *etc.*; *a corage to the cuppe* an appetite for drink 32/3

corne *n.* grain 10/9 *etc.*; *corne felde* field of grain 19/19

corps *n.* a body of persons 203/6

corrupt *adj.* rotting 4/37

Corynthyes, Corinthyes, Corynthies *n. pl.* Corinthians 4/31 *etc.*

couetyce *n.* covetousness 90/26

counsayle, counsell *n.* advice 186/22 *etc.*; council 122/24 *etc.*; *preuey counsell, pryuy counsayle* privy council 200/10, 200/32; *pl.* assemblies of ecclesiastics convened to determine doctrine or discipline 183/22 *etc.*

countenaunce *n.* demeanor 1/21

couple *v.* join 94/8

courtesye *n. See* **c(o)urtesy(e)**

cowrage *n. See* **corage**

craft(e) *n.* guile, cunning 35/8 *etc.*

cryed at the crosse 200/35. *See n.*

cunnyng(e), connynge *adj.* learned 52/34 *etc.*

cunnyng(e), connynge *n.* learning 83/1 *etc.*

cunnyngly *adv.* learnedly 17/9

cuppe *n. a corage to the cuppe. See* **corage**

cure *n.* concern 87/1

c(o)urtesy(e) *n.* bow, curtsy 99/37; courteous behaviour 99/7, 181/26; *of his courtesye* by his indulgence, by his good will 123/18

custumable *adj.* customary 207/6

custumes *n. pl.* taxes 38/8

dane *See n.* to 128/3–4

darke *adj.* obscure, hard to understand 121/17, 202/8

dayntye *adj.* precious, excellent 7/16

declaracyon, declaracion *n.* explanation 11/2 *etc.*

declare *v.* reveal, make clear 9/20 *etc.*

declarynge *ppl. a.* elucidating 83/7, 175/6

declarynge *vbl. n.* elucidation 10/11, 138/12

declynacyon *n.* decline 4/6

degre *n.* rank 90/9

dekay(e) *n.* falling off 4/6, 9/24

delectacyon *n.* pleasure 92/24

delynge *vbl. n.* behavior, conduct 85/21, 91/6

delyuereth *v. 3 pr. s.* hands over 29/29; *pt.* saved 129/18; communicated, made known 127/15 *etc.*

delyuery *n.* handing over 127/22

demaund *v.* ask 214/27

departed *ppl. a.* separated 103/22

depose *v.* testify 196/28

dere *adj* costly 7/15

derogate *v.* detract from, lessen, 188/29 *etc.*

desperate *adj.* in despair 62/31–32, 86/22

desyre *v.* ask, request 48/29 *etc.*

desyryng *vbl. n.* requesting 61/19

deteccyon *n.* exposure 10/34

detect(e) *v.* reveal, expose 4/13, 10/27

determinacyon, determynacyon *n.* decision, resolution, 59/8 *etc.*

determyned *pp. refl.* resolved 58/27

determynynge *ppl. a.* deciding 107/17

deuour *n.* best effort 86/24, 86/28

deuyce *n.* contrivance 62/26, 81/21; *pl.* plans, opinions 64/19 *etc.*

deuyll *n. what deuyll* what the devil 139/15

dew(e) *adj.* proper 38/8 *etc.*

diffidence, diffydence, dyffydence, dyffydens *n.* lack of faith 61/25 *etc.*

discerne *v. See* **dyscerne**

discordeth *v. pr. 3 s.* is not in accord (with) 73/20

disposycyon *n.* tendency 24/17

dispyse *v.* treat with contempt 186/26; *pr. 3 s.* **dyspiseth, dyspyseth, dispyseth** 105/27 *etc.*

diuers(e) *adj. See* **dyvers(e)**

diuine *v.* conjecture 90/6

do *v.* perform 35/21 *etc.*; *pr. 2 s.* **doste** 88/13; *pt.* **dyd** *etc.*; *pp.* **done** exerted, used 12/5; *done on* put on 13/5, 219/20

doctour *n.* father of the church 52/34 *etc.*; *pl.* **doctour(e)s** 11/33 *etc.*

doctryne *n.* action of teaching 23/18 *etc.*

dole *n.* distribution of alms 198/17

dome *n.* doom, the Last Judgment 24/9; *domys daye* doomsday, and day of the Last Judgment 141/4 *etc.*

done *pp. See* **do**.

done *v.* do 39/33, 64/28

doste *v. pr. 2 s. See* **do** *v.*

dowble *adv.* doubly 130/19

dowtfully *adv.* apprehensively 173/16

doynges *vbl. n. pl.* deeds, actions 23/19

draue *v. See* **dreue**

draueth *v. pr. 3 s. See* **draw(e)**

draw(e) *v.* pull, attract 6/20 *etc.*; proceed 33/22; *pp.* **drawen** 86/30; *falsely drawen out* taken out of context 75/3; *pr. 3 s.* **draweth, draueth** 20/5 *etc.*; *pt. cond.* drew 87/9

drawynge *vbl. n.* inducing, attracting 48/5 *etc.*

dress *v.* prepare; *pr. 3 s.* **dresseth** 97/11; *pp.* dressed 220/5

dreue *v.* drive, force 66/30; *pt.* **draue** 33/22; *pp.* **dreuyn** 33/13 *etc.*; *pr. 3 s.* **dryueth** 6/19, 175/1

dreuyn *v. See* **dreue**

dronken *ppl. a.* drunk 72/5 *etc.*

druggys *n. pl.* medicines 120/24

dryft *n.* scheme 187/5

dryuynge *ppl. a. dryuynge furth* whiling away 33/18

durst *v. pr. 3 s. and pl.* dares 6/4 *etc.*

dyffydence *n. See* **diffidence**

dyffydens *n. See* **diffidence**

dymencyoned *ppl. a.* having material dimensions 129/11

dyryge *n. See n. to* 186/29–32

dyscerne, discerne *v.* separate 39/9, 39/14; determine 60/33; perceive by distinguishing 73/15, 94/23–24

dyscharge *v.* disburden, clear 5/26, 119/24

dysclosed *v. pt.* revealed 92/9

dyshe, dishe *n.* course (of a meal) 7/8, 7/15

dysimuleth *v. pr. 3 s.* pretends not to see 52/3

dyspicion, dyspycyon *n.* disputation, discussion 13/8 *etc.*; *pl.* **dyspycyons, dyspytyons** 195/2, 195/26

dyspiseth *v. pr. 3 s. See* **dispyse**

dysplesaunt *adj.* unpleasant 32/15–16

dysplesauntly *adv.* unpleasantly 52/29–30

dysproue *v.* refute 203/4

dyspycyons *n. pl. See* **dyspicion**

dyspyghtfull *adj.* insulting 223/19

dyspytyons *n. pl. See* **dyspicion**

dyssemble *v.* conceal, feign 57/12 *etc. See n. to* 126/4–27

dyssemblynge *vbl. n.* ignoring 20/34

dyssimulacyon, dyssymulacyon *n.* disguise, concealment 13/5, 115/28

dyssimulynge *ppl. a. See* **dyssymylyng**

dyssymulacyon *n. See* **dyssimulacyon**

dyssymylyng, dyssimulynge *ppl. a.* dissembling 5/35; concealing, disguising 13/5–6, 213/11

dystruste *v.* doubt 70/13

dyuers(e), diuers(e) *adj.* several, sundry 7/34 *etc.*; separate, distinct 18/3 *etc.*

dyuersyte *n.* difference 138/32

ease *v. refl.* relieve (one's bowels) 12/24

Ecolampadius *n.* Oecolampadius 220/20

effecte *n.* aim, intention 10/4 *etc.*

effectuall *adj.* producing an effect 73/30 *etc.*

effectually *adv.* in a manner producing an effect 72/28 *etc.*

efte (sonys) *adv.* a second time, again 107/25, 110/12

egall *adj.* equal 45/26 *etc.*

eleccyon, eleccion *n.* special choice by God 86/14 *etc.*

encompanied *ppl. a.* accompanied 120/1

ende *n. make an ende* conclude 50/18

endeuour *v. refl.* to exert oneself 28/17, 40/34

enforce *v. refl.* force oneself, endeavor strongly 19/34

enlengthed *pp.* lengthened 7/30

ensample *n.* example 53/24 *etc.*

enstructe *pp.* taught 141/22

entent *n. to thentent* (*that*), *to the entent that* in order that 20/18 *etc.*

entre *n.* introduction 25/25, 37/21

equyte *n.* fairness 152/3

ere *conj.* before 20/36 *etc.*

ere *prep.* before 3/24 *etc.*

ernest peny pledge 28/24 *etc.*

Esay(e), Esaie *n.* Isaiah 64/18 *etc.*

escewe *v.* eschew 5/17

espye *v.* discover, detect 199/2 *etc.*

Ester *n.* Easter 205/24

estimacyon, estymacyon *n.* reputation 9/21–22; valuation 46/34

ethe *adj.* easy 172/7

euerychone, euerichone *pron.* everyone 123/7, 164/30

euyl(l) *adj.* morally depraved, impious, wicked 4/4 *etc.*; wrong 21/8 *etc.*; *euyl wylled* malevolent, ill-willed 48/18; *euyll fauored* ugly 219/28

euyll *adv.* badly, wickedly 89/26

euyn *adv.* precisely 31/34, 70/19

exacteth *v. pr. 3 s.* requires 39/8

exalted *ppl. a.* raised high 64/20, 64/21

examynacyon *n. make examynacyon of* examine 151/26

except(e) *conj.* unless 6/35 *etc.*; *except that* unless 69/33

excepte *prep.* except for 4/19, 21/1

exercysed *ppl a.* trained 130/33

expedient *adj.* fitting 152/15

exposycion, exposycyon, exposcion *n.* explanation, interpretation 11/20 *etc.*; *theyr such exposycyon* that interpretation of theirs 112/20

expositours, expositours *n. pl.* commentators, exegetes 54/34 *etc.*

expowne, expoune *v.* expound, explain (to) 11/1 *etc.*; *expowneth . . . forth* goes on expounding 16/27

expownynge *vbl. n.* expounding, explaining 18/18 *etc.*

expresse *adj.* exactly resembling 30/24

expressely *adv.* exactly 30/35

eyen *n. pl.* eyes 21/2 *etc.*

eyther *adj.* each 11/15; **eyther other** either the one or the other 89/18

face *n.* mask 13/1 *etc.*

face *v. face . . . out* impudently controvert 181/13 *etc.*; *faceth . . . a lye . . . vppon* tells a manifest untruth 209/4, 219/12–13

facynge *vbl. n. facynge . . . out* impudent controverting (of the truth) 210/8

fader *n.* father 83/28 *etc.*

faithfully *adv.* with full faith or belief 29/35

fall *v.* descend, lapse 4/1 *etc.*; *fall to* begin, start 47/24 *etc.*; *fal in his own necke* descend on him 157/27; *pt.* **fel(l), fyll** 3/32 *etc., pp.* **fall(en)** 3/9 *etc.*

false *adv.* falsely 41/12

fals(e)(h)ed *n.* falsehood 9/32 *etc.*

fantasy *n.* illusory imagination 62/26; *pl.* **fantasyes** 116/6

fareth *v. pr. 3 s.* behaves, acts 12/23, 133/28

farpassynge *ppl. a.* surpassingly great 28/27, 31/8

farre *adj.* long 138/32; *for so farre. See* **for**; *comp.* **ferther** 60/26 *etc.*

farre *adv.* far 3/25 *etc.*; widely 4/7; *comp.* **ferther, forther** 4/37 *etc.*

farre fet *adj.* farfetched 193/23

fas(s)hyon *n. on . . . fasshyon* in . . . way 119/21, 120/7; *turne the fashyon* invert the process 178/5–6

fas(s)hyoned *ppl. a. thys fasshyoned* made in this way 30/26–27; *that fashyoned* fashioned in that way 177/34

fast(e) *adv.* firmly 4/18 *etc.*; tightly 19/28; quickly 175/4

faste *adj. firm* 80/8, 149/21

fastely *adv.* steadfastly 118/11

fastidyouse *adj.* disgusted 103/29

fastynge *ppl. a.* observing a fast 5/7

fauerours *n. pl.* promoters 221/33

fawt(e), fau(e)t(e) *n.* fault, sin 11/27 *etc.*

fay *n.* faith 163/1

fayne *adj.* glad, willing 37/9 *etc.*; obliged, constrained 100/8 *etc.*

fayne *adv.* gladly 32/36 *etc.*

fayne *v.* invent fictitiously, falsify 56/30 *etc.*; *refl.* make oneself appear 126/11

fayned *ppl. a.* hypocritical, insincere 75/28, 76/8

faynt *adj.* weak 5/9 *etc.*

faynynge *vbl. n.* creation (of the mind) 185/36

fayre *adv.* completely 165/2

faythfull *adj.* believing the true faith 4/20

faythlesse *adj.* not believing the true faith 4/20

felow *n.* partner, equal 5/10 *etc.*; *pl.* **felowes** 8/23 *etc.*; worthless people 18/17 *etc.*

felyng(e) *ppl. a.* deeply felt 86/15 *etc.*

fere *v. I fere me* I am afraid 70/1

ferther *adj. comp. See* **farre**

ferther *adv. comp. See* **farre**

festue *n.* small stick or pin for pointing out letters to children learning to read; pointer 149/17

figure, fygure *n.* type 23/22 *etc.*; form, image 30/27 *etc.*; emblem, symbol 52/13 *etc.*

figured *pp.* prefigured typologically 68/14, 79/11

fleshelynes *n.* corporeality 26/6

fle(s)sh(e)ly *adj.* carnal 4/9 *etc.*; bodily 17/23 *etc.*

flesshely *adv.* carnally 69/14

fleynge *vbl. n.* fleeing 204/24, 204/25

flitteth, flytteth *v. pr. 3 s.* flees 20/16, 52/3

floodes, flodys *n. pl.* rivers 19/1 *etc.*

floryshe *n.* rhetorical embellishment 125/10

floryssheth *v. pr. 3 s.* expresses in flowery language 178/22

floure *v.* flower 174/30

flytteth *v. pr. 3 s. See* **flitteth**

fole *adj.* foolish 8/35

folke *n.* people 17/1 *etc.*

folosophers *n. pl.* foolish philosophers 179/31. *See n.*

fond(e) *adj.* foolish, silly 8/23 *etc.*

for *prep.* in spite of 3/6 *etc.*; *for all (that)* notwithstanding 8/32 *etc.*; *for al(l) this* nevertheless 40/3, 40/32; because 5/25 *etc.*; as 7/12 *etc.*; by 16/17, 127/34; *for so farre* to that extent 96/8, 200/16

for *conj. phr. for that* because 7/20 *etc.*; *for as mich as, for as mych as* considering that, since 37/19 *etc.*

forbede *v.* forbid 34/11; *pt.* **forbode** 131/17; *pp.* **forboden** 6/12

forbere *v.* abstain from, refrain from 3/32 *etc.*; spare 6/25; do without 7/2; avoid, shun 38/7, 90/8 *pp.* **forborne** abstained from 31/30 *etc.*

forbode *v. pt. See* **forbede**

forboden *pp. See* **forbede**

forborne *pp. See* **forbere**

force *v.* care, take heed of 12/21 *etc.*

fore fygurynge *ppl. a.* prefiguring 23/22

for prophecyeng *ppl. a.* prophesying in advance 23/23–24

foresayd *ppl. a.* aforesaid 133/16

fore se *v.* foresee 84/31, 84/32; *pp.* **forsene** 195/10

forewatched *ppl. a.* weary from staying awake 33/27

forsoth *adv.* truly 116/8

forth(e), furth *adv.* forward 40/27 *etc. See* **expowne, helpe, put(te)**

forther *adv. comp. See* **farre**

forthwyth, forthwith *adv.* at once 42/23 *etc.*

fowle *adv.* shamefully, foully 212/18, 216/15

fownde(n) *v. pt.* found 8/3 *etc.*; *pp.* **founden** 8/3 *etc.*

foxly *adj.* foxlike 19/27

fransyes *n. pl. See* **frenesie**

frantike *adj.* insanely foolish 179/24

frantykely *adv.* insanely 9/12

frayed *v. pt.* frightened 187/22

frenesie *n.* madness 99/5; *pl.* **fransyes** 9/7

frere *n.* friar 9/13 *etc.*; *n. pl. and poss.* **frerys** 106/24 *etc.*

freteth *v. pr. 3 s.* is eaten away 188/20

fro(m), from(e) *prep.* from 7/10 *etc.*; above 64/20

frowarde *adj.* perverse 69/31

frowardnesse *n.* perversity 201/35

ful(l) *adj.* complete, perfect 6/11 *etc.*

fulfyll *v.* fill 192/26; *fulfylled wyth* filled by 91/29

full *adv.* quite, very 9/8 *etc.*; fully 48/15 *etc.*; *at the full* fully 219/35

fundacion *n.* foundation 178/1

furth *adv. See* **forth(e)**

fygure *n. See* **figure**

fyll. *See* **fall**

fynd *v.* provide 47/6

fyrste *adv. at the fyrste* at first 46/12

galles *n. pl.* oak-apples 121/23. *See n.*

gamyng(e) *vbl. n.* amusement 33/19 *etc.*

garlandes *n. pl. See* **wyne garlandes**

garnessheth *v. pr. 3 s.* decorates, adorns 15/25–26

garnyshe *n.* embellishment 158/9

garnys(s)hynges *n. pl.* embellishments 12/17, 16/35

general(l) *adj. general(l) resurecci(y)on* universal, as distinct from individual, resurrection 4/32, 24/9

generalty *n. in a generalty* in general 93/2

gentylly *adv.* courteously 98/36

gentylys *n. pl.* gentiles 112/9

gere *n.* worthless stuff, nonsense 81/13, 194/37

gete *v.* beget 60/8, 60/27

gettynge *vbl. n.* begetting 59/28

geuynges *vbl. n. pl.* acts of giving 56/23 *etc.*

gladeth *v. pr. 3 s.* gladdens 103/12

glasse *n.* glass jar 104/12; mirror 206/16 *etc.*; *pl.* **glassys** 209/11, 209/13

glose *n.* gloss, interpretation 37/10 *etc.*

go *v. go about* attempt, strive 61/12; *go to come*, come! 160/11; *pp.* **gone** 6/17; *gone aback. See* **aback**; *pr. 3 s.* **go(e)th** goes 16/16 *etc.*; *go(e)th about* 18/30 *etc.*

gob(b)ettes *n. pl.* chunks, pieces 58/12 *etc.*

goodly *adj.* splendid 12/17 *etc.*; handsome 60/38

good man *n. phr* 196/30. See n.

go(o)st(e) *n.* spirit 42/3 *etc.*

gostely *adv.* spiritually 142/2

go(e)th *v. pr. 3 s. See* **go**

goyng(e) *vbl. n.* walking 21/9, 25/9; leaving 87/29, 105/18

Gracian *n.* Gratian 117/13

graciouse, gracyouse *adj.* endowed with grace, pious 3/6 *etc.*

gracyousely *adv.* through divine grace 41/1

grauntynge *vbl. n.* concession 157/18, 157/20

great *n. all in great* all told, in all 11/13

gret *adj.* great 177/5, 187/5; *comp.* **gretter** 81/18

grinnes *n. pl.* snares 175/26

growen *pp. growen on* advanced 4/8

grudg(e) *v.* complain 81/5, 171/28

grudge *n.* murmuring, grumbling 49/22, 129/15

gryefe, grief *n.* physical suffering 32/14 *etc.*

gryffed *ppl. a.* grafted 100/20

gynnys *n. pl.* stratagems 175/26

habyt *n.* disposition of faculty of the soul. *See n.* to 122/4

halowed *ppl. a.* sanctified, blessed 186/26

halowyng(e) *vbl. n.* blessing 185/21, 205/15

halte *adj.* lame 198/16

halted *v. pt.* limped 198/17

hand crafted *adj.* manually skilled 65/30. *See n.*

hande *n. hath . . . hadde in hande* has had in his possession 7/28; *be . . . in hande wythall* are dealing with 162/15; *out of hande* immediately 34/23, 174/34

hande crafte *n.* handicraft; *men of hande crafte* skilled artisans 64/25–26; *pl.* **hande craftes** handicrafts 206/9

handefull *n.* four inches 123/12

happe *v.* chance, happen (to) 33/7 *etc.*; *pr. 3* **hapen** 60/9

happely *adv.* perhaps 46/30 *etc.*

harde(e) *v. pt. and pp. See* **here**

hard(e)ly *adv.* boldly 110/33 *etc.*; rigorously 158/18

hardnesse *n.* difficulty 113/22

harneyse *n.* armor 198/9, 19

haserder *n.* player at hazard or dice, gamester 119/10

hatered *n.* hatred 126/10, 126/11

Helias *n. See* **Helyas**

Heliseus *n.* Elisha, disciple of Elijah 140/15, 140/18

helpe *v. helpe forthe* help out 7/21

Helyas, Hely, Helias *n.* Elijah 140/15 *etc.*

hepe *n.* mass, heap 112/4 *etc.*

here *v.* hear 3/17 *etc.*; *pt.* **herd, hard(e)** 9/26 *etc.*; *pp.* **herd(e), harde** 18/26

herre *adv.* here 137/22

heuy *adj.* doleful 188/2, 198/32

Hierom(e) *n.* Jerome 213/29, 214/11

Hireneus *n.* Irenaeus 136/25 *etc.*

his, hys *poss. pron.* its 12/24 *etc.*

hit *pron.* it 120/24

holde *n.* support 189/32, 208/31; *take . . . holde* emphasize 53/11; *one handefull holde* a handhold 146/30–31

holde *v. hold problems vppon* hold a scholastic dispute on 187/24–25; *hold on* side with 203/25; *refl.* keep oneself, remain 38/11; *pp.* **holden** held 78/7; *pr. 3 s.* **holdeth** coheres 208/24

hole, whole *adj.* healthy 66/8 *etc.*; whole, entire 30/30 *etc.*; *the . . . hole, the whole* all the 112/15, 136/22; *those whole wordes* all those words 132/3–4

homely *adj.* blunt 100/3

homely *adv.* bluntly 4/31

honest *adj.* honorable, virtuous 3/24, 3/30

ho(o)ste *n.* victim 116/10 *etc.* See note at 116/8–25

how *n.* question asking "how?" 63/25 *etc.*

how(e) be yt, how be it *conj.* however, nevertheless 7/22 *etc.*

howsle, howsyll *n.* the eucharist 52/30, 223/28

hurte *n.* injury 5/11

Huskyn, Huyskyn *n.* Hausschein, Oecolampadius 53/13 *etc.*

Huyskyns *n. pl.* followers of Hausschein (Oecolampadius) 41/9

hydde *v.* hide 99/30

hygh(e) *adj.* exalted, lofty 18/2 *etc.*; *an hygh on high* 190/8–9

Hyrineus, Hireneus, Hyreneus *n.* Irenaeus 136/25 *etc.*

hys *poss. pron. See* **his**

hystorycall *adj. hystorycall fayth* that faith concerned only with historical facts; intellectual belief or assent, as distinct from faith that is practically operative on conduct 121/2

Iamys *n.* James 37/2, 38/36

Iay(e), Ioy(e) *n.* George Joye 7/23 *etc.*

Ieryco *n.* Jericho 65/12

iest *v. iest on* joke about 223/7

iester *n.* jokster 148/6

Iewis, Iewes, Iewys *n. pl.* Jews 16/17 *etc.*

illude *v.* delude 60/16

imaginacion, imagynacyon *n.* invention, fanciful idea 51/29 *etc.*

immedyate *adj.* direct, unmediated 70/37

immedyately *adv.* without mediation, directly 29/8–9, 96/19

imperfyte *adj.* imperfect 107/24, 110/15–16

imperfytely *adv.* imperfectly 195/1–2

importune *adj.* importunate, troublesome 67/3

in *prep.* into 3/9 *etc.*; at 3/30 *etc.*; with, by 5/13 *etc.*; in reference to 7/32 *etc.*; on 9/11 *etc.*; in the course of 9/25 *etc.*

incarnate *pp.* made flesh 42/5

incidently *adv.* in a casual manner 15/6

inconuenience *n.* incongruity 193/4

incorporacyon *n.* unification 28/25 *etc.*

incorporate *v. refl.* unite one's body with 44/8, 75/11; *pp.* **incorporate** united in one body 39/7 *etc.*

inculketh *v. pr. 3 s.* inculcates 67/36; *pt.* **inculked** 144/22

induccyon, induccion *n.* preface, preamble, introduction 133/3 *etc.*

induce, enduce *v.* introduce 25/18; persuade 173/9

indurate *ppl. a.* hardened 177/26

indyfferent *adj.* regarded as neither good nor bad 111/12

indyfferent(e)ly *adv.* in an undiscriminating manner 73/21; impartially 98/32

indyghted *pp.* composed 17/30

inexpugnable *adj.* impregnable 65/12

infatuated *pp.* reduced to foolishness 199/1

inferred vppon *phr.* added to 85/3

infidelyte, infydelyte *n.* unbelief 38/22 *etc.*

infoundeth *v. pr. 3 s.* pours in, infuses 121/24, 121/27; *pp.* **infounded** 122/50

infydelyte *n. See* **infidelyte**

infyxed *ppl. a.* fixed 174/14

ingredyence *n. pl.* ingredients 120/22

iniquite *n.* unfairness 152/4

inough, ynough *adv.* enough 7/4 *etc.*

inquysycyon *n.* scrutiny 171/33–34

institucion *n. See* **instytucyon**

instytucyon, institucion *n.* establishment 69/18–19 *etc.*; establishment of the eucharist 217/25 instruction 17/24, 123/33

instytute *v.* institute, found 10/22 *etc.*

into *prep.* until 21/25; to 26/7; unto 39/6 *etc.*; with a view to 133/13

inuencyon *n.* contrivance 50/14 *etc.*

iolyly *adv.* spiritedly 193/26

Ionas *n.* Jonah 131/6

iugelynge *vbl. n.* deception, trickery 142/18, 147/16

iugle *v.* play tricks so as to cheat or deceive 121/21 *etc.*

iug(e)ler *n.* one who deceives by trickery 122/12 *etc.*; performer of legerdemain 133/21; *pl.* 129/9, 130/4

iuglyng(e), iugling *ppl. a.* cheating 151/7; *iugling boxes* 133/29; *iuglynge stycke* 133/25, 133/36

kepe *v.* keep 5/19 *etc.*; *pp.* **kepte** maintained 3/8; *pr. 3 s.* **kepeth it awaye** holds it back 12/19

kepyng(e) *vbl. n.* upkeep, maintenance 33/11, 60/29; preserving 195/14

knitte *ppl. a. See* **knytte**

know(e) *v.* have carnal knowledge of 58/24 *etc.*; *pt.* **knew(e)** 58/34 *etc.*; *pp.* **knowen** 22/14

knowlege *n.* carnal knowledge 58/36

knowlege *v.* acknowledge 49/1 *etc.*

knytte, knitte *ppl. a.* joined 29/9 *etc.*

large *adj.* licentious 4/10

large *adv.* unrestrainedly 98/9

laste *adv.* most recently 6/31 *etc.*; *at (the) laste* finally 38/18 *etc.*

late *adv.* recently 4/9 *etc.*

latenye *n. See* **letany**

later *adj. comp.* latter 11/1, 15/5

latyn(e), laten *adj.* Latin 52/35 *etc.*

law(e) *n.* Mosaic law 39/10, 39/13

lay(e) *v.* attribute, allege 15/25 *etc.*; advance, cite 15/20 *etc.*; *lay(e) . . . charge* charge . . . with 97/14 *etc.*; *lay it in the necke* blame it on, impute it to 113/19; *laieth out (abrode)* displays, exposes 99/13, 217/5; *layed open* revealed 119/6

layenge *vbl. n.* attributing 130/15

leche *n.* physician 5/7

lenger *adj. comp.* longer 100/14, 175/6

lenger *adv. comp.* longer 32/5 *etc.*

lepry *n.* leprosy 65/4

lerned *pp.* taught 48/21

lese *v.* lose 22/8 *etc.*

lesse *adj. comp.* lesser 25/24 *etc.*

leste wyse *n. at the lest(e) wyse* at least 69/31 *etc.*

let *n.* obstacle, hindrance 59/18, 77/32; *pl.* **lettes** 86/34

let(te) *v.* hinder, prevent 3/20 *etc.*; allow, permit 6/18 *etc.*; bar 85/26; forbear, refrain 4/9 *etc.*; lose 194/24

letany, latenye *n.* litany 186/29, 205/23

lettes. *See* **let**

lettynge *ppl. a.* allowing 37/16; hindering 90/30

leue *n. geve . . . leue* grant permission 57/1 *etc.*; *take . . . leue* bid farewell 191/16

leue *v.* stop, desist 5/3 *etc.*; *leue of* abandon 59/37 desist from 90/36

leuer *adv. comp.* rather 46/12 *etc.*

lewd(e) *adj.* ribald, vile 4/5 *etc.*

lewd *adv.* ignorantly 20/34

leysoure *n.* opportunity 211/21

lo *interj.* see, behold 5/15 *etc.*

lofe *n. phr.* **syngynge lofe, singyng lofe** wafer used in the celebration of the mass 129/10, 130/5

loke *v.* look 6/5 *etc.*; expect 6/34 *etc.*; beware, take care 41/4, 55/28; *pt. loked for* expected 6/33 *etc.*; *pr. 3 s. loketh to* attends to 125/35

longeth *v. pr. 3 s.* pertains 143/23; desires 160/9

losed *pp.* released 103/21

loth *adj.* reluctant 3/16 *etc.*

lothely *adj.* loathsome, disgusting 80/36 *etc.*

lothsomnes *n.* repugnance 138/25

loude *adv.* flagrantly 219/14

lowde, loude *adj.* flagrant 178/1, 219/24

lowsy *adj.* afflicted with lice 32/18

lumpyshe *adj.* clumsy 7/14

lybertye *n.* license 3/32

lycence *n.* permission, leave 97/15

lyefe *adj. had as lyefe . . . as* would as gladly . . . as 205/19–20

lyfte *n.* emergency 177/9

lyfted *v. pt.* excited 93/3

lyght *adj.* insubstantial 50/31; frivolous 60/2

lyght *adv.* lightly 60/1

lyghtly, lyghtely *adv.* in all probability 6/14 *etc.*

lyke *adj.* similar 10/25 *etc.*; probable, likely 59/20, 177/23; *lyke to* analogous to 209/13

lyke *adv. lyke as, like as* just as 37/17 *etc.*; *lyke to* in the manner of, 12/23; *lyke wyse as, lykewyse as* just as 33/36 *etc.*

lyke *v.* please 152/30

lykelyhed *n. by lykelyhed, of lykelyhed* in all probability 6/23 *etc.*

Lyre *n.* Nicholas de Lyra 89/32

lyst(e) *v.* wish, want 21/1 *etc.*; *pt.* **lysted** 220/33; *pr. 3 s. impers.* **lyste** pleases 207/26

lyste *n.* desire 9/15

lytell, lytle *n. lytell and lytell* little by little 38/17, 123/6; *setteth . . . lytell by. See* **set(te)**

lyuely *adj.* vital, living 18/1 *etc.*

lyuynge *vbl. n.* manner of living, way of life 3/25 *etc.*; livelihood, subsistence 33/15, 34/17

mache *n.* equal 193/2; *pl.* **matchys** 3/19

madde *adj. madde ordered* madly arranged 34/3

magry *prep. magry your teth* in spite of your resistance 47/34

maior *n.* first premise in a syllogism 168/32 *etc.*

maker *n.* author 10/1

maketh *v. pr. 3 s.* pretends 15/6 *etc.*; *maketh vs* composes or constructs for us 109/18; *maketh . . . agaynst* is unfavorable to, tells against 161/18, 164/26

malapert *adj.* impudent 176/29. *See also*
  sawse
maner *n.* manner, way 4/37 *etc.*; manner
  (of) 18/13 *etc.*; kind (of) 19/25 *etc.*; *pl.*
  morals 4/5 *etc.*; *in maner* as it were 8/35,
  35/20; *in one maner* in one way 12/13, 50/
  34–35
manhed, manhode *n.* humanity, manhood
  18/18 *etc.*
marke *n.* token 8/5
markynge *vbl. n.* observing 54/16, 151/8
marmole, marmoll *n.* inflamed sore,
  especially on the leg 119/27 *etc.*
marre *v.* impair, ruin 4/4 *etc.*
maruayle *v. See* **merueyle**
mary *interj.* indeed, to be sure 19/6, 163/33
maske *n.* masked ball 12/34. *See n. to*
  13/1–10
masker, maskar *n.* masquerader 13/10
  etc.
matched *ppl. a.* paired, in competition 5/9
matchys *n. pl. See* **mache**
matens *n. pl. our lady*(e) *matens* the first hour
  of the office of the Virgin Mary 186/30,
  205/23–24
mater *n.* subject 15/16 *etc.*
Mathy *n.* Matthias 91/29
maundy(e) *n.* Last Supper 10/21 *etc.*
Mawdeleyn *n.* Magdalene 104/10
mayntenaunce *n.* support 32/29 *etc.*
mayny(e) *n.* masses, common herd 164/32,
  186/4
maystershyppe *n.* the personality of a
  master 165/4, 169/6
maystry *n.* achievement, feat 81/18, 113/26
meane *adj.* intervening 187/10
meanes, meanis, meanys *n. pl. See*
  me(a)ne
meat(e), mete *n.* food 16/11 *etc.*; **salt**
  meate meat preserved with salt 32/3
medle *v.* deal 5/5 *etc.*
membre, member *n.* limb 44/6 *etc.*; *pl.*
  membrys, membres 39/7 *etc.*
memoryall, memoriall *n.* reminder 7/12
  etc.
mende *v.* reform 90/29
me(a)ne *n.* intercession, influence 7/25;
  means 17/36 *etc.*; *pl.* **meanes, meanys,**
  meanis means, methods, stratagems 3/14
  etc.

merely *adv.* merrily 99/32
meruelouse *adv.* amazingly 79/24, 79/27
merueyle, meruayle, meruaile, mar-
  uayle *v.* marvel, wonder 48/2 *etc.*; *mer-*
  ueyle . . . of wonder at 48/8 *etc.*; *pp.*
  meruayled amazed 136/8
messe *n.* course, dish 7/14; *pl.* **messys**
  136/32
Messyas *n.* Messiah 27/2
mete *adj.* fitting, appropriate 25/5 *etc.*
mete *n. See* **meat(e)**
metely *adj.* appropriate, fitting 38/15 *etc.*
metely *adv.* suitably 9/31 *etc.*
metropolytanys *n. pl.* bishops having the
  oversight of the bishops of their provinces
  128/6
mich *adj. See* **mych(e)**
minor *n.* second premise in a syllogism
  168/32, 168/33
minorite *n.* inferiority 41/26
minyshe, mynysshe *v.* diminish, reduce
  99/2, 188/29
minystreth *v. pr. 3 s.* administers 29/24; *pp.*
  mynistred 117/25
missed *pp. See* **mysse**
misteries, misteryes, mysteryes *n. pl.*
  sacramental rites, especially the eucharist
  17/36–18/1 *etc.*
mo *adj. comp.* more, 4/20 *etc.*
mo(o) *adv.* more, in addition 6/19 *etc.*
mocke, mokke *n.* an act of mockery 8/10
  etc.
mocke, mokke *v. mocke it out* to evade an
  argument by mockery or trifling 8/10
mocyon *n.* prompting 93/20
mokke *n. and v. See* **mocke**
more *adj. comp.* greater 23/24; *more than that*
  besides that 110/30
Moris, Morys *n. poss.* More's 151/11 *etc.*
morow(e) *n.* morning 5/22; next day 21/11
  etc.
mortefyeng *ppl. a.* denying (by abstinence)
  120/17, 125/6
Morys *n. poss. See* **Moris**
mot(t)en *n.* mutton 58/14 *etc.*
moue *v.* affect with emotion 186/16; *pp.*
  troubled, perturbed 42/17
moweth *v. pr. 3 s.* makes grimaces 206/18
Moyses *n.* Moses 21/33 *etc.*; *poss.* 36/7 *etc.*

mummer *n.* actor in a dumb show 13/1. *See n. on* 13/1–10

mummery *n.* dumb show 119/10

mummynge *vbl. n.* **a mummynge** like a player in a dumb show 99/29

murmur(e) *n.* grumbling, protest 49/22 *etc.*

murmur(e) *v.* grumble, protest 22/15 *etc.*

murmuryng(e) *vbl. n.* protesting, grumbling 47/24 *etc.*

muse *v.* marvel, wonder 133/24

mych(e), mich *adj.* much 3/8 *etc.*; many 6/13 *etc.*; *mych ye more* even more 4/24; *for as mych as. See* **for** *conj.*

mych(e) *adv.* greatly 3/31 *etc.*

mydde *adj.* middle 65/7

mynde *n.* attitude, intention 3/6 *etc.*; opinion 19/6 *etc.*; *put . . . in mynd* remind 35/23

mynded *ppl. a.* inclined, disposed, determined 26/9 *etc.*

mynistred *pp. See* **minystreth**

mynseth *v. pr. 3 s.* palliates 194/5

mynysshe *v. See* **minyshe**

myscheuouse *adj.* harmful 10/32 *etc.*

myschyefe *n.* evil, harm 84/12 *etc.*

mysse *v.* fail 97/24; *pp.* **missed** 176/32

mysse conceyued *pp.* misunderstood 80/15

mysse constrewyng *vbl. n.* misinterpretation 158/13

mysse happe *v.* happen unfortunately (to) 75/1 *etc.*

mysse lyked, mysselyked *pp.* disliked 209/21

namely *adv.* especially 61/10, 124/32

narowly *adv.* closely 212/22, 214/16

nat *adv.* not 217/3

nathelesse *adv.* nevertheless 222/10

natural(l) *adj.* drawn from nature 59/23 *etc.*; inherent 83/23 *etc.*; *naturall fole* fool or simpleton by birth 221/11, 221/19

naturally *adv.* by nature, normally 9/1 *etc.*

naught *n. See* **nought**

naye *adv.* no 157/3, 158/25. *See n. to* 158/35–159/7

necessare *adj.* necessary 173/29

necessyt(i)e *n.* compulsion, 33/14 *etc.*

nedes, nedys *adv.* necessarily 20/32 *etc.*

nedeth *v.* is required 101/23

nere *adv. I wote nere* I know not 100/1, 126/7

neuer *adv. neuer so* ever so 8/18 *etc.*

new(e) *adv.* newly, freshly 9/36 *etc.*; *of new* anew 115/34

neyther *adv.* either 8/30 *etc.*; *neyther nother adj.* not the one nor the other 203/30

nonce *See* **nonys**

none *adj.* no 5/1 *etc.*

nonys, nonce *n. for the nonys, for the nonce* for the express purpose 31/14 *etc.*

notably *adv.* conspicuously 11/15

noted *pp. noted you* pointed out to you 128/27

notes, notys *n. pl.* stigmas 15/24

nother *adj.* other 6/36 *etc.*; *neyther nother. See* **neyther**

nothyng(e) *adv.* not at all 15/17 *etc.*

nought *adj.* immoral, vicious 50/21 *etc.*

nought, naught *n.* nothing 6/28 *etc. fell . . . to naught* became wicked 94/4

noughty *adj.* wicked 60/15, 123/26

noughtynesse *n.* wickedness 92/7, 94/20

noyouse *adj.* harmful 33/9

nyce *n.* foolish 99/29

obiecte *v.* bring forward in opposition 118/2, 118/12

obstynacyon *n.* obstinacy 133/13

obumbracyon *n.* overshadowing 78/8

occasion, occasyon *n.* opportunity 4/24 *etc.*; *takynge occasion* taking advantage of the opportunity 16/2; *wyth occasyon of* by reason of 223/17

of *adv.* off 3/25 *etc.*

of *prep.* about, with regard to 4/9 *etc.*; for 5/2 *etc.*; by 4/26 *etc.*; in 6/11 *etc.*; with 3/18 *etc.*

ofte *adv.* often 97/34; *comp.* **ofter** 106/13, 183/1

on *prep.* of, about 38/25 *etc.*; over 219/24

onely *adj. onely fayth* faith alone 39/24; *onely power* power alone 29/17; *onely exposycyon* explanation alone 168/18; *onely worde* word alone 168/19

open *adj.* obvious, clear 56/4 *etc.*

openeth *v. pr. 3 s.* reveals 147/14; *pt.* **opened** explained 24/11, 67/10; *pp.* revealed 50/8

openyng *vbl. n.* revealing 17/36

operacyon *n.* working 27/30, 48/6

opposycyon *n. pl.* **opposycions** counter-propositions 159/24; *myn opposycyon* the rebuttal of me 158/27

oppugneth *v. pr. 3 s.* assails 183/27

ordered *ppl. a.* arranged 34/3

orders *n. pl. See* **ronne**

other *adv.* otherwise, differently 37/14 *etc.*

other *pron.* each other 203/19; *pl.* **other** others 3/9 *etc.*

ouer *adv.* excessively, too 5/5 *etc.*

ouer *prep.* in addition to 11/4 *etc.*

ouer laded, ouerladen *pp.* overloaded 198/8, 198/19

ouer seen *ppl. a.* versed 132/35

ouer seen *pp. refl.* fallen into error, blundered 151/30 *etc.*

ourshette *pp. refl.* overreached (oneself), fallen into error 212/18, 216/15

pageaunt *n.* part acted to deceive, trick 18/8, 18/28

papystes, popystes *n. pl.* papists, followers of the pope 52/36 *etc.*

parte *adv.* partly 17/24

parte *n.* side in a dispute or question 9/30 *etc.*; *for my part* in support of my position 57/1 *etc.*; *for . . . parte* on (one's) own account 12/17 *etc.*

parteners, perteners, partiners *n. pl.* partakers, receipients 25/11 *etc.*

particypacyon, partycypacyon *n.* partaking of the substance, quality, or nature of something or someone 29/7 *etc.*

part takers *n. pl.* partakers 117/25

passe *v.* surpass 64/24

passyble *adj.* capable of suffering 42/29

passyon *n.* suffering 44/24 *etc.*

paste *prep.* beyond 219/31

patched *pp. patched in* added 7/31

paynted *ppl. a.* gaudy 17/3

Paynyms, Paynims *n. pl.* pagans, non-Christians 112/1–2, 112/35

peny *n. ernest peny* pledge 28/24 *etc.*

peraduenture *adv.* perhaps 60/3 *etc.*

perdye *interj.* by God 120/2, 211/19

perfyt(e), perfite, perfayt *adj.* perfect 27/11 *etc.*

perfyted *pp.* perfected 117/23

perfytely *adv.* perfectly 43/11, 166/28

perseuerauntly *adv.* continually 77/12–13

personage *n.* identity 99/30; person 99/35

persuasyble *adj.* persuasive 111/225, 111/26

peruse *v.* expound critically 15/12; *perused you* expounded for you 96/3

perys(s)h(e) *v.* perish, die, decay 16/11 *etc.*; *pr. 3 s.* **peryssheth** 27/13

perys(s)hyng(e) *vbl. n.* decay, dissolution 27/34 *etc.*; *pl.* **peryshynges** 27/29

pestylence *n.* plague 5/6

pestylent *adj.* pernicious, noxious 3/22 *etc.*

pestylently, pestilently *adv.* noxiously 151/12 *etc.*

peuyshe *adj.* foolish 221/35

Phylistyes *n. pl.* Philistines 19/17

plaster *n.* dressing for a wound 99/12 *etc.*

plastered *v. pt.* covered with a bandage 120/6

playn(e), plain *adv.* plainly, clearly 43/5 *etc.*

pleasure *n. hath . . . pleasure* enjoys 12/13 *etc.*; *his pleasure was* it pleased him that 59/34

plentuouse *adj.* abundant 17/29

poll *v.* despoil 47/4

Pomeran *n.* Johann Bugenhagen, known as Pomeranus 128/4 *See n.*

pontyfycall *adj.* popish 206/28

pooreblynde *adj.* obtuse 97/22

popystes *n. pl. See* **papystes**

possyble *adj.* able 64/25

postles *n. pl.* apostles 128/6

poticary *adj.* apothecary 120/24

pottes *n. pl.* grimaces 206/19

powderynge *ppl. a.* seasoning 97/11

poysen *adj.* poisonous 68/17

pratynge *vbl. n.* prattling 135/5

prent *n.* imprint 30/13, 30/21

presently *adv.* so as to be present in person 191/8 *etc.*

prety(e) *adj.* clever, fine 153/20 *etc.*

pretyly *adv.* prettily, nicely 9/8, 153/21

preue prove 167/22 *etc.*

preuent *v.* anticipate 40/24 *etc.*

preuented *ppl. a.* met beforehand 48/7

probleme *n.* question proposed for academic discussion or scholastic disputation 189/26; *pl.* **problems** 187/24

processe *n.* discussion, discourse 17/3 *etc.*; story 18/34

progresse *n.* development 17/2

proper, propre *adj.* fine, admirable 9/23, 193/37; appropriate 9/30; particular, characteristic 28/36 *etc.*; *propre vnto* peculiar to 42/8

proper *adv.* excellently 197/23

properly, proprely *adv.* excellently 209/7 *etc.*

property(e) *n.* essential quality 26/27 *etc.*

proponynge *vbl. n.* proposing 25/3, 161/17

proporcionable *adj.* corresponding 169/15

propose *n.* subject 188/22

proues *n. pl.* proofs 204/33

purpose *n.* discourse 10/4 *etc.*; *for our purpose* to support our argument 117/13; *fro(m) the purpose* away from the point 17/10 *etc.*; *cometh . . . nere the purpose* is pertinent 50/23

purpose *v.* propose, intend 9/29 *etc.*

pursueth *v. pr. 3 s. pursueth forth* proceeds 132/13

put(te) *v.* set, place 6/23 *etc.*; *put . . . away(e)* reject 33/6; dispel 129/15; *put forth(e)* publish 8/3; advance, propose 10/6 *etc.*; *putte . . . in mynde* remind 86/31–32; *put of* takes off 99/33; *put(te)(. . .) out(e)* publish 12/31 *etc.*; gouge out 21/2, 198/29; *put . . . out of* rid of 187/6; *putte . . . to sale* set out for sale 222/17–18; *pp.* put; *put . . . in my choyce* asked me to choose 184/31; *putteth . . . to* adds 8/9

pyecemele *adv.* piece by piece 151/3

pyked *pp. pyked out* gleaned 11/14, 11/25

pyll *v.* plunder, 47/4

pystle, pistle *n.* epistle, letter, 4/30 *etc.*

pyth *n.* force, substance 139/9, 156/26

quatreble *adj.* quadruple 159/30

questyon *n. out of all questyon* indisputable 4/23, 106/5

quod, quoth *v. pt.* said 213/3 *etc.*

quycke, quicke *adj.* alive, living 39/22 *etc.*

quycken *v.* give life to 36/28; *pr. 3 s.* **quyckeneth** 80/2, 82/35; **quycketh** 82/10

quyknesse *n.* liveliness 70/35

rate *n.* degree, extent 90/20, 90/23

rawnson *n.* ransom 44/15

rayle, raile *v. rayle vp(p)on* inveigh against 114/32 *etc.*

realeth *v. pr. 3 s.* rails 117/8

reason, reasyn *n.* statement used as an argument 59/29 *etc.*; *pl.* arguments 8/3 *etc.*; *by reason wherof, by the reason that, by reason of* because 9/20–21 *etc.*; *it were reason,* it would be reasonable 35/18; *of reason* by the dictates of reason 105/36 *etc.*; *out of reason* unreasonable 179/7; *more reason it was* it was more reasonable 91/14; *reason is it, reason it is* it would be reasonable 111/34 *etc.*

recorde *n. be(a)re . . . recorde* bear witness 57/33–34 *etc.*

recyteth *v. pr. 3 s.* quotes 117/13

recytynge *ppl. a.* quoting 189/7

referred *pp.* directed 39/12

refrayne *v.* restrain 6/13, 94/9

regarde *v.* respect 9/25

rehersall *n.* recitation 188/18

reherse *v.* relate, recount 4/4 *etc.*; cite, quote 51/37 *etc.*

reken *v.* regard, consider 7/19 *etc.*; *pp.* **rekened** reasoned, believed 61/28 *etc.*

relygyone *n.* See **ronne**

remembraunce *n. putteth . . . in remembraunce* reminds 66/5–6 *etc.*

remoue *v.* move away 93/10

replycacyon *n.* reply 161/9; *pl.* **replycacions** 159/23

reproue *v.* condemn 37/4; *pr. 3 s.* **reproueth** refutes 74/24, 148/21

reprouyng *vbl. n.* condemning 5/2

repugnaunce *n.* contradiction, inconsistency 100/6 *etc.*

repugnaunt(e) *adj.* contradictory 12/6 *etc.*

repugne *v.* contend 160/20–21; be contradictory 188/27

resort *n.* recourse 16/6

respecte *n.* consideration 82/3; *pl.* reasons 59/24; *haue respecte . . . to* have an eye to 91/14–15; *in . . . respecte thereof* in comparison to it 35/35–36

reteyned *pp.* kept back 7/26

reyse, rayse *v.* raise 22/8 *etc.*

rochell *adj. rochell wyne* wine from Rochelle (a seaport of western France) 152/7

ronne *v.* run; *pr. subj. 3 s.* **runne** spreads 6/35; *runne out of (. . .)* orders, *runne out of relygyone* break religious vows 106/27 *etc.*

rose *v. pt.* originated 61/25

rough *adj.* acid or harsh to the taste 152/7
rude *adj.* ignorant, unskilled 8/14, 220/5
ruffle *n.* disorder 119/8
ruffleth *v. pr. 3 s.* shakes up in a rough or careless manner 121/8
ruffyn *n.* devil 220/5 *See n.*
ryall *adj.* royal 147/8
ryally *adv.* royally 64/13, 159/17
rybaldyousely *adv.* scurrilously 220/6
rydde *v.* get through 34/23
ryght, right *adv.* altogether, quite 19/6 *etc.*; rightly, correctly 62/21 *etc.*
ryght *n.* justice 91/9
ryghtuouse *n. pl.* those who are righteous 134/2, 165/39
ryghtuousnes *n.* righteousness 194/11
ryghtwyse *n. pl.* those who are righteous 133/19
ryotte *n. runne all at ryotte* run rampant 82/32
rype *adj. See* **bedelem**
rysen *pp.* which originated 194/37
ryueled *ppl. a.* wrinkled 206/20

saciate *ppl. a.* satiated 103/37
sacryfyed *pp.* offered as a sacrifice 117/4
sad(de) *adj.* serious, earnest 8/12, 99/24
sadnes *n. seriousness* 99/25
salt meate *See* **meat(e)**
Samary *n.* Samaria 31/27 *etc.*
sample, somple *n.* example 11/27 *etc.*; specimen 50/17
satisfaccion, satysfactyon *n.* performance by a penitent of the penal and meritorious acts enjoined by his confessor as payment of the temporal punishment due his sin 187/4–5
saturyte *n.* satisfaction 104/3–4
satysfye *v.* answer 129/19
saue *conj.* except 8/14
saue *prep.* except 91/33
saued *ppl. a.* preserved 61/27
saufe *adj.* delivered from sin 119/17; protected 120/5
sauour *n.* aroma 46/30
Sauygate *n.* Saviour's Gate at St. Saviour's Monastery, Southwark 99/15. *See n.*
sauyng(e) *conj.* except 6/23 *etc.*
sawse, sauce *n.* sauce 33/32 *etc., sawce malapert* impertinence 33/35

sayd *ppl. a.* aforesaid 16/24 *etc.*
say(e)ng(e) *vbl. n.* statement 23/1 *etc.*
scald(e) *adj.* affected with a scaly disease of the skin, scabby 120/23, 220/5
scant *adv.* scarcely 47/6 *etc.*
scape *v.* escape 158/18, 158/22
science *n.* knowledge 64/10
scolematter *n.* scholastic theology 194/26
scolers *n. pl.* pupils 37/28
scoles man *n.* one who is expert in school-divinity 195/18
scryptured *adj.* learned or versed in the scriptures 130/34
season *n.* time 36/14 *etc.; out of season* at the wrong time 67/2–3, 110/35
seasoned *ppl. a.* imbued 140/22
self(e) *pron.* selves 3/18; *adj:* selfsame 80/25 *etc.; one self worde* the same word 208/1; *the selfe gyftes* the gifts themselves 120/10, 121/16
seme(n) *v.* seem 5/23 *etc.; me semeth, semeth me* it seems to me 61/9 *etc.*
semely *adv.* handsomely 15/26
sene *pp.* versed 213/30
sensuall *adj.* physical 44/21
sensyble *adj.* perceptible by the senses 24/31 *etc.*
sentence *n.* sense, meaning 43/28, 55/135; opinion, interpretation 50/15 *etc.*
set(te) *v.* affix, set down 8/24 *etc.; set(te) at nought* consider worthless 65/15 *etc.; sette . . . at lyght* undervalue 188/8–9; *sette forth(e)* advance 11/4 *etc.; pp.* **set** ordered 61/1; *sette a wurke, see* **a wurke**; *sette v(p)pon* fixed upon 7/17 *etc.; pr. 3 s.* setteth *. . . about* urges to 34/31–32; *setteth . . . lytell by* disregards 48/27; *set . . . myche therby* regard it highly 48/29; *setteth out* displays 15/26, 53/23
seuerall *adj.* different, separate 42/8 *etc.*
sext *See* **syxt(e)**
shamefastnesse *n.* modesty 3/30–31
shammellys, shamell(e)s *n. pl.* shambles, butcher's stalls 69/10 *etc.*
shere thursday *n. phr.* Holy Thursday 10/21
shew(e) *v.* demonstrate, show 3/21 *etc.*; reveal 76/9 *etc.; shewe forth* display 99/3, 133/31
shewer *n.* attendant at a meal 7/7

sholdren *n. pl. See* **shuldren**

short *adj.* brief 113/26

short(e)ly *adv.* briefly 121/9, 203/23

show *n. to the show* to all appearances 15/26

shrew(e) *n.* villain 87/22 *etc.*

shuldren, sholdren *n. pl.* shoulders 197/29, 198/8

shyft *n.* stratagem, sophistry 203/20, 219/12

shyfte *v.* substitute deceptively 13/2

sinificacyon *See* **sygnyfycacyon**

skabbed *adj.* covered with scabs 119/27

skoruy *adj.* scurfy, covered with scabs 32/19

slake *v.* slacken 90/36; *pp.* **slaked** allayed 101/36

slenderly *adv.* feebly 113/16

sleyght *adj.* slight, negligible 15/16 *etc.*; wily, dextrous 142/18, 147/15. *See n. to* 129/9

sleyghtly *adv.* cleverly 129/9

slongen *pp.* slung 198/34

slyper *adj.* slippery 92/22

smale *adj.* of low alcoholic strength 152/6

smoky *adj.* obscure and objectionable 3/23

so as *conj.* in such a way that 75/9, 140/38

sodden *adj.* boiled 46/29

solucion *n.* explanation 206/10; *pl.* **solucyons** 118/36 *etc.*

soluted *pp.* cleared up 129/7

somme, summe, *n.* sum 16/1 *etc.*

somple *n. See* **sample**

som(e)tyme *adv.* sometimes, often 5/6 *etc.*

somwhat, some what *n.* something 12/12 *etc.*; *adv.* a bit 21/9 *etc.*; to some extent 50/2 *etc.*

sophims *n. pl.* ingenious arguments 70/12

sophystre, sophyster *n.* sophist 160/9

sore *adj.* diseased 66/8 *etc.*

sore *adv.* harshly, severely, grievously 6/12 *etc.*

sort *n. of that sort* such 7/1

sorys *n. pl.* diseases 32/12

soth *n.* truth 201/5

so that *conj.* provided that 18/21

soule, sowle *n. soule fode* food for the soul 47/35; *soule helthe* health of the soul 85/34–35

sowne *v.* tend (toward) 118/6, 124/12

sownes *n. pl.* sounds 206/39

sownynge *ppl. a.* tending (to or with) 124/31

sowsed *ppl. a.* soaked 199/25

soyle *v.* refute, solve 7/31 *etc.*

soylynge *vbl. n.* refuting, solving 12/2 *etc.*

spake *v. pt.* spoke 20/28

specyall *adj. in specyall* in particular 11/9–10 *etc.*

specyall *adv.* especially 15/10 *etc.*

specyally, specially *adv.* especially 4/28 *etc.*

specyfyed *pp.* related in detail 10/12

spede *n.* success 5/22

spiryng *vbl. n.* blowing 63/1

spyghtfull *adj.* contemptuous 147/32–33

stablyshement *n.* establishing 186/17

stablysshe *v.* establish 185/18, 186/15

staggred, stagerd *pp.* wavered 168/26, 170/20

standynge *ppl. a.* static 39/21

star(c)ke *adj.* unmitigated 154/27 *etc.*

stauncheth *v. pr. 3 s.* quenches 100/21, 101/30

stede *n.* place 87/22 *etc.*

stere . . . vp. raise up 129/23

stickyng *vbl. n.* hesitation 183/31

stockes, stockys *n. pl.* blocks of wood 102/17, 185/21

stongen *pp.* stung 68/18

stonied *pp. intr.* marveled 166/35

stonn(i)e *v. intr.* be astounded 171/31 *etc.*; *pp.* **stonned** 168/26, 170/20

stonned *v. tr. pp.* amazed 171/28

store *n. good store* abundance 97/16

strayn *v.* restrain 47/33

strayte *v.* limit 189/21

strength *v.* strengthen 166/6, 190/30

styrynge *ppl. a.* active 39/22

study *n.* deliberate effort 92/21

stycke *v.* remain fixed 113/29

styffely *adv.* obstinately 84/7, 127/27

styl(l)(e) *adv.* always, continually 4/18 *etc.*

substaunce, substauns *n.* wealth 6/25; essential part 17/4 *etc.*; majority 24/32

succeded *ppl. a. is succeded into the place of* has followed and replaced 117/18

suertye *n. See* **surety**

sufferaunce *n.* forbearance 5/35; suffering 91/11

sundry *adj.* various 17/36

suppe *v.* dine 86/1

sure *adj.* safe 111/25 *etc.*

surety, suertye *n.* certainty 77/18; security 158/28, 160/32

Suynglyus *n.* **Zwingli** 217/24

swagyng *vbl. n.* alleviation, relieving 32/15

syde *n.* page 212/11 *etc.*

sygned *ppl. a.* marked with a sign 30/13

sygnifyeng *ppl. a.* indicating 87/31

sygnyfycacyon, significacion, sinificacyon *n.* sign, intimation 63/9 *etc.*

syn *prep.* since 169/36

synnes, synnys *adv.* since 24/18 *etc.*

synnys *conj. synnys that* since 106/12

systern *n. pl.* sisters 9/14

syth *conj.* since, because, seeing that, inasmuch as 4/20 *etc.*

syxt(e), sext *adj.* sixth 10/18 *etc.*

take *v.* receive 5/11 *etc.*; understand 161/4 *etc.*; *take . . . leue. See* **leue** *n.*

takyng(e) *vbl. n.* capture 24/6; interpretation 202/16, 203/22

tale *n.* count 184/1

tayed *ppl. a.* tied 19/22 *etc.*

tayeng *vbl. n.* tying 19/26

tayenge *ppl. a.* tying 19/15

temporaltye *n.* body or class of secular persons 170/4

tempte *v.* test 61/18

than *adv.* then 4/2 *etc.*

thanke *n.* thanks 11/25; *can . . . thanke* offer thanks 99/6

that *pron. in that that* inasmuch as 19/24

the *pron.* thee 21/30 *etc.*

them selfe *pron. pl.* themselves 3/7 *etc.*

therby *adv.* by that 8/19 *etc.*

there *pron.* their 109/31

there as there where 21/20, 81/25

therfor(e) *adv.* for it 35/25

therin *adv.* in that matter, particular or circumstance 6/17 *etc.*

therof *adv.* of that 4/23 *etc.*; thereby 4/28 *etc.*; at that 26/19 *etc.*

therto *adv.* to that point or thing 8/26 *etc.*; to it 7/16 *etc.*

therevnto *adv.* to it 52/16

therwyth, therwith *adv.* with it 34/1 *etc.*; with that, after that 60/6 *etc.*

therwythal *adv.* with that 217/7

thorow(e), thorough *prep.* through 27/30 *etc.*

thorow out *adv.* thoroughly 72/15

thyder, thyther *adv.* thither 40/19 *etc.*

thynketh *v. pr. 3 s. impers. me thynketh* it seems to me 8/5 *etc.*

to *adv.* too 4/13 *etc.*

to *prep.* for 6/24 *etc.*

to burste *v.* burst asunder 194/35

tone *adj.* one 10/17 *etc.*

tote *v.* gaze 12/25

tother *adj.* other 5/11 *etc.*

touchyng(e), towchyng(e) *ppl. a.* concerning 9/13 *etc.*

tourne *v.* change 27/32; search through 216/26

towarde *adj.* promising 9/23

towardnesse *n.* inclination 48/7

transfygure *v.* transform 60/16

trayned *pp.* enticed 175/27

trayning *vbl. n.* enticing 176/33

trew(e) *adv.* truly 61/33 *etc.*

troub(e)lous(e) *adj.* troubled, disordered 140/28, 188/2

trouth(e), treuth, trewth, trowthe, *n.* honesty 15/30, 127/34; *of trouth(e)* in fact, indeed, truly 7/23 *etc.*; *very trewth* in all honesty 26/21

trow(e) *v.* trust, believe, suppose 17/27 *etc.*

trybute *n.* taxation 47/5

tryed *pp.* ascertained, determined 9/9, 153/24

tryfleth out *v. pr. 3 s.* dismisses with mockery 136/8

trymtrams *n. pl.* absurdities 175/27

trynclettes *n. pl.* trinkets, paraphernalia 133/22

tryppe *n. See n. to* 133/9

tunne *n.* large cask 151/10

turned vppe *pp.* overturned 71/27

twayn(e) *adj.* two 10/26 *etc.*

Tyndalyns *n. pl.* followers of Tyndale 41/19

vayn(e) *adj.* idle, worthless 6/7 *etc.*

vayn gloryouse *adj.* vainglorious 193/34

verely *adv. See* **veryly**

veri *adv. See* **very**

verified, veryfyed, verifyed *pp. See* **verifye**

verifye, veryfye *v.* prove 100/36; *pp.* **verified, veryfyed, verifyed** proven true 4/25 *etc.*; made true 42/19, 42/34

verily *adv. See* **veryly**

vertuouse *See n.* to 38/30

very *adj.* true, real, actual 10/14 *etc.*

very, veri *adv.* fully, truly 4/20 *etc.*

veryfye *v. See* **verifye**

veryly, verily, verely *adv.* truly 7/35 *etc.*

virtually *adv.* as far as essential effects are concerned 73/32

visour, vysor *n.* mask, disguise 12/27 *etc.*

vnclennesse *n.* moral impurity 3/28

vncontrolled *ppl. a.* unchecked 4/22

vndeclared *ppl. a.* unexplained 113/28

vnderpropyng *ppl. a.* supporting 9/30

vnderstanden *pp.* understood 18/36 *etc.*; implied 56/37, 57/2–3 *etc.*

vnderstanding, vnderstandynge *vbl. n.* meaning, sense 18/11–12 *etc.*

vndiuisyble *adj.* indivisible 209/29

vned *ppl. a.* united 42/18, 174/4

vnfaithfulnes *n.* lack of true belief 80/7

vnfallyble *adj.* irrefutable 77/18

vngracyouse *adj.* devoid of spiritual grace 185/6

vnmarkyd *ppl. a.* unnoticed 104/35

vnmete *adj.* unfit 90/12

vnminyshed *adj.* undiminished 137/32

vnperfait, vnperfyte *adj.* imperfect 27/10 *etc.*

vnreasonale *adj.* irrational 179/30–31

vnseparable *adj.* inseparable 77/34, 125/25

vnseparably *adv.* inseparably 29/9

vnsoyled *ppl. a.* unresolved, unanswered 63/12, 63/25–26

vnthryftes *n. pl.* dissolute persons 119/23

vnuowed *ppl. a.* not bound by a vow 59/37

vnware *adv.* unwittingly 47/20

voide, voyde *v.* avoid 5/17 *etc.*

vowesse *n.* a woman who vows chastity 60/2 *etc.*

voyde *v. See* **voide**

vp(p)on *prep.* for 85/35 *etc.*; of, about 85/16 *etc.*; on the basis of, from 16/12 *etc.*

vsage *n.* custom 23/20

vse *v.* be accustomed 12/29 *etc.*; *refl.* conduct (oneself) 4/9

vttre *v.* divulge 142/18 *etc.*

vysor *See* **visour**

wade out *v.* escape 57/8

wake *v.* stay awake 33/24

walwarde *adv. to the walwarde* toward the wall 12/24

wambled *v. pt.* felt nauseated 46/25

wan(ne) *v. pt.* won 71/25, 91/26

wantonesse *n.* licentiousness 4/9

wantonly *adv.* frivolously 99/28

ware *adj.* wary, watchful 4/11 *etc.*; cognizant, aware 88/32 *etc.*

warned *pp.* informed 200/39

wasted *v. pt.* worn out 9/14

watch *v.* stay awake 33/28

watche *n.* vigilance 92/21

wax(e) *v.* grow, become 9/11 *etc.*; *pp.* **waxed** 90/26, 93/14; **waxen** 9/15

way(e) *n.* path 38/23 *etc.*; *by the way(e)* in the process 10/7, 15/6; *in the waye* in method 18/3; *by way(e) of* by means of 20/3 *etc.*; *walke theyr way* walk away 83/14; *go (one's) way(es)* go away 23/10 *etc.*; *in waye of* as an instance of 98/31

wayeth ... downe *v. pr. 3 s.* forces down 106/9

weale, well *n.* well-being 38/31, 91/7

wel(l) *adv.* very 4/1 *etc.*

welbe *adv. and v.* well be 58/30

well *n. See* **weale.**

well wurkyng(e), well workynge *ppl. a. See* **wurkyng(e)**

welth *n.* well-being 32/15

wene *v.* think, suppose 5/30 *etc.*; *pp.* **went** 9/7 *etc.*

went(e) about to *v. pt.* set about to 25/2 *etc.*

wenynge *ppl. a.* believing, thinking 36/5 *etc.*

were *v. pt. subj:* would be 135/10

wex *n.* wax 72/14

whan y^t, whan that *conj.* when 26/5 *etc.*

wherby *conj.* by which 10/12 *etc.*

wherfore *adv.* for which reason 20/18 *etc.*

wher(e)of *adv.* for which 184/33; from what 62/17; in which 94/36; of which 7/35 *etc.*; on which 36/26

wherto *adv.* to what point, to which 17/4

wherupon *adv.* for which reason 65/16

wherwyth, wherwith *adv.* with which 6/32 *etc.*

whiche, whych(e) *pron.* who 3/5 *etc.*

whither, whyther *conj.* whether 20/11 *etc.* *See n. to* 162/28

whole *adj. See* **hole**

who so *pron.* whoever, whosoever 11/22 *etc.*

whurleth, whyrleth *v. pr. 3 s.* twirls 133/24, 133/36

whyche *pron. See* **whiche**

whyle *n.* time 24/13 *etc.*; *for the whyle* for the time being 38/14 *etc.*; *in that whyle* at that time 3/30; *means whyle* meantime, 6/36 *etc.*

whyrleth *v. pr. 3 s. See* **whurleth**

whyther *adj.* whichever 89/19, 187/16

whyther *adv.* to which 40/15

whyther *conj. See* **whither**

will *v. pr. 3 s. See* **wyll**

wise, wyse *n.* manner, means, way 6/30 *etc.*; *in diuerse wyse* in several ways 73/1; *in lyke wyse* in similar fashion 10/25–26 *etc.*

wist *v. pt. See* **wyt(te)**

with all *adv. See* **wythall**

woer *n.* wooer, suitor 60/39

wold(e) *v. pt. modal and pp. See* **wyll**

wonder *v. refl.* wonder 194/26

wonderfull *adv.* wonderfully 107/10 *etc.*

wont *adj.* accustomed 76/10 *etc.*

woo *adj.* wretched 223/16

worke *v. See* **wurke**

worker *n.* maker 64/30

workynge. *See* **wurkyng(e)**

worlde *n. it is a worlde* it is a marvel 125/19, 193/10

worshypfull *adj. See* **wurshypfull**

wote *v.* know 33/32 *etc.*; *pr. 3 s.* **woteth** 53/26 *etc.*

wowyng *vbl. n.* wooing 61/6; *a woynge* wooing 106/14

wrabelynge *ppl. a.* wriggling 19/28

wronge *adv.* incorrectly 3/18 *etc.*

wrought *pp. See* **wurke**

wryte *ppl. a.* written 35/13

wull *v. pr. 3 s.* will 121/31

wurke *n.* action 49/13

wurke, worke *v. trans.* get by labor 21/24 *etc.*; *pp.* **wrought** performed 16/3 *etc.*; brought about 24/16, 186/10

wurkyng(e), workynge *ppl. a.* active

39/19; *well wurkyng(e)*, *well workynge* doing good works 38/26 *etc.*

wurshypfull, worshypfull *adj.* notable, distinguished 137/18

wyll, will *v. pr. 3 s.* wishes, desires 34/28 *etc.*; *pt.* **wolde** wished 17/20 *etc.*; *wolde god* oh that it were God's will 3/4; *pp.* **wolde** 143/36

wyne garlandes *n. pl.* tavern signs in the form of garlands or bushes of ivy 223/11

wynke *v. intrans.* shut the eyes 21/2 *etc.*; *trans. pp.* **wynked** closed the eyes against 57/12

wyse *adv.* wisely 200/30

wyse *n. See* **wise**

wys(s)h(e)ly *adv.* steadfastly, longingly 212/19 *etc.*

wyst(e) *v. pt. See* **wyt(te)**

wyt(te) *n.* intellect, judgment 8/28 *etc.*; *pl.* **wyttes** 9/14

wyt(te) *v.* know 34/22 *etc.*; *pt.* **wyst(e), wist** 8/18 *etc.*; *wist to wyn* knew that they would win 60/5–6

wytches *n. pl.* sorcerers 68/11

wyth, with *prep.* in addition to 39/25; to 52/33

wythall, wyth all, withal, with all *adv.* besides, moreover 9/2 *etc.*; therewith 9/29 *etc.*

wythstande *v.* hinder 3/20

wytnesseth *v. pr. 3 s.* testifies 146/3–4

wytte *n. See* **wyt(te)**

wytted *ppl. a. well wytted* of good understanding 9/1

wyttes *n. pl. See* **wyt(te)**

ye *adv.* yea, truly 3/5 *etc.*; yes 157/4, 158/26–34 *See n. to* 158/35-159/7

ye *pron.* you 9/8 *etc.*

yender *adj.* yonder, other 163/3

yere *n. pl.* years 12/8 *etc.*

yet *adv. See n. to* 5/31–32

yie *n.* eye 7/17; *pl.* **yien** 150/4, 206/32

ynough *adv. See* **inough**

INDEX

INDEX